Families, Professionals, and Exceptionality

Positive Outcomes Through Partnerships and Trust

Fifth Edition

ANN TURNBULL
University of Kansas

RUD TURNBULL
University of Kansas

ELIZABETH J. ERWIN
City University of New York, Queens College

LESLIE C. SOODAK
Pace University

PEARSON

Merrill
Prentice Hall

Upper Saddle River, New Jersey
Columbus, Ohio

Library of Congress Cataloging-in-Publication Data

Families, professionals, and exceptionality: positive outcomes through partnerships and
  trust / Ann Turnbull . . . [et al.].—5th ed.
     p. cm.
  Each ed. has a different subtitle that highlights the underlying themes.
  Includes bibliographical references and index.
  ISBN 0-13-119795-9
  1. Parents of exceptional children—United States. 2. Exceptional children—United
States—Family relationships. 3. Counselor and client—United States. I. Turnbull, Ann P.

HQ759.913.F36 2006
649'.15'0973—dc22   2004059285

Vice President and Executive Publisher: Jeffery W. Johnston
Acquisitions Editor: Allyson P. Sharp
Editorial Assistant: Kathleen S. Burk
Production Editor: Sheryl Glicker Langner
Production Coordination: Amy Gehl, Carlisle Publications Services
Design Coordinator: Diane C. Lorenzo
Cover Designer: Ali Mohrman
Cover Image: Getty One
Production Manager: Laura Messerly
Director of Marketing: Ann Castel Davis
Marketing Manager: Autumn Purdy
Marketing Coordinator: Brian Mounts

This book was set in Garamond by Carlisle Publishers Services, Ltd. It was printed and bound by Courier Kendallville, Inc. The cover was printed by Coral Graphic Services, Inc.

Photo Credits: Photos of the Berg family by Rud Turnbull and Clara Berg; photos of the Cortes family by Rud Turnbull and Norma Cortes; photos of the Doleman family by Mary-Margaret Simpson (Beach Center on Disability, University of Kansas); and photos of the Holley family and students by Mary-Margaret Simpson and Leia Holley.

Pearson Prentice Hall™ is a trademark of Pearson Education, Inc.
Pearson® is a registered trademark of Pearson plc
Prentice Hall® is a registered trademark of Pearson Education, Inc.
Merrill® is a registered trademark of Pearson Education, Inc.

Pearson Education Ltd.
Pearson Education Singapore Pte. Ltd.
Pearson Education Canada, Ltd.
Pearson Education—Japan

Pearson Education Australia Pty. Limited
Pearson Education North Asia Ltd.
Pearson Educación de Mexico, S.A. de C.V.
Pearson Education Malaysia Pte. Ltd.

10 9 8 7 6 5
ISBN: 0-13-119795-

Dedication

The Turnbulls dedicate this book to their three children, Jay, Amy, and Kate, and to their son-in-law Rahul Khare—Ovid's amor omnia vincet *is precisely the right characterization of their relationships; and to their friends Susan and Fred Irons, and Dot Cansler, exemplary godparents and steadfast friends throughout life's joys and sorrows.*

Elizabeth Erwin dedicates this book to her family, Mark and Alyssa, for their laughter, love, and the sacred journey that they share as a family.

Leslie Soodak dedicates this book to her husband, Ian, and her daughter, Gaby, for their never-ending love, and in remembrance of her father, George, for his love and inspiration.

Educator Learning Center: An Invaluable Online Resource

Merrill Education and the Association for Supervision and Curriculum Development (ASCD) invite you to take advantage of a new online resource, one that provides access to the top research and proven strategies associated with ASCD and Merrill—the Educator Learning Center. At *www.educatorlearningcenter.com*, you will find resources that will enhance your students' understanding of course topics and of current educational issues, in addition to being invaluable for further research.

HOW THE EDUCATOR LEARNING CENTER WILL HELP YOUR STUDENTS BECOME BETTER TEACHERS

With the combined resources of Merrill Education and ASCD, you and your students will find a wealth of tools and materials to better prepare them for the classroom.

Research

- More than 600 articles from the ASCD journal *Educational Leadership* discuss everyday issues faced by practicing teachers.
- A direct link on the site to Research Navigator™ gives students access to many of the leading education journals, as well as extensive content detailing the research process.
- Excerpts from Merrill Education texts give your students insights on important topics of instructional method, diverse populations, assessment, classroom management, technology, and refining classroom practice.

Classroom Practice

- Hundreds of lesson plans and teaching strategies are categorized by content area and age range.
- Case studies and classroom video footage provide virtual field experience for student reflection.
- Computer simulations and other electronic tools keep your students abreast of today's classrooms and current technologies.

LOOK INTO THE VALUE OF EDUCATOR LEARNING CENTER YOURSELF

A four-month subscription to Educator Learning Center is $25 but is **FREE** when packaged with any Merrill Education text. In order for your students to have access to this site, you must use this special value-pack ISBN number **WHEN** placing your textbook order with the bookstore: 0-13-186210-3. Your students will then receive a copy of the text packaged with a free ASCD pincode. To preview the value of this website to you and your students, please go to *www. educatorlearningcenter.com* and click on "Demo."

Preface

THREE THEMES AND FOUR FAMILIES

Welcome to *Families, Professionals, and Exceptionality: Positive Outcomes Through Partnerships and Trust.*

This is the fifth edition of *Families, Professionals, and Exceptionality.* Like the previous editions, this one describes how members of families affected by disability, including students with disabilities, and professionals in special and general education and related services personnel can enter into partnerships with each other. It also has a subtitle that highlights the underlying themes. This edition features three different themes.

The first, *positive outcomes,* emphasizes that special education and related services are now part of the entire school reform movement. By "entire," we refer to the reform of general education and special education alike. The reform has occurred for two principal reasons. First, our nation has experienced more than two decades of consistent efforts to improve America's schools. Second, the federal general-education law, No Child Left Behind Act, drives all schools, all educators, and all students and their families in a single direction: to secure demonstrable outcomes in students' academic skills. (We describe the school reform movement and the No Child Left Behind Act in chapter 6.)

The second theme, *partnerships,* focuses on how families and professionals can enter into trusted relationships with each other. Although this has been the theme of each of the four previous editions of this book, what is new is the recent research literature that we cite and our new or revised ideas arising from the research literature and our own experiences working with families and professionals.

The third theme, *trust,* introduces a concept that only recently has found its place in the research and theory about schools, outcomes, and family-professional partnerships. We take that construct, ground it in the research literature, and modify and extend it to the realm of family-professional partnerships in education.

You will note the illustration of an arch on the cover and in the text. Inside the arch are seven blocks, each representing the partnership principles that derive from theory, research, and best practice. Trust is the keystone in the arch, signifying its vital role in partnerships and as a theme of this book.

This edition also continues our practice of featuring families and professionals who exemplify the practices and theories that we are teaching you. In all previous editions, we highlighted a different family-professional team for each chapter. In this edition, however, we focus on only four families and their professional partners. As always, we dare not write about families and professionals without their authentic voices being integral parts of our work.

ORGANIZATION

Usually, students and instructors regard a book's prologue and epilogue as "nice to read but not necessary to read." To regard our prologue and epilogue that way would be a big mistake. These are essential parts of the book.

We have organized the book into the following parts:

The prologue introduces the four families and their professional partners. You will need to read this in order to know "who's who" when you read the rest of the book.

Part I explains the family systems perspective. That perspective is simple and essential to your understanding of how to be a partner with families: Whatever happens to one member of the family happens to all. This becomes clear as you read about family characteristics (chapter 1), family interaction (chapter 2), family functions (chapter 3), and family life cycle (chapter 4).

Part II discusses the roles that families have played with respect to professionals (chapter 5) and the policies that shape school reform: namely, the Individuals With Disabilities Education Act and No Child Left Behind Act (chapter 6).

Part III describes six elements of partnerships (chapter 7) and how trust is the keystone to an effective, outcome-producing partnership (chapter 8).

Part IV points out how you can implement the family systems perspective (part 1), the policies (part 2), and the partnership and trust principles (part 3) as you work with families. We get to the nitty-gritty of family-professional partnerships, namely, communication (chapter 9), meeting families' basic needs (chapter 10), families as partners in student evaluation for special education services (chapter 11), individualizing education in partnership with families (chapter 12), and supporting students' achievement and performance (chapter 13).

Finally, in the epilogue, we connect the families' lives to each other, giving you a sense of how no family is like any other but how nearly all families share certain elements that are important to your partnership with them.

THREE SPECIAL FEATURES

Our book contains three special features:

The Essential Elements of Today's Schools

We bring together theory, research, and best practices in special and general education. By merging these five elements (theory, research, best practice, special education, and general education), we make this book useful to all professionals in today's schools. It does not matter whether a professional is categorized as a special or general educator because so many students with disabilities are now participating in general education. Their teachers are general and special educators, and related service professionals. What ultimately does matter is that all of these professionals know the theory, research, and best practices for being trusted and trustworthy partners of the families of their students.

Four Families That Teach Important Lessons

You will note that two of the families are from metropolitan New York City, and two are from eastern Kansas. You may ask: Aren't these families too limited by their geographic location to be examples of theory, research, and best practice?

We think not. The families have children with different disabilities; the families are from different cultural, ethnic, linguistic, or religious backgrounds; the families have different characteristics and are at different life stages.

We do not present them as "typical." No family is exactly like any other, but many families are substantially like each other. So, we ask you to meet four different families, to learn what is different and alike about each of them, and to learn how each of them became partners with trusted and trustworthy professionals.

Pedagogical Features

We begin each chapter with "Framing Questions." These two or three questions ask you to think about the issues we discuss in the chapter. They are advance prompts for you.

We follow these with the vignette in which we portray the families and their professional partners. In some chapters, we portray all of the families; in others, just some of them. These vignettes provide you with a real-life context for the theory, research, and best practice that we highlight in the chapter.

In each chapter, we include three features that amplify the text itself. "My Voice" is a first-person narrative, by either a family member or professional, that relates to the topic of the chapter. "Tips" is a practical, how-to guide on applying the theory, research, and best practice that we discuss in the chapter. "Advocacy Partners" tells you how families and professionals have become partners to advocate and secure positive outcomes for students, families, and professionals.

ACKNOWLEDGMENTS

All of us have been gratified, more than we are able to express, by the generosity of the families and professionals whom we feature. We did not know these people before beginning to write this book. As we wrote, however, and as we (Rud Turnbull and Mary-Margaret Simpson) visited them in their schools, homes, or neighborhoods, we began to feel that we were trustees of their narratives, of the stories of their lives.

Here, then, is that construct that we call "trust" and that is the keystone of partnerships. This "thing" called trust involves those who give trust (the families and professionals) and those who receive the trust (the authors).

We describe each of the four families and their professional partners in the prologue. It is impossible to describe each of them fully; this is a book about partnerships, not a biography of four families and their allies in school. Nevertheless, we hope that the prologue and the epilogue do justice to them and convey how very much we respect and have great affection for each and every one of them.

The Turnbulls have been privileged to work with a team of unusually talented people.

Lois Weldon, who assisted us on the previous edition of this book, has been our mainstay in producing this one, preparing draft after draft, never once failing to produce work of the highest quality, never complaining about our repetitive attempts to make this book the best it can be, and always celebrating the point when we reach the "final" version. We could not do this book or any other of our books and research without her. She is an indispensable colleague and valued friend.

Mary-Margaret Simpson joined the Beach Center as an editor just as we were beginning to put words to paper. She has been more than an expert wordsmith. She is a thoughtful author in her own right and brought to bea her own creativity, as well as strong organizational and follow-through skills, as we worked on the manuscript and came to know and then write about the Doleman and Holley families in Kansas.

Ray Pence is a super-sleuth in that, together with Mary-Margaret, he tracked down references and reprint permissions. But he also joined her in making our writing as clean and clear as possible. He brought to the book a perspective as a doctoral student in disability studies (at the University of Kansas) that helped us ground our own thinking in the current understandings of disability as a contextual, environmentally shaped phenomenon—one that responds to trusted and trustworthy partnerships.

Amber Olsen, an undergraduate student at the University of Kansas, mightily assisted Lois in preparing the manuscript, and Ray and Lois in making sure that all of the references were in good order. She is a valuable asset at the Beach Center.

Jay Turnbull, our son, now 37 years old, is a veteran of the first cadre of students who entered public schools with the protection of the Individuals with Disabilities Education Act. He is our greatest teacher, though we sometimes wish he would give us "the course" before he gives us the "final examination" in living in a family affected by a disability.

Amy Turnbull Khare and Kate Turnbull, our now-grown daughters, have been our partners ever since they were quite young. They taught us much about "family systems," even more about being a partner with them in their lives, and the greatest amount about how trust grows through so many expected and unexpected ways. Amy's husband, Rahul Khare, has enlarged our understanding of effects of cultural similarities and differences on families and helped us to become ever more sensitive

to those effects. We are grateful to our children and our son-in-law for all they have been, are, and will be.

Elizabeth Erwin acknowledges the faculty, staff, and students at Queens College, New York, and all of the families who have shared generously their personal lives with us through guest lectures, field work assignments, and course projects.

Leslie Soodak acknowledges four colleagues who have provided her with support and guidance in her work on this book and in other professional endeavors. They are Dean Jan McDonald of Pace University's School of Education; Rita Silverman and Mary Rose McCarthy, also at Pace; and Linda Fiore, the graduate assistant who helped Leslie see this project through to completion.

At Merrill/Prentice Hall, we have been skillfully guided by our editor, Allyson Sharp. She understands the ingredients of an effective book and conveyed those to us in ways that made it easy to follow very willingly.

Allyson's team consists of Sheryl Langner, who, once again, proved herself to be the consummate production editor and a loyal and cheerful ally; Emily Wilson, who assisted us in various stages of getting the book into production; and Kathy Burk, who is Allyson's efficient assistant.

We appreciate the individuals who opened doors for us, especially the remarkable Beth Mount of Capacity Works, Inc., in New York City. We also appreciate those who reviewed our previous edition and made helpful suggestions for this one. They are Kimberly Farrington, Southern Illinois University; Monica Brown, The University of Kansas; Mary O'Brian, Illinois State University; Helen Hammond, University of Texas at El Paso; Rachelle Bruno, Northern Kentucky University; Mark Mostert, Old Dominion University; Marci Greene, Florida Gulf Coast University; and Maureen Angell, Illinois State University.

Discover the Companion Website

Technology is a constantly growing and changing aspect of our field that is creating a need for new content and resources. To address this emerging need, Merrill Education has developed an online learning environment for students, teachers, and professors alike to complement our products–the *Merrill Education Resources for Special Education* Website. This content-rich website provides additional resources specific to this book's topic and will help you–professors, classroom teachers, and students–augment your teaching, learning, and professional development.

Our goal is to build on and enhance what our products already offer. For this reason, the content for our user-friendly website is organized by topic and provides teachers, professors, and students with a variety of meaningful resources all in one location. With this website, we bring together the best of what Merrill has to offer: text resources, video clips, web links, tutorials, and a wide variety of information on topics of interest to general and special educators alike. Rich content, applications, and competencies further enhance the learning process.

The *Merrill Education Resources for Special Education* Website includes:

Resources for the Professor—

- **Syllabus Manager**™ an online syllabus creation and management tool, enables instructors to create and revise their syllabus with an easy, step-by-step process. Students can access your syllabus and any changes you make during the course of your class from any computer with Internet access. To access this tailored syllabus, students will just need the URL of the website and the password assigned to the syllabus. By clicking on the date, the student can see a list of activities, assignments, and readings due for that particular class.

- In addition to the **Syllabus Manager**™ and its benefits listed above, professors also have access to all of the wonderful resources that students have access to on the site.

Resources for the Student—

- Video clips specific to each topic, with questions to help you evaluate the content and make crucial theory-to-practice connections.
- Thought-provoking critical analysis questions that students can answer and turn in for evaluation or that can serve as basis for class discussions and lectures.
- Access to a wide variety of resources related to classroom strategies and methods, including lesson planning and classroom management.
- Information on all the most current relevant topics related to special and general education, including CEC and Praxis standards, IEPs, portfolios, and professional development.
- Extensive web resources and overviews on each topic addressed on the website.
- A message board with discussion starters where students can respond to class discussion topics, post questions and responses, or ask questions about assignments.
- A search feature to help access specific information quickly.

To take advantage of these and other resources, please visit the *Families, Professionals, and Exceptionality: Positive Outcomes Through Partnership and Trust,* Fifth Edition, Website at

www.prenhall.com/turnbull

Brief Contents

Contents

Note: Every effort has been made to provide accurate and current Internet information in this book. However, the Internet and information posted on it are constantly changing, so it is inevitable that some of the Internet addresses listed in this textbook will change.

Prologue

FOUR FAMILIES AND THEIR TRUSTED AND TRUSTWORTHY PARTNERS

One of the best ways for you and us to be partners in the teaching-and-learning enterprise is to ask actual people to be models for the lessons we offer in this book. On your behalf, we have done just that.

We use four different techniques to introduce you to four people with disabilities, their families, and the educators and other professionals in their lives.

We introduce these people in this prologue, highlighting aspects of their lives and relationships that will acquire significance as you read the 13 chapters that follow. We write about not just the student who has a disability and the student's family members but also about the educators and other professionals who are their partners.

In each chapter, we feature one or more of the partners, emphasizing how the lives and relationships of the student, family members, and professionals exemplify the major points of the chapter.

In the epilogue, we describe the common themes—the shared narratives—of the four different sets of students, family members, and professionals, drawing your attention to the connections between such diverse families and suggesting that you may find those themes in the lives of the students and families with whom you will become a partner.

The title of this prologue uses the words "trusted and trustworthy partners," and these words follow "four families." The title calls your attention to the underlying theme of this book: Students need family members to help them prevail in life and in school.

- Family members need professionals to help the students and themselves enhance their children's education.
- Professionals can and should be partners with students and families.
- Partnership, at its best, rests on trust and trustworthiness.
- Students and families must be able to trust educators and other professionals.

- Educators and other professionals must be worthy of that trust.

As you read the next 13 chapters and the epilogue, please bear in mind those three words: families, partnership, and trust. They are the themes of our book and indispensable keys for your success as an educator. You will fully appreciate that fact after you read the book and especially if you read the epilogue.

UNEXPECTED JOURNEYS: KENNY BERG, HIS FAMILY, AND THEIR PARTNERS

Who would have expected Kenny Berg, now 23 years old, to have been a poster boy in a *Life* magazine article about students who, like him, are deaf and blind, and, later, to have been featured in books and on New York City television stations? Who would have expected Clara, his mother, to have journeyed from her home in Montevideo, Uruguay, to New York City, en route to Israel, and there to have met and married Jake Berg? Who would have expected Jake to have survived the Nazis from the 1930s to mid-1940s and, after fleeing from Poland, Russia, and France, to have found sanctuary in the United States?

Kenny Berg.

FIGURE P–1

The Berg Family and Its Professional Partners in New York City and Queens, New York

Kenny is 23 years old and deaf-blind.

Clara and Jake are his mother and father. Clara works at Columbia University's Teachers College. Jake is a retired accountant.

Sheldon is Kenny's brother, a vice president of Citibank. Karen is his sister and is a writer for *Access Hollywood,* a daily television show.

Carole Gothelf is the former principal of the Guild School, where Kenny was a student. She hired Clara Berg to work with her on behalf of families who have deaf-blind children.

Beth Mount holds a doctorate in special education and bases her work on Making Action Plans: MAPs. She operates a transition-planning program and a publishing house, Capacity Works (*www.capacityworks.com*).

Arnie Mejia is Kenny's job coach at Adriance Farm in Queens, New York.

Who would have expected these journeys? Certainly not Clara or Jake, and certainly not Kenny. Yet here these three are, in New York City, supported in extraordinary ways by three professionals, Carole Gothelf, Beth Mount and Arnie Mejia.

Let's begin with Kenny, who was born prematurely and was not expected to survive. He is a survivor although his prematurity caused him to be deaf and blind. Shuffled from one ineffective program to another during the first several years of his life, he was finally enrolled in the Perkins School for the Blind at age 6, but only because Clara would not take no for an answer from school administrators. When Kenny was photographed by *Life* for its 1991 article on the Perkins School and the students there, he was portrayed in the photograph with a helmet on his head, curled into a fetal position, his hands pressed to his face, lying inside a large plastic bubble, fully dressed but for the telltale absence of one sock—the symbol of a not-quite-fully-cared-for young boy, a portrait of "the other" person, the one who none of "us" wants to be. Kenny was at Perkins for 8 years. Each weekend, Clara bundled up her two other children and drove from the family home in New York to Boston and the Perkins campus to be with her son, to have her three children come to know each other, to maintain a family already beset by journeys away from their roots, and to advocate for changes in a standard Perkins program so it could benefit Kenny. Later, Kenny was enrolled in the Jewish Guild School. There, he was taken under the special auspices of Carole Gothelf, di-

rector of education and later principal of the school. He was nourished by the visions that resulted from the Bergs' work with Beth Mount, a consultant who worked with people graduating from New York City schools. Home at last, at Adriance Farm in Queens, New York, Kenny tends to the chickens, assembling the eggs that the farmers sell.

Now, let's bring Clara and Jake into the picture. Clara's unexpected journey was not so much her trip from Montevideo to New York and meeting and later marrying Jake as it was and continues to be her journey as Kenny's mother. Jake's journey was more predictable, his family fleeing the persecutions of Jews, coming to New York, and settling into his job as an accountant.

Let's complete the profile of these sojourners. Carole Gothelf holds a doctorate in special education. While operating a technical assistance program in New York City for families of children who are deaf and blind, she employed Clara to assist families who spoke only Spanish. More than that, Carole is a justice-driven person; she regards her work on behalf of people with disabilities from the social-justice perspective, as a "right" activity. Asked why she is so imbued with the justice mentality, she replies, in words that Jake and Clara can identify with, "In my neighborhood in Brooklyn, when I was growing up in the 1950s, many of my parents' friends and neighbors had tattoos on their arms." Yes, the same tattoos that the Nazis branded onto those they held in the infamous concentration camps. Tattoos: the stigma of difference, of being "the other," of discardable and dispensable. There are no tattoos on Kenny Berg's arms. There is, however, the scar that traverses his head, a reminder of the 8 months in the hospital following birth. Not that Kenny needs a visible sign of his difference. One notices at the first sight of him that he is deaf and blind.

Beth Mount has made a journey, too, from Georgia and North Carolina, where she was born and educated, to New York. She is a person who knew what "is" but asked the "why not" question. She knew about the dismal outcomes for students with disabilities but insisted that, when they, their family, and their friends plan a journey that builds on the strengths and choices of the person with a disability, profoundly unexpected trips occur and remarkable destinations are reached. How else to explain how Kenny, supported by Beth, transitioned from the Jewish Guild School to being a farmer in Queens, New York?

And then there is Arnie Mejia, a Filipino born and raised in California, who worked in special education, and found beauty in the simple life as Kenny's job coach at Adriance Farm in New York. Arnie has taken an even more unexpected journey than as a bicoastal traveler. He converses in languages known to only a few, made famous by Helen Keller, the deaf-blind graduate of Radcliffe College, and her teacher, Annie Sullivan, who communicated through touch sign language. Arnie and Kenny speak to each other with their fingers, holding each other's hands and signing out words into each other's palms. They do more than converse; they also travel—for conversing is communicating, and communicating is traveling along the paths of ideas and feelings with another.

The unexpected journeys that these six people have made landed them all in the same place, at Adriance Farm. There, Kenny is a member of a community of farmers. He is proof that his family's great expectations, coupled with their fierce dedication and buttressed by a few effective advocates, can lead to a world barely mapped, for who would have thought Kenny to be capable of working? Who but these partners?

"Mapping" is an appropriate metaphor for these journey takers. When Kenny was still enrolled at the Jewish Guild School, it was not altogether obvious that he and his family would have taken a journey from school to the farm. What made that journey possible was Clara's understanding that Kenny loved horses. When he was at Perkins School, he groomed and rode them. It pleased him to be able to touch them, to feel their muscles ripple below their hides, to be able to move with his hands on them, without having to use his cane or to shuffle carefully along unfamiliar landscapes, and to smell them. It also helped to abate his self-injurious behaviors, those manifestations of his desire to speak his mind and of his inability to do so. Clara took careful note of Kenny and the horses and had it in mind to buy a farm in upstate New York, miles from the city, where Kenny might live and work.

No need to go so far, cautioned Beth Mount, when she, Clara, and Carole sat down to map out Kenny's future. Why not find some horse stables nearby? If not stables, then someplace with animals, where Kenny could work in that environment where he is comfortable and comforted. And so began the mapping that culminated in Kenny volunteering at Adriance Farm and, upon his graduation from the Jewish Guild School, becoming a paid worker.

Kenny, Clara, Jake, Carole, Beth, and Arnie each have experienced an unexpected journey, and each has arrived in a single place, in a world that they created, not by themselves but together. None of them had the patience to wait; their journeys had to occur when they occurred—Jake's very existence depended on his journeying from place to place, much as Kenny's and his family's lives also depended on their deliberate movement from one school to another and then from one place of comfort, the Guild School, to another, Adriance Farm.

These six travelers remind us of the wisdom of the ancient Rabbi Hillel: "If I am not for myself, then, who will be for me? If I am not for others, what am I? And if not now, when?"

"If I am not for myself?" If Kenny had not injured himself to protest his inability to stand up for himself, to be the self-determined person he clearly is. Not the *Life* magazine "other," but one of us. Not the dispensable person to whom others may be indifferent, but the essential person who commands our attention and earns our respect.

"Then, who will be for me?" Yes, Kenny is different, but he connects with others and we with him. The latent oneness—the tattoo, the stigma of difference and disability—becomes a patent togetherness. If we are not for each other, then no one will be for us when we need them.

"If not now, when?" Clara never waited for tomorrow; each of her days since Kenny was born has been spent in diligent pursuit of a life that he would lead happily. Jake knew that action today can prevent tragedy tomorrow; Carole learned, through her family's friends, that she must confront injustice at its very first appearance.

So, Kenny speaks to us, in his way, the words of the ancient rabbi. Put your hands together with mine, he signs. Life is not a solo journey. We are all interdependent. We need partners and we need to be partners with others, and we need to be able to trust each other, even as I, Kenny Berg, deaf and blind, trust you five fellow travelers. One can almost hear him say, "We shall commune with each other. More than that, we shall find and preserve that sanctuary—that togetherness and this life—that is the land's end of our journeys."

IT'S A FAMILY AFFAIR: JOESIAN CORTES, HIS FAMILY, AND THEIR PARTNERS

What's a family? It's two or more people who perform the functions that typically are associated with "family." The functions are easy enough to identify. They include raising children, making sure they are educated, and giving them moral standards by which to live.

Joesian Cortes (far right) with (left to right) Norma Cortes, Lourdes Rivera-Putz, and Martha Viscarrondo.

FIGURE P–2

The Cortes Family and Its Professional Partners in Brooklyn, New York

> Joesian is 17 years old and is in special education because he has difficulty reading. He also receives speech-language therapy.
>
> Norma and Joaqin are his mother and father. Norma does not work outside the home; Joaqin and his sister-in-law, Alicia, run a grocery store.
>
> Juan, 11, and Tatiana, 15, are Joesian's brother and sister.
>
> Lourdes Rivera-Putz is the executive director of United We Stand of New York.
>
> Martha Viscarrondo and Lori Rosenfeld are staff members.
>
> Emily Rodriguez was the assistant principal of Bushwick High School, where Joesian is a student.

Who is in the family? That is a harder question to answer. Indeed, there is no single answer. Even blood and marriage do not serve as the only tickets that admit a person to a family. Neither blood nor marriage admitted Lourdes Rivera-Putz, Martha Viscarrondo, or Lori Rosenfeld to Joesian Cortes's extended family. And yet, they are important family members.

How that came to be depended completely on serendipity. It depended on the chance that Lourdes's and Martha's families came to New York City from Puerto Rico, where Norma Cortes, Joesian's mother, was born; on the chance that Lourdes and Martha have children with disabilities and that Lori's sister and niece have disabilities, and that Norma's son Joesian has a disability, too; on the chance that all of them live in Brooklyn, New York; on the chance that an assistant principal at Joesian's high school, Emily Rodriguez, is a descendant of Puerto Ricans and, like Lourdes and Martha, a self-proclaimed Christian Latina; and on the chance that the person who evaluated Joesian for a speech-language and reading problem referred Norma to United We Stand of New York, the family-directed community-based parent resource center in Brooklyn that Lourdes and other Latina women created 14 years ago.

So much hangs on the thin threads of chance and on those threads being connected. But from the thin threads and their connectivity Joesian has, at long last, derived a benefit in school and now can look forward to a career that is connected to his family. After many years in school, he is learning the trade that his uncle practices—plumbing.

Who, then, is in a family? Obviously, there is Norma and her husband Joaqin, and their children, Joesian, Tatiana, and Juan; Joesian's uncle, the plumber; and Alicia, who is

both sister-in-law and business partner with Joaqin. Now, is it permissible to add Lourdes, Martha, and Lori, of United We Stand? It is not entirely clear whether those three good women should be included in the Cortes family. They do perform some of the roles of a family member, advocating for Joesian and supporting Norma in her role as his mother, but otherwise they do not perform any family roles. And it is not clear whether Norma and the other members of her blood-and-marriage family would regard the three as members of the Cortes family. In the end, the answer depends on how the Cortes family—mother, father, children, and uncles and aunts—would answer the question. It is not for any of us to answer it, and certainly not for any of Joesian's teachers to answer it.

How this family formed is, of course, related to Joesian's disability. Joesian is 17 years old and enrolled in the 11th grade. But he is known as a "nonreader." He has a speech impediment. It may be that his speech impediment contributes to his poor reading skills; it also may be that the reason he cannot read does not lie within Joesian himself. At the request of United We Stand, he was evaluated by a reading and speech specialist who is not employed by the schools. The specialist concluded that Joesian has the ability to read at the 11th-grade-level. The discrepancy between his ability and his demonstrated skill is clear, but the reasons for the discrepancy are not. Norma firmly believes that the reasons lie in the school system itself. She thinks that many of Joesian's teachers simply ignored him, year after year. Not all of his teachers did that, she is quick to note, but many did.

Joesian can make himself readily understood. He translates for his mother, English to Spanish and reverse. He is soft-spoken, well mannered, and attentive as he is spoken to, speaks to others, and translates for Norma.

On one level, it matters greatly why Joesian cannot read at the 11th-grade-level, receives speech therapy, and is in special education. His future depends on his ability to read and speak clearly. That is true whether he will join his uncle's business as a plumber or hold down his dream job as a New York City firefighter. Asked why he wants to be a firefighter, when he knows very well how many of them lost their lives in the September 11, 2001, assaults on the World Trade Center, Joesian says, "Because firefighters are the best people. They risk their own lives to help other people."

On another level, what matters more to Joesian and his family is that his education is driven by a value system that Joesian can articulate very clearly: "to help other people." Joesian's value-driven education derives directly from his mother, from a few of his teachers, and from the staff at United We Stand. Of course, there is undeniable value in being able to read. But reading alone does not ensure that Joesian will have opportunities that make a difference to him and his family after he leaves the city's school system. Reading counts, but only if it also combines with values that can be felt and realized in the work Joesian will do.

Focus for a moment on Norma. Born in San Sebastian, Puerto Rico, Norma left school after the third grade to help her parents raise her many brothers and sisters. Denied an opportunity to learn English in New York because adult-education programs are few and rarely last long enough to bring their students to even a conversational-English level, Norma knows the value of an education. It is the means whereby her other children will enter their hoped-for careers, Tatiana as a lawyer and Juan as a veterinarian.

But "value" carries a special meaning for Norma, just as it does for Joesian. It means to place a value on some commodity—on a service, for example. Norma's service to this book lay in consenting to be interviewed, along with Joesian. When, after being interviewed for 3 hours, she was offered a consulting fee in an amount totally unknown to her, she adamantly refused the envelope containing the money.

Turning to Lourdes, she began an extremely animated conversation. After they had talked for nearly 10 minutes—truthfully, Norma talked and Lourdes listened, cried, and hugged Norma—Lourdes turned to me and said, "Norma says she gives her son and his story to you. She gives it. You cannot pay for this gift. She wants his story and hers to help others and they cannot pay, either. She wants you and new teachers to have the story. It is a gift, and this gift cannot be bought."

Education, then, is about giving freely, about taking actions that are beyond value but that are nevertheless highly valued. Education entails working with others, for others. And it entails teaching and living by moral standards.

If that makes education seem like a family affair, well, it is, at least in the lives of Norma and Joesian Cortes, the three women of United We Stand, and Emily Rodriguez.

To live a life in service of other people, a life that is beyond a standard measure of value, may well be in Joesian's future. Undoubtedly, it is the present reality for Norma, Lourdes, Martha, Lori, and Emily, as partners for Joesian's benefit.

Their reality also teaches that education, when driven by values and carried out by partners, is a family affair, where "family" includes those who are not related by blood or marriage.

People define *family* in their own lives, by ways that are idiosyncratic to them. Some, such as Norma, will define it broadly, inviting us to enter her life because it is the right thing to do. "You cannot buy this gift," she says, and she might just as well tell us, "A job and money do not create a partnership." There must be something more, something that is created from the chances and happenstances

of life and from taking deliberate action to turn the serendipitous into a sustaining system.

THE PHOENIX PHENOMENON: NICKY DOLEMAN, HER FAMILY, AND THEIR PARTNERS

Thousands of children are born every day, free of any innate disabilities. A relatively few children, however, are born with disabilities. Some of those disabilities could have been prevented, either by better prenatal care or by prenatal medical interventions. Some of those disabilities can be minimized by medical interventions provided in the first hours, and even in the first weeks, after a baby is born.

Other children acquire disabilities after they are born. Some experience disabilities as a result of accidents, such as in automobiles or swimming pools; in these cases, human error, which the law calls negligence, is a factor. Other children acquire disabilities as a result of maltreatment; in these cases, deliberate or intentional behavior is a factor. Among these few cases is the life of Nicky Doleman.

Like most newborns, Nicky was born free of disabilities. That happy state, however, lasted for only about 6 months. By then, she had been rendered nearly deaf, almost completely blind, and completely dependent on technology to receive food and liquids. The cause of her disability was maltreatment by her father.

There are many consequences of his action, but perhaps the most unusual result is that Nicky's maternal grandmother, Vera, is now her legal mother. That's right: Nicky's biological mother is Charolette, Vera's daughter. Odd as it may seem, Vera is also Nicky's legal mother. There's a story behind that story.

After Nicky was injured at home and then treated at Children's Mercy Hospital in Kansas City, she was released to the custody of a temporary foster parent, for safety's sake.

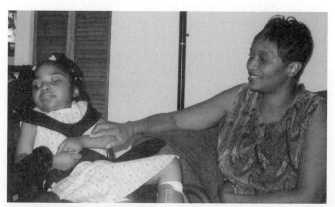

Nicky and Vera Doleman.

FIGURE P–3
The Doleman Family and Its Professional Partners in
Lawrence, Kansas

> Nicky is 6 years old and has severe and multiple
> disabilities.
>   Charolette is her biological mother.
>   Vera is her biological grandmother and her legal
> mother through adoption.
>   Altevis ("Joe") is Vera's other child, Nicky's uncle.
>   Tavion is Charolette's other child, a 4-year-old boy.
>   Marie and Aaron are Nicky's great-grandparents,
> Vera's mother and father, and Charolette's
> grandparents.
>   Pam Shanks was Nicky's teacher at Raintree
> Montessori School in Lawrence, Kansas.

Instincts drive behavior, and so Vera petitioned the local
courts to adopt Nicky, believing that adoption would forever sever the father's rights and thus protect Nicky. Given
that Charolette and the state child protective agency supported Vera's petition, the court granted it. Thus, Vera is
both Nicky's biological grandmother and legal mother.

Charolette remains heavily involved with Nicky. She
has her own apartment in Lawrence. She comes to Vera's
home every morning to bathe, dress, and groom Nicky.
She works full-time at a steady job, and is enrolled in a
nurse-training program at a nearby community college.

The ancient Greek legend of the phoenix seems so
apt: The bird, nearly destroyed, rises from the ashes. The
life that nearly ended, Nicky's, is completely safe. The life
that seemed to be free of the daily duties of parenthood,
Vera's, now includes Nicky. Vera and Nicky are now supported by a host of other Doleman relatives. The myth of
the ancient phoenix is a current reality.

One of the maxims in Vera's African American culture
is familiar to most of us: "It takes a whole village to raise
a single child." And so it does.

Both Vera and Charolette needed help to care for Nicky
and to raise Nicky's brother Tavion. Charolette called her
grandparents (Vera's parents) and asked, "I need help.
Mother needs help. What can you do?"

Without so much as a second thought, Charolette's
grandparents, Aaron and Marie, sold their home outside
Greenville, Mississippi, and moved to Lawrence, Kansas,
permanently.

Now, the "village" consists of Nicky, Charolette, Vera,
Vera's son Altevis ("Joe"), Aaron and Marie, and Vera's sister. These are the villagers who raise Nicky.

We are obliged to regard Nicky as a child with multiple disabilities. She is surrounded by family and, as you

will soon learn, she is the beneficiary of the skills, respect, commitment, and advocacy of a large number of
professionals.

There are physicians, nurses, dietitians, and occupational and physical therapists who attend to Nicky's health
needs. There are teachers who have included her in their
classes ever since she was about a year old.

That is when Nicky entered the preschool programs
operated by faculty and staff at the University of Kansas
in Lawrence. She spent a year there and then transferred
to Raintree Montessori School across town.

Raintree Montessori School had long been committed to
including young children with disabilities in its programs
for students without disabilities. A University of Kansas faculty member, Barbara Thompson, together with Raintree's
coprincipals, Lleanna and Keith McReynolds, had started a
program called "Circle of Inclusion" to carry out their commitment to inclusion.

Belief without action, and values without techniques,
are not worth too much. That is why Pam Shanks, Raintree's lead teacher, played such an important role in Nicky's
education. She earned degrees in early education and special education at KU and has continued to study there; she
also is certified as a Montessori teacher.

Although no student with such severe disabilities had
been at Raintree and part of its inclusion program in a
long time, Pam had no qualms about teaching Nicky: "If
I can teach her to respond, that in itself is worthwhile.
If I also can teach the other students in her class to respond to her with compassion, that makes my job all the
more worthwhile."

Surrounded by family, professionals, and peers without disabilities, Nicky lives in a "village" where everyone
depends on everyone else. Should anything go wrong
with Nicky's health, her medication regimen, or the gas-
trointestinal tubes on which she depends for liquid nutrition, almost everything would go wrong at home and
school. Health-care distress will disrupt all other facets of
her life.

In depending on each other, Nicky's villagers—especially the adults—have to communicate daily and candidly. They have to be professionally competent. They are
committed to Nicky and each other, respect each other's
perspectives, deal with each other as equals, and advocate for Nicky and each other.

But most of all, they trust each other. Vera puts it this
way, speaking about only one group of the villagers: "I
have no choice but to trust the visiting nurses, and I'll trust
anyone else who does not try to second-guess me." Trying
to second-guess Vera disrespects her, because she knows so
much about Nicky that others do not know. Everyone is
committed to Nicky, and Vera is the villager-in-charge.

How to conclude the story about Nicky Doleman? Why not listen for that ancient bird, the phoenix: "Out of the ashes rises a new village, Nicky's very own."

THE OLYMPICS: SEAN HOLLEY, HIS FAMILY, AND THEIR PARTNERS

We wrote this book in 2004, the year of the Olympic Summer Games, held in Athens, the cradle of democracy. You, however, are reading it in the years following the games. For us, the games are events yet to be held; for you, they already are history. The future and the past are periods of time, passages in each of our lives.

Symbols accompany passages. Religious rites yield religious symbols, some written, some iconic. Secular rites produce their own peculiar symbols: diplomas, the framed first-dollar-earned, the retirement watch.

And so it is with the Olympic Games. Many of us are familiar with the Olympic symbol—the five interlocked circles representing the five continents.

Few of us imagine those circles as symbols of the stages of life. Let us, however, adopt the Olympic rings as symbols of Sean Holley's life and those closely associated with him. We begin in a most unlikely location, not the site of any kind of Olympics.

In Bonner Springs, Kansas, there lives a family whose life fits the five circles that represent the stages of life. The Holley family consists of Sean, now 11 years old; his brother James Paul III (JP); his father Jamie, a major in the United States Army stationed at Ft. Leavenworth, just a few miles north of Bonner Springs, but previously posted for a year to South Korea; and Leia, a mother with a mission.

This is the story of the five circles of their lives. Two of the circles are full of life's events; they are the already-lived circles. One of the circles is about to be lived; within a very few months, it will begin to be filled with events. The other two circles are distant and barely discernible.

Sean Holley with his mother, Leia.

FIGURE P–4

The Holley Family and Its Professional Partners in Bonner Springs, Kansas

> Sean is 11 years old and has autism and epilepsy.
>
> Leia and Jamie are his mother and father. Leia works for Families Together, the Kansas Parent Training and Information Center. Jamie is a major in the United States Army.
>
> JP is Sean's brother.
>
> Tierney Thompson has been Sean's teacher ever since he enrolled in Bonner Springs Elementary School.
>
> Tammy Eldridge is the principal of Bonner Springs Elementary School.

One of the filled-in circles represents various episodes in Sean's life. Call it the Circle of Tears. In it are the early diagnoses of Sean's disabilities; the frequent episodes of self-injurious behaviors brought about because Sean has problems in communicating what he wants and so he acts out; the brain surgery to correct the neural misfirings that caused his epileptic seizures; and the anger that his parents, especially Leia, and teachers, especially Tierney Thompson, felt toward each other because none seemed to be able to fully satisfy the requests, which escalated into demands, of the other.

The second filled circle represents the period immediately following the Circle of Tears. Call it the Circle of Triumph. In it are the laborious efforts that Leia, Tierney, and the staff at Bonner Springs Elementary School exerted to triumph over their anger and despair with each other. Also in it are the many ways in which Sean's school mates welcome him into their lives.

The circle that is soon to be filled represents the period that will begin in just a few months. Call it the Circle of Transition Terror. In it is the uncertainty of middle school. Who will Sean's teachers be? Will they have the skills to teach him effectively? Will they enter into their relationships with Leia as equal partners? Will his schoolmates include him in their activities?

Beyond these questions lies one that goes to the very heart of schooling. It involves the different cultures of public schools. The elementary school is nurturing; the middle school is controlling. Leia and Tierney know how Sean has flourished in the elementary school; what strikes terror in their hearts is whether he will fit into the middle school and be able or willing to conform to its culture.

The other two circles represent two predictable periods. One will begin as Sean leaves school and lives as an adult. The other will begin as he ages and then comes to the end of his life. We cannot begin to know what will happen to Sean and his family during those last two periods, so we dare not name them.

We can, however, reflect on the first two circled periods—the Circle of Tears and the Circle of Triumph; and we can begin to project some parts of his life into the Circle of Transition Terror.

We must acknowledge that Sean's life, like the Olympic Games, is a contact sport, replete with struggle that is nearly physical in its dimensions.

But also like the Olympic Games, Sean's life is one in which the participants collaborate as members of a team to defeat the odds against them. Their opponent is adversity, not other individuals.

Take the metaphor of a physical struggle against combatants. There have been two principal combatants in Sean's life. One consists of disabilities, for Sean has autism and epilepsy.

Another has been the team of professionals against whom Sean and his family, captained by his mother Leia, struggled during the Circle of Tears.

Now take the metaphor of a struggle against odds, waged by a team. The odds were that Sean would not overcome many of the effects of his disabilities, that he would not attend school with students of his own age who do not have disabilities, and that he would not learn to communicate and socialize.

What team might beat those odds? A team that predictably consists of Sean and his family, that paradoxically consists of the professionals who were once combatants against Sean and his family; and that joyously includes those students without disabilities with whom Sean spends his school days and summers. Sean's family and his teachers, therapists, classmates, and physicians allied themselves with each other during the Circle of Triumph.

Having passed through the Circle of Tears and Circle of Triumph and fresh from some victories over great odds, Sean and his allies now face the prospect of leaving Bonner Springs Elementary School, the arena in which they have been triumphant, and of entering a different arena, Bonner Springs Middle School. In preparing to shift from elementary to middle school, they enter the Circle of Transition Terror, not knowing whether they can overcome the challenges of education in a different arena and at a more competitive level. The stages of their lives are marked by obligatory transitions: Sean must move on. How he does so, and with what results, depends on whether he and his family will have partners such as they have recruited out of the Circle of Tears and into the Circle of Triumph.

■ ■ ■

We do not suggest that these four families are "typical." Perhaps they are, but perhaps they are not. We do assert that their stories are instructive. The narratives that involve the teachers and other professionals involved with them are even more helpful for us to teach and you to learn about partnerships that are based on trust. As you read the 13 chapters and epilogue that follow, please bear in mind that the central theme of this book and the common narrative of these four families is all about partnership and trust.

Rud Turnbull
Lawrence, Kansas
June, 2004

Families, Professionals, and Exceptionality

PART I

TRUST

COMMUNICATION

PROFESSIONAL COMPETENCE

RESPECT

COMMITMENT

EQUALITY

ADVOCACY

INTRODUCTION TO PART I

The Family Systems Perspective

As we mentioned in the prologue, it is best to enter into trusting partnerships with families by understanding that families are systems. Whatever happens to one of the family members happens to all of them. The metaphor we use to describe the family systems perspective is a mobile. If you put one part of a mobile into action, you will create motion in all of the other parts. That is how it is with families, too: the characteristics of family members (chapter 1), their ways of interacting with each other (chapter 2), the functions they perform for each other (chapter 3), and how they move through various stages of their lives (chapter 4).

1

Family Characteristics

CHAPTER ORGANIZATION

FRAMING QUESTIONS

1. Why do some families grow stronger as a result of raising a child with a disability, whereas other families become more vulnerable?
2. On what basis can educators begin to individualize their responses to families?
3. How do cultural and linguistic diversity affect family priorities?

VIGNETTE

What characterizes each of the four families you met in the prologue? All families have several characteristics; each can affect how you relate to a family and how you can be a trustworthy partner.

One way to characterize the families in the prologue is by identifying their members; membership defines the size and form of each family. Counting only those members who are related by blood or marriage, each family has more than two members. You may want to refer to Figures P–1 through P–4 to refamiliarize yourself with the families.

Blood-and-marriage relationship is too narrow a definition of family, however, because each of these four families relies greatly on people who are not related by blood or marriage. These reliable allies regard themselves as family members and are included by the blood-and-marriage family into the family circle.

May we characterize these four families based on their cultural backgrounds and geographic affiliations? Most assuredly. To do so, we have to take the Bergs' self-definition: "South American, of the Jewish faith." And then we add to it "international"—Jake Berg, the deliberate American, the immigrant who chose to be an American; and Clara, the accidental American, the Uruguayan who met and married Jake and adopted his nationality and our country as her own. The Corteses are American,

hailing from Puerto Rico, but they are Hispanic. Spanish is the language of their home, for Norma speaks very little English. Yet English is the language of their interactions with Joesian's teachers at school. Their faith, Roman Catholic, is one of the two characteristics that connect them to Emily Rodriguez, the assistant principal at Joesian's school, and to Lourdes Rivera-Putz and her colleagues at United We Stand. The Dolemans are African American, now Midwesterners in Kansas but originally southerners from Mississippi. The Holleys are White, Anglo, and, for at least the past 4 years, Kansans.

Professionals working with the Berg family have become longtime trusted friends. Here, Beth Mount (far left) enjoys a group hug from Kenny Berg, Clara Berg, and Arnie Mejia.

Sean Holley (right), shown with his brother, JP, on a family outing several years ago.

May we classify the families according to their socioeconomic status? That, too, is illuminating. Clara and Jake Berg are professionals; she is a staff member at Columbia University's Teachers College who was educated at a French school in a South American country, and he is a retired accountant.

May we characterize them by their children's disability? Yes, for that is how many professionals and service systems characterize and relate to families. Thus, we should say that three of the families have children with a very high degree of need: Kenny Berg is deaf and blind, Nicky Doleman has great physical and mental challenges, and Sean Holley has autism and epilepsy that impair his cognitive functioning. By contrast, Joesian Cortes is on the cusp between disability and nondisability because, though he reads poorly and is receiving speech therapy, he can read, is bilingual, and speaks quite clearly when he is comfortable.

None of these families presents the special challenges of being homeless or having a parent with a disability. Each is stable and has competent and involved parents.

To be a teacher is to encounter students who have many different characteristics. To be a teacher of a student with an exceptionality is to meet and greet the opportunity to be a

younger Joesian Cortes on a field trip in Manhattan.

partner with the student's family. That partnership begins by understanding how to characterize families and valuing the many chracteristics that you can attribute to them.

INTRODUCTION

This chapter focuses on the first component of the family systems framework: the family's characteristics, which are the *inputs* into the family system. Figure 1–1 shows you the family systems framework, highlighting the family characteristics. These include (1) the characteristics of the

family as a whole, (2) the characteristics of individual members, and (3) special challenges. The characteristics of the family as a whole include its cultural background, socioeconomic level, and geographic location. In addition, each member of the family varies in individual characteristics related to exceptionality, coping styles, and health status. Finally, many families face special challenges such as homelessness, parents with disabilities, and teenage parents. Every family is a unique mixture of characteristics.

To develop trusting partnerships with families, you need to understand what makes each family unique. You

FIGURE 1–1
Family Systems Framework: Emphasis on Family Characteristics

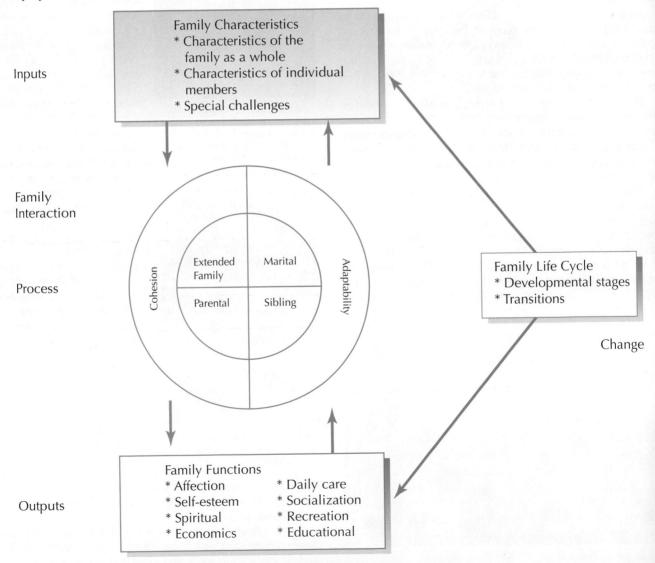

Source: Turnbull, A. P., Summers, J. A., & Brotherson, M. J. (1984). *Working with families with disabled members: A family systems approach* (p. 60). Lawrence: University of Kansas, Kansas Affiliated Facility. Adapted by permission.

may begin that understanding by focusing on the family's characteristics.

CHARACTERISTICS OF THE FAMILY AS A WHOLE

A family shares many characteristics as a single entity. Some of these characteristics are the family's size and form, cultural background, socioeconomic status, and geographic location. To build a trusting partnership with each family, you will want to take each characteristic into account.

Family: Definition, Size, and Form

Before discussing family size and form, we need to define the term *family*. Before we do, answer this question: Who are the members of your family? Now, define family on the basis of your own family.

Your definition is a starting point, at least for our work together in this book. The U.S. Census Bureau defines family as a group of two or more people related by birth, marriage, or adoption who reside together (Iceland, 2000). Does this definition fit how you define your own family? It does not fit our experiences with families. As a professional, you will encounter people who define family by including individuals who do not share the same household or are not related by blood, marriage, or adoption. Do all of your family members live in the same household? Are all the members of your family related by blood, marriage, or adoption?

We define family as follows (Poston et al., 2003): Families include two or more people who regard themselves as a family and who carry out the functions that families typically perform. These people may or may not be related by blood or marriage and may or may not usually live together. Does the composition of your family fit this definition?

Each family's size and form depends on its own definition of family—whether it is as exclusive as the Census Bureau's definition or as inclusive as ours. Family size and form refer to the number of children, number of parents, presence and number of stepparents, extensiveness of the extended family, and number of live-in family members who are unrelated by blood or marriage.

The effect of a child's exceptionality on the family can vary, depending upon the family's size and form. In large families, more people are often available to help with the chores and any special supports and resources the child needs. Other children may serve as frames of reference, reminding parents that their child with an exceptionality is more like than unlike his or her brothers and sisters and that all children have various combinations of strengths and needs. For example, a father of an adolescent daughter with mental retardation noted that her problems are often no greater and perhaps even less difficult than the problems his other children experienced during adolescence.

> Adeliza had been, in many respects, the easiest of our six children. As she was the fourth daughter with two younger brothers, we as parents were "old pros" at raising teenage daughters by the time Adeliza turned 13. She doesn't date and is not as rebellious as our other three daughters. Instead of being another stressful situation, her teenage years have, in general, been a very positive experience for our entire family.

Note the importance of birth order. This father suggests that being experienced at raising teenage daughters influenced him and his wife during Adeliza's adolescence. What if Adeliza had been their first child? How might their perceptions of her strengths and needs have been similar and different?

Just as the number of children is an important consideration related to family size and form, the number of parents (single parent or two parents) also may influence a family's reaction to the exceptionality. Figure 1–2 compares the size and form of families who have youth with disabilities with the size and form of families who have youth who do not have disabilities. What similarities and differences do you detect between these two sets of families? One of the biggest differences is that far fewer youth with disabilities live with both biological parents, and more youth with disabilities live with neither biological parent. In a two-parent family, a coalition of parents can potentially share responsibilities and support each other emotionally during the ups and downs of child rearing (Scorgie, Wilgosh, & McDonald, 1998). A supportive husband—even one who does not participate in child care—seems to be an important predictor of a mother's sense of well-being (Crnic & Booth, 1991; Nagy & Ungerer, 1990).

You are certain to have students in your class whose parents are single. As Figure 1–2 depicts, 36% of youth with disabilities live in single-parent families, contrasted to 26% of youth in the general population. Figure 1–2 also reveals that students are more likely to live with their biological mother than with their biological father. Although single mothers are more prevalent than single fathers, the number of father-only families has substantially increased since the mid-1990s ("Single Fathers," 1998). A father of two young children who had only seen his own father once every year or so when he was growing up described his decision to be the primary caregiver of his children:

> The day my baby was born, I said, "I gotta find a better life." I had always said that I was not going to be like my daddy. I mean, I had the idea, the dream, as a kid because of some of the things my mother went through. I said, "I don't want my kids to go through any of this shit. I'm going to get married

FIGURE 1–2
Household Composition of Youth with Disabilities and Youth in the General Population

Individual Characteristics	Youth with Disabilities	Youth in the General Population
Percentage of households with:		
No biological parents present	19	3
Biological father present	4	3
Biological mother present	35	21
Both biological parents present	42	73
Percentage living in a single-parent household	36	26
Average number of children in the household	3	2

Source: U.S. Department of Education. (2002). *To assure the free appropriate public education of all children with disabilities: Twenty-fourth annual report to Congress on the implementation of the Individuals with Disabilities Education Act.* Washington, DC: Author.

the right way." But, of course, that didn't happen as far as the marriage. But I just said I was not going to abandon my kids . . . . I just wanted—because I never had the opportunity to be with my dad. I just did not want to be like my father. (Coles, 2003, p. 255)

Although households headed by only a father are growing in number, Figure 1–2 shows that approximately one third of youth with disabilities live in a single-parent household where the parent is their biological mother. The poverty rate among families headed by a single, female parent is almost 40% when a child in the family has a disability (Fujiura & Yamaki, 1997, 2000). Of the 3.2 million single-parent/female households in poverty, approximately 1 in 5 has a member with a disability. Clearly, two of the characteristics that contribute to the likelihood that families will experience poverty are single-parent, female-headed households and the presence of children (particularly more than one child) who have a disability.

Some single parents may have neither the time nor the emotional energy to be heavily involved in their child's education; however, other single parents are active partners with their children's teachers (Cigno & Burke, 1997). A study of single mothers of children with learning disabilities revealed that the lack of in-home, partner support strongly influences how single parents carry out their roles and responsibilities (Cigno & Burke, 1997). Single parents ranked contact with the school and the need to connect with families in similar circumstances as even more important when they did not have a partner at home with whom to share parenting roles. These parents also needed assistance with transportation and in planning for the future.

If the major characteristics of single-parent families are that they are headed by females, face economic challenges, and are short on time and energy, then surely Marie Manning and her family are typical. Read Figure 1–3 for a glimpse into her family.

A different pattern of family size and form—more than two parents—exists when one or both parents in the original family have remarried. The new blended family may include children from two or more marriages. Children may regard their acceptance of a stepparent as a sign of disloyalty to their biological parent. They may have to abide by different rules in two different households, adapt to two different lifestyles, or surrender the adult roles they may have assumed while their custodial parent was single. Stepparents may be uncertain about their authority. Because they have a ready-made family from the first day of their marriage, parents may not have the privacy or time to establish their new relationship. Finally, negotiations among all of the adults—the former and current spouses—may be necessary to resolve conflicts over the children and their visitation schedules, discipline, lifestyle, and so on. On the positive side, a wide circle of interested family members may be able and willing to support both each other and the member with the exceptionality.

A national survey of parents of students enrolled in grades 1 through 12 indicated that biological parents are more likely than stepparents to attend school meetings, parent-teacher conferences, and school events (U.S. Department of Education, 2001). The lowest level of involvement is from stepfathers; approximately two thirds of students living with stepfathers have a stepfather who participated in one or no school activities.

You would do well to be sensitive to the various roles that adults play in single-parent or remarried families in making decisions about a child's education. When the adults convene, they may engage in an amiable discussion about the child's best interests. Or, they may create a family power struggle, requiring you or other professionals to mediate differences and state what you believe is best for the child. You may want to consult the school social worker or school counselor for suggestions on

FIGURE 1–3
My Voice: A Single Parent Amidst the Challenges

"I need $6 for a shirt for school, Mom," my 11-year-old son, Zack, declared one afternoon after school. For the first time in 4 years, he was able to participate in field day, having surmounted his autism and behavioral challenges with the help of a classroom assistant. The celebration was bittersweet for me, however. There was no doubt that he deserved a team shirt, but money is always in short supply for a single mother with two children.

Moreover, the personal anxiety of caring for Zack's every single need, maintaining every single appointment for him, and putting out every single fire with the school while juggling every financial burden often seemed insurmountable.

Zack's aggressiveness was erratic at times and required many teacher conferences, IEP meetings, and appointments with behavior specialists and psychiatrists to regulate his behavior and monitor his medication. I found myself leaving work early at least once a week to take him to appointments or attend conferences with the school. Ensuring that my son's needs were met forced me to be in two places at once: he needed me, and I had to work to support us.

The substantial child-support checks that I had been receiving had dissipated and I couldn't even make enough to cover our medical insurance premiums or offset the lack of child support. Financially, we were quickly falling behind in our obligations. My only option was to continue my education full-time, in hopes of a better life in the future. Not only would going to school full-time accelerate my career, but it also would allow me to take advantage of a full scholarship at a local university and free me up to help ensure that Zack's needs were met. But that option posed a great financial burden and presented unforeseen challenges.

One challenge was to detangle the maze of public services that could assist us while I was in school. It was imperative that my son would not run out of medication so I had to turn to the state's Mental Health and Mental Retardation (MHMR) program and the federal Supplemental Security Income (SSI) benefits for help. Qualifying Zack for these benefits took excessive amounts of patience and energy. Although the services helped us survive, they also caused additional strain that never had to be tackled in the past. The systems are so overtaxed that one mishap, such as arriving late for an appointment or not locating a correct document, caused extreme delays or even potential loss of benefits.

Another challenge was getting Zack to the counseling and psychiatry appointments and minimizing their domino effect on the structure and routine of our daily schedule. When he left school early for an appointment, he lost class time and was assigned additional homework, creating havoc with his nightly routine. There were periods when there was no relief from the negative phone calls from school, the worry of missing an appointment, and the anxiety of whether the public services would pull me through. Challenges such as helping Zack with hours of daily homework conflicted with simpler things such as coaxing him to eat, encouraging him to take a shower, helping him to brush his teeth, and vainly attempting to spend a few minutes with my daughter so she would not get lost in the chaos of disability and financial stress.

During these times, we were a family on a limited income and borrowed time. Additional complexities left me with little wiggle room both financially and emotionally. My stomach would churn with anxiety when any additional costs arose, including the much-needed extracurricular activities and even the $6 shirt. One spring, I held my breath as I wrote out a check for my son to join a soccer team for students with special needs. I was concerned about both his behavioral concerns and our family's financial issues. Past experiences had proven that not everyone was compassionate enough to work with students with special needs, and throwing money in the street would have been less painful than to spend it on a doomed-to-fail extracurricular activity. The previous fall, Zack had taken an interest in baseball and asked me to put him on a team. I spent over $200 for baseball enrollment fees and equipment, and he didn't even remain on the team long enough to get a uniform before the coach asked me not to bring him anymore. My anxieties about soccer were answered when he played his first game with the team.

"That's the most fun I ever had losing!" Zack exclaimed as he ran off the soccer field. My heart was overfilled with joy, and tears trickled down my face. I was overwhelmed with his success and completely understood his exuberance. Although I am fighting a losing battle financially and the daily stresses drain the energy out of me, being a parent of such a dynamic child overshadows all of it.

His spirit and personality shine through everything else. Our daily successes allow me to recharge. I get excitement out of the simple things like watching him tie his own shoe or cook his own Pop-tart.

These small achievements and others, such as Zack's remembering to bring his homework home or talking about his day, often appear to other people as

(continued)

FIGURE 1–3
Continued

commonplace events, but they allow me to put our financial strain in perspective and help me to recharge emotionally. In a world where daily struggles are a fact of life, the simple celebrations of minor achievements can be of major importance.

There is nothing more exciting to me than when someone else tries to grasp the complexities of a life as a single parent who has a child with special needs. The teachers who have had the most success with Zack have overlooked inconsequential issues, such as whether he uses a pen or pencil on an assignment, and

instead celebrated the fact that he completed his assignment and turned it in on time. We have found that Zack's small steps often cause goals that were considered unobtainable and that such non-issues as pencil or pen lead to needless and hurtful confrontation and conflict. It is better to celebrate than criticize, especially when a family has only one parent and few resources other than themselves.

Marie Manning
University of North Texas

how to be most supportive in especially challenging situations.

Cultural Background

Cultural and Microcultural Characteristics.

Just as your own cultural background influences what you value, how you think, and how you behave, so each student and family will also be highly influenced by their own cultural backgrounds.

The term *culture* refers to the foundational values and beliefs that set the standards for how people perceive, interpret, and behave within their family, school, and community. Sometimes people refer to culture as consisting only of a person's race or ethnicity (generally defined to include one's national origin, religion, and race) (Gollnick & Chinn, 2002). Although race and ethnicity are major influences in one's culture, many other influences constitute one's cultural identity. These multiple influences are *microcultures* (Gollnick & Chinn, 2002). Figure 1–4 illustrates the microcultures that create a person's overall cultural identity.

Each of these microcultures influences family-professional partnerships in many different ways.

- *Religion,* as well as beliefs and customs, influences the holidays that families celebrate and thus the appropriateness of your communication with them concerning holiday events, schedules, and rituals.
- *Language* influences all aspects of communicating with families, especially when families do not speak English at all or are unable to read in English or any other language.
- *Gender* influences beliefs about the roles that various family members should take in communicating with professionals.

- *Race* increases the likelihood that people will experience racism and discrimination, which fosters skepticism about trusting others of a different race.
- *Ethnicity* influences whether people think they belong or whether they perceive themselves as outsiders in schools.
- *Age* influences the experiences parents have, as in the case of teenage mothers who suddenly find themselves with parental responsibilities.
- *Geography* poses certain opportunities and barriers to partnerships, such as in rural settings when families live a long distance from school without public transportation.
- *Income* influences the resources available to families and the extent to which their housing, medical care, and nutrition are adequate.

Microcultures shape the particular cultural beliefs of families. For example, a White religious fundamentalist from the Midwestern Bible Belt who is the father of a child with a learning disability may have world views that differ from those of an African American Muslim from the inner city of a large Eastern metropolis whose child is deaf. Similarly, the African American Muslim may have world views different from those of newly immigrated intact Vietnamese family members who were highly paid professionals and leaders in their Roman Catholic church and whose child has extraordinary mathematical or scientific talents.

Different cultural attributes (not just racial or ethnic) exist in each of these three families. These attributes may change over the family's lifespan. One family may change its religion or choose atheism; another's economic status may improve or decline precipitously. Still another family may be influenced by racial or religious intermarriage. Disability status also can influence one's cultural affili-

FIGURE 1–4
Cultural Identity Shaped Through Microcultural Groups

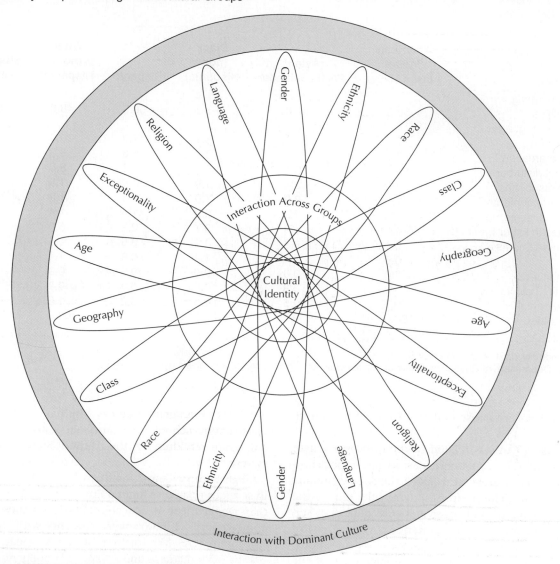

Source: From Gollnick, D. M., & Chinn, P. C. (2002). *Multicultural education in a pluralistic society* (6th ed.), © 2004. Reprinted by permission of Pearson Education, Inc., Upper Saddle River, NJ.

tions, such as the strong group identity known as *Deaf culture* (Scheetz, 2004).

Racial/Ethnic Composition of Special Education.   Figure 1–5 sets out the percentages of students in special education according to different racial/ethnic groups and categories of exceptionality. Compare and contrast the information in this table. Note the disproportionate representation of students—particularly African American students (who comprise 16% of children and youth in the general population)—in the categorical programs of mental retardation and emotional disturbance.

As you will see from the data, African American students are approximately twice as likely to be enrolled in programs for students with mental retardation than in any other program (U.S. Department of Education, 2002). They also are more likely to be identified as having emotional disturbance than other students. They are only half as likely to be enrolled in programs for students who are gifted and talented (Daniels, 1998; Ford, 1998). Ford (1998) cited data from the 1992 Office of Civil Rights Study indicating that African American, Hispanic, and Native American students were underrepresented by 40% to 50% in gifted education. In contrast, European American

FIGURE 1–5

Percentage of Students Ages 6 Through 21 Served Under the Individuals with Disabilities Education Act (IDEA) During the 2000–2001 School Year

Disability	American/ Indian Alaska Native	Asian/ Pacific Islander	Black (non-Hispanic)	Hispanic	White (non-Hispanic)	All Students Served
Specific learning disabilities	56.3	43.2	45.2	60.3	48.9	50.0
Speech or language impairments	17.1	25.2	15.1	17.3	20.8	18.9
Mental retardation	8.5	10.1	18.9	8.6	9.3	10.6
Emotional disturbance	7.5	5.3	10.7	4.5	8.0	8.2
Multiple disabilities	2.5	2.3	1.9	1.8	1.8	2.1
Hearing impairments	1.1	2.9	1.0	1.5	1.2	1.2
Orthopedic impairments	0.8	2.0	0.9	1.4	1.4	1.3
Other health impairments	4.1	3.9	3.7	2.8	5.9	5.1
Visual impairments	0.4	0.8	0.4	0.5	0.5	0.4
Autism	0.6	3.4	1.2	0.9	1.4	1.4
Deaf-blindness	0.0	0.0	0.0	0.0	0.0	0.0
Traumatic brain injury	0.3	0.3	0.2	0.2	0.3	0.3
Developmental delay	0.7	0.6	0.7	0.2	0.6	0.5
All disabilities	100.0	100.0	100.0	100.0	100.0	100.0

Note: Does not include data for New York State.
Source: U.S. Department of Education, Office of Special Education Programs, Data Analysis System (DANS).

students were overrepresented by 17% and Asian American students by 43%.

An analysis of trends related to the disproportionate representation of African American students in special education revealed a great deal about the socioeconomic status of students. The poorer the family, the greater the chances the student will receive special education services. Further, families who experience poverty often live in communities that lack resources for schools (National Research Council, 2002). The positive interaction of culture, socioeconomic status, and geographic location underscores that family characteristics are not discrete but are highly interrelated and overlapping (Oswald, Coutinho, Best, & Singh, 1999).

Immigration and Limited English Proficiency. Immigration trends strongly influence the extent of cultural diversity in schools. The 2000 U.S. Census revealed that approximately 10% of the population has immigrated and accounts for approximately 28.5 million individuals (approximately 8.5 million are school-age children), the highest percentage of immigrants in 70 years. The number of school-age children who are immigrants is predicted to double in the future, based on the

number of immigrant mothers who have young children approaching school age (Camarota, 2001). Over half of immigrant children in the United States experience poverty.

Slightly more than 2.5 million students were enrolled in services related to limited English proficiency in 1997 (U.S. Department of Education, 2001). Of these, 5.5% or approximately 145,000 were students with disabilities. Approximately 73% of the students speak Spanish, 4% speak Vietnamese, and 2% speak Hmong. Additionally, approximately 2.5% of the students with limited English proficiency speak one of 29 different Native American languages (Fleischman & Hopstock, 1993). Approximately three fourths of students with limited English proficiency are eligible for free or reduced-price lunch as contrasted to about one third of all students. It is especially important to ensure that students with disabilities who have limited English proficiency are fairly evaluated for special education services and also in documenting their educational achievement. Because of the differences in culture, language, learning, and behavior, sometimes students with limited English proficiency are particularly vulnerable for discrimination in evaluation processes (U.S. Department of Education, 2001).

FIGURE 1–6

Tips for Communicating with Parents Who Are Immigrants and Do Not Speak English Through Using Interpreters

- Learn proper protocols and forms of address (including a few greetings and social phrases) in the family's primary language, the names they wish to be called, and the correct pronunciation.
- Introduce yourself and the interpreter, describe your respective roles, and clarify mutual expectations and the purpose of the encounter.
- Learn basic words and sentences in the family's language and become familiar with special terminology they may use so you can selectively attend to them during interpreter-family exchanges.
- During the interaction, address your remarks and questions directly to the family (not the interpreter); look at and listen to family members as they speak, and observe their nonverbal communication.
- Avoid body language or gestures that may be offensive or misunderstood.
- Use a positive tone of voice and facial expressions that sincerely convey respect for and interest in the family. Address the family in a calm, unhurried manner.
- Speak clearly and somewhat more slowly but not more loudly.

- Limit your remarks and questions to a few sentences between translations and avoid giving too much information or long, complex discussions of several topics in a single session.
- Avoid technical jargon, colloquialisms, idioms, slang, and abstractions.
- Avoid oversimplification and condensing important explanations.
- Give instructions in a clear, logical sequence; emphasize key words or points; and offer reasons for specific recommendations.
- Periodically check on the family's understanding and the accuracy of the translation by asking the family to repeat instructions or whatever has been communicated in their own words, with the interpreter facilitating, but avoid literally asking, "Do you understand?"
- When possible, reinforce verbal information with materials written in the family's language and visual aids or behavioral modeling if appropriate. Before introducing written materials, tactfully determine the client's literacy level through the interpreter.
- Be patient and prepared for the additional time that will inevitably be required for careful interpretation.

Source: Lynch, E. W., & Hanson, M. J. (1998). *Developing cross cultural competence: A guide to working with children and their families* (2nd ed.). Baltimore: Paul H. Brookes Publishing Company. Reprinted by permission.

Many families of children with disabilities who have limited English proficiency identify communication as a huge barrier to developing trusting partnerships. Research with Latino parents has consistently revealed that limited English proficiency is highly influential in the extent to which the appropriate supports are provided to students and families (Bailey et al., 1999; Lian & Fontánez-Phelan, 2001; Shapiro, Monzo, Rueda, Gomez, & Blacher, 2004). Research with Korean families reached a similar conclusion; language limitations are very significant. A Korean mother of a student receiving special education services described this challenge as follows:

A bunch of papers are coming from the school. I don't know what is important and what is not. So, I always stack them on the table, hoping my husband can read them to find really important papers. My child often misses field trips because I could not read the directions and the papers. English is such a problem. (Park & Turnball, 2001, p. 137)

To foster trusting partnerships, some special education professionals will need to be multilingual or have access to interpreters (Al-Hassan & Gardner, 2002). All professionals need to honor cultural diversity and develop cultural competence. Figure 1–6 includes tips for communicating with parents who are immigrants and do not speak English.

Differences in Cultural Values. Language and communication challenges are not the only factors that affect your relationships with families. Cultural values play a huge role. In this section, we will address two of the fundamental values that typically come into play as you work with families from different cultures. Some families will adopt an *individualistic perspective,* in contrast to a *collective perspective;* and some families will have less confidence in *system-centered solutions* than in *relationship-centered solutions.*

Individualism Versus Collectivism.   The most dominant racial/ethnic microculture in the United States is European American. This microculture typically values individualism, self-reliance, early achievement of developmental milestones, and competition with others (Hanson, 2004; Kalyanpur & Harry, 1999).

> For example, politicians today still strive to point to humble roots and their climb to a higher status, much like heroes such as Abraham Lincoln. As Althen (1988) related, Americans revere those who do things the biggest, the best, or first; hence, the fascination with sports legends such as Jesse Owens, Jackie Robinson, and Babe Ruth; aviator heroes such as Charles Lindbergh, Amelia Earhart; and astronauts such as Neil Armstrong and Sally Ride. (Hanson, 2004, p. 91)

The individualistic perspective is a fundamental premise of special education (Kalyanpur & Harry, 1999). As you will learn in chapter 6, federal policy requires that special education instruction focus on *individual* outcomes. Students with disabilities have individualized education programs that target their individual levels of performance and then specify goals and objectives to be achieved. A state-of-the-art curriculum emphasizes self-determination, fostering autonomy and individual decision making (Wehmeyer, 2002). That curriculum may be countercultural for some families but highly culturally valued by others. Culture will influence not only what the family wants for their child's curriculum, but also, as we point out in chapter 10, whether the family chooses to be a partner with professionals or to defer to professionals.

Similarly, students who are gifted are rewarded in highly individualistic ways by winning contests (for example, national essay contests), achieving National Merit status on the college board examination, and earning admission to prestigious colleges and universities. These educational practices strongly influence families' expectations for their children and their own child-raising practices.

By contrast, some racial/ethnic microcultures emphasize *collectivism*, which values the group more strongly than the individual (Frankland, Turnbull, Wehmeyer, & Blackmountain, in press; Kalyanpur & Harry, 1999). Within the African American culture, a group orientation seems to be valued over private gain (Logan, 2001; Willis, 2004). Similarly, in Asian cultures, individuals are expected to have the family as the central focus of their lives and to engender ". . . primary loyalty, mutual obligation, cooperation, interdependence, and reciprocity" (Chan & Lee, 2004, p. 252). The Middle Eastern belief that "children are like canes in the hands of old parents" expresses quite well the collective obligation that family members have to each other (Sharifzadeh, 2004, p. 391).

What is the relevance of individualism and collectivism for developing trusting partnerships with families? There are two implications—one affecting process and the other affecting curriculum and outcomes. With respect to process, some families may regard individualized education programs as contradictory to their orientation of collective, cooperative, and mutually reciprocal priorities. With respect to curriculum, some families may not be interested in their child's accomplishing developmental milestones or specific academic tasks if the accomplishment singles out their child for special attention, acclaim, or recognition. Similarly, some families may be far more interested in having their children learn to take care of the home and elderly family members rather than acquiring job skills in a competitive industry (Frankland et al., in press).

System-Centered Versus Relationship-Centered Approaches.   Members of the dominant racial/ethnic group—European Americans—typically expect solutions for disability-related problems to be system based; that is, they expect solutions to be guided by federal and state policy and to be implemented at the state and local levels. This viewpoint emphasizes two contrasting theories of normalcy: the pathological model from medicine and the statistical model from psychology. The pathological model seeks to identify the "pathology" within the child and to "fix" it through technological and knowledge-based solutions. The statistical model seeks to identify an individual's deviations from those projected on the normal curve and to provide remediation to the individual to make up for the deviation (Kalyanpur & Harry, 1999; Turnbull & Stowe, 2001). It is no surprise that this value is reflected in the legal underpinnings of special education and that the vast majority of families who participate in policy-reform advocacy are European American, middle class, and upper-middle-class families (Turnbull & Turnbull, 1996; Zirpoli, Wieck, Hancox, & Skarnulis, 1994).

By contrast, members of many diverse racial/ethnic groups regard personal relationships, not policies and procedures, as the bases of decision making (Harry, Kalyanpur, & Day, 1999; Kalyanpur & Harry, 1999; Lynch & Hanson, 2004; Shapiro et al., 2004).

> Manifesting real interest in the client rather than gaining data via referral sheets or obtaining many behavioral details about a problem is essential given the Mexican American emphasis on *personalism,* or building personal relationships. Similarly, a therapist who suggests an explicit contract about number of sessions or treatment goals may be too task—rather than person—oriented.
>
> The therapist might assign "conditional homework," that is, asking the family to think about or to engage in a particular task should the occasion arise. Such a technique is co

sonant with a culture that values serendipity, chance, and spontaneity in interpersonal relationships. Conversely, Mexicans would not be comfortable with the idea of scheduling certain times to be intimate, express affection, or resolve problems. (Falicov, 1996, p. 177)

Similarly, the native Hawaiian culture emphasizes relationships with other people but also with the community at large, the land, and the spiritual world (Mokuau & Tauili'ili, 2004). And Native American cultures strongly prize relationships with nature, especially those that promote a sense of harmony (Joe & Malach, 2004).

What does this mean as you seek to develop partnerships with families? For one thing, the legal and bureaucratic referral and evaluation process to determine whether a student has an exceptionality, and the educational implications of that finding and of individualizing special education services (chapters 11, 12, and 13), may be culturally inappropriate for families who approach their child's education from a relationship orientation. You may need to spend significant time establishing genuine relationships before you and the family start making educational decisions. This has major implications for your time—a rare commodity for many professionals— and your willingness to establish personal familiarity as the basis for trust. Whereas many European American professionals and families may be eager "to get to the bottom line" in a meeting, many families from culturally diverse backgrounds may prefer to spend much more time, especially up-front time, on building relationships. In addition, people with an established personal relationship with the family can be part of their circle of support in collaborating with you and other professionals. Not all encounters need to be two-way (between an educator and a parent only); rather, the family's other trusted partners—members of the family's cultural communities and tribes—can make valuable contributions to family-professional partnerships (Frankland et al., in press; Zuniga, 2004).

We have discussed two ways that cultural values may differ, but other variations occur within and across microcultures and cultures (Kalyanpur & Harry, 1999; Lynch & Hanson, 2004). You will learn about many other cultural variations in chapters 2 through 13.

To appreciate the significance of a cultural variation, reflect on how your brothers or sisters, cousins, or other family members are like or unlike you. Are you sometimes surprised that people who are members of the same microcultures and who even share family experiences can have remarkably different values?

Because it is essential to honor families' cultural diversity in order to be partners with them, we will repeatedly suggest how you can develop trusting partnerships with families who have diverse cultural traditions. Bear in mind that, whatever a family's stereotypical cultural characteristics may be (that is, whatever they "should" be if they meet all or most of the characteristics of families from the same microcultures), some families will defy the stereotype. They will display traits from their own cultural traditions, as well as personal traits not strongly associated with their cultural traditions. We caution you against pigeonholing a family solely on the basis of certain microcultures; that is too simplified an approach.

Socioeconomic Status

A family's socioeconomic status (SES) includes its income, the level of family members' education, and the social status associated with the occupations of its wage earners. Here, disability and SES factors interact with each other quite dramatically. Figure 1–7 provides data comparing the economic status of households of youth with disabilities with the status of families who have youth in the general population.

What are the similarities between youth with disabilities and youth in the general population for head of household's education, annual household income, and percentage of households receiving government benefits? Youth with disabilities typically come from families with less education and less family income. Families with a higher socioeconomic status have more resources available to them to address exceptionality issues. Indeed, the ability to pay for services and a higher level of education are resources that can help families solve their problems successfully.

As you learned when reading about cultural diversity, a strong relationship exists between the identification of children as having a disability and some racial/ethnic groups, with poverty a confounding factor. The National Research Council (2002) documented that children from racially/ethnically diverse backgrounds are much more likely to be members of families with low income. Given the higher rate of African American students placed in special education, it is noteworthy that African Americans have been approximately 2.5 times more likely than European Americans to experience poverty (Fujiura & Yamaki, 2000). The higher disability rate among children from diverse racial groups appears to be primarily associated with a higher incidence of families who experience poverty and who are headed by a single parent.

Although nearly one in five American children lives in poverty (Children's Defense Fund, 1999), the poverty rate is even higher for families who have children with disabilities (Fujiura & Yamaki, 2000). Figure 1–8 indicates that approximately one third of students with disabilities come from a household where the annual

FIGURE 1–7

Profile of Household Socioeconomic Status of Youth with Disabilities and Youth in the General Population

Individual Characteristics	Youth with Disabilities	Youth in the General Population
Head of household's education (percentage)		
Less than high school	21.5	13.3
High school graduate or GED*	41.4	29.7
Some college	23.6	28.8
Bachelor's degree or more	13.6	28.3
Annual household income (percentage)		
Less than $25,000	34.9	19.8
$25,000 to $50,000	30.4	25.5
More than $50,000	34.7	54.7
Percentage recently receiving:		
AFDC**/TANF***	10.5	8.6
Food Stamps	16.2	14.2
Head of household's employment (percentage)		
Not employed	18.4	NA
Part-time	7.9	NA
Full-time	73.8	NA

Source: U.S. Department of Education (2002). *To assure the free appropriate public education of all children with disabilities: Twenty-fourth annual report to Congress on the implementation of the Individuals With Disabilities Education Act.* Washington, DC: Author.
*GED = General Education Degree
** AFDC = Aid to Families with Dependent Children
*** TANF = Temporary Assistance for Needy Families

income is less than $25,000 (U.S. Department of Education, 2002).

According to the U.S. Department of Education (2002), the odds that a child will receive special education services are 1.5 times greater for children living in poverty than for children who do not live in poverty. Poverty typically does not occur in isolation; it is associated with a number of other demographic characteristics related to the parents' education and the family structure (single- or two-parent families).

- The IQ scores of children who live in poverty average about 5 to 13 points lower than IQ scores of children from middle-class backgrounds (Kaiser & Delaney, 1996; Korenman, Miller, & Sjaastad, 1995).
- The size of a student's vocabulary is the most important predictor of reading success, but families from lower SES backgrounds are much more likely to have children with reduced rates in vocabulary growth and use (Hart & Risley, 1995).
- The high school dropout rate is approximately 11% for students whose family incomes are in the bottom 20% of the income distribution, 5% for students from middle-income families, and 2.1% for students in the

top 20% of family income (Kaufman, Kwon, Klein, & Chapman, 2000).

The impact of family income occurs not only at the student and family level but also at the school level. Schools are often characterized as low SES or high SES schools; as you will learn in chapter 6, the federal No Child Left Behind Act characterizes these schools as Title 1 or disadvantaged schools. The National Research Council (2002) reported that schools with a high concentration of children from low-income background have lower per-student expenditures and fewer experienced, well-trained teachers than schools with a high concentration of children from middle-income and upper middle-income backgrounds. They also reported that parent advocacy is less likely to occur in schools with a high concentration of students from poverty backgrounds.

Some family researchers have theorized that families with limited SES resources may be well justified in believing that they have little control over their environment (Kaplan & Girard, 1994; Sidel, 1996), so very few will plan for any child's future, let alone the future of a child with an exceptionality. Some families with lower SES re-

FIGURE 1–8

Advocacy in Action: Being a Hero for Homeless Families and Their Children

Do homeless children, especially those with disabilities, receive the same quality of education as children who live in stable homes? If you said, "Of course they don't," you would be correct. Compared to their peers who are not homeless, these children change schools more often, face unique legal and transportation barriers to school enrollment and attendance, receive fewer services to address their academic and social/emotional needs, and have parents who face challenges, particularly poverty, that are more pressing than their children's education.

Do homeless families participate in their children's education in the same ways as families who can provide a stable home? Again, the answer is self-evident: No. If a parent has to choose between finding a place to live and food to eat, on the one hand, and being a partner with educators, the parent will be a provider before being a partner.

The challenge, then, is to develop a system that enhances the opportunities for the children and their families to receive a free and appropriate education, consistent with federal special education and homeless-services laws. These laws require state and local educational agencies to provide an appropriate education to students with disabilities and to students who are homeless.

In Nashville, Tennessee, the Home, Educator, Readiness, and Opportunity (HERO) program operates out of the school district's social work and school attendance division and addresses the many needs that families and children have. There are two overriding needs.

The first relates to the families' many needs and how service agencies operate. Like many families and students with disabilities, but more so because of their poverty and mobility, the families and students have "horizontal" needs but live in a world where responses are "vertical." They need to benefit from school but they also need access to social services, public health services, and mental health centers. All the needs are connected—they are horizontal. Without good physical and mental health, for example, it is unlikely that the students will get as much out of being in school as they might otherwise. Yet schools and other agencies are organized as separate systems; they are vertical systems, relatively separated from each other. So, HERO helps coordinate the services; it makes the vertical systems less vertical and helps families and children meet their horizontal needs.

The second overriding need relates to the students' educational needs and their families' participation in their education. The HERO program operates at many different levels. It tracks school attendance of children who are admitted to the city's homeless shelters, identifies truancy, and tries to learn why a student is truant and then to correct the causes. It informs parents about the rights that their children have to remain in their "school of origin" and not be bounced from one school within the district to another as their parents move from shelter to shelter. It helps arrange or pay for transportation so students can go from any shelter to their schools of origin. It provides for after-school tutoring in the shelters and for holiday and summertime recreational opportunities. It collects school supplies and clothing from the schools' clothing centers and delivers them to the students. Finally, it shows parents how they can support their children to do homework and develop socially and emotionally, assisting the parents to follow up on their children's schooling and increasing the students' attendance rates.

Coordinating services between agencies and *home*—that's the "H" in HERO. Supporting students to receive an appropriate *education*—that's the "E" in HERO. Making sure they are *ready* to attend school and have the clothing and supplies they need—that's the "R" in HERO. And making sure that all agencies work together so the students and families have *opportunities*—that's the "O" in HERO.

Put these four elements together, and add "A" in front of them—to stand for *advocacy*—and you get a personalized message: A HERO is anyone who identifies a great need and responds to it.

Source: Adapted from Davey, T. L., Penuel, W. R., Allison-Tant, E., & Rosner, A. M. (2000). The HERO program: A case for school social work services. *Social Work in Education, 22*(3), 177–190. Copyright 2000, National Association of Social Workers, Inc., Social Work in Education.

ources, these theorists argue, may have difficulty considering future options for their child and may be caught unprepared when it is time for their child to enter new programs (for example, finding a long waiting list at a child-care program). Furthermore, because families with lower SES resources may believe it is useless to try to plan ahead, theorists believe these families may be relatively inactive in working with professionals to make plans for their children's education and transition from school to adulthood.

Other researchers have pointed out that many families from low socioeconomic backgrounds are vitally interested in special education issues (Harry, 1992a, 1992b). An in-depth study of 12 Puerto Rican parents from low-income backgrounds revealed the parents' cogent insights about labeling, curriculum and bilingual issues, efficacy of special versus general education placement, and methods for teaching reading (Harry, 1992b) and concluded:

> This study shows that the power of parents may be seriously undermined by culturally different ways of understanding. Yet it also shows that poor parents, with little formal education, and a different language and culture, may, through their own analysis of their children's difficulties, have a significant contribution to make to current debates in the field of special education. (Harry, 1992b, p. 38)

In every relationship with families, including those from low-income backgrounds, we encourage you to demonstrate respect, be nonjudgmental, and recognize their unique strengths and important contributions. That is the point made by an inner-city mother of an infant as she described the importance of a home visitor's informality and nonintrusive questions:

> She [the previous early intervention specialist] came out to the house when [the child] was 8 months [old], and she said, "He has problems," and I said, "No, he don't, he's just a baby".... She asks me all kinds of stuff like if I have a crib, how many people live here, and she writes it down. She was a nosy lady, nosy, nosy! I kept hiding from her, and finally I moved so they wouldn't bug me....When she [the current specialist] came out, I thought, "Oh, gee, here we go again." So I asked her, "What's wrong?" and she just says, "Nothing, I just want to know if you need anything." (Summers et al., 1990, p. 87)

As you become a trusted partner with families, you will become less like the previous early intervention specialist this mother described and more like the specialist who sought to find a relevant connection with her. In chapter 9, you will learn more about communicating with families, including those who experience poverty; in chapter 10, you will learn how to help families connect with community agencies that can assist them to meet their basic needs.

Parents who have children without disabilities who are from working-class backgrounds differ from parents of upper-middle-class backgrounds with respect to partnerships between homes and schools (Lareau, 1987, 1989). Working-class families tend to defer decision-making responsibility to educators. By contrast, upper-middle-class parents tend to believe it is important to be informed of their children's progress and to be involved in educational decision making. A key difference in these orientations is the perceived control that the families anticipate having over their child's education and within the family-professional partnership.

Indeed, Head Start children who had parents who were more responsive to them and more frequently communicated the importance of their schoolwork had higher academic outcomes than Head Start children whose parents were less responsive and less intent on academic achievement (Robinson, Weinberg, Redden, Ramey, & Ramey, 1998). The families of students who were more high-achieving still had a low SES level (the majority had monthly incomes of less than $1,000), but the mothers reflected values that are typically more associated with families at higher SES levels.

The theory that families at lower SES levels may perceive less control and be less interested in educational partnerships may hold true for some families. But for others, the theory simply does not apply—nor should it. In our experience, a family's SES is not a wholly reliable indicator of its motivation or knowledge/skills to develop family-professional partnerships.

Your role as a professional is to encourage predictable, nonjudgmental, and trusting partnerships that convey to all families regardless of SES that you respect them and recognize their strengths. You will learn more later in this chapter about special challenges associated with homelessness, and you will learn in all chapters how to establish trusting partnerships with families from all socioeconomic levels.

Geographic Location

As a result of electronic media and increased mobility in most segments of society, regional differences in family values and forms are receding. Yet regional patterns remain; Southern hospitality, Yankee stoicism, Midwestern conformity, and Western independence remain attributes of many families (McGill & Pearce, 1996). Rural and urban factors also significantly influence service delivery and family life (Kozol, 1995; U.S. Department of Education, 1995, 1996).

According to the U.S. Department of Education (1995), approximately 475,000 students with disabilities receive special education services in rural school districts. As compared to their peers in urban areas, students in rural areas tend to experience more poverty over a longer period of time. In addition, their special education services may suffer because of particular challenges. The population of rural areas may fluctuate as local industries close, reducing the tax base and talent base simultaneously. It is difficult to provide appropriate services in the least restrictive environment when students are far-spread. Many school districts create consolidated (jointly operated) special education programs and transport students to them rather than dispersing the specialists across the school district's entire, widespread area. Distance impedes opportunities for teachers and families to enter into face-to-face partnerships. Life in a rural environment also hinders the recruitment and retention of highly qualified teachers and other specialists. On the other hand, rural areas often provide social support from informal networks such as neighbors, churches, and civic/social organizations (Thurston, 1996). Some school districts use video- and teleconferencing to link teachers, specialists, and parents.

Urban areas have their own set of challenges (U.S. Department of Education, 1996). Schools in urban areas enroll almost twice as many African American and Hispanic students as do nonurban areas (U.S. Department of Commerce, 1992) and have a much larger percentage of students of limited English proficiency than other schools (Valdés, Williamson, & Wagner, 1990). It is sometimes difficult to evaluate whether urban students have a disability, given the complicated effects of poverty, race/ethnicity, and limited English proficiency. Inner-city school districts struggle to recruit and retain qualified personnel. Living in a complicated, energy-draining urban environment makes teacher-parent partnerships difficult to create.

> So long as the most vulnerable people in our population are consigned to places that the rest of us will shun and flee and view with fear, I'm afraid that educational denial, medical and economic devastation, and aesthetic degradation will be virtually inevitable . . . so long as there are ghetto neighborhoods and ghetto hospitals and ghetto schools, I'm convinced there will be ghetto desperation, ghetto violence, and ghetto fear because a ghetto is itself an evil and unnatural construction. (Kozol, 1995, p. 162)

Not all families are locked into a particular place, and some families move in order to find services. A mother of two children with hearing impairments remarked:

> We lived in a small town where they had almost nothing . . . in the schools. We decided that if our children were to get an education, we would have to move; so we started looking at programs all over the country . . . . Finally we settled on Starr King because it had a first-rate oral program. My husband had to quit a good job; we moved to [another town and], he had to search for another job and take a cut in pay. But it was worth it! (Spradley & Spradley, 1978, pp. 214–215)

Military families, migrant farm workers, construction workers, corporate executives, and others have jobs that require them to relocate frequently. How can you minimize the worries that often accompany a family's reloca-

tion? Communicate with and secure records from the student's previous school. Avoid asking routine family and medical history questions except when the information you absolutely need is not in the records or when families want to retell their story. Offer relocated families a tour of the school their child will attend; describe its programs; introduce the family and student to the staff and other families in the program. When working with families who have immigrated into the United States, determine how much English they know and, if their English is limited, what their native language is; some of them may not be literate in their native language and may try to conceal that from you. Smoothe out their relocation in every possible way.

In describing family characteristics, we have emphasized how families are the same yet different. Their size and forms, cultural backgrounds, socioeconomic levels, and geographic locations each present unique challenges. Yet the underlying common themes in your effort to build partnerships with them are constant: (1) respect their values, (2) try to understand the many issues they face, in addition to their child's exceptionality, (3) be creative as you try to capitalize on their strengths and resources, and (4) be open to forming partnerships that address their greatest needs.

CHARACTERISTICS OF INDIVIDUAL MEMBERS

The commonality and diversity of families persist when we take into account the individual characteristics of each member of the family. These personal characteristics include the child's exceptionality, each family member's skills in managing life, mental and physical health, communication style, and motivation. These characteristics can either strengthen or limit the family as a whole. They affect the family's response to the exceptionality of one of its members and the family's inclination and ability to be partners with professionals. We will focus in this section on the characteristics of the child's exceptionality and the life management skills of family members.

Characteristics of a Child's Exceptionality

The family as a whole and each of its members respond to a family member's exceptional characteristics. These characteristics include (1) the nature of the exceptionality (for example, is the student gifted?) and (2) the extent or degree of the exceptionality (for example, is the student's disability mild or severe?).

Nature of the Exceptionality. The nature of the exceptionality influences the family's response to it. For example, the families of children who have medically complex needs often adapt their routines to provide continuous care. They often have special needs for illness-specific information, equipment, and financial assistance (Batshaw, 2002). A child with a hearing impairment needs communication accommodations that may include interpreters or equipment such as special telephones and captioned television (Jackson & Turnbull, in press). Families who have a child who is gifted may feel unusual responsibility to help their child reach his or her highest potential. The family also may experience social challenges when peers and even siblings become jealous of their child's success (Friedman, 2000). Likewise, the primary concerns of parents of children with emotional disorders, attention deficit/hyperactivity disorder, head injury, and autism often relate to the child's problem behavior and the family's appropriate response to it (Baker et al., 2003; Fidler, Hodapp, & Dykens, 2000; Hastings & Brown, 2002; Stein, Efron, Schiff, & Glanzman, 2002). Regardless of the type of disability, if the child has problem behavior, the family undoubtedly will benefit from a supporting partnership to minimize the problem behavior and to teach their child appropriate behavior (Turnbull & Ruef, 1997).

There is no clear-cut evidence that the particular nature of the disability alone can predict how parents, siblings, or extended family will respond and adapt to the disability (Blacher & Hatton, 2001). Each exceptionality poses its own special needs, including the need to form partnerships with specialists and with other families similarly affected.

If you assume that a disability invariably burdens a family, you would be wrong. Children and youth with disabilities make their own positive contributions to their families (Hastings & Taunt, 2002; Scorgie & Sobsey, 2000; Summers, Behr, & Turnbull, 1988; Turnbull & Turnbull, 1978). Indeed, more than 1,200 birth parents, foster and adoptive parents, and legal guardians have affirmed that their children with disabilities are sources of happiness and fulfillment, strength and family closeness, and opportunities to learn through experiences associated with disabilities (Behr & Murphy, 1993). Moreover, they have reported stress and well-being levels similar to those of adults in the general population. Skeptical? Here's a typical affirmation of the research results, from the mother of a child with a disability:

> I've had by-pass surgery, three husbands, a son who left for the army and never came back, a pile of bills that never got paid and Colin, who was born with microcephaly. I've had lots of troubles in my life but Colin sure hasn't been one of them. Troubles with doctors, neighbors, late SSI payments, wheelchairs that won't move, and funny questions I never felt like answering. But never had any trouble with Colin. Churches that never came through, relatives that never came

> by, one grandbaby I've yet to meet, and heartburn must be since the day I was born. And Colin, he was my sweet-boy. Light my day with that funny smile, and how he'd make up to me when I came to get him in the morning. Why, if it weren't for Colin, I'd have thought life had pulled a dirty trick. (Blue-Banning, Santelli, Guy, & Wallace, 1994, p. 69)

Extent and Age of Onset of the Exceptionality. You might assume that a severe disability always has a greater impact, but again you would be wrong (Scorgie, Wilgosh, & McDonald, 1999; Shapiro, Blacher, & Lopez, 1998). The extent of the child's disability and when the child acquired the disability—the age of onset—are often highly related. For example, the diagnosis of a severe disability in a newborn requires the parents to deal immediately with what typically is an unexpected shock. When, however, a disability such as an emotional disorder or a learning disability manifests itself later in a child's life, the parents may feel a sense of relief—the diagnosis may affirm that they have been justified to be concerned about their child. These families may have to cope with a complex set of mixed emotions. Some families of a child with a learning disability, for example, may be confused and frustrated upon learning that their child, who appears capable in so many ways, indeed has a disability (Shapiro, Church, & Lewis, 2002). Others may be relieved to learn that there are reasons for the problems they have observed in their child and yet feel guilty for not identifying their child's disability earlier.

Another factor is the gradualness or suddenness of onset. Often the families of children with learning disabilities have a gradual awareness that the child has special needs. A very different circumstance occurs with a sudden onset such as a head injury resulting from an adolescent's diving accident. In those circumstances, families are thrust immediately into the world of trauma and rehabilitation units and often receive highly ambiguous prognoses (Michaud, Semel-Concepcíon, Duhaime, & Lazar, 2002). These families often have to make a series of ongoing readjustments as their child's characteristics fluctuate.

Severe disabilities or exceptional and early-blooming talent are often more apparent than milder disabilities or average or latent talent. The obvious disability may enable family members to accommodate readily to the child's special needs; however, it may stigmatize the entire family and result in their social rejection. In contrast, milder exceptionalities may be invisible, leading siblings to worry whether "something is wrong" with them, too (Powell & Gallagher, 1993). A family may develop a more definitive understanding of the child's support needs when their child has a severe disability. When, however, a child has a milder disability, the family may find its hope for the future alternately raised and dashed as the child progresses or falls back.

The nature of the student's exceptionality and the age of onset greatly influence when a student receives special education and the type of services that schools will provide. As you develop partnerships with families, we encourage you to be sensitive to how students' individual characteristics shape families' priorities, resources, and concerns. We also encourage you to highlight the student's strengths and preferences, to prevent the child's exceptionality from obscuring these and other characteristics.

Life Management Skills

The term *life management skills* refers to the techniques that people use to solve their problems (Scorgie et al., 1999). Olson et al. (1983) categorized the skills as follows: reframing, passive appraisal, spiritual support, social support, and professional support. We briefly define them here, including citations to the research literature related to families who have a member with an exceptionality. As you read about these life management skills, consider how they apply to professionals as well as families. How do you use these skills to solve your own problems?

1. *Reframing:* changing how you think about a situation in order to emphasize its positive aspects over its negative ones (Hastings & Taunt, 2002; Lin, 2000; Scorgie et al., 1999).

   My only daughter is profoundly retarded. She's loved and in return she's lovely. She's not able to walk or talk, but she can smile and laugh. She is loved. (Turnbull, Blue-Banning, Behr, & Kerns, 1987, p. 130)

2. *Passive appraisal:* setting aside your worries.

   I try not to worry about where Eric will get a job after he graduates from high school. I try not to think about what his adult life will be. It works best for me to just take a day at a time. There is no use getting all upset over something that is years away. (Poston & Turnbull, 2004)

3. *Spiritual support:* deriving comfort and guidance from your spiritual beliefs (Poston & Turnbull, 2004; Scorgie et al., 1999; Skinner, Correa, Skinner, & Bailey, 2001).

   I have faith in God, and word of God's faith. He'll never forsake you, or leave you, so whatever you're going through, he's going through with you. And you'll never get more than you can handle. So, having the faith draws things into focus, the peace, the joy, the happiness. (Beach Center, 1999)

4. *Social support:* receiving practical and emotional assistance from your friends and family members (Ain-

binder et al., 1998; Bailey et al., 1999; Brown, Anand, Fung, Isaacs, & Baum, 2003).

   At a critical time, one of my good friends said, "Don't give up, don't lose faith." It was real energizing to know that others believed in my daughter, too. (Turnbull & Ruef, 1996, p. 287)

5. *Professional support:* receiving assistance from professionals and agencies (Elliott, Koroloff, Koren, & Friesen, 1998; Romer, Richardson, Nahom, Aigbe, & Porter, 2002; Soodak & Erwin, 2000; Zoints, Zoints, Harrison, & Bellinger, 2003).

   It was the first day of summer vacation and my son was off the wall, because he really needed structure. I was freaking out, and I couldn't deal with it. I called the teacher and told her I didn't know what to do. She came across town and took him to her house and said, "Do something fun for two hours." (Turnbull & Ruef, 1997, p. 219)

We want to add a caveat, however, about the term *life management strategies:* The professional literature typically uses the term *coping strategies* instead. Families, however, talk about *coping* less often than professionals. Also, coping typically refers to dealing with a crisis situation; many family challenges, however, occur daily and weekly (Scorgie et al., 1999). Additionally, coping sometimes has a negative connotation for families (Vohs, 1997), as this mother pointed out:

   For the first 33 years of my life I wasn't once accused of coping, not even well. I just got on with, actually enjoyed it, and did many things with varying degrees of success. Then my daughter with Down syndrome was born and ever since I've been coping well. Mind you, that's not how it felt. After the initial vacuum of shock I thought I just went on getting on with life with the usual success-failure rate. But I must have been coping well because everybody kept telling me I was. . . . Why do I feel so offended by the praising people who tell me I'm coping well? I guess because I see it as an attempt to reduce me to a unidimensional figure—the mother of a child with Down syndrome who copes. . . . Cope comes from an Old French word meaning to strike (a blow) and I still feel like coping the next well-meaning person who says it to me. (Boyce, 1992, p. 37)

The words you use in your work—your professional terminology—can be barriers to your partnerships with families. We encourage you to use terms that do not stigmatize them or their children or suggest that they or their children "suffer" from some kind of pathology.

Family members vary in the number of life management strategies they use and in the quality or effectiveness of each strategy (Bailey et al., 1999; Lin, 2000; Sandler & Mistretta, 1998; Scorgie et al., 1999; Turnbull et al., 1993). Within the same family, some members may have strong life management capabilities, and others may need much more support because their own capabilities have not yet been developed fully. Think of life management capacity metaphorically: For each member of the family, "The end of the rope is the end of the rope, regardless of how long the rope is" (Avis, 1985, p. 197). Individual family members have ropes of differing lengths.

Avoid judging one family member in relation to another and wondering, much less asking, why one finds a situation so problematic that another finds so benign. Remember, the length of everyone's rope varies and depends on all the situations they are handling in their life. As a partner, regard yourself as a "rope lengthener," supporting everyone involved (families, professionals, friends, and community citizens) so that they will increase their capacity to address and resolve their priority concerns.

SPECIAL CHALLENGES

Families face challenges over and above a child's disability or extraordinary gifts and talents. Indeed, the presence of a disability may not be the family's most significant challenge. A family may have such special challenges as addiction to alcohol or drugs, abuse and neglect, exposure to violence and other fearful experiences, imprisonment, and chronic illness. In this section, we will address the special challenges associated with homelessness and with a parent having a disability. We use the term *special challenges* to refer to the conditions, separate from the disability, that are also influencing how family members interact (chapter 2), carry out their functions (chapter 3), and change across the life cycle (chapter 4).

Homelessness

Earlier in this chapter you learned that poverty is more closely associated with students in special education than with those in general education (U.S. Department of Education, 1992) and with single-female head of families than with two-parent families (Fujiura & Yamaki, 2000).

Homeless families, generally headed by women, are a subgroup of families in poverty (Butera & Maughan, 1998; Dubus & Buckner, 1998; Riley, Fryar, & Thornton, 1998). The National Coalition for the Homeless (2002) documented that approximately 4% of the people who become homeless are children and that children are the fastest growing group of the nation's homeless population.

A study of homeless families in New York City revealed a typical demographic profile:

Almost 100 percent of all families were headed by single women. The majority of these single mothers were younger than 25 years of age—an average of 22 years old. Most of these families have never had a traditional family structure, and almost 90 percent have never consisted of married parents. African-Americans constituted the largest racial group among the families; two-thirds were African-American, roughly one-fourth were Hispanic, and less than seven percent were from other racial groups. (Homes for the Homeless, 1992, p. 3)

In his book *Rachel and Her Children: Homeless Families in America*, Kozol (1988) wrote about the lives of homeless people he had interviewed and quoted a child as she described the room in which she was living with her mother and three other children.

Ever since August we been livin' here. The room is either very hot or freezin' cold. When it be hot outside it's hot in here. When it be cold outside we have no heat. We used to live with my aunt but then it got too crowded there so we moved out. We went to welfare and they sent us to the shelter. Then they shipped us to Manhattan. I'm scared of the elevators. 'Fraid they be stuck. I take the stairs. (Kozol, 1988, p. 62)

Homelessness has devastating effects on children's well-being, including their education. Children who are homeless often move from shelter to shelter, disrupting their school attendance (Institute for Children and Poverty, 2001). One study reported that one half of children who are homeless have developmental delays compared to 16% of children who experience poverty but who have houses (Kelly, Buehlman, & Caldwell, 2000). These children also experience emotional and behavioral problems 3 to 4 times more frequently than children in the general school population.

Developing partnerships with parents who are homeless poses unique challenges, but they are not insurmountable. A highly successful program in Tennessee provides training to parents, after-school tutoring at shelters, convenient and safe places where students can play, clothing, and school supplies (Davey, Penuel, Allison-Tant, & Rosner, 2000). Figure 1–8 describes this program that has effectively met the needs of parents and children who are homeless.

As a teacher, you might wonder how you will ever find the time to be an advocate, start a new program, or meet the special needs of families who are homeless. You can start by considering who among your professional colleagues could best address these special challenges; you might begin by enlisting the help of school counselors (Strawser, Markos, Yamaguchi, & Higgins, 2000) and school social workers (Markward & Biros, 2001).

Parents with Disabilities

As people with disabilities begin to lead more typical lives, more are likely to become parents. When a parent has a physical disability, the effects on your relationship with him or her primarily involve such logistics as providing accessible meeting rooms or perhaps communicating through the most accessible and convenient means (the telephone).

By contrast, parents with visual impairments often rely on their children. For example, they may ask their children to read prices in grocery stores and otherwise guide them through daily transactions. They may depend on an older child to provide care for younger siblings, expecting the older child to take on parental roles. Whether this reliance is detrimental depends, of course, on the individual family and whether the children have the time to be "just kids."

The child of a parent who is deaf often is the parent's communication link. That is the reality for a student, Jeannie, her deaf mother, and her teacher:

> We didn't have anybody who had sign language because our district's deaf education teacher was strictly from the oral school. So I asked Jeannie to interpret at our conference, since I knew she was very good at sign language. Unfortunately, what I needed to tell Jeannie's mother was that I had some concerns about her behavior in class. . . . The mother just nodded and smiled. I didn't understand her reaction. . . . It was only later that I discovered that Jeannie had not, to say the least, translated accurately what I was saying!

Although it might have been convenient to involve Jeannie, doing so presented obvious problems.

Of course, parents who have disabilities also have strengths, just as their children who have disabilities have strengths. Often the disability itself does not interfere with how the family functions. The disability may actually enhance the parent's understanding of the child as, for example, when deaf parents raise deaf children (Jackson & Turnbull, in press): "In many ways they could not be happier than they are now that what to others might seem a world of terrible isolation is in fact a world of contentment with its own vibrant language and culture" (Hewitt, 2000, p. 138).

Special issues arise in the family when mothers (Nicholson, Sweeney, & Geller, 1998a, 1998b) or fathers (Nicholson, Nason, Calabresi, & Yando, 1999) have mental illness. They may struggle with day-to-day parenting. They may be hospitalized and then face the stigma that is sometimes associated with hospitalization. They may face the threat of their children being placed in foster or adoptive care, or be obliged to consider surrendering custody to the state to receive disability-related services for their children.

What happens when adults with mental retardation have children? Researchers estimate (based on U.S. Census data) there are approximately 1.4 million parents with mental retardation in the United States who have children under the age of 18 (Holburn, Perkins, & Vietze, 2001). Typically, more women than men who themselves have mental retardation are parents, and typically these parents tend to have 2 to 3 children. Among the conclusions of a comprehensive synthesis of research related to parents with mental retardation are these (Holburn et al., 2001):

- Approximately one quarter of the children of parents with mental retardation will have mental retardation. When both parents have mental retardation, the risk doubles.
- Challenges in parenting tend to increase as children get older.
- Mothers with mental retardation rarely abuse their children but often unintentionally neglect them; some mothers with mental retardation provide adequate care.
- A parent's competence is influenced by the motivation to learn; background and current life circumstances; particular strengths, needs, and future plans; and how the parent interacts with his or her children.
- The most successful programs for increasing parenting skills are home based, long term, and based on a partnership between the parent and a professional in which the professional teaches the parent how to plan and make decisions.
- Parents with mental retardation often have other challenges, such as unemployment or underemployment, substandard housing, inadequate health care, and problems with money management.

Researchers who interviewed 30 adults who had been raised by at least one parent with mental retardation (Booth & Booth, 2000) concluded that the children generally demonstrated resilience as adults. The availability of friends and family to assist the parent with mental retardation was a key factor in achieving positive outcomes. The children had a close emotional bond with their parents, but the lack of services and supports contributed to challenges and limitations of the family. To increase the likelihood of successful parenting by adults with mental retardation, successful programs have used extensive analyses of child-care tasks, line drawings illustrating each of the steps of the task analysis, manuals written at around the third grade level, audiotapes of the manuals, and home visits to facilitate parents using these training materials. By combining these approaches, a recent research study reported that 96% of the skills were learned to criterion level, and 80% of those skills were maintained in a follow-up phase (Feldman, 2004).

SUMMARY

What affects families' adjustment and their willingness to develop partnerships with you and other educators? Clearly, the family's own characteristics do—its size and form, cultural background, socioeconomic status, and geographic location.

Of course, the individual characteristics of each family member come into play. The nature and severity of the child's exceptionality are important but not always in predictable ways. The family's need for support is also influenced by the age of onset and the suddenness or gradualness of the emergence of these special needs. And the family members' life management skills (reframing, passive appraisal, spiritual support, social support, and professional support) influence family well-being. Family members can vary widely in the extent to which they develop effective life management skills.

Some families face special challenges separate from their child's exceptionality, requiring professionals to be responsive and helpful as they work with families. Homelessness is a special challenge to a child's well-being; it also affects parents' quality of life and their ability to be an educational partner. A second type of special challenge occurs when parents have disabilities. Parents with disabilities have strengths as well as special needs. Professionals can develop trusting partnerships with parents who face uniquely challenging situations.

Whatever a family's characteristics might be, you can respond to them in your role as a partner. Just as you must take every child's unique strengths and needs into account in planning the child's curriculum and how you will teach the child, so you must consider each family's strengths, needs, and characteristics as you develop a partnership with them.

REFLECTING ON THE VIGNETTE

1. What are the most significant characteristics of each of the four families described in the prologue? Is there any one characteristic that stands out about each?
2. What characteristic most distinguishes each family from the others? The nature of their child's disability? Their ethnic, cultural, or linguistic traits? What are the characteristics that each family shares with the others?
3. Who are the members of each family with whom you, as a teacher or other education professional, expect to become a partner?

ENHANCING YOUR SELF-AWARENESS

One way to gain a greater understanding of family characteristics is to reflect on your own family. By recognizing the family patterns that you have experienced, you are more likely to understand how your own values can influence ways in which you interact with other families.

Family culture

Describe the culture of your family of origin to a classmate. Explain how cultural values were embedded in the ways you celebrate holidays, your spirituality/religion or lack of it, and the foods that you ate as a child. What advice did you hear repeatedly from the adults in your family? How did your family's cultural values influence the nature of this advice?

Life management skills

You read about five life management skills—reframing, passive appraisal, spiritual support, social support, and professional support. What one or two life management skills were most frequently used in your family? Which were rarely used and why?

Special challenges

Either in your family of origin or in the family that you have established as an adult, reflect on at least one special challenge and how it affected your family. In what ways did your family seek assistance? Overall, was your family more strengthened by the experience or weakened by it? Describe why you think your family was more strengthened or weakened.

RESOURCES

You can find a link to these resources on the Companion Website at *www.prenhall.com/turnbull*.

1. Early Childhood Research Institute on Culturally and Linguistically Appropriate Services (CLAS)
   University of Illinois at Urbana-Champaign
   61 Children's Research Center
   51 Gerty Drive
   Champaign, IL 61821
   217-333-4123, 800-583-4135
   www.clas.uiuc.edu/links.html

   CLAS identifies, evaluates, and disseminates effective and appropriate early intervention and preschool practices that are responsive to the needs of children and families from culturally and linguistically diverse backgrounds. They provide extensive lists of materials and resources in various languages.

2. National Center for Children in Poverty
   Columbia University
   Mailman School of Public Health
   215 W. 125th Street, 3rd Floor
   New York, NY 10027
   646-284-9600
   info@nccp.org

   NCCP has the mission to conduct policy analysis and academic research to prevent child poverty and improve the quality of life of children and families who experience low income.

3. Through the Looking Glass
   2198 6th Street, Suite 100
   Berkeley, CA 94710-2204
   1-800-644-2666
   TLG@lookingglass.org

   Through the Looking Glass supports parents with disabilities by conducting research, describing adaptive parenting equipment, and producing resources that enable parents with disabilities to be successful.

4. National Coalition for the Homeless
   1012 14th Street, NW, #600
   Washington, DC 20005-3471
   202-737-6444
   info@nationalhomeless.org

   The National Coalition for the Homeless focuses on public education, policy advocacy, and technical assistance to end homelessness and increase economic and social justice for all citizens.

Family Interaction

CHAPTER ORGANIZATION

1. What are the subsystems within a family and how does a child's exceptionality influence them?
2. How can family-professional partnerships enable marital, parental, sibling, and extended family subsystems to be more successful?
3. How can teachers increase the likelihood that families will have balanced levels of cohesion and adaptability?

VIGNETTE

Imagine a baby in a crib. She looks up and sees a toy above her. It is a mobile. She reaches out, touches one arm, and watches, fascinated, as all of the pieces move, not just the one she touched.

The baby has learned a lesson about mobiles and about families. Pieces of the mobile are connected to each other, just as members of a family are connected to each other. What happens to one, happens to all.

Who are the all? And how is it useful to describe them and their relationships, their connections with each other, their "mobile-ness"? Family-theory literature gives us two frameworks to answer those questions.

One framework describes relationships according to the subsystems of a family. Thus, members are related through marriage and they interact with each other as husband and wife: Clara and Jake Berg, Norma and Joaqin Cortes, and Leia and Jamie Holley.

Family members also are related and interact with each other as parent and child: Clara, Jake, and Kenny Berg; Norma, Joaqin, and Joesian Cortes; Vera, Nicky, and Altevis Doleman; Leia, Jamie, Sean, and JP Holley.

Brothers and sisters have legal relationships with each other. Kenny Berg and his brother, Sheldon, live in their parents' home, and, although Kenny's sister, Karen, is in Los Angeles, she has her own relationship with Kenny. Nicky Doleman's older brother, Altevis, lives at home with her and Vera. Both Tatiana and Juan Cortes live in their parents' home with Joesian; similarly, Sean and JP Holley live with their parents.

Family refers to two or more people who regard themselves as family and who perform some of the functions that families typically perform. Family, then, includes people who are not related by blood or marriage if they function as family members. Carole Gothelf, the principal of the Guild School, Clara Berg's colleague and always Kenny's advocate, clearly qualifies; Beth Mount, the future-planner who became a friend to the Bergs, probably does, too. It is not clear whether the Corteses regard the three women at United We Stand as family, whether Vera Doleman regards her close friends and fellow parishioners as family, or whether Leia Holley regards Tierney Thompson, Sean's teacher, as a member of her family.

To describe these four subsystems—marital, parental, sibling, and extended—does not, however, suffice to portray how family members relate and interact with each other. Two questions remain. First, are the family members "tight" with each other—do they experience cohesion? The answer for each of the four families is a resounding yes. Take just the Dolemans. When Charolette (Nicky's biological mother) called Vera's mother and father (Charolette's grandparents) at their home in Mississippi and said, "I need you in Kansas," they came running. Consider the Corteses. Joesian's uncle is teaching him the plumber's trade, and Joesian's father works with his sister-in-law.

The Berg family gathers for a family snapshot. Pictured, left to right, are Jake and Clara Berg with their children, Kenny, Sheldon, and Karen.

Three generations of the Doleman family mingle on the front porch of Vera's home. Shown, left to right, are Vera's mother, Marie Doleman; Vera's sister, Joyce Williams; Vera; Vera's father, Aaron Doleman; and Vera's children, Tavion (on Aaron's lap), Joe, Charolette, and Nicky.

The second question is whether the family is adaptable. Can it change to meet the circumstances created by a disability or other exceptionality? Once again, the answer for the four families is yes. The Bergs have persevered through different infant-toddler programs, Kenny's placement at the Perkins School in Boston, his return to New York and enrollment at the Guild School, and his employment at Adriance Farm. Vera Doleman and her family also illustrate adaptability; Vera adopted Nicky, and Vera's parents became working members of the Doleman family in Lawrence.

When you begin to work with families, you will notice how they (perhaps like your own family) create subsystems, are more or less cohesive, and adapt well, poorly, or not at all. Just remember to look at them as the baby in a crib looked up at the toy: An inert toy is not nearly so fascinating as one whose every part moves when only one part is activated.

INTRODUCTION
ASSUMPTIONS OF FAMILY SYSTEMS THEORY

In chapter 1, we defined family as two or more people who regard themselves as a family and who perform some of the functions families typically perform. This chapter is about the people who regard themselves as a family. Here, we discuss family members' *interactions* within the family and how their relationships to each other come into play as you develop partnerships with them.

The family systems framework (the circle within Figure 2–1) shows four basic types of interactions or relationships—marital, parental, sibling, and extended family. We display the types of relationships in the inner quadrants of the framework and their qualities—cohesion and adaptability—in the outer ring.

During the past several years, special educators, particularly early childhood special educators, have shifted from focusing primarily on the child or on the parental subsystem (especially the mother and child subsystem) to focusing more broadly on the family as a whole (Bailey et al., 1998; McWilliam, Snyder, Harbin, Porter, & Munn, 2000; Turnbull, Turbiville, & Turnbull, 2000). As we suggested earlier, the whole-family approach and the effect of the child with an exceptionality on the entire family system brings to mind the metaphor of a mobile:

> In a mobile all the pieces, no matter what size or shape, can be grouped together and balanced by shortening or lengthening the strings attached or rearranging the distance between the pieces. So it is with a family. None of the family members is identical to any other; they are all different and at different levels of growth. As in a mobile, you can't arrange one without thinking of the other.[1] (Satir, 1972, pp. 119–120)

[1]Copyright © 1972. Reprinted by permission, Science and Behavior Books.

A single mother of several children, one of whom is an elementary-age son with attention-deficit/hyperactivity disorder, enlivens the mobile metaphor:

> Quality of life for me is being happy and that means doing what makes me feel happy, because if I'm happy, then it comes across and falls into my children's lives. If I'm not happy, then it creates a whole lot of chaos, and a negative, negative environment. So I've learned to let go of things, and concentrate on what makes me happy, so in turn, my kids will be happy. And it's working. (Beach Center, 1999)

Family systems theory provides a framework for understanding what a family is and how it functions (chapters 1 through 4) and shows you how to establish trusting partnerships with families (chapters 5 through 13). Systems theory in general and family systems theory in particular make three assumptions relevant to your partnership with families; these assumptions address (1) the input/output configuration of systems, (2) the concepts of wholeness and subsystems, and (3) the role of boundaries in defining systems (Whitechurch & Constantine, 1993).

Input/Output

The first assumption of systems theory in general and family systems theory in particular is that certain characteristics are inputs into the system. The system then responds to these inputs, and the interaction produces outputs. Systems theory focuses primarily on "what happens to the *input* as it is processed by the system on its way to becoming an *output*" (Broderick & Smith, 1979, p. 114, italics added). As shown in Figure 2–1, a family's characteristics (chapter 1) are the inputs into family interaction. The family interaction occurs as families perform roles and interact with each other. The output of these roles and interactions is related to family functions, which we discuss in chapter 3. Thus, inputs interact with the system and produce outputs; the outputs relate to how the family functions. As we describe inputs, outputs, and functions, we tend to portray a strict linear model: in, out, result/function. However, we are describing the mobile: a slight push (input) on one part (member or characteristic of a family) produces an effect (output) on one or more other members or characteristics, with a change in the movement (function) of the entire mobile. Every arm of the mobile—every member and characteristic of the family—moves whenever any one characteristic or member moves. In this chapter we describe the way those characteristics influence how family members interact with each other and with others outside the family.

FIGURE 2–1

Family Systems Framework: Emphasis on Family Interaction

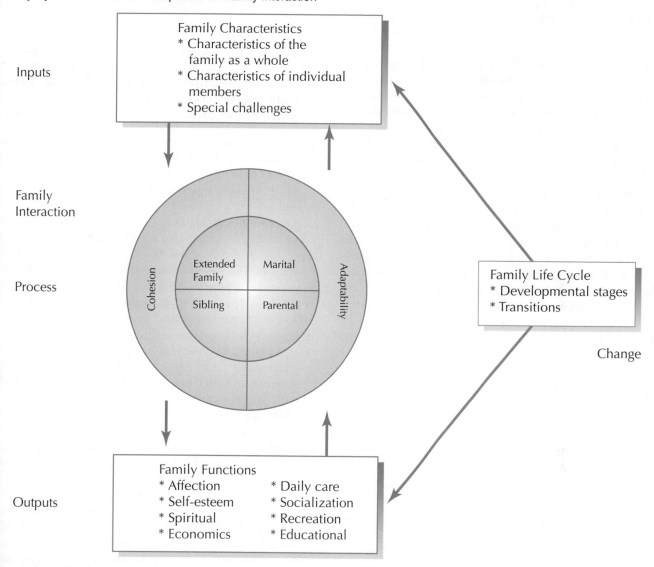

Source: Turnbull, A. P., Summers, J. A., & Brotherson, M. J. (1984). *Working with families with disabled members: A family systems approach* (p. 60). Lawrence: University of Kansas, Kansas Affiliated Facility. Adapted by permission.

Wholeness and Subsystems

The second assumption of systems theory in general and family systems theory in particular is that the system must be understood as a whole and cannot be understood by only one or more of its parts, or members (Whitechurch & Constantine, 1993). Simply understanding the child with an exceptionality does not mean that you will understand the family, yet understanding the family is necessary to understanding the child.

Many professionals assume that they can establish trusting family partnerships if they know only the mother's or the student's perspective. This is a mistake because the family consists of the sum of its members' interactions with each other. Professionals should focus on the reciprocity within the family—the aggregated inputs and the combination of interactions that constitute the whole family.

Boundaries

The third and last assumption of systems theory in general and family systems theory in particular is that boundaries exist between family subsystems, resulting from the interaction of family members with each other and from the family unit as a whole in its interactions with outside influences. From your own life, you probably know of boundaries between parents and children and between the children themselves. You may also observe boundaries between the family and the educators with whom they are involved, and note that those boundaries differ from those between the family and its friends, the leaders of its religious/spiritual communities, other professionals, or people with whom the family conducts business.

Families vary in the degree to which their boundaries are open or closed to educators or any other nonmember. This affects how much the family will collaborate with educators or others. Some boundaries are porous; others are not.

The boundaries within a family also define its members' roles with respect to each other. In some families, extended family members take on the parents' roles because the boundary between the two subsystems (extended family and parental) is open. In other families, grandparents meet resistance when they make suggestions about child rearing. In those families, the boundary between parental and extended family subsystems is closed.

In this chapter, we describe the four family subsystems and the two "operating boundary rules" of family systems and subsystems. We call these rules cohesion and adaptability.

FAMILY SUBSYSTEMS

Within the traditional nuclear family, there are four major subsystems (see Figure 2–1):

1. *Marital subsystem:* interactions between husband and wife (or same-sex partners)
2. *Parental subsystem:* interactions among parents and their children
3. *Sibling subsystem:* interactions among the children in a family
4. *Extended family subsystem:* interactions among members of the nuclear family, relatives, and others who are regarded as relatives

Interactions within one family will, of course, be different from those within another family; interactions vary according to the subsystems within each family and the membership within each subsystem. For example, a family with only one child has no sibling subsystem. Similarly, a single parent does not have a formal marital subsystem but may have the equivalent if the parent has a long-term partner. You should simply ask the student's parent or parents to tell you about their family and listen carefully to the people they mention. These people may be key to establishing a trusting partnership with the student and family. You should ask the parent or parents, because the federal special education law grants rights to parents, not

grandparents or uncles or aunts, to make decisions about the child's education (see chapter 6).

Marital Subsystem

Interactions within the marital subsystem involve marital partners or significant others who function as marital partners. When the adults who function as parents have a child or youth with an exceptionality, you can be sure that the child influences their relationship. The question is, how?

Impacts: Negative, Positive, and Mixed. Are marriages on the whole hurt, unaffected, or improved by the presence of the child with a disability? As confusing as it may be, research gives a yes answer to each of those questions.

Some studies indicate that a child or youth with an exceptionality has a negative impact on the parents' marriage. According to some research, the rate of divorce, marital disharmony, and desertions by husbands is higher in marriages where there is a child or youth with an exceptionality (Gath, 1977; Hodapp & Krasner, 1995; Murphy, 1982) than in other marriages. One group of researchers assessed marital harmony in 59 couples soon after the birth of a child with spina bifida and again nearly a decade later (Tew, Payne, & Lawrence, 1974). The researchers maintained contact with these couples as well as with 58 comparison couples (those who did not have a child with spina bifida). The couples who had a child with spina bifida had less marital harmony and twice the divorce rate as the control group couples. Thus, it appeared that the birth of a child with spina bifida presented a serious challenge to marital stability and caused many marital needs and activities to be subordinated to the child's needs. As Helen Featherstone (1980), the parent of a child with a disability, has noted: "A child's handicap attacks the fabric of a marriage in four ways. It excites powerful emotions in both parents. It acts as a dispiriting symbol of shared failure. It reshapes the organization of the family. It creates fertile ground for conflict" (p. 91).

However, the majority of studies report that the divorce rate is not higher when a family has a child with an exceptionality (Benson & Gross, 1989). Indeed, some husbands and wives report higher levels of marital adjustment, partially because of their shared commitment for their child (Raghavan, Weisner, & Patel, 1999; Sandler & Mistretta, 1998; Scorgie & Sobsey, 2000). A survey of parents of adults with disabilities still living at home was revealing: 44% of the parents reported that they believed their marriage has been strengthened because of their experience as parents of a son or daughter with a disability (Sandler & Mistretta, 1998). Elsie Helsel (1985) reflected this perspective when she described her marriage

FIGURE 2–2
Robin's Positive Contributions

Professionals are constantly probing and asking questions concerning how Robin's constant presence and problems affect our marriage. Once again, there are pluses and minuses. I really don't believe any one factor in a marriage can be pinpointed as a strengthener or strainer. There are too many variables affecting a marriage for such a simplistic explanation. The temperament of the individuals; the physical, emotional, and financial strengths; the problem-solving and coping skills; the commitment people bring—all have some bearing on the strain a handicapped child places on a marriage. From my point of view, Robin has added more strength than strain. At least my husband and I are still living together after 37 years of marriage! For one thing, at those points in a marriage when you are contemplating divorce (intellectually, emotionally, or actually), the presence of a child such as Robin is a major deterrent. The focus quickly changes from your own needs, wishes, and desires to our responsibilities, commitment, and the needs of the child. Somehow this helps you work through a problem, and you find another way. I have never bought the argument that the presence of an adult person in a family, handicapped or not, is a disruptive factor. I feel society has lost a mooring with the breakdown of the extended family. Romantic twosomes are great for novels and certain periods of our lives. I do not see such a pattern as essential for a successful marriage. My husband and I will not have a footloose, carefree, romantic retirement lifestyle, but we will have something else—the opportunity to feel needed.

Source: Helsel Family (1985). The Helsels' story of Robin. In H. R. Turnbull & A. P. Turnbull (Eds.) *Parents speak out: Then and now* (2nd ed.) (pp. 85–86). Upper Saddle River, NJ: Merrill/Prentice Hall.

and the contribution to it by her son, Robin, who has cerebral palsy (see Figure 2–2).

Other research has found no difference between families with and without a child with a disability: The child does not affect marriage positively or negatively. After comparing 60 families who have children with and without disabilities, Abbott and Meredith (1986) found no significant differences between the two groups on measures of marital strength, family strength, or personality characteristics. Young and Roopnarine (1994) reported similar findings in their research on families who have preschool children with and without a disability. Furthermore, research suggests that issues associated with the disability can *simultaneously* strengthen and impair a couple's relationship (Singer & Nixon, 1996).

The child is not the only input into a marital relationship; other characteristics constitute inputs. One consists of the family's cultural values. Tremendous cross-cultural variation occurs when marriages are formed, lived out, and disrupted (McGoldrick, Giordano, & Pearce, 1996). Among Middle Eastern families (that is, Arab, Iranian, Lebanese, and Armenian), for example, tradition dictates that parents pick the marriage partner for their son or daughter. There also is a tradition of marrying within the same lineage (cousins) to ensure economic and blood kinship, of allowing men to have up to four wives, and of strongly discouraging divorce (Abudabbeh, 1996; Dagirmanjian, 1996; Jalali, 1996; Simon, 1996). How do these values differ from those of European Americans? Reflect on what you have already learned about the different ways that family characteristics can vary (chapter 1); many characteristics within families, not just the child with a disability, influence the stability of a marriage.

Marital Satisfaction. Research consistently finds that a strong marriage makes a difference in the overall well-being of a family (Scorgie, Wilgosh, & McDonald, 1998; Simmerman, Blacher, & Baker, 2001; Willoughby & Glidden, 1995). In a study of the significant and positive changes that occurred in the lives of parents of children with disabilities, a parent underscored the critical importance of marriage to the family's quality of life: "Your marriage is foundational to everything. It was our love that carried us through" (Scorgie & Sobsey, 2000, p. 202). At the same time, a strong marriage is not an essential for positive family outcomes. Many single parents of children with a disability also experience strong family well-being.

Within any marriage, the partners have specific needs for themselves and specific roles to fulfill for their partners (such as affection, socialization, and self-esteem). It makes good sense to respect and enhance the marital relationship as you form partnerships with parents or people acting as parents. Figure 2–3 suggests how you might do that.

Some couples can benefit from marital counseling or other therapy from psychiatrists, counselors, psychologists, and social workers (Lichtenstein, 1993). If you believe that a family might benefit from marital counseling or therapy, two approaches are available. First, determine which issues are appropriately handled by you as a teacher (or in another role) and which by professionals who specialize in family counseling or therapy and then make an appropriate referral. Second, discuss your perspectives with the school social worker or counselor and ask for advice on how best to proceed. In some cases, the social worker or counselor might take the lead and have an initial conversation with the family.

FIGURE 2–3
Enhancing Marital Interactions

- Encourage parents to consider activities they may wish to engage in separately from their child or children.
- Make information available to couples on child care and companionship services.
- Consider the time and energy implications of homework and home-based teaching on the needs of the parents to spend quality time together as a couple.
- Seek ways to offer flexible scheduling or alternatives if a planned school activity conflicts with a couple's plans.

Parental Subsystem

The parental subsystem consists of interactions between parents or other couples acting as parents and their children. Couples can be biological, step, adoptive, or foster parents. Some stay married to each other; some divorce. Some remarry; others do not.

Regardless of how couples come to be parents, many parents of children with disabilities have higher stress levels and face more challenges than parents who do not have children with disabilities (Blacher & Lopez, 1997; Hoare, Harris, Jackson, & Kerley, 1998; Olsson & Hwang, 2001; Warfield, Krauss, Hauser-Cram, Upshur, & Shonkoff, 1999). Other researchers however, have reported no differences in the stress (Gowen, Johnson-Martin, Goldman, & Appelbaum, 1989; Harris & McHale, 1989) and depression (Singer, 2004) of families of children with and without disabilities. Parents of students who are gifted and talented also experience special challenges such as confusion, uncertainty, and even intimidation (Friedman, 2000; Stephens, 1999).

In this section, we will discuss issues associated with (1) foster parents, (2) adoptive parents, (3) gay or lesbian parents, (4) fathers, and (5) mothers.

Foster Parents.   Foster parents have the permanent or temporary custody of children who are in the care or custody of a state's child protection agency because they have been abused, neglected, or otherwise maltreated by their natural parents. The foster parents do not have the same legal status as the children's natural parents or of parents who legally adopt a child. Their authority is limited by the state agency or by the order of the court that places a child into foster care. You should always deter-

mine the legal power of the foster parent before you rely on that person's authority with respect to the child's education.

Approximately 600,000 children are in foster care in the United States (Emerson & Lovitt, 2003). Alarmingly, infants and young children who have physical, cognitive, and health-related disabilities constitute the fastest growing population of children in need of foster care (Benton Foundation, 1998). Approximately one fifth of children in out-of-home placements have developmental disabilities (Kocinski, 1998). Even more children in foster care have emotional or behavior disorders. One sample of children in foster care identified nearly half as needing mental health services (Leslie et al., 2000), and another study found that 75% to 80% of school-age children in foster care had emotional or behavior disorders (Clausen, Landsverk, Ganger, Chadwick, & Litrownik, 1998). It is more likely that a child will be in an out-of-home placement when the child's parents abuse alcohol or drugs, have mental health challenges, abuse and neglect their children, have children who are adjudicated to be juvenile delinquents, or are poor (Barbell, 1996; Humphrey, Turnbull, & Turnbull, in press; Kupsinel & Dubsky, 1999; Moore & Vandivere, 2000).

During the school years, children and youth in foster care have high rates of absenteeism, midyear changes from one school to another, discipline suspensions from school, and a need to repeat one or more grades (Emerson & Lovitt, 2003).

Children of non-European ethnic descent typically make up approximately two thirds of the foster care population (Behrman, 2004). Of all racial groups, African American children and youth are the most prevalent in foster care and represent 38% of the foster care population. Given that African American students are disproportionately represented in special education, you will likely encounter students who move from school to school because they are in foster care.

Approximately one fourth of the children and youth in foster care are placed with relatives, and approximately half are placed with nonrelatives. Others usually are placed in group homes or institutions (Behrman, 2004) spending an average of approximately 33 months in foster care. The longer children stay in foster care, the greater the likelihood that they will experience many different foster care placements ("foster care drift").

What happens after foster care? Slightly more than half of the children are returned to their birth families, about one fifth are adopted, and one tenth live with relatives.

The postschool outcomes for youth in foster care are cause for great concern.

- Approximately 25% of foster children end up home-less and one third end up on welfare 1 to 1½ years after leaving foster care at 18.
- Approximately 40% of youth in foster care had held a job for at least 1 year when they were surveyed 2½ to 4 years after leaving foster care (Child Welfare League of America, 2002; Emerson & Lovitt, 2003).

We encourage you to make special efforts to develop trusting partnerships with foster parents. Typically they are either left out of the educational decision-making process or included at only a superficial level (Altshuler, 1997). Figure 2–4 includes tips for establishing partnerships with foster parents.

FIGURE 2–4
Tips for Developing Partnerships with Foster Parents

- Collaborate with your school social worker and/or school counselor to seek advice about legal arrangements that govern foster care placement and how you can best comply with those arrangements.

- Communicate with foster parents and ask them what arrangements they would prefer in how they communicate with you and the extent to which you communicate with any other adults in the child's life, including birth parents or the student's social worker.

- Ask foster parents what they know about any background information that is available on the student, especially school and immunization records. Seek to obtain this information as soon as possible to help ensure a smooth transition to the new school placement.

- Inform the foster parents about extracurricular activities and make any suggestions about how the student in foster care might make friends and find a niche at school with peers who share similar interests.

- If foster parents have not had any experience with special education in the past, make sure that they have information about the nature of the student's program and also refer them to the programs and resources that you will learn about in chapter 10 that provide support to parents of children with special needs.

Source: Emerson, J., & Lovitt, T. (2003). The educational plight of foster children in schools and what can be done about it. *Remedial and Special Education, 24*(4), 199–203. Copyright by PRO-ED, Inc. Adapted with permission.

Adoptive Parents.   Research with mothers who have adopted children with mental retardation shows that adoptive families typically experience a high level of well-being (Glidden, 1989; Glidden, Kiphart, Willoughby, & Bush, 1993; Todis & Singer, 1991). A recent study followed families for 12 years who had adopted children with developmental disabilities (Glidden & Johnson, 1999). The study concluded that the mothers were generally positive about the outcomes for themselves and their children and that the adopted children experienced good outcomes. The mothers reported that the strongest benefits were giving and receiving love, positive child characteristics, pride in the child's achievement, and happiness. They reported major problems around negative child characteristics; worry, anxiety, or guilt; and developmental delay. Benefits were consistently rated as higher in importance than problems. Interestingly, 50% of the families had adopted at least one additional child since their first adoption of a child with developmental disabilities.

A higher incidence of disabilities is found among children who are adopted. Approximately 10% to 15% of children in residential treatment facilities for emotional disorders are adopted, contrasted to about 2% of adopted children under 18 in the general population (Brodzinsky, 1993). Adopted children are referred for psychological treatment 2 to 5 times more frequently than their peers who are not adopted (Grotevant & McRoy, 1990; McRoy, Grotevant, & Zurcher, 1988).

In Figure 2–5 a parent who adopted a son with emotional disorders describes some of the special issues that arose in raising her son and trying to get appropriate services and supports. As you read her story, consider what you might have done if you had the opportunity to develop a trusting partnership with the individuals identified in the figure. What difference might you have made in their family quality of life?

Gay and Lesbian Parents.   Gay and lesbian parenthood is no longer novel. It includes homosexual men, lesbians, bisexuals, and transgendered people who have children (Lamme & Lamme, 2001). The number of gay or lesbian parents is difficult to determine; societal barriers and discrimination inhibit many people from disclosing their sexual orientation. Estimates are that the number of children and youth in the United States who have gay parents ranges from 6 million to 12 million (Lamme & Lamme, 2003). Children enter gay families in many different ways, including birth to parents when they have been in heterosexual relationships, adoption, surrogate parenting, foster parenting, and artificial insemination.

FIGURE 2–5
My Voice: Speaking Out on Adoption

I met Dennis when he was nearly five-years-old and in the legal custody of my state's Department of Health and Welfare. Dennis is Native American. He is the youngest of six brothers and sisters. I was a professor of social work, single and had always loved and worked with children as a teacher, as a therapist and as a parent. Not one of these experiences had prepared me for how much I longed to be the mother of this little boy.

I was told that Dennis was "normal." Despite chronic neglect and some abuse in his birth home he had adapted well to foster placement. The worker said that Dennis was "delightful and engaging" and that if I didn't want him somebody else would "snap him up" quickly. I didn't need to be told that twice.

Dennis' problems began right away. He had bedtime fears. He screamed and cried for hours, hid food under the mattress and prowled through the house in the middle of the night. . . . He had tantrums that lasted for hours. He secretly drove knives into the furniture. One time Dennis hid in the ceiling of his bedroom; another time he hid within the frame of his bed. . . . I now know that Dennis lived in terror throughout the first few years of our lives together as a family. . . .

I was frequently asked about what I had done in Dennis' early years to give him these problems.

I had been given no history of Dennis' family. . . . I had no way of knowing about his family history of chronic mental illness and chemical dependency. I didn't know about the family's history of sexual abuse. And I certainly didn't know that at least one of the foster families had physically and emotionally abused Dennis.

I did know that one of the foster families had told Dennis that he had to be white to go to heaven.

I learned about that when I found Dennis—a handsome Chippewa-Cree boy—washing himself in bleach when he bathed trying to become white.

. . . I had come to realize that I had two full-time jobs: social worker/therapist and parent/therapist. The enormity of it hit me. . . .

I naively thought that I would tell people what had happened, and that they would help me find services to correct his problems. State officials said that they had no help to give. I had adopted Dennis and—as a parent—I had full responsibility for his care and well-being.

We have found a private case manager to help us identify whatever services may be available. The state vocational rehabilitation agency is involved. . . . A dedicated adult educator tutors Dennis on a weekly basis.

Dennis is slowly accumulating the necessities to move toward independent living (supported housing) within the next year or so. Things are certainly not perfect, nor do I expect them to ever be perfect. I no longer feel isolated. I am blessed to be able to attend a support group for families of chronically mentally ill young people and to count these families among my friends. I am beginning to be active in the Alliance for the Mentally Ill.

There is actually a bittersweet quality to life now. My life has been explicably changed by being family with Dennis. I am honored to have been trusted by a child who had absolutely no earthly reason to trust anyone. I am pleased to have come to love and trust Dennis as an honorable and compassionate young man. I know we are real family and I know we are not alone.

Source: Ward, S. (1996). My family: Formed by adoption. In *Focal Point, 10*(1), 30–32.

Opinions vary about the impact of gay and lesbian parenting on children. Setting opinions aside, what do we know from research concerning the development of children with gay parents? Two comprehensive reviews of research conducted over the last two decades came to the same conclusion: Children raised by gay and lesbian parents do not significantly differ from children raised by heterosexual parents with respect to their gender roles and social and emotional development (Fitzgerald, 1999; Tasker, 1999). Both reports pointed to the much greater likelihood that these children will experience stigma, bullying, and societal discrimination. They also pointed out several positive outcomes of growing up with gay and lesbian parents, including a wider exposure to diversity, a more open climate about sexuality issues, and less emphasis on gender-defined roles within the family.

Australian researchers interviewed more than 100 gay and lesbian parents and 48 children and youth with gay or lesbian parents (Ray & Gregory, 2001). Their findings document the societal discrimination that these parents and students faced.

- Seventy-three percent of the parents said their most common concern was whether their children would be teased or bullied.
- Sixty-two percent were concerned that there would be no discussion in the preschool or school curriculum about gay and lesbian families.

■ Slightly more than half of the parents worried that their children would have to answer difficult questions.

The actual experiences of children in this study were particularly revealing. Bullying was a major problem, as reported by the students. Bullying usually started around grade 3 and became harsher as students proceeded through middle and high school. Slightly less than half of the students had experienced bullying by grades 3 to 6. Elementary students who were bullied generally sought teacher intervention, but many teachers did not take sufficient action to stop the bullying.

From grades 7 to 12, bullying was also common, although it seemed to subside in grades 11 and 12. When bullying did occur, it was more escalated than at the elementary level, as described by one girl: "I had apple cores and banana peels and rocks thrown at me every time I walked past them. 'Dyke, dyke, dyke' they'd call at me. I used to get very scared; very frightened" (Ray & Gregory, 2001, p. 32). High school students expressed disappointment that their teachers did not provide any kind of discipline for homophobic taunting. They also underscored the benefits of being raised in gay and lesbian families, including having a greater appreciation of diversity, participating in events for gay people such as the Gay Pride March, and feeling special.

Figure 2–6 includes tips on how you can help create a respectful school environment for students who have gay or lesbian parents. These suggestions relate to all children—those with and without disabilities or giftedness—who have gay or lesbian parents.

Fathers.   Is it typical for fathers of children with disabilities to experience more favorable outcomes than mothers, for mothers to experience more favorable outcomes than fathers, or for mothers and fathers to experience about the same outcomes? The research is mixed:

■ Some studies report more favorable outcomes by fathers (Trute, 1995).
■ Other studies report that mothers experience more favorable outcomes than fathers (Kazak & Marvin, 1984; Olsson & Hwang, 2001; Veisson, 1999).
■ Studies report that mothers and fathers have experienced the same outcomes although their stress comes from different sources (Roach, Orsmond, & Barratt, 1999).
■ Still other studies indicate no significant differences between outcomes of fathers and mothers (Ainge, Colvin, & Baker, 1998; Dyson, 1997).

If you are interested in the father's perspective, we encourage you to read some first-person accounts (Greenwald, 1997; Meyer, 1995; Naseef, 1997; Stallings & Cook, 1997).

FIGURE 2–6

Tips for Creating a Respectful School Climate for Gay and Lesbian Parents and Their Children

- Seek out experiences where you interact with people who have diverse sexual orientation, and enhance your own comfort level in being with others who are different from you.

- Just as you would celebrate Black, Hispanic, and women's history months, also celebrate Gay Pride week. Encourage parents and other community citizens who are gay to speak at an assembly, provide audiovisual resources about gay issues, and highlight famous gay and lesbian people (Walt Whitman, Oscar Wilde, Alexander the Great, Billie Jean King, Gertrude Stein) in the curriculum.

- Encourage students to do book reports and research projects on gay issues.

- Point out gender stereotypes in books and encourage students to recognize diversity within gender roles.

- At middle and high school levels, encourage activism in combating harassment.

- Encourage students who appear to be the target of discrimination and harassment related to homophobic language to receive support from school counselors. Provide discipline to students who harass or bully others in a homophobic way.

- Find out about local support groups, and encourage students who are dealing with their own sexual orientation issues or those of their parents to consider attending these support groups.

- Display gay-affirmative symbols in the school such as rainbow stickers.

Source: Adapted from Lamme, L. L., & Lamme, L. A. (2003). *Welcoming children from sexual-minority families into our schools.* Bloomington, IN: Phi Delta Kappa Educational Foundation; and Lamme, L. L., & Lamme, L. A. (2001/2002). Welcoming children from gay families into our schools. *Educational Leadership, 59,* 65–69.

As you learned in chapter 1, many family characteristics influence how a family adjusts to having a child with a disability. One of those characteristics is the type of disability. Research has shown that fathers (and mothers) of children with Down syndrome experience less stress from child-related factors than fathers of children whose disabilities are not associated with a particular etiology (Ricci & Hodapp, 2003). Certainty about the cause and nature of a disability makes a difference for fathers. Other factors also influence fathers, including income, education, and the use of particular coping strategies (Gavidia-Payne & Stoneman, 1997).

The father-child relationship has many potentially positive outcomes for children and youth. Fathers positively influence their children's cognitive, personal-social, and sex-role-identification development (Grossman et al., 2002; Roggman, Boyce, Cook, Christiansen, & Jones, 2004). Recent research shows that when fathers are involved with children at age 7, the children have better psychological adjustments in their teenage years (Flouri & Buchanan, 2003). Furthermore, when fathers are involved when their children are 16 years old, the children have few psychological problems when they are in their 30s. Clearly, fathers' involvement provides psychological protection for their children.

Research has focused on the types of activities that fathers do with their children. A study of the fathers of children in kindergarten through third grade reported that fathers of children with and without disabilities spend a comparable amount of time caring for their children. This study also found that fathers of both groups of children assess their level of competence as a parent in a similar way (Turbiville, 1994). Fathers of both groups reported spending similar amounts of time in school-related activities, but they indicated that they often do not complete the activities that teachers send home. Perhaps the activities suggested by teachers are not consistent with fathers' preferences. The activity these fathers most often shared with their children was watching television; thus, a likely avenue for enhancing father-child interaction may be supporting fathers to be more actively engaged with their children around television shows. Another study that focused only on families of children with severe disabilities found that fathers primarily were involved with their child with a disability in the areas of playing, nurturing, discipline, and deciding on services (Simmerman et al., 2001).

Research has identified how fathers in low-income families want to be involved in Early Head Start and Head Start programs. Both programs are designed for low-income families with preschool children, and both emphasize the child's early development. Research has shown that approximately half of the fathers participate in the programs in one way or another (Fagan, 1999). Slightly less than one fifth participate at levels that are considered high involvement. Interviews with 575 men whose children attended Early Head Start revealed that juggling work and other demands is the primary barrier to paternal involvement in a child's educational program (Summers, Boller, & Raikes, 2004). Fathers also said they need information about parenting and expressed their preferences for receiving information through parenting classes, written information, or a telephone hotline. A typical comment was:

Yeah, I could use help with everything. I could probably use some classes. I don't know what kind of classes are there, but I'd certainly be willing to go to a few to get some pointers on working with kids and how to raise them up as good as you can. . . . I could use some hints on how to get them to do what you want. How to make discipline more . . . of a forethought than an afterthought, if you know what I mean. And I just need help with day-to-day operations. (Summers et al., 2004, p. 70)

A group of fathers also responded that there were no barriers to their participation in their child's educational program, and they were not interested in any resources. When one father was asked if there is anything that human service agencies could do to help him as a father, he replied, "I don't ever go to any of that stuff. I'm on my own. I'll [take care] of my child on my own. I'd rather do it on my own instead of letting them people tell me what to do with my child. I do it on my own" (Summers et al., 2004, p. 71).

Because fathers have tended to be the "less apparent parent" (Turbiville, 1994), professionals should make an extra effort to establish partnerships with them (Frieman & Berkeley, 2002; Rump, 2002; Turbiville, Umbarger, & Guthrie, 1998). Figure 2–7 provides suggestions for how educators might reach out to fathers. Remember, there can be a number of significant men in the lives of children who do not have a formal father figure. Grandfathers and nonpaternal males such as male partners of mothers, teachers, men from the religious community, brothers, and neighbors can bring an important male presence into the lives of children. If you develop trusting partnerships with only one parent (or only one of several family members), it will probably fall short of being a family partnership. Be inclusive; reach out to all parents and to all family members if you have permission to do so.

Mothers.   Although the trend is for mothers and fathers to share parenting roles, mothers typically assume the larger part of the responsibility of tending to family needs (Renwick, Brown, & Raphael, 1998; Simmerman et al., 2001; Stoller, 1994; Traustadottir, 1991, 1995; Voydanoff & Donnelly, 1999). What are the consequences of this disproportionate responsibility?

Singer (in preparation) conducted a meta-analysis of studies that focused on maternal depression and concluded that 18% of mothers of children without disabilities and 32% of mothers of children with disabilities scored over the cutoff for minor depression. He noted that the majority (approximately 68% of mothers of children with disabilities) do not show elevated symptoms of depression. Singer also concluded that there is a far more pessimistic view of how mothers function when they

FIGURE 2–7

Tips for Developing Trusting Partnerships with Fathers of Children with Exceptionalities

- Policies in Practice
  - ✔ Include information about the importance of men in children's lives in mission statements, family handbooks, and family communications.
  - ✔ Involve the father during family/child program intake. If a father is not present, inquire about him or other significant male figures in the child's life, and stress their important roles in the family.
  - ✔ Arrange a time when both parents can participate when scheduling an IEP or IFSP meeting, teacher-parent conference, home visit, or family meeting.
  - ✔ Talk with the father as well as the mother when telephoning a family at home.
  - ✔ Review policies on how noncustodial parents can participate in program activities.
  - ✔ Ensure that program print materials communicate to men as well as women by monitoring the choices of paper color, graphics, topics, and language.
  - ✔ Learn the names of the father and other significant men in each child's life and take the time to talk with them individually.
- Education That Broadens Thinking
  - ✔ Conduct staff in-service programs about improving the quality of service delivery to fathers/males, with some of the training being provided by fathers themselves.
  - ✔ Survey men whose children are in the program to find out their interests and concerns.
  - ✔ Establish locally available father support groups.
  - ✔ Make available a quality library of print, audio, and video resources.
  - ✔ Display pictures and read books to children that portray men and children in a variety of settings.
- Organization to Make Involvement Work
  - ✔ Get fathers to serve on the agency/organization board and standing committees.
  - ✔ Involve fathers in physical, occupational, and speech therapy and in the classroom. For example, (1) offer an evening therapy and classroom time; (2) ask fathers to volunteer in the classroom; (3) teach fathers how to work with their child at home through play and other naturally occurring activites—swimming, on the playground, bath time, mealtime, and so on; or (4) videotape classroom activities and therapy so the father can follow his child's progress.
  - ✔ Recruit and employ male staff.
  - ✔ Encourage male participation by planning special "Dad and Me" or "Me and My Guy" events.

Source: Rump, M. L. (2002). Involving fathers of young children with special needs. *Young Children, 57*(6), 18–20. Adapted and reprinted with permission from the National Association for the Education of Young Children.

have children with disabilities than their real-life circumstances warrant. To address whether more mothers have symptoms of minor depression (but not at the level of clinical concern), he urges responsive services, supports, and resources to alleviate the additional challenges these mothers face.

An in-depth qualitative study of 14 mothers showed that mothers who provide care for children with severe disabilities organize their lives around their caring role and provide that care in three ways (Traustadottir, 1991):

1. *Caring for:* taking care of the child; in particular, acquiring the specialized knowledge and management procedures necessary for the child's development

2. *Caring about:* loving the child as a way of caring

3. *Extended caring:* performing collaborative advocacy roles that address the broader community and societal concerns related to issues of exceptionality

The majority of the mothers were full-time homemakers and mothers. The one exception was a mother who combined parenting responsibilities with a professional career in medicine at a large research university. She commented on the pressures she felt were pushing her to abandon her career and become a full-time caretaker:

The agency; the care giver; the doctor; the physical, occupational, and speech therapists with whom I came in contact, and with whom I continue to come in contact, assume that I, not my husband, am responsible for this child. But if anything has to be done in order to take care of her, I am the one who is responsible for that. It was assumed by almost everyone that I would give up my career. (Traustadottir, 1991, p. 223)

The mothers also identified the roles appropriate for fathers: (1) providing financial support, (2) supporting the mother's caretaking of the child and family, and (3) discussing with the mother what she learns from investigating services and programs and contributing to joint decision making. In the families where the fathers helped in these roles, the mothers described the marriage as being good; when fathers did not support these roles, mothers frequently expressed disappointment and frustration with the fathers' involvement.

Other research has documented that the more fathers help with child care, the more each parent is satisfied with the marriage (Willoughby & Glidden, 1995). A key factor appears to be the mother's satisfaction with the father's role in child care. Thus, for many families it is not the actual extent of child care by the father but that the mother and father agree on the father's role (Simmerman et al., 2001). We discussed single mothers in chapter 1 and pointed out the potential drawbacks and benefits of meeting family responsibilities without a marital partner.

Annually more than 1 million American teenagers become parents (Alan Guttmacher Institute, 1996). The United States has the highest rate of live births to teenagers in the postindustrialized world; the rate is 55 per 1,000 females between the ages of 15 and 19. In addition to taking on the responsibilities of parenting, teenage mothers often experience low income, single parenthood, low educational levels, and poor health outcomes associated with pregnancy (Furstenberg, 2003). Parenting programs aimed at teenage mothers may be delivered in a group or on a one-to-one basis. They also vary in the intensity and duration of the programs (Barlow & Coren, 2000; Barlow & Stewart-Brown, 2000; Coren, Barlow, & Stewart-Brown, 2003). Programs are offered in schools, homes, health clinics, and family support centers. Overall, researchers conclude that parent programs for teenage mothers have produced positive changes in both parent and child outcomes. The most typical programs appear to be group based and offered over a 12- to 16-week span. Researchers speculate that a group setting enables teenage mothers to benefit from peer perspectives and support. A concern in many programs is the high dropout rate, ranging from about one third to nearly one half. If you are working with teenage mothers, ask those who drop out from the programs or seem unwilling or unable to partner with you to identify the barriers they encountered. Structure programs and interactions to facilitate their retention in the program and heighten their involvement with you.

Almost all of the literature related to teenage parents of children with disabilities focuses on mothers, and very little attention is given to teenage fathers (Coren et al., 2003). Figure 2–8 includes tips for developing successful partnerships with teenage parents of children with disabilities. Many of these tips apply to both mothers and fathers, and some are specific to one or the other.

We encourage you to read first-person accounts written by teenage mothers. Excellent sources include Gill (1997), Leff and Walizer (1992), Miller (1994), and Rose and Gallup (1998).

In summary, the parental subsystem is complex. There are different types of parental units, each unit is influenced by cultural considerations, and each member of the parental unit has different strengths and needs.

Sibling Subsystem

The sibling subsystem consists of the interactions between brothers and sisters. One of the most obvious interactions relates to socializing; brothers and sisters often provide the first and perhaps the most intense peer relationships that their siblings experience (Powell & Gallagher, 1993). Through their interactions, brothers and sisters give each other opportunities to experience sharing, companionship, loyalty, rivalry, and other feelings. As with all family relationships, the nature of the brother-sister bond is culturally rooted. Different cultures have different expectations for siblings, and those expectations often depend on age, birth order, and gender (Harry, Day, & Quist, 1998).

Although siblings can be socialization agents (Gallagher et al., 2000) and even tutors (Tekin & Kircaali-Iftar, 2002) during their younger years, they often are increasingly responsible for providing care and coordinating services for their brother or sister with a significant disability. These roles increase as their parents age. In fact, research on families whose members with a disability have lived with their parents well into their early and middle adulthood shows that siblings, especially sisters, provide caregiving and companionship when their parents are in the later stages of life (Krauss, Mailick-Seltzer, Gordon, & Haig-Friedman, 1996; Orsmond & Seltzer, 2000). Although parents consistently identify siblings as the ones who will assume the parental role, families often have a hard time talking about future plans; there are simply too many unknowns. Yet many brothers and sisters of children with disabilities worry about future caretaking roles when their parents are no longer available (Damiani, 1999).

Brothers or sisters with an exceptionality influence their siblings in many different ways (Damiani, 1999; Fisman, Wolf, Ellison, & Freeman, 2000; Heller, Gallagher, & Frederick, 1999; Lardieri, Blacher, & Swanson, 2000; Stoneman & Waldman-Berman, 1993). Some siblings benefit from the relationship. Benefits include enhanced maturity, self-esteem, social competence, insight, tolerance, pride, vocational opportunities, advocacy, and loyalty

FIGURE 2–8

Tips for Developing Trusting Partnerships with Teenage Parents

---

- Suggestions for Developing Trust
  - ✔ Provide consistent teachers to young children whom the teens can count on to communicate with them on a regular basis.
  - ✔ Schedule teens as active participants in the center so that they can regularly see what is going on.
  - ✔ Find ways to identify with the teens by engaging in shared, enjoyable activities.
  - ✔ Address individual teens' needs and concerns by scheduling regular appointments and opportunities to communicate.
  - ✔ Respect confidentiality and privacy to ensure that you do not betray teens' confidences.
- Suggestions for Developing Autonomy
  - ✔ Provide teens with power and choice to increase the likelihood that they have some control in their lives.
  - ✔ Provide a classroom structure that fosters safe exploration so that teens will feel safe taking risks.
  - ✔ Help teens demonstrate and manage responsibility as a precursor to developing more independence.

- Suggestions for Developing Initiative
  - ✔ Help teens make plans and set goals to encourage enhanced development.
  - ✔ Practice, model, and teach positive discipline to encourage teenagers to incorporate positive discipline at home.
- Suggestions for Developing Industriousness
  - ✔ Provide opportunities for teens to demonstrate competence as a foundation for encouraging more success in the future.
  - ✔ Provide recognition to teens for their accomplishments to enhance their self-esteem.
- Suggestions for Developing a Positive Identity
  - ✔ Provide opportunities for teens to be reflective to enhance the likelihood that they are sensitive, responsive caregivers.
  - ✔ Provide resources and supports that connect teens to the future to increase the likelihood that they will work toward education and employment goals.

Source: DeJong, L. (2003). Using Erikson to work more effectively with teenage parents. *Young Children, 58*(2), 87–95. Adapted and reprinted with permission from the National Association for the Education of Young Children.

Others experience negative effects. Those include embarrassment, guilt, isolation, resentment, increased responsibility, and pressure to achieve. Still others regard having a brother or sister with a disability as a neutral experience. Like all sibling relationships, positive and negative reactions occur simultaneously. There is no single definitive impact; impact depends on the size of the family, birth order, gender, the nature of the exceptionality, coping styles, and other special challenges occurring within the family.

Some studies have found that brothers and sisters who have a sibling with a disability have a higher incidence of negative outcomes, such as their own emotional/behavioral problems (Fisman et al., 2000; Orsillo, McCaffrey, & Fisher, 1993). Other research has not found significantly greater emotional/behavioral problems (Hannah & Midlarsky, 1999). Indeed, some studies have found these siblings to have fewer behavioral problems and even more positive qualities, such as empathy, than siblings of children who do not have disabilities (Carr, 1988; Cuskelly & Gunn, 2003).

Another area with conflicting research is the extent to which brothers and sisters experience self-esteem or self-efficacy. Some research indicates that children who have brothers and sisters with exceptionalities experience lower self-esteem or self-efficacy than children who do not have such a sibling (McHale & Gamble, 1989). Other research, however, indicates no difference in self-efficacy (Dyson, Edgar, & Crnic, 1989; Dyson & Fewell, 1989; Grissom & Borkowski, 2002; Hannah & Midlarsky, 1999; Van Riper, 2000). Research also points to a significantly higher locus of internal control (perceived control) in children who have a sibling with an exceptionality (Burton & Parks, 1994).

Sibling effects also occur when one of the children in the family is identified as gifted or talented. The other siblings may be jealous and become more competitive with the sibling who is regarded as gifted, or they may be competitive with each other if each is gifted (Stephens, 1999). Birth order appears to be an important factor, creating greater sibling problems when the second-born sibling is identified as gifted and fewer problems when the labeled child is first born (Tuttle & Cornell, 1993).

Don Meyer, a national leader in creating support programs for siblings of children with exceptionalities, has created a model known as "Sibshops." These workshops provide information and emotional support for brothers and sisters (Meyer & Vadasy, 1994). If your community does not sponsor Sibshops, you might collaborate with families, educators, people with disabilities, and other community citizens to start one. An evaluation of a program (similar to Sibshops) for school-age siblings found that siblings learned how to improve their relationships with their brother or sister with a disability and had become more aware of special needs (Dyson, 1998). Go to *www.seattlechildrens.org/child_health_safety/special_needs/sibshops.asp* for more information.

Figure 2–9 describes the Sibshop model and how one community worked together to start this program.

Can siblings be helpful in promoting the successful inclusion of their brother or sister with a disability? Yes, according to one research study (Gallagher et al., 2000). Siblings offer valuable perspectives on how to include their brother or sister with a disability in school and other activities. The child with a disability often wants to emulate his or her brother or sister or at least be in the same school. Brothers and sisters can ensure that their sibling with a disability receives opportunities and encouragement at school and in community activities. Siblings can serve as a conduit of information between the school and their parents.

Because brothers and sisters carry out important roles within a family, it behooves professionals to include them in family partnerships. Read first-person narratives for additional insight into sibling perspectives (Gans, 1997; Meyer, 1997; Meyer & Vadasy, 1994).

Extended Family Subsystem

Think of each person in your extended family and then total how many there are. Reflect on the role that they have had in your life, beginning when you were a young child until the present time. What factors have either increased or decreased their availability and support?

The answers to these questions may depend upon your cultural background. Cultures tend to define the composition of extended family and the frequency of contact between the nuclear and extended families (Lynch & Hanson, 2004; McGoldrick et al., 1996). Consider these two examples:

In most American Indian families, the concept of family is defined broadly to include extended family members and fictive kin (i.e., nonfamily members incorporated into the family network) in addition to the immediate family (Malach et al., 1989). Other members of the family's tribe may be included as well. In many cases, extended family members rather than the biological parents may hold primary responsibility for care of the children. Often, grandparents or other extended family members willingly assume child-rearing responsibilities so parents of young children can be employed. Furthermore, parents may seek the advice and assistance of older family members and elders in the larger family network, given the value placed on age and life experiences. In interventions, these extended family members may act as service coordinators for child and family to obtain needed services. (Joe & Malach, 2004, pp. 117, 119)

Latinos, as a whole, adhere to a collective sense of family, often resulting in extended family configurations that offer valuable support services (Vega et al., 1983). Moreover, the godparent or *compadre* system offers support by adding to the family via marriage and the use of godparents at baptism, confirmation, and the *quinceañeras*, the coming-out celebrations for 15-year-old girls. (Zuniga, 2004, p. 196)

Although many diverse cultures historically value the support of extended family members, you should not assume that every family from a culturally or linguistically diverse background gains its greatest support from extended family members (Bailey et al., 1999). The collective orientation of extended family support, for example, with Latino families, does not always hold true:

I've got brothers and a half-sister. If I go ask for help, they'll say why do you need help? You've got money, you go hire somebody or go get somebody or a specialist or whatever. Why do you come to me? What can I help you with? . . . That's the way they are. That's the way I feel with my family. If I had a choice between a brother and a pastor or a president or anything, a stranger, I think I would prefer to go to a stranger than my brother. (Blue-Banning, 1995, p. 11)

From the outset, then, ask the parents to define which family members they want to involve as they work with you and other professionals. Only after they identify these extended family members should you try to identify culturally sensitive ways for including them in partnerships.

Grandparents can make life easier or harder for families (Hastings, 1997). When 120 mothers of a child with moderate to profound intellectual disability were asked to describe the grandparents' role, 45% said they received help with child care from grandparents, 40% received advice and encouragement, 16% had help with household tasks, and 15% received financial assistance (Heller, Hsieh, & Rowitz, 2000). Other studies have also reported support from grandparents (Able-Boone, Sandall, Stevens, & Frederick, 1992; Sandler, 1998; Seligman, Goodwin, Paschal, Applegate, & Lehman, 1997). One study, however, documented that approximately one fourth of the

FIGURE 2–9
Advocacy Partners: Siblings Go Shopping

When teachers go shopping for information about how to teach, they have readily available resources—universities, colleges, bookstores, professional workshops, colleagues, and the Internet. When parents of children with disabilities go shopping for information or emotional support, they too have access to scores of resources—federally funded parent training and information centers, Parent-to-Parent chapters, local associations of families interested in particular types of disability, and, of course, universities, colleges, bookstores, and the Internet.

But where do the brothers and sisters of children with disabilities go to shop for information and support? Yes, some of them can find what they want from schools or colleges, bookstores, and the Internet. And, if they are lucky, they also can go shopping and come home with an armful of support if they land in a "Sibshop." Yes, that's right: a shop for siblings of children with disabilities.

Sibshops are like other stores. They offer something that particular shoppers need. When the shoppers are brothers and sisters, Sibshops offer a day to meet other brothers and sisters and a place to discuss the issues on which brothers and sisters often speak out openly and those about which they remain silent, bothered, and bewildered.

Sibshops operate under the joint supervision of Don Meyer—who started the Sibshops in his hometown of Seattle, Washington, in the 1980s—and of adults who work in schools or other disability agencies in a community. They are open to children who are in the same age brackets (elementary school, middle school, and high school). For example, one Sibshop could be for brothers and sisters who are ages 6 to 9, and another for those ages 10 to 13. It does not matter what kind of disability a brother or sister might have; siblings' experiences include living with a person who has chronic health, mental health, learning, and developmental disabilities.

When they come together, the brothers and sisters talk about those easy-to-mention topics such as how they have become more mature, insightful, tolerant, and socially competent because they are growing up with a brother or sister who has a disability. They learn where to get information about disability and where they might find support for themselves outside a Sibshop, such as on the Internet or through "SibKids," the worldwide Listserv. And they have fun activities . . . lots of them, so that they learn to trust each other with their thoughts.

And then they begin to talk about those silent, troublesome, perplexing, and often shameful aspects of life with a brother or sister who has a disability. About embarrassment in public; guilt because they don't have a disability or because they resent the amount of family resources devoted to the member with a disability; feelings of being isolated, lonely, and different because their brother or sister is different; unwillingness to take on the additional responsibilities, now and perhaps in the future, that come with having a brother or sister with a disability; and increased pressure, actual or perceived, to achieve at their fullest capacities or even beyond because their brother or sister is not likely to be a high achiever.

Sibshops are an international phenomenon. They occur in large cities, suburbs, and rural areas. Their curriculum has been used all across the United States and in such diverse countries as Mexico, Argentina, and Guatemala in Central and South America; England, Canada, Australia, and New Zealand in the British Commonwealth countries; Croatia and Iceland in Europe; and Japan in East Asia.

So, the next time you hear your students with a disability or their parents complain about a brother or sister, or when you hear a brother or sister responding one way or another to disability in the family, pause and ask yourself: Where could the sibling go shopping for information and support? And then, turn into a Sibshop starter, because education and advocacy involve the whole family.

Source: Adapted from Meyer, D. J., & Vadasy, P. F. (1994). *Sibshops: Workshops for siblings of children with special needs.* Baltimore: Paul H. Brookes Publishing Company; and The Sibling Support Project online at *http://www.thearc.org/siblingsupport/*

rents said the grandparents' attempts to be helpful actually produced more stress (Hornby & Ashworth, 1994). describing their experiences with their child's traumatic brain injury, a parent commented:

You have your extended family who is there grieving also, and sometimes I think you want to say, "What are you feeling sorry for yourself about? I'm the one in this situation." You

have to deal with their grief when you aren't even through dealing with your own grief, so sometimes it's harder to have them around depending on the relationship. (Singer & Nixon, 1996, p. 27)

A different kind of stress occurs when the child is diagnosed with a genetic condition (Bailey, Skinner, & Sparkman, 2003). Typically, parents receive genetic counseling and then must explain these findings to grandparents, uncles, aunts, or other members of their extended family. One study investigated the perspective of parents who had children with the genetic condition known as Fragile X syndrome. Nearly all of the parents reported that either they or their spouse informed extended family members of the genetic test results. Approximately two thirds of the parents described this experience as either somewhat stressful or very stressful since extended family members needed to consider the meaning of the results for themselves. This was especially true for siblings of the parent who was the genetic carrier of the condition.

Families typically have more than one grandparent from whom they might receive support. Researchers who collected information from 42 mothers of children with varying disabilities reported that mothers said their own mothers were more supportive of their child with a disability than their spouses' mothers (Seligman et al., 1997). This study also found that grandmothers were generally more supportive than grandfathers, and grandparents provided more emotional support than help with daily care tasks.

A study of the extent of grandparent support (Heller et al., 2000) reported that parents of children with a disability received less practical help with everyday tasks than parents of children without disabilities; however, both groups received the same amount of emotional support.

Grandparents and other extended family members of children with exceptionalities need information and support to deal with their own feelings and to know how to provide care for the rest of the family (Janicky, McCallion, Grant-Griffin, & Kolomer, 2000; Nicholson, Sweeney, & Geller, 1998; Sandler, 1998). Grandparents' or family members' ideas about people with disabilities may be more traditional than those of the child's parents. For example, a Latino mother of a young child with a disability described how her own mother agreed to make a *mandos* (bargain) related to her grandchild. She promised the Virgin of Guadalupe (Mexico) that she would visit the basilica and wear the colors of the Virgin every day if the Virgin would heal her grandchild. The child's own mother did not subscribe to her mother's approach; the differences were more generational than spiritual.

Up until this point, we have focused on grandparents as part of the extended family; however, many grandparents assume the parenting role. In 1999 approximately 1.4 million children lived in households headed by grandparents (Force, Botsford, Pisano, & Holbert, 2000). The number of grandparents who are care providers for their grandchildren has increased substantially over the last 10 years (Janicky et al., 2000). Some of the reasons include teenage parents, unemployment, poverty, substance abuse, maternal incarceration, and child abuse and neglect. Grandparent-headed households occur across all racial/ethnic groups, but grandparents assume the role of primary care provider more frequently in African American and Latino families (Smith, Dannison, & Vach-Hasse, 1998).

A study of 164 grandparents providing primary care to grandchildren with disabilities in New York revealed that 96% were female and 80% were African American (Janicky et al., 2000). Grandparents identified two reasons for assuming caregiving duties: to cope with substance abuse by the child's mother and to prevent the child from being placed in foster care because of parental child abuse and neglect. Approximately three fourths of the grandparents reported that the children experienced problems in school, and two thirds said the children had challenging behavior and developmental delays. The researchers concluded:

- Caregiving was an all-consuming role in their lives,
- Their days were fraught with uncertainty because they generally could not access proficient formal and informal supports, and
- They were constantly worried about remaining alive long enough to provide care for their grandchildren into adulthood (Janicky et al., 2000, p. 49).

A comparison of grandparents who were raising a grandchild with a disability and those raising a child without a disability revealed that both groups were caring for an average of two children (Force et al., 2000). Although grandparents raising children with and without disabilities had many similarities, they also differed. Grandparents who had a child with a disability reported a greater need for help from schools, a greater need for transportation, and greater use of speech therapy services. Few other significant differences emerged between the groups. Only about 10% of the grandparents raising a grandchild with a disability had contact with disability service agencies. It is important for schools or other service-providing agencies to reach out to grandparents who are the primary care provider, especially since both groups of grandparents had symptoms of depression.

Figure 2–10 includes suggestions on providing information and skills that can assist extended family members to support the child and family.

COHESION AND ADAPTABILITY

We have just described the subsystems—the people who interact in the family. Now it is time to consider how they interact. We will start by explaining two elements

FIGURE 2–10
Enhancing Extended-Family Interactions

- Provide parents with information to help them better understand the needs and reactions of extended-family members.

- Provide information about exceptionality, the needs of children, and the needs of families that parents can give to extended-family members.

- Encourage the development of grandparent or extended-family–member support groups. Those groups might be facilitated by school social workers, psychologists, PTA volunteers who are grandparents, or extended-family members of students with an exceptionality.

- Encourage extended-family participation in IEP conferences, classroom visits, school events, and family support programs.

- Provide library materials and resources for extended-family members.

of interaction—cohesion and adaptability. The degrees of cohesion and adaptability in a family describe (1) the ways that members of family subsystems interact and (2) the nature of boundaries among family subsystems and among family members and nonmembers (Olson, Russell, & Sprenkle, 1980). We then will discuss the implications for your partnerships with families.

We issue a significant caution. As you learned in chapter 1, the rules governing family interaction are rooted in one's culture (for example, individualism or collectivism). Your students' families will vary in cohesion, adaptability, and what works for them (Lynch & Hanson, 2004; McGoldrick et al., 1996).

Because many of the studies and research about family systems have been conducted by European American researchers with European American research participants (Scott-Jones, 1993), some professionals think that the level of cohesion and adaptability acceptable to European American families is the level to which all families should adhere. As you learned in Chapter 1, however, culture and other characteristics significantly affect families, and professionals must honor each in developing partnerships.

Cohesion

You have already learned that certain boundaries serve as lines of demarcation between people who are inside and outside a subsystem. The roles that members of a subsystem play often define these boundaries (Minuchin & Fish-

man, 1981). For example, the two adult members in a traditional nuclear family may interact with each other in the roles of husband and wife and with their children as father and mother. Boundaries may be open or closed; that is, they may or may not be accessible to interaction with people outside the subsystem. From a European American perspective, subsystems are typically open enough to allow individual autonomy and closed enough to provide support for each family member (Summers, 1987).

These boundaries also help define families' bonding relationships. Family members typically feel closer to each other than to those outside the family or its subsystem relationships. This element of family bonding relates to cohesion (Olson, Sprenkle, & Russell, 1979).

Family cohesion refers to family members' close emotional bonding with each other and to the level of independence they feel within the family system (Olson et al., 1980; Olson, 1988). Cohesion exists across a continuum, with high disengagement on one end and high enmeshment on the other. One author used the physical metaphor of "the touching of hands" to describe cohesion in the family:

> The dilemma is how to be close yet separate. When the fingers are intertwined, it at first feels secure and warm. Yet when one partner (or family member) tries to move, it is difficult at best. The squeezing pressure may even be painful. . . . The paradox of every relationship is how to touch and yet not hold on. (Carnes, 1981, pp. 70, 71)

Some families may perceive themselves or be perceived by others as not touching enough or as being highly intertwined. Most families, however, operate somewhere in the center of the cohesion continuum.

Range of Cohesion. When families are highly cohesive, boundaries among their subsystems are blurred or weak (Minuchin & Fishman, 1981). For example, a mother with many physical-care demands for a child who is deaf and blind may delegate some of the responsibilities to an older daughter. The daughter may have fewer parent-child and other-sibling interactions because she has been drawn into the parental subsystem. Her own needs as a child and a sibling may be overlooked or subordinated.

Your challenge is to identify the appropriate extent of cohesion and protectiveness according to each family's cultural beliefs. What may appear to be overprotection in one culture may be appropriate protection, nurturance, and affection in another. For example, Latino families may find it acceptable for preteens or even adolescents to sit on their mother's lap or for preschoolers to drink from a baby bottle long after European American parents would consider those actions inappropriate (Zuniga, 2004).

When you honor families' cultures, you provide the context for trust to evolve in your partnerships with them.

What happens when families have low degrees of cohesion, even to the point that children with exceptionalities are isolated from other family members? Limited interaction leaves children without the support, closeness, and assistance needed to develop independence. Disengaged family interactions include underinvolvement, few shared interests or friends, excessive privacy, and a great deal of time apart. Few decisions require family input and involvement. For all family members, particularly the member with an exceptionality, low cohesion can be both lonely and difficult.

Disengaged relationships can take place within and among subsystems. For example, disengagement within a subsystem exists when a father denies the child's exceptionality and withdraws from parental and marital interactions. Disengagement among subsystems occurs when the members of the extended family cannot accept the child and that part of the family subsystem is excluded from family celebrations.

Implications of Cohesion. Positive outcomes accrue for families when family cohesion is balanced (Dyson, 1993; Gavidia-Payne, & Stoneman 1997). A high level of cohesion is an early predictor of children's growth and communication, social skills, and daily living skills (Hauser-Cram et al., 1999). By contrast, low family cohesion is a predictor of greater parenting and child-related stress at important transition points, such as leaving early intervention programs and entering kindergarten (Warfield et al., 1999). Low family cohesion is a much stronger predictor of parenting and child stress than such characteristics as the child's age or level of cognitive impairment. These generalizations have exceptions; one study of families of adult children with mental retardation did not find a significant relationship between family adjustment and cohesion (Lustig & Akey, 1999). Moreover, studies of the positive contributions that individuals with disabilities make to their families have revealed that parents especially value the increased family unity and closeness that comes from the disability (Behr & Murphy, 1993; Summers, Behr, & Turnbull, 1989; Stainton & Besser, 1998; Turnbull, Guess, & Turnbull, 1988).

You should help families establish a comfortable level of cohesion for two reasons. First, by recognizing the levels of cohesion between and within subsystems, you can create a context that supports the family as a whole to meet its needs as well as the child's.

Second, by considering the degree of family cohesion, you can provide appropriate services and supports or refer the family to those services (Taanila, Järvelin, & Kokkonen, 1999). For example, you will know to ask whether a particular program encourages a culturally appropriate level of cohesion. Or you will be competent to make appropriate early education recommendations. Mothers who are highly involved in early childhood programs are sometimes unintentionally reinforced for establishing highly cohesive relationships with their young children. They are encouraged to spend considerable time in the classroom, attend mothers' groups, provide home teaching, and transport children to various services (Turnbull et al., 2000). When they spend all this time with the child, what happens to their own needs and the needs of other family members? Obviously, you will want to be sensitive to the implications of your professional recommendations.

Adaptability

Adaptability refers to the family's ability to change in response to situational and developmental stress (Olson et al., 1980; Olson, 1998). As with a family's cohesion, its adaptability is influenced by family values and cultural background. Adaptability can be viewed on a continuum: at one end are families who are unable or unwilling to change in response to stress; at the other end are families who are constantly changing, so much so that they create significant confusion (Olson et al., 1979). Again, most families fall somewhere in the center.

Ranges of Adaptability. At one end of the adaptability continuum, families demonstrate a high degree of control and structure, and their interactions involve many strictly enforced rules. These families firmly delineate the hierarchy of authority along with the roles that each person plays. Negotiating authority and roles is rare and usually intolerable. Consider the example of a son who sustains a brain injury and accompanying physical disability. The family must deal immediately with crisis intervention in the trauma setting (Cope & Wolfson, 1994) and later with many new demanding physical, economic, and emotional needs to provide both acute and long-term care (Kreutzer, Serio, & Bergquist, 1994; Singer, Glang, & Williams, 1996). If, in the past, the child's mother was primarily responsible for meeting the child's needs, the added caregiving demands may be more than she can handle. If the family has difficulty sharing new responsibilities with collaborators outside the family, the added demands can create stress for the mother as well as other family members.

There are two reasons to consider high degrees of control in the family power hierarchy as you propose educational programs. First, many families gradually adapt their power hierarchies to support their child or adolescent to become a self-determined adult. As noted earlier, self-determination is culturally rooted. Some families place great value on their children's increasing autonomy, whereas others consider self-determination culturally inappropriate (Kalyanpur & Harry, 1999; Turnbull & Turnbull, 1996). You need to be sensitive while negotiating the degree of student decision making that the family considers appropriate.

Second, it is helpful to identify the person or persons who have primary control over family decisions and rules. For example, if you ask a mother to implement a home-based language program but do not take into account the husband's decision-making power and possible rejection of your request, it is unlikely that the program will be effective. Indeed, if the mother carries out the intervention against her husband's wishes, the program may create marital and parental conflict. You should examine how any recommendation for home teaching will affect each family member. Work with the family to develop options consistent with its values, goals, and ability and willingness to adapt.

In contrast, other families demonstrate a low degree of control and structure. Their interactions often are characterized by few rules, and even these are seldom enforced. Promises and commitments are often unkept, and family members learn that they cannot depend upon one another. Frequently, there is no family leader, negotiations are endless, and roles are unsure and often changing.

All families can experience periods of chaos during stressful life events. But when chaos is a consistent way of life, the consequences can be negative for the family and the student with an exceptionality. Consider the example of a mother with a son who has attention-deficit/hyperactivity disorder. The child has difficulty academically and socially. The mother has a live-in boyfriend who is the family's primary source of financial support. During the last 2 years, the boyfriend has begun to drink heavily and abuse family members. When the boyfriend begins to fight, existing rules are suddenly harshly interpreted for the child. When the fighting escalates, the rules change; survival is the main concern. Later the remorseful boyfriend becomes extremely indulgent, creating a third set of rules. The instability and chaos continue. Because of his disability, the youngster already experiences difficulty interpreting social cues accurately, and his ever-revolving family lifestyle only exacerbates his problems.

Implications of Adaptability. Well-functioning families typically strike a balance between the extremes of high or low adaptability (Olson et al., 1980). A study of the adjustment of parents of adult sons and daughters with

mental retardation showed that families' adaptation is a key factor contributing to positive adjustment (Lustig & Akey, 1999). Family members often value debating a wide range of choices (adaptability) while also maintaining their ties of commitment (cohesion).

There are three ways to support those families who are dissatisfied with their current level of adaptability. First, help families plan for change. If possible, discuss schedule changes and transitions well in advance. Ask yourself: Is this change too sudden or radical for this family's current level of adaptability? Some students and families may benefit from gradual transitions. When a student will be changing classrooms or school buildings, it may be helpful to start with a gradual transition, one day a week, before making the complete transition. If a child needs to learn how to ride the bus, intermediate steps may be reassuring: riding only part of the way, riding with a friend or family member, or bringing the bus driver into the planning team.

Second, encourage families to examine alternatives. Many families who lack adaptability may not know how to examine alternatives (Shank & Turnbull, 1993; Summers, Templeton-McMann & Fuger, 1997). They might benefit from learning a problem-solving process. A service coordinator in an early intervention program described the perspectives of a parent who could benefit from problem-solving support:

> One woman finally decided to kick out her abusive boyfriend. We talked about arranging for him to pack his things and leave while she was gone. But she says to me, "What if he takes all the food with him?" And I respond, "Well, we'll have to think about things like the food pantry, or something." And then she says, "I don't know how to keep him out because he has keys." So I say, "Well, call your landlord and see if you can change the locks." (Summers et al., 1997, p. 41)

Third, if a family may be interested in receiving services from the school counselor, school social worker, or other community professionals, collaborate with the school counselor or social worker on how to approach the family and suggest these alternatives. If a family asks you about possible resources, refer members to those resources. Remember, however, that family dynamics are complicated and often require highly specialized professionals to provide the most appropriate and personalized supports. Knowing when to refer a family is critical for all professionals in special education.

SUMMARY

The best way to understand family interactions is to view the family as a system. There are three major assumptions in family systems theory. First, in a family, as in most systems, there are inputs. The family responds to and interacts with the inputs and as a result creates certain outputs in carrying out its family functions.

Second, the family system must be understood as a whole entity; it cannot be understood by examining only its component parts. The family consists of subsystems (marital, parental, sibling, and extended). The child with an exceptionality can have negative, positive, and mixed impacts on each of these subsystems.

Third, family subsystems are separated by boundaries that define the interaction family members have with each other and with people outside the family. The family's cultural heritage and other characteristics (see chapter 1) affect family members' interactions and the nature of boundaries.

Two elements of family interaction are cohesion and adaptability. The term *family cohesion* refers to the emotional attachment that family members have toward each other and the level of independence each feels within the family. Some families are extraordinarily cohesive; they are enmeshed with each other. Other families are quite the opposite; they are disengaged from each other. Although some families are characterized by excessive degrees of closeness or disengagement, most find a balance between these two extremes.

Similarly, some families are extraordinarily adaptable; they seem to have an unlimited ability to change in response to situational and developmental stress. Others are quite unadaptable; the least amount of stress is unsettling and disruptive. Again, most families strike a happy medium.

ENHANCING YOUR SELF-AWARENESS

As you reflect on your own family's interactions, think about what has worked well for you and what has not. Families with whom you develop partnerships will have their own style of family interaction. What can you learn from your personal experiences to help families have the most positive interactions possible?

Cohesion

How would you describe your family's cohesion during the years when you were a young child, and how did that cohesion change or not change over your family's life cycle? How did your family's cohesion affect you in establishing more independence as a young adult?

Adaptability

Did your family ever face a stressful situation that required every member to adapt to change? What helped your family be successful with change? What were the barriers? How will your own experiences with adaptability enable you to understand the stress that your students' families face?

Siblings

How did your birth order influence your relationships with your siblings? How did they provide a positive and not-so-positive influence? Based on your own experiences, how can siblings be helpful when they have a brother or a sister with an intellectual or physical disability?

REFLECTING ON THE VIGNETTE

1. Are family interactions always clear to an outsider? How could a school administrator know, for example, how Tatiana and Juan Cortes support Norma when she has to meet with Joesian's teachers? How could a physician know, for example, that Nicky's aunt is a registered nurse and translates much of the medical jargon to Nicky's other family members, especially Vera?

2. Are family interactions always clearly demarcated, even within a family? Do the brothers and sisters of Joesian and Nicky play some roles that are nearly indistinguishable from their parents' roles?

3. Does the fact that Clara Berg placed her son Kenny at a school far away from their home mean that her family is not cohesive?

RESOURCES

1. American Association for Marriage and Family Therapy
   112 South Alfred Street
   Alexandria, VA 22314–3061
   703–838–9808
   www.aamft.org

   The American Association for Marriage and Family Therapy (AAMFT) is a professional association with more than 23,000 marriage and family therapists as members. Its major mission is to increase education, understanding, and research related to the priorities of couples and other family members. AAMFT hosts an annual conference and training institutes and produces publications (journal, magazine, brochures).

2. Family Living Programs
   University of Wisconsin Extension
   637 Extension Building
   432 Lake Street
   Madison, WI 53706
   608-263-1095
   www.uwex.edu/ces/flp/

   As part of the University of Wisconsin Extension Service, Family Living Programs provides extensive information to promote family well-being. One of their special programs is called Grandparenting Today. They have fact sheets, newsletters, curriculum, videos, books, and manuals related to grandparents in a traditional role, as well as grandparents who have taken on the parenting role of their grandchildren.

3. Families Like Mine
   1730 New Brighton Boulevard, PMB 175
   Minneapolis, MN 55413
   866-245-4281
   www.familieslikemine.com

   Families Like Mine is designed for mature teens and adults who have parents who are lesbian, gay, bisexual, or transgender. Extensive print and media resources are available from their Website as well as opportunities to share insights and get advice.

4. Woodbine House
   6510 Bells Mill Road
   Bethesda, MD 20817
   800-843-7323
   http://woodbinehouse.com

   Woodbine House specializes in topics related to disability. They have first-person books and essays written by mothers and fathers of children with disabilities. They also have children's books that focus on sibling issues.

3

Family Functions

CHAPTER ORGANIZATION

1. What are all the different responsibilities that families must assume for their members?
2. How does a child with a disability impact each of these areas of responsibility?
3. What can educators do to enable families to be as successful as possible in meeting their responsibilities?

VIGNETTE

Remember the baby in the crib with a mobile above her? How all of the mobile's arms moved when she touched only one arm? The metaphor of a mobile serves not only to help you understand family interactions, but also to introduce the concept of family functions.

The mobile has a single, central arm, typically perpendicular, hanging from a support and pointing downward toward the ground. Branching off that central arm are other smaller arms. The central arm serves the unifying function; the branched arms serve the movement function.

Likewise, in families, the child's disability or other exceptionality serves a unifying role, helping us to understand how other members of the family function. What are those functions, and how are they manifested in the four families you met in the prologue?

Let us begin with the function we call *affection*. It's the nearly smothering hugs that Clara Berg bestows on Kenny when he returns home from work at Adriance Farm; it's the love that Vera

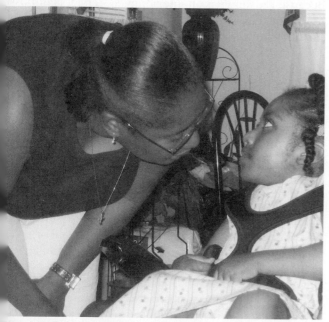

Charolette Doleman takes special pride in dressing her daughter, Nicky, for school each day.

Doleman brings to Nicky and the careful grooming with which Charolette Doleman prepares Nicky for school each morning.

With affection comes a sense of worth, the beloved comes to love himself. To ask Joesian Cortes why he is in special education and to hear him say, without shame, that he reads slowly and has trouble speaking is to understand just how highly he regards himself. He accompanies his answer with an enthusiastic explanation: He works with his uncle, he spends hours riding his bike throughout New York's five boroughs, and he takes the subways and buses to and from Bushwick High School and his vocational training program in Manhattan.

Not every family has an instinct toward a Supreme Being, but many do and enliven that instinct in their daily lives. Vera Doleman describes her faith as a "centralizing factor" in her life, as the element that reminds her why she lives and to whom Nicky belongs. Norma and Joesian Cortes most likely would not have found it so easy for Joesian to be admitted to the Manhattan vocational education program had it not been for the fact that Norma, Martha Vizcarrondo at United We Stand of New York, and Emily Rodriguez, the assistant principal at Bushwick High School, were of the same faith. Martha and Emily were involved in missionary work in the Caribbean. To have a meal with the Bergs in their home is to see icons of their faith on the walls of their dining room. To hear Clara Berg and Carole Gothelf speak about "surviving" and "survivors" is to know that these two words carry Holocaustic references.

On more practical levels, families are economic units. They are consumers and providers. They are consumers of school and disability services. They are providers of food, clothing, shelter, education, and other benefits for their family members. Jake Berg is retired but Clara works, and so does Kenny. Norma Cortes does not work outside the home, but Joaqin does, and both of them expect Joesian, Tatiana, and Juan to work. Vera Doleman works the evening shift at the local Hallmark Card production site but can do that only because Charolette and grandparents Aaron and Marie take care of Nicky. Leia Holley has transformed her advocacy for Sean into a full-time job with the Kansas parent and training center, and Jamie Holley serves his family and his country as a major in the United States Army.

Families look after their own. Caregiving is the daily role for each of the four families although the type of care varies. Kenny's parents ensure that all of the services he needs are consistently provided and mutually complementary. Joesian receives advocacy and direction both at home and from United We Stand and Emily Rodriguez. Nicky needs to be bathed, toileted, dressed, and tube-fed, but she also needs Vera to be her case manager, the central part of the mobile that consists of educators, social workers, and physicians. Sean needs Leia as his case manager, advocate, and caregiver; he is still learning about such rudimentary skills as toileting, a delicate matter given that all of his staff at Bonner Springs Elementary School are females.

Gina McMahan, a paraprofessional at Bonner Springs Elementary School, chats with Sean Holley at lunchtime.

Families socialize their children, turning them from ungoverned infants into self-governed children and youth. Norma's innate sensitivity, her ability to "read" others, helps her teach Joesian to stand when an adult enters the room, to shake hands, to look a person in the eye, to say "Yes, ma'am" or "No, sir" when asked a direct yes/no question, to speak only when another person has finished speaking, and to say "My mother says" when he translates for her to a person who does not speak Spanish.

Families simply have fun together. Call it recreation or by another name, it's all about enjoying each other's company. Would Vera take the family's regular vacation to Las Vegas to visit her brother and leave Nicky behind? Absolutely not; they put Nicky into a rented van and take off, across the Kansas and Colorado prairies to the Nevada desert and then to Las Vegas. Would any of the Bergs go swimming without including Kenny? No way, for it is in the water that Kenny is freer of his blindness and deafness than any other place, so long as he keeps his feet off the bottom of the pool.

And families teach their children, not just about giving and receiving love, not just about the spirit or the duty to work or how to care for one's self without help. There is no doubt that Kenny would not have learned how to collect the eggs at Adriance Farm unless Clara had worked alongside him, and Joesian would not have become a better reader had it not been for the tutoring he received from Tatiana and Juan.

No function is free of costs to the family's time, energy, resources, and other priorities. That's true as you will learn when you teach; every new duty, new teaching method, new curriculum imposes its own costs and its own benefits. Bear that in mind when you work with families: whatever you ask them to do, however important your request may be, requires them to find the time to respond, often at the expense of changing another function to meet the one they want to carry out with you.

INTRODUCTION

In chapter 1, we defined *family* as two or more people who regard themselves as a family and who perform some of the functions families typically perform. In this chapter, we focus on the second part of that definition, the functions that families typically perform.

The tasks that families perform to meet the individual and collective needs of their members are referred to as family functions. We identify eight categories of family functions: (1) affection, (2) self-esteem, (3) spiritual, (4) economics, (5) daily care, (6) socialization, (7) recreation, and (8) education (Turnbull, Summers, & Brotherson, 1984). The family systems framework calls these the family's outputs (see Figure 3–1). We will briefly review each of the eight family functions and discuss some of their common themes and implications.

A family generally tries to engage in activities that reasonably satisfy its members' wants and needs. One role of the family is to show the younger members how to meet those needs and perform these functions so that responsibilities can be transferred from the older to the younger generation, consistent with the cultural values and traditions of the family.

As you will learn in chapter 4, family activities and individual member contributions are strongly influenced by the family's life cycle stage. Additionally, the family's characteristics (chapter 1) and interactions (chapter 2) influence how functions are addressed within the family. Because the family is an interacting system, it is impossible to consider family functions (outputs) without taking the other portions of the family systems framework into account. Likewise, it will be much easier to create a trusting partnership with families when you understand the way that they address these eight functions and the impact of their cultural values and personal preferences.

IMPACT OF EXCEPTIONALITY ON FAMILY FUNCTIONS

Each category of family functions is distinct; however, problems or assets in one family function usually affect other functions. For example, economic difficulties can have a negative effect on family members' social or recreational activities. Likewise, stress related to financial worries can have a negative impact on affection and self-esteem. Alternatively, a child's positive contribution to household chores (that is, daily care) can enhance self-esteem, affection, and recreational outcomes.

Each of the family functions is affected by every family member, including the member with an exceptionality. This influence may be positive, negative, or neutral.

FIGURE 3–1

Family Systems Framework: Emphasis on Family Functions

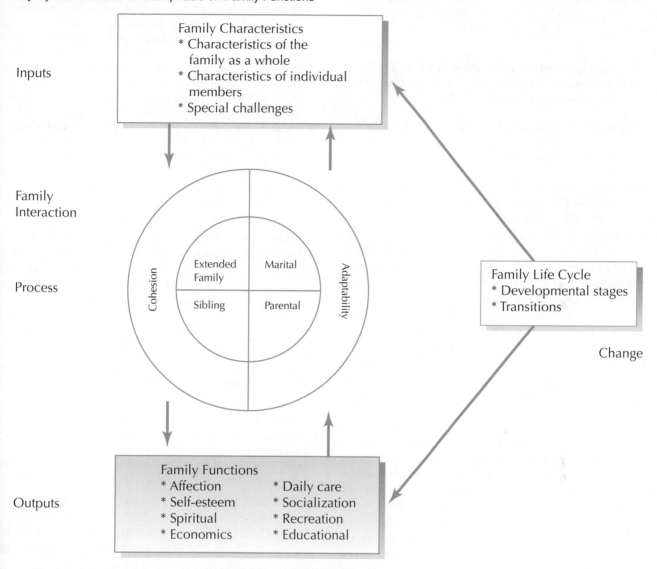

Source: Turnbull, A. P., Summers, J. A., & Brotherson, M. J. (1984). *Working with families with disabled members: A family systems approach* (p. 60). Lawrence: University of Kansas, Kansas Affiliated Facility. Adapted by permission.

Blacher & Hatton, 2001; Brown, Anand, Fung, Isaacs, & Baum, 2003; Singer, 2004; Turnbull, Turnbull, Agosta, Erwin, Fujiura, Singer, et al., 2004). Many people erroneously assume that a child or youth with a disability generally has a negative impact on the family. However, research has documented many positive contributions that children with disabilities make to their families (Sandler & Mistretta, 1998; Scorgie & Sobsey, 2000; Summers, Behr, & Turnbull, 1988; Taunt & Hastings, 2002). What positive contributions can you identify so far in the four families?

As you read this chapter, consider the following questions. What are the family's priorities for achieving balance in carrying out family functions? What cultural values and personal preferences influence these priorities? The more you respond to each family's priorities, the more likely you are to develop a trusting partnership with them.

Affection

Studies report that families who consider themselves successful in being a family emphasize positive family interaction, including sharing affection (Poston, 2002).

Affection can be characterized in many different ways, but especially important are (1) exchanging verbal and physical affection and (2) exchanging unconditional love (Poston, 2002; Summers, 1987).

Exchanging Verbal and Physical Affection.
Families have many different ways of exchanging affection. One mother commented:

> I hug my son. I embrace my son. I tell him I love him. And same way with my daughter. So it's not uncomfortable for me to do that. (Poston, 2002, p. 193)

Exchanging verbal and physical affection correlates to the attachment that family members have between and among each other. Much of the research has particularly focused on the bond between mothers and children (Osofsky & Thompson, 2000). From a family systems perspective, attachment between and among family members is a priority and consists of encouraging interactions between parents and children that deepen their emotional commitments to each other. "Human development occurs in the context of an escalating psychological ping-pong game between two people who are crazy about each other" (Bronfenbrenner, 1990, p. 31). As you learned in chapter 2, attachment usually works best in families when emotional-bonding relationships are balanced.

Cultural influences strongly determine how families display affection. For example, Asian families often provide very close physical contact with infants, carrying them even during naps and having infants and toddlers sleep in the same room or bed with their parents and other siblings until they are school age or older (Chan & Lee, 2004). Middle Eastern families also are characterized as very affectionate: "Middle Eastern mothers . . . are much more permissive than their Western counterparts in allowing their infants and young children to be kissed, held, or hugged" (Sharifzadeh, 2004, p. 394).

A major but natural issue for families is their child's evolution from expressing physical affection within the family to expressing physical affection and sexuality with one or more chosen partners (see chapter 4). Read Figure 3–2 and consider this issue from the perspective of an adult with physical disabilities.

Exchanging Unconditional Love.
All children have basic needs for acceptance, appreciation, and love (Turnbull, Blue-Banning, Turbiville, & Park, 1999). Exchanging unconditional love is an essential ingredient of family affection, as Harriet Rousso (1984), a social worker with a physical disability, noted:

In particular, disabled children need to have their bodies, disability and all, accepted, appreciated, and loved. Especially by significant parenting figures. This will solidify the sense of intactness. For all children, disabled or not, the "gleam in the mother's eye" in response to all aspects of the child's body and self is essential for the development of healthy self-esteem. This includes the parent's ability to show pride and pleasure in the disabled part of the body, as one valid aspect of the child, and to communicate appreciation and respect for the child's unique, often different-looking ways of doing things. . . . Parents too often communicate to their child, directly and indirectly, that the disability should be hidden or altered, if not purged the child should strive toward appearing as "normal" and nondisabled as possible. This attitude can put the child into an identity crisis, causing him or her to push that feeling of intactness way underground. (Rousso, 1984, pp. 12–13)

Families and professionals may need to examine their own values. How much do they and you expect a child's achievement, normalcy, success, attractiveness, or progress to be prerequisites for unconditional acceptance, appreciation, or love? Within a family, unconditional love for all members, whatever their respective characteristics, cannot be taken for granted, nor can it be underestimated. A number of families have described their child as a major catalyst for enhancing family love (Behr & Murphy, 1993; Summers et al., 1988).

> Anyone who feels that someone else is a burden has not yet learned to love. Love feels someone else's need above their own. My son, Matthew, was not useless. . . . If he served no other purpose than to give me love, then he served that one and if he served no other purpose than to teach me love, he served that one. (Turnbull & Turnbull, 1986, p. 112)

No family role is more important than the expression of affection. Figure 3–3 provides tips for addressing families' affection needs. The more you express unconditional love for the child, the more likely you are to encourage high-quality affection within the family.

Self-Esteem

One family member's exceptionality can have an impact on the self-esteem of all. For example, new parents may have anticipated raising children with typical abilities. When they are confronted with raising a child who is gifted, they may feel uncertain and even threatened (Friedman, 2000; Stephens, 1999).

Parents of children with disabilities may have self-esteem challenges, such as feelings of guilt, if they believe their own genetic makeup or their personal misconduct caused the disability (Bailey, Skinner, & Sparkman, 2003). Likewise, their self-esteem may be affected when their infants do not respond readily to

FIGURE 3–2
My Voice: Jennifer Malatesta Speaks Out on Relationship Realism

"Ninety-nine.nine [99.9] percent of guys would not want to date, let alone marry, someone in a wheelchair." My well-meaning mother offered this unsolicited assessment to me during my impressionable preteen years. Eleven years of marriage and two children later, most people think I have proven my mother wrong and that this statement should not still be replaying itself in my mind every day. But it does.

My parents, like many others, thought it was best to prepare me for the harsh realities of the world by focusing on the more dire possibilities for my future. Life is tough, and they wanted to make sure I did not enter into it clinging to fairy tale fantasies of love, joy, and Prince Charming. They knew that many opportunities most young women take for granted would only be acquired through a lot of extra work and determination. They strove to build up my emotional armor by encouraging me to prepare for the worst . . . .

Luckily, the number of people who would never consider dating a person simply because they are in a wheelchair is less than my parents had construed. When discussing the topic of dating with a young person with a disability, there must be a balance. Attention needs to be paid to what the individual can offer to a relationship, not what he or she is lacking. He or she needs to be encouraged to develop personal interests, hobbies, and knowledge, so that a well-rounded personality can be offered to the world. It can even be pointed out that being a person with a disability has its own advantages in courtship. It often "weeds out" potential mates who choose their partners based on superficial attributes. For example, I will never live up to the American prototype of physical beauty; but I also do not want to be married to someone who bases his affection on fleeting visceral attention . . . .

Having a negative self-image can cause people with disabilities to settle for less-than-desirable—even dangerous—mates. During my time in the dating scene, I contemplated marrying everyone from a man I was not attracted to at all to a man with a photo album filled with pictures of his female conquests. I even thought about being the chaste matriarchal figurehead in a "family" with my gay friend and his lover. I also toyed with the idea of marrying many different "druggies" and "burn-outs." After all, I was convinced I only had one-tenth of 1 percent of the male population to consider. I had not been encouraged to be choosy. Fortunately, I escaped these situations and married a very caring and giving man, who views me as an equal partner with valuable opinions . . . .

I am glad that my parents did not present me with a happy fantasy world where everything would work out fine and I would be guaranteed to meet my own knight in shining armor. I also realize that it must have been quite a shift in their expectations to watch their daughter, who was not expected to live past the age of two years, grow up, date, marry, and have children of her own. Nonetheless, I do wish my parents had presented the possibilities of intimate relationships in a more balanced and positive way. Life with a disability is more difficult in some ways, but it needs to be pointed out that everyone has some sort of disability. Some are just more obvious than others. Everyone has gifts and creativity to offer to others in loving relationships. Each and every person is worthy of love, and no physical, emotional, or mental disability should preclude it.

Source: From Klein, S. D., & Kemp, J. D. (2004). *Reflections from a different journey: What adults with disabilities wish all parents knew.* New York: McGraw-Hill.

soothing or stimulation or when they deal with existential issues of why the child has a disability. Leah Ziskin (1985), mother of a daughter with a severe intellectual disability, commented on the impact that her daughter's birth had on her own self-esteem:

. . . I remember feeling that I had become a completely different person, I felt that my ego had been wiped out. My superego with all of its guilts had become the most prominent part of my personality, and I had completely lost my self-esteem. Any credits of self-worth that I could give myself from any of my personal endeavors meant nothing. Graduating from college and a first-rate medical school, surviving an internship, practicing medicine, and having two beautiful sons and a good marriage counted for nil. All I knew at this point was that I was the mother of an abnormal and most likely retarded child.

It took about a year until I came home from working in a clinic and said to my husband, "today I had a problem that was greater than Jeannie." My very wise husband said, "That must mean you're getting better." It did mean that I was getting better, but it took a few more very painful months, and easily another two years, until I believed again that I was more than a mother of a retarded child. . . . I finally was able to pick up the pieces of my life and proceed. (Ziskin, 1985, pp. 68–69)

The mother in this example, Leah, is a physician who has been accustomed from an early age to high achievement. A different dilemma occurs for families who have

FIGURE 3–3
Tips for Addressing Families' Affection Needs

- Recognize the needs that all family members have for affection. For example, if a parent-child home teaching program each night interferes with a busy family's only opportunities to catch up on the day's events, play games, or snuggle on the couch together, reconsider the plan to achieve a balance in meeting affection needs, not just educational needs.

- Work with students to be able to express verbally and in writing their affectionate feelings toward their family. Students might make up stories, poems, or even a family portfolio that includes writing and other related projects focusing on affection.

- Provide materials in a resource library and arrange discussion groups involving resource persons who can help parents and students with an exceptionality gain a better understanding of sexuality and affection. Young adults or adolescents, depending on age, type, and severity of exceptionality, benefit from accurate and sensitive information about sexuality and affection.

- Help parents identify their child's positive contributions to affection as well as other family functions. Encourage family members to discuss what positive contributions each makes. For example, at dinner encourage family members to share at least two things they appreciate about each of the other members. They can also highlight the similarities and differences in each person's list.

faced multiple challenges and low levels of self-esteem for most of their lives. Many women who experience poverty, substance abuse, and mental health challenges are highly vulnerable to demoralization, depression, and low expectations for the future (Furstenberg, 2003; Kaplan-Sanoff, 1996). Self-esteem is susceptible to many challenges across the lifespan (including the special challenges we described in chapter 1) and is not reserved for exceptionality considerations alone. Nonetheless, professionals who have trusting partnerships with mothers facing multiple challenges typically affirm and build on the mothers' strengths.

Building on strengths is a way to solidify partnerships. One such strength can be a mother's persistence. Professionals have reported being genuinely respectful of and impressed by families' abilities to endure in the face of events that the professionals did not believe they, themselves, could survive.

I see them as survivors. They go through hell and back. They can do things that I couldn't stand. They are strong. If we were suddenly thrown into their situations, well, I would probably die. They don't see that, they don't see it as a strength. In addition to their tenacity, an important strength shared by most of these families was their commitment and sense of identity with their children. For many, thier ability to have children was their only source of positive self-esteem. (Summers, McMann, Kitchen, & Peck, 1995, p. 15)

A family's self-esteem can depend on whether its members see the connections between their actions and good things that happen. Note, for example, how a professional interacts with a mother with multiple challenges in an early childhood group. This mother historically had not seen herself as a strong person:

One example of the success is (a mother) who sees something happening. Not only is she getting good things in response to efforts, she is learning not to be helpless. That is helping you get rid of some of that learned helplessness. She hasn't had a lot of things handed to her. So I talk to her. I ask her what was that a result of, can she see that was connected to her efforts? (Summers et al., 1995, p. 20)

Self-esteem is important not only for parents but also for young children with disabilities and those who are gifted. Families, educators, peers, and others influence their self-esteem from a young age (Gilson, Bricourt, & Baskind, 1998; Maxwell, 1998; Plucker & Stocking, 2001). For children and youth who are gifted, parents can positively influence self-esteem by setting high standards of achievement and providing close, flexible relationships while guiding children to achieve their goals (Friedman, 2000). Addressing the self-esteem needs of gifted females is especially important because they often have lower self-esteem on a number of dimensions as contrasted to gifted males (Luscombe & Riley, 2001). Factors that can influence gender differences include a tendency for gifted females to perceive that others are critical of them and a tendency to conform to gender-role stereotypes.

The self-esteem of students with learning disabilities has been the focus of considerable research. Some studies have found that children with learning disabilities have a lower self-concept than their peers without learning disabilities (Ayres, Cooley, & Dunn, 1990; La Greca & Stone, 1990); other studies have found just the opposite (Bear, Juvonen, & McInerney, 1993; Sabornie, 1994).

Most research on self-concept of students with learning disabilities has been carried out at school. A recent study examined the self-concept, academic self-perception, social competence, and behavioral problems of children with learning disabilities and their siblings without learn ing disabilities (Dyson, 2003). This study found no significant differences in self-concept between the two groups nor were there differences in their academic self-perception. Parents did, however, rate their children with learning disabilities as having lower social competence and more behavioral problems compared to their siblings without learning disabilities. Parents who were more stressed themselves tended to rate their children as having less social competence. When family-professional partnerships are strong and families get the support that they need, they are more likely to enhance the social competence of their children.

A research study comparing the self-esteem of students both before and after they were identified formally as having a learning disability found that students reported higher levels of self-esteem following diagnosis (MacMaster, Donovan, & MacIntyre, 2002). The researchers attributed this increase to students perceiving that their learning problems were ". . . limited in scope and manageable through remediation" (MacMaster et al., 2002, pp. 104–105).

Judith Heumann, an adult with a physical disability and a national policy leader in special education and rehabilitation, shared her perspective:

> The most significant goal for parents of disabled students is assuring that their children maintain the sense of self-esteem with which we are all born. Parents are their children's most important role model. If disabled children know their parents have great expectations for them, they will have great expectations for themselves. (Heumann, 1997)

A key is ensuring that the exceptionality does not overshadow other individual traits, interests, and attributes. Just consider how Norman Kunc, a family therapist and a person with cerebral palsy, describes how people often see him and how he regards himself (see Figure 3–4).

One program has been developed to prepare parents of children with physical disabilities and mild cognitive impairments to enhance their children's self-esteem. The program includes six weekly lessons in which parents meet as a group. Through presentations, discussions, and individual and group activities, they learn how to help their children develop independence, participate in leisure activities, interact with peers, be assertive, cope with tough situations, and practice self-advocacy (Todis, Irvin, Singer, & Yovanoff, 1993). As a result of the training, parents' self-esteem increased; children gained self-care skills, completed chores more often, and became more assertive; and the parents became more likely to support their child's request for autonomy and independence.

What are the implications of these self-esteem issues for family-professional partnerships? A family's and stu-

FIGURE 3–4

My Voice: Shadows or Sun on the Sundial

When people first meet me, they tend to see me as 9/10 disability, 1/10 person. What they see as paramount are the things that mark me as "different"—the way I walk, speak, and move. The disability expands in their eyes, throwing a shadow over me and my life in the same way that shadow on a sundial widens in the afternoon light. My disability is perceived as being more influential than it actually is.

Let me counteract that view for a moment, and describe myself to you—as I see myself. First, I am a white male who grew up in Toronto, Canada. My father is Polish, my mother is English. . . . I like sailing, and used to compete in local and regional races. I'm married to Emma, and live in Port Alberni, British Columbia. I am a step-dad to Jodi, Erinn, and Evan. We live in an old house we renovated and love. Emma and I have our own business as consultants. We share a passionate interest in social justice and conflict management. I enjoy computers, classical music and Greek food. I play the drums, although not well. I have an uncanny ability to remember phone numbers and jokes. I also have cerebral palsy.

Source: Kunc, N., & Van der Klift, E. (1995). Voice of inclusion: In spite of my disability. In R. Villa & J. Thousand (Eds.), *Creating an inclusive school* (pp. 163–164). Alexandria, VA: Association for Supervision and Curriculum Development. Copyright © 1995 ASCD. Used by permission.

dent's self-esteem can be influenced by how you affirm their strengths in a genuine way; sadly, many families and students are much more accustomed to having their weaknesses and needs pointed out. You can be an affirmer of strengths. Figure 3–5 provides other tips for addressing families' self-esteem needs.

Spirituality

We use the term *spiritual* to refer to beliefs associated with spirituality and religion. Spirituality usually refers to how people find meaning in their lives, how they respond to the sacred, and how they perceive the connections between themselves, others, and the universe (Canda, 1999; Gaventa, 2001).

For example, many Native American belief systems are highly spiritual in tying human beings to the larger universe.

The Hopis (a Pueblo tribe in northern Arizona), believe that the original spiritual "being" shared with the Hopi people certain rules of life and placed spiritual helpers,

FIGURE 3–5
Addressing Families' Self-Esteem Needs

- Affirm all family members' strengths and positive contributions.

- Underscore links between family members' actions and the positive results that accrue.

- Encourage children and youth with exceptionalities to identify and develop interests that give them pride. One strategy might be to place the student with an exceptionality in the role of helper rather than the recipient of help.

- Encourage children and youth with exceptionalities to express their own choices as a strategy to enhance their self-esteem. Encouraging children and youth to choose what is important to them affords them greater control and independence.

- Ensure that children and youth have school opportunities, consistent with their preferences, to establish relationships with friends and mentors who share similar exceptionalities and ones who do not.

Source: Adapted from Stainback, S., Stainback, W., East, K., & Sapon-Shevin, M. (1994). A commentary on inclusion and the development of a positive self-identity by people with disabilities. *Exceptional Children, 60*(6), 486–490.

the Kachinas, near the tribe to protect and help them maintain that way of life. The Kachinas, therefore, help teach and guide the Hopis through their songs, prayers, and ceremonies (Titiev, 1972). Among the Apaches, the Mountain Spirits have a similar role to that of the Kachinas. Appropriate members of the respected tribes impersonate these deities during special ceremonies. (Joe & Malach, 2004, p. 122)

Not all spirituality is religious. Religion is typically defined as the organized patterns of beliefs, rituals, and social structures to which people adhere in fulfilling their spiritual quest (Canda, 1999; Fitzgerald, 1997). People explore the spiritual meaning of their lives and achieve a sense of spirituality through a broad range of activities. For example, a mother of a young child with a disability described her spiritual journey as follows:

I'm getting back into my artwork, because that was a form of getting into my spirituality. Making me, you know, all one—mind, body, and soul. And it comes across. I'm happier, work is going better, things are just coming into my life, you know, happiness. (Beach Center, 1999)

Although spirituality and religion are manifested in multiple ways across different cultures (Gollnick &

Chinn, 2002; Lynch & Hanson, 2004; Uphoff, 1999), a common theme is the role of the family in transmitting spiritual beliefs from one generation to another (D'Antonio & Aldous, 1983). A family's spiritual perspectives can vastly impact their values, beliefs, and rituals. Consider how Confucianism affects family life through its strong emphasis on filial piety:

Filial piety consists of unquestioning loyalty and obedience to parents and concern for and understanding of their needs and wishes. It also includes reverence for ancestors whose spirits must be appeased. Filial piety further extends to relations with all authority figures and defines a social hierarchy of allegiance and reciprocal moral obligations characterized by the "five relations": 1) king/justice, subject/loyalty; 2) father/love, son/filiality; 3) elder brother/brotherly love, younger brother/reverence; 4) husband/initiative, wife/obedience; and 5) friends/mutual faith. (Chan & Lee, 2004, pp. 225–226)

You might consider your own spiritual beliefs regarding these issues and how similar or different they are from Confucian principles.

Research consistently finds that children with disabilities are a catalyst for a family's increased spirituality (Poston & Turnbull, 2004; Summers et al., 1988). The spiritual function of the family often comes into play in terms of (1) interpreting the meaning of the child's exceptionality and (2) having a religious community that provides concrete and emotional support.

The spiritual function of the family is critically important as a basis for interpreting the meaning of disability (Poston & Turnbull, 2004; Rogers-Dulan, 1998; Skinner, Bailey, Correa, & Rodriguez, 1999). Interviews of Latino mothers about their spiritual interpretations revealed that approximately three fourths reported that their child was a blessing or a gift from God (Skinner et al., 1999; Skinner, Correa, Skinner, & Bailey, 2001). These mothers felt they were the recipient of God's blessing or gift either because they were especially worthy or because God was trying to teach them to be better people through the experience of raising their child. These mothers tended to have higher levels of faith than fathers, and parents who are not so acculturated in the majority culture had higher levels of faith than those who are not so acculturated.

A study of 137 parents of children with and without disabilities was equally revealing. Parents of children with disabilities frequently emphasized that their child was a gift from God and that their spiritual/religious faith plays a major role in understanding the meaning of their life and in having hope for the future (Poston & Turnbull, 2004). One mother characterized this perspective as follows:

I have to say for all parents that have kids with disabilities, or exceptionalities, I think you have to look at that as a gift from God as a blessing, as a test of your faith. If you have faith, it's going to work out. (Poston & Turnbull, 2004, p. 16)

Kalyanpur and Harry (1999) described the situation of a 7-year-old child, Kou, who is Hmong. Social workers brought a suit against Kou's parents for refusing corrective surgery on his two clubfeet. Consistent with their spiritual beliefs, Kou's parents interpreted his condition as a "sign of good luck" and as an indication that "a warrior ancestor whose own feet were wounded in battle could be released from a sort of spiritual entrapment" (p. 16). As families interpret disability positively and within a spiritual framework, opportunities will occur for their beliefs to be sources of comfort and motivation as they address various support issues. Undoubtedly, families and professionals sometimes have very different religious/spiritual interpretations. How might you react if you were Kou's teacher and his parents refused corrective surgery? In chapter 9, you will learn ways to resolve conflict when team members have very different beliefs and priorities.

Alternatively, there are spiritual interpretations that lead families to the belief that the disability is a punishment for past sins or transgressions.

. . . A Korean mother of two boys with mental retardation claimed that the spirit of a dead horse that had entered her sons' bodies during her respective pregnancies caused their "sickness." She, in turn, sought the cure for their affliction by resorting to daily prayer and meditation. Another mother (Chinese) insisted that her daughter with severe developmental delays was possessed by a ghost and would regularly bring her to a monk who sang chants (a series of repetitive choruses), gave offerings to appease the spirits, and provided the mother with a "lucky charm" made from special herbs to hang around the child's neck. (Chan & Lee, 2004, p. 267)

As you develop a reliable alliance with families by honoring their cultural traditions, we encourage you to be open to their interpretations of their child's disability. Their religious/spiritual beliefs do not necessarily have to be consistent with yours. Your role is to seek to understand how they bring meaning to their life experiences. Many families derive tremendous instrumental and emotional support from their religious communities. For example, Hornstein (1997) described how the Jewish religious community provides support for families of children with disabilities through Jewish day and supplemental schools, community centers, camps, and social service agencies. Figure 3–6 provides tips for increasing the likelihood that spiritual/religious organizations will

FIGURE 3–6

Tips for Addressing Families' Spiritual/Religious Needs

- Encourage families who are interested in spiritual/religious support to set aside time for this family function, ask for support from their spiritual/religious community, and ask for support from professionals with whom they work.

- Encourage churches in your community to provide supports for individuals with disabilities and their families, which might mean including the young person in religious education and social activities.

- Invite the individuals who are responsible for religious education to the student's IEP meeting if this is agreeable with the student and parent.

- Encourage special education teachers who may be interested to take an active part in the religious education program that they attend to promote inclusion for individuals with disabilities.

- Check out the resources at the end of this chapter, which provide information on the Religion and Spirituality Division of the American Association on Mental Retardation. Inquire whether religious organizations in the community have accommodations and programs that are particularly geared to the needs and interests of your students.

Source: Adapted from Poston, D. J., & Turnbull, A. P. (2004). The role of spirituality and religion in family quality of life for families of children with disabilities. *Education and Training in Developmental Disabilities, 39*(2), 95–108.

provide appropriate and accessible supports to children and youth with exceptionalities and their families.

In a survey of local church support, 81% of the churches had people with developmental disabilities in their congregation, with an average of five people with developmental disabilities per congregation. Most of these congregations said they included people with a developmental disability into their regular classes and services and made an effort to provide social and emotional supports (McNair & Swartz, 1995).

Many families, however, have trouble finding a religious community that can respond to their child's needs (Poston & Turnbull, 2004). As a father of a young child with autism stated:

I just don't have the energy to look around through 30 churches in the area to find the one that is right for Jason and then make all the efforts to make all the contacts. . . . It is just one more mountain that you choose to go around instead of to climb. (Turnbull & Ruef, 1997, p. 216)

When families find an accepting spiritual or religious community, many positive experiences can accrue. A father described the joy that his daughter with a disability derives from the music at church:

> Church experience is just wonderful. I mean, it just takes over. I don't know. I mean, once you walk through the door, that's it. And well, she love music, so, that's it. Once she walks in the door . . . she goes straight to the front, she can sit on the organ. She doesn't touch the keys or nothing. But she just sit there, long as the organ's playing, she sitting there. She gets up once it stops and get up and go and sit down. And, you know, that's the most, best place I think she's not being, not just tolerated. (Poston & Turnbull, 2004, p. 103)

Some people mistakenly assume that children and youth with intellectual disabilities might not be interested in religious or spiritual participation because of their inability to comprehend abstract concepts. On the contrary, research has shown that adults with mild and moderate disabilities report that religion is a very important part of their lives (Shogren & Rye, 2004). The majority of participants in this study indicated that they regularly attended religious services; in fact, participation in the religious organization was their most community-oriented activity. These individuals attended worship services but were not as inclined to be included in social or educational activities of the church, perhaps because of inadequate accommodations for people with disabilities. The majority of participants said they thought about God on a regular basis, believed in God, and prayed to God. An intellectual disability does not preclude individuals having clear conceptions of religion as well as identifying symbols associated with their beliefs (Kregel, Wehman, Seyfarth, & Marshall, 1986; Riordan & Vasa, 1991).

Much has been written about the role of the church in the lives of African American families (Willis, 2004). Many African American churches currently provide educational, recreational, and social service supports for families in addition to religious/spiritual support. Later in this chapter, you will learn how the Men's Fellowship of an African American Baptist Church in Ohio launched an after-school program to provide tutoring, recreation, and moral/social skill development for children while their parents were working.

Given the constitutional separation of church and state, you may ask whether it is your role to help families address their spiritual/religious needs. We believe many families benefit from their beliefs and derive concrete and informational support from their religious communities (Hughes, 1999; Poston & Turnbull, 2004). You can help families if you collaborate within their spiritual/religious communities to create the adaptations and ac-commodations they need to participate in their community. In chapter 12, you will learn in more detail about conducting comprehensive IFSP/IEP conferences. These conferences could be ideal opportunities for family contacts with spiritual/religious programs to learn about adaptations and accommodations for children and youth with disabilities.

Economics

Nearly all families need to earn money; only a few have the luxury of being supported by unearned income. Many families of children with disabilities qualify for government benefits because of the presence of disability. In chapter 10, you will learn more about family support programs that provide financial subsidies—Supplemental Security Income (SSI) and the Home and Community-Based Services (HCBS) Waiver Program. One of your professional roles is to know about available financial resources and where to refer families for more information.

Whatever their sources of income, all families must decide how to handle their money. Family resources vary tremendously, and finances affect how families respond to the challenges of their children's exceptionality. You should not assume that families who cannot spend at the level you want them to are less committed to their children than more affluent families. That is the point made by an African American single mother:

> You've got bummy blacks and bummy whites and you are saying, everybody black is stupid, and you are bums, and you are not good. That's not true. I am a single parent and I am trying to do the best I can with John. I don't send him to school dirty; he don't go hungry. When they need money and stuff for school, I do without. These are white people born with money. They are not struggling. I can't tell you what to do unless I wear your shoes. (Kalyanpur & Rao, 1991, p. 528)

Research shows that families spend more money on their children with disabilities than on their other children. In other words, a child's disability—especially autism, mental retardation, spina bifida, cerebral palsy, and health conditions requiring technology support—creates excess costs (Birenbaum & Cohen, 1993; Fujiura, Roccoforte, & Braddock, 1994; Knoll, 1992; Swensen et al., 2003).

Data also show that the largest expense categories for families with children with autism or mental retardation are food (specialized diets), transportation (to service providers), recreation, clothing (specially adapted or tailored), durable consumer items, medical care, specialized services, personal care, and "other" (Fujiura et al., 1994).

In addition, many families with children with developmental disabilities, hearing loss, chronic health conditions, or technology support needs must administer medications, monitor medical procedures, provide specialized treatments, and carry out behavioral intervention and other habilitative programs (Darling & Peter, 1994; Knoll, 1992; Leff & Walizer, 1992). A Korean father who came to the United States to be a university student lamented that lack of citizenship left him without access to the common financial benefits other families of children with disabilities might receive. He described his situation as follows:

> Doctor says that my daughter's hearing problem is progressive which means that her hearing ability gets worse and worse gradually. In this case, we were told that a hearing aid would not be useful. Doctors recommend surgery for her. Of course, we were concerned about the cost . . . approximately $40,000. Even before discussing about the surgery, we already spent considerable money to see the audiologist. It cost us about $400 each time. (Park & Turnbull, 2001, p. 139)

There is another aspect of the costs of exceptionality. Some families have *increased consumptive demands* and *decreased productive capacities*, also known as lost opportunities, because of their children's disabilities (Birenbaum & Cohen, 1993). According to a special disability supplement of the National Health Interview Survey, which provided a national description of the status of Americans with disabilities, parents of children with both intellectual disabilities and developmental disabilities made many job accommodations to address their child's special needs (Research and Training Center on Community Living, 2002):

- Thirty-six percent did not take a job.
- Twenty-nine percent changed work hours.
- Twenty-six percent worked fewer hours.
- Seventeen percent changed jobs.
- Seventeen percent quit a job.
- Seventeen percent turned down a better job.

Nine percent of the families reported that their child's disability led to severe financial difficulties within their family.

A comparison study reported that approximately half of the mothers with adult children with disabilities worked outside of the home for an average of 9 hours per week, as compared to three fourths of the mothers of adult children without disabilities who worked outside of the home for an average of 22 hours per week (Einam & Cuskelly, 2002). The primary reason for unemployment of the mothers of adult children with multiple disabilities was the caregiving demands associated with their child's condition. Parents who work outside of the home were found to have better mental health, which suggests that work provides a break from caretaking responsibilities. Fathers of adult children with multiple disabilities tended to work either fewer hours or longer hours than fathers of young adults without disability. The wives of the husbands who worked longer hours said they believed their husbands had retreated from caretaking and immersed themselves in more intensive work outside of the home.

Consistent with previous research on the positive contributions of children with disabilities to their families (Summers et al., 1988), some of the parents described how their career had been enhanced because of issues associated with their child's disability.

> It is actually because of Salma's disability that my career has been enhanced. You get involved, because parents should be educating themselves, and that's where you as a person can grow and benefit. Despite a disability or difficulty, you can strengthen yourself in different ways, and that's how I became a special education teacher. (Brown et al., 2003, p. 221)

A major consideration for family job opportunities is finding satisfactory child-care arrangements. One research study reported that mothers of young children with developmental disabilities encountered more difficulty finding child care, and mothers of children with more severe disabilities and behavior problems reported more difficulty than mothers of children with milder problems (Warfield & Hauser-Cram, 1996). Other research has documented that parents of children with disabilities have a difficult time finding child care not only in the early years, since their needs for child care might extend for more years than parents of children who are typically developing (Kagan, Lewis, Heaton, & Cranshaw, 1999). Mothers in this study reported a general assumption that their role was to stay at home and take care of their child with a disability rather than to pursue employment. In some families, grandparents stepped in to provide needed child care.

One might assume that mothers who are employed full-time and have children with disabilities experience higher levels of stress than mothers who work part-time or are unemployed. Surprisingly, one research study found no differences in child demands, family support, or stress according to employment status (Warfield, 2001). This research focused on mothers of 5-year-old children, and most of the children were in school for a portion of the day. Mothers who were more interested in their jobs reported significantly less parenting stress. Parents whose children needed more assistance with basic caregiving and who had children with problem behavior experienced more absenteeism from work (which can have an impact on family income).

You might consider how you can help families find successful child-care arrangements and how you can collaborate with child-care providers to support students with special needs (Brennan & Freeman, 1999; Brennan, Rosenzweig, & Ogilvie, 1999). Remember to provide families with general information about financial benefits to which they might be entitled or to at least refer them to a source from which they can get that information. You will learn about these resources in chapter 10.

Daily Care

Another basic function of families consists of meeting their members' physical and health needs. This includes the day-to-day tasks of living: cooking, cleaning, laundry, transportation, obtaining health care when needed, and so forth. A substantial portion of family life is devoted to attending to these needs. Daily care is one of the significant outputs of family interaction. Family members often work together to carry out their roles and responsibilities in meeting daily care needs.

Up to 30% of all children and youth will experience a childhood chronic illness lasting 3 months or longer (Kliebenstein & Broome, 2000). During the 2000–2001 school year, approximately 292,000 children and youth ages 6 to 21 were identified as having a health impairment. The Individuals with Disabilities Education Act (IDEA) (1) 1997 regulation (1) defines health impairment as conditions that limit strength, vitality, and alertness due to acute or chronic asthma, attention deficit disorder, diabetes, epilepsy, a heart condition, or other similar conditions. Health impairments of children, in addition to other types of disabilities, can greatly increase daily caregiving needs. Research has revealed how children with developmental disabilities and chronic medical conditions affect their families with daily care issues (Knoll, 1992):

■ Approximately 50% of the families gave their child extensive assistance with toileting, bathing, grooming, and medical monitoring.
■ Approximately one fourth indicated their child needed 24-hour-a-day monitoring.
■ Slightly more than half reported they had experienced some sort of crisis requiring extraordinary intervention within the last month.

These daily care issues can manifest themselves in frequent everyday routines such as sleeping and eating. Consider the situation of the family whose child has a chronic health problem and needs special assistance while eating. As his mother explained:

I can get the most bottle into him if I start before he's totally awake. . . . I guess I spend about 1 1/2 hours in the morning and it's closer to 2 hours at lunch. That's when I get William to eat something besides just milk or formula. . . . He goes to the school in the afternoon, and I'm always late getting him there because it takes so long for him to eat. (Martin, Brady, & Kotarba, 1992, p. 10)

The child's father explained his role:

I'm not as good as Betty when it comes to feeding William, but by 6:30 she needs a break. She eats her dinner while I feed William. I eat when I get to it. It takes about 2 hours to feed him. . . . I hadn't realized it took so long. I just know it's about 10:00 before I get to the grocery store. (Martin et al., 1992, p. 10)

Another significant daily care issue for parents of children with medical needs is dealing with the medical equipment, specialized procedures, and medical appointments (Leff & Walizer, 1992).

Respiratory therapy 3 times a day normally. When sick or congested, 4–5 times a day, plus medications. She takes 11 different kinds of medicine, including 5 vitamins. Need to monitor stool samples daily to make sure they are solid. The inhalation therapy is not disturbing, but when we're both tired it's no fun—sometimes it's a bother. Takes a half hour, 15 minutes on mask, 15 minutes pounding. It depends on her mood—if she's tired at night, she'll sleep through it. Sometimes she'll fight all the way. (Knoll, 1992, p. 26)

In addition to managing the logistical tasks associated with caregiving, the family must also deal with health insurance policies (if they have insurance) to access needed services and secure reimbursement of expenses. A national study of more than 2,200 parents of children with special health care needs in 20 states revealed that approximately half reported problems with accessing services, especially home health and mental health services (Krauss, Wells, Gulley, & Anderson, 2001). As one mother commented:

The most important need is more home nursing so that I can get some sleep at night. Insurance companies claim "custodial" care is not covered. She requires "skilled nursing." Her trach needs to be changed often, ventilator alarms throughout the night, etc., yet I must work in order to provide the things she needs. (Krauss et al., 2001, p. 176)

Aside from health issues, some extraordinary care considerations arise for children with exceptionalities. Some of the issues of daily care are age related; as children with exceptionalities grow and develop, most gain an increasing and sometimes wholly independent capacity to carry out responsibilities. You can teach children and youth daily care skills as part of their IFSP/IEP if those goals are appropriate for the student's strengths, preferences, and needs. Brothers and sisters can also be collaborators. School-age children can help their brothers or sisters with exceptionalities carry out and develop basic self-help skills. "Sometimes we ask the older girls to check the batteries in Mary Pat's hearing aid, put in new ones, help her dress or undress, monitor a bath, get her safely down the stairs. They read and sign stories, help out in a thousand other ways" (Luetke-Stahlman, Luetke-Stahlman, & Luetke-Stahlman, 1992, p. 10).

Although some children create greater daily care needs, others do not. In fact, children with exceptionalities can make many positive contributions by helping with housekeeping, yard work, laundry, or the needs of younger siblings. As a single mother reported:

> Of my three children, the one with autism is my lifesaver when it comes to housework. He believes that everything has a place and belongs in it. His room would pass any army inspection. He organizes drawers and pulls weeds out of the flowerbeds. On the other hand, the clutter and mess in the bedrooms of my normal kids is shameful. When I ask for their help, they consider it an infringement on their social life. (Beach Center, 1999)

Given the increasing number of children who are home alone after school, including those who have exceptionalities, some schools are teaming with community organizations to provide self-care instruction for parents and children. The goal of these programs is to prepare children to handle emergencies, prevent accidents and sexual abuse, manage their time, learn leisure skills, and practice good nutrition. Staying home alone or with other siblings can be particularly challenging for students who experience exceptionalities such as learning disabilities or attention-deficit/hyperactivity disorder. These impairments might make it more challenging for children to make quick decisions in threatening circumstances or to use their time in a constructive way. Moreover, students who experience asthma, epilepsy, or diabetes need to know how to respond to an emergency situation, as do brothers and sisters and other people who may be available to provide assistance (Eisenberg, 2000; Roberts, 2000).

After-school programs are especially important in low-income neighborhoods where parents are less likely to have money to pay for child care and where neighborhood crime is often higher (Halpern, 1999; Marshall et al., 1997). As a result of a partnership with Columbus Public Schools and Ohio State University College of Education, the members of the Mt. Olivet Baptist Church Men's Fellowship donated their time and money to start an after-school program for young urban at-risk students (Gardner et al., 2001). The program emphasized academic skill instruction, homework completion, recreation, and moral/social skill development. An evaluation of the program outcomes indicated that the students made substantial gains in academic skills. This is a good example of how partnerships with community programs can help meet the daily care needs of students. What other family functions do you think a program like this could positively influence?

Socialization

Socialization is vital to the overall quality of life for most individuals. Persons of all ages with exceptionalities need opportunities to experience both the joys and disappointments of friendships (Meyer, Park, Grenot-Scheyer, Schwartz, & Harry, 1998). Many families experience stress in meeting the socialization needs of their child or youth with an expectionality. In one study, the majority of parents of children, youth, and adults with problem behavior expressed disappointment and lack of hope about their son's or daughter's lack of friends (Turnbull & Ruef, 1997). In another study, parents of young children with disabilities or at risk for disabilities placed a strong priority on their children's social interactions and friendships (Guralnick, Conner, & Hammond, 1995). Forty percent of the mothers in this study expressed concern about their children being rejected by peers and the impact of that rejection on their children's self-esteem.

Many individuals with disabilities have concerns about their lack of friends or the motives that people have in being friends with them. Students with learning disabilities have reported more loneliness and lower peer acceptance than their peers whose school achievement is in the average range (Malka & Meira, 1996). On the issue of motivation for friendship, individuals with disability have pointed out insightfully that friendship is not always the outcome of relationships where people are paid helpers or regard the friendship as a "special friendship" rather than a real one (Van der Klift & Kunc, 2002). Liz Obermayer, an adult with a development disability, shares her perspective on special versus authentic friendships in Figure 3–7.

Some families and professionals may welcome your encouragement and guidance on friendships. Often, families and professionals focus on other important areas of the child's development and unwittingly ignore the social dimensions. A study of the adequacy of IEPs in documenting students' present levels of performance related to peer interaction and in providing appropriate instruction indicated that teachers need to know more about how their instruction can foster peer interaction (Gelzheiser, McLane, Meyers, & Pruzek, 1998). The IEPs were found to describe adequately the student's current level of performance; unfortunately, this accurate assessment did not lead to instruction and support. Teachers noted that the

FIGURE 3–7
My Voice: A Special Friend Versus a Real Friend

Everybody needs and deserves to have a friend, including people with disabilities. However, for a person with a disability we may never truly know whether the friendship is genuine. The friendship could start with a paycheck, or as a civic duty. What I need in a friend is someone who just enjoys the company of Liz Obermayer, and is not thinking about "How much am I getting paid to be with her?" or "Will this count toward my civic duty?"

When I used to live in New Jersey and was a part of a program there, I remember a lot of the support people who would say, "Liz, you are my friend, and I like you." Well, at that time, because I didn't understand the difference between "paid friends" and friends, I said, "Thanks, you are also my friend."

I remember when I moved out of town, a support person promised to keep in touch. We exchanged information, and I just assumed that we would. However, the only time that we had some contact was when she was picking me up so I could speak somewhere. In my mind, that isn't friendship, that's just someone who did me a favor.

I meet a lot of people—both professionals and family members—who tell me that people with disabilities can only be friends with other people who have the same label. I tell them this is just not true. You may ask how I know this. The answer is because one of my friends is someone who used to be a person who was paid to be in my life. However, now I am proud to say that she isn't paid—she is just my friend.

I think because it is not common for a person without a disability to want to be a friend to someone who has a disability, it can be scary for families due to a lot of concerns. When I told my parents I wanted to start up a friendship with my friend, my parents questioned her motives. I think there were several reasons for this reaction. They might have thought why should a person without a disability be bothered with someone like me? My answer is what gives a person the right to assume how another person would feel when he or she is in a relationship? I know one thing for sure, all of my friends want to be my friend or I don't want to be their friend. My parents might have also been reacting this way out of caution. I ask why don't you trust people's judgments in making friends? Yes, there's always the risk of being harmed, but that's a strong reason why people need to learn how to be a friend and who you can trust.

One of the things I think is a very sad sight to see is a person who gets served by an agency and has as their only friends either other people with disabilities or people who support the person. The reason is because then people with disabilities will never have an opportunity to make friends in the community. I also wonder if some agencies don't promote friendships in the community on purpose. One reason could be that they want to segregate people.

Sometimes, I feel the need to "interview" people as to their desire to be my friend. I know this is very insulting to the person, but isn't it just as insulting to me to know that after their project is over, or are they tired of being a friend to a person with a disability, they'll say "goodbye" to our friendship? I hope someday there won't be that division. But, for the time being, be careful in picking your friends.

Source: Obermayer, L. L. (2004). A special friend versus a real friend. *TASH Connections, 30*(1–2), 18. Adapted with permission.

---

assignment of a one-on-one aide appeared to limit the student's opportunities for peer and teacher interaction.

It may well be that social dimensions are underemphasized because many families and professionals are unsure how to facilitate relationships. There are some compelling examples, however, of professionals and families who have been successful (Turnbull, Pereira, & Blue-Banning, 1999, 2000).

The Circle of Friends approach has been successful with many students with disabilities (Falvey, Forest, Pearpoint, & Rosenberg, 2002; Turnbull, Pereira, & Blue-Banning, 1999). Professionals or parents typically initiate a Circle of Friends by inviting peers to form a support network to provide advice, insight, and opportunities for a *focus child* with a disability who would like to have more friends. Emphasis is placed on the focus child's strengths and preferences. Peers and the focus child work together with an adult to set and implement goals that will increase both the quantity and quality of friendships.

One study used the Circle of Friends approach with 20 children between the ages of 6 and 12 years with emotional and behavior disorders (Frederickson & Turner, 2003). The findings indicated that the Circle of Friends approach enhanced the social acceptance of the focus children within their classroom peer groups. This study also investigated whether the focus children perceived that their behavior improved and whether teachers perceived an improvement in behavior. Results indicated that although social acceptance improved, no concomitant improvement occurred in perceptions of behavior.

A helpful resource for preparing families and professionals to facilitate relationships is the guidebook *Connecting Students: A Guide to Thoughtful Friendship Facilitation for Educators and Families.* It suggests the following three steps (Schaffner & Buswell, 1992):

■ Find opportunities. Bring students together so they will have an opportunity to know each other.

■ Make interpretations. Support the student, to the degree appropriate, and make connections with others in an enhancing way.

■ Make accommodations. Adapt the physical environment so individulas with disabilities have a greater opportunity to participate in a meaningful way.

Research shows how parents have been particularly successful in promoting friendships for their child with a peer who did not have a disability (Turnbull, Pereira, & Blue-Banning, 1999). Figure 3–8 highlights the friendship facilitation strategies that these families used. We encourage you to collaborate with families who are interested in friendship facilitation and to help them carry out these strategies.

Many families do not perceive that they have the time or energy to take on friendship facilitation. You and other educators can be strategic friendship facilitators by finding opportunities, making interpretations, and fostering accommodations to support the evolution of friendships (Calloway, 1999). Some teachers have found that a very successful strategy is to encourage participation in extracurricular activities so students with exceptionalities have more opportunities for informal interaction. A different strategy used by an urban school district was to provide a tutor/mentor for students with significant emotional and behavior problems who did not have positive peer interaction (Turnbull et al., 2000). One of the major roles of the tutor/mentor was to help students meet new peers involved in sports and other positive activities.

Recreation

Recreation, play, and enjoying leisure time are important components of life for individuals with expcetionalities and their families (Mahon, Mactavish, & Bockstael, 2000). Recreation includes sports, games, hobbies, or play that can be done outdoors or indoors; as a spectator or a participant; and in an independent, cooperative, or competitive manner. A family's culture influences its views about the role of recreation and leisure. An African American cultural scholar describes play as necessary for promoting children's well-being:

Play is seen as important for both social (to have friends and fun) and physical (to have a strong body) well-being. In

FIGURE 3–8

Friendship Facilitation Strategies Foundation Theme

Foundational Theme

• Accepting the child/youth unconditionally (for example, loving the "disabled portion" of the child/youth and perceiving her or him as "whole" rather than "broken")

Creating Opportunities

• Advocating for inclusion in the neighborhood school (for example, working to have the child/youth attend the neighborhood school rather than be bused to a school across town)

• Supporting participation in community activities (for example, enrolling the child/youth for a First Communion class and supporting the instructor to engage in comfortable interaction)

• Initiating and facilitating a Circle of Friends (for example, starting a Circle of Friends to encourage friendships within the school and community settings)

• Setting sibling-consistent expectations (for example, in light of how siblings call their friends on the phone, encouraging the child/youth and his or her friends to call each other)

Making Interpretations

• Encouraging others to accept the child/youth (for example, discussing their child's/youth's strengths and needs with others and supporting others to know how to communicate comfortably)

• Ensuring an attractive appearance (for example, ensuring that the child/youth is dressed and groomed in a way that is likely to draw positive and appropriate attention)

Making Accommodations

• Advocating for partial participation in community activities (for example, encouraging an instructor of community activities to know how to adapt expectations to enable partial participation in completing them)

Source: Turnbull, A. P., Pereira, L., & Blue-Banning, M. J. (1999). Parents' facilitation of friendships between their children with a disability and friends without a disability. *Journal of the Association of Persons with Severe Handicaps, 24*(2), 85–99.

contrast with cultures that push children toward early adulthood, in African-American families there is a belief that a child should be a child; and getting "grown" too soon is frowned on, especially if older family members live in the home or have influence in the family. (Willis, 2004, p. 162)

Another cultural interpretation emphasizes not so much the importance of play as the appropriate age for children or youth to participate in recreation separately from other family members. A Middle Eastern woman describes her culture's perspective on this issue:

Middle Eastern parents, particularly mothers, rarely have social and recreational activities separate from their children. Family gathering, picnics, cinemas, and, to a lesser extent, sports events are among the most common social events in the Middle East; children are usually included in all of them. Most Middle Eastern boys do not start to have activities of their own until after puberty; for unmarried girls, this may come even later. (Sharifzadeh, 2004, p. 334)

Depending upon the nature of the child's exceptionality, the family's recreational role may be expanded, unaffected, or curtailed (Schleien & Heyne, 1998). Some children and youth have special gifts related to sports, athletics, or games (for example, chess or bridge), and a significant portion of family time may be devoted to supporting their interests and involvement. The priority given to recreation may be a positive experience not only for the child with exceptionalities but also for the family's overall interaction.

Because of Susan's reading disability, school has always been very hard for her. She reads slowly now but for a long time she never thought she would read at all. To make matters worse, Della and Melinda, her younger sisters, have always been star students—both of them are in the gifted program at their school. Because of these things, I really wanted to find the places where Susan could shine too. When she showed an interest in swimming, I encouraged her. She took swimming lessons at the YWCA, and we all started swimming a lot as a family. Now she swims on a team for the city during the summer, and next year she's decided to try out for the swim team at her high school. She has a lot of confidence in this area. She swims circles around most of her friends and all of her family! But I'm a lot better swimmer today than I would have been without her influence. (Beach Center, 1999).

Some families' recreation is curtailed because of the nature of their child's exceptionality, the unavailability of community resources, disapproving public reactions to their son or daughter, or general lack of accommodations. Families have reported substantial curtailment of activities such as going outside the home, eating in a restaurant, taking a vacation, shopping, and participating in general recreational experiences (Traustadottir, 1995).

One mother noted that she would drive her daughter with autism to the beach but neither of them would get out of the car because of the stares and disapproving looks her daughter would receive (Turnbull & Ruef, 1996). Similarly, a father described issues that arise in taking his 2-year-old son who is blind to a restaurant:

We can't just pick up and go out to eat after church, our friends can't understand that. . . . Matthew doesn't sit in a highchair, and he gets overloaded by the noise in a restaurant, he gets afraid. He can't sit for one to two hours; he can't deal with the noise of the dishes, and it's hard to entertain yourself when you can't see. (Martin et al., 1992, p. 11)

Families and professionals alike have sponsored "special populations" recreation programs rather than include children and youth with exceptionalities in typical community opportunities. A mother of a daughter with mental retardation shared how she purposely abandoned special programs in favor of inclusive ones:

A long time ago I stopped looking at newspaper listings of special programs. . . . Now I just notice what Kathryn might like. All kinds of courses are given by community schools, YMCAs, or churches. Grandparents and teenagers, beginners, or those with some familiarity with the subject all take the same course. Though there may be beginning, intermediate, or advanced levels, nobody would notice or care if someone took the same course several times. For most of us . . . taking enough time is more important than special techniques. (Bennett, 1985, p. 171)

Consistent with this mother's philosophy, which she shared approximately 20 years ago, the field of early intervention currently is emphasizing natural learning opportunities that occur as part of family, neighborhood, and community routines and traditions (Dunst, Bruder, Trivette, Humby, Raab, & McLean, 2001; Dunst, Hamby, Trivette, Raab, & Bruder, 2000). Many of the activities identified in this research were recreational ones:

- Family outings—shopping, going to restaurants, going to friends' houses
- Play activities—playgrounds, ball fields, gyms
- Community activities—fairs, libraries, recreational centers
- Recreation activities—swimming, softball, horseback riding
- Children's attractions—petting zoos, parks, pet stores
- Art/entertainment activities—music activities, art centers, children's theater

Leaders in early intervention are advocating a natural learning orientation. This involves:

- Identifying the settings that most interest a child and family,

- Identifying the learning opportunities that are most consistent with the child's strengths and preferences and that provide a source of strong motivation,
- Providing supports and services from the early intervention program to enable the child and family to be successful in that setting, and
- Encouraging the family to provide naturally occurring learning opportunities in the same settings.

This approach is highly relevant to facilitating family recreation since supports and services target the places where families would like to be included in their community.

Model programs are also being developed beyond the early intervention years to focus on providing supports and services for community recreation. Figure 3–9 describes how a partnership among recreation agencies, a school, a university, students, and families led to inclusive and enjoyable community recreation, including swimming and gymnastics (Fennick & Royle, 2003).

Leisure and recreation should be an important part of each child's curriculum (Schleien, Green, & Heyne, 1993). You will want to find out from families what recreational hobbies and interests they particularly enjoy and

FIGURE 3–9
Advocacy Partners: Inclusion Beyond the School Yard

It's summertime in Saginaw, Michigan, and the families of children with autism and developmental disabilities face the dilemma that confronts every other family with a school-aged child: What will my child do this summer?

Families who have children without disabilities can look confidently at community recreation programs and assume that their children will take swimming or gymnastics lessons.

But families who have children with disabilities can make no such assumption. Instead, they must assume a summer of idleness. Unless, of course, they are in Saginaw or a community that, like it, simply will not accept a "less-than" assumption—the idea that students with disabilities are "less than entitled" when compared to students with disabilities.

In Saginaw, university faculty in special education offered their knowledge about disabilities and their university students to three nearby communities and their summer recreation programs.

"Here's the deal," they said. "We'll provide the specially trained instructors, whom we will call activity coaches. We will match an activity coach to each youngster with a disability. The parents will not have to pay for the coaches; we'll cover that expense. But the families will have to transport their children to the programs. You, the communities, will help us recruit families and their children, reduce the participation fees to meet families' income and disability-related expenses, and open your programs to the students with disabilities. The activity coaches will individualize swimming and gymnastics for the students with disabilities and support them to participate with students who do not have disabilities. Agreed?"

"Yes," said the communities. YMCAs, Boys and Girls Clubs, recreation and community centers, and even arts centers helped recruit families and students. Special outreach to students from diverse families failed to promote any results, but six students from the majority culture, ages 6 to 13, enrolled. Five of them had autism and one had challenges associated with both hearing and dwarfism.

Three students in occupational therapy and three in teacher education were the activity coaches; two of them were men and four were women. Swim programs were less accommodating than gymnastics programs, for reasons that are unclear.

Families and coaches met before the activities began, to plan how to accommodate the student, arrange transportation and regular communication, and identify the criteria for evaluating the program. At the end of the summer, coaches, families, and community agencies evaluated the program on how it met various challenges (for example, the students' communication limitations and the attitudes of some of the directors of swimming activities) and how it contributed to the students and their families (for example, developmental improvement and enjoyment) and the coaches (knowledge about disability).

Do families have to live by the "less-than" assumption? Do their children have to face summers of enforced idleness and possible regression in their skills? Do families always have to be the advocates for their children? The answer to each question is "No."

Somewhere, beyond the school yard, there is a place for every child, a place that acknowledges disabilities but does not cave in to them. But going beyond the school yard, beyond the "less-than" world, requires partners in advocacy.

Source: From Fennick, E., & Royle, J. (2003). Community inclusion for children and youth with developmental disabilities. *Focus on Autism and Other Developmental Disabilities, 18*(1), 20–27. Copyright 2003 by PRO-ED, Inc. Adapted with permission.

where in the community they would especially like to pursue these activities. Then the IEP team can consider how the skills needed to participate successfully might be taught as part of the student's curriculum. In addition to strengthening recreational skills, this approach can enhance self-esteem and opportunities for friendships. If the community recreational opportunities are free, it can also ease the stress of daily care demands without imposing additional economic responsibilities on the family.

Education

Families generally place a strong emphasis on education. Within the European American culture, education is typically seen as the key to success in employment, financial, and quality-of-life opportunities (Hanson, 2004). A similar Asian perspective appears in this Chinese proverb (Chan & Lee, 2004, p. 253):

> If you are planning for a year, sow rice; if you are planning for a decade, plant trees; if you are planning for a lifetime, educate people.

Families from diverse cultural and linguistic backgrounds often encounter educational and social barriers in attaining equal opportunities for their children (Kalyanpur & Harry, 1999; National Research Council, 2001). As a Native American grandparent stated:

> I had children and grandchildren who are really gifted. At one time they brought home a lot of high marks from school, but they learned that if they were good achievers they would be harassed at school, so they didn't want their peers to know about their good grades. The school talks about this, but they don't know what to do about it. There should be something we could do to stop this trend and turn these other kids around. Some parents, who have money or were in education and knew their child was gifted, would pull their children out of the school and send them to a white school. (U.S. Department of Education, 1990, p. 5)

Throughout this book, you will learn about families' roles in meeting their children's educational needs. Here we will emphasize the importance of maintaining balance in family functions rather than overemphasizing education to the detriment of other functions. In chapter 4, we will describe two educational tasks that many families assume at four different life cycle stages. One of the fundamental premises of a family systems approach is the importance of maintaining balance in carrying out family roles. As we will discuss in chapter 5, professionals sometimes emphasize the role of parents as teachers or tutors. That emphasis is appropriate if it is consistent with a family's values, priorities, and available time. If it is not, the differences among the focus of school, other service agencies, and home can impair the development of trusting partnerships. Many parents and students with exceptionalities respond negatively to professional overemphasis on educational needs. Professionals should remember that educational needs are only one of eight functions that families must address. As Maddux and Cummings (1983) warned:

> If academic learning is required in both the home and the school, a child who has difficulty learning gets very little relief. The home ceases to be a haven from scholastic pressures. Imagine how most of us would feel if the most frustrating, least enjoyable, and most difficult thing about our work were waiting for us when we came home each day. (p. 30)

Beware of the "fix it" approach whereby children and youth with exceptionalities are almost continuously placed in quasi-teaching situations by well-intentioned teachers, family, and friends. These perpetual educational efforts to make the child "better" may have a negative impact on self-esteem, as Harriet Rousso (1984) noted when writing about her mother's approach to her physical therapy:

> Being disabled and being intact at the same time is an extremely difficult notion for non-disabled people to make sense of. I kept thinking of my mother's words: Why wouldn't you want to walk straight? Even now, it is hard to explain that I may have wanted to walk straight, but I did not want to lose my sense of myself in the process. Perhaps the best I can say is that my perspective on disability, from the inside out, is different from my mother's, from the outside looking in. In our work with congenitally disabled clients, we must always be receptive and respectful of that difference. (Rousso, 1984, p. 12)

Professionals and families need to be keenly aware of a perspective on disability from the inside out. Adults with disabilities can be valued mentors, role models, and consultants in assisting professionals, families, and young children with disabilities to gain such a vital perspective (Klein & Kemp, 2004).

Encouraging educational achievement is particularly prevalent in the homes of students who have been identified as gifted and talented (Friedman, 2000). Parents tend to emphasize the particular area of their son's or daughter's special interest and provide early and continued opportunities for growth and development (Friedman, 2000; Moon, Jurich, & Feldhusen, 1998). One study reported that 70% of artistically talented students indicated parental support for their artwork and 65% had place to do their art at home (Clark & Zimmerman, 1988).

According to Friedman (1994), many low-income parents of students who are gifted do not place as much emphasis on educational achievement; however, the additional attention that these families must devote to housing, dangerous neighborhoods, unemployment, and other stressors should not be interpreted to mean that the families do not support their children who are gifted.

TIME AS A FACTOR IN MEETING FAMILY FUNCTIONS

Review the eight functions that we have just discussed, and imagine yourself as Sean's mother. If you were Leia Holley seeking to raise two boys while your husband was stationed overseas, and meet all of the duties of your own job, participate in your community, have a little time for yourself, and meet the partnership responsibilities to ensure that Sean's great expectations come true, when would you find time to address all eight family functions? How would you want Sean's teachers to support you and your family? Would you want them to judge you as not caring enough about Sean to meet 100% of his needs, or would you hope that they would recognize that you are juggling as many responsibilities in a 24-hour day as possible?

Undoubtedly, time is a major issue for many families. Approximately two thirds of all employed parents with children under 18 report that they do not have enough time to meet their children's needs (Families and Work Institute, 1994), that they often leave their children unattended at home, and that they rely on their children to be occupied by watching television. If this is the report mainly from parents who have children without exceptionalities, what impact on the family do some of the tasks associated with exceptionality have?

In Figure 3–10 you will read the words of Helen Featherstone, the mother of a son with a severe disability, who had no unclaimed time for her day or night. Helen poignantly described the impossibility of adding a 15-minute request from the occupational therapist to help with the problem of Jody's gums. What would you have expected of the Featherstone family if you had been Jody's occupational therapist, teacher, or dentist? What balance should be struck between meeting Jody's disability-related needs and the needs of the entire family?

In chapter 2, we discussed how mothers and fathers distribute household duties. Traditionally, attending to the daily care needs of family members has been "women's work," and female caring roles often expand when the child has an exceptionality (Traustadottir, 1995). Mothers expressed a commitment to maintain an

FIGURE 3–10
My Voice: Where Will I Find the Time?

I remember the day when the occupational therapist at Jody's school called with some suggestions from a visiting nurse. Jody has a seizure problem, which is controlled with the drug Dilantin. Dilantin can cause the gums to grow over the teeth; the nurse had noticed this overgrowth, and recommended innocently enough, that [his] teeth be brushed four times a day, for 5 minutes, with an electric toothbrush. The school suggested that they could do this once on school days, and that I should try to do it the other three times a day; this new demand appalled me; Jody is blind, cerebral palsied, and retarded. We do his physical therapy daily and work with him on sounds and communication. We feed him each meal on our laps, bottle him, bathe him, dry him, put him in a body cast to sleep, launder his bed linens daily, and go through a variety of routines designed to minimize his miseries and enhance his joys and his development. (All this in addition to trying to care for and enjoy our other young children and making time for each other and our careers.) Now you tell me that I should spend 15 minutes every day on something that Jody will hate, an activity that will not help him to walk or even defecate, but one that is directed at the health of his gums. This activity is not for a finite time, but forever. It is not guaranteed to help, but "it can't hurt." And it won't make the overgrowth go away but may retard it. Well, it's too much. Where is that 15 minutes going to come from? What am I supposed to give up? Taking the kids to the park? Reading a bedtime story to my eldest? Washing the breakfast dishes? Sorting the laundry? Grading students' papers? Sleeping? Because there is not time in my life that hasn't been spoken for, and for every 15-minute activity that is added one has to be taken away.

Source: Excerpted from *A Difference in the Family* by Helen Featherstone. Copyright © 1980 by Basic® Books, Inc. Reprinted by permission of Basic Books, a member of Perseus Books, L.L.C.

ordinary family life (Traustadottir, 1995) by simply being able to carry out their daily routines without the child's exceptionality limiting those routines. Rather than assessing the severity of their child's exceptionality according to traditional standards, they more frequently interpreted severity according to the limitations and constraints placed on family life. As one mother described, "I feel like a wishbone being pulled apart in different directions" (Renwick, Brown, & Raphael, 1998, p. 13).

No generalizations can describe the limitations and constraints that children and youth with exceptionalities place on family living. It all depends upon the family's characteristics, interactions, functions, and lifespan issues. Clearly, a significant factor is the family's level of adaptability, as you learned in chapter 2. Consider two families: one that maintains a very strict schedule and is quite frustrated by any change, and another with a balanced level of adaptability characterized by flexible rules and routines. If these two families had children with identical characteristics, the family with more balanced adaptability probably would have less difficulty carrying out family functions than the family whose roles and routines are strictly implemented.

In one study, parents identified four barriers to their efficient and effective use of time (Brotherson & Goldstein, 1992, p. 518):

1. The inability of professionals to coordinate their activities among themselves
2. The overwhelming number of tasks parents were asked by professionals to complete
3. The lack of local and accessible services
4. A lack of flexible and family-centered scheduling of services

You can make a significant contribution to the quality of family life by helping to remove time barriers and by facilitating ways to use time efficiently and effectively. In the same study, parents' suggestions for effective time use included the following:

> Parents wanted education and therapy for their child to be part of their daily routine and environment. They wanted to work well with professionals to provide care for their children: Time was wasted if activities were learned in artificial settings or if the knowledge of parents was ignored. They wanted professionals to aid their efficiency and effectiveness by using current technology when it is applicable. Further, they wanted to be given more time to develop rapport with professionals. (Brotherson & Goldstein, 1992, p. 515)

One of the greatest lessons you can derive from understanding family functions is how busy family life is. Educational issues are one of eight functions; families may or may not be able to devote the time to educational issues that you, as an educational professional, might deem desirable. As you pursue your career and your own family life, it is likely that you will experience these same time crunches. Particularly for families who have a child with a severe disability, it is critical to recognize that they are dealing with lifelong issues that require the endurance of a marathon runner, not a sprinter. Professionals, however, often are tempted to urge the parents to make substantial investments of time over the short term (like a sprinter) to enhance what the child might be able to learn. "Parents think of time as daily routine, they also see the care of their child as an ongoing, life long, ever-evolving commitment, not a short-term education or therapeutic contact. This is a significant difference in time orientation that should be highlighted for professional understanding of families" (Brotherson & Goldstein, 1992, p. 523).

SUMMARY

Families exist to meet the individual and collective needs of their members. The tasks they perform to meet those needs are referred to as family functions; in a family systems framework, they are the outputs. There are eight categories of functions or outputs: affection, self-esteem, spirituality, economics, daily care, socialization, recreation, and education.

When partnering with families around these functions, bear the following in mind:

- Families' cultures influence the ways they carry out these functions.
- Families may or may not spend the amount of time on each function that you assume you would spend if you were in their situation.
- The child with an exceptionality as well as every family member influences how the family performs each of these eight functions.
- The child's impact can be both positive and negative and will depend in part on the family's characteristics (chapter 1), interactions (chapter 2), and life cycle stages and transitions (chapter 4).
- The family members' motivation, knowledge, and skills will influence how they carry out their functions and how you can most successfully develop a trusting partnership with them.
- There are some concrete steps you can take as you develop partnerships with families around each of these functions.
- Family life is busy, and time is a valuable and limited resource.

REFLECTING ON THE VIGNETTE

1. Which of the eight family functions does each of the four families NOT perform?
2. Which of the functions does each family seem to perform more than all other functions?
3. Which of the functions could any of the families eliminate or minimize?

ENHANCING YOUR SELF-AWARENESS

What have been your own family experiences while carrying out the eight family functions? Being in touch with what works and does not work for your family will enable you to identify and evaluate your own assumptions about what might be best for your students' families. However, the families with whom you develop partnerships may attend to their functions in ways that may not be the ones you have used or would recommend. All families are different.

Affection

As you were growing up, who were the members of your family who expressed verbal and physical affection to you? Was the exchange of affection in your family excessive, about the right level, or insufficient? How do your own experiences affect your beliefs about the role of families in expressing affection?

Spirituality

What are your religious/spiritual values and beliefs? Were these values and beliefs shaped during your childhood or developed more during adulthood? How do you rely on religious/spiritual values and beliefs when you face particularly challenging situations? How do your values and beliefs influence the extent to which you are comfortable conversing with families about their spirituality?

Daily care

As you have gotten to know children and youth with exceptionalities and their families, have you ever encountered a situation in which you felt that, given similar circumstances, you would not be able to handle the daily care requirements? What made you think that the daily care requirements would be too time-consuming and challenging? What supports and services might you and other professionals provide to enable a family to carry out their daily care responsibilities in a reasonable way?

Education

What one or two educational activities or experiences helped improve family functions within your own family? How might the education that you provide to students also enable them to be more successful with one or more family functions?

RESOURCES

You can find a link to these resources on the Companion Website at *www.prenhall.com/turnbull*.

1. Family Voices
   3411 Candelaria NE, Suite M
   Albuquerque, NM 87107
   505-872-4774
   Kidshealth@familyvoices.org

   Family Voices is a national network of families, friends, professionals, and advocates who focus on health care services. The focus is on providing health care that is family centered, community based, comprehensive, coordinated, and culturally competent.

2. American Association on Mental Retardation
   Division on Religion and Spirituality
   444 N. Capitol Street, NW, Suite 846
   Washington, DC 20001
   202-387-1968
   www.aamr.org/Groups/div/RG/index.html

   The Religion and Spirituality Division of AAMR provides national and international leadership in fostering opportunities to promote the spiritual growth of individuals with disabilities and their families. They publish the *Journal of Religion, Disability, and Health.*

3. Family Village
   www.familyvillage.wisc.edu

   This comprehensive Website provides extensive information for families of children with disabilities related to recreation and leisure, education, health, and daily living. They provide both print and electronic resources.

4. Disability Studies for Teachers
   www.disabilitystudies forteachers.org

   This Website provides extensive resources for teachers to introduce topics of disability into social studies, history, literature, and related subjects in grades 6 through 12. Lesson plans, essays, and other materials are available. When a disability studies curriculum is well implemented, it may lead to a greater readiness on the part of professionals to advance community participation and friendships for people with disabilities.

Family Life Cycle

CHAPTER ORGANIZATION

FRAMING QUESTIONS

1. What is meant by life cycle stages and transitions?
2. How do family responsibilities and priorities change over time?
3. How can family-professional partnerships enable families to experience more successful transitions?

VIGNETTE

There are many adages about time. The ancient Romans declared that time flies: *tempus fugit.* The early English poet Chaucer wrote that time abides no man. In the seventeenth century, another English poet, Andrew Marvell penned that, at his back, "I always hear time's winged chariot hurrying near." And the modern poet T. S. Eliot reminded us all, "Hurry up please, it's time." So it is with families; time passes, and the stages of their lives move inexorably from one to another.

Nicky Doleman was the perfect baby at birth—healthy, whole, and happy. Now, as a result of being abused, she has experienced life cycle transitions that no one anticipated: from the newborn nursery to home, and then back to the hospital for lifesaving surgery, then the early intervention program at the University of Kansas and thereafter the inclusion program at Raintree Montessori School, and now into first grade at Woodlawn Elementary School. Nicky's

and Vera's transitions are *off-time;* the unexpected, off-schedule ones necessitated solely because Nicky has a disability.

Sean Holley faces the "transition terror" of leaving Bonner Springs Elementary School and entering a new school, where the culture may not be so nourishing and more controlling. The unknown always gives a family a reason for concern, a justification to pause and ponder.

Joesian Cortes has a few years left at Bushwick High School, but soon he, too, will face the transition that comes to every student—commencement exercises, graduation diplomas, and life after high school. Will he qualify to be a firefighter, to hold the job where he can help people in distress? Or will he work with his uncle as a plumber, in a trade that will also enable him to help people? Uncertainty about the future is the norm in the Cortes family.

Kenny Berg is the old-timer among these four people, a graduate of the Jewish Guild School, a farmer in Queens, New York. His next transition will not occur for many years: retirement from work. By then, Clara and Jake will have predeceased him, but his brother and sister, Sheldon and Karen, most probably will still be alive. They, not his parents, will face Kenny's future as a senior citizen.

It is doubtful that any of these four families ever expected the lives they are living. Vera says that she "took life for granted" and that "God would not do me any better than anyone else." Nor any differently or any worse. Did Clara and Jake

vion Doleman sits in his great-grandfather's lap while Vera Doleman looks on.

Kenny Berg's longtime love of horses sparked his ultimate vocation at Adriance Farm in New York.

Kenny Berg's siblings, Karen and Sheldon Berg.

expect Kenny to be born premature and to lose his sight and hearing? Did Norma and Joaquin expect Joesian to be a slow reader and to have a slight speech impediment? Did Leia and Jamie expect Sean to have autism and epilepsy? No.

No family with a child with a disability can assume much. They can, however, take this for granted: Their life cycle stages will differentiate them from families who do not have children with disabilities. "Normal" means something profoundly different for these families.

As you enter into partnerships with families such as these four, you will learn to ask: What is the norm? What is normal? And you will answer these questions in part by learning about the life cycle stages.

INTRODUCTION

In the previous three chapters, we discussed the family system and how it is affected by a member with an exceptionality. The dominant image is one of multilayered complexity. First, families differ in their characteristics to such an extent that every family is unique. Second, every family is an interactive system: Anything that happens to one person affects the whole family. Third, every family is engaged in a variety of functions designed to fulfill a number of tangible and intangible needs.

A fourth layer of complexity—called life cycle changes—affects the family system (Carter & McGoldrick, 1999). The first three layers—family characteristics, interactions, and functions—provide only a snapshot of what should more accurately be portrayed as a full-length motion picture. All families progress through stages and transitions as their members are born, grow up, leave home, bring in new members through marriage or other permanent relationships, retire, and die. Families may also experience unexpected or sudden changes that drastically alter their lives, such as divorce, death, separation by military service, immigration, job transfers, unemployment, a windfall inheritance, or natural catastrophes. Whether the change is expected and "on cycle," or unexpected and "off cycle," the family changes. As it does, so do its characteristics (chapter 1), interactions (chapter 2), and functions (chapter 3). In Figure 4–1, we show how the four components of the family system, including family life cycle changes, relate to each other.

FAMILY LIFE CYCLE THEORY

Family life cycle theory seeks to explain how a family changes over time (Carter & McGoldrick, 1999; Rodgers & White, 1993). The theory is that each family experiences certain predictable stages. As the family moves from one stage to the next, it enters an interim phase known as transition. For example, families typically experience a childbirth and child-raising stage. The parents learn to care for the child and understand what parenthood really entails, and the child typically learns how to talk, walk, and explore the environment of home and perhaps preschool.

The individual life cycle stages vary within and across cultures. Leading family theorists have identified six stages (Carter & McGoldrick, 1999):

- Leaving home as single young adults
- Marriage and the new couple
- Families with young children
- Families with adolescents
- Launching children
- Families in later life

It is insufficient, however, to focus solely on one family member's life cycle. The family life cycle encompasses the interactions among all changes in the family (Carter & McGoldrick, 1999; Olson, 1988). A father who was simultaneously caring for his 81-year-old mother, 21-year-old son with a developmental disability, and 13-year-old daughter while also working 50 hours a week commented: "I felt whipsawed. No matter how much I did for one generation, there was always another whose need cried out to me with such fervor that I felt I couldn't fulfill all of them. In a sense, my mother had become my son because she had the greater disability and because he was becoming more independent."

Beyond the developmental tasks that the family and individual members must accomplish at each stage, transitions occur from one stage to another. Transitions are the periods between stages when the family is adjusting interactions and roles to prepare for the next developmental stage (Carter & McGoldrick, 1999; Rodgers & White, 1993). When an infant leaves the birth and early childhood stage and enters the childhood stage, the child and the family embark on a transition. With that transition come changes in the following:

- *Family characteristics.* For example, the personal characteristics of the child change.
- *Family interactions.* For example, the parental subsystem changes as the child matures and communicates with the parents in a different way.

FIGURE 4–1

Family Systems Framework: Emphasis on Family Life Cycle

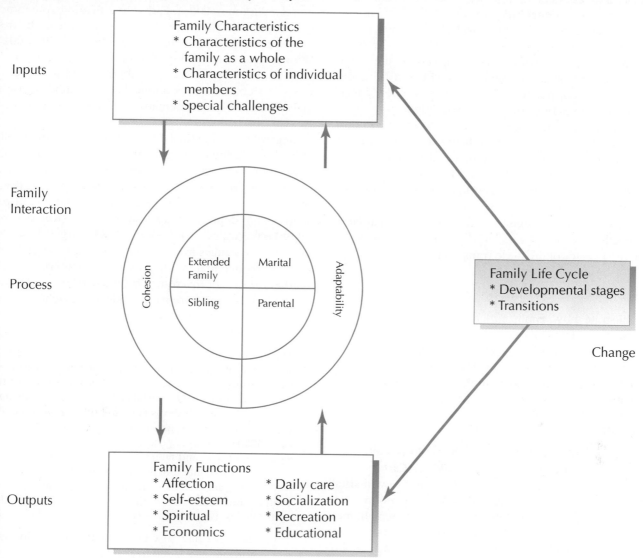

Source: Turnbull, A. P., Summers, J. A., & Brotherson, M. J. (1984). *Working with families with disabled members: A family systems approach* (p. 60). Lawrence: University of Kansas, Kansas Affiliated Facility. Adapted by permission.

Family functions. For example, the child spends more time in school and on homework and contributes more to daily care.

When the transition is complete, and the transition itself may take a while—the family has reached the next stage. [It] performs tasks and has interactions appropriate to that stage.

Transition periods are usually briefer than the stages to which they relate. But because these shifts may result in confusion and conflict, transitions are almost always times of heightened stress (Carter & McGoldrick, 1999; Olson et al., 1983).

Using life cycle theory to understand family change has at least two advantages: (1) It highlights similar family rhythms over time, and (2) it helps to understand the continuity of family life. But life cycle theory has been criticized for not sufficiently taking into account varying norms across different cultural groups, family forms, and disability-related factors (Rodgers & White, 1993; Turnbull, Summers, & Brotherson, 1986). For example, some ethnic groups place a strong emphasis on close extended families and less value on independence; thus, adults may not leave their parental home to set up a separate household (Kalyanpur & Harry, 1999; Turnbull & Turnbull, 1996).

In remarried families, particularly those with older children from a previous marriage, several life cycle stages may occur simultaneously as children from the first marriage approach adulthood while the newly married couple gives birth to their own children.

We will concentrate on the four life cycle stages during which the family is most likely to experience contact with schools: birth and early childhood, childhood, adolescence, and young adulthood. Then we will discuss transition from one stage to another and how exceptionality affects the family's ability to adjust to change. As you read, keep in mind the energy and persistence that families need as they run the marathon of life cycle stages and face the hurdles of life cycle transitions.

LIFE CYCLE STAGES

To illustrate how family functions and their priorities change as the family moves through the life cycle, we will highlight two educational issues many families encounter during each of the four stages. That way, we will concentrate on one of the eight family functions—education (chapter 3)—across each of the four lifespan stages.

Birth and Early Childhood

During the early childhood years, the family is likely to be intensely absorbed with its inner workings (Carter, 1999). If not a previously married family (in which new marital partners already have children), the childless couple (assuming it is a couple rather than a single-parent home) probably has explored the parameters of its relationship. The couple also has begun to blend the norms of two families into one and has learned how to respond to each other's needs. Sometimes, children arrive on the scene, dependent on the parents for their physical and emotional well-being. While children learn to master their bodies and their immediate environment, parents face the task of nurturing their children and meeting their own needs. A family that has a member with an exceptionality confronts a number of educational challenges. Two of these challenges are (1) discovering and coming to terms with the exceptionality and its implications and (2) participating in early childhood services.

Discovering and Coming to Terms with Exceptionality. Infants with severe and multiple disabilities, in contrast to those with mild disabilities, typically are identified at birth as having special needs.

In one or more states, screening currently exists for about 30 metabolic and genetic diseases (Bailey, Skinner, & Sparkman, 2003). Early identification sometimes occurs prenatally, with fetal therapy possible in the first 3 or 4 months of pregnancy (Schonberg & Tifft, 2002). With such advanced identification, some families decide to have an abortion whereas others use advanced diagnosis to prepare for the coming birth of a child with special needs (Bell & Stoneman, 2000; Roberts, Stough, & Parrish, 2002).

Regardless of whether the diagnosis occurs prenatally, at birth, or during the early years, some professional literature holds that families may experience a grief cycle. The cycle has been likened to stages of dealing with the death of loved ones. It includes shock, denial, guilt and anger, shame and depression, and acceptance (Kübler-Ross, 1969; Leff & Walizer, 1992; Moses, 1983). Largely based on clinical case studies in the 1960s and 1970s, some literature has concentrated on grief stages experienced by mothers. However, this research has since been described as sorely lacking in empirical evidence (Blacher, 1984a, 1984b). Nonetheless, you will encounter the literature and the theory behind it, as stated by Ken Moses (1983):

> The grieving process . . . is a feeling process that permits the parent of a developmentally disabled child to separate from dreams and fantasies generated in anticipation of the birth of that child. The inability to successfully separate from such a dream is devastating to both parent and child. If the parent does not generate new dreams that the child can fulfill, then each day the child would be experienced as a disappointment and failure in the eyes of the parent. . . It is within this context of development that the concept of facilitating grief becomes an important tool in the intervention and habilitation of developmentally disabled children. (Moses, 1983, pp. 27–28)

A parent who had just given birth to a child with Down syndrome described her feelings:

> Shock, grief, bitter disappointment, fury, horror, my feelings were a mixture of all these after my doctor told me that our new little son, Peter, was born with Down syndrome. I was afraid to have him brought from the nursery. . . . I didn't want to see this monster. But when the nurse brought in this tiny, black-haired baby with up-tilted, almond-shaped eyes, my heart melted. . . . But the grief and fear didn't go away just because we fell in love with our son. They came in great, overwhelming waves. I felt a deep need to cry out, to cry and cry until I had worked this immense sorrow up from the center of my being and out into the open. . . I think we should give honest and full expression to our grief. I suspect that when, in our attempts to be brave and face the future we repress our feelings, these feelings of pain and sorrow last longer. All I'm trying to say is that there's a time for weeping and then a time for pushing

ahead, and I don't think you can do the second without going through the first. (Vyas, 1983, p. 17)

Although the grief cycle conception is firmly rooted within much of the professional literature, many professionals question whether parents must pass through sequential stages to reach a stage of acceptance (Gallagher, Fialka, Rhodes, & Arceneaux, 2001; Howard, Williams, Port, & Lepper, 1997; Miller, 1994). Clinical descriptions of parental grief have failed to document how and what "grieving" parents were initially told about the nature of their child's exceptionality (Lee, 1994). Ruth Johnson, mother of a 15-year-old with Down syndrome, describes how she learned about her son's exceptionality: "About 8 p.m. the doctor came in and said abruptly: 'Read the numbers on the baby's ID bracelet and the one on your wrist. See, it's the same. This baby is yours. This happens to women your age. You may want genetic counseling, and you'll probably want to put it in a home.'"

One study involved interviews with parents about how the prenatal diagnosis of Down syndrome was shared with them. Six of the 10 mothers who were interviewed reported that their obstetrician or obstetrical nurse reflected negative attitudes when discussing the diagnosis with them (Helm, Miranda, & Angoff-Chedd, 1998). One mother said the obstetrician commented, "This child will not accomplish anything. Everyone [in my practice] has aborted" (Helm et al., 1998, p. 57).

From this same study, mothers offered advice to professionals about how information should be given to parents who undergo prenatal testing (see Figure 4–2). This advice is just as applicable to families hearing a diagnosis after the child is born.

How would a family's emotional reactions differ if information was shared with them in a supportive way? What if the family was immediately linked to resources? What differences would it make in their hope, sense of self-efficacy, and coping skills? See Figure 4–3 for Diane Gerst's (1991) personal view of the grief process.

Judy O'Halloran, the mother of a son with a disability, counters the grief perspective by describing a "celebration process" of reflecting positively and hopefully on the emotions associated with the diagnosis of disability. The celebration process moves beyond mere acceptance or adaptation. It emphasizes how negative emotions and behaviors can serve as catalysts for energy and presistence. For example, negative emotions can be transformed as follows (O'Halloran, 1995):

Shock over the disability leading to numbness and withdrawal can be a time to question previous beliefs and to transition between getting the news of the disability and moving into action.

FIGURE 4–2

Tips for Sharing Prenatal Testing Results with Families

- Make sure parents understand all prenatal tests.
- Give the diagnosis in person if possible.
- Give the news to both parents at the same time.
- Do not make assumptions about the parents' decision.
- Do not make judgments about the parents' decision.
- Give nonjudgmental information on all three options: continuation of pregnancy and parenting, continuation of the pregnancy and adoption placement, and termination of pregnancy.
- Give up-to-date printed material on Down syndrome.
- Make referrals to Down syndrome programs.
- Do not accentuate the negative.
- Do not use negative terminology.
- Do not pity parents, but do recognize that they may feel a loss.

Source: Helm, D. T., Miranda, S., & Angoff-Chedd, N. (1998). Prenatal diagnosis of Down syndrome: Mothers' reflections on supports needed for diagnosis to birth. *Mental Retardation, 36*(1), 55–61.

- Fear can be a catalyst to reach out to family members and friends for support to learn how to take back control.
- Denial may lead to taking action to create change that will bring better opportunities for children with disabilities.
- Anger can be energizing when it is used in a rational and reasonable way.

A recent article explores the range of interpretations of parents "being in denial." One of the authors, the parent of a child with a disability, described her husband's reactions when she asked him to recall his early impressions of their son, who is now a teenager. Her husband remembered a much more optimistic view of their child's development than she did. "She asked her husband if during those early years, he was 'in denial.' He paused and replied, 'No, I wasn't in denial. I was in hope'" (Gallagher, Fialka, Rhodes, & Arceneaux, 2001, p. 14). These authors encourage professionals to affirm parents' dreams and hopes for their child throughout the adjustment process.

Much of the literature on grieving comes from European American professionals and families writing about cultural peers. The initial diagnosis and the impact on families from multicultural perspectives are not yet well

FIGURE 4–3
Trevor Is a Citizen, Why Grieve?

I have never had a professional who had high expectations for Trevor tell me I was in denial or that I needed to grieve the loss of my dream. But I have had (more than one) professionals try to get me to accept a lower standard for Trevor by using denial, anger, guilt, and grief to invalidate my opinion and convince me to accept segregation and/or poor services. In the first six months of Trevor's life, I was presented with a grieving process over and over. I experienced stress over the fact that it did not represent what I felt and confusion because other parents felt that it did. I also felt anger with early intervention staff who insisted that *I was grieving* but refusing to acknowledge it.

What would have helped me during the days, weeks and months following my son's diagnosis? First, it would have been helpful if people had seen what I was going through, and helped me to see it, as a crisis, rather than as grief. I've lived through my share of crises, but no one helped me to see that the things I had learned from previous crises could get me through this one.

It would have been helpful if someone had paid attention to what I was feeling. While judgments were abundant, careful, empathetic, respectful, nonjudgmental listening was in short supply. My feelings were often categorized, but they were not often heard and understood. . . .

And then there was the absence of "congratulations on your new baby" cards, and the "friends" that didn't come to see him. Of all the things that happened, one of the most meaningful for me was a certificate I received from a Congressman, Jack Cera. It said that Trevor was a citizen.

. . . One of the things that helped was a celebration—in spite of the disability, not in ignorance of it— because if the child is not celebrated as he/she is, the parents feel the rejection of a palpable part of the identification crisis. Having gone through other crises in my life, I can say that during those my thinking was not discredited or denied. Even through "things had to be worked through," people did not invalidate my ideas or reactions during times of crisis, or dismiss them because I was in an "anger stage." Trevor's a gift, as my other children are. He has never been a source of grief, either now or at his birth. I had indeed been through a crisis and had experienced pain, but he was not the source. He has many times been the consolation.

Added note: Diane wrote these feelings when Trevor was very young. Trevor is now fully included in elementary school. He is not only a citizen but also a Boy Scout and a T-ball player. Diane reports that all is well with him, but the crisis more recently has focused on his younger sister who has leukemia. Diane knows how to survive and prevail when she faces crises, and her children are all the consolation.

Source: Gerst, D. (1991). *Trevor is a citizen: Why grieve?* Unpublished manuscript.

understood. From a Native American orientation, one might expect the following:

> When a family member has a disability or illness, traditional ceremonies are conducted to begin the healing process and to protect the individual and the rest of the home from further harm. For that reason, an Indian family may want to complete traditional ceremonies before they become involved in a regimen recommended by physicians or other service providers. (Joe & Malach, 2004, p. 125)

Developmental milestones also have cultural variations. In a European American culture, a major milestone occurs as the child begins to walk, whereas a first laugh, first hunt, first dance, or ear piercing may have similar priority for some Native American tribes (Joe & Malach, 2004; Sipes, 1993).

Children who are highly gifted are frequently identified during the infancy and early childhood years (Dalzell, 1998). Often these children show fast development in verbal and mathematics skills, which sometimes creates difficulty for families and professionals in providing adequate educational stimulation (Dalzell, 1998; Maxwell, 1998).

In chapter 11, we will suggest how to inform families about the presence of an exceptionality and how to foster a trusting partnership. At this point, just remember that discovering the exceptionality and beginning to come to terms with it are part of a major life cycle task for many families, especially during the early childhood years. (A significant number of students with mild exceptionalities, however, are not identified until they are in elementary school; for their families, discovery and its associated feelings come at a much later time but pose similar challenges.

Participation in Early Childhood Services

Learning about the child's exceptionality is only the first of a lifelong series of interactions with professionals. Families with young children whose disabilities have already been identified are likely to enter the world of early intervention and preschool education. Early intervention often described as "Part C programs." As you will learn in chapter 6, Part C of the Individuals with Disabilities Education Act (IDEA) regulates serving children from birth through 2 years of age (sometimes called "zero to three"). The most recent data indicate that approximately 231,000 infants and toddlers are served in early intervention; approximately two thirds are European American, 17% Hispanic, 16% African American, 4% Asian/Pacific Islander, and 1% American Indian/Alaskan Native (U.S. Department of Education, 2002). Nine states have laws that enable them to serve infants and toddlers who would be at risk for disability if early intervention were not provided.

Part C of IDEA requires states to provide early intervention services in the child's natural environments. These include the child's home, a community-based setting with children who do not have disabilities, or a community-based setting that serves only (or primarily) children with disabilities (Dunst, Hamby, Trivette, Raab, & Bruder, 2000; Dunst et al., 2001; Stowe & Turnbull, 2001). Approximately two thirds of all early intervention services took place in the home during the 1999–2000 school year; by contrast, approximately 14% of the children were served in specialized programs for children with disabilities (U.S. Department of Education, 2002). As you learned in chapter 3, *natural environment* is increasingly being interpreted by leaders in the early intervention field as supports and services in the community settings that children and families most prefer.

The U.S. Department of Education (2001) is carrying out a national study to document the progress of infants and toddlers in early intervention programs. Encouraging findings point to children's developmental progress and families' satisfaction with services. Data indicate substantial child progress in key developmental areas—motor, self-help, communication, and cognition. Over two thirds of families reported the early intervention program had significant impact on their child's developmental gains. In addition, the majority reported satisfaction with both the quality and quantity of services they received. They indicated greater confidence in their parenting roles, helping their child learn and develop, and working with professionals to advocate for their child's needs. Families from culturally and linguistically diverse backgrounds, families with low incomes, and families in which the mother had less formal education tended to be less satisfied with early intervention than their counterparts (Bailey, Hebbeler, Scarborough, Spiker, & Mallik, 2004). Clearly, families have affirmed the value of early intervention. Still, there is a need to document the less positive perspectives of families from diverse backgrounds and to ensure that their concerns are addressed.

When children reach the age of 3, they transition from the Part C early intervention programs to Part B preschool programs. This transition is a significant one. Early intervention programs focus more strongly than preschool programs on family-centered services, as reflected in the individual family service plan (IFSP) (Hanson et al., 2000; McWilliam et al., 1995). A study of 22 families geographically dispersed throughout the United States reported their experiences when they transitioned from early intervention to preschool services (Hanson et al., 2000). Although some families reported positive experiences, the majority cited a number of significant problems stemming from not knowing what to expect. One parent described the information void as follows:

> But what the teacher did was she just rang me up. She said, "We need it. We're going to do a transition meeting. Can you make Thursday afternoon?" And I said, "Yes." And, you know, I never thought to say, "Oh, what does that exactly mean?" . . . So, I didn't know what it [the meeting] was about. (Hanson et al., 2000, p. 285)

The recommendations from this research study include (1) viewing transition as a process that starts early with planning and collaboration, (2) exchanging information with families in advance of meetings and visiting preschools that might be options for placement, and (3) identifying a key person or guide to facilitate the process and ensure that parents are told the full range of options available (Hanson et al., 2000).

Ideally, early intervention professionals collaborate with families as they prepare for the marathon ahead, namely, the full life cycle of the family. By focusing on long-range needs, professionals enable families to enhance their quality-of-life outcomes and avoid the burnout that can occur when families exert all their efforts during the "100-yard dash" of an early intervention program (Turnbull, 1988). Figure 4–4 lists tips to help families develop resilience and pace to attain their goals over a lifelong marathon.

Childhood

Entry into elementary school typically widens the horizons of both children and families. For families who have a child with an exceptionality, entry into school may mark their first encounter with many of the issues we discuss in this book. For example, often with the support of professionals, the elementary years are when many parents acquire (1) a vision for their child's future and (2) a perspective on the appropriateness of inclusion.

Developing a Vision for the Future. Sally Sloop, the mother of Peter, an 8-year-old who has autism,

FIGURE 4–4

Tips for Encouraging Success Beginning in the Early Childhood Lifespan Phase to Continue Throughout the Family Marathon

- Meeting basic needs for food, shelter, health, and security.
- Taking time to reflect on the strengths and limitations of the family.
- Loving the child with an exceptionality unconditionally.
- Establishing relationships that will provide the foundation for future support.
- Experiencing and benefiting from the wide range of emotions that accompany having a child with an exceptionality.
- Learning to collaborate to enhance the child's education and development.
- Anticipating the future and learning transitional planning.
- Establishing balance and equity in the family by learning to juggle time and attention among the members.

Source: Adapted from Turnbull, A. P. (1988). Accepting the challenge of providing comprehensive support to families. *Education and Training in Mental Retardation, 23*(4), 261–272.

envisioned Peter's future when he is 25 years old: "He works where he wants to work, receives a decent paycheck, gets help from the job coach, and is a taxpayer. He has his own apartment and a roommate or partner so he can continue down life's road without undue loneliness" (Turnbull, Turnbull, Shank, & Leal, 1995, p. 24). Is it realistic for parents and professionals to develop such optimistic visions when children have significant disabilities? In Figure 4–5, Sally Sloop now describes what is actually happening in Peter's life as a 21-year-old. How does his actual life at 21 compare and contrast with her early visions, most of which others thought to be unrealistic?

Parents of children with a disability typically want the same things that almost all parents want for their children: a home, friends, happiness, and a chance to contribute to their community (Turnbull & Turnbull, 1999).

How do families and professionals develop visions? To appreciate fully the importance of visions, start by being skeptical about the traditional desires of special educators, other professionals, and families to "be realistic." What if Helen Keller's parents had been realistic about the profound impact of deaf-blindness on her development? Although they were frequently accused of being

unrealistic, their visions for her future helped her become an outstanding stateswoman.

Janet Vohs, the mother of a young adult with multiple disabilities, described how important it is for families of children with disabilities to have a future vision:

Families of children with disabilities are not allowed—or at least not encouraged—to have a dream or a vision for their children's future. What the past has given as possible outcomes for people with disabilities is far less than inspiring. If all we have to look forward to is an extension of the past, I should think we would want to avoid the pain of that future as long as possible. But I have a motto: Vision over visibility. Having a vision is not just planning for a future we already know how to get to. It is daring to dream about what is possible. (Vohs, 1993, pp. 62–63)

How can the power of one person's vision be multiplied through synergy? Synergy occurs when at least two people act in concert with each other for mutually compatible purposes. As powerful as one's own sense of vision can be, even more powerful is a collective and mutually developed future vision. Senge (1990) underscored the importance of collaborative envisioning:

A shared vision is not an idea. . . . It is rather a force in people's hearts, a force of impressive power. It may be inspired by an idea, but once it goes further—if it is compelling enough to acquire the support of more than one person—then it is no longer an abstraction. It is palpable. People begin to see it as if it is this. Few, if any, forces in human affairs are as powerful as shared vision. (Senge, 1990, p. 206)

Synergy results when the partnership between families and professionals moves the individual visions ahead in the same direction. By contrast, when individuals are without partnerships, they may proceed with a different agenda and in a different direction. When people have the benefit of trusting partnerships, individual efforts are united and the collective whole becomes more powerful and effective than any disparate effort.

Susan Rocco, a parent of a son with autism, learned early about the benefits of creating visions through synergy with partners:

As the parent . . . I had experienced most points on the power continuum. The unequal power relationship with Jason's teachers and therapists generally put the burden on me to wheedle, cajole, threaten, flatter—in essence, work harder at the relationship than anyone else—to get the desired outcome. The few times I have experienced true synergy, when we partners are working from our strengths and shared values, the burden has fallen away. The beauty of the synergistic model is that there is no more "them" and "us." "We" pool our resources and our creative juices, and "we" all celebrate in the success. (Turnbull, Turbiville, & Turnbull, 2000, p. 645)

FIGURE 4–5
My Voice: Peter Prevails

When my son Peter was 8½ years old, I wrote in a previous edition of this book that it was "both exciting and anxiety-producing to gaze into Peter's future." It was exciting because Peter was benefiting from early intervention and anxiety-producing because "we understand that these are the cute 'puppy-dog' days of our son's life."

I looked down the road to Peter's 20s and saw a handsome, well-dressed man who would be employed, pay taxes, rent his own apartment, have friends, and, with the help of others, be honored for surmounting his disability (then diagnosed as autism).

Little did I realize how well I imagined Peter's future. Today is Peter's 21st birthday, a day of triumph in so many ways. This fine son of ours, who we were once told would never be going to high school, has not only received his public school diploma through great perseverance but has also completed a 2-year certificate program from the Threshold Program of Lesley University in Cambridge, Massachusetts, some 15 hours away from our family home in Raleigh, North Carolina.

To date, Peter has met two of his major personal goals: to get a diploma and to go to college. Other life goals of his remain: to work and live independently, get a driver's license, get married, and have children. As his parents, we are no longer as stunned or surprised by Peter's accomplishments; he is clearly orchestrating his own life.

As we drive to the church camp where Peter will be employed as a "general duty" staff member for the summer, he asks me: "Should I tell them I have a slight learning disability or something?" I encourage him to share whatever he is comfortable sharing.

In the spring, we had attended Peter's job interview at camp with him. The director had carefully studied Peter's school records and evaluations to better understand the scope of his potential needs. This is the same camp that long ago, under different leadership, rejected Peter's application as a camper because his disability was "too much of a liability." Now the camp is hiring him! The director's stance was open: "We feel that Peter has as much to offer us as we do him."

I also shared with Peter that I've been asked to write about his life now in comparison to when he was 8 years old. "What are some words I could use to describe you?" I asked. He immediately offered "complicated" and "fight."

I found myself duly impressed with his insightful (by my standards) choice of the word *complicated* and was quickly brought back to reality with his choice of the word *fight*. He chose that word in reference to the ever-present role of TV wrestling characters and the dozens of toy wrestler figures that he owns and that have ongoing importance to him. Peter then added, "If I give a sermon someday, I will call it 'Never Misjudge Anybody by Their Learning Style.' " His choice of a title reflects that he is increasingly comfortable with his differences and has become a promising advocate for himself and others.

My husband and I are now able to see ongoing horizons for Peter rather than anxious, hoped-for possibilities. Peter is in charge of his own life, with support and backup guidance. In the fall, he will sign a lease for his first apartment in the Boston area and live with a roommate of his choice. He will receive guidance from the Threshold Program in helping secure full-time employment. Peter's job skills have been cultivated for specific work, possibly in a library. He has a full circle of friends of his own choosing and access to a vast system of public transportation to connect with them. He confidently gets to the Boston airport on his own, flying back and forth to North Carolina. A first significant girlfriend was in the picture for a while, so just perhaps that longed-for life partner will come along.

To quote a song from an earlier generation: What a wonderful world this would be.

Sally Sloop

At the elementary level, you will likely give many parents—especially those whose children have mild disabilities—information for the first time about their child's special needs. Consistent with the expectations of the No Child Left Behind Act for student progress (as you will learn in chapter 6), you will be in a position to emphasize the more challenging academic standards for all students and IDEA's long-term outcomes (further education, employment, and independent living). You and other professionals can offer yourselves as trusted partners in creating and achieving the visions. Almost all visions are easier to create and achieve when people work together.

Families of elementary students often develop low expectations as a result of negative thinking by professionals, other families, and outdated public attitudes (Ivey, 2004; Mutua, 2001). Professionals play a critical role in igniting visions for the future within a family (Turnbull,

Turnbull, & Blue-Banning, 1994). So, too, do family and friends. Helping families develop positive visions of the future encourages them to push the limits of what is possible, rather than being trapped by learned helplessness. It is a matter of motivating everyone who works with a student and family to achieve more progress than they might even think possible.

Developing a Perspective on the Appropriateness of Inclusion. As we will discuss in chapter 6, IDEA creates a presumption in favor of educating students in least restrictive, more inclusive environments. To what extent are students ages 6 through 21 placed in general education classrooms as contrasted to separate environments? Figure 4–6 reports on placement trends during the 1999–2000 school year.

What are your predictions about the extent of inclusion across the different school-age levels? Do you think there is more, about the same, or less inclusion as students age? Based on the most current data available, the most inclusion (57% of all students) occurred for students

ages 6 to 11 who were served in regular classrooms for most of the school day (80% or more) (U.S. Department of Education, 2002). As students grow older, their percent of inclusive placements decreases. For example, 61% of students ages 12 to 17 were served in the general education classroom for most of the school day (80% or more).

Students with speech or language impairments and students with specific learning disabilities are most likely to be served for the greatest percentage of time in the general education classroom (U.S. Department of Education, 2002). Students who are less likely to spend more time in general education classrooms include those with deaf-blindness, autism, mental retardation, and emotional disturbance.

Interestingly, IDEA does not explicitly define *least restrictive environment* or *inclusion*. Instead, it provides that the student with a disability must be educated with students who do not have disabilities to the maximum extent appropriate and that the student may be removed from that type of education only when the nature and extent of the student's disability is such that education of the child in regular classes with supplementary aids and services cannot be achieved satisfactorily (20 U.S.C. Sec. 1412 (a) (5)). We will describe IDEA's provisions in greater detail in chapter 6. At this point, we will focus on inclusion. A consistent definition of inclusion's four key characteristics is as follows:

- All students receive education in the home school they would have attended if they had no exceptionality.
- Consideration is given to placing students in classrooms according to the principle of natural proportions.
- Teaching and learning is restructured for all students so that special education supports exist within general education classes.
- School and general education placements are age- and grade-appropriate (Turnbull et al., 2004, p. 66).

As children with exceptionalities enter elementary school, many parents begin to carefully weigh the benefits and drawbacks of inclusion. Some families pursue inclusion earlier, however, during early intervention and early childhood years (Erwin, Soodak, Winton, & Turnbull, 2001; Erwin & Soodak, 1995).

After reviewing 17 studies that address the perspectives of parents of children with disabilities toward inclusion, Duhaney and Salend (2000) reached the following conclusions:

- Although parents vary in their opinions, most parents are generally positive about inclusive placements.
- Parents perceive that general education classrooms contrasted to more specialized settings, do a better jo

FIGURE 4–6

Percentage of Students Ages 6 Through 21 in Different Education Environments During the 1999–2000 School Year

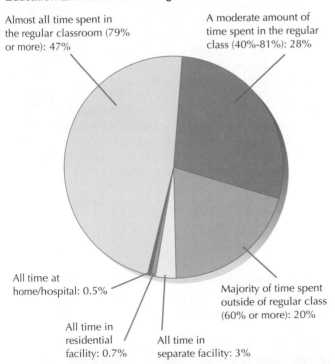

Almost all time spent in the regular classroom (79% or more): 47%

A moderate amount of time spent in the regular class (40%-81%): 28%

All time at home/hospital: 0.5%

All time in residential facility: 0.7%

All time in separate facility: 3%

Majority of time spent outside of regular class (60% or more): 20%

Source: U.S. Department of Education. (2002). *To assure the free appropriate public education of all children with disabilities: Twenty-third annual report to Congress on the implementation of the Individuals with Disabilities Education Act.* Washington, DC: Author.

of (1) enhancing their child's self-esteem, (2) enabling their child to have more friendships and peer role models, (3) making their child happier, (4) helping their child make academic progress, and (5) preparing their child for life in the real world.

■ Parents have concerns related to the qualifications of teachers and availability of individualized services, and they are frustrated about having to advocate so intensely for inclusive programs.

On this last point, many families lament how hard they must work for inclusion, which they see as one of their child's educational rights (Erwin et al., 2001; Grove & Fisher, 1999; Soodak & Erwin, 1995; Soodak et al., 2002). Parents report that often their first information comes from disability-issue conferences they attend. As they pursue inclusion, they need to convince educators that inclusion is appropriate for their child (Grove & Fisher, 1999). The mother of a child with cerebral palsy illustrated this point:

> I felt the special education class left something to be desired; it could be a lot richer. We called a new IEP with inclusion as our goal. And the district contacted the school and they assigned an itinerant. I was the one that said, "Let's talk about what equipment he needs, can we talk about what teacher might be best for him, can I meet with the administration at the school site?" Although there was supposedly an itinerant to arrange things, I had to tell them (the school site), "You need to find out about bathroom facilities and we'll need an aide." On the whole, in terms of school information for teachers, there has been nothing. Any specific information they have about Tom has come from myself or handouts about inclusive education that I shared with them. (Grove & Fisher, 1999, p. 212)

This mother, like so many other parents, would greatly value a trusting partnership with professionals in implementing state-of-the-art inclusion.

Parents of children with disabilities have wide-ranging opinions on every topic, including the appropriateness of inclusion (Lindsay & Dockrell, 2004). As one parent who objected to inclusion said:

> I have a fear of security and safety, and I felt that he needed to be in a more confined, limited environment where he could get the attention that he needed. (Poston, 2002, p. 293)

Another group of parents express strong opinions about inclusion—the parents of children who do not have exceptionalities. Obviously, they have a stake in the quality of education provided in general education classrooms. Based on a review of the research of these parents' perspectives, Duhaney and Salend (2000) drew the following conclusions:

■ Parents of children without disabilities reported that general education classrooms were meeting their children's educational needs with greater acceptance of diversity.

■ They perceived that the presence of children with disabilities in classrooms had benefits for their own children, including being more sensitive, being more helpful to classmates, having a greater acceptance of diversity, displaying fewer behavior problems, and having better self-concepts.

Adolescence

Adolescence is the next life cycle stage in the family's development. Perhaps more than any of the life cycle stages, adolescence is strongly influenced by cultural context values (Preto, 1999). For example, many European Americans generally think of their children becoming adults at around the age of 18; whereas many Navajos perceive that adulthood starts just after puberty (Deyhle & LeCompte, 1994).

In addition to various ethnic/racial interpretations of adolescence, religion also defines adolescent-related rituals to signal increasing maturity. Many world religions conduct ceremonies to mark life's passages, although they remain largely unfamiliar to the U.S. dominant culture. An example is the Hindu *upanayâna* ritual (investiture with sacred thread) signifying the transformation of Brahman (upper-class) boys into young men. This ceremony combines a religious perspective with a social class perspective. The timing of the sacred thread ritual varies from between the ages of 8 and 16 to the time just before a young man is married.

> Just before the sacred thread ritual begins, the boy takes his last meal as a child from his mother. Shaving the boy's head and giving him a bath traditionally mark symbolic distancing from childhood. Special clothes (girdle, deerskin, staff, and the sacred thread) then demarcate the liminal state. The teacher takes the boy's "heart" into his own and a symbolic father and mother usher in the rebirth to student status. The transition from one life stage to the other is a symbolic gestation process in which the teacher becomes "pregnant" with the boy and, by virtue of sacred sound (*mantra*), gives him a second birth (*Dvija*). (Forman, 1993, p. 9)

To honor a family's cultural diversity, we encourage you to discover the family's own interpretations and traditions associated with adolescence.

Adolescence can be stressful for youth and other family members. In a national study conducted with more than 1,000 families in the general population, parents reported that the life cycle stages of adolescence and young adulthood were the two stages with the highest amount of overall family stress (Olson et al., 1983).

An exceptionality may either mitigate or compound some of the typical adolescent issues. For example, parents might experience only minor rebellion and conflict because their children may have fewer peers after whom to model such behaviors, fewer opportunities to try alcohol and drugs, or decreased mobility and, therefore, fewer chances to take dangerous risks. In other cases, adolescence may bring greater isolation, a growing sense of difference, and confusion and fear about emerging sexuality. Some pertinent educational issues during the adolescent stage include (1) sexuality education and (2) self-determination skills.

Sexuality Education.   Many adolescents are sexually active and need sexuality education as part of their school curriculum. By the time students graduate from high school, one half to almost three fourths have become sexually active. The most rapidly increasing age for sexual activity is under 14 (Petosa & Wessinger, 1990).

A survey of female adolescents with developmental disabilities reported that a large percentage were sexually active, with half of the sample reporting intercourse and condom use at least once during intercourse (Scotti et al., 1997). Similarly, research has documented that adolescents with chronic health problems (for example, diabetes or asthma) and disabilities (for example, cerebral palsy or muscular dystrophy) were found to be similar to individuals without disabilities in the proportion who had sexual intercourse, patterns of contraceptive use, age of sexual debut, pregnancy involvement, and sexual orientation (Surís, Resnick, Cassuto, & Blum, 1996).

Is sexuality education necessary? As one teacher explained: "We see sexual problems among our students all of the time and, although we gossip about them, we do nothing to help students understand their feelings or drive. Really, we avoid getting involved. It's easier for us that way" (Brantlinger, 1992, pp. 9–10).

A professional who provides vocational preparation commented:

> The classic word around here is "redirect" to be interpreted as "you can't do it here" or "that is not appropriate here." The problem is there is nowhere where sex is appropriate. "Redirect" sounds objective, but it is really oppressive. The administrators talk out of both sides of their mouth. They sound like they are for normalization but, in truth, they're not. At least they're not when it comes to sexual behavior. (Brantlinger, 1992, p. 11)

Sadly, only about 5% of students receive sexuality education during their public school career. Only 19 states require sexuality education, a decrease from a decade earlier (Haffner, 1998). Viewpoints vary over whether sexuality education should focus on abstinence-only or in-

clude an abstinence-plus curriculum which explores birth control. Research studies that have focused on one of these approaches or a comparison have shown that an abstinence-plus sexuality program of instruction results in more positive long-term outcomes while not increasing sexual intercourse among adolescents (Kirby, 2000).

Researchers recently reviewed sexuality curriculum guides recommended by the Sexuality Information Education Center of the United States (SIECUS) for use with students with disabilities, concentrating on those available through the SIECUS library (Blanchett & Wolfe, 2002). Figure 4–7 lists the reviewed curriculum guides that they identified as comprehensive. We encourage you to read the entire article to learn more about curricula that were rated highly.

These researchers found that just 2 out of the 12 curricula included suggestions for parent-professional communication related to sex education. It is especially important for teachers to have a solid grasp of sexuality content to teach the subject effectively, but they also must be comfortable talking to students and families about the topic.

In chapter 2, you learned about some of the issues with establishing partnerships with gay and lesbian parents. You also read about the taunting that some children of same-sex parents face at school. Sexuality education needs to be appropriate for each student's sexual orientation. Approximately 10% of students who have disabilities have a gay, lesbian, or bisexual orientation (Blanchett, 2002). A teacher commented:

> I am a gay teacher who has noticed the lack of tolerance and support for students with any [disabilities, race, sexual orientation, etc.] difference from the average student, and I'm trying to arrange a forum/support service in my middle school to support these students. Of course, in trying to make this happen, I must overcome all of the obstacles involved in initiating something like this (Blanchett, 2002, p. 84)

We encourage you to prepare all students to live in a diverse society for disability and sexual orientation, as well as for other microcultures you learned about in chapter 1. The more that educators, students, and families who are heterosexual and homosexual work together to address these issues, the more likely the sexuality supports and services will be accepted throughout the school community.

Nearly all parents worry that their child—especially one who has a disability—may be a victim of sexual abuse. It is extremely disconcerting that estimates suggest that women with developmental disabilities are as much as 50% more likely to experience sexual abuse as others in the population and their abuse typically goes

Curriculum Information on Sexuality for Students with Moderate and Severe Disabilities

Curriculum Title	Publication Date	Publisher	Cost	Targeted Audience (Age Level)	Targeted Audience (Disability Level)	Usability and Type
Life Horizons I: The Physiological and Emotional Aspects of Being Male and Female: Sex Education for Persons With Special Needs and II: The Moral, Social, and Legal Aspects of Sexuality: Sex Education for Persons With Special Needs	1988	James Stansfield Co., Inc., Drawer: WEB, P.O. Box 41058, Santa Barbara, CA 93140	$699 for the pair	Not given	All intellectual levels of individuals with disabilities	Comprehensive
Life Planning Education: A Youth Development Program	1995	1025 Vermont Ave., NW, Suite 200, Washington, DC 20005	$60	Grades 7–12	None	Comprehensive
Sexuality and Relationships: Choosing Health	1997	ETR Associates, P.O. Box 1830, Santa Cruz, CA 95061-1830	$27	High school students	Not given	Comprehensive
The Comprehensive Health Education for Middle Grades: Puberty and Reproduction	1996	ETR Associates, P.O. Box 1830, Santa Cruz, CA 95061-1830	$27	Middle school	Not given	Comprehensive
The Family Education Program: A Curriculum and Training Manual for Teaching Sexuality, Self-Esteem, and Abuse Prevention to Students With Developmental and Learning Disabilities	1990	The Family Stress Center, Planned Parenthood: Shasta-Diablo, 2086 Commerce Ave., Concord, CA 94523	Not given	Not given	Not given	Comprehensive
The New Positive Images: Teaching Abstinence, Contraception, and Sexual Health	1995	The Center for Family Life Education, Planned Parenthood of Greater Northern New Jersey, 575 Main St., Hackensack, NJ 07601	$25 plus $4 S&H	Not given	Not given	Comprehensive

Source: Blanchett, W. J., & Wolfe, P. S. (2002). A review of sexuality education curricula: Meeting the sexuality education needs of individuals with moderate and severe intellectual disabilities. Journal of the Association for Persons with Severe Handicaps, 27(1), 43–57. Adapted with permission.

unreported (Petersilia, 2000). A study that analyzed patterns of sexual abuse of adults with mental retardation over a 5-year period reported that almost three fourths of the victims were characterized as having mild mental retardation and had an average age of 30 (Furey, 1994). Approximately one fourth of the abuse incidents occurred in institutions, and another one fourth occurred in group homes. In the remaining situations, the location of the incidents included the victim's own home, a work setting, or a vehicle. The perpetrator was known to the victim in the vast majority of cases; this also is the case in sexual abuse of people who do not have an exceptionality. Although many families may expect abuse from a stranger or in an unsupervised situation in a public place, this research indicates that sexual abuse is far more likely to occur from a known person in a known place.

Families and youth need accurate information about the likelihood of sexual abuse and its prevention (Lesseliers & Van Hove, 2002). The skills and knowledge to prevent sexual abuse should be a key topic in sexuality training during the adolescent years (Lee & Tang, 1998).

Expanding Self-Determination Skills. Definitions of self-determination vary depending upon the developers of various approaches (Algozzine, Browder, Karvonen, Test, & Wood, 2001; Powers et al., 2004; Wehmeyer, Agran, & Hughes, 1998; Wehmeyer & Sands, 1998). We define self-determination as living one's life consistent with one's own values, preferences, strengths, and needs (Turnbull & Turnbull, 2001).

Culture plays a special role in self-determination. It also affects how children and youth express preferences and solve their problems (Frankland, Turnbull, Wehmeyer, & Blackmountain, in press; Kalyanpur & Harry, 1999). Some cultural norms strongly favor individualism, while others favor collectivism, as you learned in chapter 1.

Cultural norms aside, child development theory (Marvin & Pianta, 1992) and research (Algozzine et al., 2001; Field & Hoffman, 2002; Wehmeyer, 2002) show that building on a student's interest and direction is critical for self-determination. It is especially appropriate for adolescents and is also desirable for very young children who should be encouraged to express their choices and act on their preferences (Abery & Zajac, 1996; Cook, Brotherson, Weigner-Garrey, & Mize, 1996; Erwin & Brown, 2003; Palmer & Wehmeyer, 2002). Research has documented that self-reliance competence during infancy lays the foundation for later self-reliance competence during adolescence and adulthood (Marvin & Pianta, 1992).

Over the last 15 years, a major initiative has focused national attention on self-determination for individuals with disabilities. Starting in 1990, the U.S. Department of Education funded 26 model demonstration programs and 5 curriculum-development projects to promote self-determination for youths with disability (Ward, 1996; Wehmeyer, Bersani, & Gagne, 2000). These projects have produced numerous training guides, curricula, and literature aimed at self-determination enhancements (Algozzine et al., 2001; Field, Martin, Miller, Ward, & Wehmeyer, 1998; Sands & Wehmeyer, 1996). A comprehensive literature review drew the following conclusions about the current state of the self-determination interventions and curricula (Algozzine et al., 2001):

- The majority of self-determination interventions have been developed for individuals with mental retardation or learning disabilities. The most frequent subtopics within self-determination curricula are self-advocacy and choice making. The topics least represented are self-advocacy knowledge and self-efficacy.
- More then 60 self-determination curricula have been developed, but these curricula have been evaluated in only 12 studies. Instructional methods for teaching the curriculum included large group instruction, small group instruction, and one-to-one instruction.
- Research methods for evaluating self-determination skills included observations, written assessments, reports from parents or teachers, and simulations involving role plays.
- Researchers investigated quality-of-life outcomes in 7 studies. These outcomes included postsecondary education, access to social support, and increase in inclusive activities.

Several studies found that teachers overwhelmingly support the importance of self-determination; however, a significant gap exists between that stated importance and the incorporation of self-determination instructional goals into student IEPs (Agran, Snow, & Swaner, 1999; Hughes et al., 1997; Wehmeyer, Agran, & Hughes, 1998).

One of the leading model curricula is the *self-determination learning model of instruction*. It consists of three phases—setting a goal, taking action, and adjusting the goal or plan. For each of these phases, student questions, educational supports, and teacher objectives are specified (Wehmeyer, Palmer, Agran, Mithaug & Martin, 2000; Wehmeyer, Agran, Palmer, Martin, & Mithaug, 2003). Figure 4–8 illustrates phase 1, which focuses on goal setting.

As illustrated in Figure 4–8, students are provided with educational support to learn to ask and answer questions that will enable them to set a preferred goal for themselves. The second phase enables students to learn skills to problem-solve in order to develop a successful plan for meeting their goal. Finally, in phase 3, students learn t

FIGURE 4–8

The Self-Determination Model of Instruction—Phase 1

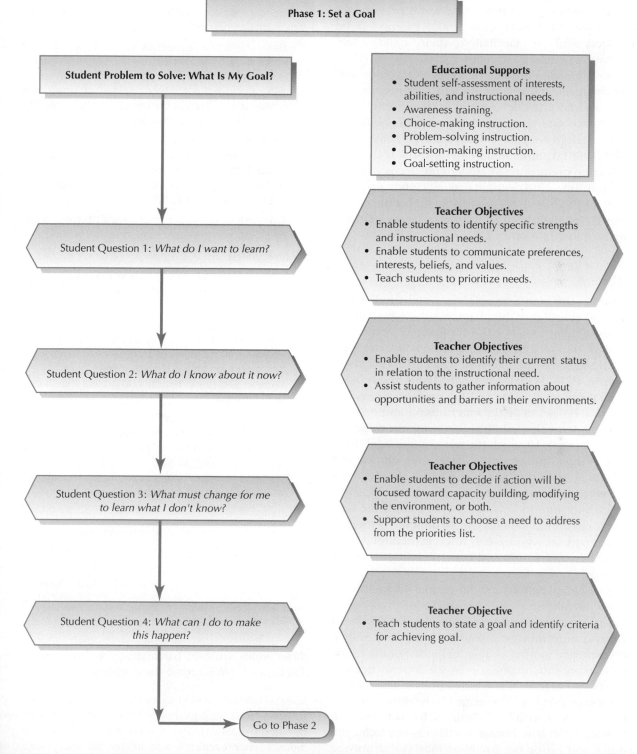

Source: Wehmeyer, M. L., Sands, D. J., Knowlton, H. E., & Kozleski, E. B. (2002). *Teaching students with mental retardation: Providing access to the general curriculum* (p. 246). Baltimore: Paul H. Brookes Publishing Company. Reprinted with permission.

evaluate their actions and make improvements based on feedback. Research has reported encouraging findings: About 55% of the students achieved the goal they set or exceeded it, while about 80% made some progress toward their goal (Wehmeyer et al., 2000). Parents can be quite successful in facilitating their child's self-determination (Palmer & Wehmeyer, 2002).

Self-determination results in many positive outcomes. Students with mental retardation and learning disabilities who are more self-determined achieve more favorable outcomes one year after high school graduation, especially related to paid employment (Wehmeyer & Schwartz, 1998). Another important outcome is that self-determination predicts active student involvement in educational planning and decision making (Sands, Spencer, Gliner, & Swaim, 1999). We will discuss this concept, as it relates to individualized education program (IEP) development, more in chapter 12.

Adulthood

Adulthood is the next life cycle stage and the last one that we will consider in this chapter. Although attaining the status of adulthood is taken for granted by most individuals in our society, for many reasons it cannot be taken for granted by people with disabilities (Ferguson & Ferguson, 1993). With the move into adulthood comes the general expectation for meeting one's own needs in the eight categories of family functions (chapter 3); but for some adults with disabilities, carrying out these duties is problematic. Although the transition to adulthood typically brings opportunities for greater choice and control, those opportunities may be hard to obtain for people with disabilities. Deciding how to divide independence and support among the young adult, the family, and other support systems can be difficult. Letting go is hard for parents who have devoted extra attention to their children and youth. And it is sometimes hard for professionals, too, to let go.

Figure 4-9 highlights three dimensions of adulthood: autonomy, membership, and change (Ferguson & Ferguson, 1993). For many people, especially those of European American culture, moving into adulthood means finding employment and moving away from home. For the young adult, this represents attaining greater independence and responsibility. For parents, it means a process of letting go of their son or daughter. This stage can be difficult in any family, but it is especially challenging for families with young adults who have disabilities. Two issues facing the individual and his or her family include (1) identifying postsecondary educational programs and supports and (2) accessing supported employment options. In both of

FIGURE 4–9
Three Dimensions of Adulthood

Autonomy is being one's own person. It is expressed through symbols of:

- Self-sufficiency—especially economic self-sufficiency, or having the resources to take care of oneself. Self-sufficiency includes emotional self-sufficiency, or the ability to "make it" on one's own. It makes a shift from economic consumption alone to production and consumption.

- Self-determination—assertion of individuality and independence. Self-determination is the ability to assure others that one possesses the rational maturity and personal freedom to make specific choices about how to live one's life.

- Completeness—a sense of having "arrived," a shift from future to present tense, no more waiting.

Membership

Membership is community connectedness, collaboration, and sacrifice. It is expressed through symbols of:

- Citizenship—activites of collective governance from voting and participating in town meetings to volunteering for political candidates to expressing one's position on issues with money, time, or bumper stickers to recycling to protect the shared environment.

- Affiliation—activities of voluntary association, fellowship, celebration, and support from greeting the new family in the neighborhood with a plate of cookies to being an active member of the church, a participant in the local service or garden club, or an entrant in area road races.

Change

Change is adulthood as an ongoing capacity for growth rather than the static outcome of childhood.

Source: Ferguson, P. M., & Ferguson, D. L. (1993). The promise of adulthood. In M. Snell (Ed.), *Instruction of persons with severe disabilities* (4th ed., p. 591). Upper Saddle River, NJ: Merrill/Prentice Hall.

these issues, trusting partnerships among professionals and families can increase the likelihood of success.

Identifying Postsecondary Educational Programs and Supports.   Postsecondary education is pursued for many reasons, such as to gain better employment, higher earnings, and an overall more successful adult life (Getzel, Stodden, & Briel, 1999; Gilmore, Bose, & Hart, 2001; National Council on Disability and Social

FIGURE 4–10

Percentage of Students Age 14 and Older with Disabilities Graduating with a Standard Diploma or Dropping Out, 1999–2000

	Graduated with a Standard Diploma	Dropped Out
Disability Category	**1999–2000**	**1999–2000**
Specific learning disabilities	62.1	27.6
Speech or language impairments	66.1	24.6
Mental retardation	39.5	26.0
Emotional disturbance	40.1	51.4
Multiple disabilities	48.0	16.1
Hearing impairments	68.4	14.8
Orthopedic impairments	62.5	15.4
Other health impairments	67.7	22.4
Visual impairments	73.4	11.9
Autism	47.3	11.1
Deaf-blindness	48.5	10.3
Traumatic brain injury	65.3	18.1
All disabilities	56.2	29.4

Source: U.S. Department of Education, Office of Special Education Programs, Data Analysis System (DANS).

Security Administration, 2000). The opportunity to attend postsecondary educational programs is influenced by the ability of students to graduate from high school. Although it is typical for approximately three fourths of high school graduates to enter some type of postsecondary education, only approximately one third of high school graduates with disabilities do so (Blackorby & Wagner, 1996).

For the 1999–2000 school year, students with disabilities had a 56% graduation rate for receiving a standard diploma (U.S. Department of Education, 2002). Wide variability exists in the graduation rate across disability categories. Figure 4-10 reports the percentage of students with disabilities graduating with a standard diploma or dropping out. As you review the data, what can you learn about the likelihood of graduating for students with different types of disabilities? Where is the greatest disproportionality, and why do you think it exists? It is especially problematic that the dropout rate for youth with behavior and emotional disorders was about twice as high as any other disability category. Additionally, approximately 11% of youth with disabilities received an alternative credential rather than a diploma (Government Accounting Office, 2003).

Disparities exist based on disability category as well as race/ethnicity. Figure 4-11 presents the number and percentage of students graduating with a standard diploma and dropping out according to different racial/ethnic groups. What patterns do you detect, and what are the factors that you believe contribute to such a wide range in student outcomes?

The vast majority of students with disabilities who graduate with a standard diploma have a learning disability. Students with learning disabilities constitute approximately one third of all college students reporting a disability (Mull, Sitlington, & Alper, 2001). In fact, the number of college freshmen with disabilities increased tenfold in the last quarter century. One study reported that 5 years after high school, 80% of the students with learning disabilities had not graduated compared to 56% of youth with no disabilities (Murray, Goldstein, Nourse, & Edgar, 2000). Ten years after high school graduation, 56% of the youth with disabilities had not graduated compared to 32% of individuals without disabilities.

A review of 26 articles, published from 1985 to 2000 and describing postsecondary education services for students with learning disabilities, identified the following shortcomings in the research literature:

- Fifty percent of the articles did not address program modifications, substitutions/waivers of courses, or degree requirements.
- The greatest emphasis on assessment was on documentation of a learning disability, but only 65% of the articles

FIGURE 4–11
Number and Percentage of Students Age 14 and Older with Disabilities Graduating with a Standard Diploma or Dropping Out, by Race/Ethnicity, 1999–2000

Race/Ethnicity	Graduated with a Standard Diploma		Dropped Out	
	Number	Percentage	Number	Percentage
American Indian/Alaska Native	1,823	48.2	1,666	44.0
Asian/Pacific Islander	2,531	56.3	896	19.3
Black	23,652	39.7	22,051	37.0
Hispanic	16,802	51.8	10,745	33.1
White	117,605	62.5	29,768	26.5

Source: U.S. Department of Education, Office of Special Education Programs, Data Analysis System (DANS).

discussed testing accommodations and only one article discussed increasing the frequency of tests or using alternative forms.

- Seventy-nine percent of the articles did not discuss program evaluation.
- Sixty-two percent did not discuss qualifications of the instructional staff.

In light of the low graduation rates and the lack of detail in the literature about secondary accommodations and supports for students with disabilities, it is especially important for teachers and families to form a partnership for postsecondary preparation.

For a long time many people assumed that a postsecondary education was entirely appropriate for a student with a milder disability, such as learning disabilities, or with a sensory disability, such as blindness or deafness. Success in postsecondary education was not considered possible for students with significant intellectual disabilities. Leaders in the field of significant cognitive disabilities refer to a new paradigm for postsecondary educational opportunities for students even with severe and multiple disabilities (Stodden & Whelley, 2004). They describe three models that have been used to date:

- A substantially separate model in which students with significant intellectual disabilities attend a separate program on a college campus (much like a separate class in an elementary or secondary school)
- A mixed program model that includes a combination of separate programs to learn life skills and opportunities to integrate into campus courses
- The individualized support model, building on students' preferences for creating individualized services

and supports consistent with their educational and career goals

A number of postsecondary programs have been designed for students with mental retardation, autism, and other developmental disabilities (Hart, Mele-McCarthy, Pasternack, Zimbrich, & Parker, 2004; Zafft, Hart, & Zimbrich, 2004). Figure 4–12 provides a snapshot of a successful postsecondary program for students with developmental disabilities. If such a program does not exist in your community, we urge you to consider working with other partners to start one.

You should help students and families identify the appropriateness of postsecondary career goals, ensure that students develop prerequisite skills, and teach students to complete applications and access services consistent with their support needs. Parents and students need advice about scholarship opportunities, loans, work-study programs, and disability-related funding opportunities (such as Social Security and Vocational Rehabilitation benefits). Resource guides in a school or local library and workshops on college planning and academic and financial issues can be helpful for families and high school students.

Students and families will also need your support in considering a variety of other special needs when selecting a postsecondary institution. Does the postsecondary institution provide special assistance, such as tutoring programs for students with learning disabilities or interpreters for students who are deaf or hard of hearing? Is the campus accessible for wheelchair users? Does the state vocational rehabilitation program provide financial assistance for personal care attendants while the student is attending college? Does the postsecondary institution

FIGURE 4–12
Advocacy Partners: Students, Families, Schools, and Colleges

Transition stages are stressful. They are especially so when a student is about to leave secondary schools, where services are mandatory, and enter the world of adulthood, where services are optional and, if available at all, offered by many different agencies that often do not collaborate with each other.

What can students, their families, and professionals do to ease the challenge of transition to postsecondary education?

They do not have to accept the status quo. Instead, they can emulate the consortium of 12 school districts and a community college in Los Angeles County, California.

The districts agreed to develop a jointly operated transition program open to all of the districts' 1,500 students with IEPs who are between the ages of 18 and 21. The college agreed to enroll the students, provide them with individualized support as they take courses for high school or college credit, and accommodate them in the college's extracurricular and social activities.

To carry out the agreement, the districts pooled their resources to hire a dozen transition specialists to work with the students, their families, and the college's faculty and other staff. These specialists develop individually tailored transition and postsecondary programs that include college enrollment, job training, independent living, and transportation training. The students take college courses; the college's faculty and staff do not substantially change the nature of a course and course standards but receive assistance from the transition staff to tailor it to a student.

Through this joint agreement, transition becomes a step-by-step process for the students; they receive support from the districts and college alike to navigate the adult world.

Why is this program significant? It is not because it is unique; other secondary school and college transition programs exist.

It is significant because the program demonstrates that no one has to accept the status quo. Here, students, families, school faculty, and college faculty looked at Los Angeles as it was and said, "That is not acceptable." Then they made it acceptable.

That's one point; but there's another one, too: Advocacy entails collective dissatisfaction and collaboration to achieve satisfaction.

Source: Adapted from Pearman, E., Elliott, T., & Aborn, L. (2004). Transition services model: Partnership for student success. *Education and Training in Developmental Disabilities, 39*(1), 26–34.

have an office that oversees the provision of reasonable accommodations for students with disabilities? Is there a published and well-enforced plan for complying with the Americans with Disabilities Act? In other words, does the postsecondary institution provide the type of empowering context that you try to provide?

Although families are their children's primary advocates during the elementary and secondary years, colleges expect students to take on this responsibility. One of the best preparations for postsecondary educational success is to prepare students and families during the elementary and secondary years in self-determined decision making and self-advocacy skills, particularly concerning disability and educational needs.

Accessing Supported Employment. The 2000 National Organization on Disability/Harris Survey of Americans with Disabilities surveyed 997 adults with disabilities and 953 adults without disabilities on 10 key measures of quality of life.

■ Considering all working-age people with disabilities (ages 18 to 64), only about 32% are employed full- or part-time compared to about 80% of working-age people without disabilities. This gap is very problematic.

■ For people with disabilities ages 18 to 29, 57% are working compared to 72% of individuals without disabilities.

■ Among people with disabilities who are unemployed, more than two out of three indicate that they want to work.

Employment is the area where individuals with disabilities experience the widest gap between themselves and those who do not have a disability.

Individuals with severe disabilities face particular challenges. The traditional employment option has been sheltered workshops, typically large, segregated work centers for people with more significant disabilities. The average wage for individuals in sheltered workshops is $2.40 an hour. The lowest wages typically have been earned by individuals with mental retardation who average around $52.00 a week (Wehman et al., 2004). Unfortunately, sheltered employment and services that lack genuine work opportunities are still the way individuals with disabilities typically receive employment and day services. Almost three fourths of individuals served in rehabilitation programs are either in segregated nonwork day programs or sheltered workshops (McGaughey, Kiernan, McNally, Gilmore, & Keith, 1994). The most frequently cited reason for individuals remaining in segregated day services is they are "not ready" for more complex employment settings. The thinking is, if they stay in these settings long enough, they might "become ready." Despite a strong push for inclusion of individuals with disabilities across all sectors of society, state and federal funding for segregated employment services has either remained stable or increased over the last 10 years (Butterworth, Gilmore, Kiernan, & Schalock, 1998).

Supported employment developed in the early 1980s as a way to provide long-term support for individuals with severe disabilities in integrated work settings, work stations in industry, enclaves, or work crews. The goal of supported employment is to develop independent work skills and the ability to earn competitive wages in an inclusive job market (Wehman, Bricout, & Kregel, 2000). People with disabilities who engage in supported employment frequently have a job coach who provides direct training and assistance to enable them to fully carry out the job responsibilities.

The average hourly wages in supported employment are at least 2.25 times the average hourly wage in sheltered employment (Coker, Osgood, & Clouse, 1995). Long-term studies have clearly documented the benefits of supported over sheltered employment for individuals with disabilities, their families, and taxpayers. Accordingly, the number of people in supported employment increased by more than 200% from 1998 to 1999. Approximately 32,400 individuals were in supported employment in 1988, while approximately 107,800 were in supported employment just 10 years later (Wehman et al., 2004).

The findings of research on factors associated with successful supported employment include:

- Employees with disabilities are more likely to earn high wages and to be more integrated at work when they have similar work roles to other employees and when the initial training and orientation of supervisors and coworkers is positive.
- Employees with disabilities in supported employment have more inclusive participation in social activities when coworkers receive training by supported employment personnel (Mank, Cioffi, & Yovanoff, 1997).
- Employees with more severe mental retardation have better outcomes when they have positive coworker relationships and when they have fewer hours of job coaching support from supported employment person-

nel outside of the employment setting (Mank, Cioffi, & Yovanoff, 1998).
- Employees with disabilities have better outcomes when coworkers and supervisors have specific information about providing support to the employee early on (Mank, Cioffi, & Yovanoff, 1999).
- Employees with disabilities have better outcomes when they have a combination of job coaching and when their coworkers are trained to provide support to them. Without the coworker training, greater hours of job coaching do not lead to outcomes that are nearly as positive (Mank, Cioffi, & Yovanoff, 2000).
- The field of supported employment is growing as evidenced by the number of people with severe disabilities who have been employed more recently and who show improvements in job acquisition, job roles, job orientation, and relationships with coworkers (Mank, Cioffi, & Yovanoff, 2003).

One of the newest types of employment is self-employment for people with and without disabilities (Wehman et al. 2004). Self-employment enables adults with disabilities to retain government benefits they sometimes lose under other employment options. It also can be individualized to particular strengths, interests, talents, and marketplace demands. Some disability organizations provide assistance with start-up costs to enable adults with disabilities to launch a business. In Figure 4–13, you will learn about the entrepreneurship of a young adult with autism.

What can you do to support families who are seeking employment for their son or daughter with a disability? Consider motivating families by providing them with comprehensive information about the benefits of employment. Families can be major resources not only by helping to prepare their family member with a disability for employment but also by helping to locate employment options. One study revealed that approximately 80% of the jobs secured by former special education students were obtained through a family connection (Hasazi, Gordon, & Roe, 1985). Just as people without exceptionalities find jobs through family and friendship networks, so do people with exceptionalities.

LIFE CYCLE TRANSITIONS

As we noted at the beginning of this chapter, life cycle stages are like plateaus between the peaks and valleys of transitions, from one life cycle to another such as from adolescence to adulthood (Carter & McGoldrick, 1999). Transition times often are the most challenging period for families because they are characterized by the most change (Falicov, 1988). Two factors tend to reduce the

FIGURE 4–13
Aaron: An Entrepreneur with Autism

Aaron Williams is a young adult with autism who is living out his dream as a small business entrepreneur. Aaron's strong will first surfaced in his preschool days. He liked watching television while sitting on the floor 2 feet away. His mother thought that was too close, so she put a piece of masking tape on the floor about 6 feet away. She told Aaron he could watch television only when he sat behind the tape. Several days later his mom got up in the morning and found him watching television from his usual 2-ft distance. He had moved the tape to accommodate his watching custom while complying with his mom's rule.

Aaron has a keen sense of humor and deep respect for working with others to meet his goals. As a teenager and young adult, Aaron built a history of participating in work experiences and community activities that helped others see and appreciate his skills and helped him to accept assistance from others when needed. Together, he and his team crafted and executed a deliberate plan that has allowed him to reach his dream. Aaron is the proud owner of Aaron's Fast Snacks.

Aaron's Fast Snacks now owns, stocks, and services eight soda and candy vending machines in three locations around his Lapeer, Michigan, community. Aaron's brother Jason drives Aaron from location to location to stock and service the machines, while his parents help him manage the money and keep his accounting books. His business is only a year old and he is implementing plans to expand both the number of locations and the number of machines his business owns and services.

Aaron's process in starting his business took more than just a dream. It took courage, determination, and the ability to focus his strengths. His autism sometimes led him to focus on narrow issues and concerns. Aaron used that trait to help him grasp the finer details of operating a business. His family helped Aaron learn about inventory control by having him monitor the contents of his refrigerator and schedule shopping trips to keep certain refrigerated items in stock. Aaron's dad helped Aaron to operate a citywide paper route with 260 customers.

Aaron knew business and personal skills alone would not lead him to his goal. He knew he had to involve himself in the community and draw community support. He went to his local Chamber of Commerce to introduce himself and tell them about his business plans. Several Chamber members immediately voiced their support for his efforts when he handed out business cards with his picture on them, calling himself a "Future Entrepreneur." His will to succeed later led to Aaron's introducing then gubernatorial candidate and now Michigan Governor Jennifer Granholm to a crowd of several hundred members of the disability rights community.

Aaron's success story happened because Aaron had the ability to convince those around him to believe he would succeed. He and his team confronted many challenges and adapted his plans as needed. His business cards still have his picture on them, but he is no longer a "future" entrepreneur. He IS Aaron's Fast Snacks.

---

amount of stress most families feel during a transition. First, in most cultures the roles of the new stages are fairly well defined. Thus, the transition may be marked by some kind of ritual such as a wedding, bar mitzvah or bat mitzvah, graduation, or funeral. These ceremonies serve as signals to the family that their relationships following the event will be changed. The interactions and roles for the new stage are modeled by other families with the same experiences. Second, the timing of transitions within various cultural contexts is also fairly well expected. In European American culture, for example, children are often expected to leave home after they graduate from high school. In Latino culture, however, it is typical for children, especially daughters, to live with their parents until they marry (Falicov, 1996). As three Latino parents stated:

■ It is against the family for the children to live alone as adults.

■ Young married couples live at the parents' home; it is Latino tradition.

■ Families live in the same house . . . always has been that way. (Turnbull & Turnbull, 1996, p. 200)

The expected roles as well as the future of a family member with an exceptionality may not be clear, and a ritual to mark the change may be absent. Life cycle transitions seem to be much more stressful when they occur at times other than when expected. In this section, you will learn about (1) the implications of uncertain futures and (2) off-time transitions.

Uncertainty About the Future

For many families of children and youth with exceptionalities, the future is a frightening unknown. Few norms and models of expected behavior may be available for either the child or the family. The common admonition to "take things one day at a time" is welcomed by many families, not only because more than enough responsibilities confront the family in the present but also because the future is so ambiguous.

A sometimes complicating factor is that rituals marking transitions for youth without disabilities may be blurred or nonexistent for youth with disabilities. The time when a transition occurs—or should occur—may be marked not with a celebration but with chronic frustration that supports are not in place. Not only is the family uncertain about how and when their interactions will change, but they may lack cues that interactions will change.

A study of the perspectives of students with disabilities revealed major lack of attention to future planning (Morningstar, Turnbull, & Turnbull, 1995). The majority of high school students had only a vague sense of future planning. They reported that their families were the major source of helping them develop a vision for the kinds of jobs that they would like to have and where they would like to live. Only a very small percentage of these students said their school-based vocational training had been helpful in planning for the future. Vocational and transitional support services are critically needed by secondary students with exceptionalities and their families (Bullis & Cheney, 1999; Dunn, 1996; Shafer & Rangasamy, 1995).

Students living in underserved areas can encounter heightened challenges during transitions. A follow-up study of students who left school on the Fort Apache Indian reservation revealed that less than one third of the graduates were employed. Most continued to reside in their parents' home, primarily due to lack of employment opportunities (Shafer & Rangasamy, 1995). Two thirds of the students reported that they experienced substance abuse, particularly alcoholism. Almost half had been arrested, mainly for driving while intoxicated. The authors pointed out the catch-22: Economic opportunity came at the cost of leaving the reservation, so students were forced to choose between economic self-sufficiency and confronting " . . . a world for which they are not prepared" (Shafer & Rangasamy, 1995, p. 64).

IDEA requires that transition services be offered to families at two different lifespan stages. It first requires transition planning as part of the IFSP process for toddlers at the age of 3 when they are moving from early intervention services to preschool services. The IFSP must include the steps that early intervention and preschool staff will undertake to support the child's transition. The other lifespan stage that IDEA specifically addresses is the movement from high school to adulthood. It requires that schools offer transition services, which means:

> . . . a coordinated set of activities for a student, designed with an outcome-oriented process that promotes movement from school to postschool activities, including postsecondary education, vocational training, integrated employment (including supported employment), continuing in adult education, adult services, independent living, and/or community participation. (Section 300.18)

The *coordinated set of activities* must be based on the student's preferences, strengths, and needs (Garay, 2003; Thoma, Rogan, & Baker, 2001). As you will learn in chapter 12, IDEA requires that the IEP include a statement of transition services when the student is 14 years old. The IEP must also state the interagency requirements and linkages needed to implement the transition plan when the student is 16. Thus, transition planning is a fundamental right of students and families, and teachers have the benefit of the full IEP committee, including representatives from multiple agencies, to implement these requirements (Certo et al., 2003). We encourage you to develop trusting partnerships with families and students that will enable you to pinpoint educational goals and objectives that best propel the student toward a desirable future (Wehmeyer, Morningstar, & Husted, 1999). Visits to new classrooms, colleges/universities, or places of employment, and meetings with future teachers, adults with disabilities, and parents of older children with similar exceptionalities can all help to reduce the fear of the future. Figure 4–14 offers some suggestions for easing the transitions between each of the life cycle stages discussed in this chapter.

Off-Time Transitions

Families with a member who has an exceptionality are likely to experience a life cycle transition at a time other than what is expected. Transitions are often delayed or fail to occur. For example, a young adult might remain at home well into his or her parents' elderly years (Essex, Seltzer, & Krauss, 1999; Magaña, 1999). Although European American culture generally regards this type of living arrangement as an off-time transition, research indicates positive outcomes for elderly parents who have provided care across the decades of their family life. A study of more than 200 aging mothers of adults with mental retardation who were living at home led the researchers to the following conclusion: "Specifically, the women in our sample were substantially healthier and had better morale than did other samples of caregivers for elderly persons and reported no more burden and stress than did other caregivers" (Seltzer & Krauss, 1989, pp. 309–310). Within the Puerto Rican culture, the role of

FIGURE 4–14
Enhancing Successful Transitions

Early Childhood

- Advise parents to prepare for the separation of preschool children by periodically leaving the child with others.

- Gather information and visit preschools in the community.

- Encourage participation in Parent-to-Parent programs. (Veteran parents are matched in one-to-one relationships with parents who are just beginning the transition process.)

- Familiarize parents with possible school (elementary and secondary) programs, career options, or adult programs so they have an idea of future opportunities.

Childhood

- Provide parents with an overview of curricular options.

- Ensure that IEP meetings provide an empowering context for family collaboration.

- Encourage participation in Parent-to-Parent matches, workshops, or family support groups to discuss transitions with others.

Adolescence

- Assist families and adolescents to identify community leisure-time activities.

- Incorporate into the IEP skills that will be needed in future career and vocational programs.

- Visit or become familiar with a variety of career and living options.

- Develop a mentor relationship with an adult with a similar exceptionality and an individual who has a career that matches the student's strengths and preferences.

Adulthood

- Provide preferred information to families about guardianship, estate planning, wills, and trusts.

- Assist family members in transferring responsibilities to the individual with an exceptionality, other family members, or service providers as appropriate.

- Assist the young adult or family members with career or vocational choices.

- Address the issues and responsibilities of marriage and family for the young adult.

familism (direct caregiving provided by family members) is extremely strong, and families expect to take care of their members over the full lifespan (Magaña, 1999).

Some transitions may occur earlier than the expected time. For instance, researchers have found that placing a child in a living situation outside the home can create a range of emotions that include stress and burden as well as relief (Baker & Blacher, 2002). Another off-time transition is premature death. Illness and death may be expected parts of life for an older person; when they happen to a child, they are seen as cruel twists of fate. In Figure 4–15, Tricia and Calvin Luker, the parents of Jessica, describe their family's life cycle with Jessica that was, sadly, all too brief.

Finally, off-time transitions occur when students who are gifted advance in grade placements, even to the point of leaving secondary schools before their peers go to college. Although there are diverse opinions about the accelerated placements of students into higher grade levels (Feldhusen, Van Winkle, & Ehle, 1996; Plucker & Taylor, 1998), advancement does occur and can be in the student's and family's best interests. A very unusual example

is Michael Kearney, who entered college at age 6 and graduated several years later. Michael described his experiences shortly after his college graduation at 9 years of age:

> . . . Growing up, I have dealt with teachers who have never knowingly met, much less talked, to someone like me. . . . I remember going to the hallways, looking at the faces of . . . students, and listening to them refer to me as Doogie Howser. . . . Another issue that I had to deal with while attending college was the chatter of my classmates. They thought that my parents had pushed me; I beg to differ. My parents have done their best to see that I am a well adjusted and a loving human being. For example, when I decided to go to college, they had to deal with the unexpected financial cost of early college attendance. They have been behind me 100 percent.
>
> I started out, at the age of 6, as a child who thrived on learning and craved a stimulating educational system that would enhance my academic spirit. At the University of South Alabama, I was allowed the freedom to think, act independently, and pursue my educational excellence even though I was only 8. These educators believe that children like myself have the potential to excel in an appropriate education. (Turnbull et al., 1995, p. 389)

FIGURE 4–15
My Voice: Grieving for Our Precious Daughter

Our precious daughter Jessica Patrice tiptoed into the arms of the angels on September 10, 1999, at age 24. Parents and friends of families have contacted us asking how a parent or family member can survive the death of a child. We do not believe there is a single right answer. You just survive because you have to.

Jessica had significant health and intellectual disabilities. Our home and work habits and efforts were built around awareness of Jessica's scheduled and unscheduled activities and needs. Our daily schedules began and ended with helping her care for herself. When we weren't with her ourselves, we still had a crisis mindset that we might be needed at a moment's notice regardless of what we were doing or where we were doing it.

Our lives stopped when Jessica died. It wasn't just because she was gone and we missed her. It was that helping her meet her needs flowed through and powered us like gasoline powers a car. We did not know how to live life without her. We had to learn new routines and find new ways to power and motivate ourselves.

We still felt like we needed to take care of Jessica. Her gravesite became a focal point for our grief and need to support her. We awoke every morning, got dressed and drove to the cemetery. Relatives and close friends worried for us, thinking our visits were too frequent. We later realized, however, that the visits were our new ways of starting the day and without them we likely would have stayed locked up in our room at home.

A large maple tree protects Jessica's gravesite. On the morning of her funeral we gathered under the tree and hung a wind chime in a low branch so that Jessica would always have music. In the following months and years we brought wind chimes to hang in the tree much as we had brought gifts directly to Jessica when she was home with us. At some point we realized that we had stopped looking down at her headstone while weeping, and began looking up into the tree and the skies beyond. We began looking at what was around us rather than at the hurt that was inside us. Our senses and sensitivity slowly began to return.

We were not alone in our grief, nor did we begin the healing process alone. Jessica was at the center of our partnerships with her school professionals. Our contacts with them revolved around Jessica. Her passing was a sudden loss not just to us but to her educational team as well. The educator's role in family healing is part of the recovery process for the professional as well. For example, Jessica's special education director, Mike Dombrowski, called every Monday morning at 8 a.m. for months without fail to see how we were and if we needed anything. Here are some strategies we suggest educators use to help families address the loss of a child.

- Order a memorial package of school photographs.

- Save student work and preserve it in a memory scrapbook for the family.

- Share a list of grief support groups and books.

- Share a favorite memory or memories of the child, either in writing or verbally.

- Reassure the parents that they were good parents.

- Do not be afraid to talk about the students or to mention his or her name. Families need to know their children will be remembered.

- Be available and willing to listen to family members who want to share their memories and thoughts with you.

- Be sensitive to those family members who are not comfortable with talking about their grief or loss.

- Do not be afraid to show your emotion and to share the fact that you hurt, too.

We have learned one absolute truth about the grieving process. It is that we all have our own ways to grieve. Educators need to recognize and address their own grief and understand that their partnership with the family remains important.

Michael's father, Kevin Kearney, added:

. . . We now allow Michael at age twelve to attend the graduate school in chemistry at Middle Tennessee State University in order to help him become as normal an individual as he is likely to be. Those on the teaching staff who have got to know us realize we don't consider Michael a genius. He is probably a prodigy, but on the other hand, he may in fact be the century's Aristotle, Plato, or Einstein. We still don't know. . . . We continually ask ourselves, "What does a suc cessful person really need to know?" By success, we mean that Michael will be a happy, social, productive twenty-five year-old. If anyone has proven ideas on how to successfull raise a possible genius, we are most ready to listen. Unti then, we intend to continue with our own program o ensuring Michael is comfortable, happy, challenged, an emotionally secure about planning appropriate childhoo activities for him. As a secondary issue, somewhere down the line he'll earn a master's degree or Ph.D. or two. (Turnbull, Turnbull, Shank, & Leal, 1999, p. 302)

Regardless of the reason that children make off-time transitions, families deserve your support and assistance. They deserve your allegiance in creating a trusting partnership that can help them get what they want in dealing with the unexpected.

SUMMARY

Families change; the mere passage of time causes changes in their characteristics (chapter 1), interactions (chapter 2), and functions (chapter 3). The changes over a family's life cycle typically occur during four stages—birth and early childhood, childhood, adolescence, and adulthood. In this chapter, we highlighted the following key issues at each of these four life cycle stages:

- Birth and early childhood
  - ✓ Discovering and coming to terms with exceptionality
  - ✓ Partcipating in early childhood services
- Childhood
  - ✓ Developing a vision for the future
  - ✓ Developing a perspective on the appropriateness of inclusion
- Adolescence
  - ✓ Providing sex education
  - ✓ Expanding self-determination skills
- Adulthood
  - ✓ Identifying postsecondary educational programs and supports
  - ✓ Accessing supported employment opportunities

Sometimes these events happen "on cycle." Sometimes they are "off cycle." Whenever they occur, the period leading up to and just following the change in a life cycle stage is the transition time, a period when families usually experience heightened stress. In each of these stages, you can support the family to take action to get what they want and need. You can be a trusted partner by being especially sensitive to life stages and transitions.

REFLECTING ON THE VIGNETTE

1. What life cycle stage do you think has been the most challenging for each of the four families?
2. Do any of the four families have any uncertainty about the future? If so, what is the nature or cause of each family's uncertainty?
3. Which of the families has experienced off-cycle transitions, and is it likely that any of them will experience off-cycle transitions in the future?

ENHANCING YOUR SELF-AWARENESS

The life cycle that you have experienced within your family of origin and within any family that you have created as an adult will help you develop partnerships with families during the particular life cycle in which you encounter them.

Early childhood

Many decisions about treatment for children with genetic disabilities occur during the prenatal period. The most typical practice is for parents to be told that their child has a developmental disability and then be offered the option of abortion and even encouraged to elect that option. What do you believe about abortion because of a certain diagnosis of disability?

Elementary

One of the tasks of the elementary-education life cycle phase is to begin to develop a vision for the future. In your own life, to what extent do you conduct long-range planning for the future? To what extent have you formulated a vision for your life 10 years from now?

Adulthood

Nowdays, many individuals with moderate and severe disabilities are supported to live on their own. Should secondary schools be responsible for preparing young adults with significant disabilities for both residential living and employment after high school? What are the relative advantages and disadvantages of group homes and "home of my own" options?

RESOURCES

You can find a link to these resources on the Companion Website at *www.prenhall.com/turnbull*.

1. Division for Early Childhood (DEC)
   634 Eddy Avenue
   Missoula, MT 59812
   406–243–5898
   dec@dec-sped.org
   www.dec-sped.org

   DEC is one of 17 divisions of the Council for Exceptional Children. It focuses on children with special needs from birth through 8 and their families. It sponsors a couple of journals, a national conference, and many relevant products.

2. National Clearinghouse on Postsecondary Education for Individuals with Disabilities at the American Council on Education
George Washington University HEATH Resource Center
2121 K Street, NW, Suite 220
Washington, DC 20037
800-544-3284
askheath@heath.gwu.edu
www.heath.gwu.edu

The HEATH Resource Center serves as a national clearinghouse for postsecondary education for individuals with disabilities. This clearinghouse provides an information exchange related to postsecondary training options, support services, policies, reasonable accommodations, and opportunities for colleges, universities, and vocational-technical schools.

3. National Center on Accessing the General Curriculum (NCAC)
CAST
48 Harvard Mill Square, Suite 3
Wakefield, MA 01880
781-245-2212
chitchcock@cast.org
www.cast.org/ncac

The National Center on Accessing the General Curriculum (NCAC) provides research-based guidance on developing curricula, instructional practices, and policies enabling students to access and make progress in the general curriculum as it is provided in inclusive settings. NCAC has a wide range of publications, including a comprehensive Website addressing topics with data, practical examples, and visual illustrations.

4. Sexuality Information Education Center of the United States (SIECUS)
SIECUS NY Office
130 West 42nd Street, Suite 350
New York, NY 10036-7802
212-819-9770
siecus@siecus.org

SIECUS DC Office
1706 "R" Street, NW
Washington, DC 20009
202-265-2405
www.siecus.org

SIECUS is a national clearinghouse of information on sexuality education, sexual health, and sexual rights for the general population, including individuals with disabilities. It provides print and electronic resources on topics such as research, curriculum, and program development.

5. Self-Advocacy Synthesis Project
College of Education
University of North Carolina at Charlotte
9201 University City Boulevard
Charlotte, NC 28223-0001
704-687-3731
dwtest@email.uncc.edu
www.uncc.edu/sdsp

The Self-Determination Synthesis Project has conducted comprehensive reviews and syntheses of research and best practices related to self-determination and self-advocacy. In addition to research, their Web site includes information on curriculum and instructional materials designed to teach self-determination and self-advocacy skills to students with disabilities.

PART II

COMMUNICATION

PROFESSIONAL COMPETENCE

RESPECT

TRUST

COMMITMENT

EQUALITY

ADVOCACY

INTRODUCTION TO PART II
Family Roles and Policies

Obviously, families are not the only people who are involved in their children's education. The most important other people are teachers, administrators, providers of specialized services in the schools, and other professionals.

In chapter 5, we describe the roles that families have played. We focus on how those roles relate to their children's education and to the professionals who are involved with their children.

In chapter 6, we describe the two federal education policies that are the backbone of efforts to reform America's schools and that provide the structure within which families and professionals enter into partnerships with each other.

5

Historical and Current Roles of Families and Parents

CHAPTER ORGANIZATION

FRAMING QUESTIONS

1. How have the roles of parents varied over the last 100 years?
2. What have been some of the benefits and drawbacks of each of the phases that characterize the roles of families?
3. What is the current role of families and how does that role influence the process of providing state-of-the-art special education services?

VIGNETTE

Parents are actors, in at least two meanings of that word. Like the actors in a play, they assume roles, "strut" their stuff, and take their directions. They give voice to the playwright's words, amusement or angst to the audience, and performances that are alive when the curtain is up and finished when it is down. In many respects, actors are the instruments for others' work, impermanent means for the expression of permanent ideas and emotions. As much as their interpretation of a role or even of a single line of a play may be their very own, they are more directed and vocal because of others, not because of themselves.

But parents are actors in a different, nontheatrical sense. They are people who take action. They are the original source of the energy that propels their lives, and respond to the circumstances of their lives, to circumstances not always of their own choosing. But it is their choice whether and how to respond.

So it has been for parents and other family members of people with disabilities and other exceptional traits. They have been both passive, acted-upon actors; and active, initiating actors.

Sometimes they have been wrongly blamed as the cause of their children's disabilities. Surely that is not accurate in the case of the Bergs, Corteses, or Holleys, but it is accurate in the Dolemans' lives.

Recognizing that they needed support to control at least some aspects of their lives, and that the best support would come from others in their own circumstances, these families organized around various disabilities or across disabilities. Clara Berg helped Carole Gothelf form a disability-specific support group for parents of deaf-blind children in metropolitan New York. Leia Holley works across disabilities in her role as a trainer for Families Together.

To organize is one kind of action. To use organizations to provide services to themselves or their children is to take a different kind of action. It was Beth Mount who suggested to Clara and Jake Berg that Kenny might work at a farm; it was Clara who paved the way as Kenny's first job coach at Adriance Farm.

Disabilities puzzle even the most well-trained professionals. Why does Sean Holley hit his head? Why does he not hit his head if someone is pressing hard on the steel plates in his

Arnie Mejia (left) helps Kenny Berg gather eggs.

head? Answers to these questions confound researchers, teachers, physicians, and other experts, just as they confound parents. So parents such as Leia, Clara, Norma, and Vera have turned to the experts for advice; they have deferred to the experts' judgments.

Often, the experts prescribe regimens that require families to become follow-through providers. Vera Doleman's skills in tube-feeding Nicky relate to Nicky's health and are prescribed by her physicians. Leia Holley's duties and skills in shaping Sean's language and behavior convert her into a teacher who has talent to guide and instruct as any member of the Bonner Springs Elementary School faculty.

Sometimes, what the experts recommend is so undeniably correct that there is no need to challenge it. Sometimes, however, professionals' advice is so insufficient that it has to be challenged, especially by the parents themselves. Some parents, such as Clara Berg and Leia Holley, had to advocate long and hard for appropriate programs for their children. Others, such as Vera Doleman, had no occasion to advocate against any professionals or systems. Some, such as Norma Cortes, turned to other family members, such as those at United We Stand of New York, to advocate for her and Joesian.

Advocacy can create adversarial relationships between families and professionals and experts. That is why families and experts have evolved into still other roles.

Parents are now members of the school teams that make decisions about their children's education. Whenever Nicky Doleman's team of nearly a dozen professionals meets, Vera

United We Stand staff members (left to right) Martha Viscarrondo and Lori Rosenfeld.

is there. Likewise, when Sean Holley's "dutiful dozen" convene, they always include Leia. It is not just that parents participate in meetings. Often, they decide where their children will attend school, as when Vera chose the inclusion program at Raintree Montessori School or when Clara Berg decided to enroll Kenny at the Perkins School.

To be a member of their children's education teams creates yet another role for parents. They now are partners with professionals in making decisions about their children. These include decisions not just about education, but about every facet of their child's life. No, Vera does not decide what kind of medication Nicky needs, but she meets regularly with Nicky's physicians at Children's Mercy Hospital in Kansas City to learn why Nicky needs certain medications or nutritional supplements and how to administer them.

Someday, you will come face to face with parents who fill one or more of these roles. For example, a pregnant woman who ingests alcohol and drugs that damage her baby fits the "role" of the cause of the disability. Another parent may want to be an advocate and join your team but be absolutely out of time, given the demands of home and work. How should you respond to these different parents?

INTRODUCTION

Why is it important to know about the history of family and parent roles in the care and education of children and youth with exceptionalities? First, history helps us understand contemporary issues and approaches, many of which are legacies from the past. Second, many of the challenges that families and professionals now face can be overcome if we heed history's lessons. And third, history teaches us that today's approaches may seem as improbable to the next generation as earlier approaches seem to us now.

Parents have played eight major roles over time: (1) the source or cause of their child's disability, (2) organization members, (3) service developers, (4) recipients of professionals' decisions, (5) teachers, (6) political advocates, (7) educational decision makers, and (8) partners with professionals. These roles do not represent discrete eras, each with a clear beginning and end. Rather, the roles overlap. There is, however, a general chronological order to them.

PARENTS AS SOURCE OR CAUSE OF THEIR CHILD'S DISABILITY

The eugenics movement (1880–1930) accused parents of being the source or cause of their child's disability (Barr, 1913). To eliminate or reduce the number of "unfit" parents, the eugenicists argued, would improve the human race through selective breeding. The eugenics movement

was based on (1) genealogical investigations such as Goddard's (1912) study of the Kallikak family, (2) Mendel's laws of heredity, and (3) studies (MacMurphy, 1916; Terman, 1916) indicating that delinquent behaviors were strongly associated with "feeble-mindedness" (Scheerenberger, 1983).

The eugenics movement resulted in laws restricting people with intellectual disabilities from marrying and compelling them to be sterilized and institutionalized (Ferguson, 1994). In upholding a compulsory sterilization law, Justice Oliver Wendell Holmes, Jr., wrote for the Supreme Court: "Three generations of imbeciles are enough" (*Buck v. Bell*, 1927). Gould (1981) and Smith (1985) have documented that the eugenics movement was misdirected; it was not so much about preventing another generation of "imbeciles" as about controlling the reproductive capacity of the poor. Wehmeyer (2003) pointed out that, however misdirected the movement was, it resulted in the involuntary sterilization of more than 50,000 Americans with intellectual disabilities. A California law reflects the attitude toward sterilization during this period. The statute authorized the board of trustees of a state institution, on the recommendation of the superintendent, a clinical psychologist, and a physician, to sterilize involuntarily institutionalized "feeble-minded, chronic manic and demented people, with or without their consent, before discharging them" (Landman, 1932, p. 59).

The eugenics movement also justified the institutionalization of persons with mental retardation. Only 9,334 persons with mental retardation were institutionalized in 1900, but 68,035 were in institutions in 1930 (Scheerenberger, 1983).

The parents-as-cause perspective extended beyond mental retardation to autism (Bettelheim, 1950, 1967), asthma (Gallagher & Gallagher, 1985), learning disabilities (Oliver, Cole, & Hollingsworth, 1991; Orton, 1930; Thomas, 1905), and emotional disorders (Caplan & Hall-McCorquodale, 1985).

Nowhere has professional blame been more directed than regarding autism. In the 1940s and 1950s, professionals typically described parents of children and youth who had autism as rigid, perfectionist, emotionally impoverished, and depressed (Kanner, 1949; Marcus, 1977). A leading professional, Bruno Bettelheim (1950, 1967), contended that a child who had autism and who exhibited severe withdrawal from his or her parents and other people was responding to the stress created by the parents' "extreme and explosive" hatred of the child. Bettelheim even advocated a "parentectomy"—namely, institutionalizing the child and thereby replacing natural parents with institutional staff and professionals who allegedly would be more competent and caring.

By contrast, the current definition of autism states that "no known factors in the psychological environment of a child have been shown to cause autism" (National Society for Autistic Children, 1977). This definition is accepted by professionals, families, and Congress (in the federal special education law). Frank Warren (1985), the father of a young man with autism and a national advocate, commented on and rejected Bettelheim's position in light of the new definition (see Figure 5-1).

Congenital malformations occur in approximately 3% to 5% of all births (Schonberg & Tifft, 2002). Only 25% of those malformations have genetic causes. Another 10% have environmental causes, and 65% have causes that are unknown (Beckman & Brent, 1986; Buyse, 1990). Some disabilities in children may be traced to the parents. For example, some conditions (such as cystic fibrosis) are clearly genetic in nature. Excessive use of alcohol or drugs by pregnant women may cause children to have disabling conditions such as fetal alcohol syndrome or cocaine addiction (Wunsch, Conlon, & Scheidt, 2002). Likewise, pregnant women who use intravenous drugs put their children at risk for HIV, the cause of AIDS. In fact, more than 90% of children with pediatric AIDS acquired HIV from their mothers during gestation or birth, or postnatally (Spiegel & Bonwit, 2002). Malnutrition during pregnancy or in the child's early life may lead to mild mental retardation or motor impairment (Baumeister, Kupstas, & Woodley-Zanthos, 1993). Some children who are exposed to extremely detrimental environments early

in life develop relatively unscathed, whereas other children who are subjected to less stressful environments may fail to thrive and experience developmental delays (Flach, 1988; Werner & Smith, 1992).

Our best advice to you is this: Avoid blaming parents. If you need to know the cause of a disability, investigate it. If you learn that the parents may have been a cause, use that information to design supports for the family. Identify and affirm the family's positive contributions to their child. You may be able to help prevent disabilities in their other children and avoid exacerbating their child's existing disability. Blaming can create a barrier to trusting partnerships between you and the family. Without a partnership, you will be less effective in supporting the family, and they will derive less benefit from you.

PARENTS AS ORGANIZATION MEMBERS

Parents and other family members began to organize on a local level in the 1930s and on the national level in the late 1940s and 1950s (see Figure 5-2). They were motivated by (1) their belief that public and professional responses to their children's educational and other needs were inadequate and (2) their desire to share emotional support with others who were facing similar challenges.

The United Cerebral Palsy Associations (UCPA) was founded in 1949 largely through the efforts of Leonard H. Goldenson, the father of a child with cerebral palsy. Here is how he described UCPA's beginnings:

> One day, realizing the cost of driving our child into New York City from Westchester, my wife said to me, "Leonard, I know we can afford to do this but what about the poor people? How can they afford to do it?" And she added, "Why don't we look into the possibility of trying to help others in this field?"
>
> It was on that basis that I started to investigate the whole field of cerebral palsy.
>
> Upon investigation, I found there were probably only twenty-some-odd doctors in the entire United States who knew anything about cerebral palsy. I found there were only a few local parents groups in the country that were trying to do something about it. But the parents were so involved with their own children and had to take so much time with them, they could not get out to raise money and inform the public about the subject. (Goldenson, 1965, pp. 1–2)

Other parent groups include the National Society for Autistic Children, founded in 1961 and now called Autism Society of America; the National Association for Down Syndrome, founded in 1961; the Association for Children with Learning Disabilities, founded in 1964;

FIGURE 5–1
My Voice: Shame on You!

That means we didn't do it . . . We, the parents of autistic children, are just ordinary people. Not any crazier than others. Not "refrigerator parents" any more than others. Not cold intellectuals any more than others. Not neurotic or psychopathic or sociopathic or any of those words that have been made up. It means, Dr. Bettelheim, that you, and all those others like you who have been laying this incredible guilt trip on us for over 20 years, you are wrong and ought to be ashamed of yourselves.

Source: Warren, F. (1985). A society that is going to kill your children. In H. R. Turnbull & A. P. Turnbull (Eds.), *Parents speak out: then and now* (2nd ed., p. 217). Upper Saddle River, NJ: Merrill/Prentice Hall.

FIGURE 5–2
Advocacy Action: A History of The Arc (originally called National Association for Retarded Children)

To name the time and place of the beginning of this movement is like trying to isolate the first growth of grass. For truly, this is a grassroots movement. Parents, in reaching out—seeking resources to help them meet this critical personal and family problem—found each other. Small groups huddled all over the country (and all over the world, we now find) but as nearly as can be told, the movement in this country had its beginning in the early 1930s.

At least among member groups of NARC, the Council for the Retarded Child in Cuyahoga County (Ohio) holds the record in seniority. This group was founded in 1933 to assist children of the area who had been excluded from the public schools. More than 10 other organizations were established in the 1930s and one in 1942.

After World War II, the first organizational date seems to be 1946, and each succeeding year recorded an increasing number of groups. A survey published by Woodhull Hay in August, 1950, revealed . . . 19,300 dues-paying members, located in 19 states. . . .

In 1950, two sessions were planned, with parent participation, at the American Association on Mental Deficiency meeting in Columbus, Ohio, for the consideration of the activities and problems of this growing phenomenon. Following these sessions, a handful of parents from East Coast to West Coast met, saw their destiny, and went to work.

And there in Columbus the drama started to unfold. In the words of a parent who was there:

"Imagine it! Practically every parent there thought his group was the pioneer. Most of us were strangers to each other—suspicious of everyone's motives and jealous of their progress." But the strange atmosphere soon changed. A steering committee was established, Miss Mildred Thomson's invitation in the name of the Minnesota group was accepted, and the date set for September (1950)—in Minneapolis. Ninety persons registered at the convention. Of these, 42 were delegates from 23 organizations in the states of California, Connecticut, Illinois, Massachusetts, Michigan, Minnesota, Missouri, New Jersey, New York, Ohio, Texas, Vermont, Washington, and Wisconsin.

A masterful statement of purposes emanated from the labors of that first convention. These were parents with a purpose. No money, no precedent, no policy to follow. The officers and directors, in most instances, were strangers to one another—but strangers with a common goal—to help ALL retarded children and their parents. (Formal ratification of the constitution by the necessary 20 local groups was accomplished on February 6, 1951.) In installing officers on that memorable Saturday night (September 30), Luther W. Youngdahl, then Governor of Minnesota, said: "Our great democracy can be measured best by what it does for the least of its little citizens." He turned a small hotel auditorium into a cathedral as the hearts and souls of misty-eyed parents echoed those words.

Source: NARC. (1954). Blueprint for a crusade. *Publicity and publications manual*. Washington, DC: The Arc.

and the Federation of Families for Children's Mental Health, founded in 1988. The federation's mission statement appears in Figure 5–3.

Despite their impact on service delivery and political advocacy, parent organizations cannot be all things to all parents. The late Elizabeth Boggs, one of the founding members of The Arc, wrote the following concerning her role as a parent advocate:

I am proud to be the only person who has been continuously active in some volunteer capacity with the National Association for Retarded Citizens [now called The Arc] since I participated in its founding in 1950. . . . The cause has taken me to 44 states, plus Puerto Rico and 10 foreign countries. It is hard to put a job title on the role I've played. One could say that I've been a social synergist with a predisposition toward communication and collaboration rather than confrontation. (Boggs, 1985, pp. 39–40)

Janet Bennett, also a parent, described organizational membership in a much different light:

My first phone call to my local unit produced a pleasant enough response from the office secretary and a promise of some information to be mailed. This material consisted of short summary of the unit's programs and services and long questionnaire on which I could indicate areas in which I would be delighted to volunteer. . . . The message was clear: a parent in my circumstances, trying to cope with trauma of uncertain dimensions, should marshal her forces muster her energies, and get out and work for the cause. . .

If I had had an unretarded baby, I'd never in a million years have thought of volunteering for anything during that period. Now that I had Kathryn, why in the world would be expected to do anything of the kind? Yet in the face of minimal help from the organization, it was telling me I should help it. And numb from shock and diminished self-confidence, I did my best to comply. (Bennett, 1985, pp. 163, 16–

FIGURE 5–3

Federation of Families for Children's Mental Health Mission
Statement

- To ensure the rights to full citizenship, support, and access to community-based services for all children and youth with emotional, behavioral, or mental disorders and their families.

- To address the unique needs of children and youth with emotional, behavioral, or mental disorders from birth through the transition to adulthood.

- To provide information and engage in advocacy regarding research, prevention, early intervention, family support, education, transition services, and other services needed by these children, youth, and their families.

- To provide leadership in the field of children's mental health and develop necessary human and financial resources to meet its goal.

Source: Steering Committee for the Federation of Families for Children's Mental Health. (1989, March). *Mission statement*. Alexandria, VA: Author. Reprinted by permission.

Many parent organizations consist primarily of White, middle-class parents. Parents from culturally and linguistically diverse backgrounds typically have not been members of the mainstream parent organizations. The Arc's last membership survey revealed that 95% of the respondents were White and only one fourth of all members had yearly incomes under $20,000 (Haller & Millman, 1987). An exception is the Federation of Families for Children's Mental Health. At their annual conference held each fall, approximately half of the participants are from culturally diverse backgrounds.

Furthermore, the federation has demonstrated cultural sensitivity by providing sessions in Spanish, having conference materials available in English and Spanish, having programs particularly targeted for Native American families, and having entertainment and social opportunities that build on the traditions and priorities of various cultures. Those accommodations enable families from culturally and linguistically diverse backgrounds to experience authentic participation. If they are interested in organizational affiliation, they are not blocked by cultural barriers.

Some parents, not all, find it helpful to belong to parent organizations. You should share information with parents about appropriate local, state, and national organizations and encourage them to determine the level and type of their own participation.

One caution: Despite the increased emphasis on non-categorical services in schools and special education, most parent organizations are based on disability categories. If you teach in schools that do not categorize students by type of disability, parents may need information about the type of disability their child has so they can find support in appropriate parent organizations.

PARENTS AS SERVICE DEVELOPERS

Parents have played a major role in developing services for children at all life stages. During the 1950s and 1960s, they and the organizations they created established education programs for children who were excluded from public schools solely because of their disabilities. These parents organized classes in community buildings and church basements, solicited financial support from charitable organizations, and did the job the schools should have been doing. During those two decades and especially since then, parents and their organizations have spearheaded the development of recreation, residential options, and employment services. In all of these endeavors, parents have assumed five jobs: creating public awareness, raising money, developing services, operating services, and advocating for others to assume responsibility for service operations.

Samuel Kirk (1984), a distinguished special education pioneer, described the profound impact of parent organizations:

> I found a satisfaction in associating with many intelligent and knowledgeable parents in these organizations. I found that through association with other parents they learned what the best programs were for their children. If I were to give credit to one group in this country for the advancements that have been made in the education of exceptional children, I would place the parent organizations and parent movement in the forefront as the leading force. (p. 41)

Although some family members prefer to develop, operate, and control the services their children receive, professionals should not expect them to start and maintain services that are the professionals' responsibility. For example, you should not expect parents to start integrated or supported employment or adult education programs for students and young adults with disabilities. After all, parents of children without disabilities are not expected to start and maintain a college-preparatory curriculum in their local high school. Families should have full opportunities to partner with professionals in creating educational, vocational, and recreational programs; but they should not have to assume the full responsibility. There is one very good reason for this: Many parents simply do not have the time to develop and operate services. As you learned in chapter 3, they often devote an extraordinary amount of time to meeting their family functions and satisfying the demands of their for-pay jobs. You should support parents to be parents, first and foremost, not service providers. For parents, service development should be an option, not an expectation.

PARENTS AS RECIPIENTS OF PROFESSIONALS' DECISIONS

As recently as the 1970s, professionals generally expected parents to comply passively and gratefully with decisions about the programs in which their children should participate. As Kolstoe (1970), an author of an early leading textbook on the methods of educating students with disabilities, wrote:

> Should it be judged that special class placement will probably be of most benefit to the child, then placement should be made without delay. Both the child and his parents should be told that the child is being transferred into the special class because the class is special. . . . The entire program should be explained so the parents will understand what lies ahead for the child and so they can support the efforts of the teachers with the child. (p. 42)

This was also a common perspective for students who were regarded as gifted, as a typical 1960s text shows:

> Some "guts" to speak straight from the shoulder would be helpful to the educators in this situation. Then the lay groups probably would realize they must delegate some of their authority to the educators to make necessary decisions for improving the education of students. For example, an overwhelming majority of parents do not have the sophistication in educational matters to decide whether or not their youngster would be better off educationally if placed in a differential program for the gifted. . . . Parents could better spend their time: a) supporting parent organizations for raising funds and influencing state and federal legislation, and b) learning techniques to aid their own youngsters toward high achievement. (Lucito, 1963, pp. 227–228)

Some professionals still believe that they know what is best for a student, so they expect families to defer to professional judgment, especially regarding the student's evaluation, individualized program, and educational placement. These expectations place professionals at the center of the decision-making team, directing parents and families about the child's education. (Later in the chapter, we will contrast professionally centered decision-making teams with family centered decision-making teams and with family-professional partnership decision-making teams.)

Professionals who believe that they are the center of the decision-making team can create a psychological barrier to effective family-professional partnerships by inadvertently (or sometimes deliberately) intimidating parents or even angering them by being so authoritative (Turnbull, Turbiville, & Turnbull, 2000). This barrier can be particularly problematic for families from diverse backgrounds whose culture clashes with that of the professionals (Harry, Kalyanpur, & Day, 1999; Kalyanpur & Harry, 1999). Try to be an equal partner with families when making decisions, and try not to expect them to be the passive recipients of your decisions. Throughout this book, we will provide information about how you can establish trusting partnerships. Understanding and applying these principles will give you the ability to assist parents in significant ways.

PARENTS AS TEACHERS

The role of parents as teachers emerged during the 1960s, peaked during the 1970s, and was moderated during the mid to late 1980s. At the root of the parent-as-teacher role was a large body of evidence showing that a family's environment influences their children's intelligence (Hunt, 1972). In particular, the data showed that families from economically deprived backgrounds had problems associated with their home lives, and that these child-rearing environments lacked the opportunities typically available in middle- and upper-class homes (Zigler & Muenchow, 1992). Thus, President Kennedy's New Frontier and President Johnson's Great Society initiatives (for example, Head Start) included programs that trained parents to teach their children. The children were expected to make more progress because of their enriched home environments. The theory of environmental enrichment is largely credited to researcher Urie Bronfenbrenner:

> Bronfenbrenner's notion of parent involvement and the ecological (environmental-influence) model of child development emerged from two sources—his own childhood and his cross-cultural research. Born in Moscow, he emigrated to the United States in 1923. His father, a physician, took a job as director of an institution for the "feeble-minded" in Letchworth Village, New York.
>
> From time to time, Bronfenbrenner's father would anguish over the institutionalization of a person who did not have mental retardation. Sadly, after a few weeks there these people of normal intelligence would begin to mimic the mannerisms of the residents who inarguably had cognitive limitation. When one of the nondisabled "patients" came to work in the Bronfenbrenners' household however, she gradually resumed a "normal" life, accidentally teaching young Urie an important lesson in how family and

community expectations and environments influence human behavior.

Given his background, Bronfenbrenner decided to become a psychologist. During the course of cross-cultural studies in western and eastern Europe, he observed that Russian parents, both fathers and mothers, seemed to spend more time with their children than did American parents. As a result of presenting his findings at a National Institute for Child Health and Human Development meeting in 1964, Bronfenbrenner was soon describing his observations on Russian childrearing to President Johnson's wife and daughters. The Johnsons were impressed, especially by the pictures of Russian preschools. One of the Johnson daughters asked, "Why couldn't we do something like this?" (Zigler & Muenchow, 1992, pp. 16–17)

Thus began the American policy initiatives directed at enriching children's home environments.

Bronfenbrenner's approach—called ecological because it linked family environment to human development—was the basis on which professionals prepared parents for increasing their children's progress and achievement. In the 1970s, the emphasis was on parents applying behavioral principles and child development techniques. Enthusiasm for the ecological approach was sparked by research showing that parents can be effective teachers of their children (Bricker & Bricker, 1976; Shearer & Shearer, 1977). Because parents could be effective teachers, many professionals believed that parents *should* be teachers. They also believed that good parents were those who frequently acted as teachers, not "just" parents. This role is also strongly rooted within a professionally centered orientation (Turnbull et al., 2000). The emphasis was on professionals directing parents, and the goal was to increase parents' competence to educate their children.

The use of the term *parent* is actually a misnomer in this context. It is more correct to substitute the term *mothers* because literature of this period contains almost no reference to the role of fathers in their children's development (Turbiville, Turnbull, & Turnbull, 1995).

Given the optimism that the research data justified (Baker, 1989), it was only natural for early childhood education programs to insist that parents should be effective teachers of their own children (Shearer & Shearer, 1977). During the height of the parent-training era, Karnes and Teska (1980) identified the competencies that parents needed to acquire to fulfill their "teacher" role:

The parental competencies required for direct teaching of the handicapped child at home involve interacting with the child in ways that promote positive behavior; reinforcing desired behavior; establishing an environment that is con-

ducive to learning; setting up and maintaining a routine for direct teaching; using procedures appropriate for teaching concepts and skills; adapting lesson plans to the child's interests and needs; determining whether the child has mastered knowledge and skills; keeping meaningful records, including notes on child progress; participating in a staffing of the child; communicating effectively with others; and assessing the child's stage of development. (p. 99)

These are fewer than half of the skills the authors regarded as essential to the parent-as-teacher role. Compare these skills to the ones you have to master in your own professional training program. Is it realistic to expect parents to develop so many teaching skills?

Some parents find teaching to be very satisfying. Others say it produces guilt and stress if they are not constantly working with their son or daughter with a disability. Another unintended consequence is the impact that instruction from parents, provided even within the context of typical routines, can have on the self-esteem of children and youth with disabilities. Diamond (1981) described her experiences with her parents as a child with a physical disability:

Something happens in a parent when relating to his disabled child; he forgets that they're a kid first. I used to think about that a lot when I was a kid. I would be off in a euphoric state, drawing or coloring or cutting out paper dolls, and as often as not the activity would be turned into an occupational therapy session. "You're not holding the scissors right," "Sit up straight so your curvature doesn't get worse." That era was ended when I finally let loose a long and exhaustive tirade. "I'm just a kid! You can't therapize me all the time! I get enough therapy in school every day! I don't think about my handicap all the time like you do!" (p. 30)

Many of today's parents of children and youth with disabilities, unlike parents during the 1970s and early 1980s, seem to place less importance on their roles as teachers (Turnbull, Blue-Banning, Turbiville, & Park, 1999). Instead, many families want more information (not necessarily formal training sessions) on various topics. Many families welcome information on topics such as advocacy, homework, and future planning. If you want to be guided by parents' current preferences, consider offering opportunities for parents to exchange information with you and other professionals. You also will want to find out from not only mothers—but also fathers, brothers and sisters, and extended family members—what they prefer as they seek helpful information.

In situations in which parents are helping their children learn, partnerships will do everyone more good than a professional-knows-best approach.

PARENTS AS POLITICAL ADVOCATES

Parents have been successful advocates at the federal, state, and local levels and in legislatures, courts, and executive agencies. Because educational services for most students with disabilities were woefully inadequate throughout 1950 to 1970, parents took on a new role as political advocates. In the early 1970s, parents of students with mental retardation and the Pennsylvania Association for Retarded Children won a lawsuit against the state to obtain a free, appropriate education for children with mental retardation (*Pennsylvania Association for Retarded Citizens (PARC) v. Commonwealth of Pennsylvania*, 1971, 1972).

Thereafter, parents and their organizations brought right-to-education suits in almost every state, usually successfully. Buoyed by their success, parents sought federal legislation to implement the courts' decisions (Turnbull & Turnbull, 1996). Parent organizations representing all areas of disability, particularly The Arc, joined forces with professionals, particularly the Council for Exceptional Children, and successfully advocated for comprehensive federal legislation requiring the states to provide all students with disabilities a free appropriate public education.

The parent groups were immensely successful as political advocates, convincing Congress to pass the Education for All Handicapped Children Act (P.L. 94-142) in 1975 and six major amendments since then (1978, 1983, 1986, 1990, 1997, and 2004). We discuss this legislation, now referred to as the Individuals with Disabilities Education Act, in chapter 6. It is a tribute to parent advocacy—always greatly aided by and sometimes led by professional organizations—that Congress passed these laws, that the parent organizations were able to form coalitions with each other and professional groups, and that all of this has been accomplished over such an extended period in a continuous and consistent manner. Tom Gilhool, the attorney representing parents in *Pennsylvania Association for Retarded Citizens (PARC) v. Commonwealth of Pennsylvania* and a leading national advocate for individuals with disabilities, described his perspectives on these significant accomplishments (see Figure 5–4).

Lowell Weicker (1985), a former U.S. senator and the father of a son with Down syndrome, played an important role in the advocacy movement. In the mid-1980s, he described the impact of political advocacy on attempts by the Reagan administration to de-emphasize the federal role in special education, attempts that he and the parent advocacy movement thwarted:

> The administration did not get its way. Why? Because the disabled people in this country and their advocates repudiated a long-held cliché that they were not a political constituency, or at least not a coherent one. It was assumed that in the

FIGURE 5–4

My Voice: Tom Gilhool Speaks Out on Significant Accomplishments of Parents As Political Advocates

The parents and families on whose shoulders we stand reversed in this century, and most particularly in the past three decades, the weight and the pattern of the historical legacy that the start of the century left for us. It is entirely correct, and a gentle understatement, to say that the parent movement has nearly eliminated segregation of disabled people into large, separate, horrific public institutions. . . .

Indeed, in 1970, just prior to the PARC decision and the decisions in the other 37 court cases which led to the passage of The Education for All Handicapped Children Act of 1975 [also known as P.L. 94-142], some 12,000 children of school age had been committed to institutions in that year. That was the annual rate of admission. In 1981, three years after the effective date of P.L. 94-142, fewer than 1,200 were admitted. . . . The parent movement has reversed the course of history in this century by insisting that these segregated institutions cannot stand and must go.

Second, the opening of the schools and the requirement that schools provide to every child, including every child with a disability, a strong, effective education are the work of the parent movement. Seymour Sarason regards P.L. 94-142 as one of just two significant changes in all of public education in the last 75 years and the only one to come in an Act of Congress. The change he refers to, of course, is the empowerment of parents, putting parents and families in charge of the education of their children. This change was birthed by The Education for All Handicapped Children Act and, so far, remains a keystone of IDEA. (The other significant change referred to by Sarason was collective bargaining.) Both of those accomplishments are signal, resonant achievements in the name of the American commitment to equality. They have advanced, and promise to advance still further, equality for very, very many American citizens. Thus far, they have been sustained even while the American politic in the last two decades has moved so strongly away from equality, even against it.

Source: Gilhool, T. (1997, Spring). Tom Gilhool speaks out on significant accomplishments of parents as political advocates. In *The Parent Movement: Reflections and Directions. Coalition Quarterly, 14* (1).

rough and tumble world of politics they would not ho their own as a voting block or as advocates for their caus But that assumption was blown to smithereens in the bud; and policy deliberations of 1981, 1982, and again in 1983.

fact, I would be hard-pressed to name another group within the human service spectrum that has not only survived the policies of this administration but has also defeated them as consistently and as convincingly as the disabled community has. Indeed, it has set an example for others, who were believed to be better organized. (p. 284)

As the federal role in disability services changes and as state and local governments and even the private sector play more significant roles in implementing disability policy and funding services, parents have been obliged to continue to be advocates. However, not all parents have the time, interest, or resources to be political advocates.

PARENTS AS EDUCATIONAL DECISION MAKERS

The Individuals with Disabilities Education Act (IDEA) was revolutionary when enacted because it grants parents a right to participate with educators in making decisions about their children. The law recognizes the critical role that families play in their children's development and the necessity of subjecting schools to parental oversight. Although children who are gifted are not included in the federal laws for children with disabilities, approximately two thirds of the states have mandates, accompanied by some level of funding, for gifted education (Council of State Directors of Programs for the Gifted and National Association for Gifted Children, 2003).

In granting these rights to parents, Congress adopted the basic premise that families of children and youth with disabilities could make no assumptions that the public schools would enroll their children, much less educate them appropriately (Turnbull, Turnbull, & Wheat, 1982). Congress regarded parents as persons who could ensure that professionals would provide an appropriate education to the children. This view reflected a major reversal in expectations about parents' roles. No longer were parents expected passively to receive professionals' decisions. Now, they were expected to make educational decisions and to monitor professionals' decisions.

Parents' relationships with professionals may have become more equal than a couple of decades ago; however, the majority of parents participate in educational decision making in a more passive than active style, as we will discuss in chapter 12. Sometimes parents do not have the motivation to be educational decision makers; at other times they have the motivation but do not have the knowledge and skills. Even those parents who have motivation, knowledge, and skills face an educational context that inhibits rather than facilitates their role as partners. This is particularly so for parents from culturally and linguistically diverse backgrounds (Harry, Kalyanpur & Day, 1999; Kalyanpur & Harry, 1999). As you learned in chapter 3, many families have no unclaimed time to add more responsibilities.

In the field of early childhood education, the role of parents as decision makers took a new direction in the 1980s with the introduction of a family-centered model. The role of parents as the recipients of professionals' decisions is professionally centered. Similarly, the role of parents as teachers also is professionally centered. Over time, however, practitioners, policy leaders, and researchers, especially those in early education, began to move from professional-centeredness to family-centeredness (Dunst, Trivette, & Deal, 1988; McWilliam et al., 1995; Murphy, Lee, Turnbull, & Turbiville, 1995; Turnbull et al., 2000).

The three basic characteristics of family-centeredness are (1) building on family choice by ensuring that families are the ultimate decision makers, (2) capitalizing on families' strengths, and (3) making the family the unit of services and support, instead of centering services and support on only the child or the child and mother (Allen & Petr, 1996).

The first characteristic, family choice, is especially notable. The emphasis in family-centered services is for professionals to defer to the family in decision making regarding the nature and extent of services and supports for the young child and for other family members. Family-centeredness is stronger as a philosophy than as a practice in early intervention services (Dunst, 2002; Katz & Scarpati, 1995; McBride, Brotherson, Joanning, Whiddon, & Demmitt, 1993). Furthermore, family-centeredness is less favored and practiced at each lifespan stage, starting with early intervention and continuing through secondary school programs (Dunst, 2002).

FAMILIES AS PARTNERS

In this book, we focus on the role of families as partners. An important word in that sentence is families. As we stated earlier, until early intervention developed a family-centered approach, almost all emphasis was on parents and not on families. Under family-centered approaches, the whole family, not just one or more of its members, receives support and services (Allen & Petr, 1996). Policy makers and professionals now recognize that partnerships should not be limited to parents only (especially to mothers only). Partnerships can and should involve relationships between professionals and other family members, such as fathers, grandparents, brothers and sisters, and even close family friends. Each of these people can support and enhance the educational outcomes for students with exceptionalities.

Merriam-Webster's Collegiate Dictionary (2003) defines partnership as "a relationship . . . involving close cooperation between parties having specified and joint rights and responsibilities." This definition places families, students, and professionals into a relationship where each has rights and responsibilities toward the other.

In this text, we define partnerships as relationships between families and professionals in which they mutually agree to defer to each other's judgments and expertise, as appropriate for the purpose of securing outcomes for the student, the other family members, and the professionals. Key principles of partnership are communication, professional competence, respect, commitment, equality, advocacy, and trust.

Our definition retains the idea of joint action, but it does not confer any more decision-making power on the families than on the professionals, or vice versa. Instead, our definition describes a relationship in which the families and professionals work together to achieve a collective wisdom.

We will expand on our definition in chapter 7. For now, pay close attention to its basic characteristics: mutual action, collaboration, and collective wisdom for outcomes that benefit all members of the partnership.

Partnerships can benefit many stakeholders—students with exceptionalities, families, classmates, teachers, administrators, paraprofessionals, and related service providers. Family members benefit when the student is educated effectively, and professionals benefit when they derive support and assistance from professional colleagues and families. For example, a general classroom teacher who is responsible for educating a student with autism is not left alone to solve all of the challenges facing the student. Instead, the teacher can rely on a dynamic team of partners to find the most successful solutions to those challenges.

Students with exceptionalities can be part of the partnership that their parents, other family members, and professionals form; their participation is one way for practicing self-determination. As you learned in chapter 4, self-determination means choosing how to live one's life consistent with one's values, preferences, strengths, and needs (Turnbull, Blue-Banning, et al., 1996; Turnbull & Turnbull, 1996). For too many years, it has been assumed that either the professionals or the parents, or both, know what is in a student's best interests and that they should make decisions about the student's education. Research shows, however, that many students can make quite defensible decisions about their education and participate effectively in developing and carrying out their education programs (Allen, Smith, Test, Flowers,

& Wood, 2001; Martin et al., 2003). Some families believe that self-determination is a culturally inappropriate goal (Kalyanpur & Harry, 1999).

Family-professional partnerships have two important benefits. First, they benefit the student by bringing to bear on the student's behalf the partners' multiple perspectives and resources. Second, they benefit the partners by making available to each the resources, motivation, knowledge, and skills of the others (Blue-Banning, Summers, Frankland, Nelson, & Beegle, 2004; Turnbull, Turnbull, Shank, & Smith, 2004).

Because partnerships occur in a school context, we describe in the next chapter the policies that most directly affect students, families, and professionals who are involved in special education.

SUMMARY

Parents and families have played many roles, some unwelcome or unjustified, some born out of necessity, and some eagerly embraced. In these roles, parents have been regarded as the sources of their child's problems, organization members, service organizers, recipients of professionals' decisions, learners and teachers, political advocates, educational decision makers, and partners (with all family members being potential partners).

No one role can fully and perfectly characterize all parents, and some parents have played all or most roles. Parents and other family members vary in the roles they assume, and professionals vary in the roles they consider appropriate and recommend to and expect from families. However, it is clear that roles have changed in the following ways:

■ From regarding parents and other family members as part of their child's problem to regarding them as partners in addressing the challenges of exceptionality

■ From insisting on passive roles for parents to expecting active partnership roles for families

■ From regarding families as consisting only of a mother-child dyad to recognizing the preferences and needs of all members of a family

■ From responding to family needs in a general way to individualizing for the family as a whole and for each member

Families and professionals may feel caught up in time zone changes, much like world travelers. Dorothy "Tof" Avis (1985), a parent who is also a professional in the disability field, described the concept of "deinstitutionalization jet lag," referring to parents who were told years ago that the state institution was best for the child and who now are told that the community is preferable. Nowadays, families and professionals experience "family-role jet lag." Expectations and philosophies have drastically changed since the days when the eugenics movement was in full cry. If you can appreciate the distance that families have traveled, you will be better prepared for the journey into mutually beneficial family-professional partnerships.

What does it mean to have time-traveled and role-traveled? It means to have understood the roles that families have played and to assume that they and the professionals who work with them will have different roles in the future.

Very little about family-professional relationships is static. Among the most dynamic aspects of the relationships are those that rely on partnership, not professional dominance or parent dominance within the relationships.

REFLECTING ON THE VIGNETTE

1. Do you characterize each of the four families as passive players who act out roles that professionals create for them, or as active players who take charge of their lives and relationships with professionals? Or is each family both an active and a passive player?
2. Given what you know about family characteristics, interactions, functions, and life cycle stages, what roles would you recommend to each of the families in their present life cycle and circumstances?
3. Which role did each family most eagerly adopt? Which role did each family resist?

ENHANCING YOUR SELF-AWARENESS

As a professional, it is particularly important that you know the field's history. If you will be teaching older students, their families will have played many different roles before they have an opportunity to develop a partnership with you. Even if families are younger, they often have heard the "stories" about when times were different. For these reasons, you should not only be aware of historical roles but also reflect on your own values and opinions that relate to these roles.

Families as the source or cause of their child's disability

What are your views about the eugenics movement and the forced sterilization of many people with mental retardation or other disabilities? Recently self-advocacy groups

and professionals have asked the governors of states and the officers of professional organizations to apologize. Do you believe it is appropriate for people who are in professional roles today to apologize and thus assume some accountability for their predecessors' decisions?

Parents as recipients of professionals' decisions

Is it ever appropriate for parents to be recipients of professionals' decisions without having any way to determine whether they believe the decision is sound? If you are working with a parent who automatically accepts everything you say, would you be comfortable or uncomfortable? What steps might you take related to your comfort level?

Parents as political advocates

If you were a member of the U.S. Senate, would you place more credence in parents' or in school superintendents' testimony about how to revise IDEA? How important is it to you that people have had personal experience with the issues on which they give advice?

RESOURCES

1. The Arc of the U.S.
   1010 Wayne Avenue, Suite 650
   Silver Spring, MD 20910
   301-565-3842
   info@thearc.org
   www.thearc.org

   The Arc of the U.S. focuses its advocacy on children, youth, and adults with intellectual and developmental disabilities. It is particularly effective in political advocacy to enact new laws and improve existing laws at the federal level.

2. Federation of Families for Children's Mental Health
   1101 King Street, Suite 420
   Alexandria, VA 22314
   703-684-7710
   ffcmh@ffcmh.org
   www.ffcmh.org

   The federation is run by families of children with mental health needs and focuses on how to enable children and their families to experience a better quality of life. The federation provides support to a nationwide network of state-run organizations. Special emphasis is placed on ensuring that families from culturally and linguistically diverse backgrounds are welcomed to be part of this organization.

3. Minnesota Governor's Council on Developmental
   Disabilities
   370 Centennial Office Building
   658 Cedar Street
   St. Paul, MN 55155
   651-296-4018
   admin.dd@state.mn.us
   www.mncdd.org

The Website of the Minnesota Developmental Disabilities Council features a section called Parallels in Time. This section provides a history of the field of developmental disabilities, including more than 150 pages of information in addition to numerous video and audio clips.

Policies Shaping School Reform

1. What are the major federal polices that influence the delivery of special education services and what are their key requirements?
2. What are the benefits and drawbacks of federal control of education versus local control of education?
3. What are your responsibilities as an educator in implementing federal policy?

VIGNETTE

Prehistoric humans conquered nature when they first learned to make a fire. They began the technological revolution when they invented the wheel. And, most relevant to this chapter, humans began to be civilized when they sought to resolve their disputes with others, not by using violence but by seeking the judgment of an independent party.

To become civilized by resorting to an independent person and then by agreeing with those who disagree with you to abide by that person's judgment is the hallmark of law. Law is the secular institution that regulates the affairs of one person with respect to others and that regulates the affairs of all people with respect to their common government.

Let's make these abstractions concrete. What establishes the rights of Joesian Cortes, Nicky Doleman, and Sean Holley to attend school? Law does. The Constitution of the United States and the state constitutions proclaim their fundamental rights and the reciprocal obligations of the federal and state governments. The statutes enacted by Congress and by state legislatures create further rights, including the right to a free appropriate public education. The regulations promulgated by the U.S. Department of Education and state educational agencies implement the statutes. Federal and state courts adjudicate disputes between these students and their educational agencies.

Do these three students have a right to go to school, without regard to how great their disabilities are? Can even Nicky, with her great disabilities, attend? Yes.

Do these have the right be evaluated for their strengths and needs? Yes. Should Joesian be evaluated only in English, or should Spanish also be used to evaluate him because that is his mother's language? Probably not, because he speaks English well.

Do these students have a right to benefit from school? Should Nicky's school assist in her health care so she can attend? Should Sean's address his problem behavior? Should Joesian's provide him with vocational training along with instruction in reading? Yes.

Do these students have a right to be in school with peers who don't have disabilities? To be in the classrooms even though Nicky can barely communicate, even though Sean has difficulty in communicating, and even though Joesian reads slowly? Yes.

Vera Doleman (left) visits with Annie Bowersox, a social worker at Woodlawn Elementary School.

Norma Cortes laughs with her son, Joesian.

Do these students have the right to have their parents become partners with their teachers? Even though Joesian's mother, Norma, does not speak English? Even though Vera Doleman and Leia Holley work and cannot easily meet with their children's teachers? Yes.

Finally, do these students have the right to have an independent person adjudicate their disputes with the school? To allow Norma Cortes to bring United We Stand into a mediation meeting with Joesian's school administrators and—over a period of 4 hours of accusations, tears and, finally, problem solving—to reach a decision about Joesian's education? Yes.

Why "yes" in every case? Because "the law" says so. Because there must be some means for regulating the relationships between these students and their parents on the one hand and the student's teachers and school administrators on the other. That means, of course, is the law.

In these relationships of the governed (students and families) and the government (the schools, acting through their teachers and administrators), there are rights and responsibilities, claims and duties. The students and their families have rights; the schools, teachers, and administrators have the responsibility to satisfy those rights. That is why Vera Doleman can compel the schools to accept Nicky and why Norma Cortes can require Joesian's school

The door to Tierney Thompson's classroom at Bonner Springs Elementary school reflects what the school calls its "core virtues."

meet with her and United We Stand to resolve a dispute about his education.

But teachers also have rights. For example, they do not have to tolerate violence. As Joesian so accurately noted, "Bushwick High School doesn't allow bad behavior." That is why he did not fight back when a fellow student assaulted him. Nor do teachers have to "go it alone" when carrying out their duties to their students. They should be supported by their colleagues and their students' families. Support from peers and parents is exactly what makes Nicky's and Sean's teachers so effective.

Teachers, students, and families have the same goal: to engage in the teaching and learning relationship safely and effectively. They also share the same purpose: to achieve that goal and thereby ensure that every student will benefit from their education and be able to use it in their lives after school.

It all seems so civilized, this business of legal rights and responsibilities. Equally civilized are these expectations that families and professionals will support each other. And so it is, but it has not always been this way for students with disabilities, nor is it always this way nowadays.

INTRODUCTION

In chapter 5, we highlighted eight roles that parents and families of students with disabilities have played and we concluded that families and educators are expected to be partners to enhance student outcomes. Although we briefly discussed how IDEA has influenced families' roles, we did not explore the most powerful factor that now affects families' roles: the nation's efforts to reform its schools.

SCHOOL REFORM

School reform is one of the most recurring and perplexing domestic public policy issues facing our nation and its educators, families, and students. During the past 50 years, at least four major recurring developments have influenced school reform (Burello, Lashley, & Beatty, 2001; Fullan, 1999; Goldenberg, 2004; Koret Task Force, 2003; Loveless, 2003; Senge, 2000):

- Advances in technology by economic competitors such as Russia, Germany, and Japan
- Low achievement scores of American students when compared to those of students in other nations
- The need for a well-trained domestic workforce
- The civil rights movement, which advocated for equal opportunity and excellence in education for students from culturally and linguistically diverse backgrounds and for students with disabilities

School reform is more than a recurring issue. It also is a perplexing one because our nation's many different approaches to school reform arguably have not reassured policy makers in Washington or the state capitals that the reforms will produce students who will be able to safeguard American economic and national security interests. Nor have efforts to improve the educational opportunities through remedial and compensatory programs for students in poverty been as effective as their sponsors had hoped. (As you learned in chapter 1, there is a higher rate of poverty among families of students who have disabilities than among families of students who do not have disabilities.) In an increasingly globalized world, our nation looks to its schools to educate the youth for their future roles. More than that, our nation looks to its schools to be partners with families, so that families will reinforce the schools' efforts and so that all students, including those with disabilities, will benefit from the schools.

Finally, school reform is a domestic issue because our methods for changing our schools are influenced by two political factors. The first relates to the roles of the state, local, and federal governments. There is a powerful tradition of state and local control of education. Yet state and local educational agencies, students, and families, look to the federal government to fund school reform initiatives and to enforce the civil rights of students who have disabilities or are from culturally and linguistically diverse backgrounds. As state and local educational agencies look to the federal government for funds and enforcement of rights, however, they find that federal money and enforcement are accompanied by conditions. For example, a state or local educational agency may receive federal money only if it agrees to educate all students with disabilities or if it agrees to test students annually to determine how well they are mastering a school's curriculum. The challenge is always to balance state and local rights with federal conditions. Just where the balance lies is highly debatable and involves a contest between the advocates for state and local control and the advocates for civil rights and federalized school reform.

The second political factor arises from the American tradition of incremental reform of long-established institutions. Schools acquire traditions and customs over decades, generations, and even centuries. They become established in their ways, yet they are not inflexible institutions and they demonstrate their abilities to change to meet the nation's (and state and local) interests. Change, however, comes slowly. The challenge facing those who want a more appropriate education for students with disabilities and those who want to hold schools more accountable is to secure change without destabilizing schools' and educators' worthwhile traditions.

Two federal laws reflect the nation's efforts to reform schools. More than that, they fundamentally shape the partnerships between educators and families. One of those laws is the Individuals with Disabilities Education Act (IDEA). IDEA applies only to those students with disabilities who have been determined to be eligible for special education. The second law, the No Child Left Behind Act (NCLB), applies to all students, including those with disabilities and those who are gifted. Because IDEA applies specifically to special education, we will describe it before we describe NCLB.

SPECIAL EDUCATION REFORM: INDIVIDUALS WITH DISABILITIES EDUCATION ACT

IDEA (as reauthorized in November, 2004) requires state education agencies (SEAs) and local education agencies (LEAs) to provide to every student who has a disability a *free appropriate public education*. (All references to IDEA are to the law as Congress authorized it in November, 2004.) Under IDEA, the U.S. Department of Education allocates federal money to SEAs and LEAs to assist them in educating students with disabilities. One part of the law, called Part B, provides for the education of students ages 3 through 21. Another part, called Part C, provides for the education of infants and toddlers, birth to age 3. Part B and Part C are alike in many ways, but we will explain how they differ as we describe their basic provisions. In order to qualify for Part B and Part C federal money, SEAs and LEAs must adhere to six principles for educating students with disabilities (Turnbull & Turnbull, 2000).

The six key principles that govern the education of students with disabilities are described in Figure 6–1. With respect to each of IDEA's six principles, we will highlight (1) background problems that persuaded Congress to adopt the principle, (2) major purposes and provisions of the principle (including educators' rights), and (3) implications of each principle for family-professional partnerships.

FIGURE 6–1
Six Principles of IDEA

- **Zero reject.** Enroll all children and youth, including all those with disabilities.

- **Nondiscriminatory evaluation.** Determine whether an enrolled student has a disability and, if so, the nature of special education and related services that the student requires.

- **Appropriate education.** Tailor the student's education to address the student's individualized needs and strengths and ensure that education benefits the students.

- **Least restrictive environment.** To the maximum extent appropriate for the student, ensure that every student receives education in the general education environment and do not remove the student from regular education unless the nature or severity of the disability is such that education in general education classes with the use of supplementary aids and services cannot be achieved satisfactorily.

- **Procedural due process.** Implement a system of checks and balances so that parents and professionals may hold each other accountable for providing the student with a free appropriate public education in the least restrictive environment.

- **Parent participation.** Implement the parent participation rights related to every principle and grant parents access to educational records and opportunities to serve on state and local special education advisory committees.

Zero Reject

Background Problems. For many years before 1975, when Congress enacted IDEA, state and local educational agencies barred many students with disabilities from any kind of education whatsoever. Indeed, when it enacted IDEA in 1975, Congress found that:

- one million children with disabilities were excluded entirely from the public school system,
- their educational needs were not being met,
- more than half of them did not receive appropriate educational services and
- their families were often forced to find services outside the public school system, often at great distance from their residence and at their own expense.

As you learned in chapter 5, parents formed organizations to provide services where they were unavailable or inadequate; parents also became political advocates. To rem

CHAPTER 6 ■ POLICIES SHAPING SCHOOL REFORM

FIGURE 6–2

Related Services Required in Part B and Part C of IDEA

Parts B and C

- Audiology services
- Medical services
  (for diagnostic purposes only)
- Occupational therapy
- Physical therapy
- Psychological services
- School nurse and health services
  (for educational benefit only)
- Social work services
- Speech-language pathology
- Transportation and related cost
- Interpreting services (including
  sign language and cued speech
  under Part C)
- Early identification and assessment
  of disabling conditions
- Assistive technology services
  and devices

Part B Only

- Counseling services, including
  rehabilitation counseling
- Orientation and mobility services
- Recreation services
- Parent counseling and training

Part C Only

- Family training, counseling,
  and home visits
- Service coordination
- Special instruction
- Vision services
- Early identification,
  screening, and assessment
  services

edy these problems, Congress established the zero-reject principle.

Major Purposes and Provisions of the Principle. The principle of zero reject is that no school may exclude any student ages 3 through 21 who has a disability. Schools must educate each such student, without regard to the type or extent of the student's disability.

The zero-reject principle rests on the Fourteenth Amendment of the U.S. Constitution, which provides that no state may deny any person the equal protection of the laws (Turnbull & Turnbull, 2000). Equal protection affirms that every person has equal value and therefore should have equal educational opportunities.

The principle of zero reject applies to the provision of special education and related services. IDEA defines special education as "specially designed instruction, at no cost to parents, to meet the unique needs of a child with a disability" (IDEA, 20 U.S.C. Sec. 1401(a) (29)). Related services are those that "may be required to assist a child with a disability to benefit from special education" (IDEA, 20 U.S.C. Sec. 1401(a) (26)). Figure 6–2 describes the related services for Parts B and C.

Despite the zero-reject principle, some school districts have refused to enroll and serve students who have very severe disabilities. Administrators in these school districts have argued that the extent of the students' dis-

abilities is so great that they are not able to learn (are "uneducable") and that it is futile for the schools to try to educate them and an unwise expenditure of education funds. The issue of educability and the scope of the zero-reject principle was settled when a federal court of appeals ruled that a school district had to enroll and provide services to a student who had profound mental retardation and cerebral palsy, was deaf and blind, had no communication skills, and experienced frequent convulsions (*Timothy W. v. Rochester, New Hampshire School District*, 1989). The court found that Congress intended schools to educate all students, especially those who have the greatest limitations.

In recognition of the fact that some state and local education agencies have not chosen to provide an education to any child under the age of 6 (the typical age for starting first grade), Congress qualified the zero-reject rule in two ways. First, it provided (in Part B of IDEA) that the rule applies to all state and local educational agencies when all children with disabilities reach age 6. Second, it made it optional for a state or local agency to educate children ages birth through 2 years (infants and toddlers, to whom Part C applies) and 3 through 5 years (to whom Part B applies).

One of the most controversial issues within the zero-reject principle relates to discipline and school safety. Many educational agencies have wanted to expel students whose behavior causes discipline problems or violates schools' codes of conduct. On the one hand, state, local, and federal policies seek to create safe schools. "Zero-tolerance" policies, the federal Gun-Free Schools Zone Act of 1994, and the No Child Left Behind Act of 2000 favor a policy of safe schools. On the other hand, the zero-reject principle favors a policy of educating all students with disabilities, including those whose behaviors create unsafe conditions. Clearly, educators and parents must find ways to be partners in implementing the zero-reject principle. IDEA's discipline provisions govern a student's rights but not how educators and parents become partners in meeting the joint challenges of disability and discipline.

IDEA strikes a balance between school safety and the zero-reject principle. It requires the LEA to determine whether the student's behavior, for which the agency is disciplining the student, is a manifestation of the student's disability. The question is: Did the student's disability cause, or does it have a direct and substantial relationship to, the student's behavior? If the student's behavior is not a manifestation of the disability (the disability does not cause the behavior), *as a general rule*, the school may discipline the student in the same ways and to the same extent that it disciplines students who do not have disabilities. However, the school may not entirely terminate services to a student whom it has suspended or expelled; this is the no-cessation rule. Figure 6–3 further describes IDEA's discipline provisions.

Educators have the following rights and expectations under the zero-reject principle:

■ To be safe
■ To be a member of decision-making teams
■ To participate in a manifestation determination hearing
■ To benefit from comprehensive programs, such as schoolwide positive behavior support, to address problem behavior

Note how educators' rights and expectations support the students' education and carry out the zero-reject principle.

Implications for Family-Professional Partnerships.

Clearly, parents want to ensure that their children with disabilities not only will be enrolled in public schools but also will be secure in their placement. When students with disabilities teeter on the line between attending school and being suspended or expelled, typically the whole family is vulnerable to exclusion. Parents generally do not want to invest time and energy in advocating that their child be permitted to attend school; rather, they want to know that their child with a disability will not be excluded because of the challenges associated with the disability. When students are

excluded from school, often at least one of their parents is excluded from work or from other commitments that they have during the day. When parents are excluded from work, they are also excluded from the opportunity to economically support their family.

Some schools resort to suspension and expulsion rather than implement comprehensive, schoolwide positive behavior support (Sugai, Sprague, Horner, & Walker, 2000; Turnbull et al., 2002). Families report being frustrated when teachers call them to pick up their child when, in fact, the teachers have not developed the competencies to teach appropriate behavior and to minimize problem behavior. A mother commented on this situation as follows:

> The school is calling me to see if I could pick K up because the "aide is nervous". . . that's exactly what they said—"the aide is nervous" and [K's teacher] wants to do a lot of work. Ya know, and I couldn't believe that the school was calling me. And I told them no—first of all I asked them, "Is she okay? Is she ill?" "She's not ill." "Did she hit anybody?" "She didn't hit anybody." "Well, what are you telling me?". . . I said, "No, she needs to stay in school." (Wang, Mannan, Poston, Turnbull, & Summers, 2004)

Nondiscriminatory Evaluation

Background Problems. It has not always been easy for schools to determine whether a student has a disability, much less what kind of education to provide to mitigate the disability's effects. Too often in the past, evaluations were simply not refined enough to identify a disability or its educational consequences. The result was that schools often excluded students from special education who should have been included, or placed students into special education programs that were not likely to benefit them.

Unhappily, there was another problem. For many years, the tests that schools administered arguably discriminated against students who were from culturally and linguistically diverse backgrounds. Indeed, some courts ruled that the tests were inherently discriminatory (*Larry P. v. Riles*, 1979), while other courts found that the tests, on the whole, were not (*PASE v. Hannon*, 1980). Although IDEA does not reach any findings of fact about the tests themselves, it does acknowledge that many students from culturally and linguistically diverse backgrounds have been placed in special education (20 U.S.C. Sec. 1400 (c) (11) and (12)). Often the disproportionate placement occurred because there are not enough safeguards to (1) protect against and possible bias in the tests or in educators' testing procedures and test interpretations, and (2) ensure that the students do

FIGURE 6–3
IDEA Discipline Provisions

The "Stay Put" Rule
- As a general rule, the student has a "stay put" right to remain in his or her current educational placement during the time any mediation, due process hearings or appeals, or court trials or appeals are being conducted, but the child's parents and the school may jointly agree to waive this right and secure a different placement (20 U.S.C. Sec. 1415(j)).
- The exception to the "stay put" rule is that a due process hearing officer may place the child in an appropriate interim alternative educational setting for not more than 45 days if the officer determines that the student's current placement is substantially likely to result in injury to the child or others (20 U.S.C. Sec. 1415(k)(3)). During an appeal, the student must stay in the interim alternative educational placement, unless the parents and school agree otherwise, and the hearing officer must expedite the hearing (20 U.S.C. Sec. 1415(k)(4)).

Placement in Alternative Educational Settings
- There is a new "Case by Case" Rule—School personnel may consider "any unique circumstances on a case-by-case basis" when determining whether to change a student's placement because the student violated a "code of student conduct" (20 U.S.C. Sec. 1415(k)(1)(A)). (IDEA does not define "unique circumstances.")
- The previous "Ten Day Rule" remains—School personnel may remove a student from his or her current placement to an interim alternative educational placement for not more than 10 consecutive school days in that same school year for separate violations of a code of student conduct (20 U.S.C. Sec. 1415(k)(1)(B)).
- The previous "No Cessation" rule remains—School personnel may apply to the student with a disability the same discipline, for more than 10 schools days, that it applies to students without disabilities, but only if they determine that the student's behavior was not a manifestation of the student's disability; and the school must still continue to provide free appropriate public education to the student, albeit in an interim alternative educational setting (20 U.S.C. Sec. 1415(k)(1)(C)), and must provide a functional behavioral assessment (FBA), and behavioral intervention services and modifications, that are designed to address the student's behavior so that it does not occur again (20 U.S.C. Sec. 1415(k)(1)(D)).
- The "Manifestation" rule is different—The local educational agency, parents, and IEP team members must determine if
    # the student's conduct "was caused by, or had a direct and substantial relationship to" the student's disability (the "relationship to" language is new) (20 U.S.C. Sec. 1415(k)(E)), or
    # the conduct was the "direct result of the local educational agency's failure to implement the (student's) IEP" (the "direct result" language is more stringent than previous law) (20 U.S.C. Sec. 1415(k)(E)).
- The consequences of the "Manifestation Determination" are different – If the behavior is a manifestation, the IEP team must either (20 U.S.C. Sec. 1415(k)(1)(F))
    # conduct a functional behavioral assessment (FBA) and implement a behavioral intervention plan (BIP) (there is no provision about positive behavioral interventions and supports) or
    # review and modify, if appropriate, and re-implement any BIP
    # return the student to his or her original educational setting unless the school and parents agree to change the student's placement as part of the modification of the student's BIP, and
- The three exceptions to these rules remain basically unchanged – The local educational agency may remove the student to an interim alternative educational setting for not more than 45 school days, without regard to whether the behavior is a manifestation of disability, if the student (20 U.S.C. Sec. 1415(1)(G))
    # carries or possesses a weapon to or at school, on school premises, or to or at a school function, or
    # knowingly possesses or uses illegal drugs, or sells or solicits the sale of a controlled substance while at school, on school premises, or at a school function, or
    # has inflicted serious bodily injury on another person while at school, on school premises, or at a school function

Consideration of Positive Behavioral Interventions
- If a student's behavior impedes his or her learning or the learning of other children, the IEP team must consider the use of positive behavioral interventions and supports, and other strategies, to address the student's behavior (20 U.S.C. Sec. 1414(d)(3)).
- But there is no similar requirement that the school must consider positive behavioral interventions and supports if the student is subjected to school discipline, only that the school must carry out an FBA and develop a BIP (which may include, at the IEP team's discretion, positive or other behavioral interventions) (20 U.S.C. Sec. 1415(k)(1)(F)).

have a disability that requires special education intervention. These safeguards are the essence of IDEA's principle of nondiscriminatory evaluation.

Purposes and Provisions of the Principle.
The principle is that each student is entitled to a fair, unbiased evaluation to determine whether he or she has a disability and, if so, the nature of special education and related services that the student needs. We discuss the evaluation requirements in detail in chapter 11. At this point, we identify the four major dimensions of evaluation that IDEA addresses and an example of one of the requirements within each category:

■ *Breadth of the evaluation*—Include more than one test.
■ *Procedures*—Use assessments that are validated for the specific purpose for which they are used.
■ *Timing*—Re-evaluate the student at least every 3 years (unless the parents and school agree to waive the re-evaluation), or more frequently if the educational and related services needs of the child, including the child's improved academic achievement and functional performance, warrant it, or the student's parent and school agree to more frequent re-evaluation.
■ *Interpretation of the evaluation data*—Ensure that a group of persons consisting of educators and parents interprets evaluation data.

The principle of nondiscriminatory evaluation creates a process through which educators and families may understand the student's needs and strengths and then use the evaluation to provide the student with a free appropriate public education. Notice that the principle creates a way for educators and families to evaluate the student; nondiscriminatory evaluation provides opportunities for professionals and parents to be partners. IDEA requires schools to give notice to the parents whenever it wants to evaluate the student (whether for the first or any other time) and to get the parents' consent for each evaluation before conducting it and before placing the student into or out of special education (unless the student is graduating from high school or aging out at age 21).

Remember that students' rights create educators' duties, but educators have to benefit from IDEA or else the law and the nondiscriminatory evaluation principle will not result in fair and unbiased evaluations that are useful for deciding how and where to educate the student. Educators' rights and expectations with respect to this principle of fairness are as follows:

■ To obtain evaluations that provide a relevant basis for appropriate curriculum, instruction, and assessment

■ To have their observations and classroom-based assessments considered as part of the evaluation data
■ To participate on the evaluation team to make sure that results are helpful for planning curriculum, instruction, and assessment

Implications for Family-Professional Partnerships. The nondiscriminatory evaluation of students provides the foundation for all other education decision making (Turnbull & Turnbull, 2000). Fair procedures are presumed to produce fair results. "The importance of accurate, fair, and comprehensive educational evaluations is viewed from a domino perspective. That is, if the eligibility evaluation is flawed, the placement and resulting special education services are likely to be inappropriate" (Fiedler, 2000, p. 76).

It is important for educators and parents to work together to ensure that the evaluation will lead to sound decision making. Because technical terms and difficult concepts are involved in evaluations, it is essential for schools to communicate with parents in clear and understandable language. Chapter 11 will provide you a strong foundation for building successful partnerships with parents.

Appropriate Education

Background Problems. Even when students with disabilities were admitted to schools and evaluated fairly, there were no assurances that they would benefit. In enacting IDEA in 1975, Congress found that more than one half of all children and youth with disabilities did not receive appropriate educational services and thus did not have full and equal educational opportunity. Even though students with disabilities were admitted to school, many were still functionally excluded. They attended classes, but often the classes did not benefit them. Thus, they were excluded from the function of the school, namely, to educate students. To respond to these problems, IDEA established the appropriate education principle.

Major Purposes and Provisions of the Principle. The principle is that schools must tailor education to the student's individual needs and capacities and thereby benefit the student. These twin demands—*individualization* and *benefit*—are satisfied when professionals and parents (and students, when appropriate) partner with each other in developing and carrying out an appropriate, individualized education for the student. A student between the ages of 6 and 21 years is entitled to an individualized education program (IEP). When the child is between the ages of birth and 3 years, the child and family are entitled to an individualized family services plan

(IFSP). When the child is between the ages of 3 and 6, the IFSP may serve as the IEP or the child may receive an IEP that replaces the IFSP.

The IEP and IFSP set out the type and extent of special education and related services that the child (and family, the case of an IFSP) will receive from the school. You will learn about the specific requirements for IFSP/IEP content, participants, and time lines in chapter 12. For now, recognize that the IFSP and IEP essentially specify the content that the student will be taught (curriculum), how the student will be taught (instructional strategies), how the student's progress will be determined (assessment), and where the student will be educated (placement in the least restrictive environment). Parents are members of the IFSP and IEP teams and have the right to be full-fledged educational decision makers.

Educators' rights and expectations pertaining to the principle of appropriate education are as follows:

- To seek and expect to have reliable allies for instruction
- To secure guidance related to curriculum and instructional modifications and supports
- To be a member of the IFSP/IEP team
- To expect that the school will comply with the required participants and components of an IFSP/IEP
- To read a copy of the IFSP/IEP

Implications for Family-Professional Partnerships. IDEA sets out both a process (required meetings) and documents (IEP and IFSP) that, together, define the nature and extent of the special education and related services that each student will receive. Clearly, the implications for family-professional partnerships are vast. Chapter 9 teaches you the communication skills to use when developing the IFSP/IEP. Chapter 12 teaches you how to be an active participant in the meetings and how to develop the IFSP/IEP document. Figure 6–4 provides a glimpse into a highly successful IEP meeting in addressing the needs of a high school student. The process of developing and implementing IFSPs/IEPs provides countless opportunities to reap benefits from a partnership approach. Nowhere are partnerships more important than in implementing the principle of appropriate education.

Least Restrictive Environment

Background Problems. Historically, local educational agencies segregated children with disabilities from their age-appropriate peers who did not have disabilities. As Congress put it in 1975 when setting out its findings of fact in IDEA, students with disabilities did not have opportunities or rights to attend school with students who did

FIGURE 6–4

Advocacy Partners: Infusing Advocacy Into an IEP Conference

Greg Motley, a high school freshman who qualified for IDEA benefits, simply could not stay seated during class, keep his hands to himself, take tests in the same room as other students, or move from the "all-F (failing)" tier of his class into a "passing grade" tier. At least he couldn't until his IEP team decided that he could and that the team would transform *could* into *would* and then into *will*.

Greg himself was the team leader. He acknowledged that he needed various kinds of help "to get better, to do better." His mother Sherry, his teachers Stephen D. Kroeger and Donna Owens at Turpin High School in the Forest Hills School District in suburban Cincinnati, other teachers, and administrators at his school were his team players.

Together but following Greg's lead, they agreed on a vision for Greg. It was more than staying in his seat and so on; it was that Greg would work outdoors, perhaps as a forester, perhaps in other jobs. This vision drove the team to specify goals and objectives that would be part of Greg's IEP and would help move him toward his vision. The authentic buy-in from vision, goals, and objectives that Greg, Sherry, Stephen, and Donna made then shaped the response of the rest of the Turpin High School staff.

When Greg's IEP team meeting convened, there were a total of 15 adults, plus Greg, of course. Greg's requests—to take tests in a room by himself, to have certain kinds of teachers and to avoid other kinds of teachers, to receive counseling to improve his social behavior, and through all of those ways to boost his grades—might have seemed unreasonable to some educators, but not to those at Turpin High School. Why? Because, as Stephen put it, "The IEP is a useless document unless the student buys it." And if the student buys it, then, as Donna said, "We (are) anchored by our vision."

Stephen and Donna created a team. They advocated with Greg and Sherry when the other educators showed up for Greg's IEP. Stephen advocated on the basis that Greg owns his life and his IEP, and Donna on the basis that "we" are anchored by a common vision.

Partners? Yes: Greg, Sherry, Stephen, Donna, and others. Advocacy? Yes: Based on ownership and vision that drives goals and objectives. Results: Yes: No more F grades, a consistent string of C grades, and successful social integration.

not have disabilities. Schools assigned students with disabilities to special school districts, placed them into buildings or classrooms where the only students were those with disabilities, and otherwise physically separated them from their peers without disabilities. All too often, these settings and programs limited the students' abilities and opportunities to learn and to use their education outside of school. To remedy this problem, IDEA enacted the principle of the least restrictive environment.

Major Purposes and Provisions of the Principle. The principle is that schools must educate students with a disability alongside students who do not have disabilities to the "maximum extent appropriate" for each student with a disability. IDEA gives meaning to the concept of "appropriate" by providing that ". . . special classes, separate schooling, or other removal of children with disabilities from the regular education environment (may) occur(s) only when the nature or severity of the disability of a child is such that education in regular classes with the use of supplementary aids and services cannot be achieved satisfactorily" (IDEA, 20 U.S.C. Sec. 1412 (a) (5)).

Just how much removal does IDEA allow, and to what kinds of settings? Schools may offer a continuum of placements, from less to more restrictive (e.g., general education classrooms to home-based, hospital-based, or institutional placements) and may place students in one of these atypical (separate or segregated) settings only if the setting also provides an appropriate education.

Thus, this principle creates a presumption in favor of educating students with a disability with their peers who do not have disabilities. IDEA implements this presumption in two ways. First, the student's IEP must describe any extent to which a student may not participate in general education (IDEA, 20 U.S.C. Sec. 1414 (d) (1) (V)). Second, the IEP must describe the special education related ser-vices, supplementary aides and services, program modifications, and other supports that will enable the student to make progress in the general curriculum and to participate in extracurricular and other school activities (IDEA, 20 U.S.C. Sec. 1414 (d) (1) (VI)).

Because professionals and parents alike are members of the IFSP and IEP teams that make the placement decisions, the principle creates an opportunity for partnerships in determining the least restrictive environment for the student.

The principle of least restrictive environment also affords rights to teachers. These rights include the following:

- To have a team approach in providing academic and social benefits to students
- To experience the collaborative benefits of related services and supplementary aides and services in terms of

having colleagues provide assistance in educating students with disabilities
- To have the student's IFSP/IEP team plan program modifications and supports to enable teachers to successfully teach students with disabilities

Implications for Family-Professional Partnerships. As you learned in chapter 5, many parents have been political advocates and have sued schools to secure inclusive services for their child (Turnbull & Turnbull, 2000). One of these cases, *Oberti v. Board of Education of the Borough of Clementon School District* (1993), imposed on schools an affirmative obligation to educate students with disabilities in general education classrooms with the use of supplementary aids and services and to do so before considering more restrictive educational placements. See Figure 6–5 for Mr. Oberti's perspective.

Procedural Due Process

Background Problems. Traditionally, educators had nearly unchallenged authority to operate schools on their own terms. For students with disabilities, that kind of authority too often resulted in:

- *Exclusion*—violation of the principle of zero reject.
- *Misclassification*—violation of nondiscriminatory evaluation.
- *Denial of a genuine individualized education*—violation of appropriate education.
- *Segregated placements*—violation of least restrictive environment.

Moreover, students and their parents traditionally lacked the right to protest educators' actions. As you learned in chapter 5, parents were sometimes obliged to play the roles of service developers, recipients of professionals' decisions, and political advocates. The professionals' power, however, was inconsistent with the traditional notion of American law that those who are in public office must be held accountable to the public for their decisions.

Major Purposes and Provisions of the Principle. Professionals and parents should be accountable to each other. The principle of due process codifies the historic rule of governmental accountability to the public and the constitutional principle of fair dealing between the government and the governed (as set out in the due process clause of the Fourteenth Amendment). IDEA requires schools to provide parents with ample notice concerning the actions that they want to take, or do not want to take, with respect to the child (IDEA, 20 U.S.C. Sec. 1415 (b) and (c)). It also entitles parents to exercise

FIGURE 6–5
My Voice: My Son Rafael Will Succeed

We, the parents of children with disabilities that have had the longest amount of experience working with them from birth, know the way they learn. In my family's case, my son was doing wonderfully, growing and learning in a fully inclusive environment until kindergarten when we hit the brick wall set up by an outdated system. We found that the law is not being taken seriously and that for children with severe cognitive and/or physical disabilities, the path is already written and decided—segregated classes, often very far from their hometown, or if pressed by parents, dumping in the regular class with no supports.

The demands on a child with a disability are not so extraordinary when a group of knowledgeable professionals, together with the parents, have a genuine desire to do what is correct and meet to discuss the abilities, strengths and special needs a child may have as they develop a *fully supported inclusive educational plan*. If that is done instead of "dumping" a child in the regular classroom, and if it is done on an ongoing basis, none of the "robbing" of the rest of the students will occur.

The Individuals with Disabilities Education Act, which proclaims that all children with disabilities have the right to a "free and appropriate education" in the "least restrictive environment," is very clear and still, for too many years school bureaucrats have walked all over it. They feel that based on an IQ score they have the right to label, classify, and ship out children with disabilities to a distant segregated location.

Our son, Rafael A. Oberti, went through six different placements by the time he was seven years old and there would have been many more had we followed the "professionals'" recommendations. Looking back, our only regret is not to have taken charge of the situation sooner than we did. Please remember his name, because he will succeed and he will make a great contribution in this world. Perhaps he already has, certainly in our lives.

Source: Oberti, C. (1993 September). A parent's perspective. *Exceptional Parent,* 18–21. Reprinted with the expressed consent and approval of *Exceptional Parent,* a monthly magazine for parents and families of children with disabilities and special health care needs. Subscription cost is $28 per year for 12 issues. Call 1-800-247-8080. Offices at 120 State Street, Hackensack, NJ 07601.

two different ways for holding schools accountable. (These techniques also are available to schools, but they use them only rarely.) The Supreme Court has ruled in *Schaffer v. Weast* (2005) that the parents have the burden of proof to show that the student's initial IEP does not comply with IDEA because it does not offer the child a chance to benefit from the education the school is offering. (We discuss this decision in Chapter 12 (p. 257) when we discuss what IDEA expects parents and educators to do when they are developing an IEP.)

The first technique is the *due process hearing*. Parents or schools may require each other to go to a hearing before an impartial hearing officer, who serves as a judge to adjudicate the parents' and teachers' rights and responsibilities. The parents or schools may challenge each other's actions in providing, or failing to provide, the student with a free appropriate public education in the least restrictive environment. The hearing is a mini-trial, with the parents and school professionals each having the right to introduce evidence, present and cross-examine witnesses, be represented by a lawyer, and obtain a written or electronic record of the hearing. Parents also have the right to have their child present. Initially, the hearing is held in front of an individual called the due process hearing officer. The losing party may appeal an adverse judgment to a federal or state trial court, go to trial on the case, and then appeal still further to higher courts, including a state supreme court or the United States Supreme Court.

There are two major disadvantages to the due process provisions. One is that they can cause schools to practice defensive education, being concerned only with protecting themselves from any form of legal liability rather than with providing an appropriate education. The other is that they can create an adversarial process, involving huge financial and emotional costs to the parties and siphoning schools' and parents' resources from their major duty to educate and care for the child (Fiedler, 2000; Lanigan, Audette, Dreier, & Kobersy, 2000). That is the perspective one parent expressed:

It was torture, I'm sure it [the prospect of a hearing] was torture for them, too, because I made it miserable. You know, their misery increased every time mine did. . . . Actually it [the dispute] was settled a week before the hearing, and [the school] did everything it was supposed to do. But it took 2 years. And for that 2 years, I look back, and I wonder how I ever lived through it. It's right there in your face at the forefront of everything, all day, every day, and sleeping at night and the whole thing. It just takes over your life. (Lake & Billingsley, 2000, p. 248)

The second technique is to use alternative dispute resolution procedures. One procedure involves mediation

(20 U.S.C. Sec. 1415(e)). Mediation occurs when a disinterested third party (the mediator) meets with the parents and the school personnel to identify the issures and reach an agreement on how to resolve them. The other procedure involves a "resolution session" (20 U.S.C. Sec. 1415(f)(1)B)) at which the parent and school personnel meet with a representative of the local educatioal agency who has authority to make decisions on behalf of the agency. The parents and agency may waive either or both of these procedures and go straight to due process (34 Code of Federal Regulations Secs. 300.510).

Fortunately, the numbers of due process hearings and mediations are relatively low; there were 3,020 due process hearings in 2000 (approximately 500 fewer than in 1996) (U.S. General Accounting Office, 2003). This means that about 5 due process hearings were held per 10,000 students with disabilities. Another national study reported that the total number of due process hearings in 1998 represented less than 0.02% of all parents of students with disabilities and that a similar percent of mediation hearings were held (Feinberg, Beyer, & Moses, 2002).

It is important that IDEA confers rights and expectations on educators, so that they too can present their "case" when they disagree with parents. Educators' rights and expectations related to due process include the following:

- To participate in mediation with the support of the school in order to reach win-win solutions
- To participate in due process hearings with the support of the school in order to have one's point of view fully considered by the due process hearing officer

Implications for Family-Professional Partnerships. IDEA's due process provisions seek mutual accountability. They make it possible for parents to know what educators propose to do (the notice requirements) and to protest those proposals through mediation and hearings or to consent to them. They also make it possible for educators to seek a hearing to protest the parents' refusal to consent to a proposal that educators believe will benefit the child. The purpose of mutual accountability is to ensure that the student receives a free appropriate public education in the least restrictive environment. When educators and parents have an opportunity to review each other, the likelihood of better decisions increases.

Parent Participation

Background Problems. As you may have concluded from reading chapter 5, schools often have not shared information with parents and have excluded them from educational decision-making processes, causing parents and students often to be recipients of educators' decisions. One parent characterized parent-school relationships, especially when the child first enters special education, as follows:

> You're sort of left out there hanging. It's all new to you. . . and you're just lost. Just lost. You don't have a clue as to why your child is having a problem generally. You don't have a clue where to go; you don't know what (your child's) need(s) are. (Lake & Billingsley, 2000, p. 245)

The principle of parent and student participation challenges educators and parents to cast off the outdated role of parents as recipients of educators' decisions and to take on roles in which professionals and parents, and even students, become partners in making and carrying out decisions about the students' education.

Major Purposes and Provisions of the Principle. The principle is that parents should participate in making decisions about a student's education. This principle legitimizes parents and students as educational decision makers and enables parents, students, and professionals to establish partnerships with each other.

In addition to the opportunities for parent and student participation inherent in the other five IDEA principles, the principle of parent and student participation creates even more rights for parents and students to be empowered decision makers. Two additional IDEA requirements in this regard include the following:

- Parents have access to school records concerning the student and control who has access to those records (IDEA, 20 U.S.C. Sec. 1417 (c)).
- Parents must be invited to participate on state and local special education advisory committees to ensure that their perspectives are incorporated into policy and program decisions (IDEA, 20 U.S.C. Sec. 1412 (21)).

Figure 6–6 provides tips, based on IDEA requirements, related to parents' access to their child's educational records.

Just as IDEA seeks partnerships between parents and educators, so it also confers the following rights and expectations on educators:

- To expect all colleagues at team meetings to protect the confidentiality of information about students
- To benefit from the contributions that parents make on local and state advisory committees
- To form partnerships with parents so that parents are helpful in providing suggestions about a free appropriate public education for the child

Implications for Family-Professional Partnerships. The principle of parent and student participation pervades all aspects of IDEA. In chapters 9

FIGURE 6–6

Tips for Providing Access to Parents of Their Children's Educational Records

- Comply with parents' requests to read their child's educational records within 45 days of the request.

- Interpret or explain the records to the parents.

- Give copies of their child's records to parents who request it.

- Provide copies at no cost to the parents, if they cannot afford the cost of copies.

- Listen to parents who believe that the educational records contain inaccurate or misleading information. If they request that information in the records be changed, determine if you agree with their position. If you do agree, make the change in the records. If you do not agree, recognize that the parents may initiate a due process hearing to resolve the conflict of opinion.

FIGURE 6–7

Four IDEA Outcomes for Students

- **Equality of opportunity**—having the same opportunities in life as people without disabilities.

- **Full participation**—having opportunities to be included in all aspects of their community and to be protected from segregation based solely on their disability.

- **Independent living**—having opportunities to fully participate in decisions and to make choices about how to live their lives.

- **Economic self-sufficiency**—being provided with opportunities to engage fully in income-producing work or in unpaid work that contributes to a household or community.

through 13, we discuss in detail how parents and professionals can be partners in carrying out the principle.

IDEA Outcomes

As we have just pointed out, IDEA establishes elaborate processes for educating a student and creating family-professional partnerships.

To understand IDEA's student-related outcomes, consider what it says about disability and the rights of people with disabilities:

Disability is a natural part of the human experience and in no way diminishes the right of individuals to participate in or contribute to society. Improving educational results for children with disabilities is an essential element of our national policy of ensuring equality of opportunity, full participation, independent living, and economic self-sufficiency for individuals with disabilities. (20 U.S.C., Sec. 1400 (c) (1))

IDEA has four general long-term outcomes related to students, as we describe in Figure 6–7.

What is the evidence concerning the extent to which these four outcomes are being achieved? Data are available on three indicators: high school completion, postschool employment, and overall satisfaction with life.

The first indicator is high school completion. Slightly over one quarter of all students with disabilities graduated with a high school diploma from 1996 to 1998 (National Council on Disability, 2000). Although the overall national dropout rate is approximately 12%, students with disabilities experience a much higher dropout rate

(Kaufman, Kwon, Klein, & Chapman, 1999). The dropout rate for students with learning disabilities ranges from 17% to 42%, whereas the dropout rate for students with emotional or behavior disorders is even higher, ranging from 21% to 64% (National Center for Education Statistics, 1993, 1997, 1999). The group of students who have the highest dropout rate consists of males from backgrounds characterized by racial diversity and low income (National Center for Education Statistics, 2000).

The second indicator is postschool employment. The employment rate for individuals with disabilities is 49 percentage points lower than for people without disabilities (National Organization on Disability, 2000). Although approximately four fifths of all people without disabilities are employed, only about one third of individuals with disabilities are employed. The employment rate drops to 19% for individuals with more severe disabilities. Students from diverse racial backgrounds and from low-income families experience greater challenges in gaining employment than their counterparts (National Council on Disability, 2000).

The third and final indicator of long-term outcomes is overall satisfaction with life. Two thirds of individuals without disabilities are very satisfied with life, whereas one third of individuals with disabilities are very satisfied with life (National Organization on Disability, 2000).

Clearly, IDEA has made a difference, but there is room for the schools to improve by having high expectations for students with disabilities and ensuring their access to the general education curriculum in the regular classroom to the maximum extent possible (IDEA, 20 U.S.C. Sec. 1400(c) (5) (A)) and by strengthening parents' role and responsibility and ensuring that families have meaningful opportunities to participate in their children's education at school and at home (IDEA, 20 U.S.C. Sec. 1400 (c) (5) (B)). IDEA has the potential to be a vehicle for still better student educational results and long-term outcomes and to be a catalyst for America's public and private sectors to support people with disabilities to achieve equality of opportunity, full participation, independent living, and economic self-sufficiency.

GENERAL EDUCATION REFORM: NO CHILD LEFT BEHIND ACT

In signing the No Child Left Behind Act (NCLB) of 2001 (which amends the Elementary and Secondary Education Act of 1965), George W. Bush put his approval on efforts begun by his father and by Bill Clinton to set goals for America's students (Goals 2000; Improving America's Schools Act, 1994) and to reform our nation's schools. President Bush echoed the efforts of his predecessors but used more recent evidence to support his thesis, and the justification for NCLB, that "too many children in America are segregated by low expectations, illiteracy, and self-doubt. In a constantly changing world that is demanding increasingly complex skills from its workforce, children are literally being left behind" (Bush, 2001a). As the president put it, "We have a genuine national crisis. More and more, we are divided into two nations. One that reads, and one that doesn't. One that dreams, and one that doesn't" (Bush, 2001b). By acknowledging that decades of efforts to improve schools for all students have fallen substantially short, the president challenged the nation to engage in more aggressive school reform. Furthermore, Congress, in a bipartisan fashion, enacted NCLB to respond to the needs of all students, their families, educators, and taxpayers.

Congress intended NCLB to benefit all students, including those with disabilities and those who are exceptionally gifted, in kindergarten through 12th grade. IDEA allows a student with a disability to remain in school until age 21. If a student is covered by IDEA, NCLB applies until the student graduates from school or leaves school permanently. NCLB does not apply to infant and toddler programs operated under Part C of IDEA, but it does provide incentives for schools to develop standards and to provide early literacy curricula at the preschool level.

Figure 6–8 describes NCLB's six principles for school reform. Just as we did with IDEA, we will describe (1) the background problems that each principle is intended to address, (2) the major purposes and provisions of each principle, and (3) the implications of each principle for family-professional partnerships. Where appropriate, we will connect NCLB to IDEA (as reauthorized in 2004).

FIGURE 6–8
Six Principles of NCLB

Accountability for results. Reward school districts and schools that improve student academic achievement and reform those that do not.

School safety. Acknowledge that all children need a safe environment in which to learn and achieve. Require states to report on school safety to the public and districts to establish a plan for keeping school safe and drug free.

Parental choice. Grant parents the right to transfer their child from a "failing" or "unsafe" school to a better and safer one.

Teacher quality. Acknowledge that learning depends on teaching; students achieve when they have good teachers. Condition federal aid on states' agreement to hire "highly qualified" teachers.

Scientifically based methods of teaching. Acknowledge that teaching and learning depend not just on highly qualified teachers but also on the teachers' use of scientifically based methods of teaching. Grant federal funds to states and school districts that use only those methods.

Local flexibility. Encourage local solutions for local problems and do not hold schools accountable for student outcomes unless the schools also can use federal funds to respond to local problems in particularly local ways.

Accountability for Results

Background Problems. The U.S. Department of Education has reported that "nearly 70 percent of inner city fourth graders are unable to read at a basic level on national reading tests. Our high school seniors trail students in Cyprus and South Africa on international math tests. And nearly a third of our college freshmen find that they must take a remedial course before they are able to even begin regular college-level courses" (U. S. Department of Education, a 2001). Further, beginning with the enactment of the Elementary and Secondary Education Act in 1965, Congress has created hundreds of programs to address school problems. Despite the expenditures of $120 billion a year by 39 different agencies within the Department of Education, results have been discouraging.

- Average reading scores for 17-year-old students have not improved since the 1970s.
- In 1998, 60% of the nation's 12th graders were reading below proficiency.

- Only one third of all fourth graders can read at a proficient level.
- Although the highest performing students have improved in their abilities, the lowest performing have declined in their abilities (U.S. Department of Education, 2001, 2002a).

Major Purposes and Provisions of the Principle. The principle of accountability for results is that it is good public policy to reward states, school districts, and schools that improve student academic achievement in reading, mathematics, and other core academic subjects. Conversely, it is good public policy to punish the failure of low-performing schools to improve. To carry out this principle, NCLB makes it clear that one of its purposes is to "ensure that all children have a fair, equal, and significant opportunity to obtain a high-quality education and reach, at a minimum, proficiency on challenging state academic achievement standards and state academic assessments" (Title I, Sec. 1001). In particular, NCLB targets students who are immigrants and those whose first language is not English—those whom the law and practitioners call "limited English proficient"—so that they too may "develop high levels of academic achievement in English, and meet the same challenging State academic content and student academic achievement standards as all children are expected to meet" (Title III, Sec. 3102). To these ends, NCLB imposes various requirements on state and local education agencies.

NCLB requires each state to (1) establish academic standards in reading/language arts, math, and science for all students, (2) develop assessments to measure students' efficiency in meeting the standards, and (3) define adequate yearly progress for school districts and each school. To measure students' progress, NCLB requires each state, by the 2005–2006 school year, to test students annually in grades 3 through 8 in reading and math, and students in grades 10 through 12 at least once in reading and math. Beginning in the 2006–2007 school year, states must test students in science. Finally, every student will be assessed to meet state standards in reading/language arts, math, and science with proficiency by the end of the 2013–2014 school year.

In administering the state assessments, the state and schools must include at least 95% of all students (in the state and in each school). If the state or school does not include at least that percentage of its student population, it fails to meet an accountability standard known as adequate yearly progress (AYP). The state must disaggregate the assessment data according to subgroups of students; the subgroups are students with disabilities, those who are migrants, those who receive free and re-

duced-price lunches, those who have limited English-language usage, and those who belong to various racial/ethnic groups. The state must also disaggregate data according to students' gender. The state may set different targets for adequate yearly progress for each of these groups; if one subgroup does not make adequate yearly progress or if less than 95% of the students in a subgroup do not take the assessment, the state fails to make adequate yearly progress. So at least 95% of students with disabilities must participate in the assessments and demonstrate proficiency. IDEA provides that students with disabilities will participate, with accommodations and sometimes by alternate assessments, in NCLB assessments (IDEA, 20 U.S.C. Sec. 1412 (a) (16) (A) and 1414 (d) (1) (A) (VI)).

Students with disabilities must receive appropriate accommodations on this statewide assessment. An IEP committee must determine if each student with a disability is capable of taking the statewide assessment without accommodations or if accommodation or an alternate assessment will be needed. Assessment accommodations include any changes in testing materials or procedures that enable students with disabilities to perform at their level of proficiency. Alternate assessments are appropriate for students with significant cognitive disabilities who have a modified curriculum that has been deemed appropriate for them by the IEP committee (Browder & Spooner, 2003).

NCLB limits the number of alternate assessments that each school, school district, and state may use to compute students' and schools' adequate yearly progress. A school district may not count more than 1% of students' proficiency scores from alternative assessments in reading/language arts and in math. This ensures that schools do not use alternate assessments as a loophole to avoid having large numbers of students with disabilities meet the general curriculum standards.

NCLB requires states to hold each school district and each school accountable for the academic progress of its student body and annually to measure students' progress toward proficiency in reading/language arts and mathematics, so that all students will achieve proficiency in those subjects by the academic year 2013–2014.

NCLB requires each state to define the amount of adequate yearly progress toward proficiency in the core subjects that each school and school district must achieve. Each state must also set the minimum level of improvement, measurable by student performance on the annual assessments, that school districts and each school must achieve. Thus, the state determines the percentage of students who will score at a proficient level on the statewide assessment of these two subjects. The state develops a starting point based on the performance of its lowest achieving demographic group or of the lowest achieving schools in the state, whichever is higher. Then, the state sets the level of student achievement that a school must attain after 2 years in order to show adequate yearly progress. The state must raise the subsequent thresholds at least once every 3 years until, after 12 years (the 2013–2014 academic year), all students in the state achieve at the proficient level on state assessments in reading/language arts and math. These adequate yearly progress provisions apply to all school districts, all schools, and all students, including students with disabilities.

School districts and schools that are successful in meeting or exceeding the state proficiency standards will receive achievement awards from the state education agency. States may also use their NCLB federal funds to financially reward teachers in schools that receive academic achievement awards.

Each school district or school that does not make adequate yearly progress for 2 consecutive school years will be designated as "needing improvement." The state must take specific action to improve the district or school through the use of scientifically based instructional strategies. If the district or school continues not to make adequate yearly progress, it becomes subject to still further state oversight.

There are additional consequences for a "Title I" school. A Title I school is one in which more than 50% of its students are eligible for free school lunches; a student is eligible if the student's family meets the federal definition of poverty. Thus, a Title I school is one in which at least half of the students are from poor families.

NCLB provides for an action plan and a timetable when any Title I school fails to make adequate yearly progress.

■ If the school does not make adequate yearly progress for 2 consecutive years, the school district must identify that school as needing improvement and make sure that the school receives technical assistance to develop and carry out a plan to improve. Students in that school acquire the right to transfer from it to another public school in the same school district that has not been identified as needing to improve.

■ If the school fails to make adequate yearly progress for 3 years, it remains in "improvement" status, and the school district must continue to offer the transfer option to all students in the school. In addition, the Title I students may receive supplemental educational services, such as tutoring or remedial education, from a state-approved provider.

■ If the school fails to make adequate yearly progress for 4 years, the school district must take corrective actions to improve it. These include replacing staff or fully implementing a new curriculum. Title I students continue to have the option for transfer or supplementary services.

■ If the school fails to make adequate yearly progress for 5 years, the school district must take action to restructure the school, including converting it to a charter school (a public school that is free to operate independently of many of the school district's and state's regulations), replacing some or all of the faculty and administrators, or putting the school's operations into the hands of the state or a private entity that has a demonstrated record of school-improvement effectiveness.

Implications for Family-Professional Partnerships. The accountability principle will have massive effects on students with disabilities (Browder & Spooner, 2003; Ruppman, 2003). Because all students are included in NCLB, students with disabilities are expected to meet general education standards or at least demonstrate progress toward proficiency on state assessments that are based on the standards.

NCLB requires each school to report the results of each student's academic assessments to the student's parents. Among the assessment reports must be "diagnostic" reports. Parents will be able to use those evaluations in collaborating with teachers to design their children's individualized programs.

Schools are also required to inform parents about the performance of the whole school and their options if their child's school is not making adequate yearly progress. Schools must distribute annual report cards that enable parents, community citizens, and other concerned stakeholders to compare and contrast the performance of schools within their community and across the state. Parents are informed about their own child's performance relative to other students and about the performance of the whole student body in their child's school. Then, as you have previously learned, if a Title I school does not make adequate yearly progress for 2 consecutive years, parents may request that their child be transferred to another school in the same district that has not been identified as needing to improve. If their child's school does not make adequate yearly progress for 3 years, the parents are entitled to request that their child receive supplemental educational services, including tutoring and remedial education. The result is that NCLB empowers parents to ensure that their child makes adequate progress and achieves the expected educational goals.

School Safety

Background Problems. Are schools safe? Are the perceived as being unsafe? Unquestionably, the media coverage of tragedies such as the one at Columbine creates a sense that schools are unsafe (Garcia & Kennedy, 2003; Willert & Lenhardt, 2003). So, too, the nearly universal efforts of school districts to increase school security suggest that schools are unsafe (Garcia & Kennedy, 2003). Nearly every school is a site for bullying, teasing, verbal put-downs, harassment, clique-based exclusion, shoving, stealing, and fighting (Willert & Lenhardt, 2003); these behaviors also fuel the "unsafe schools" fire.

The question of whether schools are safe depends on the data, and the meaning of the data depends on one's perspective. Between 1997–1998 and 1999–2000, the year of the Columbine High School shootings, the number of school-associated violent deaths declined by 40% (National School Safety Center, 2000, cited in Garcia & Kennedy, 2003). Furthermore, between 1995–1996 and 1998–1999, violent deaths at school declined from 49 to 34—a reduction of 31% (U.S. Department of Education and U.S. Department of Justice, 2000). Nonfatal school crimes such as theft, sexual assault, and robbery declined from 144 to 101 per 1,000 students during 1992 to 1998. Also declining were the number of students who carried weapons to school or engaged in physical fights on school grounds (U.S. Department of Education and U.S. Department of Justice, 2000).

Nevertheless, in the year 2000 students between 12 and 18 years of age were victims of about 1.9 million crimes at school, including rape, sexual assault, robbery, and aggravated assault. Also in that year, about 29% of students in grades 9 through 12 reported that someone offered, sold, or gave them an illegal drug on school property (U.S. Department of Education, 2003). The majority of these crimes occurred in only 7% of the nation's schools, indicating that there is a critical mass of unsafe schools and that most schools are relatively safe.

Definition of Principle. The principle is that schools must be safe and drug- and alcohol-free in order to provide an effective context for teaching and learning. NCLB has two major strategies for addressing school safety. First, it provides funds to SEAs and LEAs to (1) prevent school-based violence and the illegal use of drugs, alcohol, and tobacco and (2) foster safe and drug-free teaching and learning environments. To qualify for funds, schools must:

- Address local needs as established by objective data.
- Be grounded in scientifically based prevention activities.

- Consult with parent, student, and community organizations.
- Measure and evaluate progress on a continuous basis.
- Establish a uniform system for reporting data to parents and other citizens.

The second major strategy relates to NCLB's requirement that parents can transfer their children from a dangerous school setting to a safe school setting. Parents of children who are victims of violent crimes at school or who attend "persistently dangerous schools" (as determined by the SEA) may choose to leave the school and attend a safer one. When a state identifies a school as being persistently dangerous, the state must notify parents of every student and offer them opportunities to transfer to a safe school. This is a parental choice provision, which is the third NCLB principle.

Under a different federal law, the Gun-Free Schools Zone Act, schools that receive federal money under NCLB must (1) expel for at least one year any student who brings a firearm to school or possesses a firearm in school and (2) report any such student to the criminal justice or juvenile justice system. Parents have no say about expulsion and reporting. There is no partnership opportunity here, only a duty the schools cannot avoid. The law applies to any student with a disability whose behavior is not a manifestation of the disability. If the behavior is a manifestation, however, IDEA's zero-reject rule comes into play (IDEA, 20 U.S.C. Sec. 1415 (k) (1) (E)).

Implications for Family-Professional Partnerships. There is no doubt that safe environments are better for teaching and learning. NCLB's approach to increasing school safety is to grant parents active decision-making roles. NCLB requires schools to involve parents in designing violence prevention and addictions prevention programs. It also requires schools to give parents full access to reports on the status of school safety and drug use among students. Both of these requirements give parents information and opportunities to contribute to safe school environments.

Parental Choice

Background Problems. "What's a parent to do?" is a fair question when some of America's schools fail to produce acceptable academic achievement results or when schools are found to be persistently dangerous. These two problems—academic underachievement and school violence—are the sources of NCLB's third principle, parental choice.

It seems that NCLB relies on the same strategy that IDEA proposed over 25 years earlier—parent participation to hold schools more accountable for providing an appropriate education.

Major Purposes and Provisions of the Principle.   One of NCLB's purposes is related to students' academic achievement but is specifically focused on their parents, namely, "affording parents substantial and meaningful opportunities to participate in the education of their children" (Title I, Sec. 1001(12)). Among those opportunities is the "transfer option" for good cause, and the good cause is the failure of a school to educate a student or to provide a safe environment for teaching and learning. Parents may enroll their Title I school child into another public school (including a charter school) in the district or, under limited circumstances, in another district. As a general rule, school districts must provide transportation for the transferring students. If a parent does not choose to transfer a child from a school that continues to fail to make adequate yearly progress or from an unsafe school, the child should not be penalized by that choice but should receive supplemental educational services in school. The transfer provisions theoretically increase parents' choice and thereby put pressure on the failing or unsafe schools to improve.

To provide alternatives to the existing public schools, NCLB provides funding to help charter schools pay for start-up costs, facilities, and other needs. Charter schools are public schools and must meet the same standards as other public schools, but they are chartered by parents and educators who organize them, specify their mission, and control their staffing and curriculum.

No parent can make an informed choice without information, so the principle adds requirements for schools periodically to report certain data to parents. Figure 6–9 summarizes NCLB's data-reporting and notice requirements.

NCLB also authorizes funding for Parental Assistance Information Centers. These centers provide support, training, and information to parents, professionals, and organizations that work with parents. Their goal is to increase parent-professional partnerships that will ultimately lead to improved achievement results for students.

Implications for Family-Professional Partnerships.   As an abstract principle, parent choice is appealing. After all, parents are legally responsible for their children until they reach the age of 18, and many thereafter remain financially and otherwise responsible for them, especially if they have disabilities. So, parents should be able to choose how to have their children educated.

FIGURE 6–9
NCLB Data-Reporting and Notice Requirements

- The first kind of data relates to the particular student. NCLB requires each school to measure each student's academic achievement in reading and math in each of grades 3 through 8 and at least once during grades 10 through 12 and to report the information to the student's parents.

- The second kind of data relates to the school as a whole. The parent gets a report card about the child's progress. This is the student report card. The parent also receives report about the overall achievement of students in that school, about the teacher's qualifications, and about school safety. This is the school report card.

- Each school must notify all parents (through the report cards) if their child is eligible to transfer to another school or district because (1) the student's present school or school district needs improvement, corrective action, or restructuring because of poor student outcomes in the assessments of academic achievement, (2) the school is "persistently dangerous," or (3) the student has been the victim of violent crime while on school grounds.

Two factors influence how much the principle will benefit families who have children with disabilities. First, parents must know about their choices (and NCLB requires educators to inform them), have the motivation to exercise the choices, have the skills to turn motives into actions, and have the resources to turn actions into reality (Turnbull & Turnbull, 2000). At this time, it is purely speculation just how many parents will choose different placements or supplemental services. It may be that neighborhoods and communities that are economically disadvantaged may have many, if not all, schools in a situation of not making adequate yearly progress. Thus there may be no schools in the vicinity that offer the alternatives that parents would want for their children.

Second, a parent's choice may be limited by the child's disability. The special education programs in schools making adequate progress may be full; it may be difficult for them to accommodate more students. A director of special education in an urban school district described this situation as follows:

Let's say that we get kids in our life skills program, it's our severely handicapped program. The chances are that that class is already full in many schools—that's the way it starts

So the parent's applied there under school choice, been accepted, now we go, "oops—that was a life skills kid." Then we have to find a high performing school near the one she asked for, so you get transportation patterns that didn't exist and the cost of transportation is huge. (Nagle & Crawford, 2004, p. 33)

In urban districts, transfer from one school to another may be easier than in rural districts where there may be only one elementary school, one middle school, and one senior high school.

The fundamental challenge is to convert the parental choice principle into a reality for parents and students with disabilities, especially those who also face daunting challenges related to poverty. Ultimately, the parental choice principle may help hold schools accountable because they may have a declining enrollment if many parents choose to transfer their children.

Teacher Quality

Background Problems. There is a shortage of qualified teachers; the country's schools face challenges of quantity and quality, including in special education (Abt Associates, 2002; U.S. Department of Education, 2002b). According to the U.S. Department of Education data on general education teachers, only 41% of eighth-grade math teachers majored in math in college. In history and physical science, more than half of the country's students are taught by an instructor who never studied the subject in any concentrated way; more than 4 million students in physics, chemistry, or history are taught by underqualified teachers. Data reveal that 92% of special education teachers are fully certified for their main teaching assignment (Carlson, Brauen, Klein, Schroll, & Willig, 2002). This number drops to 71% for special education teachers with less than 3 years of teaching experience. Among all teachers of students with emotional disorders, 10% have an emergency certificate. That percentage is twice the rate for teachers in any other category of exceptionality.

Definition of Principle. The principle is that learning depends on teaching, and student outcomes depend on teacher competency. It follows that student learning and outcomes will remain unsatisfactory unless there is a sufficient number of highly qualified teachers. Accordingly, one of NCLB's purposes is to provide grants to state and local educational agencies "to increase student achievement through strategies such as improving teacher and principal quality and increasing the number of highly qualified teachers in the classroom and highly qualified principals and assistant principals in the schools" (Title II, Sec. 2101).

NCLB advances this principle by requiring every state to develop plans to ensure that all teachers of core academic subjects will be highly qualified by the end of the 2005–2006 school year and that all teachers of these subjects in Title I schools are highly qualified as of the 2002–2003 school year. The core subjects are English, reading or language arts, mathematics, science, foreign languages, civics and government, arts, history, and geography. A highly qualified teacher is one who has a full teacher's certification, has a bachelor's degree, and passes a state-administered test on core academic subject knowledge. These requirements apply to teachers in general and special education and IDEA aligns with NCLB. It requires special education teachers to be highly qualified (20 U.S.C. Secs. 1401 (10) and (1412) (a) (14)). NCLB stipulates that special education teachers may participate in some instructional activities that do not require them to be highly qualified in core academic subjects. These special instructional activities include implementing positive behavior support, consulting with teachers who are highly qualified in core academic subjects, selecting appropriate curriculum and instructional accommodations, working with students to teach study skills, and reinforcing instruction that a student has received from a highly qualified teacher.

NCLB requires that paraprofessionals who teach in Title I schools must have earned a secondary school diploma or its equivalent. In general, paraprofessionals hired after January 8, 2002, must have an associate degree or higher, or they must have completed 2 years of postsecondary study at an institution of higher education. Paraprofessionals also have the option of passing a local or state examination that tests their knowledge related to teaching the core academic subjects. These qualifications must be met by January 8, 2006.

Each district and school must report its progress toward the teacher qualification goal when it issues its annual report cards on adequate yearly progress. The report must be accessible to the public.

Implications for Family-Professional Partnerships. NCLB's requirement that information on teacher qualifications be made accessible to the public enables parents to know whether each teacher is state-certified, is teaching under an emergency or provisional status, and/or has earned a bachelor's or higher degree or certificate. Parents who know the qualifications of their children's teachers presumably know what to expect when they meet with the teachers, what to request in terms of better teachers, and how to approach their partnerships with teachers. Teachers, however, who do not meet the requirements for being fully qualified may feel threatened or intimidated when this information is shared with parents. They may think that parents will be inclined to distrust their judgments. Since these requirements are new, it is too soon to tell what their effects will be.

Scientifically Based Methods

Background Problems.   Much of the impetus to use scientifically based methods derives from research about how to teach children to read (Yell & Drasgow, 2004). In 2002, the National Assessment of Educational Progress (NAED) report indicated that approximately two thirds of fourth graders on a national basis do not read at a proficient level. In addition, the vast majority of children who are not proficient readers are capable of learning to read if their teachers use empirically based instructional methods (Fletcher & Lyon, 1998). These research results undergird NCLB's commitment to scientifically based methods for instruction in all academic areas and particularly in the area of reading.

Definition of Principle.   The principle is that instruction is most effective when it proceeds from scientifically based research. Accordingly, one of NCLB's purposes is to improve student academic achievement by funding state and local educational agencies "to implement promising education reform programs and school improvement programs based on scientifically based research" (Title V, Sec. 5101). NCLB defines scientifically based research as "research that applies rigorous, systematic, and objective procedures to obtain relevant knowledge" (Title I, Sec. 1208 (6)). Some of the criteria for determining the extent to which research is ". . . rigorous, systematic, and objective. . . " include whether the researchers used empirical methods, applied rigorous data analyses to test their hypotheses and justify their findings, used multiple measures to gather data, and ensured that a peer review process evaluated the defensibility of the research methods and findings. IDEA aligns with the NCLB by excluding from special education students whose school challenges arise from lack of appropriate instruction in reading and the essential components of reading instruction as defined by NCLB; by limiting who can be classified as having specific learning disability; and by calling for scientifically based instruction (20 U.S.C. Secs. 1414 (d) (1)(A)(i)(IV) and 1400 (c) (5) (E) and (F)).

Under NCLB, the U.S. Department of Education will provide grants to SEAs and LEAs that use scientifically based methods in reading instruction. Each state is responsible for establishing a Reading Leadership Team composed of policy makers, educators, and at least one parent of a school-age student. The Reading Leadership Team is responsible for ensuring that schools that need to improve their reading achievement scores are using scientifically based instructional methods for teaching reading and that a comprehensive, seamless approach to reading instruction occurs in schools throughout all LEAs in the state. In addition, the department may require "failing" schools or districts to use scientifically based instructional methods in order to remain in business.

Implications for Family-Professional Partnerships.   In order to engage in partnerships in making educational decisions, it will increasingly be necessary for parents to be informed about scientifically based instructional methods. Parents may seek that information from their children's schools. If schools do provide that information, they should format it in a family-friendly way so as to inform but not overwhelm parents.

From the perspective of special education, there is a major challenge. The scientific base for teaching reading to students with exceptionalities sometimes differs from the scientific base for teaching reading to typical learners. It will be especially important that members of the Reading Leadership Team have a good working knowledge about scientifically based instruction relevant to the particular learning styles of students with exceptionalities.

Local Flexibility

Background Problems.   School reformers have argued that initiatives such as accountability, teacher quality, and scientifically based instruction fail because different federal, state, and local laws and regulations restrict school administrators' ability to use federal and state dollars in ways that respond effectively to local problems. The many different federal programs are often somewhat inconsistent with each other. Also, the federal programs adopt a top-down and one-size-fits-all approach. There is great inflexibility in how educators can administer the programs locally, which inhibits administrators from devising local responses to local needs.

Definition of Principle.   The principle of local flexibility is that federal programs should encourage local solutions for local problems. The principle of flexibility for accountability holds that schools should have more discretion to use federal funds, but they should also be accountable for student results. The justification for the principle is that it is inconsistent to hold state and local districts accountable for student results without giving them discretion to respond to local problems. Accordingly, one of NCLB's purposes is related to student ac demic achievement and involves having state and local agencies "bear the basic responsibility for the administration of (federal) funds" and that the responsibility "be carried out with a minimum of paperwork and that the design and implementation of programs. . . be mainly that of local education agencies. . . (and their staff) because local educational agencies and individuals have the most direct contact with students and are most likely to be able to design programs to meet the education needs of students in their own school districts" (Title V, Sec. 5101). IDEA also recognizes the primary role of state and local educational agencies (20 U.S.C. Sec. 1400 (c) (6), and reduces paperwork 20 U.S.C. Sec. 1400 (c)(16) and 1409 and allows some flexibility in using federal funds (20 U.S.C. Sec. 1411 (e)(3)).

NCLB consolidates 55 separate federal general education categorical programs into 45, reducing red tape and the costs of maintaining large bureaucracies, and allows state and local administrators to transfer money from one federal program to another. IDEA is not one of the federal programs subject to consolidation. Arguably, consolidation increases local control, flexibility, and innovation.

NCLB also permits states and school districts to designate themselves as charter states and charter districts. These states and districts will be relieved of the requirements under the many federal categorical programs if they enter into a 5-year performance agreement with the U.S. secretary of education. Under that agreement, these charter states and districts will be subject to especially rigorous standards of accountability and to sanctions (for example, loss of freedom from federal requirements) if student achievement and other performance indicators do not improve according to the terms of the agreement.

Implications for Family-Professional Partnerships. The principle of flexibility has some potentially positive implications for family professional partnerships. Parents should find it easier to know what services their children are receiving and to coordinate their partnerships with professionals because the professionals will operate under consolidated programs and not a large number of separate programs. Also, parents and professionals may collaborate to create charter schools and thus acquire opportunities for partnership and greater control over students' education.

NCLB Outcomes

Clearly, the ultimate outcome of NCLB is for *all* students to achieve at least at grade level on state assessments. This includes students with disabilities, students who are migrants, students who have limited English proficiency, students in urban and rural areas, and students from diverse racial/ethnic groups.

Given that NCLB is so new, it is impossible to judge at this time if its ultimate outcome is being met. The only data available are for 2003. Highlights of those data in reading and math are as follows:

- No significant increase was found in fourth-grade reading scores during 2003 as compared to previous years beginning in 1992.
- For both grades 4 and 8, average math and reading scores were higher in 2003 as compared to all previous years of assessment.
- For grades 4 and 8, White students and Asian/Pacific Islander students had higher average scores than students in other racial/ethnic groups. Asian/Pacific Islander students scored higher than White students.
- For grades 4 and 8, White, Black, and Hispanic students had higher scores in 2003 than they did in years since 1990. Students who are eligible for free or reduced-price lunch had lower math scores in 2003 than did students who were not eligible (NAEP, 2004).

SUMMARY

School reform is a recurring and perplexing domestic policy problem. The two federal laws that best exemplify our nation's approach to school reform are IDEA and NCLB. The six principles of IDEA are:

- Zero reject
- Nondiscriminatory evaluation
- Appropriate education
- Least restrictive environment
- Procedural due process
- Parent participation

The six principles of NCLB are:

- Accountability for results
- School safety
- Parental choice
- Teacher quality
- Scientifically based methods
- Local flexibility

In this chapter, we provided an overview of the background problems, major purposes, and provisions of each principle, and we discussed the implications of each for family-professional partnerships.

1. Which of IDEA's six principles is more important to the students than any other, or are they all equally important?
2. Which of NCLB's principles is likely to be more important to the students than any other, or are they all equally important?
3. Which of the IDEA or NCLB principles would you change if you could, and how would you change it?

ENHANCING YOUR SELF-AWARENESS

Reflect on your own experiences related to how IDEA was implemented in the elementary, middle, and high school that you attended. Then consider what steps you can take to implement IDEA's and NCLB's principles.

IDEA principles

Recall the six IDEA principles and ask yourself: Did I observe parents and professionals implementing these principles when I was in school or during any of my teacher-training programs? If you answered yes, then ask yourself this question: How well was the principle carried out, and what more would I do, now that I know more about the principle, to assist parents and professionals to be partners to carry it out more effectively? If you answered no to the first question, then ask yourself this question: What are the reasons why I did not observe parent-professional partnerships when I was in school or during my teacher-training program?

Implementing IDEA and NCLB principles

What two actions could you take, as an educator, to be a partner with parents, implement IDEA, and not take undue time away from your work with typical students and their NCLB-related education?

Scientifically based instruction

What steps can you take to learn about scientifically based practices for educating students with disabilities, exceptional gifts and talents, and limited English proficiency? How might you become a lifelong learner about those practices?

1. Determine what your state education agency requires by way of adequate yearly progress for all students and also for those with disabilities. Determine how the agency provides for students with disabilities to be accommodated in their curriculum, instruction, and assessment under IDEA and NCLB. Consult the SEA's Website or public information office.
2. Determine what your state education agency requires by way of parent-professional partnerships in implementing IDEA and NCLB. What policies, procedures, forms, and technical assistance does the agency provide to parents and professionals? Consult the SEA's Website or public information office.

You can find a link to these resources on the Companion Website at *www.prenhall.com/turnbull*.

1. IDEA Partnerships at the Council for Exceptional Children
Council for Exceptional Children
1101 North Glebe Road, Suite 300
Arlington, VA 22201-5704
703-620-3660, 888-CEC-SPED (toll-free)
www.ideapractices.org

   IDEA Practices provides information on IDEA in terms of the statutes, final regulations, litigation log, related laws, and their related resources (for example, annual reports to Congress developed by the Office of Special Education Programs within the U.S. Department of Education).

2. Families and Advocate Partnership for Education Project (FAPE Project)
PACER Center
8161 Normandale Boulevard
Minneapolis, MN 55437-1044
952-838-9000, 888-248-0822 (toll-free)
www.fape.org
fape@fape.org

   The FAPE Project provides information to parents and advocates related to IDEA. Information is provided on the statutes, regulations, resource organizations, and best practices. Some of the online documents are available in Spanish and Hmong translations.

3. U.S. Department of Education
www.ed.gov/nclb

   This comprehensive Website provides information on NCLB's key principles. It also has a Teacher

Toolkit and Parents' Guide, as well as an opportunity to sign up to receive e-mail updates.

4. National Assessment of Educational Progress (NAEP)
   www.nces.ed.gov/nationsreportcard

NAEP is also known as the Nation's Report Card. It provides assessment of America's student progress in academic areas. It concentrates on student achievement at grades 4, 8, and 12.

PART III

COMMUNICATION
PROFESSIONAL COMPETENCE
RESPECT
TRUST
COMMITMENT
EQUALITY
ADVOCACY

INTRODUCTION TO PART III

Partnerships and Trust

In the prologue, we said that the major theme of our book is that families and professionals must learn how to create partnerships. The strength of these partnerships depends on how much trust families and professionals have for each other. Partnerships and trust constitute the archway through which families, professionals, and students pass on their way to securing satisfactory outcomes from the students' education.

In chapter 7, we describe six principles on which partnerships rest. We also offer some practical advice for developing effective partnerships.

In chapter 8, we discuss the role that trust plays among partners and how to develop trusting and trustworthy partnerships with families.

Partnerships as Archways

CHAPTER ORGANIZATION

Archways are interspersed throughout Bonner Springs Elementary, a visual reminder of what values the school considers important for students, staff, and visitors alike.

FRAMING QUESTIONS

1. What is the difference between "law on the books" and "law on the streets" when it comes to family-professional partnerships?
2. What key principles of partnerships should guide professional practice?
3. What actual practices will enable you to act on the principles of partnerships?

VIGNETTE

For as long as there has been a law regulating the relationships among students, their families, teachers, and administrators, there has been a distinction between "law on the books" and "law on the streets." Law on the books is the law as written in statutes, regulations, and court decisions. Law on the streets is the practice of the written law. It is what students, families, teachers, and school administrators do when they try to implement the law, especially as partners with each other.

The law communicates rights and responsibilities, but people have to communicate with each other about those rights and responsibilities. Communication involves words: the home-school notebook that Vera Doleman and Nicky's teachers write in every day; and the interpretation that Tatania, Juan, and Joesian Cortes provide for their mother, Norma, when she meets with teachers who speak only English.

Communication also has an affective component. Sometimes the affect is friendly, even loving, as it is between Clara Berg and Carole Gothelf. Their shared ethnic history—the

Jewish history of the 20th century—both overlies and undergirds the words they exchange with each other. Sometimes the affect is far from friendly, as it was when Leia Holley confronted Sean's IEP team in a decisive meeting in May 2000.

It makes a huge difference when those whose relationship is regulated by law bring various skills to the relationship. Nicky Doleman's teacher at Raintree, Pam Shanks, has 18 years' experience as a teacher and two advanced degrees in education. Though not as experienced, Sean Holley's teacher, Tierney Thompson, is no less qualified to teach Sean. Leia Holley has been a teacher. The other three parents—Vera

Doleman, Clara Berg, and Norma Cortes—bring to the partnership their astute and intimate knowledge of how educators can best relate to their children.

With skill comes respect, not just for the talents that each partner has but also for the origins of their concerns. A cultural hallmark of Clara Berg and Carole Gothelf is their deep commitment to social justice. Norma Cortes's ethnic heritage teaches her to defer to those in authority, such as Joesian's advocates at United We Stand, but also to stand up for what is right for her son. Vera Doleman's culture rests on the solid foundation of family unity; educators must always deal with other members of her family.

When commitment exists, respect grows. Ask Norma Cortes who Joesian's best teachers have been, and she will say it is those who stayed after school to work with him, one on one, and those who speak with her at chance encounters at a local grocery store. Ask Norma who have been the greatest disappointments, and she will say it is those who treat Joesian as dispensable, as just another failure-to-read student. Ask Carole Gothelf why she became so bonded to Kenny Berg, and she will answer, "It's because I try to walk in Clara's shoes, as I try to walk in every parent's shoes." Ask Leia Holley about committed teachers, and she will talk about their steadfastness in enduring and prevailing in the struggle to educate Sean appropriately. Ask Vera Doleman, and she will talk about teachers who are willing to try to include Nicky, even though no student with as many disabilities has attended Raintree Montessori for many years.

Respect and commitment are intertwined. The more partners respect each other, the greater their mutual commitment. The more they respect and are committed to each other, the more they will be equals.

Respect, commitment, and equality yield results for partners and the students. No one person knows all there is to know about how to keep Nicky Doleman alive and have her interact with peers who do not have disabilities. Vera, Pam, Nicky's new teachers at Woodlawn School, and her physicians must share their knowledge and power with one another. No one person can unlock Sean Holley's secret talents, eliminate his problem behavior, and forestall or treat his seizures. His parents, Leia and Jamie, his brother JP, his

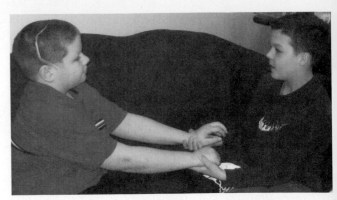

By participating in a Circle of Friends at school, Sean Holley interacts regularly with peers, among them Tyler McMahan.

teachers, especially Tierney, all members of his IEP team, and his neurologists need each other; their mutual need requires that each honors the other's contributions.

Finally, partnerships require advocacy. Kenny Berg refused to return to the Perkins School. The minute he felt its well-trod bricks beneath his feet after several years' absence, he bolted away from Clara and Carole. Such self-advocacy can accompany advocacy for others. Leia Holley insisted that Sean have an opportunity to speak by using the computer; she said Tierney needed more paraprofessionals in Sean's classroom. United We Stand and Emily Rodriguez combined to secure Joesian's admission to a vocational education program.

No law can create genuine partnerships. All the law can do is to provide rights, impose responsibilities, and create the structures within which parents, students, teachers, and administrators can relate to each other.

Beyond these essential roles, the law is relatively powerless to foster partnerships. It is up to people to breathe life into the written law, to ensure that their practice on the streets is wholesome for each other and a model for others who struggle and prevail to be authentic partners.

INTRODUCTION

You have learned about families and how they operate as a system (chapters 1 to 4), about the roles families historically have played (chapter 5), and about the policies that shape today's family-professional partnerships (chapter 6). In this chapter, you will learn about partnerships.

Among other things, the word *partnership* refers to a relationship involving close cooperation between people who have joint rights and responsibilities (Merriam-Webster's Collegiate Dictionary, 2003). As you learned in chapter 6, the Individuals with Disabilities Education Act (IDEA) and the No Child Left Behind Act (NCLB) specify the rights and responsibilities that families and educators have with respect to each other. But neither law says any

Rachel Haydon (smiling), interrelated resource teacher, moderates an IEP meeting at Woodlawn Elementary School to discuss Nicky Doleman's progress.

thing about the principles and practices that families and educators need to incorporate in order to be effective. We offer a definition that goes beyond the meaning as set out in a dictionary and those two laws. Our definition fits family-professional relationships and goes beyond the limiting concept of "joint rights and responsibilities." Our definition of partnership refers to a relationship in which families (not just parents) and professionals agree to defer to each other's judgments and expertise, as appropriate for the purpose of securing benefits for students, other family members, and professionals.

Our definition takes into account historical roles that parents and family members have played.

As you learned in chapter 5, at one time, families were the recipients of professionals' decisions. They were expected to defer unquestioningly to professional judgment. Later, families were in the role of being the central decision makers in the field of early education because family-centered service delivery systems expected the professionals to defer to the families.

Based on our definition, partnerships are characterized by seven principles: communication, professional competence, respect, commitment, equality, advocacy, and trust.

Our definition retains the idea of joint or mutual action, but it does not confer any more decision-making power on the families than on the professionals, or vice versa. Instead, it describes a relationship in which the families and professionals truly collaborate to achieve a collective wisdom.

Think of a circle in which the professionals are at the center and make all the decisions; then, think of a circle in which the families are at the center and make all the decisions. Now, put those two circles on top of each other. You have a circle in which families and professionals are in the center together. Their collective wisdom guides the actions that implement the decisions that secure acceptable outcomes (as IDEA and NCLB identify the outcomes) for students, other family members, and professionals. Each of these individuals is entitled to benefit from the others' collective wisdom.

In order to benefit, they will need to create a partnership based on the seven partnership principles. The word *principle* refers to a comprehensive and fundamental law, doctrine, or assumption. Our seven partnership principles do not constitute a law, because they do not have the power to command behavior. Nor do they constitute an assumption, because they are based on research. Instead, they constitute a *doctrine*, a body of principles in a branch of knowledge. The knowledge derives from the research and recommended practice that we report in this chapter and those that follow.

Figure 7–1 illustrates the seven partnership principles by using the structure of an arch. There are three princi-

FIGURE 7–1

The Arch and Its Seven Principles of Partnership

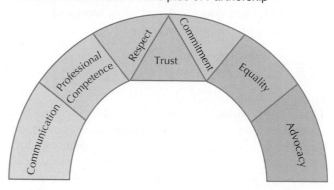

ples on each side of the arch. The seventh principle, trust, is the keystone. A *keystone* is the wedge-shaped piece at the crown of an arch that locks the other pieces into place (Merriam-Webster's Collegiate Dictionary, 2003).

To explain the arch, it is helpful to begin with a very fundamental question: Why do students attend school? No, it is not because they are required to do so. It is because, by attending school, they will learn certain skills and acquire certain habits that benefit them and society. Who is involved in their education? Families and professionals. An outcome for the family is that their child is educated. As you learned in chapter 3, educating a child is one of the family's functions. The professionals benefit because they succeed in educating their students.

Why is an arch an appropriate illustration of the seven partnership principles that lead to good outcomes for students, families, teachers, and other professionals? The answer lies in the purpose that an arch serves. Think of the students, their families, and the professionals as following a path through an arch. The path is education; the arch denotes the school. On one side of the arch is life during school, and on the other side is life outside of school. The students, their families, and professionals follow the path of education, with each other through the arch of the school, to life outside of school.

In the best of worlds, they embark on this journey in partnership. And during that entire journey they learn to trust each other. They know that none of the six other partnership principles is, alone, sufficient to sustain them. They must trust each other throughout the journey.

Without trust, the partnership is weak or may not even exist. With trust, the partnership remains strong and can sustain them; they can move along the path of education, in partnership with each other, to a life outside of school that is shaped by what happens inside the school. They can move together, on parallel paths, through school to outcomes. But they cannot do it well and joyously without trusting each other. You will learn why that is so as we define each of the other six partnership principles and the state-of-the-art practices associated with each. In the next chapter, you will learn about trust and its keystone role.

COMMUNICATION

Effective partnerships require effective communication. That is easy enough to say. What is difficult is to be a good communicator. Effective communication requires that we pay careful attention to both the quality and the quantity of our communication. Quality means that we have to be positive, clear, and respectful of the person with whom we are communicating. Quantity refers to how often we communicate and if we use our own and others' time efficiently. Research shows that the following five practices almost always are necessary for effective communication between family members and professionals (Blue-Banning, Summers, Frankland, Nelson, & Beegle, 2004):

- Be friendly
- Listen
- Be clear
- Be honest
- Provide and coordinate information

In chapter 9, we will provide even more strategies for being an effective partner through good communication, but for now it is best for you to learn about those five necessary communication practices.

Be Friendly

Some professionals mistakenly believe that being professional means they must be formal, distant, and even controlling when they communicate with family members. A survey of families and professionals, not limited to those in special education, underscored what professionals believe parents want from them and what parents actually want:

> In a classic example of misunderstood cues, the reported preferences of parents are not what school personnel think they are. School personnel passionately believe that a professional, businesslike manner will win the respect and support of parents. The response of parents to questions about their contacts with the school revealed that they view "professionalism" on the part of teachers, school psychologists, guidance counselors, or principals as undesirable. Parents mention their dissatisfaction with school people who are too businesslike, patronizing, or who talk down to us. . . . Parents reported a "personal touch" as the most enhancing factor in school relations. (Lindle, 1989, p. 13)

What is the "personal touch"? A parent whose child was receiving home-based early intervention services described it this way:

> At first, I was tense with a professional coming to my home. But it was a nice little conversation. The professional's mannerism and the way she asked questions was like we were sitting down for a cup of coffee. She got a lot of information without asking. (Summers et al., 1990, p. 87)

Simply put, the personal touch means being friendly; that is the key to helping parents feel comfortable enough to share information about a child or even about the family. Instead of "interviews," have conversations (Coles, 1989). Here's the advice of an early childhood educator:

> Professionals need to be able to be nice. In a professional meeting, we need to be able to put the family at ease by showing them that we are working together for the good of the family member that's in need. So we need to be able to be nice to each other and joke around a bit. We need to try to get the family to feel like this team is going to work. That they're going to help me. They like each other. They need to get the impression that we like each other and that we know what we're doing. (Frankland, 2001, pp. 107–108)

Listen

Listening is the language of acceptance. One of the seven habits of highly effective people, as described by Stephen Covey, is to "seek first to understand, then to be understood" (Covey, 1990, p. 237). When you truly seek to understand the other person before stating your own perspectives, you will find yourself in a listening mode; you will hear the family's "language" and you will incorporate it into your communication with them. That is what the word *acceptance* means; you incorporate the family's communication, even if you might disagree with some of their statements. Covey (1990) describes empathetic listening as "listening with intent to really understand":

> Empathetic listening involves much more than registering, reflecting, or even understanding the words that are said . . . In empathetic listening, you listen with your ears, but you also, and more importantly, listen with your eyes and with your heart. You listen for feeling, for meaning. You listen for behavior. You use your right brain as well as your left. You sense, you intuit, you feel. (pp. 240–241)

When you listen empathetically, you do not agree or disagree; instead, you simply try to understand what it means to be in the other person's shoes (sand and all). You convey genuine interest, understanding, and acceptance of the family's feelings and experiences. You will not necessarily approve of or agree with the family's point of view, but you will try to understand the family's situation from their point of view—not your own.

To understand from the family's point of view requires you to be nonjudgmental. That is not easy; we all make judgments about other people and their lives. But you still should try to accept others as they are. Suspend your own judgment of what is right or wrong, and try to relate to families' differences and values. Keep in mind that both you and the families share a common goal, namely, good outcomes for their children.

Families want professionals to be empathetic listeners. Indeed, parents have reported that professionals' refusal to listen to them escalates conflicts that, in turn, can lead to formal mediation or even a due process hearing (Lake & Billingsley, 2000). By contrast, empathetic listening can contribute to trusting partnerships and can even de-escalate conflicts, as a father commented:

> The first thing is to LISTEN to us. Because we know our kids better than anybody, ya know, they're our kids. They're part of us! And, ya know, you go to some of those places and they just fill a form, ya know, and that's it. (Blue-Banning et al., 2004, p. 175)

The more empathetic listening becomes a natural part of your communication, the more likely you are to be an effective listener as you interact with families.

Be Clear

As is true of other professions, the discipline of special education is full of complicated concepts and terms. Few of them are readily understandable by people who have not had formal training or extensive experience in special education, even when the terms and concepts are used in full. Acronyms just compound the challenge of being clear in your communications with families. In the following example of how *not* to be clear, a psychologist is explaining the results of an evaluation of a student who has a specific learning disability to the student's mother:

> I gave him a complete battery and, um, I found that, uh, he had a verbal IQ of 115, performance of 111, and a full scale of 115, so he's a bright child. Uh, he had very high scores, in, uh, information which is his long-term memory. Ah, vocabulary, was, ah, also, ah, considerably over average, good detail awareness and his, um, picture arrangement scores, he had a seventeen which is very high . . . very superior rating, so he, his visual sequencing seems to be good and also he has a good grasp of anticipation and awareness of social situations. Um, he (she is scanning her notes) scored in reading at 4.1, spelling 3.5, and arithmetic 3.0, which gave him a standard score of 100 in, uh, reading,

95 in spelling, and 90 in arithmetic. When compared with his [overall] score, it does put him somewhat ah below his, you know, his capabilities. I gave him the Bender Gestalt and he had six errors.

> And his test age was 7.0 to 7.5 and his actual age is nine, so it, uh, he was considerably beneath his, uh, his uh, age level. His, I gave him the, uh VADS and his, um (looking through notes) both the oral-aural and the visual-written modes of communication were high but the visual oral and the oral written are low, so he, uh, cannot switch channels. . . . I gave him several projective tests and, um, the things that I picked up there is that, um he [does] possibly have some fears and anxieties, uh, so I had felt ah, that perhaps he might, uh, uh, benefit, um, from special help. He also was tested, um, in 1976 and at that time he was given the WISC-R and his IQ was slightly lower, full scale of a 93 (3 or 4). His, um, summary of that evaluation, uh, was, uh, he was given the ITPA and he had high auditory reception, auditory association, auditory memory. So his auditory skills are good. He was given another psychological evaluation in 1997. He was given the Leiter and he had an IQ of 96. And, um, they concluded that he had a poor mediate recall but they felt that was due to an emotional overlay and they felt that some emotional conflicts were, uh, interfering with his ability to concentrate. (Mehan, 1993, pp. 251–252)

Little wonder that families would have a hard time understanding such an evaluation report!

Many families have learned the terms and concepts of special education; they may even use this terminology themselves when they communicate with you. Other families will be new to special education and its terminology. Still other families will face the challenge of learning English as a second language. A good way to clearly communicate with a family is to listen and pay attention to the terms that they use. You then will know what level of complexity will help you become a clear communicator with that family. You may find it helpful in communicating with some families not to use technical terms; instead, you will want to translate your information, using simple synonyms or several words to explain a concept that professionals have reduced to a single word. You will want to introduce this family and others like them—the newcomers to special education—to technical terms by using the term and then clearly explaining its meaning.

The term *jargon* refers to the technical terminology or characteristic idiom of a special activity or group. Jargon impedes communication; it creates obscurity, not clarity. An effective communicator is a "jargon buster." When you hear other professionals using terms you know the family members do not understand, ask questions that help clarify the meaning, or explain the terms yourself. Keep your communication clear and direct.

Be Honest

Being direct means being honest. Many families want you to be honest, even when you have to give them bad news. But they also need you to be tactful. Being tactful involves conveying hard-to-receive information in ways that are sensitive to how a family will react. You can be tactful by sharing information with a family in a private setting; by not blaming family members for problems; and by pointing out the strengths, not just the challenges and concerns, related to the family or the family's child (Blue-Banning, Summers, & Frankland, in press).

Being honest is especially important when disagreements occur among family members, between a family member and one or more professionals, or among professionals, as this teacher pointed out:

> Good communication means that if you disagree on something, you can say that in a tactful way, you can discuss those issues. The conversation will still go on. Everybody will still be there present and discussing and not offended, no one leaves. Everybody can discuss the positives and negatives in a tactful way without hurting someone else's ego or feelings. I think good communication means you can say "No, I don't agree with that, let's talk about that some more or let's try something else." (Frankland, 2001, p. 111)

Another dimension of honesty is being straightforward when you do not know an answer to a question. It is far better to admit you cannot answer a question and commit to securing and communicating a full and accurate answer, as this father noted:

> If she doesn't know anything, she makes sure she finds out . . . . When you ask a question, she makes sure that you get a response to it. And yeah, she's not scared to tell us up front, you know, I don't know. Which is one thing that I appreciate . . . tell me you don't know and get the information back to us. (Beach Center, 2000)

Provide and Coordinate Information

Families want and need information (Bailey et al., 1999; Scorgie, Wilgosh, & McDonald, 1999). They especially want to know about present services, future services, the nature of their child's disability, experiences of other parents who have a child with similar needs, community resources, and legal rights (Cooper & Allred, 1992; Gowen, Christy, & Sparling, 1993). They do not want the runaround from professionals:

> Well I think that the Board of Education has all of these different little programs. And apparently the only way to know about them is by speaking to other parents. And I think they are selective as to whom it is they tell. (Soodak & Erwin, 2000, p. 36)

Parents also want their children to be respected and treated with dignity, similar to the way a preschool director acts toward a child:

> She'll stop whatever she is doing if Lena asks her something. She'll stop and get on her knees and say, "Lena, tell me again. I don't hear you. Say it slow." And she'll sit there for five minutes and be late for a meeting until she can figure out what my child wants, and then answer her. (Soodak & Erwin, 2000, p. 37)

Sometimes, the very nature of the child's exceptionality can make it more difficult to locate information or make informed decisions. Moreover, there often are competing theories about the causes and appropriate interventions for some exceptionalities; autism and deafness are good examples. Especially when different factions of professionals and families strongly agree or disagree about various interventions, families face additional challenges, beyond how to raise and educate their child. Most families want to know about all the optional interventions (Jackson, Becker, & Schmitendorf, 2002). Families also want professionals to coordinate the information, not just to provide it (Kasahara & Turnbull, in press).

PROFESSIONAL COMPETENCE

In chapter 6, we compared IDEA's and NCLB's "law on the books" about highly qualified teachers with the realities about the teacher workforce. What are the implications for "law on the streets"? Being qualified and competent means that you know how to:

- Provide a quality education.
- Continue to learn.
- Set high expectations.

Provide a Quality Education

What is a quality education? As you learned in chapter 6, IDEA approaches quality by requiring schools to provide an individualized appropriate education to students with disabilities. NCLB approaches quality by requiring schools to enhance students' achievement in core academic subjects using scientifically based instructional strategies. These two laws aside, however, parents report that quality instruction begins when professionals recognize their child as an individual and then plan a curriculum, its method of instruction, and its assessment to build on the child's individual strengths (Blue-Banning et al., in press; Kasahara & Turnbull, in press; Lake & Billingsley, 2000). Here is how one parent expressed this perspective:

(My son) needs to be recognized as an individual, with in-dividual strengths and abilities. . . . There was only room for what they wanted to provide and what they felt was ade-quate. It wasn't adequate for him. . . . I realized these peo-ple had no ability to look at him as an individual, and help him as an individual strive for what he wanted to get. They were interested in keeping him where they thought he be-longed. (Lake & Billingsley, 2000, p. 244)

In a nutshell, parents want educators to have the knowledge and skills to individualize instruction to meet their child's special needs and to provide the ap-propriate supports and services (Summers et al., in press). This means that you must master the content of your undergraduate or graduate program and also be-come a lifelong learner, continuing to build on your present strengths.

Continue to Learn

State education agencies require teachers to renew their teaching certificates periodically, believing that mastery of new curriculum and methods of instruction will result in better student outcomes. Teachers generally have for-mal requirements to participate in continuing education programs.

In addition to these formal opportunities to learn, every interaction you have with a family gives you an op-portunity to examine your present skills and to reflect on how you can improve them. In the short run, it may be easier not to take the time for self-reflection or to invite the perspectives of other educators or of families. In the long run, however, it is highly time efficient to learn from every situation. You need not repeat your mistakes and spend additional time correcting them.

To continue to learn, you will need to seek feedback about your work with families and to be nondefensive. Being nondefensive means that you are open to others' perspectives about your performance and feel little, if any, need to defend or justify yourself.

You also may want to ask your students' families and your colleagues—those whom you can trust and who have expertise that you want to acquire—for pointers on how to improve your teaching and your partnerships.

Set High Expectations

As you learned in chapter 4, when families first learn that their child has a disability, they often fear the future, as-suming that their child may not be able to make sufficient progress in school, participate in typical experiences with peers, or even enjoy a high quality of life. Similarly, many students may fear the future. Both families and stu-dents need to be hopeful about what lies ahead; hope is

a powerful motivator for them to take action to get what they need and to live the kind of life they want to live.

To help families and students set high expectations for themselves, you would do well to be skeptical when pro-fessionals encourage families to "be realistic." That per-spective can limit the family's ambition, goals, and sense of well-being.

A different perspective adopts a theory of "positive il-lusions" (Taylor, 1989). This theory helps to explain how people adapt to threatening situations. Some people tell themselves or others that they have to be realistic and therefore should not have "false hope" about themselves and their world. Others, however, regard themselves, their world, and the future with positive, self-enhancing illusions. We use the term *great expectations*, not illu-sions. But, name aside, such an outlook does not deny the truth; instead, it creates a reality by promoting, rather than undermining, good mental health.

> Overall, the research evidence indicates that self-enhance-ment, exaggerated beliefs in control, and unrealistic opti-mism typically lead to higher motivation, greater persis-tence at tasks, more effective performance, and, ultimately greater success. A chief value of these illusions may be that they help to create self-fulfilling prophecies. They may lead people to try harder in situations that are objectively diffi-cult. Although some failures are certainly inevitable, ulti-mately the illusions will lead to success more often than will lack of persistence. (Taylor, 1989, p. 64)

When reflecting on his treatment for the cancer that eventually took his life, Norman Cousins (1989), a distin-guished editor of a major literary magazine, deplored the fact that many professionals were worried about giving him and others "false hope." Cousins said that these pro-fessionals never realized how frequently they gave "false despair" (p. 100) and how false despair can dissuade peo-ple from creating any kind of desirable future: "Perhaps the most important of these characteristics (of people who vigorously pursue active treatment) is the refusal to accept the verdict of a grim inevitability. . . . What it means is that any progress in coping . . . involves not de-nial but a vigorous determination to get the most and the best out of whatever is now possible" (pp. 76, 78).

Many students with disabilities and their families are frequently given false despair. Far too often, it limits their sense of the future and constitutes a major barrier to se-curing desired outcomes.

Janet Vohs, a parent of a daughter with significant dis-abilities, shared her perspective on the power of a posi-tive vision of the future:

> Families of children with disabilities are not allowed—or at least not encouraged—to have a dream or a vision for their

children's future. What the past has given as possible outcomes for people with disabilities is far less than inspiring. If all we have to look forward to is an extension of the past, I should think we would want to avoid the pain of that future as long as possible. But I have a motto: Vision over visibility. Having a vision is not just planning for a future we already know how to get to. It is daring to dream about what is possible. (Vohs, 1993, pp. 62–63)

Having a vision for the future fuels great expectations. When you develop and communicate high expectations for students and families, you will be a catalyst for them to develop their own high expectations. When people are enthusiastic about their future, they are far more likely to work hard to achieve their goals.

What if you had high expectations for yourself but found, once you started teaching, that you were deluding yourself, that you were not as competent as you thought you were, that your own great expectations seemed to be unrealistic? How could you transmit to your students and their parents a sense that they should expect much when you did not have that same expectation for yourself? You may well have that experience one day. In Figure 7–2, a teacher describes what she did and what happened to her relationships with her students' families.

RESPECT

Respect in partnerships means that members regard each other with esteem and communicate that esteem through their words and actions (Blue-Banning et al., 2004). A respectful professional will:

- Honor cultural diversity.
- Affirm strengths.
- Treat students and families with dignity.

Honor Cultural Diversity

In chapter 1 you learned how cultural characteristics can influence family-professional partnerships. Take a moment to review the information about the racial/ethnic profiles of students in special education, and pay particular attention to the data about immigration and limited English proficiency and the differences that often exist in cultural values. Think how you can best honor each family's cultural beliefs as a way of demonstrating your respect for them. Honoring cultural diversity begins with understanding the family's culture and its related microcultures. Figure 1–4 (in chapter 1) depicts the broad range of family perspectives stemming from cultural and microcultural beliefs. Where do your beliefs fall? By answering that question, you will know where to focus

your attention to honor families' cultural diversity. For example, "equality" reflects a belief that it is important for individuals to have equal rights and opportunities, including the opportunity to be an equal member of a team that makes decisions about a student. Equality is just one example of how practices in the field of special education are rooted in cultural beliefs strongly associated with a European American tradition (Hanson, 2004).

What if you are trying to develop a partnership with a family who does not believe families should have equal rights and responsibilities when working with professionals? Instead, the family may want the professionals to control the decision making and give the family guidance, even directives. Figure 7–3 provides tips for how you can enhance your own cultural competence and honor families' cultural diversity.

In addition to their cultural values, families also have personal values (Kalyanpur & Harry, 1999), such as a preference for communicating with a teacher through e-mail rather than face-to-face meetings. You need to take multicultural issues and personal preferences into account as you develop partnerships with families.

Affirm Strengths

Many families find that the professionals who work with them and their children focus on only the family's or the child's weaknesses, not their strengths. Sadly, many families are accustomed to getting bad news about their child or hearing a litany of problems. That emphasis on weaknesses can cause families to feel sad, frustrated, and defensive. In turn, these feelings can impede effective communication. One parent put it this way:

I often think if [school staff] could do one-on-one instead of [coming] with five people, telling me Susie can't do this and Susie can't do that, and Susie can't this, and Susie can't that. And I am thinking, What about "Susie *can* do this and Susie *can* do that"? (Lake & Billingsley, 2000, p. 245)

Parents appreciate hearing about their child's strengths and hearing other positives, as one parent described:

The last two years have been like in a dream world. It is like I want to call them up and say, "You do not have nothing (sic) negative to say?" This educational system—this school itself has worked wonders with my son. It has taken a lot of stress off ME, so that when I go home, I do not have to get into it with him and say, "Oh, you know, the school called me today about this and that." They will call me, but they have already worked it out. Or they will call me to praise him and tell me how wonderful and how positive a role model he is now, and it's because they have worked with us. It is like I said, it has been a dream world to me. (Beach Center, 2000)

FIGURE 7–2
My Voice: Competence, Confidence, and Confiding Communication

My first year as a teacher was filled with many learning experiences. I will share with you one of the greatest lessons I learned that year: Professional competence is an all-encompassing phenomenon. As I reflect upon my experiences, I now realize it is impossible to be professionally competent unless you believe in your abilities and are a confident decision-maker. So much of the success of our students depends upon our own success as a teacher. How competent I felt as teacher had a profound impact on my relationships, both with my peers and with the parents of the children I served.

While a student teacher and a beginning teaching professional, I taught several students with rare disabilities. At first, I felt very guilty that I had not heard of their disability. Several thoughts and questions circulated in my mind. Perhaps, I didn't study enough while a student. Why hadn't I heard of these disabilities? Would the parents think I was incompetent to teach their child? Admitting lack of knowledge was my first step, and deep down I knew it was the right thing to do. Upon confiding in the parents, I found my fears were unwarranted. I was not chastised for my ignorance, and oftentimes, the parents were still learning about their child, too. They were appreciative of my honesty and were eager to share with me knowledge about their child and also their frustrations of sometimes just not knowing what to do.

Personally, I had to accept that it was unrealistic for me to have a full understanding of all the possible disabilities that exist. While my education degree provided me with a good foundation of best practices, I realized it would not prepare me for every possible teaching opportunity. It was now up to me to continue my professional growth so I could provide the best services for my new students. As a professional, I had to be comfortable with learning as I went. I had to be confident as I shared information with peers, parents, and paraprofessionals, and I had to trust in the decisions I made. What was most important, though, was how the parents made me feel—they valued my judgment and my teaching expertise despite my not knowing about their child's specific disability. I believe this was possible because my outside persona represented confidence.

The partnerships I had with families seemed to click much more easily than those I shared with professionals. I was very comfortable conversing with parents and being an advocate for all of my students, but sometimes this stance negatively impacted my relationships with my peers. I thought of my students as my own children, so my goals, hopes, and dreams were in line with those of their parents. I never gave up hope of progress despite some of the negative research reported, especially the research surrounding autism. My unabashed optimism and willingness to try new things was sometimes met with skepticism from my peers. At times I felt challenged during interchanges to defend my actions, while at other times, I could sense that my peers felt that I challenged their work, too. In this mode, we were no longer focused on producing the best educational outcomes for the child but were, instead, embroiled in a competition of purporting ideas or ideological viewpoints. This situation illustrates just how expansive the concept of professional competence is. Professional competence includes not only knowing your content area, but also knowing how to apply good partnership skills. This represented an area of growth for me. I had to work on my interpersonal skills, diplomacy, and patience to ensure that my partnerships with my peers were productive and respectful.

Many individuals immediately associate professional competence with earning CEUs/PDUs, but this alone does not ensure professional competence. Professional competence also entails how you view yourself as a professional and the image you project to others as a professional. Sometimes, I think we all get bogged down with the numerous professional development classes and we forget one of the simplest ways to improve our performance is to improve our confidence, our well-being, and the well-being of those around us. There is always something to improve upon, even if it is as simple as smiling to those with whom you work. Ensuring continued professional growth is a daily job. My most valuable learning experience was connecting my academic professional growth with my personal growth. The greatest wisdom is not learned from books alone.

Nina Zuna
Lawrence, Kansas

Note the two important points that this parent makes. The first is that she appreciates the focus on strengths rather than weaknesses. The second is that she finds it helpful when she does not need to "get into it" with her son in the evening by following up on a problem that the school identified. Reflect on the information you learned in chapter 2 about family interaction—especially the parental subsystem—and consider the potential for conflict between parents and children when educators share only negative information.

FIGURE 7–3

Tips for Honoring Cultural Diversity

General Tips

- Gain insight from talking with families, talking with colleagues, reading, and other opportunities provided through the school and community to learn how education is perceived in the cultures of the students in your class related to issues such as teacher authority, discipline, academic success, homework, and peer relationships.

- Tie the content of the general curriculum to the particular skills and knowledge that are especially valued in your students' cultures.

- Incorporate projects into the curriculum that enable students to reflect on their culture, relate their culture to what they are learning, and share information about their culture with their classmates.

- Invite parents of students in your class to share information with the class about their culture.

Specific Tips for Communicating About Cultural Values

- Learn about the family's strengths, needs, and expectations by communicating with families consistent with their preferences (see chapter 9).

- Determine the family's priorities and preferences for their child's nondiscriminatory evaluation (chapter 11) and IFSP/IEP (see chapter 12). Seek to understand and honor the family's cultural values and priorities.

- Talk with the family about the assumptions that underlie their cultural values and priorities. Seek to find out about the reasons for their priorities and preferences.

- As you reflect on their priorities and preferences, identify any disagreements or alternative perspectives that you or other professionals have associated with providing educational supports and services to the student or family. Identify the cultural values that are embedded in your underlying interpretation or in the interpretation of other professionals. Identify how the family's views differ from your own.

- Respectfully acknowledge any cultural differences you have identified and share your perspectives on cultural values related to your and other professionals' assumptions.

- Brainstorm and then determine how you and the family can find "common ground" in your understanding.

Source: Adapted from Kalyanpur, M., & Harry, B. (1999). *Culture in special education: Building reciprocal family-professional relationships.* Baltimore: Brookes.

Just as it is critical to affirm students' strengths, it is also important to affirm the strengths of families. As you learned in chapter 5, at one time professionals regarded families as the source of a child's problems; indeed, some professionals still do. It may be that families with whom you seek to develop a partnership have had the painful experience of being blamed for their child's problem. They may not tell you this directly, but they nevertheless may fear that you will criticize or blame them.

Even families who face special challenges (for example, substance abuse) have strengths. In your communication with all families, try to genuinely affirm their strengths and let them know that you notice and appreciate the positive things they do for their child. Figure 7-4 includes examples of families' strengths.

Treat Students and Families with Dignity

Treating students and families with dignity—treating them as honored, worthy, and esteemed—shows how you respect them. Families want you to regard their child as a person rather than as a diagnosis or a disability label, as this mother says: "If they perceive someone as being less than human, then they are going to treat that someone as an object . . . I want my son to . . . feel like he belongs to the human race, like there's a place for him, like he fits in" (Blue-Banning et al., 2004, p. 179).

Another aspect of treating a family with dignity is to treat them as decision makers without condescension, as happened to one parent:

> Instead of making accommodations for him, it was just a lot of deception, a lot of manipulation, and a lot of head patting. I felt like I was constantly being just patted on the head and told to go home and everything would be fine. And they hardly ever listened to the concerns with an open ear at all. It was just "go away, you're bothering me." I think they were trying to humor me and they wanted me to just be happy with what they wanted to give. (Lake & Billingsley, 2000, p. 247)

Treating people with dignity involves honoring their cultural diversity; what one person considers appropri-

FIGURE 7–4

Samples of Families' Strengths

- Lots of caring, extended families
- Being very optimistic
- Being very knowledgeable
- Making the child feel loved and accepted
- Maintaining an orderly, well-organized, and safe home
- Having a yard or park for playing
- Encouraging the child to notice, hear, and smell different interesting things around the house
- Encouraging wellness and health in all family members through exercise, balanced diet, and healthy habits
- Seeking out support from friends or counseling as needed
- Finding unique ways to use informal teachable moments as part of a typical home life
- Communicating thoughts and feelings to family members in a supportive and authentic way
- Having a sense of humor
- Being persistent in seeking help and support from others
- Having a strong religious faith
- Having interesting hobbies to share with children

Source: Adapted from Turbiville, V., Lee, I., Turnbull, A., & Murphy, D. (1993). *Handbook for the development of a family friendly individualized service plan (IFSP).* Lawrence: University of Kansas, Beach Center on Families and Disability.

ate, dignified treatment may be offensive to someone else. For example, the formality of the relationships you establish with families and how you address them (first name or last name, title or not), the nature of your eye contact with them, and how you arrange a room when you meet with them should reflect respect but also be shaped by a family's culture. Remember, if you make unintentional mistakes, you can learn from them and avoid them in the future. In this way you can teach yourself to become culturally competent; certainly it is worth the effort to try.

COMMITMENT

Commitment occurs when professionals consider their relationship with a child and family to be more than an obligation incurred through work. It occurs when they feel loyal and are sensitive in working with the child and the family (Blue-Banning et al., 2004). To demonstrate commitment, you should:

- Be sensitive to emotional needs.
- Be available and accessible.
- Go "above and beyond."

Be Sensitive to Emotional Needs

Life is complicated enough without being responsible for a child who has exceptional needs. Add disability or giftedness to the life of a professional or family and the complications intensify. The child might be teased, be excluded from social groups, or face architectural and other societal barriers. The family probably worries greatly about locating resources to meet the future.

Professionals, too, have complicated lives. As many will say, "We're only human." Some professionals interact with students and their families by focusing on only the student's developmental/academic priorities; they distance themselves from any of the extraordinary circumstances that accompany having an exceptionality. Others invest in a different kind of relationship with students and families. Demonstrating one facet of partnership, they embrace the full reality of the student's and family's life. That full reality includes the need for emotional support as well as academic support.

A parent described a benefit of receiving emotional support from her child's teacher as follows:

> It was such a relief that I didn't have to try to fake my emotions when I was around my son's teacher. If I got choked up with tears, I knew that it was going to be okay to do that. In most of my relationships with teachers in the past, I have always felt that they expect me to "keep a stiff upper lip" and always be objective when I hear bad news about my son. I can't separate myself from my emotions, and I'm so glad that I finally found a teacher who is comfortable with me expressing my true feelings. (Beach Center, 2000)

There are many ways to demonstrate sensitivity to a family's emotional needs. These include empathetic listening, connecting families to other families who have experienced similar emotional issues (you will learn about the Parent-to-Parent program in chapter 10), and seeking assistance from school counselors or social workers when more emotional support is needed than you as a teacher can provide alone.

Be Available and Accessible

Availability and accessibility occur when professionals arrange their schedules so families can reach and communicate with them. Families often praise professionals who are available for guidance or conversations "off hours"—at those times when parents are free from their work or other responsibilities. A parent described available and accessible educators as follows:

> The teachers here aren't just your 8:30 to 2:30 people. They are involved in the lives of the children and their well-being—not just education. They are interested in their education, but it doesn't stop there. And they have also made themselves available to us as a family that other teachers wouldn't. (Nelson, Summers, & Turnbull, 2004, p. 153)

Being available and accessible means being there. Many parents have expressed frustration about IEP or other school meetings that professionals do not attend; they also become frustrated when professionals come in and out of a meeting (Salembier & Furney, 1994). A parent described the situation as follows:

> I had to leave my job to go to the [IEP] conference. . . . Do you want to know how many educators came in and had me sign something and walked out? And I just, I thought that was so rude . . . they do not give me or my daughter the respect that we need. . . . It's like you're just being brushed through like an assembly line. Or they were like scanning you through the grocery line. And then, they leave. (Beach Center, 2000)

Although it is difficult to schedule meetings that are convenient for everyone, the IEP meeting absolutely requires the availability and accessibility of professionals who have responsibility for providing an education to the student. An option that you will learn about in chapter 12 is to hold meetings at times and in locations better suited to parents' needs (Gomby, Culross, & Behrman, 1999; Jordan, Reyes-Blanes, Peel, Peel, & Lane, 1998).

Go Above and Beyond

When describing the professionals who are effective partners with them, families frequently use the following phrases:

- "More than a job." Professionals undertake an obligation to enter into a reliable alliance with the family.
- "More than a case." Professionals recognize the student and family as real people, not just one more group to which they reluctantly owe a duty.
- "Going the second mile." Professionals provide assistance to the student and family beyond their job description (Blue-Banning et al., 2004; Kasahara & Turnbull, in press).

Some parents even describe professionals going "above and beyond" when professionals speak to them while in community settings other than the school. These professionals

demonstrate a genuine interest in the student and family as *persons,* not as *objects* of their job.

Professionals who, themselves, were identified as exemplary collaborators described going above and beyond in these terms:

- "Those who give the sweat equity"
- "Doing the extra step that may not be required"
- "Putting your all into your work"
- "Working outside the parameters of the job description"
- "Taking it to the next level and not just doing what you need to do, but going a little beyond" (Frankland, 2001, p. 130)

In this same study of exemplary professionals, an audiologist described how going above and beyond worked as part of a team effort with educators:

> The team was not trying to squeeze these children into any square pegs. They viewed the child as primary, not the process. They were all committed to that idea. It was the child that was primary, and they made the process work for the child. As silly as that may sound, many teams that I have worked with, because of the sheer volume (of students), have to make the child fit the process. My experience was just the opposite with this team. They also followed up with things that were not mandated by any guidelines. They worked through the IEP process, and they advocated for the kids. That is a true sign of commitment, going beyond what is required for compliance. (Frankland, 2001, pp. 130–131)

Going above and beyond within a school context yields "extracurricular" (outside of school) benefits for the professionals. They have the satisfaction of being included in family events such as birthday parties, weddings, and funerals. Listen to what one professional said:

> Parents can really tell when you truly believe in them . . . I mean, we don't just go in, sit down, and start . . . doing paperwork. . . . We may talk about soap operas or. . . one of the kids we're working with, the parents are getting married, we're going to the wedding. We're going to the shower. I mean it's just stuff like that. Because you talk about other stuff that's happening in their lives. I'll tell them about, ya know, I'm doing this, I'm doing that. So it's not just professional. (Nelson, et al., 2004, p. 160)

Going above and beyond to participate in family events raises the issue of boundaries in family-professional partnerships. Some human service professions, such as social work and counseling, have explicit guidelines for ethical and unethical practice related to professional-family relationship boundaries (American Counseling Association Foundation, 1995; National Association of Social Workers, 1996), although the field of education does not (Cobb & Horn, 1989; Keim, Ryan, & Nolan, 1998; Nelson et al., 2004).

Is it appropriate to question the traditional belief that professionals should keep their distance from families? To encourage professionals in education to cross boundaries that professionals in other disciplines must not cross? You will remember that one of the indicators of communication is being friendly. Being friendly suggests an informal rather than formal relationship. Schorr (1997) visited many programs nationally and synthesized what works for students who face the greatest vulnerabilities—students who experience poverty and the challenges that are associated with it. What works, she wrote, is " . . . a new form of professional practice" (p. 12), going beyond the traditional boundaries of professional norms to establish closer and friendlier relationships with families. She believes that this approach is particularly effective for families from poverty backgrounds who are accustomed to having unequal relationships with professionals.

EQUALITY

Equality refers to the condition in which families and professionals feel that each of them has roughly equal power to influence a student's education. They will not feel equal unless they believe that each of them is being fair with the other (Blue-Banning et al., 2004). To establish the condition of equality, effective professionals:

- Share power.
- Foster empowerment.
- Provide options.

Share Power

As you learned in chapter 5, family-professional relationships historically placed the professionals at the top of the relationship and the families at the bottom; you also learned that, nowadays, best-practice partnerships occur when all team members collaborate and enter into trust-building relationships.

Hierarchies and professional dominance reflect how power is distributed within relationships. Power is the ability and intention to use authority, influence, or control over others. Many forms of power can greatly influence the extent that equality exists in partnerships. Just consider two of them: *power-over* and *power-shared* relationships.

In power-over relationships, professionals typically exert decision-making control over families. These relationships reflect vertical hierarchies, with professionals on top. A mother described what it was like for her to experience power-over relationships in an IEP conference:

I was told that this is a room full of professionals. All these people have college degrees. She told me, there's an MSW, and there's a Ph.D., and I mean she was naming off more initials than I even know what they mean. . . . And I'm just sitting here, nobody looked at me as the professional of knowing how these boys live. (Wang, Mannan, Poston, Turnbull, & Summers, in press)

One of the major outcomes of a power-over relationship is conflict within the family-professional relationship. Many families feel anger when they find that professionals are relating to them from a hierarchical position of power. Unfortunately, anger often begets still more anger, and anger leads to conflict and can cause partnerships to dissolve. A parent described his anger cycles as follows:

No matter how angry I got, the angrier they got back. The angrier I got, the worse the response was. I'm sure I was very annoying to them, . . . but they're very good at wearing you down. And I was worn down a number of times. It was fighting, all the time. It was like pushing back the water. No matter where you pushed, you were met with resistance everywhere. (Lake & Billingsley, 2000, p. 247)

In power-over relationships, it is ultimately the student and family that will experience the consequences of decision making. Whenever you are in situations where professionals are forcing their judgments on families, you would do well to remember the perspective that a parent has offered:

I said, you intend to do this regardless of what I say. I said, if you made the wrong mistake, what will happen to you? Nothing. I said, I have to live with the outcome of any erroneous decision for the rest of my life because I will be caring for my child until I'm gone from this planet and I have to reap the consequences . . . I said, I want to make the decisions about my child and I'll live with the consequences if I happen to make the wrong one. But it's difficult to live with the consequence for the decision you made that I was against. (Beach Center, 2000)

An alternative to power-over is a power-shared partnership. Power-shared partnerships are horizontal, not vertical. Imagine a team of professionals and family members all sharing their talents, time, and resources so that the whole is greater than the sum of the parts. Greater power is generated because everyone is working together toward mutual goals, and individual energy becomes group synergy. Each person's efforts significantly and exponentially advance individual and group goals (Senge, 1990; Turnbull, Turbiville, & Turnbull, 2000). A parent describes the synergistic benefit of power-shared partnerships as follows:

It has been WONDERFUL. It has absolutely been the best thing. Not only have there been benefits and services that have come, but all of the people that we deal with have got to where there's relationship there with everybody and there's this bonding, and we're getting to where we're on the same page and . . . nobody gets 100% of their way. It's everybody there, you put it in a pile, and it's give and take. (Wang et al., in press)

Figure 7–5 includes the perspectives of a mother from South-Central Los Angeles. She describes a situation when her son's early intervention teacher shared power with her and another experience when a social worker exercised power over her. Compare and contrast these different relationships, identifying the partnership benefits when power is shared and the partnership limitations when it is not.

It is important not to share so much power with families that they feel they have more responsibility than they have the time, energy, or desire to handle. One mother made an incredibly important point about the meaning of an equal partnership:

In the beginning I was an insignificant member of this team. But as the years go on, I do find myself taking more leadership in this. But that bothers me because I don't want the leadership role. I want an equal partnership. (Soodak & Erwin, 2000, p. 37)

Foster Empowerment

Empowered people strive to have control over their lives; they take action to get what they want and need (Akey, Marquis, & Ross, 2000; Turnbull et al., 2000); they know what action to take to solve the problems they face. Empowerment is the opposite of being stuck with a problem and having no motivation or capacity to resolve it.

As you become a partner with families and earn their trust, you will be an agent of their empowerment, demonstrating how you and they can take action to get what both of you want for the student. But you also will be an

FIGURE 7–5
Advocacy Partners: The Good and Not-So-Good

To ask Hortense Walker about the family and context factors and collaboration as a connector, it is best to ask about the characteristics of the most and least effective professionals she and her family have worked with.

Their best experiences came with Eric's teacher in an early intervention program. Before Eric entered the program at age 18 months, Marlene (the teacher) visited the Walker home and quickly became encouraging so that she and Hortense easily bonded.

How was she encouraging? By not being a "hammer" and insisting that Eric should be in the program but by explaining how the program would help Eric and the whole family and then letting the family decide whether to enter it. She gave them a reason to enroll Eric (motivation) and information on which to make a decision. She acknowledged to them that they have the power within themselves to be empowerful to make decisions. How was she able to create a bond? She was considerate of the family, keeping her appointments and gently prompting Hortense and her husband Michael to ask questions they were afraid to ask, questions about Eric and his impact on the family.

"We came to see Marlene as a person whose first objective was to meet the needs of our family as a whole. She emphasized the positives of the program for us and for Eric. We just ate up her time and her knowledge. She felt appreciated by us, and she was. That made the difference."

In a very real sense, Marlene became the context: She offered herself as a resource, and in doing so she created opportunities for partnerships. Clearly, by her

offer and especially the manner in which she made the offer, she displayed her sense of obligation to be a reliable ally.

By contrast, the least effective professional, a social worker at the regional service center, never asked Hortense and Michael what they needed. "Eric was very young, throwing up everything he ate, very skinny, and never asleep. I'd work all day and then sleep just an hour a night," recalled Hortense. But the social worker visited only once and never asked if Hortense needed respite. "She was rationing the respite to families whose children were more severely involved than Eric."

Yet in Hortense's mind, Eric was indeed a child with a severe disability, and Hortense herself was fast approaching the end of her rope.

The result of that interaction with the social worker? "I grew up in a home that respected professionals. I was raised by my grandmother and oldest sister; my mother died at childbirth, and I was the last of nine children. My oldest sister is 20 years older than I. They taught me to respect doctors and teachers and to do as they say."

The social worker taught Hortense just the opposite. Now, Hortense questions everyone closely and doesn't let anyone take her or her family lightly.

Well, almost everyone. With Marlene, it's not necessary to question closely. After all, Marlene acknowledges Hortense's and her family's power. In doing so, she creates a different kind of life for them, one in which they are invited by her to be collaborators and in which they gladly accept the invitation.

agent of your own empowerment, learning what you want and how to get it. The first step toward self-empowerment is to consider how to build your self-efficacy and to expand your capacity for persistence.

As you will learn more about in chapter 8, self-efficacy refers to the belief in your own capacities (Bandura, 1997; Hoy & Miskel, 2001). People tend to avoid activities and situations in which they believe they cannot succeed. They tend to undertake those activities and situations in which they think they can be effective. Thinking you can be effective is the core of self-efficacy. It also is a technique for adding to families' "empowerment quotient." Teachers who have a relatively strong sense of self-efficacy tend to encourage families to believe more in their own capabilities; the teachers augment families' self-efficacy. Family-augmented self-efficacy, in turn, encourages teachers to be even more efficacious. If you believe in your own effectiveness, the actions you take will probably encourage others to be more effective. This mutuality between families and professionals can foster empowerment for all partners.

Another key aspect of taking action is persistence—putting forth sustained effort over time. Persistence requires tenacity. It entails refusing to give up when your initial efforts do not immediately produce the desired results (Scorgie et al., 1999). Sometimes certain goals, such as finding the best medication regimen for a child with diabetes or working through problem behavior for a youngster with an emotional disorder, are especially elusive. Families and professionals will go through periods of trial and error before obtaining a successful solution. Persistence is required to work through seemingly insoluble challenges as well as to solve discrete, time-limited, or relatively short-term challenges. Empowered people typically refuse to give up until they find a solution to a challenge.

We encourage you to foster empowerment within yourself, your professional colleagues, students, and families by promoting self-efficacy and being persistent to achieve outcomes. When all of the partners in a student's life are more empowered, it is far more likely that each of them will feel relatively equal to the others. Each is capable of solving challenges, influencing outcomes, and participating in joint decision-making activities.

Provide Options

Solutions to challenges often do not come quickly and easily. One response to a challenging situation is to be inflexible and absolute:

- "I'm sorry but we have never done that at this school."
- "The rules and regulations say that is impossible to consider."

- "You have to be realistic and accept the fact that what we are offering you is all there is."

Another response to a challenging situation is to be flexible and creative. Just because one possible solution has never been tried before is not a good reason not to try it. Indeed, the mere novelty of a possible solution may be just the reason to try it. Committed professionals do not allow their thinking to be restricted. They embrace the complexity of challenges and the contexts in which challenges arise. They thrive on flexibility and creative options.

Equality is promoted when many options are available rather than backing families into a corner with only one alternative. People who have choices are able to be more powerful decision makers (Petr, 1998; Turnbull et al., 2000).

ADVOCACY

Advocacy refers to speaking out and taking action in pursuit of a cause. Advocacy is problem oriented; it identifies the nature of a problem, the barriers to solving it, the resources available for solving it, and the action to be taken. Your advocacy on behalf of a student or family leads to partnerships because it demonstrates your commitment to them. To be an effective advocate and a partner, you should:

- Prevent problems.
- Keep your conscience primed.
- Pinpoint and document problems.
- Form alliances.
- Seek win-win solutions.

Prevent Problems

We reviewed some of the problems in education in chapter 6. They are worth a closer look in light of the partnership principle of advocacy. A recent national random-sample survey of over 500 parents of children in special education reported the following results:

- Forty-five percent of parents believe their child's special education program is failing or needs improvement when it comes to preparing them for life in the real world after high school.
- Thirty-five percent believe their child's special education program is failing or needs improvement when it comes to being a good source of information about learning problems and disabilities.
- Thirty-five percent believe it was frustrating to get the special education services their child needed.

■ Thirty-three percent believe their child's current school is doing a fair or poor job when it comes to giving their child the help that they need (Johnson, Duffett, Farkas, & Wilson, 2002, p. 23).

Sixteen percent of parents reported that they have considered legal action because of the lack of quality in their child's special education program. Thirty-one percent of parents of children with severe disabilities indicated that they have considered suing, as contrasted to 13 percent of students with mild disabilities.

Would the survey have reported such discouraging results if professionals regarded themselves as advocates and acted accordingly? Most likely not. An effective advocate seeks to prevent problems; only when prevention fails does the advocate then have to seek to remedy any violations of a student's rights or to solve problems.

As a professional, you will encounter many situations in which you have the opportunity to pass the buck. But you also will have an opportunity to take responsibility. The advocating professional—the one who is a partner to students and families—tries not to pass the buck to someone else. That professional does not want to be labeled as Everybody, Somebody, Anybody, or Nobody:

> This is a story about four people named Everybody, Somebody, Anybody, and Nobody. There was an important job to be done, and Everybody was asked to do it. Anybody could have done it, but Nobody did it. Somebody got angry about that, because it was Everybody's job. Everybody thought Anybody could do it, but Nobody realized that Everybody wouldn't do it. It ended up that Everybody blamed Somebody when Nobody did what Anybody could have done.

Keep Your Conscience Primed

Keeping your conscience primed means feeling a sense of concern, irritation, and sometimes even outrage when children and youth with exceptionalities and their families face injustice. The opposite of a primed conscience is indifference to the circumstances of students and families. Try to stand in the shoes of the two parents whose feelings are expressed below. Think about whether your professional duty is to advocate for them as a partner, or to be indifferent to their concerns.

> Those of us that have older kids, it was a struggle. You have to basically get on your knees and crawl every step to get one thing. (Beach Center, 2000)
>
> And they wanted me to sign a paper that he would never talk. I said how do you know he'll never talk—I said I'm not signing anything so I went over the teacher's head to speech therapist and they were very angry with me and I went to the principal and he said—who told you to sign the paper—

I said the teacher did—well, she was outraged. But they did reprimand the teacher, and I wish I could find her today now. He's a motor mouth. We call him motor mouth. (Beach Center, 2000)

The more you prime your conscience to these types of injustices, the more likely it is that you will be an effective and motivated advocate.

Pinpoint and Document Problems

Effective advocacy requires you to develop a clear and detailed description of the nature of the problem you, a student, and a family face. It is not enough to describe a problem in a general way; you also need evidence about the nature and extent of the problem. Figure 7–6 includes tips for pinpointing and documenting problems.

Broaden Alliances

An old adage advises, "Lone wolves are easy prey." The opposite statement assures, "There is safety in numbers." Effective advocacy occurs when there are alliances among individuals who have similar concerns and interests—teachers, related service providers, principals, families, students, community citizens, and others. You will learn more about the positive outcomes of strong alliances in chapter 8.

A parent described the strength of her child's team, composed of professionals and family members who have formed a strong alliance:

> We're getting strong and what we're doing is we're forming this circle of strength around John and John is in the middle, he can't break through this. He's just surrounded by this wall of togetherness and strength. (Beach Center, 2000)

FIGURE 7–6
Tips for Pinpointing and Documenting Problems

- Observe the behavior of the people who seem to contribute to the problem and of those who seem to contribute to its solution.

- Keep data charts that reveal the frequency and types of problems that occur.

- Supplement these data charts with notes about what you observe; interview students, families, and colleagues and make notes of your conversations with them.

- Ask your professional colleagues for second and third opinions about the nature of the problem and the possible solutions.

Create Win-Win Solutions

Advocacy, within a partnership context, emphasizes the creation of win-win solutions; everyone who has a stake in a problem has a way of winning through the particular solution. A win-win satisfies everyone; it solidifies a partnership. The opposite is a win-lose situation. Hardly conducive to partnership, it pits one person against another.

The win-win approach is consistent with conflict resolution programs that focus on using communication skills to prevent, manage, and peacefully resolve conflict (Jones, 2003). When the other five principles of partnership are in place and when trust has evolved, it is much more likely that parties can negotiate to identify solutions everyone can endorse.

Communication can lead to win-win results; and the earlier the win-win results occur, the more likely it is that the final result will satisfy all parties. Consider a situation in which a parent asks the principal of his son's school to place the child into a private school, at public school expense, because the education the child is receiving in the principal's school seems to be inappropriate. Under IDEA a public school system must pay for the tuition of a private school placement if the public school does not offer an appropriate education but the private school does. Sometimes it is necessary for the parent to have an administrative or judicial due process hearing to prove that the public system must pay the private school tuition. Few principals want to admit that the school cannot offer an appropriate education; few want to be identified as the chief of a school that costs the public system even one private school tuition. So, what process of communication will enable the parent and professionals to create a win-win situation? A mediator suggested:

> Ask questions. If a parent comes in and says I found this new program down the road 50 miles, and I want that for my child, it's an error to say we don't do that or we're not going to provide that. The best response is, "Come in. Have a cup of coffee. Tell me about it. What did you like about the program? You went and saw it, did your son see it? What did he like? How were you treated? What did you see there that particularly impressed you?" Because it's the answers to those questions that reveal a person's needs and interests. . . . So try to think of our negotiation without walls, without artificial boundaries between what you can do and what you can't do. (Lake & Billingsley, 2000, p. 246)

How might a win-win situation be created by handling the situation this way as contrasted to immediately engaging in a power-over approach? Which approach is most likely to strengthen partnerships and build trust?

SUMMARY

The seven principles of effective partnerships with families include:

- Communication
- Professional competence
- Respect
- Commitment
- Equality
- Advocacy
- Trust

The principles of partnerships form an archway where trust is the keystone—the principle that supports all of the others.

Partnerships are mutually supportive interactions among families and professionals in which all parties agree to defer to each other's judgments and expertise, as appropriate for the purpose of securing benefits for students, other family members, and professionals. What you have learned in this chapter and what you will learn in chapters that follow should enable you to develop skills and to enhance motivation so you will be an effective partner with families.

REFLECTING ON THE VIGNETTE

1. Which of the seven partnership principles was most important for each of the four families? How did the principle play a significant positive or a significant negative role in their relationships with professionals?
2. If you were a professional working with each family, which partnership principle would you want to practice the most? Or are all of them important to practice simultaneously?
3. Which of the partnership principles did each family practice with the professionals in their lives? Which did they not practice?

ENHANCING YOUR SELF-AWARENESS

Review each of the seven principles of partnerships presented in this chapter and reflect on your own experiences, preferences, areas of comfort, and areas of discomfort with respect to each. Knowing yourself and developing goals for enhancing your capacities will substantially influence your own success and family-professional partnerships.

Communication

Reflect on your relationships with others and identify the people who bring out the best in your ability to listen empathetically. Who brings out the worst in how you listen?

What characteristics are associated with each of those two groups of people? What do your reflections teach you about improving your capacity to listen?

Professional competence

Describe a situation in which you felt a great deal of pity for a person with a disability. What was the source of that pity, and how could you transform that pity into a sense of high expectations for that person's future?

Respect

Identify a person who seems to you to be without many strengths. What might you do to find a strength of that individual, no matter how many challenges that person faces?

Commitment

How would you react in a situation in which you want to be available and accessible to a family, but the best time for them to meet with you conflicts with a planned get-together with your family or friends? How should you handle this situation and how can you create a win-win situation?

Equality

Describe a situation in which you have sought help from a professional who ultimately used a power-over approach with you. How did you feel in that relationship? How did it influence the trust you placed in the professional and the extent to which you followed the professional's advice? What implications does this experience have for you in developing your professional skills?

Advocacy

Do you perceive yourself as a loner or as a person who naturally seeks alliances with others to solve problems? How does your own comfort as a team member affect your tendency to broaden alliances in order to be a more successful advocate? What steps can you take to foster your capacity to form alliances with both professionals and families?

SUGGESTED ACTIVITIES

1. Identify all of the jargon in the quoted passage on p. 143. In that passage, a psychologist is explaining test results to a parent. Rewrite all or even a small portion of this passage to enhance its clarity. Try to stand in the shoes of the mother. List the questions that you think she might have after hearing this information.

2. Have an extended conversation with the parent of a child with an exceptionality about the parent's experiences with educators. What was the most beneficial partnership that the parent has ever had with the child's teachers? What made the partnership work and what difference did it make for the parent? Ask the parent to contrast that relationship with one of the least beneficial experiences that the parent has ever had with one of the professionals who works with the child. What led to this second experience being so unsuccessful, and what suggestions does the parent have for educators to avoid having such unsuccessful partnerships?

RESOURCES

You can find a link to these resources on the Companion Website at *www.prenhall.com/turnbull*.

1. Children's Defense Fund
   25 E Street, NW
   Washington, DC 20001
   202-628-8787
   www.childrensdefense.org

   The Children's Defense Fund provides effective advocacy for all children in America, with a particular attention on the needs of children who are poor and who are from culturally and linguistically diverse backgrounds. It offers current data related to trends of children's well-being and highly relevant publications.

2. Quality Mall Website
   www.qualitymall.org

   This Website specializes in information related to providing support to people with developmental disabilities in respectful and empowering ways. The Website is organized as a mall with many stores or topics such as Health and Safety, Housing Office, Life and Future Planning, Family Place, and Cultural Place. The values on which the Website is based are highly consistent with the partnership elements.

3. Beach Center on Disability
   The University of Kansas
   1200 Sunnyside Avenue
   3111 Haworth Hall
   Lawrence, KS 66045
   785-864-7600
   beachcenter@ku.edu
   www.beachcenter.org

The Beach Center, cofounded and codirected by Ann and Rud Turnbull, conducts research, produces publications, and provides master's and doctoral training to students related to implementing state-of-the-art programs for individuals with developmental disabilities. The Beach Center's Website has many full texts, research articles, and two- to three-page research briefs on these articles that provide a broad overview of priority issues, including those facing families.

Trust as the Keystone for Partnerships

CHAPTER ORGANIZATION

FRAMING QUESTIONS

1. Should educators expect parents of children with exceptionalities to trust them?
2. What can educators do to establish trust with parents who have had negative experiences with the educational system in the past?
3. What difference does trust really make in family-professional partnerships?

VIGNETTE

Some people begin their relationships with others by instinctively trusting them. Others begin by trusting because they have reason to trust.

Leia Holley did not begin her relationships with the Bonner Springs Elementary School staff by instinctively trusting them. She had had so many connections with schools that she knew better than to trust simply on the basis of instinct. Instead, she began by trusting on the basis of instincts as buttressed by facts.

Leia had heard that the Bonner Springs Elementary School had a teacher who was qualified to teach students with autism and who used a particular method for overcoming their communication barriers. That hearsay alone was sufficient for the family to move to Bonner Springs.

Leia's instinct was also visceral. It was the look in Tierney Thompson's eyes when Leia first met her: "We came here because I met Tierney, and I saw the look in her eyes. I heard her voice when she talked about the kids. She never said a name, she never described a kid but I could see those kids and I could see every element of Tierney in those kids and that's why we brought Sean here. . . . I didn't need anything else, I've seen Tierney's eyes, I've looked at her, I've seen her heart, and if she's got a school that will support her and give her the elements she needs, Sean's going to succeed."

The instinct to trust, even when it rests on a factual foundation, is fragile. It is particularly fragile when the factual foundation begins to crumble, and even more so when the trusted professionals and the trusting parents miscommunicate about a matter of great importance to both of them.

In this case, the miscommunication was about a video of Sean that Leia wanted the school staff to make. Leia wanted a video of Sean in class to show to his neurologist, providing some evidence on which the physician might adjust Sean's medications.

So Leia prevailed on Tierney to videotape Sean. And videotape is exactly what Tierney did—all of Sean's day, all activities except his using the toilet, even though Sean had problems with bladder control and with letting others know when he needed to go to the bathroom.

When, however, Leia used the videotape to confront the school staff about how it was, in her opinion, inadequately educating Sean, Tierney was justified in accusing Leia of misrepresenting why she wanted the videotape.

It does not matter now whether Leia explained fully why she wanted Tierney to videotape Sean, whether Tierney fully understood Leia, or even whether Leia had another reason in mind. What does matter is that neither of them was fully clear; their communication channels were flawed.

Was it the video episode alone that turned the instinct and factual foundation for trust into distrust? No. Other patterns convinced Leia that she could not trust Bonner Springs Elementary. The turning point, of course, was Sean's seizure and Leia's sense that the school did not have a plan, or even the staff capabilities, to respond rapidly to Sean's seizures. As she often told the staff, she was "scared to death" and "panicked." But there had been other turning points—untrained bus drivers, too few paraprofessionals to assist Tierney, and no consultants to conduct a functional behavioral assessment. Leia's trust dissolved over time.

Trust, however, is a two-way relationship: The trusting or distrusting person must place trust or refuse to place trust in one or more other people.

As Leia's trust began to dissolve, so too did the trust in Leia that the school faculty, staff, and especially Tierney and the assistant principal had enjoyed when Sean first enrolled.

It was not as though they lacked a reason to distrust Leia. Indeed, they had many reasons. In their view, Leia misrepresented how she would use the videotape. She often quoted federal law and implicitly threatened them with a lawsuit. She challenged them about their preparedness for dealing with Sean's seizures.

Here, then, were two former allies who were now adversaries, neither trusting the other, and each having reason to be distrustful. It was not that any one person was at fault. Sadly, many events conspired to destroy the initial trust.

That which is destroyed is often rebuilt, sometimes in the same shape, sometimes in a different and often better form. So it was with Leia and Bonner Springs Elementary.

After the May 2000 IEP meeting, Leia withdrew Sean from school 4 days before the end of the semester. Both Leia and the school staff drew back from each other, allowing a vacuum to develop in their relationships. Whether this was deliberate

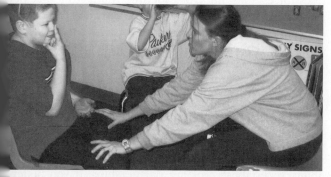

Tierney Thompson provides hands-on guidance to Sean Holley.

Jackie Bennett, a social worker at Bonner Springs Elementary School, encourages Sean Holley to mix a bowl of cookie dough during a Circle of Friends gathering.

Sean Holley and his teacher, Tierney Thompson, formed a close, personal bond during their time together at Bonner Springs Elementary School.

or merely instinctive, we can only guess. Everyone, however, knew it was necessary to create space. The implicit message of the IEP meeting was simply that everyone needed to cool down. Fortunately, the creation of space was mutually agreed on. If either Leia or the staff had pursued the other, no good would have come from any new confrontation.

The summer months passed. Sean attended summer school and made some gains. Tierney, exhausted from the school year and wary of any further struggle with Leia, sought sanctuary outside of school.

And then Leia called Tierney, just before the beginning of the fall semester. "Let's start over again," was her simple plea. Tierney's response was equally simple: "Yes, it's water under the bridge. Let's focus on Sean, not on you and me, not on who said what to whom."

Without saying it, Leia and Tierney mutually committed to civility and collaboration—no more yelling, no more tears, no more having to leave an IEP meeting to collect one's feelings and thoughts, no more anger. How to build trust again? Leia's idea was to supplement the IEP process with a different one: Making Action Plans (MAPs) (see chapter 12).

This process involved the following steps: Bring together everyone who is involved with Sean. Focus on what he wants, what he can do, and what he needs to learn to achieve his vision for himself. Make a map for Sean's future and put him at its epicenter.

A change of school personnel helped; Tammy Eldridge moved from the position of assistant principal to principal. A change of school culture also helped. During the summer, the entire faculty had agreed to a four-part ethic for Bonner Springs Elementary: culture, character, curriculum, and community.

So, when the MAPs meeting occurred, Leia felt burdens fall off her shoulders. Everyone cared for Sean, everyone fo-

cused on him. "We were beyond IEPs, money, and resources." And beyond accusation, blame, and insistence on meticulous compliance with law and forms.

In their place were many seemingly small actions that collectively created trust: Leia offered to demonstrate the MAPs process to other teachers and schools in the Bonner Springs district; food appeared on the table when Leia and the staff gathered. Those kinds of activities brought individuals together as a team.

All that, plus honest and civil communication, enabled Leia and the staff to enter into an equal relationship, respecting each other's skills and commitment to Sean, advocating as much for each other as for Sean, and going beyond the call of duty.

Now Leia and Tierney can say anything to each other without offending the other. Neither has to guard what she says; neither grabs hold of every word from the other and parses it for its offending content.

Among the dozen staff who are directly involved with Sean, there is consensus. Trust began with two people and spread to the entire team. Trust is twice-blessed: It blesses those who give and those who receive.

INTRODUCTION

In chapter 7, you learned about six of the seven principles of partnership: communication, professional competence, respect, commitment, equality, and advocacy. For each, you learned about state-of-the-art partnership practices.

We now turn our attention to the seventh principle. We begin by defining trust and explaining why trust is the keystone for partnerships. We then review the key practices for establishing trust, identify the factors that persuade families and teachers to trust each other, and explain how these factors produce distrust, conditional distrust, and unconditional trust. Of course, trust refers to individual partnerships between families and professionals. But many factors at the school building level—the school climate related to trust—can make it easier or more difficult to establish partnerships with families. We explain how trust reflects school climate. Finally, we discuss how the interaction between your beliefs about yourself and others' beliefs about themselves affects your ability to establish trusting partnerships. If you believe that you can establish trusting partnerships, and if other believe that they also can establish trusting partnerships, then trust is more likely to flourish, and student outcomes are more likely to improve.

DEFINING TRUST AND DESCRIBING PRACTICES FOR ESTABLISHING TRUST

Defining Trust

There are many different definitions of trust. *Merriam-Webster's Collegiate Dictionary* (2003) defines it as an assured reliance on the character, ability, strength, or truth of someone or something. One literature review reported nearly 20 definitions (Tschannen-Moran & Hoy, 2000). These definitions generally share some common elements, but they contain unique aspects, as well. We define trust as having confidence in someone else's reliability, judgment, word, and action to care for and not harm the entrusted person. It exists when people believe that the trusted person will act in the best interests of the person extending the trust and will make good faith efforts to keep their word (Baier, 1986; Rotter, 1967; Tschannen-Moran & Hoy, 2000).

Trust is as simple as this, expressed in the terms of the metaphor of the arch (chapter 7): "I, a parent, trust you, an educator, to teach my child and not to harm her in any way. I think you are reliable, will exercise good judgment, will keep your word, and will act in my child's best interests. I trust you to walk with me and my child through the process of educating her in school so that she will have skills and habits to use outside of school. I trust that we will walk through the arch together." Or it can be as simple as this: "I, a teacher, trust you, a student or a parent, to walk with me down the paths that we call education, through the arch that we call school, and to outcomes that will occur inside and outside of school."

Trust as the Keystone

Trust is the keystone in the arch that illustrates the partnership principles. Take a look at some arches, usually found in campus buildings or houses of worship. You will see that several stones on the left, and the same number of stones on the right, rest on top of each other and lean toward each other. These inclining stones meet at a center point, and the stone at the center is the keystone. Without it, the left and right sides of the arch will not connect. When the left and right sides connect, they do so at the point of the keystone. Figure 8–1 illustrates the central role that trust plays in family-professional partnerships.

What is the practical significance of the arch metaphor? How you carry out each of the six other partnership principles significantly influences the extent to which families trust you. Some examples of trust as the

FIGURE 8–1

Trust as the Keystone for Partnership Practices

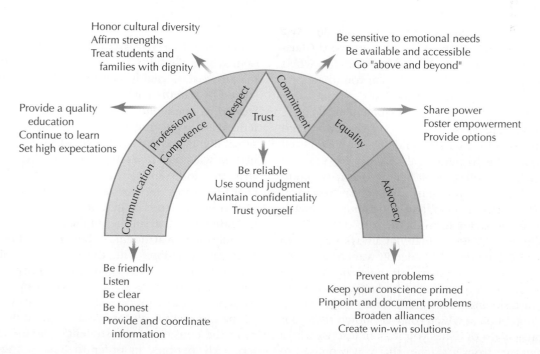

keystone of partnerships are as follows (Blue-Banning, Summers, Frankland, Nelson & Beegle, 2004; Frankland, 2001; Tschannen-Moran & Hoy, 2000):

- *Communication.* You build trust when you exchange information in open and honest ways.
- *Professional competence.* You build trust when you are skilled in providing a quality education to their child.
- *Respect.* You build trust when you treat people with dignity and honor their cultural values.
- *Commitment.* You build trust when you go "above and beyond" in meeting the priority needs of students and families.
- *Equality.* You build trust when you share power with families.
- *Advocacy.* You build trust when you take action to seek win-win solutions when students and families experience injustices.

Like the mason who builds the arch, you build trust when you practice each of these six partnership principles, for each leads to the seventh partnership principle, trust.

Trust Practices

Four practices will enable you to create trust in your partnerships with families:

- Be reliable.
- Use sound judgment.
- Maintain confidentiality.
- Trust yourself.

Be Reliable. Reliability occurs when you do what you say you will do; it means keeping your word (Blue-Banning, Summers, & Frankland, 2004; Hoy, 2002). When you are reliable, others can depend upon you to act predictably. A parent of a child with a disability put it this way: "If you tell me you're going to do something, do it . . . don't tell me you are going to do this and don't do it; and don't tell me you did it when you didn't—just don't tell me an untruth" (Blue-Banning et al., 2004, p. 179).

To be reliable, you first must believe that it is important to be reliable. Then you must want to be reliable; you must have the desire, energy, and persistence to match your words and behavior, to "walk the talk."

In a teacher's busy life, it may not always be easy to keep your word, even when you deeply want to do so. So much can get in the way; there can be a slip between what you say and what you do. To be reliable, you need to organize your tasks and your time. You may want to keep a "trust me" notebook in which you write down all of your commitments—a list of issues you want to discuss with a parent, a message from a teacher that you promised to give to a student, a phone number for a return phone call, a request from a parent to know about upcoming school holidays. The notebook can help you remember your commitments. It is a good device for combining your values and motivation with your behavior.

Use Sound Judgment. Teachers make judgment calls in countless situations, often on the spur of the moment. Families will trust you if they can rely on your good judgment in such matters as curriculum, instruction, assessment, discipline, social relationships, and particularly safety. Parents want to be assured that their child will be both physically and emotionally safe. Many parents of children with problem behavior have concerns about some of the extreme measures that schools take to discipline students, especially students with disabilities. Consider trust in light of one parent's experience: "I found out they were keeping my son in the bathroom for an hour at school because of his behavior. So I was very upset because of the time that lapsed without me finding out. I couldn't do anything about it" (Beach Center, 2000). Just how much will that parent trust a teacher or school that isolates a child and then does not tell a parent about that "treatment"?

Using sound judgment involves being competent. Professional competency, you will recall from chapter 7, is one of the principles of partnership. When teachers know how to provide scientifically based instruction and how to promote positive behavior in scientifically valid ways (not using the "bathroom isolation technique"), it is far more likely that parents will trust them.

Maintain Confidentiality. The records of a student with a disability or special gifts will contain information that is highly sensitive. Often, information is shared by parents with the understanding that it will be treated as confidential and always be protected by the federal law regulating student records, the Family Educational Rights and Privacy Act (FERPA). Some of the information will come from the nondiscriminatory evaluation that the Individuals with Disabilities Education Act (IDEA) requires. As you learned in chapter 6, the purpose of that evaluation is to determine whether a student has a disability and, if so, the implications for the student's program and placement. Other information will come from conversations with the student's family or other teachers, or from other agencies that provide services to the student (such as a mental health or social service agency). As a general rule, FERPA requires you to treat all of the information as confidential and to disclose it only with the consent of the student's parents, or as FERPA explicitly permits, in order to benefit the student in school. FERPA implicitly provides a foundation for trust because it requires you to do exactly what families and parents trust you to do, which is to maintain their confidentiality. We cannot emphasize enough how important it is to maintain that confidentiality. A teacher described her perspectives as follows:

> It's purely a matter of trust, that they can trust that person so that they can tell them whatever. I have heard all kinds of things ya know, from families and from the children that I work with, and I consider that pretty sacred, actually. It's kind of a compliment, as far as I can see, that they're willing to trust me with those kinds of things. (Blue-Banning et al., 2004, p. 179)

In your many interactions in the school building (including the teachers' lounge and school office) and even outside it, the best approach for trust building is to regard confidential information about students and their families as absolutely off-limits in any discussions. Under FERPA and IDEA, you may share information in team meetings about the individual student when the information is relevant, recent, and reliable and is necessary or desirable for making decisions about the student's education. As you will learn in more detail in chapter 10, the one exception to this rule is that, in most states, teachers and other educators are "mandated reporters," meaning that they must report to a child protection agency any abuse, neglect, maltreatment, or exploitation. If you suspect any of those, you should consult with your immediate supervisor or school principal concerning your duties and the process for reporting. Otherwise, regard information as yours to be held in a sacred trust.

Trust Yourself. Trusting yourself means that:
- You have confidence in your own reliability, judgment, word, and action.
- You know that you have the capacity to care for and not harm what others entrust to you.
- You know that you will act in the best interest of others who trust you and that you will make good efforts to follow through on your word.
- You believe in your own capacity to be trustworthy.

To trust yourself is such a critical component of the overall principle of trust that we will return to it at the end of the chapter, after we explain other issues about trust, families, and schools.

TRUST AT THE INDIVIDUAL LEVEL

No single stone builds an arch. You and your students' families will use many stones; indeed, you will bring some of them from your past as you quarry new ones. To put it another way, the values, emotions, and perspectives you and the family members bring to the partnership, as well as the experiences that you share with each other, influence your present and future partnerships (Jones & George, 1998). It is said that all politics is purely local; likewise, all trust is purely personal.

We begin focusing on trust at the individual level by identifying some of the factors that dispose families and professionals to trust each other. We then point out that trust exists on a continuum.

Disposition to Trust

Just as some people have a disposition to be cheerful and others have a disposition to be somber, so people have a general disposition to trust or to distrust. People who are inclined to trust find it natural and easy to trust others—even from their initial meeting. People who are inclined to distrust find it natural and easy to lack confidence in others and to expect negative outcomes from their relationships.

The disposition to trust and distrust derives from past experiences and personality characteristics (Erikson, 1968; McKnight, Cummings, & Chervany, 1998; Rotter, 1967). Some people have an abundance of "faith in humanity" (McKnight et al., 1998, p. 4); they expect others to be trustworthy, to care about them in respectful ways, and to act in their best interests. They also believe that life is easier and better outcomes generally happen when people deal with each other in trusting ways. People are said to have a "trusting stance" (McKnight et al., 1998, p. 7) when they believe that placing trust in others is the right approach to human relationships.

Indian nationalist leader Mahatma Gandhi exemplified a person with a trusting stance, for he believed that one should always expect the best from other human beings:

> As long as I see the slightest excuse for trusting people, I will certainly trust them. It is foolish to continue trusting after one has had definite ground for not trusting, but to distrust a person on mere suspicion is arrogance and betrays lack of faith in God. (Gandhi, 1958, p. 333)

Just as some people have a disposition to trust, others have a disposition to distrust. They "lack faith in humanity"; they assume that they cannot put their trust in others and are persuaded that better outcomes occur when they withhold trust.

To help you understand these issues, reflect on your own disposition:

- To what extent do you tend to have faith in humanity? How does your disposition affect the relationships that you establish, both initially and long term?

■ To what extent have you taken a trusting stance in relationships even when you may have lacked confidence in a particular person?

Just as your disposition to trust affects your relationships generally, so it also shapes the likelihood that students' families will trust you and that you will trust them. Two key factors influence families' disposition to trust professionals, as well as professionals' disposition to trust families. These two factors are (1) individual and collective history and (2) cultural diversity.

Individual and Collective History. Families and professionals bring their individual and collective histories to each new relationship and to each new partnership. What historical factors influence their dispositions to trust?

Families' History Influencing Their Disposition to Trust Professionals. In chapter 5, you read about the eight different roles that families and parents play, sometimes willingly and sometimes not. Families may have experienced a few or even all of these roles by the time their child becomes your student. Their experiences with any of these eight roles will dispose them to trust you or not and will affect how long it takes them to trust you.

A national survey of families (Johnson & Duffett, 2002) whose children receive special education services demonstrates that families' own experiences and the revealed experiences of other families influence their disposition to trust or not. Some of the findings were encouraging in terms of "faith in teachers":

■ "My child's teachers really care about him/her as a person." Eighty-five percent strongly or somewhat agree.
■ "My child's teachers know a lot about his/her specific disability and how to work with it." Sixty-nine percent strongly or somewhat agree.

Other findings point out families' major concerns:

■ "Too many special-needs children lose out because their parents are in the dark about the services they are entitled to." Seventy percent strongly or somewhat agree.
■ "Many students wouldn't need to be in special education if they had gotten extra help in school earlier on." Sixty-nine percent strongly or somewhat agree.

In addition to their beliefs about the quality of education in general, parents' own experiences with teachers, school-based teams, and other professionals affect each new relationship with educators, as one mother so aptly pointed out:

I was one of those parents who left . . . IEPs like someone who has left a foreign movie without the subtitles. I felt a very small and incidental part of this procedure, and at times I felt a feeling that my daughter really wasn't getting her full share or placement of services. (Sullivan, 1995, p. 108)

Foreign movies. No subtitles. Low comprehension. Feelings of distrust. They all go together, like an ill-conceived arch. Surely you have been in a class where the curriculum or instruction seemed foreign to you. If asked to answer a question, did you ever just want to hide? If you gave the wrong answer, did you feel "small" and "incidental"?

Someday, you may find yourself trying to be a partner with a parent who has felt small and incidental in IEP meetings, not only once but many times. And then, you will understand just how hard it is for that parent to be disposed to trust you even before getting to know you.

It is not just the direct personal experience of a parent that affects the disposition to trust or not. It also is what the parent hears from other parents. Disposition to trust arises from both the individual and collective experiences of parents. Like professionals who collectively may label a parent as uncooperative and not trustworthy, so too parents have a grapevine that compels them to trust or not trust a particular educator, administrator, or even an entire school district. That is the point made by one mother of a high school student with a significant disability:

We had been warned in advance by other parents that my son's teacher was secretive and dishonest. She would tell you one thing to your face in a meeting, and then she would go in her classroom, close the door, and do just the opposite. She even said that one of the reasons she liked to teach students with significant disabilities is that they "can't communicate well enough to tell their parents what's happening." A student teacher confessed to us that what was happening behind closed doors was that students spent most of the day watching TV and taking naps rather than learning. Once the word got out, parents banded together to make sure that the principal knew and that other parents would not send their child to this school. (Beach Center, 2000)

How can you secure a reputation, within the parent grapevine, of trustworthiness (McKnight et al., 1998)? Every interaction you have with every parent and student contributes to your reputation. The more you develop partnerships with families, the more they will tell other families about their positive experiences with you. The more you experience distrust with families, the more your reputation for untrustworthiness will spread.

Professionals' History Influencing Their Disposition to Trust Families. Just as families' individual and collective histories incline them to trust or distrust professionals, so professionals' individual and collective histories incline them to trust or distrust families. What are professionals' general perspectives about families who have children with exceptionalities?

These general perspectives may influence you, but even more powerful may be the quality of partnerships that you and your faculty peers have had with families. Successful previous partnerships provide a positive context for future partnerships. Just as positive experiences can lead to the disposition to trust, so can negative experiences contribute to the disposition to distrust.

Families' reputations precede them, just as yours precedes you. Your peers might warn you that one of your students comes from a "dysfunctional family" and that you are in for a "hard time" with the family. What is your disposition to trust apt to be? Will you follow Gandhi and try to find even the slightest excuse for trusting the family? If so, your inclination to trust the family may very well bring out the best in them and become the basis for a surprising partnership.

Cultural Diversity. In chapter 1, you learned that culture influences families in many important ways. Two aspects of culture relate directly to trust, namely, race and income.

Impact of Cultural Diversity on Families' Disposition to Trust Professionals. As it has been for our entire history as a nation, "race and ethnicity continue to be salient predictors of well-being in American society" (National Research Council, 2001, p. 21). Two aspects of race and ethnicity influence parents' disposition to trust professionals. These are (1) the proportion and disproportion of students identified as having a disability and (2) the degree to which families of different racial and ethnic groups place confidence in schools and other organizations that are run by European Americans.

Regarding disproportionate representation, 16% of children and youth, ages 5 to 17, in the general population are African American; however, 21% of all children and youth with disabilities are African American (U.S. Department of Education, 2002). Of all students identified as having mental retardation, 34% are African American. Of all the students identified as having emotional disorders, 27% are African American (U.S. Department of Education, 2002). Furthermore, African American, Latino, and Native American students are underrepresented by 40% to 50% in gifted education (Ford, 1998).

A national survey of parents whose children were receiving special education services reported that 44% of the African American and Hispanic parents believed that schools are "too quick to label African American stu-

dents," 33% did not agree with this tendency, and 24% reported that they did not know. Based on these data, you can anticipate that a substantial number of families will believe that racial discrimination is inherent in the process of identifying African American students for special education and providing services to them.

Racial disproportion in special education is strongly related to income. Given the higher rate of African American students placed in special education, it is noteworthy that African Americans have been approximately 2.5 times more likely than European Americans to experience poverty (Fujiura & Yamaki, 2000). The higher disability rate among children from diverse racial groups appears to be primarily associated with the higher incidence of families who experience poverty and who are headed by a single parent (Fujiura & Yamaki, 2000, p. 191).

Families from diverse backgrounds vary in how much confidence they place in organizational policies, regulations, and practices, especially when those organizations are run by European Americans (McKnight et al., 1998). A family's disposition to trust school systems often depends on whether the family is a member of the majority or minority population of the school. Approximately 14% of all special education teachers are from culturally and linguistically diverse groups, while 38% of the students in their classrooms are from diverse backgrounds (Billingsley, 2002). Olson (2000) has predicted that these data will become even more skewed, with 12% of teachers and 40% of students coming from diverse backgrounds. Furthermore, over 40% of U.S. schools had no teachers from diverse groups on their faculty as of 1996 (Riley, Fryar, & Thornton, 1998). Given that schools are primarily dominated by European Americans, families from culturally and linguistically diverse backgrounds may be cautious in their disposition to trust. Instead, they may trust teachers and administrators who share their own racial and ethnic cultural traits (McKnight et al., 1998; Zucker, Darby, Brewer, & Peng, 1996). A mother of a Korean child who attended a predominantly European American school described her concern about racial discrimination as follows:

> I feel that his teacher at the previous school was somewhat prejudiced against non-white people like us. Similarly, his teacher at the third school, the school he went right before the current school, seemed to dislike him too. When I was watching the school's Special Olympics Games, a coach would blame Bob for making troubles whenever he had problems with other American kids. Of course, when children fight, both parties are equally guilty, not just one. It made me feel that they are discriminating against him. (Park, Turnbull, & Park, 2001, pp. 162–163)

This mother's concern about discrimination obviously will affect her disposition to trust her son's teacher and others whom the teacher influences.

Families from culturally and linguistically diverse backgrounds may think that they, not just their child, bear the brunt of discrimination. They may believe that educators do not offer them the same respect they give to a family from the majority culture. A study of Puerto Rican families (Harry, 1992) indicated that parents had valuable insights about their children's education that educators generally discounted. One mother, typical of the research respondents, said:

> It is only their opinions that matter. If I do not want the child in a special class or if I want her in a different school, they will still do what they want. Because that is what I tried to do, and Vera [the social worker] talked with them too and tried to help me, but—no! Our opinions are not valued. Many parents do not want their child in a special class or in a school so far away, but they keep quiet. It is very hard to struggle with these Americans. In America, the schools are for Americans. (Harry, 1992, p. 486)

In addition to race/ethnicity, a family's disposition to trust educators and school systems also relates to the family's income. In chapter 1, you learned that the racial disproportion of African American students in special education is strongly connected to family income. Similarly, poverty affects how both students and families relate to others. As one mother explained:

> If you have no money, it's very difficult to be—to do—to be together, to do fun things, to be at peace, to come home to a haven. . . . Because if you have no money, the bills not paid, you not gonna rest when you get home. You might have a good family, you know, a good husband, whatever, whatever. But you don't have money, all that can go down the drain, so. . . . Money provides a way of release. You can go on a vacation, maybe, once a year, whereas if you don't have the money, you won't be able to do that. You can— you can pay your bills. Whereas if you don't have money, you won't be able to do that. And when you can't do those things, you have this feeling of insecurity which floods over into other problems, emotionally. Anger, bitterness, and then it jumps off on the other family members and you got chaos. (Park, Turnbull, & Turnbull, 2002, p. 151)

Anger and bitterness can also "jump off" to professionals. When people are angry and bitter about the deprivations of living due to income disparities, they may not be disposed to have faith in humanity and to trust professionals.

The impact of socioeconomic status (SES) is felt not only at the student and family level, but also at the school level. Schools are often characterized as low SES or high SES. In chapter 2, you learned that No Child Left Behind (NCLB) characterizes low SES schools as "Title I" or "disadvantaged schools." The National Research Council (2001) reported that schools with more children from low-income backgrounds have lower per-student expenditures and fewer experienced, well-trained teachers than schools with a higher concentration of children from middle- and upper-middle-income backgrounds. The council also reported that parent advocacy is less likely to occur in schools with a high concentration of students from poverty backgrounds.

In seeking to understand that parents from diverse backgrounds may be less inclined to trust professionals, it is important to understand that schools are largely based on European American middle-class values, forms of communication, and organizational expectations (Lareau, 1987, 1989). Thus it is often more challenging for families from diverse backgrounds to trust than it is for families who are similar to school professionals in culture, ethnicity, race, education, and financial power. In Figure 8–2, you will read the perspectives of two African American parent leaders from New Orleans, Ursula and DJ Markey, and how their organization, Pyramid Parent Training, seeks to bridge the gap between parents from diverse backgrounds and the city's school system.

Families' History Influencing Their Disposition to Trust Professionals. Factors related to race, ethnicity and income affect families' disposition to trust professionals, but they also affect professionals' disposition to trust families. It is easier for people to trust others who share common values, goals, and experiences (Kramer, Brewer, & Hanna, 1996; McKnight et al., 1998). When you share the same racial/ethnic background and same income level as parents, you may feel you have more in common with them and be more willing to trust them.

What can you do about your disposition to trust when you recognize that it is influenced by race/ethnicity and income differences? You can begin by examining your own values and stereotypes about people from backgrounds different from your own. Do you ever regard such families with suspicion? Do you assume they will behave in a less-than-desirable way? If so, here is our advice: The more you incorporate the seven principles of partnership into all of your interactions with families—especially families who may have a disposition for distrust—the more likely it is that your partnerships will move in a positive direction.

How do these factors about family income influence professionals' ability to trust families? The SES of students in the school population, in general, has been found to be the most powerful predictor of student achievement (Hoy, Hannum, & Tschannen-Moran, 1998). As you will

FIGURE 8–2
Advocacy Partners in Bridging the Gap of Trust for Diverse Families

We are parents, and that's what makes all the difference for us and for the families with whom we work in New Orleans.

Our first son, Duane, was born with epilepsy and autism. We lost him in December 1999, when, at the age of 26, he had a seizure in his bedroom in our house. He died in our arms; for that fact, and for his life, we can only be grateful.

Our other son, Teiko, has some learning disabilities; but he is now launched into adulthood, having graduated from the New Orleans schools and a postsecondary job-and-life skills training program in Los Angeles.

We have said that our children have made all the difference in our lives, and that is true. But we also have been heavily involved, since the early 1960s, in the civil rights movement in New Orleans.

As African Americans, we see the disability rights and civil rights movements as one movement, with the disability rights movement being an extension of the civil rights movement.

In New Orleans, discrimination in education takes two forms. First, there's discrimination based on students' races. Second, there's discrimination based on the fact that they have disabilities.

We respond to discrimination by reaching out to the parents of the children, for far too often the parents lack the resources—time, money, and knowledge of the law and the best practices that could benefit their children—to combat discrimination and get an appropriate education for their children.

To reach out to parents and to mediate between them and the schools, we formed Pyramid Parent Training Program. We offer workshops, publish newsletters, refer parents to resources, and provide one-on-one assistance. We attend their children's IEP meetings. We also attend state and local school board meetings. By working on both the individual and the system levels, we mediate—that is, we serve as a go-between. Don't get us wrong: We advocate for the parents and their children, but we can't be successful advocates unless we also understand the school system and what drives it to do what it does.

You see, there is a cultural difference between the families and their children, on the one hand, and most professionals in the school system, on the other. The families and their children are from traditionally underserved or unserved segments of our population. They have experienced so much discrimination for such a long time in jobs, housing, access to medical care, and education that they begin to believe that their children are not entitled to an education that launches them to jobs, independent living, and community participation.

Many of the schools' professionals do not or no longer relate to these experiences. Some are white; all are educated and have succeeded in the very system that employs them and that writes off children.

And the families and schools have different agendas, too. The parents want their children to get an education that makes a difference in their lives. The schools have to serve as many students as possible with an insufficient amount of money and with the greatest efficiency possible. So the schools conserve resources and increase their efficiency by placing the emphasis on budgetary constraints rather than parent priorities.

With these two different cultures and agendas, the question we faced as parents and that other families face daily is this: How can we bridge the gaps between the cultures so that the students will get what IDEA promises? For us, the answer was to mediate between the cultures by telling the families, "You are not alone," and then proving it by helping them gain the knowledge and support they need. Whatever help we provide—we call it "leadership development"—we recognize that, within each parent, there is the power to be an effective advocate for his or her child. And we have to acknowledge the parallel: Within every educator there is the power to be an effective teacher of that child.

So cultural mediation consists of recognizing the potential in everyone to become part of a team that works for a child. Thus, team building is an essential part of our work that incorporates the recognition that cultural agendas may differ and that our job is to help both the families and the schools by raising the level of effective parent participation in the education process.

Ursula and D. J. Markey, New Orleans, LA, used by permission of the authors.

earn later in this chapter, research at the building level has found that ". . . poverty more than ethnicity seems to be the culprit in hindering the trust that could lead to achievement for many students in urban schools" (Goddard, Tschannen-Moran, & Hoy, 2001, p. 15). Given that poverty and the lower SES of families affect student achievement and teacher trust, you will want to be especially mindful of all the principles of partnership as you interact with families, especially those who experience poverty.

Individual and collective histories and cultural diversity influence professionals' disposition to trust families, and families' disposition to trust professionals. As a general rule, they will influence your trusting partnerships with parents. Specifically, histories and diversity affect the level of trust that educators and families bring to their partnerships.

Continuum of Trust

A continuum is a line along which something can be measured. For our purposes, that "something" is trust. The word *continuum* also allows for trust to begin at one point or level and to evolve to other points or levels. When partnerships are successful, typically trust evolves gradually from less trust to more trust. The same is true about distrust. Different scholars describe the evolution to trust and the levels of trust in different ways (Jones & George, 1998; Lewicki, McAllister, & Bies, 1998; McKnight et al., 1998; Rempel, Holmes, & Zanna, 1985). Accordingly, we describe trust as existing on a continuum that includes distrust, conditional trust, and unconditional trust (see Figure 8–3).

Distrust. Distrust is the opposite of trust. Distrust entails lacking confidence in the reliability, judgment, word, and action of someone; it reflects the expectation that what is entrusted to someone will not be cared for and may even be harmed. It assumes that people will not act in the best interests of others and will not demonstrate good faith to follow through on their words. Often distrust reflects a lack of faith in humanity. The distrustful person believes that others are generally not trustworthy and that it is always better to distrust than to trust; distrust prevents disappointment when others prove to be untrustworthy.

Families' Distrust of Teachers. It can be especially challenging for teachers to have a strong disposition to trust and then to encounter parents who have an equally strong disposition to distrust. That can happen, as we pointed out, when race, ethnicity, culture, and poverty come into play. You may begin with a high disposition to trust but quickly move on the continuum toward distrust if you believe that the parent assumes you have stereotypical and even prejudicial views. If you encounter that situation, ask yourself the following questions: How does the parent's disposition to distrust affect you and your relationship with the parent? Do you believe you have been unfairly criticized or even stereotyped? Could the parent's perspective help you understand how your actions may have conveyed that you have stereotypical perceptions, even if you are unaware of such feelings?

It is easy to become defensive, frustrated, or angry at parents who are disposed to distrust. Try to put aside your own perspective and, however hard it is, take the parents' perspective. True, you cannot walk in the parents' shoes; you will never know all of the factors that have led them to a distrusting disposition. It is possible and even probable that you and the parents can move along the continuum from distrust toward conditional trust if you repeatedly demonstrate the partnership practices that we have described.

Is it worth it for you to demonstrate those practices and try to develop trust with a distrusting parent during the short 9 months when school is in session? Is it worthwhile to get to the point of greater trust just in time for the end of the school year? We think so.

The effort you invest in the parent and the trust you establish will make it easier for the parent and other professionals to form trusting partnerships in the years ahead. Your present effort will yield future returns. It also will enhance your own and your school's reputation for trust. That reputation, in turn, will help other parents and professionals. Figure 8–4 includes the perspectives of Carla Berg (not related to Clara Berg) concerning her efforts as a European American teacher to establish trust with parents from diverse backgrounds, some of whom were initially inclined to distrust her.

Many people will begin their partnership with you with strong levels of trust. Sometimes, however, partnerships slip into levels of less trust or even distrust. Being on a continuum means that levels of distrust can displace levels of trust, which can happen when either you or the parent breaks trust with the other.

The cost of distrust is exceedingly high. You and a parent might divert your energy to trying to protect yourselves from the other, monitoring each other's behavior and injecting formality into your interactions. Within special education context, distrust can lead to mediation, due process hearings, or both.

Once distrust occurs, it feeds on itself in such a way that educators and parents actually expect the worst from each other; indeed, they seek examples of the other's negative behavior (Govier, 1992; Holmes & Rempel, 1989). For example, a father who distrusts you may look for examples of behavior that confirm your untrust-

FIGURE 8–3

Continuum of Distrust, Conditional Trust, and Unconditional Trust

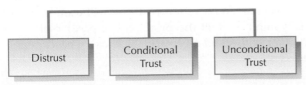

FIGURE 8–4

My Voice: A Teacher's Strategies for Building Trust

Parents and families of children with severe or multiple disabilities have had several years of "systems experience" by the time I meet them in my role as their child's elementary school teacher. In those years they have had at least as many (or more) negative experiences with professionals or systems as good experiences. They will view me through all of those experiences. Whether they are trusting by nature or not, I must prove myself to them in order to earn their trust.

I am Caucasian—my blonde hair proclaims my ethnicity—and have worked in schools that are in communities of racially, ethnically, and culturally diverse families. In these environments, I have been viewed with skepticism, many times based upon my appearance alone. As much as the children are fascinated and want to touch my hair, adults are upset and suspect my commitment to their community and their children. Even having been prejudged, I try to address all families the same . . . as unique individuals.

Parents anticipate that educators will judge them. They expect that whether they are from diverse populations or not. Characteristics such as their intellect, socioeconomic status, style of child rearing, clothing, and transportation are some bases on which they may think I will judge them. But I try, directly or indirectly, to let them know I cannot and will not pass judgment on them.

To the extent which I have control over it, I try to begin our relationship by sharing information. During our first meeting, I describe the structure of my classroom, the routines, and general class goals. I explain the activities that I use to achieve these goals. I tell them I have an open door policy to my classroom and that no appointments are necessary. I encourage their input and ask for their ideas, concerns, suggestions, and examples of previous experiences with their children in school, home, and the community. I always ask what we can work on at school to support the family's goals and needs at home. Most important, I take time to listen to the family and what they have to share—good, bad, hopes, disappointments, whatever they feel is important for me to know. This is basic strategy for building trust at the beginning of my relationship with them, being open about my work and being a good listener.

I also try to establish trust through daily or frequent communication. I prefer to use daily communication notebooks. When language or literacy are challenges for families, I use the phone or picture communication, or I find a reliable translator. However we determine works best to communicate, I always share positive messages about their child. No matter how small the progress, CELEBRATE! It may be a new experience for parents to get good news from school about their child. Parents appreciate that someone else values their child's good qualities. I also rely on open communication to share when I am uncertain, and I ask for their input, I respect their suggestions, and tell them about the outcomes of our combined efforts.

The tone of my communication is important. I ask about them and their family members in honest, conversational tone. My expression of interest in all of the family creates an opportunity for us to have a relationship that extends beyond the child.

Not the least, I share information about myself to the extent I am comfortable. I let parents know about a trip I am planning on or if I have been sick, and I ask for their expertise on sewing or our other common interests.

None of these strategies is limited to ethnicity, race, or culture. Given enough time and committed interest, I have found these to be successful means to be trustworthy. I believe that a trusting relationship may be the most powerful support parents and I can offer to enhance students' progress in school.

Carla Berg, formerly a teacher in Hawaii and now a doctoral student in special education at the University of Kansas.

worthiness. When you discipline his child because of problem behavior, he might think that you "have it in for my son" and that your discipline was unwarranted. This situation could become even more divisive if the father perceives that you are discriminating against his child because of racial/ethnic or income differences.

Just as trust begets trust, distrust begets distrust. Families who trust you will be inclined to find all the good you do. Likewise, families who distrust you will be inclined to identify the negative about you. Trust makes relationships pleasant and partnerships effective. Distrust makes relationships contentious and partnerships unlikely. We encourage you to take every step possible to reap the positive dividends that trust produces, avoiding the negative dividends of distrust. It is far easier to invest the time to ensure that trust continues and moves up the continuum than to repair broken trust.

Conditional Trust. Conditional trust is the broad band on the continuum in which people neither completely distrust nor unconditionally trust each other. In this situation, people generally assume that another person is trustworthy, and they seek opportunities to confirm that assumption. When conditional trust exists, educators and parents get to know each other so they can develop a sense of how reliable the other person is.

Conditional trust is like courtship; two people seek to foster trust and avoid any action that might impair it (Shapiro, Sheppard, & Cheraskin, 1992). When one party behaves in similar ways over time and in different circumstances, the other party sees predictable patterns of behavior; a sense of dependability replaces skepticism. Like some courtships, trust can develop quickly. Like others, it can take a lot of time, especially when the educators and parents bring individual and collective histories and the challenges of racial, ethnic, and socioeconomic diversity (Kipnis, 1996; Tschannen-Moran & Hoy, 2000).

Families' Conditional Trust of Teachers. Families who have not struggled with educators and schools will probably begin their relationship with you by presuming you trust one another. They will not set aside that presumption unless you give them reason to do so (Gambetta, 1988). They will be highly disposed to trust and will manifest their "faith in humanity" with a "trusting stance" (McKnight et al., 1998). Although some people need to "see it to believe it" (parents may require you to prove yourself before they believe you are trustworthy), others "believe it and then see it" (parents will believe that you are trustworthy and then note whether your behavior confirms or disconfirms their assumption). During this conditional stage, families will note how you interact with them and how you go about educating their child. As they observe you, they will develop evidence about your trustworthiness. The courtship involves gathering evidence on whether to continue it, conclude it happily, or end it. During that courtship, the stage of conditional trust, families will note your partnership practices:

- To what extent are you professionally competent?
- To what extent do you communicate with them in friendly, clear, and honest ways?
- To what extent do you treat them and their child with respect?
- What is your commitment in going "above and beyond"?
- How do you practice the principle of equality in your relationship?
- Do you speak out and advocate when injustices occur?

During the conditional trust stage, families gather impressions about you and begin to define the nature of their relationship with you. As you learned earlier, their initial impressions will be influenced by many factors, including their backgrounds, cultural compatibility, your reputation, the reputation of the school in its partnerships with families, and your behavior. Families develop expectations based on each interaction with you. They determine whether you are predictable in your behavior or if you interact with them in so many different ways they never know what to expect (Rempel et al., 1985).

If your behavior consistently confirms that you are trustworthy, parents need less behavioral evidence of your trustworthiness. Instead, they recognize that your personal and professional qualities and your character enable them to trust you as a person. The words "as a person" are important. They trust you, yourself. That is different from trusting you to take specific actions in specific situations. They come to trust you holistically, not specifically. They start to depend on you as a person in whom they can place their trust.

Teachers' Conditional Trust of Families. Just as families gather information that enables them to know "who you are," you acquire information to learn about them. The courtship works very much the same as you get to know families and discover the extent of your trust in them. You will seek information on whether a family is predictable so you can rely on them and know what to expect. As their behavior becomes more predictable, you will be able to determine if you can depend on them.

A family's reputation for trustworthiness will influence the extent of your conditional trust and if you are able to move along the continuum to unconditional trust. Similarly, your individual and collective history with families, especially families in similar situations (and with similar cultural backgrounds), will likely influence the amount of time it takes to determine if you can conditionally trust a family and if you have reason to move to unconditional trust.

A problematic situation arises if you discover that a family is abusing or neglecting their child. Abuse and neglect issues can significantly impair your ability to trust parents. In chapter 10, we will cover that topic and describe how you can communicate with families who have challenges related to abuse and neglect and still develop trusting partnerships with them.

Unconditional Trust. In unconditional trust, partners feel safe about being open with each other. They share their needs and concerns candidly because they have faith that the trusted partner will seek positive rather than negative outcomes (Jones & George, 1998). They believe the other person will represent their interests in the same way and to the same extent that the other would represent his or her own interests. Quick to overlook mistakes, they cut each other slack.

Families' Unconditional Trust of Teachers. When unconditional trust exists, families have supreme confidence in teachers' reliability, judgment, word, and action.

They are convinced the teacher will act in the best interests of the family and student and will do no harm to them or their child. They will not second-guess your judgment, worry that you will be upset with them, or calculate how they should interact with you in the future.

Understandably, a family may trust you unconditionally in some areas of your professional role but only conditionally in other areas (Tschannen-Moran & Hoy, 2000). A family may trust you unconditionally to provide instruction in reading and math, but trust you only conditionally in how you interact with them in the IEP meeting. It is unlikely that families would distrust you in some areas and trust you unconditionally in others, but they might distrust you in some areas and conditionally trust you in others. Distrust rarely coexists with unconditional trust.

Can unconditional trust evolve to a level where families trust you too much? Yes. You may conclude that a family's disposition to trust you is excessive and unwarranted. Perhaps a family has unconditional trust in your ability to prepare their son or daughter for life after high school, when, in fact, you know that you are not carrying out this task nearly as well as it needs to be. Perhaps you do not have all of the skills you need to accomplish the priority outcomes.

It is very important to be honest in your partnerships with families. That honesty extends to excessive and unwarranted trust. A trusting partnership means (among other things) that you can tell parents when and how you need more help and when they have trusted you too much. If you fail to justify their trust, even if it is excessive, they may begin to distrust you.

Your goal, then, is to establish an optimal level of trust, avoiding some of the problems associated with trusting too much or too little (Wicks, Berman, & Jones, 1999). Researchers on trust caution that partners should try to achieve the "golden mean" that the Greek philosopher Aristotle espoused.

Aristotle's work (1986) focused on individual character understood in the context of the polis (i.e., community). The highest good for human beings—eudemonia (living well)—came through cultivation of virtues or human excellence. Virtues are golden means between extremes; excess or deficiency in these tendencies represents vices. For instance, in response to danger, the extremes are cowardice and recklessness; the mean is courage. We position optimal trust as a form of the "golden mean" Aristotle discussed. From his work on the golden mean, we can infer that one ought to have a stable and ongoing commitment to trust but that judgments about trusting others should be made carefully, realistically, even prudently. Aristotle's golden mean does not dictate that there should always be "moderate" levels of a trait, such as trust. Rather, it implies that trust levels should be appropriate to the context and may fall anywhere on the spectrum, from minimal trust to high trust, depending on the person and situation. We suggest that Aristotle's "virtuous person" would be an astute creator of what we term optimal trust: knowing whom to trust, how much to trust them, and with respect to what matters. (Wicks et al., 1999, pp. 5–6)

Establishing the golden mean of unconditional trust—which is sometimes referred to as optimal trust—is a balancing act that will differ within each professional-family partnership. No specific formula helps you find that golden mean, but one of the key practices of trust—using sound judgment—will help you approach it.

Finally, unconditional trust is your best "insurance policy" when crises occur in your relationships with families and students. It is impossible to predict when a crisis is going to arise or what its causes will be. A crisis may relate to a student's academic performance, social relationships, behavior, emotional well-being, or physical health. Another crisis may result from dramatic changes in the family's life, such as death, divorce, or disability.

During a crisis, you and a family will have the greatest need for trust; trust will enable you to work with each other to address the crisis. You cannot expect families to trust you unconditionally or even to a high degree during a crisis unless they have developed their trust during "courtship" when only conditional trust existed (Adams & Christenson, 2000). The more opportunities you have to build unconditional trust with families before a crisis occurs, the more likely you will be able to address or even resolve the crisis successfully, raising the level of trust in the process.

With unconditional trust, the parties try hard to understand the challenges that professionals, families, or students face. During a crisis, those who have trusted each other unconditionally have faith that the others will act in their best interests. If you should make a mistake in judgment that has consequences for the child or family, your error will have a far different outcome if the family trusts you unconditionally than if the family distrusts or only conditionally trusts you. Unconditional trust typically leads to forgiveness and understanding (Wicks et al., 1999).

Teachers' Unconditional Trust of Parents. When you have unconditional trust in parents and other family members, you have utter and complete confidence in their reliability, judgment, word, and actions. You also, however, are conscious that you could trust them too much, so you seek Aristotle's "golden mean." You also anticipate that you and they may need to trust each other unconditionally in times of crisis, so throughout every opportunity you cultivate your understanding of them and their life circumstances.

FIGURE 8–5
My Voice: Challenging Behavior and Trust

I have often wondered how my son's teachers and their school administrators would describe my son, AJ, who is now 13 years old. Would they say he is tall, strong, polite, good-looking, and usually well-behaved? Or would they say he has autism, acts out when challenged by tough academics or teased by his schoolmates, and has been known to throw a plate of spaghetti in the cafeteria? Would they ask to have him in their classes, or would the first words out of their mouth be about his going somewhere else, such as home, and being a sure candidate for being suspended?

More than wondering how his teachers and their administrators might portray AJ, I wonder what values drive them and how I can make my values and theirs come together, on my son's behalf. Do they believe, as some of his school administrators have believed, that AJ should be disciplined like every other student and that overlooking some of his behavior is catering to his disability and teaching him and other students that disability excuses otherwise inexcusable behavior? Do they ignore the conditions in school that trigger his challenging behavior? Or do they believe that it is a moral imperative to educate AJ and all other students as effectively as they can, whether or not the students have a disability? Do they modify the academic curriculum so that it is not so difficult that he physically rebels against it? Do they seek ways to include him, such as by creating opportunities for his classmates to be his buddies?

And finally, I have wondered what the bottom line is when it comes to my son's education, and whether his teachers and their administrative officers concur with me. Do they follow the rules slavishly, or do they exercise independent judgment? Do they see every infraction of a rule as a punishable offense, or do they have their eyes set on protecting AJ and others from harm and then trying to change the school's environment, his peers' behavior, and his own behavior so as to assure safety for everyone and effective outcomes for AJ?

What I do not have to wonder about is this: When I encounter a teacher such as Deb Engstrom, a school principal such as Steve Nilhas, or a special education director such as Bruce Passman, then I can trust them. Why? Because they regard my son in a positive way and respect him for what he is and can be. They share the same values that I have. They are professionally competent and exercise professionally defensible judgments. One of them was a farmer for ten years and knows what it means to fail, despite his best efforts. All of them know about effort and failure and about being humble in the face of challenging behavior. Each of them advocates to keep AJ in school so he can continue to learn; they don't want to be the cause of his failure. They call me and take my calls anytime and anywhere. They treat each other as equals and include me in their circle of equals.

I trust them because I know that their action, even when it results in AJ being suspended or isolated, comes from a concern for AJ and for me, too. I trust them because I know that they have decided, among themselves, to back each other up so long as what they are doing helps AJ and does not result in him hurting anyone. I trust them because I know they will operate as a team, with consistent behavior that AJ and I can count on, day after day. And I trust them because AJ himself thinks of them as his allies, not his opponents.

So I don't have to confront them every time they act. I don't' have to demand that they do this or that. I avoid creating an antagonistic relationship with them, because they don't want to have that kind of relationship with AJ and me. I trust them because I know that they have to balance the needs of all of AJ's schoolmates, all 1,300 of them, with what is good for him. I know that, in striking the balance, they will consider AJ's needs, my vision for him, and the reality of AJ's school.

Denise Poston
Lawrence, Kansas

Figure 8-5 provides the perspective of a single parent of an adolescent son with autism about the process she went through to unconditionally trust her son's teachers.

TRUST AT THE BUILDING LEVEL

You have learned about two important aspects of trust between individuals—the disposition to trust and dis- trust and the continuum of trust. However, individual trust exists (or does not exist) in various contexts. For your purposes as a teacher, the most immediate context

is the school in which you teach. The school or buildin level climate influences how easy or challenging it can l to develop trusting partnerships with individual familie

Every school has its own climate—its own personali (Hoy & Miskel, 2001; Tagiuri, 1968). A school's climate personality is shaped by such internal characteristics the following:

■ Perceptions and values that the administrative lead ship bring to bear in working with faculty, parents, a teachers

- Physical environment inside and outside the school
- Competence or incompetence of the faculty (including teachers, related service providers, and other school staff)
- Nature of the rewards and sanctions that building administrators and parent-directed associations are able to bring to bear

School climate tends to be relatively stable over time unless there are systemic efforts to change it (Smith, Hoy, & Sweetland, 2001).

As you work to develop trusting partnerships with families, the school climate will either facilitate or impede your efforts and those of other families, students, faculty, administrators, and principals. That is why you should learn about the key dimensions of school climate and how they are tied to trust. If you know about the dimensions of school climate, you can either rely on them to build trust or try to prevent them from destroying trust.

Theory and research provide a foundation for understanding school climate (Halpin & Croft, 1963; Miles, 1969; Parsons, 1967). Hoy, a leading researcher in educational administration, and his colleagues have conducted extensive research on the nature and outcomes of school climate (Goddard, Sweetland, & Hoy, 2000; Hoy, 2002; Hoy, Smith, & Sweetland, 2002; Hoy & Sweetland, 2001; Smith et al., 2001; Sweetland & Hoy, 2000). Drawing from their research, we present four key dimensions of school climate:

- *Collegial leadership*—the principal's leadership style and relationship with faculty
  Faculty professionalism—the relationship among the faculty in a school
  Achievement press—setting high academic standards and providing the means for attaining those standards
  Environmental press—the relationship between a school and its community

These four dimensions influence the extent to which the context at the building level will (1) facilitate or impede your and other professionals' efforts to build trust with families and students and (2) affect student outcomes (Hoy et al., 1998). When you teach in schools that excel in these four dimensions, you are far more likely to develop trusting family-professional partnerships. It is still possible to develop trusting partnerships in schools without a positive climate, but it is much more challenging and typically takes longer. In this section we will discuss each of these four dimensions of school climate and how they can help or hinder you in developing partnerships with families.

Collegial Leadership

Collegial leadership refers to the principal's leadership style and particularly the relationship between the principal and faculty (Hoy et al., 2002). The faculty consists of general and special education teachers and other professionals such as school psychologists, speech and language pathologists, physical therapists, occupational therapists, and music therapists.

Many of the partnership practices that are important in your individual partnerships with families are also important in forming partnerships between principals and faculty members. These include avoiding hierarchies and sharing power, providing choices, setting high expectations, being friendly, and being available and accessible. When principals engage in these partnership practices, teachers are far more likely to trust them (Hoy et al., 2002; Smith, et al., 2001). A faculty member shared her perspective of how she wished her principal would demonstrate greater partnerships with faculty:

> My preference is that they would be more of a collaborating leader than ours is right now. Just because I think that that's where the push is going to come to actually collaborate with others—it's going to come from the top. Others won't care or make the effort unless somebody else is putting that pressure on (to collaborate). This will make things better and probably that authority figure is the one to do it. At the same time, the authority figure needs to also have to come down and say, "I'm going to be part of this team." I wish our administrator would be more of a collaborative advocate. (Frankland, 2001, p. 165)

The collegial leadership style of the principal makes a real difference in student outcomes. Schools with high student achievement are more likely to have a climate characterized by collegial partnerships between principals and faculty (Hoy et al., 1998). Principals in high-achieving schools are more likely to treat faculty with equality, friendliness, and consideration; the teachers are more likely to reciprocate in kind without any need for coercion or sanctions.

Faculty Professionalism

School climate research defines faculty professionalism as the relationship among the faculty in a school (Hoy et al., 2002). The partnership principles and practices we described in chapter 7 are comparable to the practices that exist when there are strong partnerships among the faculty: going "above and beyond" with students, being sensitive to each other's emotional needs, treating each other with dignity, respecting each other's professional competence, using sound judgment, and being cooperative (Hoy et al., 2002).

Cooperative teachers seek a power-shared approach rather than power-over, just as families want a power-shared approach with professionals (as you learned in chapter 7). A faculty member described the effect of an uncooperative teacher on her trust of that individual:

> She was hard to trust because she was putting me on the spot all of the time. In every situation, I felt like I was on the spot to know the exact answer. I was not as comfortable to ask questions . . . because I felt she would be looking down on me. . . . I never really shared any personal information about myself with her because of the trust factor. (Frankland, 2001, p. 136)

Focusing on the provision of special education services, a faculty team member at an IEP meeting stated her concerns about another team member who was not a trusting partner:

> I send a reminder notice that the meeting is going to be on February 8th. I send them out two weeks before (the meeting is scheduled). All professionals are okay with the date for the meeting. Then we get to the meeting and this professional hasn't even arranged to have her kids supervised while we are in the IEP meeting. None of the paperwork has been done. I don't like parents to have to wait and see how inefficient we are. So, you've got the parent there, and they have to wait 20 minutes while this teacher gets herself organized. Then she comes to the meeting and says she doesn't have this or that done. This is typical of this person. (Frankland, 2001, p. 124)

In contrast, a faculty member described what enables her to trust other educators in the school:

> When you know that they are there for the good of the student and that they will do the best thing for the student, I feel that I can trust them. They have to be committed to the children, and they have to be knowledgeable and be willing to listen. Then I feel that you can trust them. (Frankland, 2001, p. 137)

Faculty who practice partnerships are more likely to trust each other (Hoy et al., 2002). Indeed, schools with a climate of strong faculty professionalism are more likely to have high student achievement (Hoy et al., 1998). Schools characterized by strong partnerships among faculty also are more likely to provide a highly responsive context to develop trusting partnerships with families. Partnerships between and among faculty members lead to multiple positive outcomes.

Achievement Press

Achievement press, within the context of school climate research, focuses on the extent to which teachers and parents set high standards, students work hard to achieve

the standards, and principals supply the organizational resources to support teachers and students (Hoy et al., 2002; Tschannen-Moran & Hoy, 1997). You can think of achievement press as partnerships among teachers, parents, students, and principals with the primary focus on improving student achievement. Thus, we will refer to partnerships associated with achievement press as achievement partnerships.

Achievement partnerships include setting high expectations, going above and beyond, affirming student strengths, and providing quality instruction. A mother who recently immigrated to the United States described how pleased she was with the emphasis her son's teacher placed on his academic achievement:

> At the time, we had a hard time managing my son's behaviors. He sometimes did not follow directions and showed some tantrums. Of course, he did that at school, too. But he had a very good teacher at the time. If he did not finish his work or showed behavioral problems, the teacher had him stay in school even after other kids went home and worked with him until all work was done and he calmed down completely. I have never seen a teacher who tried to teach him even after school time. (Park et al., 2001, p. 165)

As you learned in chapter 6, NCLB's principle of accountability for results (adequate yearly progress) pressures schools to ensure that all of their students make academic progress. Students with disabilities are not exempt from the achievement press. Some may have a different curriculum, methods of instruction, or assessments, but they too are expected to make progress, and their schools are expected to include these students' progress when reporting the progress of all other students.

Schools with strong achievement partnerships are more likely to have faculty who trust students and parents (Hoy et al., 2002; Smith et al., 2001). In those schools, teachers are more likely to perceive that students and parents are working with them rather than against them. The teachers' perception, in turn, helps build partnerships and leads to greater trust.

> When students, teachers, and the school value academic achievement and parents press for high standards and improvement, teacher trust in parents and students is high. Perhaps it is the agreement among all groups that creates teachers a strong trust in their partners, after all, each party is committed to the same goal—academic achievement. Clearly, the achievement press of the school promotes faculty trust in parents and teachers, but such trust also facilitates a commitment to achievement excellence. (Hoy et al., 2002, p. 15)

Strong achievement partnerships are positively related to high student achievement in elementary school

(Goddard et al., 2000), middle schools (Hoy & Sabo, 1998; Sweetland & Hoy, 2000), and high schools (Hoy & Tarter, 1997). The relationship between partnerships and student outcomes exists not only in middle-class schools but also in schools in which a majority of the students come from low-income backgrounds. Based on a sample of students in which the majority were African American and the recipients of free or reduced-price lunch, researchers reported that school-achievement means averaged 11.39 points higher in schools with strong achievement partnerships. "Our results suggest that schools with strong academic emphases positively affect achievement for poor and minority students" (Goddard et al., 2000, p. 698).

Environmental Press

Environmental press refers to the relationship between the school and the community in which it exists (Hoy et al., 2002). Within the research literature about school climate, *relationship* refers to the extent to which parents and community members exert strong pressure on the school to change policy or to influence the functioning of the school (Hoy et al., 1998). Although the other three dimensions of school climate have a positive focus, this dimension sometimes results in a negative focus because it emphasizes protecting teachers from unreasonable demands. Rather than focusing on how to build productive and supportive partnerships between educators and families, the emphasis is on making sure that a few vocal parents do not interfere with school decision making.

Researchers have investigated the impact of environmental press on student achievement and trust. Schools that have vocal parents and community citizens eager to be involved in school decision making are more likely to have students who achieve at higher levels (Hoy et al., 1998). The pressure from parents and community citizens appears to be a positive catalyst for student achievement, even if educators feel the pressure is excessive.

The dimension of environmental press within the research literature does not adequately capture the possibilities for positive partnerships among educators, families, and community citizens (Hoy et al., 2002). This is an area identified for important future work.

Faculty Trust of Parents and Students. Although environmental press does not focus on the positive nature of family-professional partnerships, extensive and promising research has been conducted on faculty trust of parents and students. Similar to school climate studies, this research is done at the building level. It is clear from the research that the degree to which the fac-

ulty in your building trust parents and students will affect how easy or difficult it will be for you to develop trusting partnerships with families and students.

Initially, researchers used one measure to evaluate the level of faculty trust in parents and another measure to evaluate the level of faculty trust in students. Results showed that faculty trust in parents and students were not two separate factors but combined into a single factor. Teachers who trust students also are very likely to trust parents and vice versa (Goddard et al., 2001). Trusting partnerships with families do not happen in isolation but are linked to, in this case, partnerships with students.

In this section we will review findings related to faculty trust in parents and students and then expand upon that research to provide a stronger base for understanding faculty trust of parents and students at the building level. In review, you have learned that:

- Faculty who teach in schools led by principals with open leadership styles (collegial leadership) are more likely to place greater trust in parents.
- Faculty who teach in schools with strong partnerships among faculty (faculty professionalism) are more likely to place greater trust in parents.
- Faculty who teach in schools with strong partnerships among teachers, parents, students, and principals with an emphasis on achievement (achievement press) are more likely to place greater trust in parents and students.

Faculty trust of parents and students is a positive predictor of student achievement (Goddard et al., 2001):

> To our knowledge, this is the first study that links faculty trust in students and parents with student achievement. Our findings suggest that trust makes schools better places for students to learn, perhaps by enabling and empowering productive connections between families and schools. There seems to be a collective effect of trust; in schools where there was greater trust, student achievement was generally higher. (p. 14)

Other research also has linked trust and school achievement. In a study of trust and achievement in 400 Chicago elementary schools, researchers reported that the extent of trust among teachers, parents, students, and principals discriminated powerfully between schools that improved their achievement and schools that did not. "Most significant was the finding that schools with chronically weak trust reported throughout the period of the study had virtually no chance of improving in either reading or mathematics" (Bryk & Schneider, 2003, p. 43).

Greater trust leads to higher achievement and, in turn, higher achievement enhances trust. Unfortunately, the opposite is true as well: Low levels of trust are associated with low achievement, and low achievement diminishes trust (Goddard et al., 2001; Tschannen-Moran & Hoy, 2000).

In addition, teacher trust seems to be affected by the students' socioeconomic status. Teachers had greater trust when a higher proportion of students were not poor, and teachers had less trust when there were more poor students in the school. This finding should remind you that income (and race) can influence a teacher's or parent's disposition to trust.

A very positive finding, however, is that when trust was high in low-income schools, SES was not a significant predictor of student achievement. This means trust is more important than SES in their relative influence on student achievement. Raising trust levels of faculty at the building level is a far more attainable goal than raising the SES level of all poor children and families.

> Our findings indicate that teacher trust in students and parents is an important social feature that is distributed inequitably among the schools we studied. The need to build trust is signaled by the strength of the effect of trust on student achievement. Students have higher achievement in schools where teachers report greater trust. Our findings also suggest that teachers in schools with more low-income students seem to find trust harder to cultivate. These are the places with the most critical need to learn more about building trust. (Goddard et al., 2001, p. 14)

Parents' Trust of Teachers. You have learned about (1) the extent of trust that teachers have in parents and (2) the outcomes associated with teachers' trust in parents. What about parents' trust of teachers? A comparison of teachers' trust in parents and parents' trust in teachers found that parents tend to trust teachers more than teachers trust parents (Adams & Christenson, 1998, 2000). In this research, parents' trust of teachers was most influenced by parental satisfaction with their interactions with their child's teacher and their child's grade level. Parental trust in teachers is highest at the elementary level, substantially declines at the middle school/junior high level, and then slightly declines at the high school level (Adams & Christenson, 2000).

This same study also investigated how much a number of different factors influence teachers' trust in parents. These factors included the frequency of teachers' interaction with parents, their satisfaction with the interaction, teacher ethnicity, teacher gender, teacher education level, teachers' experience and longevity as teachers, and teachers' satisfaction with their relationship with parents. The item most associated with predicting the teachers' trust of parents was the teachers' satisfaction with their relationship with parents. Teachers' trust in parents was significantly higher at the elementary school level than at the high school level. Parents and teachers both identified the importance of communication as their top priority for improving trust.

Research has found other factors associated with trust levels between parents and teachers (Adams & Christenson, 1998):

- No differences in trust were found between parents of students receiving special education and regular education services.
- Parents of students who receive more intensive special education services had higher levels of trust than parents of students who receive less intensive special education services.
- Parents with higher trust also had higher levels of involvement with their child's teacher and school.
- Contrary to research previously reported, no differences were found in trust levels based on parent income or the ethnicity of parents.

What meaning do you draw from the finding that parents tend to trust teachers more than teachers tend to trust parents? One way to interpret this finding is that parents have more at stake in entrusting the care of their child to a teacher, especially when they do not know the teacher, than teachers do in instructing the student or interacting with the parents. Thus, parents may seek reasons to raise their trust level. Because forming a partnership depends upon reciprocal trust among all partners, consider how you can be sure your trust of parents does not get stalled but rather continues to evolve throughout your partnership with them.

No matter how much teachers, administrators, parents, and students might trust each other, one sure way to stir up distrust is through action in the political arena, especially when local school boards become involved with state education agencies, teachers and parents in the schools they serve, and local politics. To learn about distrust at the system level, see Figure 8–6.

TRUSTING YOURSELF

At the beginning of the chapter, we stated that there are four partnership practices associated with trust. We described three of those practices—be reliable, use sound judgment, and maintain confidentiality. We promised that we would come back to the fourth practice, which is to trust yourself.

Trusting yourself is tied to your self-efficacy and your own empowerment. As we have already described, the

FIGURE 8–6
My Voice: Distrusting the System

It's rare for professors to tell future teachers that the systems that will employ them are not always trustworthy and that people don't always behave the way Denise Poston describes them in Figure 8-5. But distrust is a reality, as news reports about the New Orleans, Louisiana, school board made clear during the summer of 2004.

During that summer, the state legislature was debating whether to pass a bill that would place the state superintendent of education in charge of the New Orleans schools. The reason for the bill, some said, was that the schools were failing the children. The bill, some said, is about saving the students by saving the schools.

Others said the bill was about taking control of the schools away from the elected school board. If the school board were no longer in control, it could not fire the city schools' superintendent, whom the board had hired and who had so antagonized some school board members that they now were turning against him.

Others saw something even more subtle behind the proposed state law. The law gave the state superintendent the power to enter into contracts to build or repair schools or provide services to the schools. The bill, then, was not about saving the schools, the students, or the local superintendent. It was about allocating patronage: If there were only one person who had to be paid off (assuming the state superintendent could be bribed), then a hungry contractor would not have to pay off the majority of members of the local board.

Inevitably, race enters the debate in New Orleans, because the majority of the city's students are African American. Were they again going to be shortchanged by the white legislators, a white governor, and a white state superintendent who favored the bill?

Further, were the African American parents who elected the city school board members about to be disregarded by a state takeover that, in effect, would nullify their votes?

There is an adage in politics that the person who controls the agenda and access to the meetings usually controls the outcomes of the meetings. So, when the school board met to fire its city superintendent (ostensibly because he was not competent but perhaps because he was too assertive in running the schools and

not deferential enough to some school board members), it did so after he had left the city for a vacation. It did so with less than a day's notice of the meeting. And it did so by meeting in a room that would accommodate only 65 members of the public.

Power politics evokes legal challenges, so those who favored the state takeover law (and the local superintendent) secured a court order preventing the board from firing him. The federal court (acting in matters having to do with state and local education) held that the board's "fire-the-super" meeting violated the laws requiring sufficient notice of meetings and that the meetings be held in a public place, and also because the firing would have deprived the superintendent of his legal rights without due process of law (he had no chance to defend himself and his record).

In time, the state law passed and increased the local superintendent's power. The lawsuit was settled, and the court order preventing the board from firing the superintendent was made permanent.

During all of this turmoil, parents disagreed with other parents. Some favored state takeover; others did not. "It's about our children" is what everyone said.

Was it really? Ask yourself: If you were a parent of a student or if you were a teacher in this school system, whom would you trust if you knew all of what is on the surface and below it, relative to the state takeover law?

And how would you relate to a teacher if you were a parent or to a parent if you were a teacher? Is there a role for partnership and trust on the person-to-person level when the truth about trust at the system level is that there is much more distrust than trust? Before you answer, reflect on what Denise Poston has written in Figure 8–5. Reflect, also, on the story (at the beginning of this chapter) about Leia Holley and the Bonner Springs Elementary School staff. Now, answer the question and ask yourself how you would behave if you were a parent or a teacher in circumstances similar to those in New Orleans in the summer of 2004.

Rud Turnbull
Lawrence, Kansas
Based on information in *Gambit Weekly*, June 15, 2004

school in which you teach will influence your self-efficacy and empowerment to the extent that the school's teachers, parents, students, and principal have a sense of collective efficacy. In this final section, we address self-efficacy and teacher empowerment.

Self-Efficacy

Self-efficacy refers to beliefs in one's capacities to organize and carry out a course of action (Bandura, 1997). In general, self-efficacy influences how people set expectations for themselves, the extent to which they persist in reaching goals, and their commitment to go above and beyond. We encourage you to reflect on people who have achieved important goals. How do you think their self-efficacy played a key role when compared to other characteristics such as intelligence, quality of their educational background, or assistance from others? People with high self-efficacy tend to take on challenging tasks and to persevere in order to achieve desirable outcomes.

Your self-efficacy will influence how much you trust yourself to carry out all of the partnership practices related to the seven partnership principles: communication, professional competence, respect, commitment, equality, advocacy, and trust. As you develop your capacities for each of the partnership practices and gain confidence in your own skills, you will be far more likely to believe you can develop successful partnerships, even with families who have a disposition to distrust you.

Self-efficacy is not a static characteristic; rather it can be enhanced through a variety of means. Figure 8–7 includes tips for enhancing your self-efficacy (Hoy & Miskel, 2001).

You can develop not only your competence across partnership practices but also confidence in your own competence. In other words, you can avoid distrusting yourself and even move beyond conditional trust to having unconditional trust in your capacity to develop trusting partnerships with families. You will increasingly evolve in your capacity to trust yourself. When you trust yourself, it will be far more likely that families will trust you as well.

Empowerment

As you learned in chapter 7, empowered people take action to get what they want and need (Akey, Marquis, & Ross, 2000; Turnbull, Turbiville, & Turnbull, 2000). You will be more effective in fostering empowerment of families and in earning their unconditional trust when you are highly empowered yourself.

Enhancing your own empowerment involves expanding your knowledge and skills and boosting your motivation (Akey et al., 2000; Soodak et al., 2002; Turnbull et al., 2000). You will need to refine continually and expand your competence in each of the seven principles of partnership. To stay motivated, you will need to attend to your self-efficacy, energy levels, and persistence (putting forth a sustained effort). Empowered people set high goals for themselves, gather and use state-of-the-art knowledge that helps them reach their goals, and refuse to give up until they find solutions to the problems that confront them.

We encourage you to set a goal during this course—indeed, throughout the rest of your life—to become more empowered and to support others to be more empowered. Ultimately, you will be more likely to trust yourself unconditionally and to establish the kind of partnership with families that will enable them to trust you unconditionally as well.

SUMMARY

Trust is essential to all positive human relationships, and this chapter has described why trust is especially important in your interactions with families and fellow professionals. We define trust as confidence in the character and integrity of another person or persons, and we address the concept of the continuum of trust. Also, we believe that the relationships between trust and the partnership principles of communication, professional competence, respect, commitment, equality, and advocacy must be healthy and mutually reinforcing.

Although our focus is on the role of trust in relationships, we also have emphasized individual responsibility in nurturing trust by discussing the importance of trusting yourself, and having a trusting disposition toward others. Another key issue is the special opportunity you will have for building trust when working with families of diverse cultural, ethnic, social, and other backgrounds. There is a

FIGURE 8–7
Tips for Enhancing Your Self-Advocacy

- *Mastery experiences.* The more you incorporate *partnership practices* and refine your skills related to each one, the stronger your self-efficacy will become.

- *Modeling.* The more you observe successful *partnership practices* of other professionals and families, the more likely you are to believe that you, too, can be successful.

- *Verbal persuasion.* The more you listen to the advice and experience of others, as well as read current literature on best partnership practices, the more likely you will have a strong knowledge base and greater confidence in your capacities.

- *Physiological state.* The more you can minimize your stress when engaged in partnership practices and maximize feelings of confidence and enthusiasm, the more likely you are to strengthen your self-efficacy (Hoy & Miskel, 2001).

ways a context for trust or lack of trust, and therefore we have addressed trust's role in work settings, such as schools, and in relationships between colleagues. Finally, we reemphasized the crucial need for self-trust, which empowers you to do your best for yourself, and for others.

REFLECTING ON THE VIGNETTE

1. Did either Leia or Tierney have a reason to trust each other, from the very start of their partnership and before Sean even enrolled in school? Who had that reason, and what was the reason?

2. What happened to Leia and Tierney and their trust? Who broke trust with the other, or did neither break trust? Did the school system, at one time, impinge on trust and nearly destroy it?

3. What made it possible for them to re-establish trust? Was it their individual actions alone? Was it some change in the personnel or culture of Sean's school? Was it all of the above?

ENHANCING YOUR SELF-AWARENESS

As you reflect on the content of this chapter, we encourage you to give attention to the following issues:

Practices associated with the principle of trust

Think of an experience in which you confided in a family member or friend, and that person broke your confidentiality by sharing your information with others without your consent. How did this experience influence your ability to trust that person?

Distrust and unconditional trust

Identify one professional whom you distrust and one professional whom you trust unconditionally. What factors shaped the nature and extent of your trust in each person? What do those factors teach you about your professional behavior as you try to increase the likelihood that families will trust you unconditionally?

Collective efficacy

Of all the groups with whom you have been affiliated at one time or another, which group has the highest level of collective empowerment? What factors enabled the collective empowerment to grow? How were the people associated with the organization influenced by the collective empowerment?

SUGGESTED ACTIVITIES

1. Reread the quote by Gandhi on p. 163. Of all the people you know, think of the person who comes closest to having the same trusting stance that Gandhi described. Interview that person and ask the following questions: How have you been able to develop such a trusting stance? What factors positively influence you in maintaining your faith in humanity?

2. Write a personal reaction to the quote describing Aristotle's perspectives on the "golden mean" related to levels of trust. Propose a hypothetical conflict that you might have with a family in the future and how you might use the concept of the golden mean to resolve the conflict.

RESOURCES

1. Division for Culturally and Linguistically Diverse Exceptional Learners (DDEL), Council for Exceptional Children
   1110 North Glebe Road, Suite 300
   Arlington, VA 22201-5704
   703-620-3660, 1-888-CEC-SPED
   www.cec.sped.org

   DDEL is the division of the Council for Exceptional Children that specifically addresses improving educational opportunities for students with disabilities from culturally and linguistically diverse backgrounds. It publishes *Multiple Voices for Ethnically Diverse Exceptional Learners* and the *DDEL Newsletter.* DDEL is open for membership to any member of the Council for Exceptional Children.

2. Family Involvement Network of Educators (FINE)— Harvard Family Research Project
   3 Garden Street
   Cambridge, MA 02138
   617-495-9108
   http://www.gse.harvard.edu/~hfrp/

   FINE is the national network of over 2,000 people who are committed to promoting strong partnerships between children's educators, their families, and their communities. There is no cost to join. Members receive free monthly announcements through e-mail of resources related to partnerships. Information online includes research, training tools, model programs, and other topics of interest.

3. Early Childhood Research Institute on Culturally and Linguistically Appropriate Services (CLAS)
University of Illinois at Urbana-Champaign
61 Children's Research Center
51 Gerty Drive
Champaign, IL 61821
217-333-4123, 800-583-4135
www.clas.uiuc.edu/links.html

   CLAS identifies, evaluates, and disseminates effective and appropriate early intervention and preschool practices that are responsive to the needs of children and families from culturally and linguistically diverse backgrounds. It provides extensive lists of materials and resources in diverse languages.

4. Consortium for Appropriate Dispute Resolution in Special Education (CADRE)
P.O. Box 51360
Eugene, OR 97405-0906
541-686-5060
www.directionservice.org/cadre
mpeter@directionservice.org

   CADRE is funded by the U.S. Department of Education to work with state departments of education on the implementation of mediation requirements related to IDEA. Emphasis is placed on the prevention and resolution of conflict in order to promote partnerships among students, families, and educators.

PART IV

INTRODUCTION TO PART IV

Implementing Partnerships

Professionals need strategies to be effective partners. These are the simple tools of what to do. When, however, professionals meet challenges in applying these strategies, they need problem-solving processes. In no aspect of their work is the need greater than when they are attempting to establish trusting and trustworthy partnerships with families. The next five chapters identify how professionals can use evidence-based practices to support children with disabilities and their families and how the partnership principles relate to the practices.

Chapter 9 focuses on the ever-so-important tool of communication. As you recall, communication itself is one of the partnership principles.

Chapter 10 asks professionals to bear in mind that families cannot be effective partners in their children's education if they are struggling to meet their family's basic needs. It then suggests how professionals can help address those needs.

Chapter 11 describes how teachers and professionals, such as school psychologists, can be partners with families when evaluating a student to determine whether the student is eligible for special education.

Chapters 12 and 13 describe how teachers and other professionals, such as related service providers, can be partners with families to develop and implement a student's IEP.

Communicating and Collaborating Among Partners

1. What are the communication skills and strategies that honor families' preferences, values, and beliefs?
2. How can challenges to communication be transformed into opportunities to strengthen family-professional and professional-professional partnerships?

VIGNETTE

You may have heard someone—perhaps your parents or brothers or sisters, perhaps a close friend—tell you that it's not just what you say, it's how you say it.

Communication consists of words. There are the written words in the individualized education programs for Joesian Cortes, Nicky Doleman, and Sean Holley. There are the spoken words, such as Norma Cortes, Vera Doleman, and Leia Holley exchange with the professionals who serve them and their children. There are words in one language, English, that do not translate easily into another language, such as Norma's Spanish. There are words that require explanation, such as those that physicians use when explaining to Vera about Nicky's medications. And there are words that require interpretation, such as those that Kenny Berg and Arnie Mejia sign into each other's hands.

Arnie Mejia and Kenny Berg communicate by signing.

Communication consists of more than words. Behavior is a form of communication, as when Tierney Thompson twice had to leave a heated, confrontational IEP meeting with Leia Holley. Affect is a form of communication, as when Norma Cortes raves about Joesian's education. Questioning communicates distrust, as when some professionals have asked Vera about Nicky's health, suggesting they need to second-guess her decisions.

Culture affects communication. How else to explain the bond that linked Norma, Lourdes, and Martha of United We Stand of New York, and Emily Rodriguez, the assistant principal at Joesian's school? How could there be such implicit understandings between Clara Berg and Carole Gothelf had they not both understood their common ethnic history of persecution?

Not all communication is positive. Some is filled with anger,

as was the case during the May 2000 IEP meeting with Leia Holley and the staff at Bonner Springs Elementary School. Paradoxically, anger can sometimes be a positive force for partnerships, as when it brings issues to the surface and demands the attention of parents and teachers. Sean's seizure was the catalyst for candor and, in time, civility among Leia and his educators.

So, it is not just what a person says that constitutes communication. It is also how the person says it and, just as important, how the listener hears or understands the speaker's words and affect.

Sean Holley (left) and Tyler McMahan became buddies thanks to structured peer get-togethers at Bonner Springs Elementary School.

Not all communication is face to face. Words on paper communicate, as *Life* magazine story about the Perkins School communicated to Clara and Carole how marginally Kenny was regarded. Words transmitted by telephone communicate, as is the case when Vera, never without her cell phone, stays in regular touch with Nicky's teachers. Home-to-school notebooks also link partners; not a day goes by without Vera and Nicky's teachers writing notes to each other.

Vera Doleman expresses her concerns at an IEP meeting while the professionals in the room listen intently.

Pamela Shanks (left), Nicky Doleman's preschool teacher at Raintree Montessori School, worked closely with Vera Doleman to ensure a smooth transition to kindergarten at a public school in Lawrence, Kansas.

Often, parents and professionals plan how, when, where, and why they will communicate. They are formal about communicating. But sometimes, the informal communication means the most, as Norma pointed out when she recalled the most helpful of Joesian's many teachers were the ones she met in the supermarket and who took time to ask about him.

So, it is not always "what" and "how" that affect communication; "when," "where," and "why" make a difference, too.

INTRODUCTION

Communication is essential to all interpersonal interactions. Every professional has to communicate with at least two different sets of people. First, there are students and their families. Second, there are the other professionals involved with students, especially those who design and implement each student's Individualized Family Service Plan (IFSP) and Individualized Education Program (IEP).

In this chapter, we focus on communicating as a practice for establishing solid family-professional partnerships. We also note how these skills can be used in your partnerships with other professionals. Strong professional-professional partnerships have the same seven principles as strong family-professional partnerships. All partnerships must be grounded in trust and adhere to the principles that sustain it, including respect, commitment, advocacy, equality, competence, and communication. You will have many opportunities to apply the communication skills and strategies in this chapter as you read about the processes discussed in chapters 10 to 13.

CREATING A COLLABORATIVE CLIMATE

Have you ever been in a situation where the members of a group were working in isolation from one another? Have you ever been in a group where all the members were working cooperatively and collectively toward a mutual goal? A collaborative team climate, in which everyone works cooperatively with mutual respect and equity, is essential for reaching successful outcomes for students, families, and professionals.

Communicating Within a Team Context

No matter where students receive special education and related services, their families most likely have had experiences with a group of professionals providing these services and supports. As you will learn in chapters 10 to 13, families and professionals work closely together to evaluate a student and then to develop and implement the IFSP/IEP. They constitute a group called a team. The Individuals with Disabilities Education Act (IDEA) (20

U.S.C. Sec. 1414 (b)(4)(A)) provides that a student's parents have a right to be on the team; moreover, best practice recognizes that parents (and other individuals, including family members or professionals, as designated by parents) are essential members of the team. IDEA also provides that, whenever appropriate, the student may participate. The purpose of the team is to decide whether a student has a disability and, if so, what special education and related services the student should receive through the IFSP/IEP.

Types of Teams in Schools. Many different types of teams exist. Because their purposes vary, their membership also varies and usually consists of individuals from different disciplines. The disciplines include, but are not limited to, special education, general education, speech-language-communication therapy, occupational therapy, physical therapy, school social work, school psychology, school nursing, audiology, vision and orientation and mobility, and paraprofessionals.

The number of professionals on a team is often influenced by the student's support needs. Students who have greater support needs are likely to have more professionals from different disciplines on their team.

The way that professionals provide services and interact with one another varies across models. One model is the multidisciplinary team, indicating that the team consists of members from more than one discipline. Other models imply greater interaction and cohesiveness. For example, the transdisciplinary approach is typically preferred as a model of service delivery for students with disabilities, particularly in early childhood (Friend & Cook, 2003; Hemmeter, Joseph, Smith, & Sandall, 2001; Snell & Janney, 2000). Professionals and families have a collective responsibility for planning, implementing, and evaluating services. This model recognizes families as full and active participants in the process.

A unique attribute of the transdisciplinary approach is the practice of *role release*. Team members, including the parents, cross the traditional disciplinary or other boundaries (such as parents as the passive recipients of professionals' knowledge and direction, as discussed in chapter 5) and "step out of their usual roles to become either teachers of other team members or learners taught by other team members" (Snell & Janney, 2000, p. 5). Professionals share their particular information and skills; they also share the responsibility for facilitating the student program but usually designate one or only a few members to make sure the program is executed.

Other team-based approaches to providing services and supports to students with disabilities have various titles such as collaborative teaming, collaborative consultation and integrated therapy (Friend & Cook, 2003; Giangreco, 1986; Scott, McWilliam, & Mayhew, 1999). The common thread throughout these approaches is the shared responsibility for planning, implementing, and communicating about the student's services and supports. In chapter 13, you will learn how teams can collaborate to implement students' IEPs.

Fostering Communication Within Teams. Creating a climate for partnerships from the beginning enables families and other team members to communicate openly and honestly. Without positive and consistent communication, it usually is impossible to plan and implement effective educational programs for students. One way of determining the degree to which this partnership climate exists is to examine how the team functions. Figure 9–1 offers a set of questions to help teams determine the extent to which a positive, collaborative team climate exists.

Families' Roles on Teams. As we pointed out in chapter 6, one of the purposes of both IDEA and No Child Left Behind (NCLB) is to provide parents with more rights to participate in their children's education. IDEA provides that parents have the right to various notices, to consent or withhold consent to educators' proposed action, and to be members of the team that evaluates a student and decides how to educate the student appropriately. NCLB provides that schools must notify parents concerning their child's academic progress and the academic achievement and safety level of the school as a whole. Because NCLB is a relatively new law, few data are available about its effect on the parent choice principle. Data on IDEA's parent participation principle indicate that parents' level of involvement and satisfaction with the team process varies greatly.

Some families feel they are welcomed and important members of the team, whereas other families feel that they are not part of the team at all (Johnson, 2003; Soodak & Erwin, 2000; Squires, 2000). Other parents feel they are assuming more responsibility than they want to take on, and prefer that the professionals should take more initiative (Erwin, Soodak, Winton, & Turnbull, 2001). When parents perceive they are part of a team, it seems to make all the difference. Listen to this parent's perspective:

> It is a team effort, I think because, myself, my husband, the grandparents, aunts, uncles, and the school are working together. It is like everybody is working for the best of Adam. They are all so supportive of me and my husband. It makes such a difference. (Erwin et al., 2001, p. 142)

Ultimately, parents should decide how they want to participate in teams. Some parents may want to be an active participant at every team meeting, but others may prefer a less intensive role. To honor parents' preferences and establish trust with them, you should ask parents what their preferred team role is. No matter what their preferences are, however, the most important investment you can make in being their partner is to demonstrate that you welcome them and value their contributions to the team.

Communicating with Individual Families

As we discussed in Part 1 of this book, each family has a unique set of characteristics, interactions, functions, and life cycle experiences that have shaped their identities. Because of these and other distinctive features, no two families are exactly alike. Accordingly, you will need to tailor your communication with each family.

In the following section, we describe the skills you can use to communicate positively with families in ways that develop partnerships and trust. Then we will discuss how you can tailor your communication to honor families' preferences, cultural values, and linguistic diversity. Although we describe communication strategies as they apply to partnerships with parents, the same strategies apply to your partnerships with professionals.

USING POSITIVE INTERPERSONAL COMMUNICATION SKILLS

The more accurately and constructively you, the family, and the professionals on the team communicate, the more successful your interactions will be and the more you will create partnerships grounded in trust.

We encourage you to incorporate positive communication skills into your personal style so that they become natural and spontaneous. That requires systematic practice. It also requires cultural and disability sensitivity.

Refining your nonverbal communication skills is challenging when done within a unicultural context, but it is even more so when you are developing partnerships with families from cultures different from your own. For example, looking the speaker directly in the eye is typically considered being attentive and polite within a European American culture (Gollnick & Chinn, 2002; Lynch, 1998). But eye-to-eye contact with members of the opposite sex, people in authority, or elders can be considered disrespectful within an Asian culture (Chan & Lee, 2004; Sileo & Prater, 1998).

An individual's disabilities sometimes interfere with communication skills, so you need to make accommodations. For example, a parent or team member who is deaf and communicates through sign language will need an interpreter or professional collaborators who can sign.

FIGURE 9–1
"Are We Really a Team?" Worksheet

Directions: Circle the points to the right of each question only if all group members answer yes to the question. Tally the total number of points circled. The maximum score is 100 points.

	Points
1. Do we meet in a comfortable environment?	4
2. When we meet, do we arrange ourselves so that we can see each other's faces?	4
3. Is the size of our group manageable (e.g., 7 or fewer members)?	4
4. Do we have regularly scheduled meetings that are held at times and locations agreed on in advance by teammates?	3
5. Do needed members:	
a. Receive an invitation? (Note: Needed members may change from meeting to meeting based on agenda items.)	2
b. Attend?	2
c. Arrive on time?	2
d. Stay until the end of the meeting?	2
6. Do we start our meetings on time?	3
7. Do we end our meetings on time?	3
8. Do we update tardy members at a break or following the meeting rather than stopping the meeting in midstream?	3
9. Do we have a communication system for:	
a. Absent members?	2
b. People who need to know about our decisions but who are not regular members of the team?	2
10. Have we publicly discussed the group's overall purpose?	3
11. Have we each stated what we need from the group to be able to work toward the group's goals?	3
12. Do we distribute leadership responsibility by rotating roles (e.g., recorder, timekeeper, encourager, facilitator)?	3
13. Have we established norms for behavior during meetings (e.g., all members participate, no "scapegoating")?	3
14. Do we explain ground rules to new members?	3
15. Do we feel safe to express our genuine feelings (negative and positive) and to acknowledge conflict during meetings?	3

	Points
16. Do we consciously attempt to improve our communication skills (e.g., giving and receiving criticism, perspective taking, creative problem solving, conflict resolution) by:	
a. Setting aside time to discuss our interactions and feelings?	3
b. Developing a plan to improve our interactions next time we meet?	3
c. Arranging for training to improve our skills?	3
17. Do we use a structured agenda format that prescribes that we:	
a. Have identified agenda items for a meeting at the prior meeting?	2
b. Set time limits for each agenda item?	2
c. Rotate leadership roles?	2
d. Devote time for positive comments and celebration?	2
e. Have public minutes?	2
f. Discuss group effectiveness in accomplishing tasks, communicating, abiding by ground rules, and coordinating actions?	2
18. Do we consciously identify the decision-making process (e.g., majority vote, consensus, unanimous decision) that we will use for making a particular decision?	3
19. Do we summarize the discussion of each topic before moving on to the next agenda item?	3
20. Do we refocus attention when the discussion strays from the agenda?	3
21. Do we generally accomplish the tasks on our agenda?	4
22. Do we distribute among ourselves the homework/agenda items?	4
23. Have we identified ways for "creating" time for meetings?	4
24. Do we have fun at our meetings?	4

Our score = _____   Total possible points = __100__

Source: From Thousand, J. S., & Villa, R. A. (2000). Collaborative teaming: A powerful tool in school restructuring. In R. A. Villa & J. S. Thousand (Eds.), *Restructuring for caring and effective education: Piecing the puzzle together* (2nd ed., pp. 254–292). Baltimore: Paul H. Brookes Publishing Company. Adapted by permission.

In this section, you will learn about nonverbal and verbal communication skills, how to solve problems creatively, and how to resolve conflicts and misunderstandings.

Nonverbal Communication Skills

Nonverbal communication includes all communication other than the spoken or written word. We communicate nonverbally through gestures, facial expressions, voice volume and intonations, physical proximity to others, and posture. Often, we are unaware of the many noverbal cues we transmit to others. If you wish to improve the nature of your interactions with families and other professionals, you will need to be more aware of nonverbal communication skills such as physical attending and listening.

Physical Attending.   Physical attending consists of contact, facial expressions, and gestures. The contact component involves both eye contact and the degree of physical contact, or closeness, between people who are communicating with one another. Because your eyes are a primary vehicle for communicating, maintaining culturally appropriate eye contact is a way of showing respect for and interest in another person. It is estimated that European American middle-class people look away from the listener approximately 50% of the time when speaking but make eye contact with the speaker about 80% of the time when listening. A trend for African Americans is to make greater eye contact when speaking and less eye contact when listening. Native Americans consider it a sign of disrespect to ask direct questions and to make eye contact with people in authority (Joe & Malach, 2004). Sustained eye contact between people of different ages, of different social standing, or of the opposite gender is viewed as rude, hostile, or flirtatious in South Asian cultures (Jacob, 2004).

Adjusting the physical space between yourself and family members with whom you are communicating may also convey a particular message. Proximity between European American individuals engaged in a conversation is typically 21 inches apart. Among other cultural groups, such as Latinos, Arabs, and Southern Europeans, the physical proximity is much closer (Gollnick & Chinn, 2002). As you become more culturally aware of the specific traditions of families, observe their interactions with each other and with others. Seek recommendations from professionals who have worked successfully with them.

A second component of physical attending is facial expressions. Typically, desirable facial expressions are described as being appropriately varied and animated, occasionally smiling, and reflecting warmth and empathy. Cultural groups vary in the emphasis and frequency of smiling. For example, many people from Southeast Asia tend to smile regardless of being happy or sad or even when they are being reprimanded (Chan & Lee, 2004; Sileo & Prater, 1998).

By contrast, having a stiff facial expression, smiling slightly, or pursing the lips is often considered undesirable within the European American culture. Despite these general rules, you should recognize that some people have facial differences that necessitate accommodations by them and appropriate interpretation of these accommodations by others. Some have no ability to smile, frown, or otherwise express their feelings through their face or eyes. Sandy Goodwick described her experiences as follows:

> I was born with absolutely no facial expression—smile, frown, wink, etc. Due to the "wonders" of microscopic surgery, I now can "smile," albeit artificially. I have been an elementary school teacher for 20 years. The road to a successful career was not easy. . . . Contrary to the Dean of Students' wishes [when I was an undergraduate majoring in education] I went into teaching (despite the horrific student teaching experience!) and became a well-respected educator.

Gestures are a third component of physical attending. The meaning of gestures varies across cultural groups. Some hand gestures mean one thing for one cultural group but a different thing for another group; some groups may regard "thumbs up" or "V for victory" as vulgar signs, whereas other groups may regard them as entirely positive.

Listening.   We encourage you to review the tips for effective listening presented in Figure 7–2 (chapter 7). Listening is one of the most essential ingredients of effective communication.

Unfortunately, true listening rarely occurs naturally or spontaneously. To listen with genuine, undivided attention requires diligence, practice, and an awareness of different types of listening (Covey, 1990):

- *Ignoring:*   not paying attention at all to the person talking
- *Pretending:*   giving the outward appearance you are listening but actually thinking about something entirely different or thinking about what to say in response
- *Selective listening:*   listening to only parts of what someone is saying based on your own energy, time, interests, or emotions
- *Attentive passive listening:*   listening to what the other person is saying but not using noverbal attending skills, using silence or minimal encouragement for the speaker to continue, or not communicating any acceptance of what he or she is saying
- *Active listening:*   assuming a much more involved and direct role by being animated, making comments, asking

questions, and even sharing personal experiences to foster a dialogue

■ *Empathetic listening:* standing in the shoes of the person who is talking and seeing the world and the situation as he or she sees it

Parents want professionals to listen carefully, nonjudgmentally, and without predetermined ideas, as this parent clearly articulated:

> . . . I think some of these people have preconceived notions about everything . . . So if I tried to say, to tell them [professionals] something, it'd be LISTEN TO ME. (Blue-Banning, Summers, Frankland, Nelson, & Beegle, 2004, p. 175)

Although none of us likes to admit it, we all have ignored, pretended, and selected what we have heard. Listening takes hard work but it clearly conveys our level of interest, commitment, and understanding.

Verbal Communication Skills

Although the nonverbal communication skills are effective and essential means for communicating with families, verbal responses are also essential to facilitate communication. Examples of verbal responses include (1) furthering responses, (2) paraphrasing, (3) response to affect, (4) questioning, and (5) summarization. Figure 9–2 highlights each of these communication skills and how they may be used with families.

Furthering Responses. Furthering responses indicate attentive listening and encourage people to continue to speak and examine their thoughts and feelings. There are two types of furthering responses. The first, *minimal encouragers,* includes short but encouraging responses such as "Oh?" "Then?" "Mm-hm," "I see," or "And then?" Minimal encouragers can also be nonverbal and take the form of head nods, facial expressions, and gestures that communicate listening and understanding. The second way of furthering responses, *verbal following,* involves restating the main points or emphasizing a word or phrase from what the family member has said, using the language system of the family. Verbal following not only encourages the family member to go on speaking but also provides the professional with a means of checking his or her own listening accuracy, as illustrated in Figure 9–2.

Paraphrasing. Paraphrasing involves using your own words to restate the other person's message in a clear manner. In paraphrasing, you are restating the cognitive aspects of the message (such as ideas or objects) but not necessarily the affective state of the speaker. Use language as similar to the family's as possible. Paraphrasing responds to both the implicit and explicit meanings of what is said. Its goal is to check for accuracy and make sure that there is a clear understanding of the issues, as in the example provided in Figure 9–2.

In this example, you try to comprehend the situation from the person's perspective and to sense how challenging it is to have so many different responsibilities. It is not just the words but the frustration, fatigue, and overload that is communicated. In paraphrasing, the task is

FIGURE 9–2
Interpersonal Communication Skills

Verbal Communication Skill	Example
Furthering Response	
• Minimal encourager (short, but encouraging responses)	"Mm-hm." "I see."
• Verbal following (restating main points using family's language system)	"From what you are sharing with me, it sounds like you had a really rough night."
Paraphrasing	"Let me see if I am understanding this correctly."
Response to Affect	"It seems like you are feeling very let down by a family member who you thought would always be there for you."
Questioning	"How can I be of assistance?" "What things seem to be going very well right now?"
Summarization	"Let's review our plan. By next week, I will meet with the occupational therapist and you will contact the pediatrician."

not just to respond mechanically with a rephrased statement but to let the person know you empathize with the tremendous drain on time and energy.

Paraphrasing is extremely useful in clarifying content, tying a number of comments together, highlighting issues by stating them more concisely, and—most important—communicating interest in and empathetic understanding of what the family member is saying.

Reframing is a technique you can use when paraphrasing to ensure that you maintain a positive point of view. Problems, issues, and concerns can be reframed as the goals and dreams that parents hold for their children. For example, you can use reframing by talking about a child as spirited rather than hyperactive or by describing a parent as inquisitive rather than nosy. Reframing permits a situation to be viewed constructively, fosters trust, and encourages parents to contribute their ideas and efforts to the partnership (Christenson & Sheriden, 2001).

Responding to Affect. Response to affect involves the ability to (1) perceive accurately the other person's apparent and underlying feelings and (2) communicate understanding of those feelings in language that is attuned to the other person's experience at that moment. You pay attention not only to what is said but also to how it is said. When you use this technique, try to verbalize the family member's feelings and attitudes, and use accurate responses that match the intensity of the family member's affect. Developing a vocabulary of affective words and phrases can be helpful. See Figure 9–2 for an example of response to affect.

The purpose of responding to affect is to help family members see their feelings and attitudes. Response to affect also enables you to check the accuracy of your perceptions of the family member's feelings.

Questioning. Questions generally fall into two categories: closed-ended and open-ended. Closed-ended questions are used mostly to ask for specific factual information. Skillful communicators keep their use of closed-ended questions to a minimum because this type of question limits responses to a few words or a simple yes or no. Overuse of closed-ended questions can make an interaction seem like an interrogation. Although closed-ended questions can restrict conversation and often yield limited information, they are appropriate when used sparingly and wisely. Here are some examples of closed-ended questions that are usually appropriate:

"When did Carlos first start having seizures?"
"How old is Betty Sue?"
"Would a ten o'clock meeting be okay for you?"

Unlike closed-ended questions, open-ended questions invite family members to share and talk more. Some open-ended questions are unstructured and allow family members to talk about whatever is on their mind (see the example provided in Figure 9–2).

Other open-ended questions are more structured and impose boundaries on possible responses by focusing the topic (for example, "What are some of the specific methods you've tried to help Matthew behave more appropriately?"). Open-ended questions can be formulated in three general ways:

- *Asking a question.* "How is Miko getting along with her new wheelchair?"
- *Giving a polite request.* "Would you please elaborate on your feelings about the new bus route?"
- *Using an embedded question.* "I'm interested in finding out more about Ansel's toilet training at home."

Open-ended questions generally involve using the words *what* and *how*. We encourage you to be cautious about "why" questions because they can connote disapproval, displeasure, or blame (for example, "Why don't you listen to me?" or "Why are you late?"). They may evoke a negative or defensive response.

In general, we caution you about questioning. Educators tend to phrase questions in a way that focuses on problems, deficits, and concerns:

> We often start our initial contact with phrases like "How can I help you? What are your needs as a family? What kinds of problems are you having with your child? What are your child's most immediate problems?" These words immediately focus attention on what is going wrong and on a relationship based on the professional being in a position of expertise and power. (Winton, 1992, p. 1)

Try to think of interactions with families as conversations, as distinguished from interviews. Use open-ended, opportunity-driven questions, such as "What is one of the best experiences that you have had with a professional? What can we learn from that experience about how we might best work together?" or "What would an ideal day be like in the life of your family?"

We also caution you against being intrusive. Families vary in their comfort about being asked questions. Some families believe that most or all questions challenge their competency, invade their privacy, or both. One African American parent said she was raised by her parents and she raised her own children with the firm belief that "What happens in this house stays in this house." It was totally foreign to her to go into a conference with educators and be asked questions about what happens in her house and how she raises her children.

Our advice: Respect family boundaries about what is private versus public information.

Summarizing. Summarization is the act of restating what the other person has said, with an emphasis upon the most salient thoughts and feelings. Although similar to paraphrasing, summaries are substantially longer. Summarization is particularly useful in recalling the highlights of a previous meeting, tying together confusing or lengthy topics, and acknowledging the point at which a topic has become exhausted (Walker & Singer, 1993). Take a look at Figure 9–2 to see how summarization could be used during a conversation with a family or another professional.

Whether it is a school-based management council meeting or an IEP conference, communication skills such as empathetic listening, paraphrasing, and summarizing can facilitate the relationships between and among participants. You will be able to use these communication skills frequently in your interactions with families and with other team members. This discussion has focused on skills that can be used during individual interpersonal exchanges. The next section describes skills for team meetings and other group contexts to solve problems and issues collaboratively.

Solving Problems Collaboratively and Creatively

The communication skills we have discussed can occur not only in a two-way relationship between yourself and a family member but also within group discussions such as team meetings (Lambie, 2000). In addition to noverbal and verbal communication skills, another communication option is to refine your creative problem-solving skills within a group situation.

Unfortunately, much time in team meetings is devoted to reports that were developed before the meeting instead of featuring a dynamic and creative problem-solving process (Mehan, 1993). Approaching students' educational programs from isolated perspectives can lead to fragmented and inconsistent outcomes. Working within a team context enables stakeholders to share their resources, experiences, and ideas so that meaningful and positive outcomes are achieved.

Using Cultural Competence to Seek Solutions. Service delivery for students with disabilities continues to reflect more partnership approaches today. The expert-as-decision-maker approach that guided special education practices for so long created barriers between parents and professionals. File (2001) observed:

As the early childhood field has built its identity as a profession, we've increased the distance between ourselves and families, because our society's professional models have been traditionally oriented toward the exercise of expert knowledge. (p. 71)

Although there has been a steady shift toward more partnership models across all age groups, partnership models of teaming may not be consistent with all families' beliefs or practices. As you learned in chapter 1, cultural values will influence how families make decisions about their children and themselves. Some cultural groups view professionals as the primary decision maker about their child's education (Lynch & Hanson, 2004).

Even when there may be questions or disagreements about the school's approach, some parents are not likely to communicate their perspectives. One Korean parent commented, "You know, our culture totally trusts and obeys school. We do not express even though we have complaints. There are many moms like that" (Park & Turnbull, 2001, p. 137). Betsy, an early interventionist, struggled with wanting to be respectful of the family's culture and at the same time wanting to work in partnership:

How can I be culturally responsive when I go into the homes of families from cultures that make sharp distinctions between parents and "experts"? Take Karen, for example; she's a single mother from Puerto Rico whom I see weekly. When I ask her to tell me what she'd like for Maya, she tells me that I am the "expert" and that I should tell her what needs to be done. . . . I know that Karen cares about Maya and is just expressing her respect for my professional skills, but how can I involve her more actively in Maya's activities while I am there? (Barrera & Corso, 2002, pp. 105–106)

As we have pointed out, the partnership principle of respect, particularly the practice of honoring cultural diversity, is necessary at every stage of planning and implementing students' educational plans. How can professionals creatively resolve problems and issues and at the same time honor families' cultural beliefs and practices?

Lamorey (2002) has suggested that instead of trying to persuade families to change their opinions and beliefs, professionals should consider themselves "interpreters or translators of Westernized approaches and resources available within the special education community, and as guides who respectfully offer services that families may or may not choose to embrace" (p. 70). By serving as an interpreter or translator of westernized practices, professionals can convey American practices and at the same time learn about families' practices and cultural beliefs. Only then can a meaningful dialogue begin about how to address issues or problems, because there is an equal and respectful sharing of information.

Skilled dialogue is an approach that teaches professionals to be more competent and responsive in interactions with families whose cultural perspectives vary from those of the professional (Barrera & Corso, 2002). Two assumptions guide this approach: (1) cultural diversity is a *relational reality*—everyone is diverse depending on the specific environments, and (2) cultural diversity is a positive attribute and never negative, problematic, or limiting. Skilled dialogue is highly consistent with the cultural reciprocity practices described in chapter 7 (Kalyanpur & Harry, 1999).

The skilled dialogue approach relies on two skills to address issues creatively and respectfully: anchored understanding and third space. Anchored understanding occurs when there is a "compassionate understanding of differences" that comes from truly getting to know individual families (Barrera & Corso, 2002, p. 108). You have achieved an anchored understanding when you respect and appreciate the actions, intentions, and beliefs of a particular family, even in situations where you might have acted or thought differently. The second skill used in skilled dialogue is third space. This term refers to a situation in which people creatively reframe the diverse perspectives and contradictions of each other so that these perspectives merge to address challenging issues. A third-space perspective is achieved when family members and professionals each reach a new perspective without abandoning their individual points of view. Implementing skilled dialogue during interpersonal interactions encourages you to generate questions, such as:

- What is the meaning of this person's actions?
- How does my behavior influence this interaction?
- What can I learn from this person?

Using skills such as paraphrasing or reframing allows both perspectives to be clearly communicated and understood. Think about a time when you might have used skilled dialogue to address a complicated issue with a family. How could you have achieved an anchored understanding of the family's perspective? What third-space alternatives might have been considered? What are some of the challenges and benefits you might personally face using this approach?

Using Creative Group Problem-Solving Approaches. Disagreements with families or other professionals can be viewed as opportunities for learning and can be addressed creatively within group contexts. Problem solving typically involves those techniques listed in Figure 9–3.

How might you also use anchored understanding and third space in the scenario described in Figure 9–4? This figure illustrates how group problem solving can resolve

FIGURE 9–3
Steps to the Group Problem-Solving Process

- Develop a vision.
- Agree on a specific goal.
- Brainstorm options for addressing the goal.
- Evaluate benefits and drawbacks of each option.
- Select the most appropriate option.
- Specify an implementation plan, including person responsible, resources needed, and time line.
- Implement the plan.
- Evaluate how closely the results of the action matched the goals.
- Modify the plan and continue to make progress.

a situation associated with truancy. The implementation planning form provides a structured framework for documenting next steps, the person responsible, resources needed, and time lines. The problem-solving process can be helpful in dealing with minor or major issues, but it is often especially beneficial in times of crisis. Because crisis situations often involve heightened risk, danger, or emotional turmoil, a comprehensive written action plan can help everyone collaborate and support each other. Just as the communication skills mentioned earlier in this chapter can be used with families directly, these problem-solving strategies can be used with professionals in team meetings and other group situations.

Resolving Conflict and Misunderstanding

Communication skills are particularly important during times of crisis. When in crisis, families may respond to you with anger, fear, or resistance, making meaningful communication more difficult to initiate or maintain. Likewise, when a major disagreement occurs between families and professionals, trust becomes an important factor to resolve conflicts respectfully and positively.

During difficult interactions with families, you may need to use the whole spectrum of communication skills. It is particularly helpful to examine your own behaviors and beliefs to be aware of how your actions may or may not have an impact on the misunderstanding. Sometimes, professionals who regard a parent as "high maintenance" simply fail to acknowledge their own biases and insecurities (Stonehouse & Gonzalez-Mena, 2001).

Professionals' level of awareness of parents or other professionals will influence their interactions (Ulrich & Bauer, 2003). A mismatch between a family member and

FIGURE 9–4
Solving Problems and Creating Action Plans

When Lekia came to the conference, she was frustrated and tired. James had been steadily going downhill since the beginning of the school year. It was early October and James had been in trouble for skipping classes and was not academically successful. After each time he skipped, the school had held a conference. Behavior plans were written, his schedule was changed, and his teachers were switched. Lekia really felt that the school was trying to help James but nothing was working.

Lekia had received a phone call at 10:00 A.M. from the school saying that James had been picked up by a local police officer while eating at a fast food restaurant. James knew the officer and didn't resist going back to school, but he had to be reported as truant. This was the fourth report filed. He has had 10 days of suspension and Lekia knows that this is not the answer for James's problems. She hopes that today's conference will lead toward a vision for her son that is acceptable to everyone here. **Next Steps:** In order to reach our goal and to work toward our vision, . . .

Group Action Plan

	Person Responsible	Resources Needed
Starting tomorrow, we will:		
A. Find an adult "buddy" with whom James can spend time before or after school.	Teacher	
B. Have established a safe place where James can go when he feels too much pressure at school. Document each time it is used.	Teacher	Safe place
C. Call his mom at work each day before he goes home. James will call her when he gets home. This must be documented.	Teacher/Principal, Mom, James	Phone, private place at school
In one month, we will:		
A. Formally check in with James's buddy and discuss successes and failures. Have James there for the discussion.	Buddy, James, Teacher	
B. Review how many times James has used his safe place versus skipping school. Begin to lessen the times the safe place is used.		Safe place
C. Review documentation on phone calls and revise system if necessary.	James, Mom, Teacher	Documents, phone
In three months, we will:		
A. Sit with James and his buddy. James may have made more "buddies." If not, encourage this.	Teacher, James, Buddy	
B. Wean James from his safe place almost entirely. It should be available but not consistently used.	Teacher	Safe place
C. Have James talk to Lekia about how he feels things have gone and whether he needs more supports.	James, Mom	Time to meet

professional could exist because of differences in their feelings about a disability, personal histories, prior experiences, knowledge of related issues, and cultural and personal beliefs (Ulrich & Bauer, 2003). For example, students who are gifted may demonstrate such behavior as constant interjecting, challenging authority, or anger over insignificant incidents; parents may tolerate these behaviors at home whereas educators regard them as disruptive in the classroom (Strip & Hirsch, 2000). This mismatch of perceived expectations of behavior could lead to a conflict. When professionals disagree with parents, they should try to understand why the mismatch occurs and how to address it collaboratively. The skilled dialogue approach can be quite helpful.

Conflict is a "natural part of collective human experience . . . and [has] the capacity to inform and advance our collective efforts" (Uline, Tschannen-Moran, & Perez, 2003, p. 782). Experiencing conflict need not be viewed as negative or harmful. Conflicts can lead to stronger interpersonal communication, enhanced clarity of purpose, and increased trust (Tjosvold, 1997). On the other hand, the costs of suppressed conflict can be quite significant (Uline et al., 2003). It is better to engage in a healthy disagreement that moves toward a resolution grounded in trust than not to engage in conflict at all.

Conflict resolution strategies will help you deal with challenges in a respectful and honest manner. Fisher and Ury (1991) have laid the groundwork for negotiating and resolving conflicts. See Figure 9–5 for practical and effective skills to negotiate agreements based on the method Fisher and Ury call "Getting to Yes."

Can you think of how you could have used the skills described in Figure 9–5 to positively resolve a conflict? Which of the negotiation strategies are you able to use comfortably right now? For which do you need additional practice?

Conflicts or crises offer unique opportunities to strengthen trust. Approaching a potentially challenging situation with respect is critical. Susan Rocco, a parent who chartered new territory by having her son Jason included in general education, understood the power of respect and culturally relevant communication skills. Susan knew, "You get more flies with honey than vinegar." Abandoning the mainland confrontational style, she adopted the nonassertive, nonconfrontational mores of Hawaii. She also had to trust professionals in order to secure their trust in her.

Because of their heightened vulnerability and an urgent need for collaboration, families and professionals can come through a challenging situation with a strengthened partnership. You can embrace a conflict as a unique opportunity to enhance a partnership.

Another consideration is the power of anger to motivate people. Often, anger leads to transforming events as outrage is channeled into positive action. We encourage you to view each conflict as an opportunity to get things moving in a positive direction, sometimes with a sense of urgency that is hard to establish when all is going well.

You can practice these skills throughout all of your conversations with families and other professionals, during team meetings, and even when communicating in personal relationships. Improving communication requires time, effort, attention, and a genuine desire to be the most effective communicator you can possibly be.

COMMUNICATING POSITIVELY: STRATEGIES

Communication lies at the heart of all interactions among team members. In communicating with families, you can incorporate and strengthen all other partnership practices—respect, commitment, advocacy, equality, professional competence, and trust. Communication is a means by which you can create a supportive and trusting context for partnerships among all team members. In this section you will learn to use the positive communication skills just described to enhance your partnerships with families and other professionals.

Ever since IDEA was enacted in 1975, special educators and education agencies have invested tremendous time and effort in formal team meetings, formal notices of evaluation and placement, and formal notices of legal rights (as you learned in chapter 5). Given this emphasis on formality and strict compliance with the law, it is paradoxical that parents of children with various exceptionalities frequently prefer *informal* rather than *formal* communication (Soodak & Erwin, 2000; Turnbull & Winton, 1984; Turnbull, Winton, Blacher, & Salkind, 1983). Generally, families want communication with professionals to be frequent, comfortable, nonhierarchical, and positive. The specific strategies you use to communicate must be responsive to the individuals involved in the interaction. In the following section, we will examine how you can tailor your communication strategies to individual families.

Identifying and Respecting Family Preferences

Although most families prefer informal communication to formal communication, they still vary in their preferences. To determine a family's preferences, you need to gain a family systems perspective, understand and honor the family's cultural values and traditions, and be able to make accommodations for linguistic diversity.

Gaining a Family Systems Perspective. Your best approach to gain an understanding of a family is to develop a comfortable, trusting, authentic partnership that begins informally. The more you genuinely connect with the family, the more its members will be eager to share their family story with you. As you listen to family members, you can begin to fill in the different parts of the family systems framework. Robert Coles (1989), a prominent psychiatrist and humanitarian, described the advice that was given to him by one of his mentors: "Why don't you chuck the word 'interview.' Call yourself a friend, call your exchanges conversations!" (p. 32).

FIGURE 9–5

Tips for Using a "Win-Win" Approach to Negotiate Agreement

A win-win approach to negotiation emphasizes understanding the problem from the other's perspective and identifying all existing options so everyone wins and no one loses much or at all. Strategies that can be used to arrive at a mutually empowering agreement are listed below.

Examples of the strategies are taken from Kevin's team meeting. The meeting was convened to decide whether Kevin would enter first grade in the fall. Kevin is a 6-year-old child with developmental delays; his twin brother, Kyle, appears to be typically developing. The boys' mother, Tess, wants Kevin to enter first grade with his brother. Professional members of the team feel that Kevin would benefit from an additional year in kindergarten.

STRATEGY	EXAMPLE
Separate People from Issues Try to understand the other person's point of view.	Assume that Tess wants what is best for her sons. Think about how you might feel if you were in Tess's shoes.
Practice active listening.	Ask Tess to tell you about what she would like as well as her concerns. Paraphrase what you hear Tess saying to check your understanding of her thoughts and feelings.
Allow the other person to express emotion and do not react to his or her emotions with an emotional outburst.	Acknowledge Tess's feelings with supportive words and gestures. Consider your own feelings; if you find you are angry, try to identify why.
Focus on Interests, Not Positions Identify the interests underlying each side's position.	Ask yourself *why* it matters to Tess that Kevin enter first grade. For example, does Tess highly value the twins' shared experiences? Is she concerned about Kevin's self-image as he matures?
Generate Options Generate creative options by brainstorming all possible solutions.	Invite all team members, including Tess, to "invent" creative options to ensure Kevin's success. Broaden your options; don't focus exclusively on where Kevin will be educated.
Use Objective Criteria Develop and agree on objective criteria that are based on scientific findings, professional standards, or legal precedents.	Identify objective standards that are relevant in decisions about Kevin's placement including special education laws, school policies, and research on grade retention and practices in educating twins.

Source: Excerpt from Fisher, R., Ury, W. & Patton, B. (1991). *Getting to yes: Negotiating agreement without giving in* (p. 13). Copyright © 1981, 1991 by Roger Fisher and William Ury. Adapted and reprinted by permission of Houghton Mifflin Company. All rights reserved.

There is wisdom in this statement. As you develop genuine partnerships with families, you will not need to administer formal assessment instruments or have stiff, professionally controlled interviews. The more you think of yourself as a friend or a partner and incorporate the partnership practices associated with respect, equality, and commitment, the more your exchanges will be conversations.

Connecting in a comfortable way is especially important when you work with families from culturally and linguistically diverse backgrounds. The whole special education process can be overwhelming for many families, especially families from diverse backgrounds. The more formally you present the paperwork and questionnaires, the more intimidating you are likely to be. Remember, many families do not have documented status in the United States. Be sensitive to their desire for privacy and understand that paperwork can be a special threat to families who, for whatever reason, do not wish to reveal information about themselves.

You can use the family systems framework, which you learned about in chapters 1 through 4, in your conversations with families. Families, however, do not share their stories all neatly organized according to the family systems framework. But in practically every exchange, information about that family and its system will crisscross the four components. It is your responsibility to listen carefully and without judgment. What components and subcomponents of the family systems framework do you detect in Armando Sellas's description of his daughter Angelica, who has Down syndrome?

> Our expectations of Angelica have been very, very little different between what we expect from her sister and what we expect from her. We take into account that they are two distinct individuals, and they're each going to have their own identity, but you know we expect Consuelo to do certain things in the way of chores around the house or homework and things like that, then we have the same expectations for Angelica to get up in the morning, make her bed, get freshened up, go to the bathroom, brush her teeth and get ready to go.

What did you learn from this father about sibling interaction, parental expectations, the family function of daily living, or the family cultural characteristics? Now consider a passage from a different parent:

> I was raised up in my own religion, but then just recently I stopped going. My kids already know God is very important, we were all raised that way. They know right from wrong. They also already know that they are going to experience things, and I sit and tell them I know this is wrong, because I've done it. You want to smoke a cigarette, I'll buy the pack. You know, don't do it behind my back. My daughter, if you're pregnant and you're out there, then come to me and we'll talk about it. Don't keep bringing babies because it's too hard. You want to have sexual intercourse, there's birth control. If you want to talk, we can talk. I'll try to be very open about anything you want to talk about. I advise that they learn streets, but be intelligent too. Stay in school, get an education, because that's the only way you're going to get by in this world.

What do you learn here about family cultural characteristics, the parental subsystems, family interaction in terms of cohesiveness and adaptability, and life cycle stages and transitions?

A good strategy for understanding a family and its system is using a *portfolio*. The portfolio is a folder, file, or packet where you can keep notes of your conversations, copies of correspondence, and information. You can organize the portfolio into the family systems framework. Whenever you learn relevant information about a particular component of the framework, make a note in the appropriate place. As the information accumulates, you will increasingly understand and be more able to work in partnership with the family.

Although checklists and surveys can also help you collect family information (as we will describe in chapter 11), conversations offer a more open-ended and friendly way to develop trust in your relationships. Take time to get to know a family. Follow the partnership practices associated with the principle of communication: be honest, be friendly, and listen.

Respecting Family Preferences.   To individualize your communication, you need effective positive communication skills—verbal, nonverbal, and problem solving (as you learned earlier in this chapter). You also need a keen understanding of the family's preferences for communicating with school personnel. Whenever possible, modify the strategies to suit a family's preferences and your personal style.

How do you learn about a family's preferences for communication? Simply ask. We recommend that you use open-ended questions to begin a conversation. At least three areas of questioning may be useful. First, you may want to ask, "How do you wish to communicate?" You can follow up by asking parents what they have liked or not liked about their past communications with professionals. For example, are telephone calls effective or inconvenient? Are written notices helpful?

Second, it is useful to ask, "What information is important to you to communicate about?" Some parents may want to know about their child's health status, whereas others may be interested in school activities or classroom behaviors.

Last, you may ask, "With whom would like to communicate?" Some parents may wish to be in contact with the paraprofessional who works directly with their child, while others prefer to be in contact with their child's teacher. Think about family preferences as you read Lossie's story in Figure 9-6. How would you gather information about the family's preferred way for staying in touch?

In a study of parent-professional partnerships, trust was hindered by restrictions placed on the people with whom parents could communicate (Soodak & Erwin, 2000). One parent recalled the principal's comment to her upon their introduction: "If you have any problems, go to the consultant teacher" (p. 37). Parents indicate that being asked about their preferences is an important way for professionals to demonstrate their respect and build trust with families (Zionts, Zionts, Harrison, & Bellinger, 2003).

FIGURE 9–6
Advocating for Systems Change

Although you may have the best intentions in getting to know the families of your students, you are likely to encounter some families whose past experiences have left them reluctant to communicate openly with school personnel. How might you communicate to a family that you are a partner worthy of their trust?

Consider Lossie's situation. As the granddaughter of a slave who lived to see his freedom and the daughter of a civil rights activist, Lossie was raised to be aware of what she calls "the struggle" for civil rights. From the moment Lossie learned that she had a son, Thomas, with Down syndrome, she was determined to make sure that he would receive a proper education and become part of his neighborhood school. However, according to Lossie, "While we were prepared for the world, the world was not ready to receive us."

Lossie had found professional allies and advocates along the way. She kindly refers to one particular friend and advocate, Dawn, as "my other listening ear." But,

when one of the special education teachers, a vocal advocate on behalf of Thomas, was suddenly dismissed from the school, it confirmed Lossie's growing distrust of the school administration. By the time Thomas graduated from elementary school, Lossie had grown tired of the empty promises of services, supports, and equipment her son was to receive and had successfully taken legal action against the school for its failure to implement her son's IEP.

As Lossie prepares to meet the teachers and other team members who will be working with Thomas in middle school, she wonders whether this year will be different.

What might the teachers say and do to build trust in their impending partnership with Lossie? How can they communicate their empathy and respect for Lossie and Thomas? What communication skills might they use to foster open communication?

Making Accommodations for Linguistic Diversity. You will need to develop proficiency with translations of written communications and with interpretations of oral communications. Many families with whom you will be working will have limited English proficiency because of their cultural and linguistic diversity. For these families, it will be essential to provide translations of written documents in the language in which they are proficient. You will need to talk with your school administrator and other professionals, such as teachers of English as a second language, to explore local and state resources for translation. Software programs that can aid this process are also available.

Some families are unable to read because of their own limited education or because of disabilities. That is why you should consider the reading level at which you provide written communication. Try to make it understandable and accessible to the families with whom you are working.

In face-to-face interactions, consider the occasions when you will need to have an interpreter for families who do not speak English or who are deaf. Again, you can work with your school administrators to identify local and state resources that can be used in meeting this need. Often families have preferences for interpreters with whom they have worked in the past. If those interpreters are not available, you might provide families with a few choices so that they have some control over who does the interpreting. Some families have commented that in an adversarial situation they sometimes perceive that the interpreter is "on the side" of the school. Tips for communicating with families through interpreters were presented in chapter 1. In an equal and respectful partnership, families must have confidence that the interpreter will convey both the substantive content and the emotional overtones of their messages.

Throughout the remainder of this chapter, we will focus on five major strategies for communicating with families: (1) handbooks, handouts, and newsletters; (2) letters, notes, and dialogue journals; (3) telephone contacts; (4) technology options; and (5) face-to-face meetings. In addition to whether they can read English or any other language, families vary in many other ways, including whether they have a telephone, whether they have access to and an understanding of computer technology, and whether they have transportation to come to school for a conference. Thus, you will need to adapt your communication strategies to respect the family's preferences and capabilities. Frequent, open, and honest communication is key to knowing whether the strategies you select strengthen your partnerships.

Written, Spoken, and Technology-Based Communication

Handbooks, Handouts, and Newsletters. Most school *handbooks* for families outline administrative policies and procedures but do not include information about educational services or opportunities for parent involvement. It may be helpful to develop a supplemental handbook containing information specific to your class or program, including information about personnel, classroom procedures, classroom supplies, transportation, methods of reporting progress, and topics unique to your program.

Content aside, you must also consider format. Handbooks are more enjoyable to read when they are concise, attractive, and written in simple and understandable language (Kroth & Edge, 1997). If families do not speak English or if they speak it as a second language, consider having the handbook printed in other languages. Translation services are becoming increasingly available, and sometimes bilingual parents may assist in producing the handbook in different languages.

Handouts deal with specific matters such as resources in the community, safety and travel, accessible places of leisure and recreation, sources of college scholarships, drug prevention, and summer enrichment programs. To get families to read the handouts and establish communication with you, consider whether the information is useful, affirming, and relevant.

Consider individualizing the handouts by highlighting or placing stars next to items that are particularly pertinent to specific families or family members. Ask students to help prepare the handouts by writing, illustrating, or duplicating them; their contributions can be meaningful language arts activities. Personalizing communication intended for a larger audience shows your respect for an individual family and enhances equality in your partnership.

Newsletters can be enjoyable and useful communication techniques. They can be developed by an individual teacher and class, an entire grade, or an entire school. Families, students, and school personnel can submit drawings, quotations, essays, comic strips, announcements, updates on ongoing school projects, advice, descriptions of adaptive devices, advertisements for toy swaps, methods of encouraging positive child behaviors, announcements of workshops and seminars, and "bragging" notes. Articles about homework, teacher profiles, "getting to know you" features, reports about special projects, and parenting tips are often well received by parents.

Keep newsletters brief (1 to 2 pages) and present topics that are of interest to families (Hollingsworth, 2001). Try to recruit families to help in publishing the newsletter, thereby showing that their input is valued and needed. Most people like to see their names in print; by sharing good news about families in the program, you affirm their strengths.

School newspapers that include information about exceptionality issues give a positive message about inclusion and can also address substantive family concerns. Figure 9–7 contains a letter written by Kate Turnbull, Ann and Rud's daughter, for her high school newspaper, expressing her views on using respectful language. This letter reflects her own experiences as the sister of her brother, who is 11 years older than she. Kate not only expressed her preferences about respectful language, but also educated her peers on the important topic of offensive language, showing them how to become more sensitive about disability discrimination.

Letters, Notes, and Dialogue Journals. The written communication strategies we have just described are typically used with multiple audiences. Letters, notes, and dialogue journals are strategies to exchange information with individual families.

According to parents, written communications, such as school-to-home notebooks, can provide a number of helpful functions, including letting them know what's happening in their child's day, assuring them of their child's participation, and providing opportunities for informal troubleshooting with staff (Davern, 2004). Involve families in deciding how frequently to write, who will write, what kinds of information to exchange, and whether the journal will be open to all family members, not just restricted to parents.

Some professionals and families prefer dialogue journals over notes and letters, which may be more easily lost or misplaced. Dialogue journals offer a record of communication over time and aid in end-of-the-year reports.

If you cannot use a notebook every day, you might consider alternating days or sending a notebook on a weekly or biweekly basis (Williams & Cartledge, 1997). As much as possible, use dialogue journals to communicate positive information about the student; keep negative comments to a minimum. Reread your comments to see if the tone or content of your message can be misinterpreted (Davern, 2004). Sensitive information is best shared in person when parents can ask questions and seek clarification. One parent sadly described her son's dialogue journal as a "log of sins." Each day when he got home, she dreaded pulling out the notes and reading about the 10 to 15 behavioral infractions that day. You can imagine how painful this was for her and what a strain it created between her and the teacher and even with her son. By failing to affirm the

FIGURE 9–7
Letter Published in a School Newspaper: Offensive Language Needs to Stop

The word "retard," unfortunately, has now achieved mainstream status. I have been affected by the word all my life because I have a brother with mental retardation and autism. When I was in elementary school and junior high, I was embarrassed about my brother because people always used "retard" so lightly. Now that I am no longer embarrassed, rather, I am proud of him, I had hoped to escape the word. So far at my school, I have been unable to do so.

I frequently hear "You are such a retard!" or "Gosh, I'm so retarded!" when someone has made a mistake or has said something seemingly stupid. Every time I hear the word, I cringe. I think about my brother, my greatest teacher, and know that someone is making a mockery out of his disability.

Often times the speaker does not realize the effect of their words. What happens when lower school students, walking down the hall to class, hear the word spoken by an upper school student? They are going to think that "retard" isn't a bad word. It is. The word itself is obviously derogatory to people with disabilities because it is never used to describe something or someone that is successful or intelligent.

People with mental retardation are not stupid; they are just slower at processing information, J. T., my brother, leads a completely normal life despite his disabilities. He works at the University of Kansas, rides the campus bus to work everyday, and lives in his own house with two graduate students. No one would want to approach him and call him a retard to his face so why is it O.K. to use the term so loosely behind his back? . . .

Some people might say that if they use "retard" or other offensive words in such a way that they don't mean them in a demeaning way, people should not take them offensively. If you know, however, that the words have the potential to demean someone, why use them and intentionally flare up conflict or hurt someone's feelings?

"Retard" is only one example of the offensive language circulating the halls and classrooms. Our vocabulary is filled with stigmatizing words such as "faggot," "chick," and "retard." These words have the potential to deepen the factions already apparent in the human race. They cannot possibly be doing more good than bad, so why use them?

Our school is only a microcosm for the "real" world. We hear these words from our peers and even our role models everyday, but whether or not we choose to use them is solely up to us. This is a major source of conflict for students in high schools and in our everyday society. But does it have to be?

Kate Turnbull
Editor-in-Chief

Source: From Turnbull A., & Turnbull, H. R. *Families, professionals, and exceptionality: Collaborating for Empowerment,* 4th edition, ©2001. Reprinted by permission of Pearson Education, Inc., Upper Saddle River, NJ.

child's strengths, the teacher failed to show respect, the principle that would lead to a partnership with the parent.

Telephone Contacts. The telephone can be an effective means for providing both information and emotional support. Occasional telephone calls to families may even result in improved student performance. Approximately 94% of all children live in homes equipped with telephones (O'Hare, 2001), and not all parents or other care providers are able to read or write well enough to use printed information as a communication mode. But keep in mind that not all students live in homes with telephones. Children living in poverty are four times more likely to be living in phoneless households than are children living in homes with income above the poverty line (O'Hare, 2001).

As a general rule, telephone conversations with parents should be brief and to the point. Longer, more involved conversations are more effective when conducted in person. Conversing over the telephone poses some disadvantages, such as not being able to see the parents' nonverbal reactions. Listen carefully and check out your perceptions by asking questions and summarizing. Ask families in advance about convenient times to contact them, and also share with them preferred times for you to receive telephone calls. Before calling a family member at work, ask whether that person wants to receive telephone calls there. Figure 9–8 contains suggestions for use of the telephone.

Families often appreciate it when teachers share their telephone number with them. This gives families a greater sense of connection; they regard the teacher as a partner in their child's education. One mother observed

. . . in all the previous schools, not one teacher gave me their home phone number . . . so I think one of the characteristics of these [collaborative professionals] is that they truly, truly, have a genuine interest into the well-being of that child and they believe that in order to serve the child properly they have to have a close personal relationship with the parent. (Blue-Banning et al., p. 176)

It is important, however, to consider when it is convenient for you to receive telephone calls (Lord-Nelson

FIGURE 9–8

Tips for Using the Telephone

- Treat every message (incoming or outgoing) as an important call.

- Always identify yourself as you place a call or answer one.

- Personalize your conversation at every opportunity by using the caller's name.

- Don't use the telephone for criticism. Criticism is tricky enough even in an eye-to-eye encounter. When the parent must depend completely on your voice, criticism is doubly difficult.

- Be sure to ask parents if you have called at a convenient time. If not, ask them to name a time when they'll be free to talk.

- Jot down in advance what you want to find out from the parent and what you want to tell the parent.

- When taking down information, briefly double-check your notes.

- If it is necessary to leave the line during a call, explain the reason and excuse yourself. When you return, thank the caller for waiting. (On long-distance calls, make every effort to avoid putting a parent on "hold.")

- Always offer the caller or person being called your help or assistance.

- Allow time for parents to ask you their questions.

- Return all calls promptly; the exception, of course, is if you are involved in the classroom with students.

- Give definite information and offer positive information.

- Avoid the use of vague statements that may force the caller to dig for information. Vague statements are irritating and waste time.

- As the conversation ends, thank the caller before you say goodbye.

Source: From the Parent Center of the Albuquerque, New Mexico, Public Schools. (1985). Adapted by permission.

Summers, & Turnbull, 2004). Also, when you are contacted by families, sometimes it may be hard to find the time to respond. An answering machine at the school central office or a teacher's own voice mail lets educators receive messages from parents when it is impossible or inconvenient to answer the telephone.

Speaker phones and three-way calling options allow more than two people to participate in a telephone conversation. Involving more than one parent or additional team members on the same telephone conversation may increase participation of key stakeholders and prevent miscommunication (Chaboudy & Jameson, 2001). But not everyone is comfortable with this technology. Ask parents for their permission to bring others into the conversation, and honor their preferences.

The telephone can be an efficient way to get information to several people with relatively little effort. Many schools set up a telephone "chain" whereby you telephone one or two parents with a message. Each of them, in turn, calls two or more other parents and so on until all parents have been contacted. This system has the additional advantage of providing parents with opportunities to interact.

Another way to use the telephone is to record daily messages on an automatic answering machine that parents can access. For example, you can prerecord information about schedule changes or homework assignments.

A common source of telephone information is an office secretary. Secretaries frequently take messages from families, handle small decision making on their own, call parents when they need to pick up their child, and relay significant information. Collaborate with the school secretary in discussing family preferences for communication, such as whether parents want to be called at work or which parent to call in families in which a divorce or separation has occurred.

Technology Options. Three options for using technology to communicate with families are (1) the Internet, (2) videotapes, and (3) audiotapes.

The Internet provides a growing number of ways to communicate with families. Many parents may welcome the opportunity to communicate through e-mail. An e-mail bulletin board system for all parents or a restricted e-mail system for each family may be quite effective, especially if parents are among the 63% of adults with a computer with e-mail or Internet access (Madden, 2003). Be considerate of families without computers or Internet access. For these families you will need to print and send out information (Johnson, 2000). Although less convenient than home use, you can also direct families to sources for Internet access throughout their community (Beghetto, 2001).

E-mail messages serve many of the same purposes as other forms of written communication. In addition, e-mail messages can be distributed to family members at home or at work. A middle school in Ohio e-mails a summary of its weekly team meetings to parents and extended family members so that everyone knows what is going on at school. Notes of the team meeting are taken by students and then submitted to volunteer parents who type and e-mail them to all the families on the team (Chaboudy & Jameson, 2001). If you use technology to communicate with families or other professionals, you need to consider that your e-mail message may be read by unintended audiences. It may be best to communicate confidential information about students through methods that are more secure.

Websites are being used more frequently by schools or programs to communicate with parents. Websites provide a location on the Internet for family members to visit, to access information, and, in some cases, to communicate with each other. Websites can be used by family members or others to raise questions, share ideas, plan class activities, learn about school activities, express their concerns, ask questions, or organize their own meetings or activities (Beghetto, 2001).

For those Websites that enable users to have a written dialogue, communication is typically "delayed" or "asynchronous." This gives family members time to reflect, compose, and edit their message before it is sent (Walther, 1996). There are a number of commercially available tools for setting up a Website. You may also have technology support staff in your school or program to help you.

Websites can be used to provide information in multiple formats. For example, the SPIES Website (*www.cpd.usu.edu/spies/*) provides information about recommended practices to families of young children with disabilities. This Website, which you will learn more about in chapter 10, uses both written text and videotapes to describe and model practices that parents can use with their children (Cook, Rule, & Mariger, 2003). An evaluation study of the Website indicated that parents found it to be practical, accessible, and appropriate. Although some parents had difficulty accessing the videos, many noted their usefulness: "If I wasn't sure exactly what the written description was trying to teach, I could look at the visual example" (Cook et al., 2003, p. 26).

Videotapes (used independently of the computer) are a second technological medium for communicating with parents. Videos can give parents and teachers an understanding of what children are doing, with whom they are interacting, and whether they are improving. A study of video use with families of students in three early childhood classrooms found that parents and teachers benefited from this means of communication (Hundt, 2002). One teacher noted:

> The parents have been very positive. It's the only school correspondence that _____'s family has had in two years. It also shows parents what I am talking about when I conference with them. (Hundt, 2002, p. 42)

Videotapes can be used as picture report cards, progress reports, or illustrations of instructional procedures. Because of the reduced reliance on reading and writing, videotapes provide an effective method for communicating with families with limited English proficiency or low literacy (Guidry, van den Pol, Keeley, & Neilsen, 1996). In addition, videotapes allow families who cannot come into classrooms during the school day to learn what is going on.

Portable or microcassette audiorecorders are a third means of technology-based communication. These simple, low-tech devices allow students, family members, and school personnel to exchange greetings, information, and ideas. Students can listen at home to recorded messages from friends; family members can find out from teachers what happened during the day or what has been assigned for homework. Quicker and less demanding than written communication, microcassettes are an inexpensive and quite effective way to make conversations more accessible.

Face-to-Face Interactions

Face-to-face interactions are one of the most effective and commonly used methods of family-professional communication. We will discuss three types of face-to-face interactions: (1) planned meetings, (2) unplanned meetings, and (3) group meetings.

Planned Meetings. Regularly scheduled meetings can help to maintain and enhance family partnerships (Lambie, 2000; Spinelli, 1999). Planned meetings (sometimes called parent-teacher conferences) are arranged in most schools to discuss a student's progress with an individual family. In addition, planned team meetings serve as the primary vehicle for shared decision making about a student's individualized education. (You will learn more about these particular meetings in chapter 12.) Because of their many potential benefits, meetings should not be limited to the beginning and the end of the school year.

Sometimes a family's cultural values conflict with professional expectations for participation in meetings (Jordan, Reyes-Blanes, Peel, Peel, & Lane, 1998). Some families will decline to take an active role in attending meetings about their children's education. Some families find formal meetings, particularly meetings with many participants, to be intimidating (Lake & Billingsley, 2000; Lynch & Hanson, 2004). We urge you to think about whether you have what one educator called "Westernized blinders" in your partnerships with families (Lamorey, 2002, p. 68). How do you interpret families' beliefs and practices about participating when they differ from your own? How do you honor their beliefs?

In planning a meeting, you will need to consider three major phases: (1) premeeting, (2) meeting, and (3) postmeeting.

Premeeting preparation consists of notifying families of the meeting, planning an agenda, and arranging the environment (Kroth & Edge, 1997). Consider needs and preferences for translations when working with families who are English language learners or non-English speaking. (You may review the information on the use of interpreters provided earlier in this chapter and in chapter 1.) Additional suggestions for ensuring that partnerships are strengthened by the decisions you make during the premeeting phase are included in Figure 9–9.

Use the opportunity when notifying parents to decide with the family who should attend the meeting and whether the student should attend. When appropriate, involving the student in discussion and problem solving (including IEP conferences) can help ensure that decisions are consistent with his or her preferences and interests (Wehmeyer & Sands, 1998). Be sure to communicate with the family about the cultural appropriateness of the stu-dent's decision-making role, and demonstrate respect for their personal choices (see chapter 12).

Logistical barriers prevent many families, especially those with restricted financial resources, from participating in meetings. One father noted:

> Teachers just don't understand that I can't come to school at just any old time. I think Judy told you that we don't have a car right now. . . and then I have to make sure Judy is home because I got three kids in three different schools. (Finders & Lewis, 1994, p. 51)

You can advocate for families by asking other educators at your school, student service clubs, or other community resources to help arrange child care and transportation assistance.

Another option is to consider meeting at the family's home if that is convenient for the family (Gomby, Culross, & Behrman, 1999; Jordan et al., 1998). Although home visits may mean more distractions, they provide

FIGURE 9–9

Tips for Questions to Consider in Planning Meetings with Families

Notifying Parents

- Have you notified parents of the reason for the meeting in an understandable and nonthreatening manner?

- Did you follow up written notification with a telephone call to be certain that family members understand the reason for the meeting, to answer questions, and to find out if assistance with child care or transportation is needed?

- Did you discuss with family members whether they would like their child to attend the meeting?

- Did you discuss with family members whether they would like to have professionals from specific disciplines or other individuals who are important to them participate in the meeting?

- Did you provide information to parents about what will happen at the meeting and what they might do to prepare for the meeting in advance?

- Have you considered the family's preferences in planning the time and location of the meeting?

Setting the Agenda

- Does the agenda include topics the family has mentioned as important?

- Is the agenda flexible enough to accommodate last-minute additions?

- Does the agenda allow adequate time for discussion with family members?

- Is the family comfortable with a written agenda or would they prefer that a more informal approach be used?

Preparing the Environment

- Would it be preferable to hold the meeting in a setting other than the school, such as the family's home, a coffee shop, or the community library?

- Have you made arrangements to meet in a private, comfortable, well-lighted room that has limited distractions?

- Have you gathered all necessary materials and made arrangements not to be interrupted?

- Does the room contain an adequate number of adult-sized chairs and tables?

- Is the furniture arranged in a manner that reflects equality? (Are the seats arranged to avoid having someone sitting behind a desk or at the head of the table?)

- Are all participants able to locate and access the building, parking lot, meeting room, and nearest restrooms?

- Are tissues, beverages, papers, and pens available for all participants?

FIGURE 9–10
Tips for Making Home Visits

- Talk with family members about the home visit before scheduling the appointment.
- Make home visits only if they are scheduled with the family ahead of time.
- Arrive and leave on time.
- Cancel home visits only when absolutely necessary.
- Dress appropriately and comfortably.
- Respond with sensitivity to offers of food and beverages.
- Expect distractions.
- Bring activities for the children.
- Be aware of the environment, and alter the visit if your safety or the safety of the family makes you uncomfortable.
- Leave your schedule and where you will be with someone.
- If part of your visit includes working with the child, take a blanket or tablecloth and spread it on the floor for your work area.
- Parents make choices when home visitors work with their children—some choose participation in the visit, and some use it for a few minutes of respite. Do not be judgmental of their choices.

the opportunity to gather a more complete picture of the student's environment and family life. Figure 9–10 includes tips for making home visits in a friendly and respectful manner.

The second step in premeeting preparation is to prepare an agenda. An agenda (1) helps ensure your own preparation, (2) notifies participants about what topics are to be covered, and (3) serves as a guide for structure and sequence during the conference.

Keep in mind that not all families value efficiency in their interactions with others. Often, European American professionals are eager to follow an agenda and to be as time efficient as possible. Some families, particularly from culturally and linguistically diverse backgrounds, may prefer a more indirect approach that leaves room for conversations about tangential issues, humor, and personal stories (Harry & Kalyanpur, 1994; Lynch & Hanson, 2004). By honoring families' preferences and providing options, you can foster respect and equality in your partnership with family members.

The final step in premeeting preparation is to arrange the physical environment and establish an atmosphere

that will enhance communication. Two of the most important considerations are privacy and comfort. Review the tips for selecting and preparing the setting for your meeting in Figure 9–9. How would the settings you create using these tips affect your communication with families?

In some cases, you may want to consider bringing another person (perhaps a social worker or a school nurse), particularly when the topics to be discussed may cause conflict, when there is a history of misunderstandings between the family and professionals, or when you are concerned about neighborhood safety (Harden, 1997). This person may serve as a witness to events, a support person, or a mediator in case of serious disagreements.

Effective communication during the premeeting phase can build trust in your partnership. Be friendly, be clear, and provide information to prepare families for the meeting. Consider what can happen when there is inadequate communication prior to a meeting:

> When Kristi was first evaluated for a special education program, the school social worker called to say that she was coming to our home for a visit. She did not say why she was coming, and I did not ask. I only knew that social worker normally visit a home to see if it "passes inspection." I cleaned for days, baked cookies and had coffee, tea, and homemade lemonade ready for her visit. The joke was on me. She had only come for a social history. She did not inspect my home or even eat a cookie. How much easier my life would have been if she would have explained to me why she was making her visit.

Once planning has been accomplished, you and the family members are better prepared to meet and converse. During the meeting you should focus on (1) building rapport, (2) obtaining information, (3) providing information, and (4) summarizing.

Rapport building sets the tone for the remainder of the meeting. Your genuine interest in, and acceptance of, the family builds rapport. Reflect on the professionals who provide services to you (such as physicians or other therapists) with whom you have a genuine rapport. What contributes to that rapport? How long did it take to develop? What could have been done to facilitate it more readily? By incorporating the seven partnership principles you learned about in chapter 7, you will have a better chance of establishing a positive rapport with families.

The second component of the conference, obtaining information, provides you the opportunity to practice many of the nonverbal and verbal communication skills that we described earlier in this chapter, such as empathetic listening. Encourage families to share information by asking open-ended questions. When you are unclear about a family member's point of view, ask for clarification or specific examples. Respond empathetically if failies have difficulty expressing a thought or a feeling. Provide feedback to the family regarding the ideas, and affirm their strengths and contributions.

The third component of the conference process, sharing information, requires you to use jargon-free language. Jargon limits families' ability to understand information. When you use clear and simple terms, you promote equity in your partnerships. One professional noted that "the most articulate parents tell us they believe this jargon is the interventionist's way of reminding them who is in charge" (Stonestreet, Johnston, & Acton, 1991, p. 40).

When sharing information, begin on a positive note, pointing out the student's strong points before mentioning topics that concern you or the family. Provide specific examples by telling anecdotes or showing samples of the student's work. Be aware of and respond to the impact of what you are saying on the family. If they are frowning or appear puzzled, stop for a moment to provide an opportunity for questions or comments. Ask the parents what kind of person their child is at home and to share information to assist in understanding the child (Walker-Dalhouse & Dalhouse, 2001). As much as possible, encourage everyone to exchange information and concerns. One mother, who also served as the president of the parent organization, described the critical role of two-way communication in successful meetings:

> The all-important purpose of home and school meetings should be to facilitate communication between families and schools . . . Parents need to have a voice and be able to ask questions and receive accurate, up-to-date information. This dispels rumors and builds confidence and trust. . . . With good team work, things get done. (Haviland, 2003, p. 52)

When you are summarizing or planning follow-up activities, review the high points of the meeting and emphasize next-step activities. Restate who is responsible for carrying out those tasks and the date by which they are to be completed. Discuss and agree on options for follow-up strategies. If another meeting is planned, decide on the time and place. End the meeting on a positive note. Thank the family for their interest and contributions, and offer to be available should any questions or issues arise.

After the meeting concludes, it is important to take time to share information and reflect on the team process:

Review the meeting with the student (with parental consent).

Share the outcome of the meeting with other professionals.

Record and file minutes of the meeting.

■ Evaluate your satisfaction with the meeting and seek reactions, feedback, and suggestions for improvement from other participants.

The more you reflect and invite feedback on planned meetings, the more likely it is that your partnership with families will flourish.

We now ask you to consider how the strategies you use to collaborate during planned meetings apply during your unplanned or spontaneous interactions with family members.

Unplanned Meetings. Unplanned meetings inevitably occur at any time and in any place. Parents may unexpectedly drop in at school before, during, and after school hours; you may receive telephone calls at home in the evenings and on weekends; or you may be approached by families with child-related concerns at unlikely places, such as a movie theater or a grocery store.

Although it is probably impossible to avoid being caught off guard at such times, you can prepare for these meetings and the likelihood that parents will express their most intense thoughts and feelings. Consider the following suggestions:

■ Decide in advance what is possible for you to do in response to unplanned conferences.
■ Talk with other professionals about their strategies for handling unplanned meetings.
■ Identify the topics that are open or closed for discussion at unplanned meetings.
■ Have helpful resources readily available for families seeking information (e.g., names, addresses, and phone numbers of other agencies, families, and professionals).
■ Seek advice and support from the administrator at your school.
■ Be flexible and open to special circumstances that require an immediate meeting.

Of course, you need to inform families of your preferences. Ideally, you should do this at the beginning of the year before any unplanned meetings have occurred. Communicate your preferences both verbally and in writing to avoid misunderstanding and to allow the families to ask questions. Be sure to explain your rationale regarding unplanned meetings in noneducational settings: for example, "I want to be able to meet your needs and answer your questions as well and as completely as possible; however, I am not able to do so without sufficient preparation and access to your child's records."

Practice the positive communication skills discussed earlier in this chapter during unplanned meetings. Without positive communication skills, even the best prepared professionals can fail in their attempts to meet the needs of families.

Group Meetings. Group meetings represent a third way of face-to-face interactions with families. Almost all schools have orientation meetings or open houses during the year for families to learn about their child's schedule and curriculum. Although it is difficult to connect with families individually at such large meetings, group meetings provide information to many people at one time and give families an opportunity to meet each other.

Group meetings should be arranged at a time convenient for families. Consider giving families the option of meeting during the day and or in the evening. Holding the

FIGURE 9–11
Creating Partnerships Through Trust Building: Selected Actions Leading to Trust and Distrust When Communicating with Families

Partnership Principles and Practices	Issues	Actions Leading to Distrust	Actions Leading to Trust
Communication: Listen.	You are participating in a conference with parents who are extremely angry that their gifted child is making poor grades and believe that it is your fault.	Tell the parents that they have not provided proper supervision for homework and that the poor grades are their fault.	Listen empathetically and ask if they would be willing to brainstorm options that would involve them and you collaborating to promote their child's program.
Respect: Honor cultural diversity.	The school handbook is only available in English, yet the parents speak Mandarin.	Tell the parents that maybe their child or some friends can translate parts of the handbook to them.	Talk with your administrator about getting the handbook translated into Mandarin or securing someone to explain it to the parents.
Professional Competence: Set high expectations.	Parents of a student who is failing every subject are not showing any concern about school failure.	Tell the parents that you object to their family priorities and that they are only hurting their son.	Meet with the family and find out, from their perspective, their priorities for their son, both this year and in the future.
Equality: Provide options.	A parent asks if a conference can be arranged before school to accommodate her work schedule.	Tell the parent it is against teacher-union policy.	Ask the parent if it would be possible to talk on the telephone early in the school day rather than to meet at school.
Commitment: Be sensitive to emotional needs.	The family has just moved to a new community, and neither the student nor the parents know anyone at the child's new middle school.	Assume that the parents may be interested in coming to the school open house next year; leave them on their own to make connections in the new community and school.	Call the parents, issue a special invitation to come to the school open house, and arrange with another family to meet the new parents and student and introduce them to others.
Trust: Maintain confidentiality.	The school administration asks parents to contribute to a fund to pay for the classroom newspaper, but the parents do not have money to contribute.	Tell them they'll not be able to get the newspaper, since they have to "pay their own way."	Identify a nonmonetary way for them to contribute to the class; tell them their classroom contribution represents their donation; keep everything confidential.

meeting in community locations or at work sites may make transportation and child care easier for some families to arrange. Finally, remember to inform parents of what is to take place during the meeting and how the meeting will be conducted (Lundgren & Morrison, 2003). Pena (2000) described a situation in which a school, composed primarily of Latino families, had planned for parents to move from the cafeteria to their children's classrooms on Back to School Night. Because the procedures were not made clear to parents, many simply exited the building after leaving the cafeteria, unaware that the meeting had not yet ended.

Face-to-face meetings with parents, whether planned, unplanned, or group, provide a critical opportunity for partnership building. In each situation, the communication practices of honesty, clarity, and friendliness strengthen relationships and build trust.

SUMMARY

Positive communication is a critical element to developing partnerships with families and professionals. To be an effective communicator, you will need to reflect on and develop your own interpersonal skills and tailor your communication strategies to be consistent with family preferences.

The effectiveness of your communication with families and other professionals is enhanced when you interact respectfully and positively. You send nonverbal messages about your interest and empathy by the way you physically position yourself and listen to others. The words you use in conversation with families can foster trust and openness; conversely, your words may cause parents to withhold their thoughts or feelings. Figure 9–11 summarizes how words and actions can foster positive communication.

Keep your eyes, mind, and heart open so that you promote trusting partnerships and avoid misunderstandings. When differences do arise, you will need to rely on culturally responsive strategies to resolve conflicts.

Families typically prefer informal and frequent communication with professionals. Ask family members about their preferences for different methods of communication. They may prefer—and you will need to know and practice—specific communication strategies, including those that are written, spoken, and technology based. In addition, you will need to plan, carry out, and follow up on face-to-face interactions.

Effective communication occurs when you use positive strategies to learn about students and their families, share ideas and information with them, and strengthen your partnerships with individual family members. Communication is the one partnership principle that allows you to give expression to the values inherent in the others: equity, respect, competence, advocacy, commitment, and trust.

REFLECTING ON THE VIGNETTE

1. If you had been a teacher or other professional involved with any one of the families in the vignette, what action might you have taken to improve the communication the family, or any of its members, had with the professionals?
2. If you were a specialist hired by the school district to assist its professionals to improve their communications with any of the families in the vignette, what needs (of the professionals) would you identify and what recommendations would you make?
3. What was more important in the family-professional communication for each of the families: the words, the way they are spoken, the behaviors of the families and professionals, the families' and professionals' culture, or is each of these factors equally important?

ENHANCING YOUR SELF-AWARENESS

How would you characterize your ability to communicate with others? Are you able to interact comfortably and effectively with all families? Other professionals? Do your interactions convey to others that you are a team member worthy of trust? Reflect on how effectively you presently communicate with different individuals in a variety of situations. Remember that the efficacy of your communication is not judged solely by your intent but rather by how the message you send is interpreted by others.

Nonverbal communication

Think about your interactions with other people. How do you use gestures and facial expressions to convey your empathy and understanding? What cues let you know that the other person needs more or less distance when communicating? When have different cultural perspectives influenced communication? How do you modify your physical proximity and posture to accommodate the preferences of others? Can you think of a time when your facial expressions or the expressions of the other person were incongruent with what was being said? How did this impact communication?

Verbal communication

How effectively do you encourage communication with others through your words and questions? Think about a recent conversation with a family member or colleague.

What questions were asked that opened up the dialogue? What responses led you or someone else to pull back? How do you feel when the emotions behind your words go unrecognized?

Resolving conflict

You can learn a great deal about effective communication and trust building from difficult situations. Consider a time when you held a different position than a family member or colleague. Were your respective positions shared openly? How did your ability to see the issue from the other's perspective affect your ability to see alternative solutions? Think about what you might have done differently to promote trust and enhance communication.

RESOURCES

1. Conflict Resolution Network (CRN)
P.O. Box 1016, Chatswood NSW 2057
+61 (0) 2-9419-8500
http://www.crnhq.org

   The CRN was developed to promote the theory and practice of conflict resolution. The Website contains accessible and reproducible information about conflict resolution skills, strategies, and attitudes.

2. Capacity Works, LLC
P.O. Box 271
Amenia, NY 12501-0271
888-840-8578; NY State: 845-373-4218
www.capacityworks.com

   Capacity Works was created by Beth Mount to showcase books, posters, and other works to inspire positive futures and images of people with disabilities throughout the world. Beth Mount received the TASH 2001 Award for Exemplary Achievement in Print for her work that is displayed on this Website.

3. Collaborative Problem Solving and Dispute Resolution in Special Education
Center for Appropriate Dispute Resolution in Special Education (CADRE)
P.O. Box 51360
Eugene, OR 97405-0906
541-686-5060
www.directionservice.org/cadre/resources/ contents.htm

   This manual, which is published by CADRE, is designed as an educational tool for understanding and resolving conflict. It offers state-of-the-art thinking in dispute resolution applied to special education situations.

4. Center for Nonviolent Communication (CNVC)
2428 Foothill Boulevard, Suite E
La Crescenta, CA 91214
800-255-7696
www.cnvc.org

   CNVC is an international, nonprofit training and peacemaking organization. They provide training and curriculum materials to help individuals and organizations resolve their conflicts peacefully.

CHAPTER

10

Meeting Families' Basic Needs

CHAPTER ORGANIZATION

1. What role do families' basic needs play in their over-all quality of life?
2. Why does having access to information, support, and community resources influence family-professional partnerships?
3. How do systems, and professionals within systems, support families in ways that build trust?

VIGNETTE

In his poem "Invictus," William Ernest Henley proclaimed, "I am the master of my fate, I am the captain of my soul." Certainly many families share that lofty aspiration but find it hard to attain. Their ideal does not always conform to their reality. To be their own captain, even to meet their basic needs, often means that they must rely on one or more professional partners.

Clara Berg knew that Kenny wanted to work on a farm. But it was not until Beth Mount began to work with Clara and Jake to map out Kenny's future that people realized Kenny might become the captain of his ship—or more accurately, the master of the chicken coop—at Adriance Farm.

Joesian Cortes knows he wants to be a firefighter or help people in some other important way. But it was not until the assistant principal at his school, Emily Rodriguez, opened up the doors for him at a city vocational education program that he had a realistic chance to attain that goal.

Mastering even the most ordinary parts of daily life often means that families must be partners with professionals. When Sean Holley wants to go swimming in the summer, paraprofessionals from Bonner Springs Elementary School take him to the community pool. In doing so, they offer Leia social support that benefits both Sean and her. When Norma Cortes goes into a mediation hearing with Joesian's teachers, her support comes from Lourdes Rivera-Putz and Martha Viscarrondo at United We Stand of New York.

Professionals are not the only people who support families to meet basic needs to acquire some control over their lives.

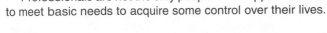
Sean Holley eats alongside classmates and teachers in the Bonner Springs Elementary School cafeteria.

Clara Berg (left) enjoys reminiscing with Carole Gothelf, former principal of the Guild School where Kenny Berg was once a student.

Joesian's brother and sister help translate for Norma whe she meets with his teachers. Carole Gothelf no longer play a professional role in Kenny's life, but her friendship with th Bergs supports them emotionally.

To get help in understanding Sean's rights to a free ap propriate public education, Leia Holley contacted the Kansa parent training and information center, which is operated b parents for parents. She now works for the center, suppor ing other parents as they and their children receive specia education.

One role of the parent training and information centers an of community parent resource centers such as United W Stand of New York is to ensure that parents get answers t their questions about disability and special education. Info mation must be relevant, straightforward, and often in lar guages other than English.

But these centers and other parent organizations focus c more than just information about education. They also refe parents to places that provide medical and other evaluatior of their children, as United We Stand did for Joesian ar Norma. They know the locations of local offices of various so cial service agencies and who are the key decision makers those offices. They help families qualify for Social Securit housing, and other benefits.

Some families experience domestic violence. Sometime as was true for Nicky Doleman, the violence creates disabi ties. When this happens, professionals are legally bound intervene. If they do not, they not only violate their legal d ties and often their professional ethical duties, but they als neglect families' basic needs for safety at home.

Nicky Doleman cuddles under a quilt as her bedtime approaches.

All families want some control over what happens to them. But more than most families, those who have children with disabilities face challenges in meeting even their basic needs. So when teachers, paraprofessionals, other professionals, and even other parents come to the families' aid, they help families meet basic needs.

Meeting basic needs means supporting families to meet social-emotional, informational, financial, safety, and health-related needs. You learned in chapter 3 that families perform eight basic but different functions simultaneously and that each function demands much of their time and attention. Their child's education is only one function. Some families cannot pay rent or purchase food; others cannot fully understand the nature of their child's exceptionality. Your support to better fulfill those essential needs can enhance greatly the child and family's quality of life and at the same time strengthen your partnership with the family.

Some educators may wonder if it is appropriate to give their time and attention to families' basic needs. They may believe that their primary role—indeed, their only role—is to teach the student. Are they mistaken? Yes. The more you support families to address their most basic needs, the more likely they will be able to respond to their children's educational priorities and their needs in other areas.

INTRODUCTION

In this chapter we will provide you with information to reflect on your role in meeting families' basic needs in ways that are both meaningful and respectful. We will also offer you an array of resources and strategies to support families' social-emotional, informational, financial, safety, and health-related needs. We encourage you to build trust with families by considering each family's individual perspectives and resources, particularly in situations that differ from your own. An informed and trusting professional is one who is more understanding, proactive, and effective in helping families access information and services to enrich their lives.

RECOGNIZING THE IMPORTANCE OF FAMILY SUPPORT

If a family has to sacrifice money to attend an individualized education program (IEP) meeting, much less a school fair, there is little choice: Work comes first and school is second. Of course, some families are able to strike a balance, but they have different life conditions than families who are served by community parent resource centers such as United We Stand of New York (we describe those centers later in this chapter).

It is regrettable that 27 million children in the United States are growing up in families with low incomes, even though the majority of them have at least one working parent. Furthermore, our nation's poverty rate is two to three times higher than most other industrialized countries (National Center for Children in Poverty, 2003). As you learned in chapter 1, there is a higher rate of poverty in families who have children with disabilities as contrasted to families whose children do not have disabilities. In addition to experiencing challenges related to disabilities, poor families also face highly stressful living conditions every day (Hanson & Lynch, 2004).

In an examination of the influences of poverty on quality of life for families with children with disabilities, Park, Turnbull, and Turnbull (2002) discovered that poverty's impact is far-reaching and directly affects such aspects of family life as the following:

- Health—hunger, limited or no access to health care
- Productivity—limited leisure or recreational activities
- Physical environment—overcrowding, safety
- Emotional well-being—high levels of stress, low self-esteem
- Family interaction—marital stress, parenting issues

Families who are *not* living in poverty also need support and services. To respond to the needs of all families, you will find that partnerships with families and other professionals are essential.

There will be many different opportunities to partner with families to meet their most basic needs. For example, you can connect them to health-care agencies. You can let them know where they can get benefits for their child (such as those available from a local Social Security office). You can be a witness if their child is involved in a juvenile justice proceeding.

Helping families meet basic needs involves more than providing information or referring them to a different service system. It is a matter of developing trust and helping families understand that you—and others in your school—will not lump them into groups that receive the same generic services. Families want individual attention and respect; each family is its own entity, not part of a conglomerate. Understanding how much or how little support a family wants is vital to the trust that grounds a true partnership.

UNDERSTANDING SELF-DETERMINATION WITHIN A FAMILY CONTEXT

Freedom, choice, and control over one's life are at the heart of understanding self-determination and children with disabilities and their families. The concept of self-determination for individuals with disabilities emerged in the past decade. As you learned in chapter 4, self-determination can be thought of as living one's life consistent with one's values, preferences, strengths, and needs (Turnbull & Turnbull, 2001).

In this chapter, we discuss how to work with families to meet their most basic needs. Self-determination is one of those needs. Parental choice is at the heart of self-determination because parents are primary decision makers for their children within the context of their values, culture, and definition of quality of life. As you learned in chapter 6, the concept of parental choice is a guiding force in both the Individuals with Disabilities Education Act (IDEA) and the No Child Left Behind (NCLB) Act.

Think about the partnership principle of respect and the practices of honoring cultural diversity and treating families with dignity. One of the most important roles you will play involves partnership with families to advance their autonomy and self-determination. Supporting student self-determination based on family preferences will also be important in your job. Research indicates that when teachers are self-determined, they are more capable of promoting self-determination in students (Field & Hoffman, 2002).

Self-determination can be powerful in the lives of individuals with disabilities. Specifically, students can develop several elements leading to greater self-determination such as choice making, self-awareness, problem solving, and self-advocacy (Wehmeyer & Palmer, 2000). Although the growing body of knowledge on self-determination has represented primarily children, youth, and adults with significant disabilities (Brown, Gothelf, Guess, & Lehr, 1998; Wehmeyer, Agran, Palmer, Martin, & Mithaug, 2003; Wehmeyer, 1998), self-determination and very young children and their families have received increased attention (Erwin & Brown, 2003; Wehmeyer & Palmer, 2000; Weigel-Garrey, Cook, & Brotherson, 1998). This literature supports the concept that skills, behavior, and attitudes of self-determination are formed early in life. As we begin to focus on self-determination in young children, we need to understand the vital role that family and home environment play in the early years and beyond.

We are just beginning to understand the central role families play in determining the meaning and impor-

tance of self-determination. Ferguson (1998) described it this way:

> It is a jointly authored account. Self-determination is not *inside* (my son) Ian. It is an expression of the relationships he has with his parents, paid supporter, friends, and neighbors that define what happens to him and the rest of us day to day. (p. 46)

As parents promote self-determination for their children with disabilities, their quest influences the whole family. Despite significant advances in understanding the concept of self-determination, "the intertwining of individual self-determination and every other family member has not been taken into sufficient account" (Turnbull & Turnbull, 1996, p. 203). By practicing the partnership principle of respect, you can affirm families' strengths, treat them with dignity, and honor their cultural diversity.

This last partnership practice, honoring diversity, needs to be considered first when addressing self-determination and students with disabilities and their families. The concept of self-determination represents a value with Anglo-European roots and often conflicts with values embraced by other cultural perspectives (Hanson & Lynch, 2004; Kalyanpur & Harry, 1999; Turnbull & Turnbull, 1996).

Kalyanpur and Harry (1999) have suggested that the self-determination concept reflects Western society's value that children are individuals with rights who should have opportunities to exert those rights to maximize their potential. However, the value ascribed to self-determination in one culture may conflict directly with values of other cultural groups such as the Hmong, who deeply value group identity and would reject freedom of choice, particularly for children. Moreover, not all families from the same cultural or ethnic backgrounds share the same values. Erwin and Brown (2003) have suggested that because "self-determination is personally and culturally determined, it is important to identify with the family the level of importance, if any, that they place on self-determination."

Have open conversations with families about the meaning and importance of self-determination in their child's life. Families exercise their choice in many different ways. Some emphasize harmony over progress; others value community over individualism (Lynch & Hanson, 2004). Figure 10–1 offers a set of questions to help you and the family identify values most important to them.

When addressing families' basic and unmet needs, remember the partnership principle of commitment. In particular, practices that foster trust include (1) being sensitive to families' emotional needs, (2) being available and accessible, and (3) going above and beyond.

FIGURE 10–1

Guiding Questions to Identify Family Values Related to Self-Determination and Family Life

Talk with families to identify how important each value below is to their family. For each of the paired words, ask them which of the two values matters most to them. Circle the star that is closest to what the family members believe is important.

1. Interdependence	*	*	Independence
2. Collective/group identity	*	*	Individual identity
3. Saving face	*	*	Being direct/open
4. Emphasis on interpersonal relationships	*	*	Emphasis on task completion
5. Spiritual/holistic orientation	*	*	Rational/logical orientation
6. Tendency toward patriarchal family structure	*	*	Tendency toward democratic family structure
7. Overt respect for age, maturity, wisdom	*	*	Interest in youth, intelligence, fitness
8. Harmony with nature	*	*	Limited interest in nature
9. Human interaction dominates	*	*	Time dominates
10. Children raised interdependently	*	*	Children raised independently
11. Family hierarchy; roles defined	*	*	Equality; role flexibility
12. Families make decisions/choices	*	*	Children encouraged to make decisions/choices
13. Families address/solve problems	*	*	Children encouraged to help solve problems
14. Fate	*	*	Personal control over environment

Source: Adapted from Lynch, E. W., & Hanson, M. J. (Eds.). (2004). *Developing cross-cultural competence: A guide for working with children and their families* (3rd ed.). Baltimore: Paul H. Brookes Publishing Company. Adapted by permission.

You can cultivate trusting partnerships with families and address their basic, unmet needs by (1) accessing social-emotional support, (2) accessing information, (3) accessing economic support, and (4) accessing support to address violence or neglect in the home.

ACCESSING SOCIAL AND EMOTIONAL SUPPORT

Social support refers to a source of comfort found within group and individual relationships. Emotional support involves caring, encouraging, and understanding. Informational support, which you will read about in the next section, provides families with knowledge, skills, and connection to services.

An assessment of the stress levels of families of children with disabilities can help match them to appropriate supports and services (Lessenberry & Rehfeldt, 2004). Social and emotional supports reduce families' stress and improve their emotional well-being (Boyd, 2002; Brannan, Heflinger, & Foster, 2003; Evans, 2003; Lustig & Akey, 1999; Singer et al., 1999). Unfortunately, families of children with disabilities often have smaller social support networks than other families and tend to receive their support from nuclear and extended family members (Bailey et al., 1999; Herman & Thompson, 1995; Kazak & Marvin, 1984). Yet when families do have access to social and emotional support, they often report greater satisfaction as parents and more positive interactions with their children (Dunst, Trivette, & Cross, 1986; Lehman & Irvin, 1996; Singer et al., 1999). Likewise, when families have greater control over managing their personal support, their satisfaction with services increases (Caldwell & Heller, 2003).

Professionals in special education may limit themselves to working directly with the student. They may choose not to try to support the student's family. They should first examine their roles and responsibilities and how and why they are held accountable for their professional actions, especially when working with families of very young children (Bailey, 2001; McConnell, 2001; Turnbull & Turnbull, 2000). According to a former teacher, who now is a professor of special education and the mother of two children with special needs, parents "need to lead the dialogue on what family outcomes could be and how they would be measured . . . parent voices have to enter this dialogue prominently and be the foundation at every level of accountability" (Brotherson, 2001, pp. 23–24). When families feel that professionals listen to them and address their priorities at every stage of family support, professionals become trusted partners. This is particularly valuable as families share what type of support is important to them and how they want to receive the support.

Within-Family Support

While some families look outside their family system for emotional and social support, others seek this kind of intimate support from within their own family unit. In chapter 2, you learned about the importance of all family subsystems. Think about how different family members could be rich sources of support, particularly because they are familiar with and part of the family context. Imagine how valuable a grandmother's advice might be to her granddaughter who is a new mother experiencing difficulty breast-feeding. Can you think of specific situations when you received emotional and social support from family members?

Many of the values, beliefs, and practices guiding special education may be in stark contrast to what families from culturally and linguistically diverse backgrounds value (Kalyanpur & Harry, 1999; Kalyanpur, Harry, & Skrtic, 2000; Singer, 2002; Turnbull & Turnbull, 1996). Professionals should recognize and honor potential within- family contributions. Within-family support is an essential source of comfort and assistance, especially for families with infants and young children, when caregiving expectations and practices are culturally determined (Bailey et al., 1999; Denny et al., 2001; Fadiman, 1997). Consider how this parent, a Mexican immigrant whose infant was hospitalized and received neonatal intensive care services, planned to follow her grandmother's advice for raising healthy babies:

> She would always say that potatoes and beans were very important because they have a lot of protein. She would say if you were going to make a dish, it would always have the three colors like the Mexican flag. Red, white, and green. (Denny et al., 2001, p. 154)

Parents who have not completed high school report that they prefer receiving support about child rearing from family and friends rather than from others (Gowen, Christy, & Sparling, 1993). Their preference acknowledges that an abundance of social and emotional support is available within the nuclear and extended members of a family.

Understanding family cohesion and the availability and value of within-family support is helpful. By promoting partnership principles and the corresponding practices of commitment (being sensitive to emotional needs) and respect (affirming family strengths), you are on the right track toward partnership with families.

Family-to-Family Support

Another excellent way to enable families to obtain social and emotional support is to connect them with other families who share similar experiences (Ainbinder et al., 1998; Santelli, Poyadue, & Young, 2001; Santelli, Turnbull, Marquis, & Lerner, 1997; Singer, 2002; Singer et al., 1999). Like so many parents, this mother wanted to talk to other parents who have walked down similar paths:

> Family and friends fell by the wayside in a fantastic pattern of despair . . . like a chain of dominoes. Many of these friends were professionals that I had the utmost confidence in. Pillars of strength and guidance drifted away like straws in the wind. . . . I knew then that from that day forward my whole life must change if [my son] were to survive. His vulnerability frightened me. I knew what I must do. I could no longer go it alone. I needed other mothers, other fathers to relate to. (Pizzo, 1983, p. 25)

Parent to Parent Programs. A widespread and popular type of social and emotional support is called *Parent to Parent*. These programs establish one-to-one matches between a trained "veteran parent"—someone with experience as a parent of a child with a disability—and a "referred parent" who is facing that kind of parenthood for the first time. The veteran parent provides emotional and informational support to the referred parent. The support is available "24 hours a day—not just Monday through Friday from 8 a.m. to 5 p.m." (Santelli et al., 2001, p. 53). Consider how one parent benefited from the advice of another couple:

> After our daughter was diagnosed with a major heart defect that would require open-heart surgery, we were matched with a couple who had a two-year-old with Down syndrome who had gone through the same surgery. They adopted us as their couple to support. Our daughter had been in hospitals constantly. Our support parents came down to see her in the hospital, called us, and sent letters. The dad even gave blood for our daughter's surgery. They took us out to dinner when our daughter was in intensive care. They came to our daughter's first birthday party. They have become our close friends. (Santelli et al., 2001, p. 53)

Parent to Parent programs, which are run by parents for parents, have increased to more than 600 active local and statewide programs with at least one in every state. More than 65,000 parents are involved across the United States (Santelli, Turnbull, Marquis, & Lerner, 2000). You will find the national Parent to Parent Website in the resources section at the end of this chapter.

Local Parent to Parent Programs. Typically, local programs serve parents without regard for the type of disability their children have. They are run by volunteer parents who match a veteran parent with a parent who is just beginning to deal with a particular challenge. Typically, matches are made on the basis of six factors: (1) a similar disability, (2) a family facing similar problems, (3) a veteran parent who can respond within 24 hours, (4) children with disabilities who are close to the same age, (5) families who live close by, and (6) families with a similar family structure.

The match often occurs just after the initial diagnosis that the child has a disability, usually within the neonatal intensive care unit of the hospital or shortly after the family begins exploring community services and supports. Most parents who are matched during the child's early years testify to the value of such early support, as this parent indicates:

When our son with Down syndrome was born three years ago, my husband and I were shocked and devastated. . . . The couple that our Parent to Parent program sent us were such warm, optimistic, "normal" people, they gave us hope. About a year later, my husband and I were trained by our program to be support parents. The Parent-to-Parent office has many requests for visits from both father and mother. My husband was one of very few men willing to go through formal training. I have also found that support for non-English speaking families is hard to come by. It has been satisfying to me to be able to serve the Spanish-speaking community.

Many referred parents evolve into veteran parent roles as they share insights and practical know-how with new parents. Veteran parents not only have the benefit of knowing they are helping others but also have an opportunity to reinforce their own learning.

University researchers and members of Parent to Parent organizations have interviewed 400 parents nationally (Santelli, Singer, DiVenere, Ginsberg, & Powers, 1998; Singer et al., 1999). More than 80% of the parents found Parent to Parent programs to be helpful. Specifically, parents who used Parent to Parent services reported feeling better able to deal positively with their child and family situation, to view their circumstances in a more positive light, and to make progress on goals that were important to them.

Parent to Parent is also a resource for professionals. Listen to what a school administrator said about the unexpected impact of Parent to Parent on his staff:

When the Parent to Parent program was established, we knew that it would be helpful for families, but we didn't realize until later that it would also be helpful to our staff. As professionals, we often feel inadequate because we cannot understand what families are going through because we haven't actually experienced what they have. Our staff became aware that the Parent to Parent program could fulfill a need for families that they could not. (Santelli et al., 2001, p. 66)

If you are in a community without a Parent to Parent program, you could convene a group of potential veteran parents and committed professionals to brainstorm about the possibility of starting a new program. Figure 10–2 describes strategies for developing a local Parent to Parent program.

You might also arrange for individualized matches among parents of children with disabilities when no programs are available. Parents of children who are gifted may also want to meet other parents with similar experiences. Unique issues facing families of gifted children may include feelings of isolation, parental self-concept, and neglect of or insecurity in nongifted siblings, leading families to seek social and emotional support (Stephens, 1999).

Statewide Parent to Parent Programs. Because local programs need support and coordination, statewide Parent to Parent programs exist in approximately 30 states (Santelli, 1999). These programs provide technical assistance to local programs and make matches on a statewide basis when a local match is not available.

Statewide programs can be centralized or decentralized. In some states, the statewide program is part of the same program as the parent training and information centers (you will read about them in the next section). In other states, the statewide program is affiliated with a parent organization, an early intervention program, or a university. No two statewide programs are exactly alike. A manual that describes best practices in statewide programs is available in the Parent to Parent section of the Beach Center's Website (*www.beachcenter.org*). We encourage you to contact these programs for information about services in your state. If you want to know about local programs in states without a statewide program, visit the Parent to Parent Website (described in the resource section at the end of this chapter).

By being a resource for providing or securing social and emotional support, you are practicing the partnership principle of commitment, specifically the practices of sensitivity to emotional needs, availability and accessibility, and reassuring parents that they are not alone.

ACCESSING INFORMATION

Families will be more empowered to help their children and themselves when they have access to relevant information (Bailey et al., 1999; Scorgie, Wilgosh, & McDonald, 1998). What are families' information needs and

FIGURE 10–2

Theory into Practice: Working with Families to Start a Parent to Parent Program

- **Identify a small group of parents who are interested in developing a Parent to Parent program.** Parent leadership, energy, and commitment are keys to the program's success. Professionals can be important guides and offer a newly developing program many important resources.

- **Determine roles and responsibilities.** Decide whether your program is going to be entirely staffed by volunteers or sponsored by a service provider agency, disability organization, existing parent group, or other group. If you take the volunteer route, you may find it useful to ask people in the community for advice and assistance. Also consider asking banks, religious organizations, libraries, and other places to donate space for your meetings or office needs.

- **Connect with established Parent to Parent programs** who might be able to offer excellent information and training materials. You can get information on local programs by visiting the Parent to Parent Website (www.p2pusa.org) or the Beach Center on Disability Website (www.beachcenter.org).

- **Establish a system to connect parents.** You will need a local telephone number, preferably available at all times, that potential program parents can call. Use an answering machine if necessary. Appoint someone to coordinate incoming referrals and establish matches.

- **Develop a record-keeping system** for keeping track of referrals and matches.

- **Let people know what you are doing.** Use flyers, brochures, word of mouth, parent speeches, radio, newspapers, doctor offices, and Internet—anything you can to promote the program.

- **Offer optional support activities,** such as ongoing consultation for veteran parents, informational group activities, social gatherings, advocacy training, and instruction for others in the community.

Source: Beach Center on Disability, University of Kansas, Lawrence.

interests? The research that was conducted in the early 1990s, shortly after IDEA authorized infant-and-toddler services, focused primarily on parents of very young children, the majority of whom were European American (Cooper & Allred, 1992; Gowen et al., 1993; Sontag & Schacht, 1994). The researchers concluded that, in gen-

eral, parents want information on child care, service availability, community resources, and parenting practices and that families differ in their preferences for having access to the information.

Access to information remains one of the greatest unmet needs of families of children with disabilities, especially those from culturally and linguistically diverse backgrounds (Al-Hassan & Gardner, 2002; Mitchell & Sloper, 2002; Park, Turnbull, & Park, 2001; Public Agenda, 2002; Shapiro, Monzo, Rueda, Gomez, & Blacker, 2004; Zoints, Zoints, Harrison, & Bellinger, 2004). A study of families, friends, teachers, and individuals with challenging behavior about access to information concluded that families want relevant, user-friendly, and easily accessible research-based information and increased support and technical assistance in using information (Ruef & Turnbull, 2001).

The partnership principle of communication helps match families' informational needs to specific resources. By providing and coordinating information for families who want information but do not know where or how to get it, you meet one of their basic needs. Of course, there may be questions that neither you nor anyone else seems able to answer. In that event, consider working with parents to find the answers; you do not have to practice the communication principle alone—indeed, you should not. Partnership means working with the families.

Even though there are more resources available to families than ever before, many families still have limited access. Some professionals will withhold information. Some families face language and communication barriers; others do not understand that they have rights to certain information about their children and their children's school (as we pointed out in chapter 6) (Al-Hassan & Gardner, 2002; Park et al., 2001; Public Agenda, 2002; Zhang & Bennett, 2003; Zoints et al., 2004). Sometimes, information about a school or other service-delivery system is not always offered by the system (contrary to IDEA and NCLB), leaving families unaware of the services to which their child is entitled (Public Agenda, 2002). Some families just happen to stumble across critical information for their child (Blue-Banning, Summers, Frankland, Nelson, & Beegle, 2004; Mitchell & Sloper, 2002).

Sometimes the information that a family does have is just not helpful. One parent summed it up this way:

> It's not simply that people aren't getting the information, it's why are they not getting it when they want it or in the form that they can absorb it, or in a way that they can act on it? . . . So it's not enough for services to simply chuck the leaflets across and say there you are, there's the information, because it doesn't work. (Mitchell & Sloper, 2002, p. 78

Think for a moment about families for whom English is not a first language. Often information does not reach them in their native language, or it is inadequate or difficult to understand (Al-Hassan & Gardner, 2002; Shapiro et al., 2004). You can help families overcome these challenges by finding ways to make information accessible to parents whose primary language is not English or to those with limited literacy skills.

At times you may notice that information is not getting to families or is not presented in an accessible format. When this occurs, you will need to consider how to use the partnership principle of advocacy and the corresponding practices of preventing problems, keeping your conscience primed, and pinpointing and documenting problems. Figure 10–3 presents you with a problem; how might you respond?

Consider this professional's perspective about the vital link between trust and sharing information with families:

> . . . I give them so much information. . . . They're really grateful about that because no one else really gives them that much information. . . . They trust me now, you know, and I can help them better if they trust me. . . I build a lot of relationships through a lot of talking and giving them information and that's important to them. (Blue-Banning et al., 2004, p. 175)

The partnership principle of trust is the key to healthy, positive partnerships with families. Having access to information enables families to make informed decisions affecting their child and the rest of the family. You are a rich source of information, particularly for parents who are new to the special education system or who do not understand how the system works.

There are several options for acquiring and sharing the information that families want. You have already learned about one important source of social and emotional support, the Parent-to-Parent programs. These also are rich sources of information for families (Santelli, Turnbull, Sergeant, Lerner, & Marquis, 1996; Santelli et al., 2001). Other sources of information include (1) federally funded parent centers, (2) clearinghouses, (3) family organizations, (4) local neighborhood resources, (5) books and magazines, (6) television, radio, and film, and (7) technology and the Internet.

Parent Centers

Recognizing that parents need training and information to help their children develop to their fullest potential and secure their rights under federal and state laws, Congress

---

FIGURE 10–3
Advocating for Systems Change

Dana, a high school dropout, has entered a GED program, because under Louisiana's welfare-reform programs, she must be in school full-time. No absences are tolerated, not even to fulfill obligations to her son Marcus, age 3. A single absence automatically requires her to perform community service, beyond the community service she already must perform to remain in a welfare-to-work program.

The vicious circle—tend to Marcus, have to do more in the program, then have less time for Marcus—has had negative consequences for her and Marcus. Dana could not be present when early intervention staff determined that he has an emotional disability. She cannot consult face to face with teachers about his behavior: fighting with other children, crying at length when he cannot get what he wants, refusing to settle down at nap time, and pitching objects when frustrated. She was intimidated by the teacher's langauge—full of words she did not understand—at the only IFSP meeting she was able to attend.

The welfare-to-work program provides Dana $10 per day for child care. Finding full-day care for Marcus at that price is nearly impossible as well as risky. The state does not license child care, and Marcus's disability makes him ineligible for many facilities and programs. Dana has been denied Medicaid benefits, and no state family support aid is available.

Unfortunately, the "target jobs" for which Dana trains—such as a nursing-home assitant—pays only minimum wage, require rotating shifts, and do not offer health insurance. Moreover, the minute Dana finds work, she loses the temporary aid she now receives. Trapped in the "working poor" category, Dana and Marcus face an uncertain future.

What would you do to advocate on behalf of Dana and Marcus? Think about the informational, social, and emotional support that Dana might want. How would you find out what is most helpful to her right now?

Introducing Dana to mothers and fathers who have faced the same kinds of challenges but who have overcome them may be a good place to start. You will need to face Dana's very challenging situation honestly and bravely. When you talk about her and Marcus, realize that you are talking about their lives. Personalize Dana and Marcus. See them as you would want to be seen. Treat them as you would want to be treated. Recognize that though they are less fortunate, they are not less worthy.

began authorizing and funding parent coalitions in the late 1960s. As a result, more organizations provide support and information to parents today than ever before. There are approximately 107 parent centers funded by the U.S. Department of Special Education, under IDEA (Technical Assistance Alliance for Parent Centers, 2003). Parent centers basically consist of Parent Training and Information Centers (PTIs) as well as Community Parent Resource Centers (CPRCs), which we describe below.

All of the parent centers across the nation are connected to a network called the Technical Assistance Alliance for Parent Centers (*www.taalliance.org*), generally referred to as "the Alliance." The Alliance coordinates technical assistance for all PTIs and has a special emphasis on enhancing the capability of PTI staff to take full advantage of computer technology to manage and provide educational support to families.

The Alliance is located in Minneapolis, Minnesota. It is affiliated with the Parent Advocacy Coalition for Educational Rights (PACER) Center (*www.pacer.org*). The Alliance has four regional PTI centers. Each regional center is administered by a state PTI that provides technical assistance and conferences for all PTIs within the region. This broad national network provides valuable information and resources. We encourage you to take advantage of this support and share it with the parents with whom you work.

Parent centers serve families of children and young adults with various disabilities from birth to age 22. These centers generally help families obtain appropriate educational services and supports for their child. They also train parents and professionals, resolve disputes between families, and identify appropriate community resources.

Parent Training and Information Centers.

PTIs support parents to:

- Understand the nature and needs of their children's disabling conditions.
- Provide follow-up support for their children's educational programs.
- Communicate with special and general educators, administrators, related services personnel, and other relevant professionals.
- Participate in decision-making processes, including development of the child or youth's IEP and the Individualized Family Service Plan (IFSP).
- Obtain information about programs, services, and resources available at national, state, and local levels and the degree to which they are appropriate to the needs of their children.

- Understand IDEA's provisions for educating infants, toddlers, children, and youth with disabilities.

Connie Zienkewicz, director of the Kansas Parent Training Center, Families Together, says that the most valuable service her organization provides is getting families through the maze of education and community services. She explains that "families [are] standing by who have the experience and expertise to help other families, one-on-one, in navigating the maze. They can address a myriad of informational needs, such as finding an expert to treat an unusual medical condition, accessing information on a child's school program, or locating a specialist in challenging behavior."

We encourage you to contact the PTI in your state to learn what services it offers. You may want to take advantage of these services for your own continuing education, and you will want to alert families about PTI activities.

Community Parent Resource Centers.
CPRCs are also funded by the U.S. Department of Education. These centers work in traditionally underserved communities to provide information, training, and other assistance to families who have children with disabilities or who have limited English proficiency. These centers include United We Stand of New York, the center that came to the aid of the Cortes family. Each center has four functions:

- Preparing new family leaders
- Providing one-on-one assistance
- Distributing family-friendly materials (including materials translated into languages other than English)
- Engaging in outreach to families in their communities

These centers are invaluable. Traditional agencies—often not led or staffed by families—have not penetrated the underserved communities sufficiently; they may not know how to do so, or they may be unwelcome. Even some family-directed associations have been unable to support families in those communities. The CPRCs know who the families are, where they are, what they need, what language and customs they use, and what approaches work in involving them.

Outcome Data on Parent Centers.
Parent centers, composed of all PTIs and CPRCs, serve more than 1.2 million parents, professionals, and families through training and telephone assistance and another 9 million individuals through newsletters and Websites (Technical Assistance Alliance for Parent Centers, 2003). Each state has at least one Parent Center, and there are also centers in Palau and Puerto Rico.

A national report documented outcomes of the parent centers from 1997 to 2002 (Technical Assistance Alliance for Parent Centers, 2003):

- Ninety-four percent of parents indicated the information learned during training was useful.
- Seventy-five percent of parents felt they became more effective or involved as a result of training and support received from parent centers.
- Seventy-two percent of parents also reported that information received from parent centers helped resolve conflicts with schools.

Data from this national report indicate that 87% of parents reported more confidence in their ability to interact with schools as a result of contact with a Parent Center. One parent commented, "I feel I am loaded with information now as I begin the new year. I am more educated now."

Data from the national report also indicate several trends in providing support to families. For example, the commitment of parent centers to serving families from culturally diverse backgrounds is growing. In 2001–2002, approximately 37% of the families that parent centers served were from culturally diverse backgrounds, compared to only 22% in 1997–1998. Parents were assisted at more than 10,000 IEP meetings in 2001–2002, a number that more than tripled since 1997–1998. You will read more about IEP and IFSP planning and development in chapter 12.

Clearinghouses

Clearinghouses of information for families and professionals receive federal funding to distribute information. Two different types of clearinghouses funded by the U.S. Department of Education are the National Information Center for Children and Youth with Disabilities (NICHCY) and the Beach Center on Families and Disability.

NICHCY prepares and disseminates free information about children and youth with disabilities and disability-related issues to families, educators, and other professionals. NICHCY is operating the National Dissemination Center for Children with Disabilities that acts as a central source of information on IDEA, NCLB, and research-based information on effective educational practices. Most NICHCY publications are available through the Internet in English and Spanish.

The Beach Center on Disability at the University of Kansas (cofounded and codirected by Ann and Rud Turnbull, two of the authors of this book) conducts research and training to enhance individual and family quality of life and to enhance public policy and professional practice. The Beach Center also disseminates information to families, individuals with disabilities, researchers, practitioners, policy makers, and the general public. The center's information covers a broad array of topics, including parent-to-parent support, family-professional partnerships, family quality of life, positive behavior support, self-determination, assistive technology, access to the general curriculum, policies involving all of those issues, and the ethical, legal, and social implications of the Human Genome Project, a federally funded effort that identified all the genes in human DNA. Some materials are available in Spanish, Chinese, and Korean. Its Website is *www.beachcenter.org*.

Family Organizations

There are more than 2,000 family organizations nationally, many with state and local chapters. These organizations vary in size, scope, and operating budgets. Most focus on specific disabilities. Some address large-population categories of disabilities such as mental retardation, and others address a rare syndrome.

One of the largest family organizations is The Arc (formerly the Association for Retarded Citizens of the United States; *www.thearc.org*). In chapter 5, you read about The Arc's critical role in advocating for individuals with mental retardation and their families and in stimulating state-of-the-art programs and support systems. The Arc produces fact sheets, pamphlets, manuals, videotapes, and posters on a wide range of topics, including HIV/AIDS prevention, the Americans with Disabilities Act, and assistive technology devices. These materials are useful to families, employers, volunteers, community citizens, and teachers.

The best way to learn about family organizations in your state is to go to the NICHCY Website (*www.nichcy.org*) and click on the State Resources link on the home page. There is a listing of resources for each state, including state chapters of disability organizations and parent groups.

Local Resources

Countless untapped resources can be found in our own communities. We noted earlier that within-family support provides social and emotional assistance. Local resources can be essential sources of support and information because parents have a history within their own communities and may have already established comfort zones and trust.

For example, children and youth with exceptionalities and their families can connect with and learn from neighbors and community members with exceptionalities who have "insider" knowledge (Powers et al., 1996). Vicki Turbiville, who contracted polio when she was 3 1/2 years old, maintains that students with disabilities should have opportunities to be with other children and adults who have disabilities.

> They also need to have an opportunity to learn from adults who have disabilities and to see us in responsible and desirable positions. Getting information directly from us also affirms our own skills and abilities.
>
> We all value competence and helpfulness. When you ask for help or information from an adult with a disability, you are affirming our contribution to the well-being of others and our place in the community.

Consider adults with exceptionalities in your community as possible mentors, guides, and sources of information and advocacy. You can contact them through a local or state independent living center, which is a community advocacy program for adults with disabilities. You can also get information on independent living centers from the NICHCY Website under State Resources.

Likewise, a doctor's office or local YMCA might be a valuable resource for information because of its familiar, nonthreatening atmosphere. The local library is a rich, sometimes underused source of information; many libraries offer free classes for community members. That is the point made by a parent who felt that information could be more accessible if it were in everyday, familiar places:

> We said we'd like to see information more in places like the post office, doctors' surgeries (clinics), because some people find clinics intimidating places to just walk in. We shouldn't really have to search out information, it should be readily available in places that you go into every day. (Mitchell & Sloper, 2002, p. 74)

As we noted earlier, information is not always reaching families when they need it. By identifying existing resources as well as developing new ones, critical information for all families can become more available and accessible.

Books and Magazines

Families, individuals with disabilities, and professionals are prolific authors of books and articles about disability, education, and families. A recent search of *www.amazon.com* using the words *disability* and *family* produced a list of more than 30,400 books. In chapter 2, we recommended several books that have been written by mothers, fathers, and siblings. You might consider working within your school district to set up a library of disability-related books that parents can check out.

Despite the large market for disability-related books and how-to guides (especially those by families for families), disability information is not widely incorporated into popular magazines (although there has been an increase in coverage in the last several years).

Exceptional Parent (*www.eparent.com*) is a magazine specifically aimed at parents who have a child with an exceptionality. Published since 1971, this monthly magazine offers practical information about the day-to-day issues of living and working with a child who has a disability or special health-care need. *Exceptional Parent* also has a library that provides easy access to a broad range of books on disability topics. We encourage you to visit the Website and become familiar with its resources.

Television, Radio, and Films

Increasingly, television and radio highlight family and exceptionality issues. A number of children's television shows, including *Sesame Street, Dragon Tales*, and *Arthur*, routinely incorporate people with exceptionalities. Radio stations are beginning to feature disability news and special disability-related programs.

Mainstream films that include individuals with disabilities are also more common. In the 1950s, very few people with disabilities or culturally diverse backgrounds were featured. Those who did appear in films were often portrayed in stereotypical rather than realistic, positive ways. More mainstream films are featuring lead characters who have exceptionalities and are exploring family relationships. For example, the film *I Am Sam* featured a man with developmental disabilities and his experiences with fatherhood. *Rain Man* portrayed the relationship between two brothers, one of whom had autism. These cinematic images shape attitudes about people with disabilities and their roles in family, work, and community life.

The Internet and Technology

There has been a dramatic shift over the last decade in how families and professionals obtain information. Technology, particularly the Internet, vastly expands access to information. The Internet also allows families to communicate with each other. Fleischmann (2004) examined personal narratives written by parents of children with autism and found that although parents first visited Websites in search of information, they often returned to assist other parents. Fleischmann also discovered that all the narratives had positive outcomes related to child progress and parents' coping and effectiveness in raising a child with autism. This finding, among others, led Fleischmann to suggest that the Internet allows ". . . parents to create, if not a full-blown virtual community, then at least a valuable networking system" (p. 41).

The Internet also gives families access to parent-friendly, research-based knowledge. One Website, Strategies for Preschool Intervention in Everyday Settings (SPIES; see *www.spiesforparents.cpd.usu.edu/Evaluation/Evalpage.htm*), is a curriculum for adults on how to use research-based strategies for interacting with young children with disabilities (Cook, Rule, & Mariger, 2003). Online evaluations of this Website conducted by Cook et al. (2003) revealed that more than half the parents who responded said that the online instructional videos (68%) and text (89%) were helpful. Seventy-four percent of parents indicated that they applied information learned from the Website to assist their child, and 79% of parents reported that what they applied was successful. These promising data suggest that the Internet is transforming how families access and use information.

There are countless ways that families can receive and share information. Computer bulletin boards offer interactive opportunities for families and professionals. Think about building your individual and school capacity to share information with families. Familiarize yourself with the informational resources this chapter discusses. Create your own personal library and make it available to families and colleagues. Recommend articles and books that have touched you. Work with school and community librarians and other educators to develop resource libraries for families. The more you develop your computer expertise, the more you will be able to communicate with major clearinghouses, Websites, and bulletin boards that can help you get information that you and families need. Knowledge is power, and shared power—a practice related to the partnership principle of equity—is central to every partnership.

ACCESSING ECONOMIC FAMILY SUPPORT

Family characteristics related to socioeconomic status, employment, and opportunities to earn income vary. In particular, households that support a member with developmental disabilities have less income and receive more means-tested benefits than do average U.S. households (Fujiura, 1998). Households headed by a single parent who has a child with a developmental disability have the lowest income of any household type. All families require adequate economic resources to meet their members' basic and disability-related needs. The major sources of financial assistance (sometimes called "income support" or "cash transfers") for families who have children with disabilities derive from the federal Social Security Act. In this section, we describe the two most significant Social Security Act programs that address the families' needs. IDEA in that respect.

Federal Programs: Supplemental Security Income and Medicaid

Supplementary Security Income (SSI).   The SSI program is administered by the Social Security Administration. SSI pays monthly benefits to individuals with limited incomes who are 60 years of age or older, individuals age 18 and older who have a disability or who are blind, and children under 18 who have significant disabilities. The SSI program is "means-tested," that is, a person is not eligible unless he or she meets the ever-changing federal standards for poverty and thus does not have the means to meet his or her basic needs. A person who meets this means test must then prove to the Social Security Administration that he or she has a significant disability.

The criteria for low income is based on a complex formula that takes into account family size, parental income, and whether a child lives at home. As of July 2003, a single parent and one child with a disability were eligible for SSI benefits if the family had a monthly earned income under $2,333 (the equivalent of a $28,000 annual gross income) and resources totaling less than $2,000 (not counting one residence and one car) (Msall, Bobis, & Field, in press). The maximum monthly SSI benefits for the family would be $609.35, of which the federal benefit is $552 and the remainder is a state supplement (Msall et al., in press). Generally, children (as contrasted to families) receive around $375 per month. The precise amount of the family or child benefit varies from state to state because the SSI program allows states to supplement federal benefits.

To meet the disability criteria, children must meet Social Security's definition of disability: a physical or mental condition that results in "marked and severe functional limitations." The child's disabling condition must last or be expected to last at least 12 months or be expected to result in the child's death. Furthermore, the child must not be engaged in any "substantial gainful activity" (a job that pays more than about $750 per month). A disability evaluation team collects evidence about the disability and makes a determination of eligibility. The team examines information to compare the functioning of a child with a disability to other children of the same age. Some disability categories entail a presumption of disability, and payments can start before the evaluation is completed. Examples of these categories include total blindness, Down syndrome, and mental retardation.

You may be able to help a family document the nature and extent of their child's disability. Families will need to provide information concerning physicians, medical treatment, and educational records. Families will also need to have their child's Social Security number and birth certificate.

When a youth with a disability reaches 18 years of age, he or she must requalify for Social Security benefits, using adult disability criteria. These criteria focus on impairments that restrict individuals from doing any substantial gainful activity (work) for at least a year or that are expected to result in death. The general Social Security definition for substantial gainful activity is a job that pays $740 or more per month.

A study of how families use these funds revealed that families pay primarily for clothing and shoes, diapers and related incontinence supplies, food, rent and utilities, transportation, and medicine (Pugliese & Edwards, 1995). It may seem that these are typical household expenditures (except for the diapers and incontinence supplies), and they are. But SSI is the federal government's "family support" program and recognizes that a family must meet basic needs to care for its child with a disability. Recent data support the idea that a general family support program, coupled with disability assistance, is well justified:

■ Slightly less than 30% of single mothers who have a disability and have a child with a disability, in addition to having a low-income, receive SSI benefits.

■ Only 20% of single mothers who have a child with a disability and who have low income receive SSI benefits.

The Social Security Administration's Website (*www.ssa.gov*) provides helpful information about eligibility. There is even an opportunity for families to enter demographic information and find out whether they qualify for SSI. We encourage you to review this Website, become knowledgeable about SSI, and be prepared to assist families who can substantially benefit from additional economic resources. The Social Security Administration has over 1,300 local offices, organized into 10 regional programs. You can visit your local office to obtain copies of pamphlets and booklets written specifically for parents who have children with disabilities. Some of these resources are available in multiple languages.

Medicaid. Medicaid is a program of medical and health-care assistance for low-income people, including those with disabilities. It is commonly known as the Title XIX program, referring to the portion of the Social Security Act that authorizes Medicaid. Title XIX was first authorized in 1965 to provide funds for the health care of individuals who are poor and who have disabilities. Congress amended Title XIX in 1971 to allow federal funding for states to improve conditions in state institutions for people with mental retardation and related developmental disabilities. These funds, however, created a federal bias in favor of institutions (Gettings, 1994), while other federal and state policy was directed at deinstitutionalization

(discharging people from institutions and preventing them from being placed there).

Accordingly, in 1981, Congress authorized a new program within the Medicaid program, called the Home and Community-Based Services (HCBS) waiver program. The HCBS program changed the pro-institutional bias by allowing states to use Medicaid funds to provide community-based residential and employment supports and services to individuals who would otherwise require institutional or nursing facilities (Braddock, Hemp, Parish, & Westrich, 1998). The major impact of the HCBS waiver was to reverse the bias toward institutional placement and to provide a catalyst for family and community supports (Parish, Pomeranz-Essley, & Braddock, 2003).

Currently, all 50 states and the District of Columbia have a waiver program (Braddock, Hemp, Parish, & Rizzolo, 2000), although the programs vary greatly from state to state. Typically, services financed by the waiver include ". . . case management; homemaker assistance; home health aids, personal care; residential habilitation; day habilitation; respite care; transportation; supported employment; adapted equipment; home modifications; and occupational, physical, speech and behavioral therapy" (Braddock et al., 2000, p. 189). Data for the federal fiscal year 2000 (October 1, 1999, through September 30, 2000) reveal that 19 states provided cash subsidies to families, totaling $69 million to 26,000 families for family support. This averages $2,650 per family (Parish et al., 2003).

An exciting new development for adults with disabilities, including students moving from high school into adulthood, is variously called consumer control, participant-driven, *individualized budgeting*, or *self-determination*. These terms refer to an HCBS program in which the person with a disability or his or her representatives (such as family members), rather than a local service-provider agency, decide whom to hire as support staff and how to spend the person's HCBS funds (Shumway, 1999). The individual or a representative develops a budget to hire staff and fit the individual's particular needs. Individuals with disabilities, in partnership with their chosen reliable allies, will be able to hire and fire support staff and purchase services that will enable them to meet their individual goals (Lord & Hutchinson, 2003; Smith, 2003), including paying for onetime investments such as a down payment on a home, business-related equipment, and assistive technology (Nerney, 1998). The National Association of State Directors of Developmental Disability Services has prepared a helpful guide on individualized budgeting strategies (Moseley, Gettings, & Cooper, 2003).

The public policy goal of the HCBS individualized budgeting and self-determination program is to maximize opportunities that a person with a disability will have to determine how to achieve outcomes that IDEA stipulates (see chapter 6): equality of opportunity, full participation, independent living, and economic self-sufficiency.

State Family Support Programs

The two federal-state programs that we have just described are not the only sources of financial support for families who have children with disabilities. The states have their own programs, called family support programs.

The largest source of funding for family support is the HCBS waiver program described above. That program accounts for about half of the family support that states provide. States that rely heavily on the HCBS waiver program also provide the greatest amount of funds for family support (Parish et al., 2003). Thus, the state's family support program uses HCBS funds but also contributes funds to make up the entire state family support program budget.

The goals for these programs are to enhance a family's ability to meet the needs of their family member with a disability within the home and community setting. Typically, states make these programs available to families whose children have developmental disabilities, although some states also assist families whose children have emotional disorders.

To empower families to carry out decisions they think are best, some states pay cash directly to the families; these are pure *cash transfer* programs. Other states give families vouchers they can redeem for services. Some states provide both cash and vouchers. Families may use the cash or vouchers to obtain a wide range of services.

In 2000, the median annual cash subsidy payment to a U.S. family was $2,607 with nearly 26,000 families benefiting (Parish et al., 2003). Some state programs reach a smaller number of families and pay at higher levels (Illinois pays the most, with an average of over $8,000 per family). Other states tend to spread their resources over a greater number of families and provide lower levels of support.

Family support programs are usually administered by the state's human resources or social/rehabilitation agency and have local councils. The local councils not only determine which families are eligible for services but also help them develop and carry out IFSPs.

On the whole, families approve of family support services, and the services effectively carry out the purposes for which they were created (Herman & Thompson, 1995; Human Services Research Institute, 1995). Because families define their own needs and spend the cash to satisfy those needs, they believe that they experience less stress and have improved quality of life (Herman, 1994). Families also report increased capacity for raising their

child at home, assistance in the child's development, and compensation to a degree for the income they lose because they care for their child instead of taking jobs (Agosta & Melda, 1995; Herman & Thompson, 1995). Respite services provided to families in an easily accessible way also help reduce stress (Herman & Marcenko, 1997). A key factor in reducing family stress is helping parents have more time for themselves. Figure 10–4 includes quotations from families in Iowa, Illinois, and Louisiana who participate in their states' family support programs.

A 2000 analysis of national trends on family support revealed expenditures of $1.05 billion; this figure represents about 4% of total spending for developmental disability services (Parish et al., 2003). In 2000, almost 400,000 families received some form of family support, a 37% increase from 1996.

Although over 60% of people with developmental disabilities live with their biological families and only 15% receive care in a formal residential service system (Fujiura, 1998), most federal and state funding for developmental disabilities still goes to institutions rather than family care (Parish et al., 2003). Over the last 15 years, there has been a growing trend toward providing families more services and cash subsidies.

FIGURE 10–4
What Family Support Means to Us

- Having a child who is quadriplegic is very expensive. I am a single mother and this money helps us get through everyday living.

- [We appreicate] the fact that we are able to spend the money on our child without being told what to buy. We feel that we are being trusted to meet the needs of our child.

- It is like a breath of fresh air to a drowning person.

- It is the only program that has been willing to help us financially and recognize our needs.

- The extra money helps us to keep our child at home.

- Our family member was able to get high-quality hearing aids that we would not have been able to afford.

- It gave us an opportunity to build a ramp which increased our child's safety and lessened physical stress on us.

Source: Agosta, J., & Melda, K. (1995). *Supplemental Security Income for children.* Boston, MA, and Salem, OR: Human Services Research Institute.

You can find the amount your state spends per family and how it compares with other states in the article by Parish et al. (2003). Another helpful contact for finding state-specific resources is your state's PTI center.

Your Role in Meeting Families' Basic Needs

As you develop partnerships with families, especially in the transition-to-adulthood years (ages 14 and older), you should know a great deal about the SSI and HCBS individualized budgeting/self-determination option. However, both programs have complicated regulations and are implemented in somewhat different ways by each state. We urge you to contact your local Social Security office for printed information and assistance in learning about funding availability in your state and community. We also encourage you to consult experts on public benefits. You may find some experts at your state PTI center. You should share with families everything you know about these programs and refer them to the Social Security Administration and state PTI offices for more information.

In chapter 7, we discussed advocacy and roles that you might take in building family-professional partnerships. Helping families meet basic needs means linking them with programs that provide economic resources or, if a state lacks a family support program, advocating for one. When you take these steps, you create an opportunity to be a partner in meeting families' basic needs.

ENSURING SUPPORT TO ADDRESS VIOLENCE AND NEGLECT IN THE HOME

A fourth way to support families to meet their basic needs is to collaborate with them in ways that build trust while ensuring their children's safety. In the following section, we provide strategies for interacting responsibly with children and their families to prevent situations that jeopardize children's health and well-being.

Addressing Children's Exposure to Violence

Violence permeates the lives of almost every family in the United States daily, and the concern over its impact on children continues to escalate. Most children are exposed to violence through television, film, video games, and even popular toys. These media often glamorize violence (physical power over another is celebrated), portray it as a source of good fun (laughing during aggressive acts), sanitize it (lack of blood or broken bones), and minimize its effects (absence of pain or suffering). According to Levin (1998), children will have witnessed about 8,000 murders and 100,000 other acts of violence on television alone by the time they complete

elementary school. Levin traced this growing trend of violence in the media to 1984, when the Federal Communications Commission deregulated children's television programming. From that point on, shows were developed for the explicit purpose of selling toys and products to children, and programming became much more violent and unrealistic.

There is cause for concern over this growing trend. The negative impact of witnessing violence in children's lives can be very powerful. A joint statement by six major medical and mental health organizations concluded that there is overwhelming evidence linking media violence and an increase in aggressive behavior, attitudes, and values (American Academy of Pediatrics, 2000). This report, in which more than 1,000 studies were examined, states, "The conclusion of the public health community, based on over 30 years of research, is that viewing entertainment violence can lead to increases in aggressive attitudes, values, and behavior" (p. 1).

Many parents feel frustrated and helpless about the influence of violence in the media and the marketing of "power" toys. One African American father expressed his concern about the toys currently available on the market:

> Of the toys marketed primarily for boys, a considerable majority are violent toys, reinforcing the concept that the bigger the gun, the more powerful the individual. What messages are these toys giving our children? If we agree that play is a child's building block for learning, then, by playing with toys of this nature, our children are building violent foundations for learning. I think this is wrong. (Beach, 1996)

How can educators and families work together to reduce or eliminate violence in children's lives? We suggest that working in partnership is the key to addressing this and other complex situations. Figure 10–5 provides a set of questions that can be used to generate a conversation with families about solutions for reducing media violence in their lives.

By applying the partnership principle of communication to reduce children's exposure to violence through the media, you implement the partnership practices of providing information and being clear. You will be well on the road to promoting children's health and well-being collaboratively with families, which ultimately improves their overall quality of life.

Facts About Maltreatment of Children with Disabilities

Whether children witness violence or are its victims, the effects can be devastating. There is probably no greater goal than ensuring the safety of all children in their com-

FIGURE 10–5

Theory into Practice: Questions to Explore with Families in Reducing Children's Exposure to Violence in the Media

1. How can we teach children how to make good choices about TV programs as well as movies, videos, and computer games?

2. How can we help children learn to plan what and when they will have television and other screen time?

3. How can we develop guidelines with children for how much TV they will watch?

4. How can we explore with children how adults in their lives deal with TV and other media?

5. How can we help children reduce their screen time and consider alternative activities?

6. How can we promote the use of children's books as an effective starting point for talking about TV-free activities?

7. How can we teach children to be responsible consumers of media and to resist potentially negative images?

8. How can we help children make informed consumer decisions rather than rely on the lure of products they see advertised?

Source: Levin, D. (1998). *Remote control childhood? Combating the hazards of media culture* (pp. 66–67). Washington, DC: NAEYC. Adapted and reprinted with permission from the National Association for the Education of Young Children.

FIGURE 10–6

Definitions of Major Forms of Maltreatment

Physical abuse: An act of commission by a caregiver that results or is likely to result in physical harm, including death of a child. Examples of physical abuse acts include kicking, biting, shaking, stabbing, or punching of a child. Spanking a child is usually considered a disciplinary action although it can be classified as abusive if the child is bruised or injured.

Sexual abuse: An act of commission, including intrusion or penetration, molestation with genital contact, or other forms of sexual acts in which children are used to provide sexual gratification for the perpetrator. This type of abuse also includes acts such as sexual exploitation and child pornography.

Neglect: An act of omission by a parent or caregiver that involves refusal to delay in providing health care; failure to provide basic needs such as food, clothing, shelter, affection, and attention; inadequate supervision; or abandonment. This failure to act holds true for both physical and emotional neglect.

Emotional abuse: An act of commission or omission that includes rejecting, isolating, terrorizing, ignoring, or corrupting a child. Examples of emotional abuse are confinement; verbal abuse; withholding sleep, food, or shelter; exposing a child to domestic violence; allowing a child to engage in substance abuse or criminal activity; refusing to provide psychological care; and other inattention that results in harm or potential harm to a child. An important component of emotional or psychological abuse is that it must be sustained and repetitive.

Source: Larner, M. B., Stevenson, C. S., & Behrman, R. E. (1998). Protecting children from abuse and neglect: Analysis and recommendations. *The Future of Children: Protecting Children from Abuse and Neglect, 8*(1), 41.

munities, at school, and at home. Both NCLB and IDEA address school safety (as you learned in chapter 6). There are also laws that control possession and use of weapons and criminalize abuse, neglect, and maltreatment of children, especially those with disabilities, who have been characterized as a "distinct high-risk group for abuse and neglect" (APA Council of Representatives, 2003).

Child maltreatment refers to a situation in which a child under age 18 is put at risk of harm or is caused harm by a person otherwise responsible for the child's care. As defined by Congress in the Child Abuse Prevention and Treatment Act (1974), the term *maltreatment* includes abuse, injury, or neglect. Figure 10–6 includes definitions of the four major types of maltreatment—physical abuse, sexual abuse, neglect, and emotional abuse.

According to the National Child Abuse and Neglect Data System, more than 12% of all children were victims of maltreatment in 2002 (National Clearinghouse on Child Abuse and Neglect [NCCAN], 2004). Children with disabilities are particularly vulnerable, and are 2 to 3 times more likely to be maltreated than are children with-

out disabilities (Sullivan & Knutson, 2000). More specifically, when compared to children without disabilities:

- Children with disabilities are 1.6 times more likely to be physically abused.
- Children with disabilities are 2.2 times more likely to be sexually abused.
- Children with disabilities are 1.8 times more likely to be neglected.
- Children with emotional disorders, conduct disorders, and autism are 7 times more likely to be maltreated.
- Children with multiple disabilities are more likely to be abused than children with single disabilities.

In addition to being more vulnerable to abuse and neglect, children with disabilities are least likely to have their stories believed or investigated, and are least likely to experience justice in having their abusers prosecuted (Oregon Institute on Disability and Development, 2000).

A troubling finding is that data on disability status are not routinely collected or reported. Disability information was not included in the two most recent federally funded studies of child abuse and neglect (NCCAN, 2001, 2004). States are not required to collect data on disability status under the Child Abuse and Prevention Treatment Act, and only 19 states do so (NCCAN, 2001). In addition, states do not typically document the number of children whose disabilities were found to be caused by maltreatment.

Identifying and Reporting Abuse and Neglect

One of your major obligations as a teacher is recognizing and reporting situations in which you suspect maltreatment of a child. Symptoms of physical abuse include bruises and injuries the child cannot or will not explain, or that the child explains implausibly. Injuries on parts of the child's body not usually damaged by a fall (such as the upper arms, face, back, thighs, stomach, or genitalia) may indicate physical abuse. In addition to signs of physical trauma, sexually abused children may show sexual behavior or knowledge that is inappropriate for their age, be overly self-conscious of their bodies, withdraw, and victimize other children. Signs of emotional abuse include being withdrawn or acting out, being overly rigid or passive, being destructive to oneself or others, and having learning problems. Signs of neglect include unkempt appearance, poor hygiene, hunger, listlessness, depression, apathy, and developmental delays.

Sometimes it is difficult to detect specific signs of abuse or neglect. Look for sudden changes in the child's emotions, behaviors, or academic performance. Be mindful of a child's regression to earlier developmental stages, which may involve enuresis (involuntary urination), withdrawal, or aggressiveness. Ask yourself whether the child has become especially shy, hypervigilant, or resistant to being touched. Be curious about whether the child has become particularly anxious or distressed in the presence of a caregiver.

Detecting maltreatment in children with disabilities is very difficult for a number of reasons. First, children may have limited ability to communicate or report abuse or neglect; they may be unwilling to just "say no, go, and report"—the three strategies that most professionals teach

children without disabilities. Second, you may tend to overlook maltreatment because you are accustomed to seeing minor injuries on a particular child. Certain physical disabilities, blindness, and epilepsy may make some children more injury-prone than others. Finally, some children and youth with disabilities are reluctant to report maltreatment because they depend on the person who maltreats them to help them meet their basic needs (Nosek, Howland, & Young, 1997).

What should you do if you suspect a child has been maltreated? First, make sure that your suspicions are based on facts and that you have reasonable grounds for concern. Second, follow your school's procedures for reporting within the school. You may be required to report to the school social worker, counselor, nurse, or principal, depending on school procedures. Third, call the local or state child protection agency; if you do not know what agency to call, contact your school social worker, counselor, or principal, or call your local district or county attorney. Every state requires people who have any child-care responsibilities to report maltreatment. If you do not report it, you may violate the law and be subject to civil or criminal punishment.

Preventing Abuse and Neglect

Your efforts to prevent child abuse and neglect should focus on both the child and the family. If you suspect that a child has been abused, neglected, or maltreated, you may find the suggestions in Figure 10–7 to be particularly useful.

Also included in Figure 10–7 are suggestions for extending your prevention efforts to the family (or other caregivers) who put the child at risk. Begin by trying to increase the family's capacity to withstand forces that contribute to maltreatment. Be particularly aware of how the family's cultural background may impact parenting, be sensitive to differences in child-care practices and aware of misunderstandings when you communicate with family members. Listen to parents when you discuss sensitive issues. Most important, recognize the family's strengths and build on them. Maltreatment often occurs because the child's, the family's, and the community's characteristics intersect in ways that can lead to maltreatment.

Teachers and other school personnel face a dilemma when confronted with maltreatment, their obligation to report it, and their desire to collaborate with a family. It is particularly challenging, but necessary to use partnership practices to restore trust with families. If you communicate honestly rather than placing blame on the

FIGURE 10–7
Theory Into Practice: Preventing Maltreatment

Working with the Child

- Help to decrease behaviors that are difficult to handle, and facilitate more appropriate and adaptive behaviors through the use of positive behavioral support (discussed in chapter 13).

- Provide sexuality education that includes self-protection behaviors and assertiveness training. This is particularly important because most programs train compliance by the child with a disability. Rather than allowing children to make their own choices or assert their own rights of assertiveness during appropriate situations, their goals are usually set up to develop compliance.

- Provide developmentally appropriate communication techniques so the child has an effective ability to "say no, go, and tell."

- Provide individual rights education.

- Provide social skills training.

Working with the Family

- Provide opportunities to increase parenting skills. (This includes fathers. Most training programs are targeted toward mothers only.)

- Link parents to other families for support to reduce the factor of isolation.

- Provide social and other informal positive supports.

- Provide information on positive parental responsiveness to the child.

- Increase parental awareness of resources.

- Ensure parental involvement in child-serving programs.

- Teach nonviolent strategies for handling aggressive behaviors.

- Teach techniques for positive behavioral support (see chapter 13).

- Enhance parental life management strategies.

- Arrange for home health visitors trained in detecting child maltreatment to visit families' homes following the birth of a new baby for up to one month and thereafter as needed.

- Facilitate intervention at birth to help ensure parent-child attachment and newborn care techniques.

- Provide community resource referrals to families who have substance abuse problems.

- Provide the support needed by parents when they themselves have a disability.

- Carefully select caregivers when the child is removed from the natural home.

Source: National Symposium on Abuse and Neglect of Children with Disabilities. (1995). *Abuse and neglect of children with disabilities: Report and recommendations.* Lawrence: University of Kansas, Beach Center on Families and Disability and Erikson Institute of Chicago.

family, you may be able to help them access the supports they need. As you discuss these sensitive issues with parents, you must disclose your responsibility to their children and the possible consequences to them if you know or suspect that abuse or neglect has occurred (Henry & Purcell, 2000). Be sure to examine carefully the resources listed at the end of this chapter that address the prevention of child abuse and how to support children and families.

Remember, the goal is establishing trust with the family so you can help them access resources for themselves and protect their child. You already are aware of the importance of including the seven partnership principles in your interactions with families. Helping families meet their basic needs creates a powerful context where trust is created and maintained.

SUMMARY

Collaborating with families to meet their basic needs may not seem to be the most pressing priority in a teacher's day, but it is one of the most important roles for an educator. We have highlighted four ways you can help families to meet their basic needs. First, you can help them access social support, particularly through Parent to Parent networks. Second, you can help them acquire information in ways they find meaningful. Third, you can link families to many economic and family support services. And last, you can work with families to eliminate violence and neglect at home.

Figure 10–8 provides an opportunity to think about creating partnerships through trust building when helping families address their most basic needs. Take a moment to think about actions that can either lead to or prevent trust.

Remember that you can create a trusting context that ultimately leads to partnership.

FIGURE 10–8

Creating Partnerships Through Trust Building: Selected Actions Leading to Trust and Distrust in Meeting Families' Basic Needs

Partnership Principles and Practices	Issues	Actions Leading to Distrust	Actions Leading to Trust
Respect: Honor cultural diversity.	A parent wants her young daughter with mental retardation to learn Spanish as well as English, but the speech-language pathologist at another agency says that two languages will be too confusing.	Advise the parent to be realistic about the fact that her child will be lucky to learn English.	Network to locate the most current information on bilingual education for children with disabilities. Review the information with the parent and plan next steps.
Communication: Provide and coordinate information.	Parents of a child with spina bifida who is in an early intervention program believe that their child will have no future.	Warn the parents that they'd better make sure that their marriage is not torn apart by the child.	Suggest to the parents that they contact the local Parent to Parent program to be matched with parents of older children with spina bifida.
Equality: Foster empowerment.	A family has just been informed that their child has been diagnosed with attention-deficit/hyperactivity disorder and is invited to an IEP conference; they do not know what this is or have any relevant information.	Send the parents a list of their legal rights even though you know the information is practically incomprehensible.	Ask the family about their preferences for information, and review a wide range of resources with them. Respond to their priorities.
Advocacy: Keep your conscience primed.	A student comes to school with unexplained bruises and cuts. He has a communication impairment and will not or cannot explain why he is so frequently injured.	Call the parents, accuse them of abuse, and threaten to call the police if their son ever shows any more signs of maltreatment.	Ask the school social worker to join you in gathering more information, filing a report if appropriate, and informing the parents.

REFLECTING ON THE VIGNETTE

1. What specific actions did professionals take to help the four families meet their basic needs?
2. How many of those professionals are educators of one type or another?
3. How many of those professionals (in education) had a job description that called for them to help families meet their basic needs?

ENHANCING YOUR SELF-AWARENESS

Each of us needs support at different times in our lives and we have our own preferences for how support is provided. What events in your life have triggered your need for support? Developing insight into your preferences for asking for and receiving support is an important first step in understanding how you might best support individual families.

Social and emotional support

Whom do you turn to when seeking support? How do these trusted allies let you know they understand your experiences and feelings? Think of a situation in which someone has turned to you for emotional support. How would you describe your sensitivity and skill in providing this person with emotional support?

Information

Think about a time when you have needed information for yourself or your family. How did you go about getting this information? Do you consider yourself familiar with resources that parents of children with disabilities may need? How might you strengthen your knowledge of local and national resources?

Economic support

In this chapter, we addressed economic resources that may be available for families of children with disabilities. Are you comfortable having discussions with families about their entitlements? How can you share information in a respectful way? How might you help families to access and assume control of the resources to which they are entitled?

Violence prevention

Think about your own viewing of television and movies and how the images affect your sense of well-being. How can you help children and families make informed decisions about television viewing without imposing your values on them? In this chapter, we pointed out that while your responsibility is the safety of the child, you should help the family access needed support when maltreatment occurs. How do your feelings come into play when you are called on to assist individuals whom you suspect have maltreated their children? What can you do when your feelings detract from your ability to be supportive of families?

RESOURCES

1. LD On Line
   2775 S. Quincy Street
   Arlington, VA 22206
   www.ldonline.org

   This is a leading Website on learning disabilities, dyslexia, attention deficit disorders, special education, learning differences, and related issues for families, teachers, and other professionals.

2. National Clearinghouse on Child Abuse and Neglect Information
   330 C Street, SW
   Washington, DC 20447
   800-394-3366
   http://nccanch.acf.hhs.gov/index.cfm

   The National Clearinghouse on Child Abuse and Neglect Information collects, organizes, and disseminates information on all aspects of maltreatment. You can download documents including *The Role of Educators in the Prevention and Treatment of Child Abuse and Neglect* (1992) and *Emerging Practices in the Prevention of Child Abuse and Neglect* (2003).

3. Parent to Parent—USA
   http://www.P2PUSA.org

   The purpose of this alliance is to help emerging and established Parent to Parent programs by providing a clearinghouse of information and support on best practices, offering networking and peer mentoring experiences, and developing key relationships.

CHAPTER

11

Families as Partners in Student Evaluation

CHAPTER ORGANIZATION

1. How can a family contribute to their child's evaluation and enrich the evaluation team's understanding of their child?
2. How can professionals honor families' preferences for participation in their child's evaluation?

VIGNETTE

There never was any question during the second 6 months of her life whether Nicky Doleman would qualify for special education services. Her vision, hearing, speech, movement, and mental capacities were all significantly impaired.

That fact, however, did not obviate the Lawrence, Kansas, interagency coordinating council on infants and toddlers (ICC) from securing Vera's consent to evaluate Nicky. The ICC became the first community-based program with which Vera, Nicky, and the entire Doleman family would have contact.

The ICC was also the first agency, other than Children's Mercy Hospital and the local child protection agency, with which Vera was about to enter into a partnership. The ICC's visiting nurses and physical therapists (who regularly came to Vera's home to serve Nicky) were the first people in Lawrence to become partners with Vera.

Seeking consent for an evaluation is more than the first point of contact between parents and special education professionals. It also is the first opportunity for them to develop partnerships. It is the gateway into a world in which disability is a significant consideration in a family's life.

So, even though Nicky's eligibility for special education was never in doubt, how the ICC staff and its contractors secured Vera's consent was the first act of partnership and trust building between the Dolemans and the professionals.

When the ICC staff secured Vera's consent to evaluate Nicky, they had to tell her the following: why they wanted her consent, what kinds of evaluations they wanted to perform, how they would use the evaluation data to develop an individualized program for Nicky and the Doleman family, what services they would probably offer, and where they would offer those services.

The ICC staff looked at Nicky as a whole person. They needed to consider at least four domains and explain each, secure consent for evaluation in each domain, and then provide data and offer a program and placement related to each.

To take a holistic view, staff had to take into account Nicky's physical, developmental, cognitive, and emotional/psychological strengths and needs. They also needed access to Nicky's medical records at Children's Mercy Hospital and to court records that explained the causes of her disability and that awarded Nicky's legal custody to Vera. Those records recited facts, but they did not provide any real sense of what Vera wanted for Nicky and the family.

So the staff began the important job of asking Vera about Nicky and collecting data. The combination of the person-centered approach, focused on Nicky, and the family-centered approach, focused on Vera and her family, increased

era Doleman (left) and Kim Gillpatrick, a paraprofessional at Woodlawn Elementary School, review a thick stack of reports and recommendations at an IEP meeting for Nicky Doleman.

Parents face a potentially intimidating group of professionals at IEP meetings, but in the case of Vera Doleman and Woodlawn Elementary School, the atmosphere is friendly and caring.

the staff's workload. The benefit, however, was that the professionals secured a holistic view of not just Nicky but also Vera and the Doleman family.

With those two different but highly related views, the professionals were able to communicate their diagnosis and prescription for Nicky and Vera. They demonstrated their commitment and competence and showed their respect for Vera. They demonstrated that they would continue to advocate for Nicky and treat Vera as their equal. More than that, they established the first foundations upon which trust would be built, so that neither the professionals nor Vera would ever second-guess or undermine their partnership.

INTRODUCTION

Evaluation is the gateway to special education, but referral charts the course to the evaluation process. In this chapter, we describe the requirements of the Individuals with Disabilities Education Act (IDEA) and today's best practices for referral and evaluation. We explain how partnership in the referral-evaluation process can benefit students, families, and professionals. We also provide strategies for fostering trust with families throughout the evaluation process, beginning with the student's initial referral and continuing to special education.

REFERRING STUDENTS FOR SPECIAL EDUCATION SERVICES

The term *referral* describes the formal request for evaluating a child. IDEA defines *evaluation* as the procedure to determine whether a child has a disability and, if so, the child's educational needs (20 U.S.C. Sec. 1414(a) (1) (C)).

Partnerships that include families in referral and evaluation usually lead to a greater understanding of the student's and family's strengths. That understanding becomes the foundation for (1) the student's individualized family service plan (IFSP) and individualized education program (IEP); (2) partnerships among the student, family, and educators as they implement the IFSP/IEP; and (3) long-term outcomes for the student such as equal opportunity, full participation, independent living, and economic self-sufficiency.

When professionals and parents have a common understanding about the student, they are more likely to trust each other and themselves. One mother concluded that the capability of an evaluator "is not about following guidelines and strategies," but rather "about what a person knows" as well as what "comes from the heart" (Turnbull & Turnbull, 2001, p. 234).

Figure 11–1 outlines eight steps in the referral and evaluation process. In this chapter, we describe each step and discuss practices that promote partnerships and trust with the families of your students. We also urge you to learn about and comply with policies and guidelines that your state department of education and local school board have adopted; these may include requirements above and beyond IDEA's. For example, states differ in their requirements for referring and evaluating students for gifted education. Thirty-two states require that schools identify students who are gifted (Swanson, 2002).

Implementing Prereferral Interventions

Prereferral intervention sometimes can prevent a student from being unnecessarily referred for special education evaluation and placement (Buck, Polloway, Smith-Thomas, & Cook, 2003). Its primary purposes are analyzing the student's strengths and needs, and providing additional individualized assistance without also providing special education (Bahr, Fuchs, & Fuchs, 1999; Bahr, Whitten, Dieker, Kocarek, & Manson, 1999; Safran & Safran, 1996). Prereferral intervention teams typically are responsible for recommending and implementing supports, strategies, and services to address a student's academic or behavioral challenges. In one approach to prereferral, educators document the student's response to increasingly complex interventions and then identify effective intervention (McNamara & Hollinger, 2003).

Most prereferral practices do not include active family and student participation (Sindelar, Griffin, Smith, & Watanabe, 1992). However, the student can avoid unnecessary evaluations if educators and family members share information about changes at school or at home and exchange ideas to support learning. To develop trust through partnership principles of communication and respect, inform families about your concerns and seek their perspective before launching a prereferral intervention.

Initiating and Reviewing the Referral

Referral is a formal request to evaluate a student to determine whether he or she has a disability and, if so, to determine what the student's educational needs are. A referral not only signals concern but also begins a process through which educators and families can fully evaluate the student.

A referral can be made by the student's parents or anyone who is concerned about the student's education. A random national survey of parents of students referred for evaluation found that 40% of the recommendations were initiated by teachers, 33% by parents, and 13% by the student's physician (Johnson & Duffett, 2002).

Usually referral takes place after a prereferral intervention. Typically, educators or other professionals identify children with severe congenital disabilities during

FIGURE 11–1
Referral and Evaluation Process

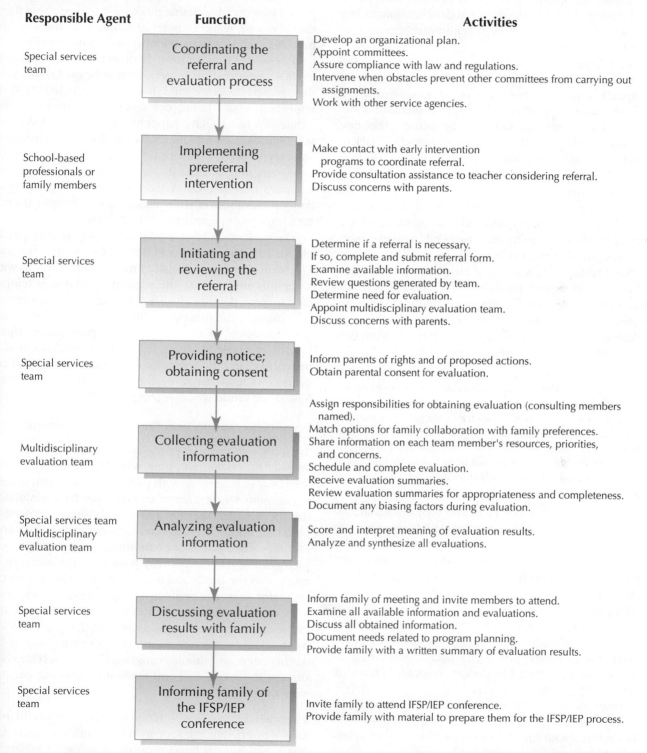

Responsible Agent	Function	Activities
Special services team	Coordinating the referral and evaluation process	Develop an organizational plan. Appoint committees. Assure compliance with law and regulations. Intervene when obstacles prevent other committees from carrying out assignments. Work with other service agencies.
School-based professionals or family members	Implementing prereferral intervention	Make contact with early intervention programs to coordinate referral. Provide consultation assistance to teacher considering referral. Discuss concerns with parents.
Special services team	Initiating and reviewing the referral	Determine if a referral is necessary. If so, complete and submit referral form. Examine available information. Review questions generated by team. Determine need for evaluation. Appoint multidisciplinary evaluation team. Discuss concerns with parents.
Special services team	Providing notice; obtaining consent	Inform parents of rights and of proposed actions. Obtain parental consent for evaluation.
Multidisciplinary evaluation team	Collecting evaluation information	Assign responsibilities for obtaining evaluation (consulting members named). Match options for family collaboration with family preferences. Share information on each team member's resources, priorities, and concerns. Schedule and complete evaluation. Receive evaluation summaries. Review evaluation summaries for appropriateness and completeness. Document any biasing factors during evaluation.
Special services team Multidisciplinary evaluation team	Analyzing evaluation information	Score and interpret meaning of evaluation results. Analyze and synthesize all evaluations.
Special services team	Discussing evaluation results with family	Inform family of meeting and invite members to attend. Examine all available information and evaluations. Discuss all obtained information. Document needs related to program planning. Provide family with a written summary of evaluation results.
Special services team	Informing family of the IFSP/IEP conference	Invite family to attend IFSP/IEP conference. Provide family with material to prepare them for the IFSP/IEP process.

Source: Adapted from Strickland, B., & Turnbull, A. P. (1990). *Developing and implementing individualized education programs* (3rd ed., 50). Upper Saddle River, NJ: Merrill/Prentice Hall. Copyright © 1990 by Pearson Education Company. Adapted by permission.

infancy. Children identified during school years generally have milder exceptionalities, experience a later onset (such as a learning disability or attention-deficit/hyperactivity disorder), or live where there is no comprehensive preschool identification program.

Referral may occur because educators, other professionals, or families suspect that a student needs specially designed instruction. Often the student is performing significantly below expectation levels, or sometimes a student's behavior is atypical. Referral may also occur because the school system is ineffective. Class size, teachers' lack of knowledge, and inappropriate instructional materials may lead staff to think that a student has special needs.

Although IDEA does not require parental consent for referral, some state and local educational agencies do. Even if consent is not required where you work, we encourage you to tell parents that their child may need specially designed instruction. In so doing, you will enhance the parents' understanding of their child's performance and grade-level expectations, reinforce benefits of evaluation and intervention, and establish the foundation for an effective partnership and ongoing trust.

Parents respond in different ways when they learn that their child is referred. Some express relief:

> It was clear to us that there was something wrong. . . . It seemed out of the ordinary compared to our experience with our other son and with other children that we had met. What was even better was we could get some early intervention and get started while he was young. . . . I have heard from other families that they got their diagnosis when their child was older and they lost so much critical time for interventions. (Nissenbaum, Tollefson, & Reese, 2002, p. 37)

Other parents may object to the formal referral and evaluation process: "My family is doing whatever we can to keep our adopted son's disability hidden from the school, knowing that once the disability is labeled . . . the expectations that will arise will not at all be positive" (National Council on Disability, 1995, p. 32).

Many parents are dismayed by the mere possibility that their child will be treated differently or separated from friends and classmates. One mother spoke of her desire to have her daughter "just [be] a part of regular life as much as possible from birth on through life" (Erwin & Soodak, 1995, p. 139).

Partnership principles of communication, respect, and commitment are particularly important when you discuss a referral with the child's family. The more you communicate honestly, show genuine interest in the student and family, affirm the student's strengths, and talk about your great expectations for the student, the more the family will see how referral can benefit their child. When parents meet with teachers who welcome their contributions and share information, trusting partnerships can grow. Once they know that professionals care about their children and respect their opinions, parents may approach evaluation in partnership with educators.

If, however, families strongly object to a referral, listen to their concerns and respect their reasons. Assume that their perspectives are valid (Barrera & Corso, 2002). Most important, avoid being defensive. Ask parents, "What would you like to have happen?" rather than "Don't you want what is best for your child?" In the spirit of partnership, try to see the situation from the parents' point of view; they may be right that a referral will not be in the student's best interest. A true partnership enables you and your evaluation team colleagues to benefit from a very important perspective, the family's.

The student's school special services team is responsible for addressing concerns that surface with a referral. The team may decide to gather more information, to wait several months in case the student's problem is temporary, to provide individualized general education rather than evaluate the student for special education, or to pursue evaluation. In the latter case, approximately three fourths of those students who receive evaluation ultimately are later determined to be eligible for special education (Christensen, Ysseldyke, & Algozzine, 1982; Ysseldyke, Vanderwood, & Shriner, 1997).

Providing Notice and Obtaining Consent

Typically, one member of the special services team is responsible for communicating with the family throughout the process, beginning with providing notice and obtaining consent. Often referred to as the service coordinator, this person may already have established partnerships with the parents, may have frequent contact or likely contact, may share values or communication styles that complement the parents', or may have the time available to work with the family and team members. The service coordinator provides ongoing family support, guides parents through the referral and evaluation process, and helps significantly to develop the IFSP/IEP. You will learn more about the service coordinator's role in chapter 12. At this point, you should recognize that the service coordinator must establish and maintain a trusting partnership with family members.

Providing Notice. IDEA requires schools to provide written, timely notice to parents in their native language when the schools propose or refuse to initiate or change the student's identification, evaluation, educational placement, or services. Figure 11-2 lists five specific information items the notice must contain.

FIGURE 11–2
Providing Written Notice to Parents

A local educational agency must provide written notice to a student's parent(s) whenever it proposes or refuses to evaluate a student, and the notice (20 U.S.C. Sec. 1415(b)(3) and (4) and (c) must:

- Describe the action the agency proposes or refuses to undertake (that is, evaluate the student for special education or not), the reasons for the proposed action, and other options that the agency considered and why the agency rejected those options.

- Describe each evaluation procedure, assessment record, or report that the agency used as a basis for its decision.

- Inform the parents that they have rights to procedural safeguards with respect to evaluation and how they can obtain a copy of a description of those safeguards.

- Describe the sources the parent(s) may contact to obtain assistance in understanding their and their child's rights.

- Describe the other options that the student's IEP considered and why the team rejected those options.

- Describe the factors that are relevant to the agency's proposed action.

FIGURE 11–3
Informed Parental Consent

According to the laws that apply generally throughout the U.S., consent consists of three components:

1. **Knowledge.** The parent has been fully informed of all information relevant to the evaluation in his or her native language or other mode of communication.

2. **Voluntariness.** The parent understands that the consent is voluntary and may be revoked at any time but not retroactively.

3. **Competence.** The parent is legally competent to give consent.

Information must be clear, accurate, and easily understood. Review your school's notice to ensure that families with whom you work can easily understand it. Share it with several parents with varying levels of education and invite their suggestions on how to make the notice clear, relevant, and jargon-free. If it is unclear to you, your colleagues, or family members, assume that it is not an effective way to foster communication and build trust. An excellent resource for information about parents' rights is the Parent Training and Information Center (PTI) in your state. You and the families you serve may want to attend the center's workshops on IDEA and other student and parent education rights.

The notice must tell parents why educators want to evaluate their child. Best practices are for educators to summarize information from the prereferral intervention or from the team's discussion and include names and purposes of the recommended tests. If the teacher or service coordinator has already contacted the family to discuss educators' concerns and options, information in the notice will seem less intimidating and legalistic.

Family members can learn more about information and evaluation from several national resources. Refer them to your state's PTI center and to Websites, books, and Parent to Parent programs.

Notification is one main reason for communicating with families. It is an important priority that fosters parent-professional respect and equality and leads to trusting relationships with families.

If parents do not respond to notices, do not presume a reason. Consider the partnership elements of respect and commitment and learn how the family wants you to communicate. Express yourself in a friendly, clear, and honest way by phoning, by making a home visit, or by consulting with other professionals involved with the family. The more you work to build a partnership, the more likely it is that families will respond to written notices.

Obtaining Consent. To protect parents' and children's rights and to secure their participation in evaluation, IDEA requires educators to secure parents' consent for each proposed evaluation, reevaluation, or special education placement (20 U.S.C. Sec. 1414(a)). Figure 11–3 contains a general definition of consent.

It is good practice to communicate clearly, even repeatedly, how an evaluation will help determine whether the child has a disability and, if so, how the child might benefit from special education and related services. If you believe that an evaluation will not help the student, it is also good and ethical practice to state your viewpoint. Listen carefully to the child's parents; understand and acknowledge their thinking and feelings about the proposed evaluation. Parents who refuse consent may be right! Their son or daughter may be harmed rather than helped by an evaluation and possible placement in special education.

If parents do not consent to the evaluation and if school personnel refuse to seek alternatives to a full evaluation, the school and the parents must first attempt to resolve the conflict (as you learned in chapter 6). They may use mediation, or choose not to. If after any mediation they still cannot agree, the school may initiate a due process hearing. If the hearing officer rules in the school's favor, the school may proceed with evaluation and notify the parents of its actions. The parents may decide to appeal the hearing officer's decision to a state-level hearing officer or a state or federal court (according to the procedure in the state's special education plan). If the hearing officer rules in favor of the parents, the school may not proceed with the evaluation unless the school successfully appeals the decision.

Supplementing Written Notices and Consent. Although the notice to the parents and their consent must be in writing, face-to-face communications at this early stage of the evaluation process are important opportunities to build partnerships and trust. It is not good practice to offer only one way of providing notice and requesting consent. You might send parents the written notice and request consent, then follow up with a face-to-face meeting to discuss your request and answer questions. Or you might share information with the parents in person, either before or when you provide written notification. Ask them which option they prefer. This shows parents that you value their preferences and want to build a trusting partnership.

COLLECTING INFORMATION FOR SHARED DECISION MAKING

A student's evaluation for special education services is designed to determine whether the child has a disability or is exceptionally gifted and, if so, what the student's special education and related services will be.

Figure 11–4 describes the IDEA requirements for nondiscriminatory evaluation. No explicit requirement states that a child's parents must be involved in collecting evaluation information, although good sense suggests that including them will ensure a full, accurate picture of the child. Under IDEA, however, parents are members of the IEP team, (20 U.S.C. Sec. 1414 (d)(1)(B)).

Parents should be involved in their child's evaluation early and often. Unfortunately, while parents can give valuable information from a unique perspective, professionals do not regularly seek their responses (National Council on Disability, 1995). One mother provided a com-

pelling reason why collaboration with families in planning an evaluation can have important outcomes:

> When Lauren was 6, the school insisted she have a standardized IQ test (Lauren has significant motor and communication challenges). I begged to be allowed to sit in on the assessment session, or at least to teach the examiner (newly out of school) how to understand Lauren's unusual way of communicating. I wasn't allowed to be there; I was told, "We don't permit parents in test sessions because they always try to help their children. It's more accurate and therefore more fair for your child if you aren't there." The outcome of the assessment was devastating to both Lauren and to us. Lauren was labeled mentally retarded and as a result, teachers expected less of her and she wasn't afforded the opportunities that she would have been given without this label. (Christy Blakely, Lauren's mother, 1997)

Listening to and valuing a parent's perspective fosters communication, respect, and equality among evaluation team members and parents.

Partnership Practices in Evaluation

If you want to create a context for shared decision making with families, think about how your evaluation practices hinder or foster trust. Approaching evaluation as a partnership means that you will involve families in decisions about whether and how the evaluation will be conducted and how its results will be used. You can enhance the partnership principles of respect and equality when you honor the family's cultural diversity, treat all family members respectfully, and give them options during evaluation.

The following passage describes what happened when a mother's preferences and concerns guided the evaluation of her preschool child, Jeff, who had been adopted at age 2:

> [The program's] approach to this community evaluation coalesced around the family's perspective and the question Maria wanted addressed. The questions raised by the primary health care provider and the school personnel were reviewed by the family. . . . A literature search on Eastern European adoptions was conducted and team members from education, nursing, psychology, and social work provided the remaining team members with literature on attachment disorders and adoption in preparation for the home and community visit. . . . The team was not proceeding with th intent to diagnose this child as having Persuasive Developmental Disorders/Autism but rather to address the primary concerns of Maria and the community providers. Team members assigned to the child and family included an SLP [speech language pathologist], a developmental pediatrician, a psychologist, and a nutritionist. (Prelock, Beatson, Contompasis & Bishop, 1999, p. 42)

In this situation, the evaluation team deferred decision about the child's diagnosis. Instead, it responded t

1. Initial Evaluation
   - Must be "full and individual"
   - Must occur before a local educational agency provides special education and related services under IDEA
   - May be initiated by the student's parent(s), the state educational agency, any other state agency, or a local educational agency
   - Must be undertaken within 60 days after the parent(s) request it (the state may establish other timelines, however), but the timeline does not apply if the student is transferring from one local educational agency to another or if the student's parents "repeatedly" fail or refuse to produce their child for evaluation
   - Determines whether the student is a child with a disability
   - Determines the student's "educational needs"
   - May not occur unless the student's parents consent to the evaluation
     + Their consent to evaluation is not a consent for their child to receive special education and related services
     + The agency must seek to obtain the parent(s)'s consent for services.
     + If the parents do not consent or fail to respond to a request for consent for evaluation, the agency may initiate mediation and due process hearing procedures.
     + If the parent(s) do not consent to services, the agency shall not provide special education and related services by initiating mediation and due process hearing procedures.
     + If the parent(s) do not consent to services or fails to respond to a request for consent to services and the agency does not provide special educa-tion and related services, the agency shall not be considered to violate a duty to provide free appropriate public education to the student and shall not convene an IEP meeting or develop an IEP for the student.
   - If a teacher or specialist "screens" a student to determine what instructional strategies are appropriate for the student, the teacher's or specialist's action is not an evaluation of the student for special education and related services.
2. Re-evaluations
   - A local educational agency must re-evaluate a student if
     + the agency determines that the student's special education and related services needs, including the student's improved academic achievement and functional performance, warrant a re-evaluation, or
     + the student's parent(s) or teacher(s) request a re-evaluation
   - The agency must not re-evaluate the student more than once a school year unless the student's parent(s) and agency agree otherwise.
   - But the re-evaluation must occur at least once every three years unless the student's parent(s) and the agency agree that a re-evaluation is unnecessary.
3. Notice for Evaluation and Re-evaluation
   - The local educational agency must give notice to a student's parent(s) whenever it proposes or refuses to initiate or change the student's identification, evaluation, or educational placement or the provision of free appropriate public education.
   - The notice must be in the parent(s)'s native language unless it is clearly not feasible to provide it in that language.
4. Two Purposes of Evaluation and Re-evaluation
   - First, to gather relevant functional, developmental, and academic information, including information provided by the student's parent(s), that assist the agency and parents to make the following determinations.
   - Second, to determine whether the student has a disability (meets the IDEA definition of a child with a disability) and, if so, the content of the student's IEP, including information that enables the student to be involved in and progress in the general education curriculum or, for preschool children, to participate in appropriate activities.
5. Types of Assessment Tools and Strategies—The local educational agency must
   - Use a "variety" of assessment tools and strategies
   - Not use any single measure or assessment as the sole criterion
   - Use technically sound instruments that may assess the relative contribution of cognitive, behavioral, physical, and developmental factors
   - Select and administer the tools and strategies so as not to discriminate on the basis of race or culture
   - Provide and administer the tools and strategies in the language and form that are most likely to yield accurate information on what the student knows and can do academically, developmentally, and functionally
   - Use the tools and strategies only for which they are valid and reliable
   - Have trained and knowledgeable personnel administer them
   - Administer them in accordance with the producer's instructions

(continued)

6. Scope and Breadth of Evaluation—The local educational agency must
   - Assess the student in all areas of the student's suspected disability
   - Assess the relative contribution of cognitive, behavioral, physical, and developmental factors
   - Use assessment tools and strategies that provide relevant information that directly assist the agency in determining that the student's educational needs are provided for
   - Coordinate assessments of students who transfer from one school to another
7. Evaluation Team—The determination of the student's eligibility and educational needs must be made by a team of qualified professionals and the student's parent(s), and the team must provide a copy of the evaluation report to the parent(s).
8. Exclusionary Criteria—A student is not eligible for IDEA services if the determinant factor for that determination is
   - A lack of appropriate instruction in reading, including in the essential components of reading instruction as defined by No Child Left Behind Act (Elementary and Secondary Education Act of 1965, Section 1208(3)), or
   - A lack of instruction in math, or
   - Limited English proficiency
9. Special Rule for Specific Learning Disabilities—To determine whether a student has a specific learning disability, a local educational agency
   - Is not required to take into account whether a student has a severe discrepancy between achievement and intellectual ability in oral expression, listening comprehension, written expression, basic reading skill, reading comprehension, mathematical calculation, or mathematical reasoning
   - May use a process that determines if the student responds to scientific, research-based intervention (as part of the evaluation and re-evaluation procedures)
10. Additional Evaluation and Re-evaluation Requirements—The local educational agency must also
    - Review existing evaluation data, including
      + Evaluations and information that the student's parent(s) provide
      + Current classroom-based, local, or state assessments and classroom-based observations
      + Observations by teachers and related service providers
    - On the basis of those data and "input" from the student's parent(s), determine what additional data

are needed to determine
  + Whether the student has a disability under IDEA
  + What the student's educational needs are or (in the case of a re-evaluation) whether the student continues to have a disability and, if so, what the student's educational needs are
  + The student's present levels of academic achievement and related developmental needs
  + Whether the student needs special education and related services or (in the case of a re-evaluation) whether the student continues to need special education and related services
  + Whether any additions or modifications to the special education and related services are needed to enable the student to meet the measurable annual goals set out in the student's IEP and to participate, as appropriate to the student, in the general education curriculum
- The agency must administer such assessments and evaluation measures as are needed to produce the data identified above.
- The agency must secure the consent of the student's parent(s) unless it can demonstrate that it has taken reasonable measures to obtain that consent and the student's parent(s) has/have failed to respond.
- If the student's IEP team and other qualified professionals, as appropriate, determine that they do not need any additional data to determine whether the student has a disability and what the student's educational needs are, the agency
  + must notify the student's parent(s) of that determination, the reasons they reached it, and the parent(s)'s right to request an assessment to determine whether the student continues to be a child with a disability and to determine the student's educational needs, and
  + is not required to conduct that assessment unless the student's parent)(s) request it to do so
11. Evaluations Before Change in Eligibility—The local educational agency must
    - Evaluate a student (following all of the requirements set out above) before determining that a student no longer has a disability (as defined by IDEA and no longer is entitled to special education and related services).
    - But the agency is not required to evaluate the student before the student's eligibility under IDEA terminates because the student will graduate from secondary school or exceeds the age eligibility (age 21) for FAPE under state law (a state may extend the age beyond 21 or, in some instances, limit the age to 18, under 20 U.S.C. Sec. 1412).

FIGURE 11–5

Tips for Conducting Evaluations with Family Members

1. Recognize family members as individuals with preferred learning styles, values/opinions on education, child-rearing practices, and parenting roles.
2. Recognize families as partners in the process and as ultimate decision makers.
3. Provide families partnership opportunities regarding the evaluation process, contexts, and participants.
4. Share information in a reciprocal, sensitive, and timely manner.
   - Provide program, state, and federal rules and regulations; community resources; and evaluation process information.
   - Explain the advantages and limitations of various evaluation and assessment measures.
   - Ask the family to describe the student's abilities/interests and their concerns/priorities.
   - Continue to share information throughout the evaluation process.
   - Present the evaluation results in a strengths-based, family-friendly, program-planning approach.
   - Provide time for the family members to ask questions and review the evaluation with team members.
   - Avoid professional jargon and acronyms.
   - Present information in the family's language, using interpreters.
   - Give information in formats and quantities that match the family's preferences and skills.
5. View evaluation as a teaching/intervention opportunity.
   - Explain the purpose of your evaluations.
   - Provide information about their child's development and the possible impact of the disability.
   - Encourage family members to demonstrate/describe their child's skills/behaviors that occur in other settings.
   - Identify the strategies you want to use to observe the child's optimal performance.
6. Identify supports for a family member's participation.
   - Provide information about their child's development, disability, or legislation.
   - Provide information about community resources (e.g., respite, utilities).
   - Encourage the participation of extended family or other family support individuals.

Source: Adapted from Woods, J. J., & McCormick, K. M. (2002). Toward an integration of child- and family-centered practice in the assessment of preschool children. *Young Exceptional Children, 5*(3), 2–11.

Maria's concerns about her son and identified supports and services to foster his development. It is particularly important to ground evaluation in the family's culture when the educators' approach to evaluation differs from the family's ideas about their child's learning and development (Schuman, 2002).

How can you create partnerships with families? Include them in decisions about the time and place of the evaluation. Identify the aspects of their child's learning and development that need evaluation. Help gather information. Confirm and interpret test results. Figure 11–5 lists tips for conducting evaluations with parents and other family members within a partnership framework.

Consider how you introduce parents and other family members to the evaluation process. Parents and other family members may enter the evaluation with limited knowledge about schools, schooling, special education, or evaluation. They may be inexperienced in procedures, terminology, and their options for participation, and unfamiliar with a team-based approach to decision making.

When it is time to introduce the family to the team and to outline what will occur, delegate responsibility to someone who knows the family well, perhaps the service coordinator or teacher.

This designated person can use information in videos, flowcharts, pamphlets, and contacts with other parents during the evaluation. Consider how you learned about referrals and evaluations. What explanations, images, and experiences helped you understand the process? The same might help the family.

Professionals and family members generally agree on evaluation practices that promote partnership (Crais & Belardi, 1999). They also agree that many highly valued practices have been underused, such as having parents describe their feelings or observe their children actively. How effectively does your program or school incorporate good partnership practices in evaluating children? To answer that question, use the self-rating tool in Figure 11–6.

Tapping into a family's knowledge about their child enhances their confidence and ability to participate, builds trust among team members, and increases the likelihood that valid information will be gathered (Woods & McCormick, 2002). Not all parents, however, enter the evaluation process with the same expectations,

FIGURE 11–6
Partnership Practices in Evaluation: Questions for Self-Reflection

	never	sometimes			always

TRUST

1. Do you offer parents a choice as to with whom and how the evaluation information will be shared? — 1 2 3 4 5

2. Do you honor parents' decisions even when you are not in agreement with them? — 1 2 3 4 5

COMMUNICATION

3. Do you offer parents opportunities to share their stories, dreams, and priorities and do you actively listen as they share this information? — 1 2 3 4 5

4. Do you clearly explain evaluation results to parents using terms that are readily understood and meaningful to them? — 1 2 3 4 5

5. Do you give parents copies of all evaluation reports before meeting with them? — 1 2 3 4 5

RESPECT

6. Do you conduct evaluations and hold meetings at times that are convenient to parents? — 1 2 3 4 5

7. Do you ask parents to help determine if a test is fair, i.e., if their child is familiar with the language or content of the test? — 1 2 3 4 5

8. Do you include in evaluation reports only information that has been discussed with and agreed upon by parents? — 1 2 3 4 5

EQUALITY

9. Do you provide parents with options for gathering and sharing information about their child or family? — 1 2 3 4 5

10. Do you ask parents which professionals or disciplines they want involved in the evaluation of their children? — 1 2 3 4 5

11. Do you offer parents the opportunity to be present at all discussions about planning their child's evaluation and the results? — 1 2 3 4 5

COMMITMENT

12. Do you notice and respond to how parents feel about information they receive about their child's evaluation? — 1 2 3 4 5

13. Do you make yourself available to parents throughout the evaluation process? — 1 2 3 4 5

ADVOCACY

14. Do you let parents know that they may have anyone else whey want present at or involved in the evaluation of their child? — 1 2 3 4 5

15. Do you think that parents would consider you to be their advocate in the evaluation process? — 1 2 3 4 5

PROFESSIONAL SKILLS

16. Do you have knowledge of and access to resources for parents? — 1 2 3 4 5

17. Do you have the skills, knowledge, and resources to contribute meaningfully to the evaluation process? — 1 2 3 4 5

Source: Adapted from McWilliam, P. J., & Winton, P. J. (1990). *Brass tacks*: *A self-rating of family-centered practices in early intervention* (pp. 9–11). Chapel Hill: Frank Porter Graham Child Development Center, University of North Carolina.

priorities, or resources. Some may choose a quieter role in their child's evaluation and may have specific preferences for how and with whom they exchange information. One mother explained her initial feelings about communicating openly with the team:

> This meant that I had to open myself up completely and let everyone analyze me and tell me things that made me feel like I was a bad mother. That is what you feel like when you see that some of your child's behavior problems happen because of things you are doing. This is not something that is easy to share with people. It was against my nature to let other people look at us so closely. It was very hard for me to do, but I did it. (Kincaid, Chapman, Shannon, Schall, & Harrower, 2002, p. 314)

When parents opt out of the evaluation process, respect their choice but encourage them to give their perspectives about their child in another way. Establish trust by providing information and options that enable parents to share what they know about their child in ways that meet the parents' preferences. This is the partnership practice of fostering empowerment, which is part of the partnership principle called equality.

Family Participation in Collecting Evaluation Information

To create partnerships that promote trust and lead to shared decision making about evaluation, invite families to (1) share their family story, (2) express preferences and great expectations and describe their child's strengths and needs, (3) help professionals evaluate and administer assessments, (4) collaborate with professionals to construct portfolio assessments, and (5) work with professionals to conduct a transdisciplinary evaluation.

Sharing the Family Story. Often the most relevant information evolves from informal conversations in which families express their hopes, worries, successes, and questions.

By telling stories in their own words, family members bring the child to "life" and authenticate the evaluation. Consider how one mother spoke of her daughter:

> Janine, Dana's mother, shared Dana's health and behavior history by describing a recent birthday party during the initial assessment at Dana's childcare center. Janine described Dana's skills in riding her bike with training wheels, her delight at having friends to her house for the first time, her improvements in playing games and sharing toys, and her subsequent asthma attack. Thus the team learned about Janine's concerns regarding Dana's development through realistic examples. (Woods & McCormick, 2002, p. 4)

Think how Dana would seem had she been described simply (and rather clinically) as "a child with autism."

Stories unfold in different ways, so it is good practice to give families choices. Some families talk openly about their child's and family's activities, whereas others prefer to prepare a memo or letter for professionals. Some families may even feel more comfortable demonstrating their routines, interactions, and activities by showing a video (Woods & McCormick, 2002)

Expressing Preferences, Great Expectations, Strengths, and Needs. Giving a student and his or her family an opportunity to share preferences, great expectations, strengths, and needs during evaluation contributes significantly to partnerships. Students and families can convey preferences about homework, school subjects, hobbies, peer relationships, future aspirations, and other relevant matters. Parents of high-ability students can provide information about a wide range of special talents and interests their child exhibits (Jin & Feldhusen, 2000). Team members should carefully pay attention to such clearly expressed preferences from the family, especially at the outset of the evaluation process.

Professionals can help students and families share information by using probe questions and through active listening. Questions should be open-ended, nonjudgmental requests for information. For example, ask, "Tell me more about. . ." rather than simply "What do you mean?" (Woods & McCormick, 2002). Effective probe questions spark conversation. You might ask: "What makes your child smile and laugh?" "What brings out the best in your child?" "What is your child especially good at doing?" or "What gets your child to try new things?" (Dunst, Herter, & Shields, 2000). Consider how you would use, modify, or add to these questions to help parents express insights into a child's strengths, challenges, and successes. Remember that you enhance the partnership principle of respect by honoring families' culture and beliefs.

You also can offer families the option of completing checklists. Among the several checklists for evaluation in early childhood are the Family Interest Survey (Cripe & Bricker, 1993), Parent Needs Survey (Seligman & Darling, 1997), Family Needs Survey (Bailey & Simeonsson, 1988), and Family Needs Scale (Dunst, Cooper, Weeldreyer, Snyder, & Chase, 1988). Families rate how items on the checklist apply to their situation. These scales, however, do not focus on the family's strengths, priorities, and resources as much as they do on the family's needs. Also, as we mentioned in chapter 9, checklists are not an interactive or personal communication. Consider whether checklists are appropriate for all families, especially those from culturally and linguistically diverse backgrounds or those in nontraditional arrangements (Barrera & Corso, 2002). For families with limited English proficiency, a checklist can be not only daunting but a professional misstep.

Evaluating and Administering Assessments.

Collaborating with families when you evaluate their child and administer assessments also enhances your partnership with them. Although some evaluation and assessment procedures feature standardized instructions, others are more flexible and can be adapted for family participation. Family members may join the professional who is evaluating their child or administering the assessment, as audiologist David Luterman described:

> . . . we all enter the testing booth. I also bring in other family members who have accompanied the parents, including grandparents and siblings . . . I proceed to start testing the child, usually giving one parent the audiogram to fill out. In this way the information they need is being incorporated into what they are doing and seeing. The audiogram becomes much more meaningful to them because they are using it. (Luterman, 1991)

If you were the parent of a child with disabilities, would you rather discover the exact nature of your child's disability through your own observation and collaboration, or would you prefer to sit in the waiting room and receive the experts' verdict? The more you involve families in collecting evaluation information, the more likely you are to develop accurate information and establish partnership with them.

Some educators believe that families cannot assess their own child's performance accurately. A number of research studies, however, have compared professional and parental ratings of child performance. Generally, parent versus teacher reports were similar in adaptive behavior assessments (Shaw, Hammer, & Leland, 1991; Voelker, Shore, Hakim-Larson, & Bruner, 1997) as well as communication assessments (Diamond & LeFurgy, 1992; Jackson & Roberts, 1999; Snyder, Thompson, & Sexton, 1993). When differences occurred, teachers typically rated the children as more skilled than did the family members. There is good evidence that parental involvement in collecting evaluation information will lead to accurate rather than subjective profiles of their children.

Constructing Portfolio Assessments.

In contrast to traditional assessments that provide a "snapshot" of a student at a specific time, portfolio assessments document student progress over an extended period (Demchak & Greenfield, 2003; Gelfer & Perkins, 1998; Salend, 1998). Portfolio items may include drafts of a student's written work, pictures of projects, excerpts from a reflective journal, a chart of student progress, videotape demon-

strations, artwork, homework, essays, and open-ended problems. Portfolios can also include students' personal reflections on their own strengths, preferences, and challenges, as well as other information they wish to share (Kelly, Siegel, & Allinder, 2001).

Because portfolio assessments can ensure a close link between typical experiences and assessment, family partnership assumes a much greater role (Demcheck & Greenfield, 2003; Lynch & Struewing, 2001). For example, all parents, especially those from culturally and linguistically diverse backgrounds, can nominate their children as gifted and organize a portfolio of work representing the student's gifts and talents (Baldwin, 2002). Family input presents a different and often more well-rounded picture of the child's development, and the method itself encourages communication, affirms the child's strengths, and fosters effective partnerships. Encouraging input from parents is essential when you evaluate students from diverse cultural and linguistic backgrounds to ensure that they gain equal access to special and gifted education programs (Artiles & Zamora-Duran, 1997; Baldwin, 2002; Subotnik, 1999).

Conducting Transdisciplinary Evaluation.

Transdisciplinary evaluation brings professionals and families together to evaluate a child across multiple domains or areas (Ogletree, 2001). Professionals and families often carry out the evaluation together, from planning to implementation.

In the transdisciplinary approach, a case coordinator or facilitator explains the process and asks the family to state their goals and priorities (Ogletree, 2001). The professionals and family observe the student in an array of play-based activities across a variety of settings and reach consensus about the child's strengths and needs (Grisham-Brown, 2000). The evaluation follows the student's lead to elicit his or her best performance. Most important, it is sensitive to the family's recommendations on how to obtain the most accurate picture possible of the student's skills and behavior.

Transdisciplinary teams also gather observational and anecdotal data to develop comprehensive understanding of the student's behavior within a variety of contexts (Rogers, 2001).

Transdisciplinary evaluation usually places the family at the center of decision making (Ogletree, 2001). One study compared a traditional multidisciplinary evaluation with a transdisciplinary play-based assessment for 40 children between birth and 3 years of age (Myers, McBride, & Peterson, 1996). The assessment increased parents' satisfaction, provided a more comprehensive perspective of the child, and was a significant aid in planning interventions based on the child's strengths and needs. Overall, a transdisciplinary approach promotes partnership components of respect and equality by treating families with dignity and fostering their empowerment.

Each of the five ways for involving families in collecting evaluation information can build partnerships. They also produce robust understanding of the student; rather than having a limited view of the child's skills and abilities on a given assessment day, the team secures comprehensive understanding of the student's and family's lives. The next section shows how team members and family can share their perspectives through an approach called person-centered planning.

Incorporating Person-Centered Planning

An effective method of involving parents, other family members, and others who care about the student is called person-centered planning. Person-centered planning elicits the great expectations of individuals with disabilities and their families and plans how to support those expectations. It is a process that supports the partnership principles of respect, commitment, equality, and advocacy.

Person-centered planning strategies include Personal Futures Planning (Mount, 1995), Making Action Plans (Falvey, Forest, Pearpoint, & Rosenberg, 1997; Forest & Lusthaus, 1990), Essential Lifestyle Planning (Smull & Harrison, 1992), Planning Alternative Tomorrows with Hope (Falvey, Forest, Pearpoint, & Rosenberg, 1994), and Group Action Planning (Turnbull, Turbiville, Schaffer, & Schaffer, 1996; Turnbull & Turnbull, 1996; Turnbull, Turnbull, & Blue-Banning, 1994). Figure 11–7 sets out the features common to all of these approaches.

Person-centered planning enables professionals and families to approach the ideal IFSP/IEP process by reframing their thinking about what they are trying to achieve: to affirm the student's strengths and have high expectations. Three mothers explained why they favor a person-centered approach to evaluation:

> At this stage in our families' development, we are looking for partners: people who appreciate our children; who can truly imagine opportunities that are not here until we make them; and who understand that families are for a lifetime and that 'goals and objectives' must be referenced to hopes, dreams, and positive futures for children. (Rocco, Metzer, Zangerle, & Skouge, 2002, p. 91)

The mothers' perspectives are consistent with the research. Research on person-centered planning (Blue-Banning, Turnbull, & Pereira, 2000; Hagner, Helm, & Butterworth, 1996; Timmons & Whitney-Thomas, 1998) indicates that shared commitment to meaningful change in a person's life and the absence of a professional hier-

FIGURE 11–7
Features of Person-Centered Planning

Key features of person-centered planning include:

- A circle of support with primary direction from the individual with a disability shaping the planning process
- Involvement of family members and friends and a reliance on personal relationships as the primary source of support to the individual
- A focus on capacities and assets of the individual rather than on limitations and deficiencies
- An emphasis on the settings, services, supports, and routines available in the community rather than those designed for people with disabilities
- Planning that tolerates uncertainty, setbacks, false starts, and disagreements
- Shared action through creative problem solving in which technical information (e.g., assessments) are subordinated to the personal knowledge of the person's history and desired future

Source: From Bui, Y. N., & Turnbull, A. (2003). East meets west: Analysis of person-centered planning in the context of Asian American values. *Exceptional Children, 38*(1), 18–31. Copyright 2003 by The Council for Exceptional Children. Reprinted with permission.

archy are the most important outcomes (Holburn, 2002; O'Brien, 2002).

When families and professionals use person-centered planning effectively, there are two major outcomes: first, positive changes in the lives of the focus persons and, second, satisfaction with the process (Everson & Zhang, 2000). In contrast to goals derived from need-based evaluations, the vision of person-centered planning teams centers on seeking (1) inclusive educational programs and (2) opportunities for more friendships and social activities.

Most writing about person-centered planning has focused on European-American families. This does not mean that the planning process does not respond to families and individuals from culturally and linguistically diverse backgrounds. In one study using focus groups to gather Hispanic parents' perspectives on Group Action Planning, parents emphasized the benefits of teamwork and flexibility (Blue-Banning et al., 2000). As one mother stated: "I can relax a little, sit back and say, 'Wow, it's not all on me now and everybody is helping me.'" The parents also identified disadvantages of vulnerability in being so open with a group of people and the time commitment that is involved (Blue-Banning et al., 2000).

Person-centered planning creates a context of belonging and reciprocity beneficial to all group members. But neither context occurs without trust. One professional said that person-centered planning "challenges everyone involved to think about themselves critically, related to how they interact with [the student]. You need to trust everybody on your team to open yourself up to that level" (Kincaid et al., 2002, p. 318).

Right of Parents to Obtain Independent Evaluations

Under IDEA, parents have the right to obtain an independent evaluation of their child and to have that evaluation and other information taken into account (20 U.S.C. Sec. 1415(b)(1) and 1414(c)(1)(A)). This right applies even if the school's evaluation has already been completed.

Why would parents seek independent evaluation? They may be concerned about the appropriateness, accuracy, completeness, or timeliness of the school's evaluation; or they may be concerned about the implications of the evaluation. In either case, it is important for professionals to communicate findings and recommendations of all evaluations to each other. Unfortunately, that type of exchange does not always occur, as a father recounted:

> We invited one of the evaluators, who had a Ph.D., at our expense to come to Dubuque to observe Alex in a school setting. . . . We were told later that the independent evaluation was considered, when honestly, it was ignored. (Testimony by Greg Omori, in National Council on Disability, 1995, p. 46)

ANALYZING EVALUATION INFORMATION

The evaluation team must determine whether the student has a disability and qualifies for special education services and, if so, what the student's educational needs are. To make these decisions, the team first scores, analyzes, and interprets results of each assessment instrument or procedure and then synthesizes and evaluates all the separate assessments. The team members usually do the first task individually or collaboratively among those members who administered the assessment procedures; by contrast, they usually do the second task at a full team meeting.

Families are rarely involved in analyzing assessment information. Many professionals assume that scoring, analyzing, and synthesizing assessments require technical expertise that most families do not have. Family members, however, can gather information and provide perspectives on what it means. Although some assessment procedures such as an IQ test must be administered and scored only by people with special training, many assessment procedures can be carried out collaboratively with family members (provided that procedures and their administration comply with the instructions of the developers of the assessments, as IDEA requires).

Some families participate by analyzing assessment and other evaluation information, but others prefer not to be involved. Some families appreciate being present at any discussion related to their child, perhaps because they think that is the best way to ensure that their perspective is considered. Others will opt out of the process. However, professionals should not consider interpretations of assessments and other evaluation information final until families have a chance to review and comment. If you want to create partnerships with families, you need to respect their perspectives and be careful to reach conclusions only when you have their input.

DISCUSSING EVALUATION RESULTS WITH FAMILIES

This section describes four ways to enhance partnerships when discussing evaluation results with parents: (1) notify parents, (2) assume the family's perspective, (3) consider the student's role in discussing evaluation results, and (4) follow an agenda for the discussion.

Notifying Parents

As we noted earlier, IDEA requires a local educational agency to notify parents in writing any time it proposes or refuses to change a student's identification, evaluation, or educational placement or the provision of free appropriate education, and why it proposes or refuses to take certain action. Schools can comply with these requirements by providing a summary or full copy of all evaluation information.

Full disclosure frequently enhances a family's trust in professionals and increases probability of informed decisions. In addition, because assessment and other evaluation information can be highly technical and written explanations may not be fully informative, explaining results face to face is good professional practice. These discussions can elicit the family's perspectives to validate or dispel tentative interpretations. Parents can share information about their son's or daughter's special needs, confirm whether the performance that professionals describe is typical, and make connections between the independent evaluations that the family offers.

One option is to hold a separate conference with the parents; another is to review the evaluation information during the IEP/IFSP. By holding a separate conference particularly for the initial evaluation, professionals on the evaluation team allow more time to discuss their findings and for parents to assimilate information before making program and placement decisions (assuming the student is eligible for special education). It is usually difficult to review and discuss evaluation data and also plan an IFSP/IEP in just one meeting. We generally recommend inviting parents to a separate conference to discuss the initial and all subsequent reevaluations.

Taking the Family's Perspective

How do families respond to evaluation results? From relief to pain, the gamut of their responses is long and varied. However sensitively you convey the information, many families—particularly those who strongly value academic achievement, success, and conformity—may be sorely disappointed by the confirmation of a disability. As we mentioned in chapter 10, many parents want and benefit from hopeful information. One mother noted that hope was "why we wake up every day. There is nothing that any of us cannot go through if we believe that there is hope for progress" (Nissenbaum et al., 2002, p. 36). Presenting information optimistically can enhance families' motivation, just as negative expectations can diminish or even quash families' hope:

> My frustration is with professionals in the field who say "she'll plateau"; she'll "like to do only routine things"; "don't expect too much"; "she's already doing better than I ever expected," etc., etc. . . . These individuals are very dangerous in the predictor's status quo that individuals [with disabilities] all fit in a neat nutshell.

Some parents may feel they have contributed to their child's exceptionality or that they should have attended to it earlier. They may worry about their child's future and fear that the child's and the family's challenges will inevitably escalate. They may doubt the credibility or expertise of the evaluation team, and they may need time to come to grips with the reality of the evaluation results. This parent reminds us to be extremely sensitive about reverting to an earlier paradigm (referred to in chapter 5) in which many parents were mistakenly blamed for their child's disabilities:

> For my family, assessments planted fear, discouragement, and lower expectations in our minds. Professionals' comments, such as 'children bring their lifestyle to school' and 'much of Glen's energy is spent in avoidance behaviors,' triggered feelings of guilt and incompetence. (Rocco et al., 2002, p. 78)

Other families feel justified and relieved to learn the results of their child's evaluation (Mallow & Bechtel, 1999):

justified because they, perhaps unlike the school, believed all along that their child had real needs, and relieved because at last they have an evaluation that can lead to effective intervention.

Parents' perspectives are likely to reflect their culture and beliefs. Different cultures ascribe different meanings to the concept of disability and even to standard terminology (Kalyanpur & Harry, 1999). For example, a Puerto Rican mother described the distinction, from her cultural and language perspective, between "retarded" and "handicapped":

> For me, retarded is crazy; in Spanish that's "retardado." For me, the word "handicapped" means a person who is incapacitated, like mentally, or missing a leg, or who is blind or deaf, who cannot work and cannot do anything . . . a person who is invalid, useless. . . . But for Americans, it is a different thing—for them "handicapped" is everybody! (Harry, 1992, p. 31)

Many traditional Native American languages do not have words for disability, handicap, or retardation (Robinson-Zanartu & Majel-Dixon, 1996). In fact, there is no overall concept for disability.

> If . . . [a] Navajo child is diagnosed with Down syndrome and is from a more traditional Navajo family, the family may disagree with school officials when their child is said to have a disability. They may welcome the child's placement in special education, but from the family's perspective, they feel that their child functions well at home and exhibits no physical evidence of a disability. In other words, all the body parts are there and are in their appropriate places. The child walks, eats, and helps others at home. (Joe, 1997, p. 254)

At no time are partnership practices of sensitivity, availability, accessibility, respect, and honesty more important than when you share evaluation information. We encourage you to reflect on your communication with families, particularly those from culturally and linguistically diverse backgrounds. Beth Harry and her colleagues, all national leaders in developing culturally sensitive services, provide tips in Figure 11–8 for evaluating students from diverse cultures.

In chapter 7, we emphasized the importance of empathetic listening, expression, and reciprocity to build effective partnerships. You should display empathy in all your communications. Linda Mitchell, a parent and speech-language pathologist whose son experiences a developmental disability, characterizes the critically important role of empathy:

> I don't want someone to feel sorry for me. Sorrow sets me up to grieve for a loss, but I don't feel that my son, John, is

FIGURE 11–8
Evaluating Students from Diverse Cultures

- Include parents in the evaluation process by inviting them to observe and/or participate in all assessment procedures, following their lead in identifying which family members to involve, and arranging meetings at convenient times and places.

- Provide extended time for explaining results to parents who hold very different values and beliefs about the meaning of disability.

- Provide an independent person who is familiar with the family's culture to interpret during conferences, and encourage families to bring friends or advocates who share their cultural beliefs with them to the conference.

- Ensure that children are evaluated in their native language.

- Consider using alternative assessment approaches, such as authentic assessment, that will best enable students to demonstrate their capabilities, strengths, and needs.

Source: Adapted from Harry, B., Grenot-Scheyer, M., Smith-Lewis, M., Park, H., Xin, F., & Schwartz, I. (1995). Developing culturally inclusive services for individuals with severe disabilities. *Journal of the Association for Persons with Severe Handicaps, 20*(2), 99–109.

any kind of a loss. He is truly a source of great happiness and a huge contributor to our family. Empathy says I feel for you because I care about you. Sympathy says I feel sorry for you. Empathy connects, sympathy disconnects. If you want to really begin to build a relationship with me, empathize with me, and then help me move on.

Considering the Student's Role in Discussing Evaluation Results

Sharing evaluation results with students can help them decide about their education and other activities, provide them with accurate estimates about their abilities, and contribute to their self-esteem (Sattler, 2001). There are a number of ways to share information with students. First, parents may share evaluation results and recommendations with their son or daughter. Second, the student may participate at the end of a conference held initially only with parents. Third, one or more members of the evaluation team may hold a separate conference with the student. This approach may prevent the student from becoming overpowered by the presence of many adults. Finally, the student can participate in the regular evaluation team meeting. In that event, prepare the student in advance, be sure the discussion at the conference is clear

to the student, and explicitly affirm the student's strengths.

Whatever the approach, remain sensitive to the family's and student's preferences and needs about how they want to receive evaluation information:

> Definitely it was better not to have [my son] there because [the diagnosis of autism] is a real big blow to give parents. They need to deal with their emotions, or at least in our case, we needed to deal with our emotions and kind of get figured out how we were going to think about this and how we were going to deal with it. We needed time. (Nissenbaum et al., 2002, p. 35)

Sharing the Evaluation Results with Parents

You should have at least three goals you discuss the evaluation results with families:

1. Ensure that they have a clear understanding of the student's strengths, preferences, great expectations, and needs.
2. Support them to adjust emotionally to the evaluation information.
3. Interpret and communicate information to lay the foundation for the student's appropriate education and for partnership among the student, family, and professionals.

You are likely to meet these goals when you follow partnership practices leading to trust. Specifically, convey information clearly, treat students and families with dignity, and respond to families' emotional needs as you discuss results, your diagnosis, and recommendations.

We recommend that you follow an agenda for discussing evaluation results with families. Organize the meeting into four components: (1) opening dialogue, (2) presentation of findings, (3) discussion of recommendations, and (4) summary. The opening dialogue should inform the family of the purpose of the conference and convey that you desire and value their contributions. Families should have the opportunity to describe their perspectives about their child's functioning, to offer their views, and to react to and reflect upon others' input. Their comments will reveal their understanding about their child and even allow you to incorporate some of the words they use (such as "lagging behind") in your subsequent explanations.

Most of the conference will be devoted to sharing results of the evaluation and discussing recommendations, which we cover in the next section of this chapter.

The final agenda item is providing a clear and concise summary of the information discussed. Describe any consensus about information or other discussions. In the spirit of partnership, end the meeting by affirming that you will continue to be accessible to parents.

Presenting the Findings. When you communicate evaluation findings, be as concrete, precise, accurate, and complete as possible. First, identify the subject or developmental area that was assessed (such as reading, social skills, communication, or mathematics) and then present your findings. Be very clear to parents about the meaning of specific test scores. For example, if a student scored at the 60th percentile on a standardized test, you may want to explain that he or she scored higher than 60% of all other test takers. Give examples of skills the student could and could not perform accurately. These examples should help identify skills in which the student excels and skills for which supports may be needed. There are several sources for clear, accurate, and informative descriptions of tests and test scores. For example, *Straight Talk About Psychological Testing for Kids* is a useful guide to testing written by two psychologists, Ellen Braaten and Gretchen Felopulos (2004).

You and your colleagues should present a composite of the student's strengths, preferences, great expectations, and needs, not just list separate and isolated discipline-specific reports. The family sees the whole child, not a child segmented into discrete parts:

> Specialists see [my daughter] from their own point of view. I guess the hardest thing is that I want answers. I wanted them to say she is going to make it or she isn't going to make it. I guess the hardest thing is not getting answers and everyone looking at their particular area and no one giving me the whole picture. Everyone is just looking at one area and forgetting she is a whole child. (author unknown)

You should do more than present a composite; you should also stimulate discussion and address the priorities and concerns of the family and other team members. But be careful: It is imperative to affirm the child's and family's strengths throughout the discussion. If you leave families without hope and optimism, they will be poorly motivated to develop partnerships with you.

When sharing findings with families, listen actively so that you can provide useful, personalized feedback. Different families will have different responses, perspectives, and schedules (Nissenbaum, 2002). Most will need time to absorb evaluation information and develop new understandings about their child. These new understandings often create disappointment as well as hopefulness or well-being (Larson, 1998).

Think about how you might incorporate the communication skills you learned in chapter 9 as you share evaluation findings with families. Figure 11–9 offers tips for sharing findings with families. Because most families ap-

FIGURE 11–9
Tips for Sharing Findings

- Create a setting that makes all participants comfortable.
- Convey the message that you have the student's and family's interests in mind.
- Be concrete and precise in your presentation of findings.
- Identify the developmental or content area assessed before presenting test results.
- Explain the text results in everyday language.
- Provide specific examples of skills the student can and cannot perform.
- Stay focused on the whole child.
- Present the diagnosis and explain terms using clear and understandable language.
- Discuss possibilities and provide hope.
- Take time to listen and respond to parents' verbal and nonverbal responses.
- Provide a list of resources and interventions.
- Offer suggestions for follow-up reading material.
- Be available and accessible to families in their requests for information.
- Take the time to find out what you don't already know.
- Schedule a follow-up meeting if you or the family needs time to reflect on or gather information.

preciate direct yet sensitive communication, consider partnership principles of communication, competence, and commitment when presenting evaluation findings.

Discussing the Diagnosis. You and other members of the evaluation team should discuss the student's performance and the type and extent of any disability or giftedness. Consider the family's personal and cultural perspectives about labeling when you present the child's potential diagnosis. Some parents may find categorical labels painful or demeaning. Others are relieved to have a name attached to a condition that has created so many concerns.

When they have a diagnosis of their child, many parents begin to take forward-looking action. The following excerpt is from a mother's story:

> I will never forget how numb I felt when they told me that [my son] was on the 'Autistic Spectrum.' I went outside and

threw up. Then I started my battle plan. (Fleischmann, 2004, p. 39)

Sometimes professionals mistakenly assume that it is best to offer services to the child without making the child's diagnosis explicit. They think that by avoiding the use of disability labels they will be able to communicate better with parents. Unfortunately, ambiguity does not usually enhance a family's understanding, as the following demonstrates:

> The disposition for 5-year-old Tyrone indicated that his disability category was "04" (speech and language impaired) and that he would continue in his present placement of "Level III services" until the new academic year, at which time he would be moved to a "Level IV" (more restrictive) placement. At the end of the meeting, after the disposition was signed, the mother, . . . asked the professional team what Level IV meant, and was told it meant that the child would have more hours of service, which meant a smaller class and more one-to-one attention. When we asked the mother in an interview what she thought the other "04" designation on the record meant, she replied: "I think that's what they call Level IV: it means 4 hours of special education a week." (Harry, Allen, & McLaughlin, 1995, p. 369)

Because the evaluator never explained the 04 code, the mother was unaware that the evaluator assigned the diagnostic category of mental retardation to her child. In an attempt to avoid labels, the professional communicated without clarity (and to some extent, without honesty) and contributed to inequity in the relationship with the family. The partnership principle of communication, and related practices of clarity and honesty, are crucial to building trust with families.

The key is to explain categorical labels to family members in a straightforward manner. Before the meeting, think about the language you will use. When you are uncomfortable using specific terminology, you may jumble words, ramble, or rush through your comments, creating tension for families and professionals alike.

> [Parents] can sense the tension in our voices and I think they react to it. They know that something is wrong with their child just by our behavior. Our anxiety brings out their own anxiety. (Nissenbaum et al., 2002, p 36)

Explain what the label or diagnosis means using clear and nontechnical language. For example, you might say that mental retardation means that the child has slower-than-average intellectual and adaptive behavior development. Because many families associate mental retardation (and other disabilities) with negative societal stereotypes, you and your professional colleagues should talk about the different degrees of mental retardation and the positive outcomes that many individuals with mental retarda-

tion experience with access to appropriate services. Connect parents to local or regional parent organizations, a PTI center, a Parent to Parent group, or other disability-specific groups. Encourage them to talk to other parents whose children experience similar disabilities, to learn about services, and to get emotional support.

Many information sources you learned about in chapter 10 (such as parent support groups, Internet sites, books, and criteria for access to funding) are organized by category of disability. When families have a label for the condition, they are likely to get information about their child's strengths and needs more easily.

Sometimes, parents will not immediately accept your evaluation results and may criticize your diagnosis. Take into account the parents' perspectives. Realize how much they love their child and how much they need to "stack the deck" in their child's favor. Your support and patience will pay off in the end.

Some parents seek additional information, perhaps from one specialist and then another, searching for answers to their questions. These parents have been unkindly labeled as "shoppers" who have failed to accept their child's exceptionality (Blacher, 1984). But consider this: They may be seeking full and complete information and investigating the widest possible range of professional resources so that they can make an informed decision about their child and about the professionals with whom they might want to form a partnership.

Unfortunately, some professionals interpret families' desire to get a second opinion as a personal challenge to their expertise. Any family who wants additional information or resources deserves immediate referrals. If you support rather than criticize their actions, you will strengthen your partnership with the family and serve as a catalyst for their empowerment.

Making Recommendations. After discussing the evaluation results, you must make recommendations. The more parents have been partners in the evaluation process, the more they are apt to trust and follow through on these recommendations.

Traditionally, evaluation conferences have been characterized by professionals agreeing in advance about their recommendations and then presenting them to families. A partnership model, however, encourages families and professionals to reflect together about evaluation data and then generate recommendations for action. The recommendations should, at the very least, enhance the student's appropriate education and, at best, help both the child and family.

The recommendations must provide families, teachers, and related service providers with detailed information about the child's participation and progress in all aspects of school, including the general curriculum. They should also show how best to promote preferences, build on strengths, and remediate needs.

Parents are most apt to carry out recommendations that they have helped develop and that they believe to be beneficial to their children (Eccles & Harold, 1996; Human & Teglasi, 1993). To ensure that all recommendations are implemented, develop a specific plan of action. Specify who is responsible for following through on each recommendation, when those people will begin and finish their duties, the necessary resources they need to perform their duties, and how everyone will know when work is completed. It also is useful to continuously reflect in subsequent evaluations or IFSP/IEP conferences about how the partnership is maturing and how professionals interact with each other and with families.

As we conclude this section on discussing evaluation results, we underscore what a formative moment it is for most parents when they first learn about the nature of their child's disability (Miller & Hanft, 1998). Bear in mind that the parents' expectations for the future, great or small, may be largely determined by words and messages you convey at this crucial time. We concur with the parent of a child who expressed her perspectives as follows:

> . . . If I could say one thing to doctors, educators and all professionals who work with families of children with disabilities it's this: they need to know their power and the effect their words can have on these families. Predictions about the child's future should not be given without great circumspection and an extraordinary degree of sensitivity for the parents' feelings. If parents lose hope, everything is lost. (Sullivan, 1995, p. 70)

FOSTERING TRUST

There are many opportunities throughout the evaluation process to build trust with families. You can build trust by using the partnership practices that support it, such as responding to parents' questions honestly and clearly, describing and giving concrete examples of their child's performance, demonstrating genuine interest and commitment to their child's success, and affirming their child's and their own strengths and abilities. You can also build trust by keeping your conscience primed at times when parents' interests in the evaluation process are overlooked, such as in the situation described in Figure 11-10.

More than that, you can be the catalyst for long-term positive outcomes, as this mother experienced through her partnership with professionals in the evaluation process:

FIGURE 11–10
Advocating for Systems Change

Although it is required that the evaluation conducted to determine a student's eligibility for special education services be nondiscriminatory, there are occasions when unintentional biases may be brought into the evaluation process. What might you do if you recognized that the findings of an evaluation underestimated a student's abilities?

Consider a situation in which you were participating with the evaluation team and the student's parents in a meeting at which the results of an assessment of a sixth-grade student were being reported. This student and his family had moved from South America 2 years earlier. A translator was also present at the meeting to assist in the dialogue with the student's parents, whose primary language was Spanish. As the results were presented, the student's parents expressed, through the translator, their surprise at how poorly their son had done. You, too, are skeptical about the accuracy of the results since you know that this student was achieving in your class in some of the areas with reported deficits.

What do you do about your concerns? We urge you to consider the principle of advocacy and the partnership practices leading to trust. How can you act in accordance with your conscience to prevent further problems for the student and his family?

The remembrance of Haley's first assessment will always linger in my mind as one of the gentle reminders that there are kind, supportive, and caring service providers who are there to give true service and support to families in times of great trial and adversity. With this session as a foundation to our experiences, we were able to weather the sporadic intense "storms" that many, many surgeries and long recuperative periods in numerous hospitals created for our family. As a parent, I know that bright beginnings are a great forecast of future happenings, and ours was certainly hopeful of what our unexpected journey might have in store for us. (Tracy Price-Johnson, Haley's mother, 1997) (Miller & Hanft, 1998, p. 57)

SUMMARY

The referral and evaluation process has many component parts:

- Coordinating the referral and evaluation process
- Implementing prereferral intervention
- Initiating and reviewing the referral
- Providing notice and obtaining consent
- Collecting evaluation information

FIGURE 11–11

Creating Partnerships Through Trust Building: Selected Actions Leading to Trust and Distrust in Student Evaluation

Partnership Principles and Practices	Issues	Actions Leading to Distrust	Actions Leading to Trust
Communication: Be honest.	In your noncategorical program, parents ask you what "functional placement" means. You know that the professional interpretation is "severe disability," but the school district forbids you to use that classification.	Tell parents that "functional placement" really does not have a meaning, and that the professionals do not associate any kind of diagnostic label with it.	Explain to the parents the rationale for noncategorical programming and share your own value. Also tell them that sometimes noncategorical labels have other connotations, and honestly share those connotations with them.
Respect: Honor cultural diversity.	Asian family members tell you that they believe their son's leaning disability is a punishment to him for not adequately honoring their ancestors.	Tell the family to discount nonscientific interpretations as groundless and foolish.	Listen empathetically to the family's perspectives and ask members what information or support you could provide that they might find helpful.
Professional Competence: Set high expectations.	Parents have just received the diagnosis that their infant is legally blind.	Encourage the parents to be realistic and to recognize that it is too much of a burden for community preschools to adapt their programs.	Ask the parents what information would be especially helpful for them as they consider their next steps. Let them know that you look forward to collaborating with them and watching their child grow and develop. Tell them that you are available to help make their dreams for their child come true.
Equality: Share power.	In the evaluation conference, the parents seem to want to "kill the messenger." They are angry at the professionals for "creating their child's problem."	Point out to the parents that they have displaced anger and that you and other professionals are doing all that you know how to help them.	Listen emphatically to the parents' perspectives and reflect on whether any of the communication used in the conference could unintentionally come across as representing a "we-they" orientation.
Commitment: Be sensitive to emotional needs.	A mother with AIDS comes to a diagnostic conference to hear the latest educational report on her child, who also has AIDS.	Tell the mother that nothing would make you feel as guilty as giving AIDS to your child.	Share with the mother one or more things that she has done that has made a difference in the child's educational progress and tell her you appreciate her efforts.
Advocacy: Create win-win solutions.	Parents are highly dissatisfied with the evaluation that you believe has been done very appropriately. They request an independent evaluation, but you do not believe one is needed.	Defend the school's evaluation and tell the parents that their request is unwarranted.	Encourage the parents to discuss with you their concerns, and ask them to describe an evaluation process that they would find satisfactory. Inform them of the process for initiating an independent evaluation.

- Analyzing evaluation information
- Discussing evaluation results with the family

We encourage you to consider how the partnership practices leading to trust can be used throughout the referral and evaluation process. As you can see in Figure 11-11, the actions you take will help you build and maintain trusting partnerships with families. Upon this strong foundation, you can develop the student's individualized education program.

REFLECTING ON THE VIGNETTE

1. What difference, if any, would it have made for Nicky and Vera if the interagency coordinating council had evaluated Nicky for only her cognitive capacities and for no other traits?
2. What difference, if any, would it have made if the evaluation had focused on only Nicky and not also on what Vera and other family members wanted for themselves?

ENHANCING YOUR SELF-AWARENESS

Reflect on your own experiences with assessments that were administered to you as a child. What was it like to be evaluated? Were your parents given the information they needed to support you and to advocate for you? Use the following questions to reflect on your own experiences with assessment and how they can be used to facilitate your partnerships with families as they participate in their child's assessment.

Initiating and reviewing the referral

Did a teacher ever suggest to your parents that you or a sibling might benefit from special education services or programming for gifted students? How was the recommendation made? Were your parents given sufficient information about the referral and evaluation? Did your parents have reservations about giving consent? If so, were their concerns adequately addressed? What might have been done differently?

Partnership practices in conducting an evaluation

We have identified practices that you can use to promote partnerships in student evaluation. These strategies em-

power families by emphasizing their perspectives and preferences in planning for and conducting an evaluation of their child. As a professional-in-training, are you adequately prepared to support and advocate for families throughout the assessment process? What would you do if you identified practices in your school that inhibited partnership?

Sharing evaluation information

Think of a situation in your own life when a professional, such as a doctor, nurse, or educator, shared important information with you about the results of an assessment that you had taken. What did the person do to share the information in a way that was useful to you? Was the information shared with honesty, empathy, and clarity? How did you feel as the diagnosis was being shared with you? What are your own preferences for receiving information?

RESOURCES

1. Families and Advocates Partnership for Education *www.FAPE.org*

   The Families and Advocates Partnership for Education (FAPE) project is a strong partnership that aims to improve the educational outcomes for children with disabilities. It links families, advocates, and self-advocates to communicate the new focus of IDEA. The project represents the needs of 6 million children with disabilities.

2. National Center for Culturally Responsive Educational Systems *www.nccrest.org*

   The National Center for Culturally Responsive Educational Systems (NCCRESt), a project funded by the U.S. Department of Education's Office of Special Education Programs, provides technical assistance and professional development to close the achievement gap between students from culturally and linguistically diverse backgrounds and their peers, and to reduce inappropriate referrals to special education. The project targets improvements in culturally responsive practices, early intervention, literacy, and positive behavioral supports.

Individualizing Education in Partnership with Families

CHAPTER ORGANIZATION

1. What factors contribute to successful partnerships in developing the individualized education program (IEP) and individualized family service plan (IFSP)?
2. How do the cultures of families and professionals affect them as they develop these individualized programs?

"Night and day, you are the one." That's a line from a Cole Porter song. The lyricist was describing his permanent longing for a certain someone. He could just as well have been describing the different IEP meetings that Leia and Jamie Holley have had with professionals at Sean's school in Bonner Springs.

Night. It really wasn't night, but a bright May afternoon in 2000 when the Holleys and the school staff had their infamous IEP meeting. Twelve people gathered, Sean and Leia plus 10 professionals. Ostensibly, they convened to develop an IEP. Truth be told, they faced off not only to decide what Sean needed and who would do what, when, where, why, and how, but also to air their grievances and frustrations. The sun may have been shining, but it was dark midnight for these 12 people.

The grievances were real. As the Holleys put it, they were "scared to death" that Sean would die from a seizure that no one at the school was prepared to prevent or treat. Their grievance was not personal in the sense that it complained about any one person. Instead, it was institutional. The entire school system was inadequate to address a life-and-death matter. They had other grievances, too, but those paled in comparison to the one about Sean's life.

The frustrations were just as real. The school staff feared the Holleys, just as they feared for Sean. To fear parents is a different matter than to fear for their son. Being fearful for Sean involves concern for his health and even his life. Fearing the parents involves being intimidated, worrying about lawsuits, fretting about administrators who would look with disfavor on a school staff that provoked a lawsuit, and being concerned that, if they were unable to come to Sean's aid, they might lose their professional licenses and the means to their livelihood.

Day. That portion of a 24-hour period that precedes and follows night. Not a period of brightness all the time.

The day dawned when Leia called Tierney, Sean's teacher, before the beginning of the fall 2000 semester. Leia's plea: "Let bygones be bygones. Let's start over." Tierney's answer: "By all means." Their approach was as follows: Reconvene the dozen people, or at least all who were still at Bonner Springs School that fall and even a few others. Focus on just Sean, mapping out his future and then committing that plan to writing in the form of an action plan, not just in the form of an IEP. Have the "function" prevail over the process and over the form. Focus on Sean, not on each other, and have the paperwork be whatever it is, whether the school district's IEP

Comfortable with the familiar surroundings of Bonner Springs Elementary School, Sean Holley and his family will face new issues when he transitions to junior high school.

form, an action plan, or both. Comply with IDEA's requirements. Have all the right people at the meeting, and then add those who are not mandated to be there but who have much to contribute. Consider all of the components of an IEP that the law requires, but go beyond ritualistic compliance and bring everyone's talents together to ensure that Sean, his parents, and the Bonner Springs School staff have a mutually enjoyable quality of life with each other.

No one puts a tune to the words of IDEA. No one rhapsodizes its requirements. Cole Porter himself could do very little, if anything, to fashion a tune that would make IDEA compliance singable and danceable.

Sean Holley (right) and friend Tyler McMahon at fifth-grade graduation ceremonies held at Bonner Springs Elementary School.

But in Bonner Springs in the fall of 2000, a dozen committed people acknowledged that they once had a partnership, that it was broken, that IDEA provided the sheet music, but that it was up to them to write their own lyrics.

They did just that. The title and principal sentiments paraphrase the first line: "Day after day, we are the ones."

INTRODUCTION

Professionals and parents can be partners in evaluations to determine whether students have disabilities and, if so, how they should provide an appropriate education. The nondiscriminatory evaluation should lead to an appropriate education and to the Individuals with Disabilities Education Act (IDEA) outcomes described in chapter 6: (1) equal opportunity, (2) independent living, (3) economic self-sufficiency, and (4) full participation. In this chapter, we describe IDEA's requirements and recommended practices for developing a program or plan for individualized education; in the next chapter, we describe IDEA's requirements and recommended practices for implementing the program or plan.

UNDERSTANDING THE INDIVIDUALIZED PROGRAM OR PLAN

IDEA Requirements

In keeping with IDEA's original intention and the best practices for evaluation, you should treat families as partners not only in developing programs and plans but also in implementing them. In chapter 6, we said Part B of IDEA regulates education of (1) children in early childhood education who are between the ages of 3 and 5 years (2) students in elementary, middle, and secondary school programs who are between the ages of 6 and 21. Part C of IDEA regulates the education of infants and toddlers (birth to 3 years). We begin by describing Part B.

Part B, Ages 3 to 21 Years.   Every student receiving special education services who has a disability is entitled to an individualized education program. Think of the IEP as the roadmap that leads professionals, parents, and students along the paths under the arch described in chapters 7 and 8. Remember that the arch consists of seven principles of partnership—six that are the foundation and the seventh that we call trust. Finally, note that the path leads to the four IDEA outcomes we just identified. The IEP can take professionals, parents, and students, in partnerships with each other, along the path to the outcomes. The IEP is a vehicle for communication, as well as a partnership principle.

Required Components.   The IEP must contain statements concerning each factor described in Figure 12–1.

Required Participants.   Certain individuals must be involved in developing the IEP, as we describe in Figure 12–2.

Important Considerations About the IEP.   The IEP is a vehicle for communication between parents and school personnel (U.S. Department of Education, 1981). In recent years, students have been enabled to meaningfully participate in their IEP process and self-advocate during meetings (Mason, McGahee-Kovac, & Johnson, 2004; Wood, Karvonen, Test, Browder, & Algozzine, 2004). IDEA does not allow schools, teachers, or other persons to be held legally accountable if students do not achieve the IEP annual goals. Educators must, however, make good faith efforts to help students master IEP goals and objectives. What do you think constitutes a good faith effort in developing an IEP?

The spirit and intent of IDEA hold that parents are valued, integral participants in IEP development. That is why IDEA requires educators to document their efforts to secure parent participation by keeping copies of letters to or from the parents, and detailed records of telephone calls and visits to parents' homes or workplaces and the results of those visits.

When developing the IEP, parents and professionals must consider the student's strengths, the nondiscriminatory evaluation of the student, the parents' concerns and input, and, as appropriate, the results of the student's performance on general state or districtwide assessments. The IEP team must also take five unique factors into account (see Figure 12–3).

The team must indicate in the IEP whether any of these five factors relate to the student and, if so, how the IEP will address them.

Part C, Ages Birth to 3 years.   As we noted in chapter 6, the individualized family service plan (IFSP) describes and shapes the early intervention process for young children with disabilities and their families. Part C of IDEA authorizes state and local education agencies to achieve four different outcomes: (1) enhance the infants' and toddlers' development and minimize their potential for developmental delays, (2) reduce the costs of special education by minimizing the need for that service, (3) minimize the need for institutionalization of people with disabilities and maximize their potential for independent living, and (4) enhance the capacity of state and local agencies to meet the needs of "under-represented populations, particularly minority, low-income, inner-city and rural populations" (20 U.S.C. Sec. 1431). To achieve this

FIGURE 12–1
Required Components of the IEP

The IEP is a written statement for each student, ages 3 to 21. Whenever it is developed or revised, it must contain statements about the following:

- **The student's present levels of academic achievement and functional performance, including:**
  - how the disability affects his or her involvement and progress in the general education curriculum (same curriculum as for nondisabled child), or
  - how the disability of a preschooler (ages 3 through 5) affects his or her participation in appropriate activities
  - a statement of benchmarks or short-term objectives if the student is to take alternate assessments.

- **Measurable annual goals, including academic and functional goals, designed to:**
  - meet the student's needs that result from the disability, in order to enable the student to be involved in and make progress in the general education curriculum, and
  - meet each of the student's other disability-related educational needs.

- **Measurement of annual goals:**
  - how the school will measure the student's progress toward annual goals, and
  - how often the school will report the student's progress.

- **Special education, related services, and supplementary aids and services, based on peer-reviewed research to the extent practicable,** that will be provided to the student or on the student's behalf, and the program modifications or supports for school personnel that will be provided so that the student can:
  - advance appropriately toward attaining the annual goals,
  - be involved in and make progress in the general education curriculum, and participate in

extracurricular and other nonacademic activities, and
  - be educated and participate with other students with disabilities and with students who do not have disabilities in the general education curriculum and extracurricular and other nonacademic activities.

- **The extent, if any, to which the student will not participate with students without disabilities** in the regular class and in the general education curriculum and extracurricular and other nonacademic activities.

- **Any individual appropriate accommodations necessary to measure the student's academic achievement and functional performance on state and local assessments** of student achievement. If the IEP team determines that the student will take an alternate assessment on a particular state- or districtwide assessment, the IEP must document why the student cannot participate in the regular assessment and what alternate assessment is appropriate.

- **Projected date** for beginning services and program modifications, and the anticipated frequency, location, and duration of each service and modification.

- **Transition plans, including:**
  - beginning not later than the first IEP to be in effect after the student is 16 or younger if determined by the IEP team, and annually thereafter
  - appropriate measurable postsecondary goals
    - based on age-appropriate transition assessments
    - related to training, education, employment, and, where appropriate, independent living skills.
  - the transition services, including courses of study, needed to assist the student to reach those goals
  - beginning at least one year before the student reaches the age of majority under state law (usually at age 18), a statement that the student has been informed of those rights under IDEA that will transfer to the student from the parents when the student becomes of age.

Part C uses a similar approach as Part B. Instead of an IEP, however, Part C provides for an IFSP.

Note the differences between the IEP and IFSP. Each has different outcomes. Unlike the IEP, the IFSP includes family outcomes. The IFSP enhances the child's development while simultaneously enhancing the family's capacity to meet the child's unique needs. Figure 12–4 shows a list of the required IFSP components.

Timing. The initial meeting to develop the IFSP must take place within 45 days after the child or family is referred for early intervention services. Thereafter, periodic review is available in two ways: (1) Every 6 months the IFSP must be reviewed for progress and appropriate revision, by a meeting or other means agreeable to participants, and (2) a meeting must be held annually to evaluate the IFSP and revise it as needed.

FIGURE 12–2
Required IEP Participants

- **The student's parents.** Parents are key decision makers in developing the IEP.

- **A regular education teacher.** At least one regular education teacher of the student if the student is or may be participating in the regular education environment. That teacher helps determine the appropriate positive behavioral interventions and supports, and other strategies, and the supplementary aids and services, program modifications, and supports for school personnel.

- **A special educator.** At least one special education teacher or, where appropriate, at least one special education provider of the child. The teacher might suggest supports for and accommodations to the general education curriculum, recommend assessment modifications, and help in individualizing the curriculum.

- **A representative of the school system** who is qualified to provide or supervise the provision of specially designed instruction, and is knowledgeable about the general education curriculum and the availability of the system's resources.

- **An individual who can interpret the instructional implications of the evaluation results**. The person may be a member of the IEP team. The individual should ensure that the evaluation results are the basis for the student's IEP.

- **Individuals with knowledge or special expertise about the child.** At the discretion of the parents or school district, other individuals with knowledge or special expertise regarding the student, including related services personnel.

- **The student (whenever appropriate).** To advance self-determination, opportunities for student contributions can be provided in key educational decisions.

FIGURE 12–3
Five Special Factors to Consider in Developing an IEP

- If a student's behavior impedes his or her learning or that of others, the IEP team must consider the use of positive behavioral interventions and supports, and other strategies, to address the impeding behavior.

- In the case of a student with limited English proficiency, the IEP team must consider the language needs of the student as those needs relate to the IEP.

- In the case of a child who is blind or has a visual impairment, the IEP team must provide for instruction in Braille and in the use of Braille. The exception to this requirement is that the team might determine that Braille is not appropriate, based on an evaluation of the student's reading and writing skills, needs, and appropriate media writing.

- For every student, his or her communication needs, and, in the case of a student who is deaf or hard of hearing, the student's language and communication needs, as well as opportunities for the student to communicate directly with peers and school personnel in the student's language and communication mode (e.g., sign language, communication board), academic level, and full range of needs.

- The IEP team must determine whether each student requires assistive technology devices and services.

If the parents agree, early intervention services may start before evaluation and assessment are finished. In that event, an interim IFSP is developed (naming the service coordinator and demonstrating that the child and family need services immediately), and the evaluation must be completed within the 45-day period.

Required Participants. The IFSP uses the term *family*, whereas the IEP uses the term *parent*. This difference reflects evolving recognition of the importance of the family systems perspective described in chapters 1 through 4. Early intervention providers must explain to families what the IFSP contains and obtain families' informed, written consent for those services. Families may consent to and receive some services but object to other services and decline them. Figure 12-5 lists required IFSP participants.

If a required person is not available for a meeting, other means for participation are required—for example, telephone conference calls, attendance by a knowledgeable representative, or access to pertinent records at the meeting. In keeping with the partnership approach, all meetings must be at times and places convenient to the family and must be arranged to allow them enough time to plan to attend. All notices to the family must be in the native language or other mode of communication. (If you are in doubt about what language to use, ask the family members.)

FIGURE 12–4
Required Components of the IFSP

The IFSP is a written statement for each infant or toddler, ages birth through 2, and the family. It must contain a statement of the following:

- Child's present levels of physical, cognitive, communication, social or emotional, and adaptive development, based on objective criteria.
- Family's resources, priorities, and concerns related to enhancing their child's development.
- Measurable outcomes for the child and family, including preliteracy and language skills, and criteria, procedures, and time lines used to determine progress and need for modifying outcomes.
- Specific early intervention services based on peer-reviewed research, to the extent practicable, to meet the child's and family's unique needs, including the frequency, intensity, location, and service delivery method.
- Natural environments in which early intervention services are provided, and why services will not be provided in those environments if the plan so provides.
- Projected dates for initiating services and the expected length, duration, and frequency of each.
- Name of the service coordinator responsible, from the profession most immediately relevant to the child's or family's needs, to implement and coordinate the IFSP with other agencies and persons, including transition services.
- Transition plan to support the child's transition from early intervention to preschool or other appropriate services

FIGURE 12–5
Required Participants in the IFSP

Participants in the initial and in each annual IFSP meeting must include the following:

- The child's parent or parents
- Professionals from more than one discipline, so that the IFSP reflects a multidisciplinary assessment of the child's unique strengths and needs and a family-directed assessment of the family's resources, priorities, and concerns, and the services appropriate to meet the child's needs and the services and supports necessary to enhance the family's capacities to meet their child's developmental needs.

they reach age 3. These programs help children adjust to a new setting, prepare service providers who will support the transition, and identify individuals responsible for helping children and families make the transition.

Transition Services and IEPs.   IDEA also requires educators to develop transition plans that prepare students for adult life and to include these plans in the IEP.

What We Have Learned Over Time

You may notice many similarities as well as differences across the IFSP/IEP. The primary common theme, regardless of the student's age, is clear articulation of partnerships among families and professionals in planning and developing these plans.

What Does IDEA Expect?   What is the significance of the requirements that the parents must be members of the team tha tdevelops the IEP? There are two answers.

> One comes from the findings of fact that Congress made when it reauthorized IDEA in 2004. Congress found that the education of students with disabilities can be made "more effective" by "strengthening the role and responsibility of parents and ensuring that families…have meaningful opportunities to participate in the education of their children at school and at home" (20 U.S.C. Sec. 1400(c) (2)(5)(B)).
>
> The second comes from a decision of the United States Supreme Court, Schaffer v. Weast (2005). The question in that case was whether a parent who challenges the child's initial IEP has the burden to prove that the IEP is legally insufficient. The Court held that the parent does shoulder the burden of proof. But the real significance, for our purposes here, of the decision is that the Court declared that the "core" of IDEA is the "cooperative process" that is inherent in the development of the IEP.

Transition Plans

Transition generally means passage from one place to another or from one time to another. We described the life cycle stages in chapter 4. Students with disabilities and their families experience several transition stages. In early childhood, an infant or toddler with disabilities transitions from receiving early intervention services to preschool special education services; the young child transitions from receiving preschool services to school-age services. When a student is older, he or she begins a transition to adulthood.

Transition Statements and IFSPs.   IDEA requires early intervention programs to develop transition plans for all children receiving early intervention services before

Thus, the "meaningful opportunities to participate" in their child's education arise when the school is evaluating the child and developing the IEP, and the process of developing the IEP should be "cooperative." Clearly, the IDEA, in its own words and as interpreted by the Court, expects that the educators and parents will cooperate to develop an appropriate IEP and to implement it in school and (as appropraite) at home.

What Research Reveals About Partnerships in Developing IFSPs/IEPs.

Since the 1980s, the research literature has been fairly consistent in acknowledging that IFSP/IEP conferences often fail to honor partnership practices. In a summary of the IEP literature from IDEA's initial enactment in 1975 through 1990, Smith (1990) concluded, "After more than a decade of implementation, research, and subsequent recommendations for improvement, substantive IEP change has not ensued" (p. 11). Although more than a decade has passed since Smith's analysis, a pressing need still exists for the IEP to reflect adequately the priorities of children with disabilities and their families. For example, IEP conferences usually do not allow enough time to plan appropriate educational programs; moreover, parents have limited roles in these meetings (Harry, Allen, & McLaughlin, 1995; Soodak & Erwin, 2000; Vaughn, Bos, Harrell, & Lasky, 1988). Conferences are usually terminated at a set time regardless of whether they are complete. The main activity within conferences consists of obtaining parents' signatures on IEP documents, not encouraging their genuine participation (Harry et al., 1995). The researchers noted, "As professionals identify with the culture of the school bureaucracy, most become entrenched in a "we-they" posture by which parents are seen as potential adversaries, rather than allies" (p. 374).

Soodak and Erwin (2000) found that while several parents were involved in a series of collaborative meetings to develop their child's IEP, other parents were asked to attend only one IEP meeting and simply to agree with decisions that professionals had previously made.

Many parents complained of computer-generated IEPs that were developed before the IEP meeting took place. Note the contradiction—how can a student's plan be individualized if developed by a commercially available computer program?

In IEP conferences, it appears professionals are the primary decision makers and families feel neither heard nor comfortable with sharing their ideas (Hanson et al., 2000; Katz & Scarpati, 1995; Salembier & Furney, 1997). Developing meaningful individualized goals is critical to IEP development (Etscheidt, 2003; Pretti-Frontczak & Bricker, 2000), so that families' contributions are articulated

clearly and accurately. How can families feel like equal partners when they are denied adequate time and opportunity to participate meaningfully?

Unfortunately, the seven principles of family-professional partnerships have not yet been realized fully. Parents are still viewed as participants, not as trusted partners in important educational planning.

Similar challenges to partnership persist for students and families as they transition from one program to another. Although research indicates that IDEA transition mandates have had a positive impact, progress remains inconsistent and slow-moving (Hasazi, Furney, & Destefano, 1999; Johnson, Stodden, Emanuel, Luecking, & Mack, 2002). For example, students with disabilities still lack access to a full range of curricular options and learning experiences in general education, and to community-based work and vocational education (Johnson et al., 2002). Choices and options remain limited for young children with disabilities and their families (Hanson et al., 2000). In addition, a dramatic shift occurs in the values of service delivery as young children and their families move from a supportive, family-centered culture to one focused more narrowly on child- and school-centered practices (Hanson et al., 2000).

Despite the importance of parent participation, cultural diversity and transition-planning issues have largely been ignored in the transition process. Indeed, "how one defines 'successful adulthood,' the end goal of transition planning, is determined by culture-specific values and expectations such as work, community integration, role expectations, and social functioning" (Geenen, Powers, & Lopez-Vasquez, 2001, p. 266). As you learned in chapter 4, each family has its own visions about the future that culture and other factors shape.

The dominant theme of the research is that schools try to comply with IDEA, and with state and local legal mandates and procedures, but seldom strive to foster trusting partnerships (Rodger, 1995; Smith, 1990; Smith & Brownell, 1995; Soodak & Erwin, 2000).

One of the most common reasons for disputes between families and schools is disagreement over developing and implementing the IEP (U. S. Department of Education, 2003). One parent described her experience as she entered the IEP meeting:

> As I walked into the room and there were eleven people sitting at the table. . . all these people with the same purpose in mind—to tell me that this was a terrible idea. (Erwin & Soodak, 1995, p. 270)

For many families, the IEP process has brought disempowerment. Although research indicates that the IFSP process comes closer than the IEP to creating partner ships, the IFSP process generally fails to fulfill the seven elements of partnerships.

Partnerships make a difference when they do occur. A mother of a young child with a disability summed up her family's positive, empowering experiences with team members after creating their child's IFSP: "[They] recognized our concern, saw it as part of our long-term vision for our child and family, and helped us work out ways to achieve our goal" (Squires, 2000, p. 11).

The next section offers practical suggestions for developing an IFSP/IEP in a collaborative way, creating partnerships and fostering trust.

MAINTAINING TRUST DURING THE PLANNING PROCESS

Unfortunately, many families and professionals regard the IFSP/IEP meeting as a "meaningless ritual in which teachers dictate the prescribed educational program and then pass the ceremonial pen to parents to secure their signatures" (Rock, 2000). You, however, should regard the meeting as an exciting, creative opportunity to generate fresh ideas, dream, and find resourceful solutions.

As chapters 7 and 8 pointed out, progressive educators are moving beyond family-centered practices to professional-family partnerships grounded in trust. Hanson and Lynch (2004) acknowledge that a "cluster of practices" are essential for healthy collaboration between families and professionals. How can you adhere to the partnership approach and engender trust? Start by paying careful attention to how you and families develop an IFSP/IEP.

Developing the Individualized Program or Plan

As chapter 11 showed, IDEA requires nondiscriminatory evaluation to determine whether students have disabilities and, if so, what special education and related services those students need. Developing the IFSP/IEP is the next step in the process of providing an appropriate education.

The process for developing a student's individualized plan is as important as the final product. Developing a family-friendly IFSP/IEP should never be rushed; you cannot hurry and listen at the same time (Turnbull, Turbiville, Jones, & Lee, 1992). The IFSP/IEP can be developed over time in a series of conferences. One mother pointed out, "because all along I've been involved, . . . we reached consensus by the time we came to the meeting" (Soodak & Erwin, 2000, p. 35). Because of time and other constraints, however, some schools may choose to develop the plan in a single conference. Whatever type or number of meetings are used to create the plan, spend the allotted time as efficiently as possible. If only one

conference occurs in which yearlong recommendations are made, you should conscientiously use all partnership elements—communication, respect, commitment, advocacy, professional skills, and trust.

All conferences should consist of these nine components:

1. Preparing in advance
2. Connecting and getting started
3. Reviewing formal evaluation and current levels of performance
4. Sharing resources, priorities, and concerns
5. Sharing visions and great expectations
6. Considering the interaction of the student's proposed goals, services, and placement
7. Translating student priorities into written goals and objectives (or outcomes)
8. Specifying placement, supplementary aids/services, and related services
9. Addressing assessment modifications and special factors
10. Summarizing and concluding

Explore the summary of these suggestions in Figure 12–6. Does the school you work in, or are familiar with, follow these practices?

Remember what you learned about families from chapters 1 through 4. The four components of the family system—characteristics, interactions, functions, and life cycle—individually and collectively influence families' preferences for participation. We offer a broad range of issues for consideration; of course, you will need to tailor this information to individual family situations. Culture plays an important role in influencing family preferences for the planning process (Bennett, Zhang, & Hojnar, 1998; Geenen et al., 2001; Hyun & Fowler, 1995; Kalyanpur & Harry, 1999; Rhodes, 1996). We urge you to apply the partnership practice of *honoring diversity* when working with parents to make IFSP/IEP plans.

Preparing in Advance. Families and educators frequently fail to prepare adequately for conferences. Primary work for conferences usually does not start until everyone sits down, which is far too late.

When preparing for the conference, implement suggestions from chapters 7 and 8 for building partnerships with families. Establishing trust at the outset is the foundation for all other partnership practices. Begin by communicating positively with families. Create a climate of respect, commitment, and equality from the start. By creating partnerships with families, you set the stage for meaningful preconference preparation.

FIGURE 12–6

Tips for Collaborating with Parents in Conferences

Preparing in Advance

- Appoint a service coordinator to organize the conference.
- Make sure evaluation has included all relevant areas, is complete, and has clearly synthesized results.
- Ask the family's preferences regarding the conference. Reflect on what you know according to the family systems consideration. Find out whom the family wants to invite.
- Arrange for a translator to attend the conference, if needed.
- Decide who should attend the conference, and include the student if appropriate. Discuss with the student his or her preferences about who should attend.
- Arrange a convenient time and location for the conference, based on family preferences.
- Help the family with logistical needs such as transportation and child care.
- Inform the family and students who are at least 14 years of age (in jargon-free language) orally and/or in writing about the following:
  - Purpose of the conference
  - Time and location of the conference
  - Names and roles of participants
  - Option to invite people with special expertise
- Exchange information in advance by giving the family and student the information they want before the conference.
- Encourage and arrange for the student, family members, and their advocates to visit optional educational placements for the student before the conference.
- Review the student's previous IFSP/IEP and document the extent to which each goal has been met. Identify factors and barriers that contributed most to these results.
- Request an informal meeting with any teachers or related service providers who will not attend the conference. Document and report their perspectives at the conference.
- Consider whether providing snacks is appropriate and possible, and make arrangements accordingly.

Connecting and Getting Started

- Greet the student, family, and their advocates.
- Share informal conversation in a comfortable and relaxed way.
- Serve snacks, if available.
- Share an experience about the student that was particularly positive or one that reflects the student's best work.

- Provide a list of all participants or use name tags if there are several people who have not met before.
- Introduce each participant, briefly describing his or her role in the conference.
- State the conference's purpose, review its agenda, and ask if additional issues need to be covered.
- Ask the participants how long they can stay, discuss the conference time frame, and, if needed to complete the agenda, offer to schedule a follow-up conference.
- Ask if family members want you to clarify their legal rights, and do so, if they request.

Reviewing Formal Evaluation and Current Levels of Performance

- Give family members written copies of all evaluation results.
- Avoid educational jargon and clarify terms that puzzle the family, student, or their advocates.
- If a separate evaluation conference has not been scheduled, discuss evaluation procedures and tests and the results and implications of each.
- Invite families and other conference participants to agree or disagree with evaluation results and to state their reasons.
- Review the student's developmental progress and current levels of performance in each subject area or domain.
- Ask families if they agree or disagree with the stated progress and performance levels.
- Strive to resolve disagreements among participants using the Skilled Dialogue or other strategy, as discussed in Chapter 9.
- Proceed with the IFSP/IEP only after all participants agree about the student's current levels of performance.

Sharing Resources, Priorities, and Concerns

- Plan how all participants can share expertise and resources to create the most comprehensive support system possible in addressing priorities and responding to concerns.
- Ask participants to share their priorities.
- Encourage all participants to express their concerns about their own roles in supporting the student, especially in areas where they believe they will need support or assistance.
- Note the resources that all committee members can contribute.

Sharing Visions and Great Expectations

- If a MAPs process has been completed, share the results with everyone.

- If a MAPs process has not been completed, consider incorporating it into the conference.
- Encourage the student and family members to share their visions and great expectations for the future, as well as the student's strengths, gifts, and interests.
- Identify the student's and family's visions and great expectations as well as those of the professionals (those attending and absent).
- Express excitement about the visions and great expectations, and about commitment to goals and objectives (or outcomes) that will be planned at the conference.

Considering Interaction of Proposed Student Goals, Placement, and Services

- Assure the family that the decisions about the student's IFSP or IEP will be made together.
- State that interactive factors between the student's proposed goals, placement, and services will be examined carefully before final decisions are made.

Translating Student Priorities into Written Goals and Objectives (or Outcomes)

- Discuss and prioritize the student's needs in light of the student's and family's visions, great expectations, strengths, interests, and preferences.
- Generate appropriate goals for all academic and functional areas that require specially designed instruction, consistent with stated great expectations, priorities, and MAPs process.
- Determine the evaluation criteria, procedures, and schedules for measuring the goals and how parents will be regularly informed.

Determining Placement, Supplementary Aids/Services, Related Services

- Identify placement options that reflect the least restrictive environment (e.g., regular class with necessary supports in the first option considered; close to student's home).
- Consider characteristics of placement options (e.g., building characteristics, staff and student characteristics).
- Specify supplementary aids/services and related services the student will receive to ensure appropriateness of the educational placement.
- Explain the extent to which the child will not participate in the general education program.
- Identify the supplementary aids/supports and related services the student will need to access education and achieve goals and objectives.

- Document and record the time line for providing supplementary aids/services and related services.
- Discuss benefits and drawbacks of types, schedules, and modes of providing related services the student needs.
- Specify dates for initiating supplementary aids/services and related services, frequency, and anticipated duration.
- Share names and qualifications of all personnel who will provide instruction, supplementary aids/services, and related services.

Addressing Assessment Modifications and Special Factors

- Determine necessary modifications for the student to participate in state or districtwide assessments of student achievement.
- If the student is not able to participate in state or district assessment, provide a rationale and specify how the student will be assessed.
- Consider the five special factors identified in IDEA (for example, positive behavioral support, limited English proficiency, use of Braille, language and communication modes for people who are deaf or hard of hearing, and assistive technology), and make plans as needed for the student.
- Identify any other modifications or special factors that apply to the student, and develop appropriate plans to address those.

Summarizing and Concluding the Conference

- Assign follow-up responsibility for any task requiring attention.
- Summarize orally and on paper the major decisions and follow-up responsibilities of all participants.
- Set a tentative date for reviewing IFSP/IEP implementation.
- Identify preferred options for ongoing communication among all participants.
- Reach a consensus decision with parents on how they will be regularly informed of the student's progress toward the annual goals and the extent to which that progress is sufficient in achieving the goals by the end of the year.
- Express appreciation to all team members for their collaborative decision-making.
- Affirm the value of partnership, and cite specific examples of how having a trusting atmosphere enhanced the quality of decision making.

Many schools have a preconference meeting to share assessment and evaluation results with families and to establish meaningful dialogue about the family's priorities for their child. Although sometimes informal, this preconference meeting shows respect for the family's right to articulate their priorities. Professionals and families can also gather and consider relevant information before making decisions.

Prior to the conference, you may refer families to Parent to Parent, and to Parent Training and Information Centers, for the emotional and informational resources they may need to feel confident and empowered at their conferences (see chapter 10). For students initially evaluated for special education services, the way in which you and other professionals facilitate the process will contribute significantly to preconference preparation. The more you incorporate partnership practices—communicating effectively with families and respecting their preferences—during referral and evaluation, the more likely it is that partnerships will coalesce before the conference meeting.

Everything you have learned from chapters 1 through 11 can become part of your preconference preparation. But you should also consider five additional issues:

- Designating a service coordinator
- Inviting participants
- Inviting and preparing students, when appropriate
- Taking care of logistical considerations
- Exchanging information in advance

Designating a Service Coordinator. Even though a service coordinator is required only for the IFSP, having a service coordinator can be just as useful when developing an IEP. The service coordinator's main responsibility at this stage is ensuring that preconference preparation is carried out and guided by students' and families' strengths, preferences, great expectations, and priorities. The service coordinator should also monitor implementation of an individualized plan. Some families find that service coordinators block access to other professionals, which is not good practice. The coordinator should ensure access and communication.

Inviting Participants. Consistent with IDEA and the practices we have described, you should learn a family's preferences for who should attend the conference, convenient times and places for scheduling, whether assistance with transportation or child care would be helpful, and the kinds of information the family wants in advance. Consult with the family in a face-to-face conference or by telephone. Do not rely on others to tell you what the family wants; others may contribute, but families are the experts.

Give families access to evaluation reports, a summary of the student's strengths and needs in each subject area, information on legal rights, descriptions of various placement options and related services, student priorities and draft goals from the professionals' perspective, options for extracurricular activities, and information on transition services. Gather this information early so there is time to make needed arrangements or changes.

Most conferences are composed of three to five professionals and the mother (Able-Boone, 1993; Campbell, Strickland, & La Forme, 1992; Goldstein, Strickland, Turnbull, & Curry, 1980; Vacc et al., 1985). Learn which family members want to participate—fathers, grandparents, brothers and sisters, cousins, live-in significant others, godparents, or other people who have family-like relationships. Remember that friends of the student or family, people who can foster community membership (such as soccer coaches, scout leaders, and religious education teachers), and people who can mentor the student to explore hobbies or career choices (such as musicians, business leaders, and mechanics) could participate and enhance quality of education (Turbiville, Turnbull, Garland, & Lee, 1996). If it is impossible for all team members to meet face to face, IDEA allows the use of video conferences and phone conferences, if both parents and schools agree to do so. If possible, the meeting should be scheduled to include all those who want to participate.

Involving Students. Equality, which is a partnership principle, involves sharing power and fostering empowerment, including a student's choice of whether to participate in the conference. In chapter 4, we discussed self-determination and adolescents. Under IDEA, all students may participate in IEP meetings "whenever appropriate." Students 16 years of age and older are entitled to voice their preferences and interests when transition services are developed. IDEA presumes that transition-age students will participate.

Although some parents feel their child should be involved in school-to-adulthood transition planning wherever possible (Goupil, Tasse, Garcin, & Dore, 2002), past experiences may discourage the students from participating:

> When I go to them meetings, I get really frustrated because it seems like if you do something wrong, you know, which everybody does, they exaggerate it. I mean you tell them the basic of what happened, but they, like, exaggerate it. Teachers are good at that. They should be salesmen. (Morningstar, Turnbull, & Turnbull, 1995)

Typically, students at the transition age have not attended IEP meetings (Getzel & deFur, 1997; Van Reusen & Bos, 1994), although this seems to be changing. There have been efforts to encourage student participation at their IEP meeting (Hammer, 2004; Van Reusen, 1998; Wood et al., 2004), and there is recent movement to encourage students to lead the meeting (Barrie & McDonald, 2002; Mason et al., 2004). When older students attend their own IEP meeting, parents report that they themselves understand significantly more and feel more comfortable contributing (Martin, Marshall, & Sale, 2004).

You will find many ways to involve students in educational planning and decision making (Mason et al., 2004; Snyder & Shapiro, 1997; Wehmeyer & Sands, 1998; Van Reusen, 1998). As chapter 10 made clear, a student's or family's cultural values may be inconsistent with special education practices, including student involvement in conferences. Cultures differ in the value they place on child and adolescent autonomy. For example, the Taiwanese mother of a junior high school student who is gifted was frustrated at the IEP conference because the professionals were more concerned with her daughter's preferences than with the mother's viewpoint:

> During the meeting [the gifted education counselor] only asked my daughter what she wanted to do in the next year, and she didn't ask me. After she asked my daughter, then she give me the papers and say, "Okay, sign your name." That was really frustrating.

A Hispanic mother agreed with this view when she added her comments:

> I think that basically the cultural differences are not being considered in these IEP meetings. And here in the United States it is like you always ask the child first, and for us it's very important for us as a parent to participate. . . I know that it's not on their mind, but it really hurts our feelings . . . why we were one way at home (in asserting parental authority) and the teachers treated them in a different way (offering them more choices).

You should consider cultural appropriateness of involving students in conferences and help students develop participation skills. By honoring the partnership practice of cultural diversity throughout the planning process, you earn trust from parents and students.

Taking Care of Logistical Considerations. Every conference requires logistical considerations such as scheduling, committee size, transportation, and child care.

Consider the size of the student's IFSP/IEP team. Some parents prefer a limited number of people at the conference, but others want everyone with a stake in their child's education to attend. Smaller conferences can be less intimidating and more focused. Larger conferences include wider ranges of expertise and provide opportunities for all professionals to develop the student plans for which they are responsible.

Time is another major logistical issue. Many professionals feel they have too little time for conferences, other professional duties, and their personal lives:

> I cannot ask my wife and children to put up with me, depressed and tense for months each spring because I must finish my testing, must begin testing with the new kids we've identified, must get the reports in on time, must complete reams of papers (the law says so, and tells me how much time I have to do it), and can't teach. When I am in class, I am tense and harried because the testing isn't getting done on time. I don't have any time to plan, to diagnose, to remediate, and I can't get on top. (Katzen, 1980, p. 582)

Clearly, the place to cut corners is not during the conference itself. You and other professionals might ask your school to (1) hire a permanent floating substitute so teachers are free to address conference tasks, (2) use administrators and other school staff to provide educators with additional release time, (3) assign weekly shared prep periods for staff collaboration, (4) create early-release days reserved only for collaborative activities, or (5) purchase laptop computers for all teachers to use in developing an IFSP/IEP (Johnson, Proctor, & Corey, 1995; Snell & Janney, 2000; Walther-Thomas, Korinek, McLaughlin, & Williams, 2000; West, 1990). You may want to hold a series of planning meetings so teachers and families feel no pressure to "get everything in" during a single meeting.

Exchanging Information in Advance. By exchanging information in advance, you and your partners can use conference time to clarify issues and make decisions. Without advance information, you may spend most of your time reviewing information, generating ideas, and perhaps rushing decisions.

Be careful to distinguish between preparation and predetermination. Parents are dissatisfied with educators who predetermine decisions (Salembier & Furney, 1997) and interfere with their ability to make decisions for their children.

Exchanging information in advance also can minimize cultural differences between families and professionals. A family's religious beliefs are sometimes overlooked as a component of cultural difference, as one teacher noted:

> Sam's expression was wide-eyed when the psychologist who was to test him walked through the door. Sam was not going to perform well for this man, I could tell. I was teaching in a private Christian school, and Sam's parents were fundamentalist Christians. The psychologist was dressed, to put it kindly, casually and very differently from the dress code we had at our school. . . . A simple phone call to Sam's administrator, myself, or his parents to ask what might prove offensive to the family's religious beliefs would have established a better rapport with all concerned and provided Sam with an opportunity to perform to his capacity during assessment.

Connecting and Getting Started.   It is important to attend to the partnership principles of trust, communication, respect, commitment, and equality. For example, the communication principle and its practice of providing and coordinating information can redirect a team toward a common goal of creating the student's program.

It is both polite and important to introduce everyone and describe the conference format and time line. Be sure to establish that each professional values the family's contributions and wants to form a partnership. This will emphasize equality, an important partnership principle. Key practices of equality are avoiding hierarchies, sharing power, and fostering empowerment. One parent commented about the differential power structure: "One group has power and the other doesn't. I think the ultimate lack of power is to have a child who has special needs" (Ferguson, 1984, p. 44).

To equalize power, start by creating a warm, relaxed atmosphere defined by the positive communication skills discussed in chapter 9. Betsy Santelli, the parent of two daughters enrolled in a gifted program, described the importance of informal sharing:

> Although anxious at first about what our roles might be, Jim and I were delighted to find a real willingness and genuine interest on the part of the staffing team to learn from us about Maren and Tami's unique and special qualities as well as those of our family. Before any assessment results were shared or questions were asked, time was allowed for informal sharing among all of us as people—not professionals, not parents—just people. Those few minutes helped set the stage for the comfortable sharing of information that followed and continues to this day.

By starting with a climate of trust, you will make great progress toward establishing partnership with families. If you genuinely connect with families, you all but guarantee a successful conference. Too many professionals err on the side of formal compliance with IDEA while neglecting trusting partnerships (Gallagher & Desimone, 1995; Harry et al., 1995; Lovitt & Cushing, 1999).

Reviewing Formal Evaluation and Current Levels of Performance.   IDEA requires that each IFSP and IEP describe the present level of academic achievement and functional performance (20 U.S.C. Sec. 1414 (d)(1)(A)(i)(I)). This information derives directly from the student's nondiscriminatory evaluation and is the foundation for the student's individualized plan and appropriate education (20 U.S.C. Sec. 1414(d)(1)(A) and (B)). You can proceed in two ways. First, you can use the conference to review the formal evaluation results and develop the actual plan. Of course, you will want the family

and other team members to agree to this approach. Second, you can hold a separate meeting (before the conference) to review evaluation results. We discussed both options in chapter 11.

When you share evaluation information, you have an opportunity to practice the partnership principles of communication, respect, and commitment. Parents may feel vulnerable or overwhelmed when hearing the information and its educational implications. Your sharing must establish or maintain the highest levels of trust. Decisions about when and how to report evaluation results should be based on family and professional preferences.

Sharing   Resources,   Priorities   and Concerns.   The referral and evaluation process can be a time for families, teachers, related service providers, friends, and other interested people (such as physicians) to identify their resources, priorities, and concerns. Identifying and agreeing to share resources, priorities, and concerns should start during the evaluation process and continue during the conference. The goal is to link evaluation information with outcomes for students and families.

How can you ensure that parents do not feel brushed aside or rushed during conferences? After reviewing the evaluation and performance information, offer family members adequate time to express their ideas fully.

As we said in chapter 11, families participating in IFSP conferences have a right to discuss their resources, priorities, and concerns. Collaboration is best when all participants (not just family members) share their resources, priorities, and concerns. Participants should start by focusing on those special contributions they can make to best support the student. Only by sharing their unique resources can they find a combination that benefits the student and each other.

Next, team members should discuss general priorities before identifying goals and objectives. By articulating their priorities, all participants will help ensure that the student's goals and objectives reflect the team's individual and collective priorities.

Team members should also discuss general concerns or potential barriers, such as whether resources are available within the team or from the family, school, or community to satisfy agreed-upon priorities. For example, general educator concerned about individualizing the curriculum for a student with a learning disability can collaborate with a consulting special education teacher. Teachers anxious about attending to the needs of students who are supported by medical equipment can receive instruction and support from parents, the school nurse, and other specialists.

By discussing special and common resources and concerns, team members can support each other. Partnership means that no one on the team must address concerns in isolation.

Sharing Visions and Great Expectations. Typically, people are more excited and motivated when working for something that genuinely sparks their hopes and dreams. A vision statement helps generate enthusiasm and inspiration for the future. This is a critical part of any IFSP/IEP process because it allows families to express their concerns and their dreams for their children. Developing a vision statement for the student is a valuable investment of time because it helps determine priorities, shape decisions, and generate goals for IFSP/IEP plan documents.

The Process of Making Action Plans and Vision Statements. The Making Action Plans (MAPs) process is one of the most effective ways to develop vision statements. MAPs is a practical, positive way to provide open-ended, intimate, and personalized views of the student and family. The process portrays the student within the full context of his or her life at home and school and within the community. MAPs is used frequently for students with severe disabilities (Mount & O'Brien, 2002; Thousand, Villa, & Nevin, 2002).

Those attending MAPs gatherings may include the student, parents, other family members, student and family friends, educators, and others interested in making the school and community as close to the student's preferences as possible. MAPs gatherings are usually held in comfortable surroundings—often the student's home or some other community setting—to encourage connections and relationships.

Seven key questions form the basis of the MAPs process (see Figure 12-7). The order of the questions can vary, but their purpose remains consistent: to stimulate dynamic, open-ended discussion among people with a major stake in the student's well-being.

In a MAPs gathering, experienced facilitators guide discussion and encourage brainstorming to generate as many creative ideas as possible. As ideas are shared, facilitators record them on a large poster board.

Ideally, the MAPs process should be complete before holding an IFSP/IEP conference. If the family has already completed a MAPs process, you may want to devote the initial portion of the conference to reviewing the MAPs plan. If the family has not engaged in a MAPs process, you might offer to incorporate it into the initial conference, recognizing that you cannot complete that activity and develop a full IFSP/IEP at the same time. Educators report

FIGURE 12–7
Guiding Questions for the MAPs Process

1. **What is the student's history or story?** Typically, the student and family share background information, highlighting triumphs and challenges associated with the student's visions, great expectations, strengths, interests, and preferences.

2. **Who is the student?** The group will use as many adjectives as it takes to get behind the exceptionality label and describe the real or essential aspects of the student's personhood.

3. **What are the student's strengths, interests, gifts, and talents?** Teachers, friends, family members, and others can lose sight of all the positive characteristics the student can bring to bear to achieve his or her dreams.

4. **What are the student's priorities?** What will it take to make the student's and family's dreams come true? What barriers exist between where the student is at the present time and having the dreams come true?

5. **What are the dreams for this student?** It is especially important for students to share their dreams for the future. Families also should share their dreams and supplement what the student is saying if the student cannot or chooses not to communicate with group members.

6. **What are the nightmares for this student?** Students with exceptionalities and their families may have fears that serve as barriers to their working toward great expectations. Identifying these fears or nightmares allows the team to put adequate supports into place.

7. **What is the plan of action?** A plan of action includes specific steps to accomplish the dream. The plan of action can involve tasks, time lines, resources, and other information that will help lead to real progress.

that the MAPs process contributes positively to developing an individualized plan. One teacher described the impact of MAPs on school personnel as follows:

> Since we're dealing with students with disabilities, you know, so often you've looked at that student with a list of they can't do this, this, this, this, and this. So it's enabled the whole group, including the school personnel, I think more than anybody, to be able to see that student in a different light, which has been extremely valuable. (Grigal, Quirk, & Manos, 1998)

A principal also commented on the benefits of MAPs:

> It's not learning just sterile facts. When you hear parents talk about their hopes and their dreams for their child, it's just like any other parent talking about their hopes and dreams. When you listen to the fears, it's the same as any other parent talking about the fears they have. The difference is that you're talking about a child with a disability. And how are we going to help this child feel good about being in a situation in a school setting and make sure that the child is viewed as other children are. (Grigal et al., 1998)

If the family and professionals forgo the complete MAPs process, they still need to make time for sharing visions, great expectations, and strengths. One student described the benefits of sharing:

> I have never in my life heard a group of adults sit around and say anything positive about me. That list is exactly right. (Kroeger, Leibold, & Ryan, 1999, p. 6)

As we discussed in chapters 4 and 10, if it is consistent with family preferences, you can promote opportunities for self-determination when you encourage older students to be an active part of this process.

The MAPs process can strengthen the partnership among professionals and family members. When everyone works as partners, dreams can indeed come true. One parent, Sara, recalled that church was a focal point in her family's life. It was important for Kimberley, her daughter with cerebral palsy and visual impairments, to go to the toddler class in the church program with her twin sister, Abigail.

> By identifying this church activity as being of prime importance to our family's happiness and well-being. . . our family was able to shape the attitudes and obtain the tools necessary to make this dream a reality. The service providers recognized our concern, saw it as part of our long-term vision for our child and family, and helped us work out ways to achieve our goals. (Squires, 2000, p. 11)

As the team's visions and great expectations become more concrete, the next step is to identify goals or outcomes that can transform the vision into a reality.

Considering the Interaction of Proposed Student Goals, Services, and Placement.

Few aspects of educational decision making are more important than determining student outcomes, related services, supplementary aids/services, and placement. However, the sequence that is usually followed in determining placement and services may jeopardize development of appropriate, individualized plans for the student, sometimes excluding parents from decision making (Giangreco, 2001).

How can you ensure that parents feel like partners in planning and making decisions about their child's education? Figure 12–8 illustrates a process in which families and professionals work together to discuss the child's goals, placement, and services.

This decision-making process reinforces the principle that families are partners in their child's education.

First, the process prioritizes learning outcomes and supports for those outcomes. (Refer to chapter 6 to review the four IDEA outcomes.) Next, the process addresses placement options and services for supporting the student in different placements. It then considers interactions between a proposed placement and necessary services. Finally, the process requires a comparison of all placement and service options. Families and professionals work as partners, identifying and examining options and making final decisions. We follow this overall model when (1) translating student priorities into written goals and objectives, (2) specifying placement, supplementary aids/services, and related services, and (3) addressing assessment modifications and special factors.

Translating Student Needs into Measurable Annual Goals.

IDEA requires the IEP to describe the student's present levels of academic achievement and functional performance (20 U.S.C. Sec. 1414(d)(1)(A)(i)(I)). Only if the student takes alternate assessments that are aligned to alternate achievement standards must the student's IEP describe the benchmarks or short-term objectives that the IEP team prescribes. The IEP of students who do not take the alternate assessments are not required to contain benchmarks or short-term objectives. IDEA does not prohibit the IEP of these students from containing them; it simply does not require it to contain them.

In addition, the IEP of every student, including those in preschool and those who take the alternate assessment, must describe the student's measurable annual goals, including academic and functional goals (and others as the IEP team determines). In addition, the IEP of every student must describe how the student's progress toward meeting these annual goals will be measured and when periodic reports on the student's progress will be provided (20 U.S.C. Sec. 1414 (d)(1)(A)(i)(III)).

The measurable annual goals (and benchmarks and short-term objectives for the "alternate assessment" student) are the core components of a student's IEP. They shape the student's involvement and progress in the general curriculum; the way the school will respond to the student's academic and functional goals and other educa

FIGURE 12–8

A Process for Considering Interactions Among Program, Placement, and Services

- Determine the student's educational program.
  - Learning outcomes: What a student will learn, stated in terms of measurable annual goals.
  - Supports: What will be done so that the student will be able to achieve those goals.

- Discuss proposed placements.
  - Annual review of placement.
  - Placement advances with the student's educational goals.
  - Placement conforms to the least restrictive environment requirements.
  - Placement considers characteristics of the specific location (e.g., building accessibility).
  - Determine the nature and extent of the general and special education services associated with the placement.

- Determine services needed to support the initial proposed placement.
  - Determine whether there is a need for nonspecialized support services (e.g., additional paraprofessional support services).
  - Determine whether there is a need for specialized related services (e.g., speech-language pathology, physical therapy, occupational therapy, school psychological services).

- Consider interactions between placement and services.
  - Consider how placement and services may interact with and impact each other.
  - If the team decides it is appropriate to consider other placement options and corresponding services, recycle through the second and third steps above.

- Finalize placement and services.
  - Compare advantages and disadvantages of placement/service options if the team has considered more than one service option.
  - Finalize a team decision about placement and services that meets the student's right to receive a free appropriate education.

Source: From Giangreco, M. (2001). Interaction among program, placement, and services in educational planning for students with disabilities. *Mental Retardation, 39*(5), 346. Adapted with permission.

onal needs that result from the child's disability; the re-
ted services and supplementary aids and services that
the student will receive; the extent, if any, that the student
will not participate in the regular class and extracurricular and other nonacademic activities; and the nature and reason for alternate assessments (20 U.S.C. Sec.
1414 (d)(1)(A)(i)).

Before discussing the student's goals, team members
should identify their own priorities. Those discussions
will reflect the individual and collective priorities of the
team. One mother, Sherry, described the IEP meeting of
her high school son:

> We discussed as a group the goals we wanted my son to
> achieve. As a group, we came to the same conclusions as far
> as strategies to implement the goals we wanted my son to
> attain. The whole process was very beneficial to me as a
> parent. We all know what our role would be to help my son
> attain his goals. The program was a complete success as far
> as I am concerned.

To begin translating the student's needs into measurable annual goals, the parents and other team members must ask: What are the most meaningful goals for
this student? The question is shaped by the student's
and family preferences, nondiscriminatory evaluation
data related to the student's academic achievement and
related developmental needs, the student's strengths
and interests, and the team's visions, great expectations,
and priorities. In partnership with families, you can begin translating the evaluation information, including
the MAPs or vision statement, into meaningful goals for
the student. Before writing those goals, think about the
questions presented in Figure 12–9. They may assist
you in identifying the student's highest-priority goals.
You may add to or modify these questions, based on
professional and family member recommendations.
Team members can rank draft goals, discuss rankings,
and then set priorities.

The student goals must be closely related to the general curriculum, which consists of three domains: academic, extracurricular, and other school activities (for
example, field trips and dances). The team must consider
access to and participation in each domain when formulating goals and objectives; it may not focus solely on academic skills. Areas often neglected in formulating
student goals include peer group membership, friendships and other social relationships, and participation in
extracurricular activities (Lovitt & Cushing, 1999; Morningstar, et al., 1995; Turnbull, Blue-Banning, & Pereira,
2000). Nonacademic opportunities related to a student's
hobbies or leisure skills are equally important.

Tony is a 17-year-old student with autism. He believes that
"music is magic." Music was identified as an important subject to include on Tony's IEP. One of the objectives was to

FIGURE 12–9
Tips for Determining the Most Essential Student Goals

Does the goal reflect:

- **Student and family visions and great expectations?** Student and family preferences and contributions are not merely represented but guide the development of goals.

- **Access to the general education curriculum and participation in inclusive settings?** The student will have consistent and frequent opportunities to learn and otherwise participate fully in typical settings.

- **The family's culture, values, and priorities?** The desired skills or behaviors must be consistent with the family's cultural values, priorities, and practices.

- **The student's interests, strengths, priorities, and challenges?** The goals must reflect a unique, personalized, and rich portrait of the student.

- **Opportunities for practice?** There are multiple, consistent opportunities for the student to practice the skill or behavior in naturally occurring situations.

- **Chronological age-appropriateness?** Behaviors, skills, or experiences are consistent with what the student's same-aged, typically developing peers are expected to do.

- **A strong generalization probability?** There is a very good chance that the skill or behavior will be used across different settings, situations, or people.

- **Enhancement of friendships, social opportunities, and membership?** The skill or behavior will promote a range of positive social experiences and relationships with others of his or her choice.

- **Enhancement of the child's and family's quality of life?** The student will have access to meaningful experiences both inside and outside of school that will contribute to an overall high quality of life.

- **A strong connection to future outcomes (e.g., lifelong habits, career, or other postsecondary opportunities)?** The skills and behaviors consider the experiences, settings, and individuals the student will likely encounter in the near and distant future.

teach Tony to play a guitar. As the year progressed the music program and the guitar, as contrasted to the independent living and career-education programs, provided the spark for Tony to turn off the alarm clock and get out of bed every morning.

If the goals are specific and personally relevant, the team members will be more accountable to each other for student progress.

We have discussed IEP goals, but what about IFSP and family (not infant-toddler outcomes). IDEA requires that each family whose infant-toddler receives services (under Part C) must have an IFSP. The IFSP must describe the family's resources, priorities, and concerns relating to enhancing the infant-toddler's development (20 U.S.C. Sec. 1436(d)(2)). The purpose of identifying family outcomes is not for staff to assign duties to families but to direct staff as they provide culturally (and personally) relevant supports and services to families and their infants and toddlers. So, professionals should write outcomes in the family's language—describing what changes families want to occur—rather than in the format of a behavioral objective (McGonigel, Kaufmann, & Johnson, 1991). For example, this could be a "professionally stated" behavioral objective:

> The siblings will attend a siblings support group for at least 80% of the meetings in order to gain a developmentally appropriate understanding of Down syndrome.

But a "family-stated" outcome might read like this:

> We want some assistance in knowing how to help our other children understand why their little sister is slow, so they can answer the questions of their friends at school (McGonigel et al., 1991, p. 58)

Developing an IFSP is as important as specifying its outcomes. To partner with families to identify outcomes related to their quality of life, early intervention program planners probably need to work with other professionals and agencies. The outcomes that educators and related service providers are prepared to address may differ from those requiring expertise or training from physicians and other health-care providers, social workers, audiologists, psychologists, and occupational or physical therapists. Early educators should inform families about other agencies or service providers who could help them meet their outcomes. By referring families, you will demonstrate the partnership practice of professional competence. You do not need to have all the answers, but you should know where to find someone who does.

Remember to address discrepancies between family and professional judgments about goals, objectives, and outcomes. By using communication skills from chapter to resolve disagreements, you help families and professionals understand discrepancies and perhaps find common ground.

The more you create partnerships with families, the more there will be mutual trust, sharing of concerns, and open brainstorming about the most appropriate out-comes for their children.

Specifying Placement, Supplementary Aids/Services, and Related Services.

As explained in chapter 6, the concept of educating children with disabilities alongside their peers without disabilities is called the principle of the *least restrictive environment*. This principle holds that students with disabilities are legally entitled to be educated with peers without disabilities, to the maximum extent appropriate for the former. IDEA requires that students with disabilities have opportunities to participate in the same general curriculum that is available to their nondisabled peers. Special education is a service, not a setting. This general curriculum is based on content and performance standards that individual states develop for students at different grade levels.

As you learned in chapter 8, support for inclusion by families varies (Duhaney & Salend, 2000; Erwin, Soodak, Winton, & Turnbull, 2001; Fisher, Pumpian, & Sax, 1998; York & Tundidor, 1995). Although more placement options are available now than ever before, many disagreements persist between parents and professionals over placement decisions. Consider the "wall" one parent faced when discussing her child's placement with professionals:

> They claimed that her disability was so severe that she could not make it anywhere else. So they have all the children with disabilities in this one classroom. And then they have an adjoining door to another classroom where typical children are. And they tried to convince me how wonderful the program was. They said, "look, there is a door that is open between children with disabilities and children that are typical." And my response was "you see the open door. But I see the wall between my child and the typical children." (Soodak & Erwin, 2000, p. 38)

Families do not always believe they have access to inclusive educational environments (Erwin & Soodak, 1995; Erwin et al., 2001; Hanson et al., 2000; Hanson et al., 2001). Consistent with this research, a parent advocate commented:

> I've been to 57 IEP meetings. Not once, not even once, did the school offer regular class placement as a placement for a child. Beyond that, they never offered, never discussed, never considered what kinds of supports, modifications, options would be necessary for a child to succeed in a regular class environment. Children are placed within existing programs, they're placed categorically and/or into existing programs. (Testimony by Laura Glomb, in National Council on Disability, 1995, p. 59)

A study of experiences of parents of children with significant disabilities across three states showed that only two out of ten parents were offered inclusive placements for their children, and one of those parents was responsible for paying the tuition (the school district offered to pay tuition if the parent chose a self-contained placement) (Soodak & Erwin, 2000). Sadly, district or school personnel often send parents the message that their children are unwanted.

However, you have a legal duty to welcome students and their families into general education settings. They have a right to be there unless they cannot benefit from academic, extracurricular, or other general curriculum activities. Ensuring that special education supports and services are provided is not enough. You must show parents and their children that they are valued members of the school community. Families hope to hear that their children are accepted. They are understandably alienated by professionals who consider their children burdens on teachers and classmates.

Educators have questioned the meaning of the least restrictive environment for students who are gifted, given those students' ability to benefit from an accelerated or enriched curriculum (Gallagher, 1997; Gallagher & Gallagher, 1994). Unfortunately, when typical general education programs do not meet unique educational needs, students often lose their enthusiasm and capacity for reflective, creative thinking (Hodge & Kemp, 2000).

By acknowledging your own and others' professional competence while you, a family, and other professionals are discussing a student's educational placement, you can use the partnership practices of continuing to learn, setting high expectations, and providing a quality education. Together with families, the team can share and then make informed decisions about placement.

IDEA requires a student's IEP to list supplementary aids and services the school will provide. This requirement reflects professionals' and families' concerns about securing program modifications and ensuring teacher competency for children's success (Erwin et al., 2001; Fisher et al., 1998).

A useful decision-making process encourages educators to consider specific physical, instructional, social-behavioral, and collaborative team-building factors. Figure 12–10 outlines factors and sample questions related to each dimension.

After carefully considering these dimensions, the team must add a statement to the IEP about the supplementary aids and services that the student will receive and about individuals responsible for providing them. For example, Greg Motley, a high school freshman, has difficulty with English and math but not with science or social studies.

FIGURE 12–10
Sample Factors and Questions for Identifying Supplementary Aids and Services

Factors	Sample Question(s)
Physical Dimension	
Mobility	Could the classroom be made more accessible to the student?
Room arrangement	Could a round table be available in the classroom for small-group work?
Seating	Does the student's desk need to be placed close to the blackboard, teacher, or other students?
Instructional Dimension	
Lesson presentation	Does the student need visual aids, large print, or alternative media?
Skill acquisition	Could the student be provided process-of-reading guides, highlighted or tape-recorded?
Assignments and worksheets	Could the student be allowed extra time for completion of assignments, have alternative assignments, or be provided a calculator or word processor?
Test taking	Could the student have take-home or alternative (e.g., oral) tests? Could the student use a study guide during the test? Could tests be divided into parts and taken over a series of days?
Evaluation	Could the student be graded pass/fail or receive IEP progress grading? Could the resource teacher and regular teacher use shared grading? Could contracting be used? Could portfolio evaluation be used?
Learning structures	Could cooperative learning or reciprocal teaching be incorporated? Could the student be assigned a partner?
Organization	Does the student need an assignment notebook or home copies of texts?
Parallel activities	Could the student work on related activities such as illustrating?
Parallel curriculum	Could the student work on alternative, functional skills (e.g., coin recognition during the unit on metric conversion)?
Assistive technology	Could the student be provided computer-assisted instruction, communication switches, or software? Does the student require electronic aids or services?
Social-Behavioral Dimension	
Skill training plan	Could the student be involved in social skill instruction? Does the student need counseling?
Behavior management	Does the student need a behavioral management plan that describes a reinforcement system, supportive signals, and corrective options?
Self-management	Could the student use self-monitoring of target behaviors?
Peer support	Could peers be used to monitor and/or redirect behavior? Could peers be used to take notes, help prepare for exams, and so on?
Class-wide systems	Could the teacher implement an interdependent group contingency for the class? Could a "Circle of Friends" be initiated?
Collaborative Dimensions	
1:1 Aide	Does the student need a paraprofessional to assist him or her?
Co-teaching	Could the regular educator and special educator team-teach? Do teachers need additional time for planning and problem-solving?
Resource room assistance	Does the student need additional strategy or study skill instruction (e.g., memory strategies, test-taking skills)?
Teacher consultation	Could the teacher receive assistance from a curriculum consultant, strategist, or behavioral specialist?
Teacher training	Could a workshop or in-service on behavior management strategies or certain topics (e.g., autism, AD/HD) be provided?

Source: From The IDEA amendments: A four-step approach for determining supplementary aids and services by Etscheidt, S. K., & Bartlett L., *Exceptional Children, 65*(2), 1999, 163–174. Copyright 1999 by The Council for Exceptional Children. Reprinted with permission.

When he is in English and has difficulty reading, Greg can ask permission to leave class and go to the resource room to read, often with one-on-one help from his English teacher. Greg knows what accommodations he needs and has asked for them; they are clearly documented in his IEP. The result: Greg's failing grades have become passing grades. He is successful in school and proud of his accomplishments. Given the fast-paced development of new technologies, families and educators will discover even more ways to provide individualized options for supplementary aids and services.

Many students require additional services and supports to ensure that they benefit from their education. IDEA requires that these related services be identified in a student's IEP.

For students ages 3 through 21, related services are any service that enhances a student's educational benefits, including but not limited to transportation, counseling, occupational therapy, physical therapy, and speech/language therapy. Figure 6–2 in chapter 6 presents all the related services available under IDEA.

The plan must specify how often and in what way the related services will be provided. Team members may choose among a variety of service delivery models. These might include consulting with general education teachers, providing therapy within general education classrooms, and working with students in one-to-one arrangements or small groups (Thousand et al., 2002; Walther-Thomas et al., 2000).

If parents choose related services not included in the IFSP/IEP, they must pay for them and may use any insurance or federal benefits to which they are entitled. For example, if they qualify for Medicaid (health-related services or parents who meet federal low-income standards, and whose children qualify for Medicaid because of their disabilities), parents may seek reimbursement from the state Medicaid agency if services are not provided for in their child's IEP.

During a conference you may be called upon to apply the partnership practices. This is likely to occur when service providers and educators disagree about who pays for related services. Figure 12–11 illustrates the advocacy principle and related practices of preventing problems, keeping your conscience primed, and pinpointing and documenting problems. Remember, the student's priorities are the primary consideration, not the availability or cost of related services.

Addressing Assessment Modifications and Special Factors. As we noted in chapter 6, the general academic curriculum sets performance standards for all students and NCLB requires periodic state or local assessments of all students to determine how well they have mastered the curriculum. The purpose of including students with disabilities in these assessments is to hold schools accountable for improving educational results, which have not been sufficiently favorable to students in the past (Erickson, 1998; McLaughlin, 1998). Accordingly, each student's IEP must describe all individual appropriate accommodations that are necessary to measure the student's academic achievement and functional performance (20 U.S.C. Sec. 1414(d)(1)(A)(VI)). If the student's IEP team determines that the student should take an alternate assessment, the IEP must state why the student cannot participate in the regular assessment and why the alternate assessment that the team selects is appropriate for the student.

Teachers of students with severe disabilities have suggested ways to carry out alternate assessments (Ysseldyke & Olsen, 1999). These include observations, interviews or surveys, record reviews, and tests. For example, students' academic or functional literacy skills can be assessed through interviews or surveys of people who are regularly involved with them, using checklists of functional skills. Assessment should be geared to meaningful community

FIGURE 12–11
Advocating for Systems Change

A student's educational priorities should be the only basis for determining the type and amount of services needed. If you find yourself in conferences in which school personnel are trying to avoid their responsibility for related services, what might you do?

What if the school in which you were working had not provided occupational therapy for a 3-year-old child in your class because they could not find a therapist to fill a maternity leave position? The child had been making significant progress when occupational therapy was provided in your classroom during cooking, art, and other related activities. Since the therapist went on maternity leave 2 months ago, the child has not received any occupational therapy. The school maintains that they have looked but can't find a replacement.

We encourage you to ask yourself, "What would I do in this situation?" The parents may not even be aware that their child is not receiving the occupational services even though it is clearly stated on the IEP. *In considering the partnership practices within the advocacy principle, what steps might you take to keep your conscience primed, pinpoint and document problems, and create a win-win solution?*

settings, be measured across time, and provide integration rather than testing discrete, isolated skills.

Summarizing and Concluding. The concluding portion of the conference should synthesize family and professional recommendations and develop an action plan for follow-up responsibility, as shown in Figure 12–6. It is crucial to acknowledge and affirm contributions from the family and others, express great expectations for ongoing collaboration in implementing the plan, and encourage the family to contact other members with follow-up questions or suggestions. One goal is to end the conference with enhanced appreciation for the team's shared commitment and hard work in creating a high-quality educational plan for the student.

SUMMARY

To individualize a student's appropriate education, the team must be committed to the student, to teamwork and collaboration, and to a lasting relationship with the family that relies on the seven elements of partnership. The team must adhere to these logical steps:

- Preparing in advance
- Connecting and getting started
- Reviewing formal evaluation and current levels of performance
- Sharing resources, priorities, and concerns
- Sharing visions and great expectations
- Considering interaction of the students' proposed goals, services, and placement
- Translating student priorities into written goals and objectives (or outcomes)
- Specifying placement, supplementary aids/services, and related services
- Addressing assessment modifications and special factors
- Summarizing and concluding

By now, you are becoming well prepared to bring partnership practices into your work with families. Figure 12–12 summarizes how to focus on the partnership principle we call trust. It is possible to maintain partnerships while individualizing for an appropriate education. Creating and maintaining a climate of trust can make developing the IFSP/IEP a positive, valuable experience for all.

REFLECTING ON THE VIGNETTE

1. Given how the Holleys and the Bonner Springs Elementary School staff faced off about Sean's education and even his lifesaving interventions, what benefit, if any, did the family or school staff derive from IDEA's strict adherence to procedures in developing his IEP?

2. What would you have recommended if you had been an outside consultant or arbitrator of Sean's May 2000 IEP meeting, in order to prevent the deterioration of the partnership? Would it have helped maintain the partnership, or at least prevent it from falling apart, if the Holleys and school staff had followed the IDEA procedures exactly?

3. Could it be that the "night" aspects of the Holley–staff relationships were necessary preludes to the "day" aspects? To what degree, if any, can feelings be submerged to the IDEA process, and is it always good for families and professionals to repress their feelings while developing an IEP? What roles do feelings have in the IEP process and in developing a trusting partnership?

ENHANCING YOUR SELF-AWARENESS

How would you want parents to describe your participation and support during the individualized planning process for their child? Think about the strengths and skills you could bring to this process. What do you think might be challenging for you? One of the best ways to reflect on these questions is to think about goal setting and transitions in your own life.

Vision statements

Think about where you see yourself 5 years from now. How about 1 year from now? How do you feel when you think about your vision? What goals do you need to set to make your vision a reality?

Who would you invite to support and share with you their great expectations for your future? Who would you not invite? Why? What does this tell you about how vital it is to provide encouragement and support?

Transitions in life

In the chapter we spoke of how plans or statements document the supports needed to ensure a smooth transition. Think about a time when you were planning for a major event in your life. Perhaps it was a new job or a change in your marital status. What plans did you make to prepare for the transition? Who played a key role?

Think about the role partnerships played during the transition process for you. What might you have done differently during the transition to promote trust? What could others have done to demonstrate their trust? How can your own experiences assist you in your work with families?

FIGURE 12–12

Creating Partnerships Through Trust Building: Selected Actions Leading to Trust and Distrust for Developing Individualized Education Programs and Other Support Plans

Partnership Principles and Practices	Issues	Actions Leading to Distrust	Actions Leading to Trust
Communication: Listen.	You are working with parents who have had past negative professional interactions; they're angry.	Tell parents that you are not the one who committed past mistakes, and you do not appreciate their taking it out on you.	Listen emphatically to their experiences; invite suggestions on making the IEP conference as supportive as possible.
Respect: Affirm family strengths.	You are developing an IFSP with parents whom you believe emotionally neglect their toddler.	Ask the parents to explain why they don't say kind things about their child and blame the parents indirectly at the conference for being the cause of their child's low self-esteem.	Highlight one or more positive contributions that the parents make to their child; alert them to community resources (including Parent to Parent) that provide parenting support and information.
Professional Competence: Set High Expectations.	A gifted student says her goal in to get a scholarship to Harvard.	Discourage the student by emphasizing the excess expense that the scholarship is unlikely to cover.	Collaborate with the student and family to research scholarship options; locate a community mentor who graduated from Harvard to provide admissions advice.
Equality: Foster empowerment.	A family wants an adolescent with mental retardation to attend a community college you and other team members do not think it is a feasible transition goal.	Redirect the conversation and ignore family members' preferences; talk with them about vocational training.	Contact community colleges and find out about their admissions policies and accommodations for persons with disabilities.
Commitment: Be sensitive to emotional needs.	The parents are very worried and sad that their child with multiple disabilities has no friends.	Inform the parents that the IEP focuses on skill development and then consider adding a specific goal, such as turn taking to the child's IEP.	Have all IEP team members share vision, goals, and strategies for increasing the child's social connections and friendships.
Advocacy: Prevent problems.	A grandparent and mother (who has a history of chronic drug abuse) attend the IEP meeting; the grandmother criticizes her daughter and preempts her contributions.	Minimize the mother's role in the IEP process. Address your comments to the child's grandmother. Assume that a mother with a history of drug abuse probably does not care about her child and is not capable of making worthwhile contributions.	Reflect on the mother's strengths and let her know the positive things that she is doing or can do. Point out the grandmother's strengths and express your desire to work together as a team.

RESOURCES

1. A Guide to the Individualized Education Program
   Office of Special Education and Rehabilitative Services, U. S. Department of Education

   www.ed.gov/parents/needs/speced/iepguide/index.html

   The guide's purpose is to help educators, parents, and state and local educational agencies implement requirements of IDEA regarding IEPs for children with disabilities, including preschool-age children.

2. Individualized Education Programs Briefing Paper

   National Information Center for Children and Youth with Disabilities (NICHCY)
   P.O. Box 1492
   Washington, DC 20013
   800-695-0285, 202-884-8200
   nichcy@aed.org
   www.nichcy.org

   This document is a verbatim reprinting of federal regulations for the IEP as contained in IDEA.

Supporting Students' Individualized Achievement and Performance

CHAPTER ORGANIZATION

It is not often that a poet expresses both a biological fact and a social reality, all in one meditation, but John Donne did just that when he wrote: "No man is an island, entire of itself; every man is a piece of the continent, a part of the main" (Donne, 1624). Donne's observation applies quite aptly to the four families and their professional partners.

Let's go to the "island" that the Cortes family occupies. One resident is, of course, Joesian. But his brother and sister also reside there, and they assist him in completing some of his homework assignments. That may seem all well and good, but unless Joesian's teachers, as well as his brother's and sister's teachers, understand that family members collaborate among themselves, they cannot accommodate the family reality to their expectations for any of the Cortes children.

Another "island" is one that the Doleman family inhabits. There, a different challenge faces Nicky's family and her teachers. It is to ensure that Nicky receives exactly the right medical and technological support to keep her healthy and even alive. Under the Individuals with Disabilities Education Act (IDEA), Nicky is entitled to "assistive technology." This kind of technology includes any item, piece of equipment, or product system (except medical implants), whether acquired commercially off the shelf, modified, or customized, that is used to increase, maintain, or improve the functional capabilities of a child with a disability. Nicky's wheelchair fits the definition of a customized piece of equipment that increases her capability to go from home to school. However, the tubes that she relies on for food and medicine do not fit the definition of assistive technology because they are directly related to Nicky's health; they are implanted medical technologies, not assistive technologies. For the purposes of their partnerships with each other, it does not matter a great deal whether the Dolemans and the professionals who serve Nicky are concerned with assistive or medical technologies. Of course, it matters who the professionals are. Sometimes Nicky's physicians will be involved with her family and teachers, and sometimes not. Her teachers will always be involved. But their common interest in Nicky requires them to monitor how she

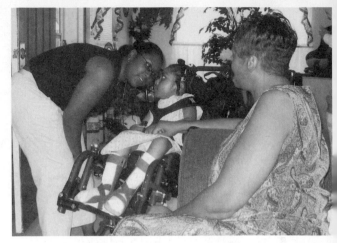

Charolette Doleman lovingly meets the gaze of her daughter, Nicky.

responds to the technologies and to determine what adjustments, if any, need to be made to provide functional and medical benefits to her and not to overwhelm her already fully occupied family.

Many families know what the Holley and Berg families learned long ago: However valuable education and social services are to their children with disabilities, it is beyond argument that social support and friendships are the ultimate safety nets for the children and their families. Special education is important, and the benefits that come from various federal and state programs are important. But without the support of family and friends, especially those in school and work, the programs are unlikely to provide the kind of life that everyone wants to have. That is why Leia Holley and Clara Berg have worked so hard to cultivate friendships among the professionals with whom they have contact and to make it possible for their children to have friends and advocates in

Norma Cortes (left) continues to advocate for her son Joesian as he explores vocational education.

Kenny Berg completes his chores, guided by Arnie Mejia.

Sean Holley's adjustment to junior high school will be guided by a committed team of parents and professionals.

school and on the job. Leia has found her reliable ally in the staff at Sean's school, especially Tierney Thompson. Clara's reliable ally is Carole Gothelf, who has played many different professional roles in Kenny's life.

Leia and Clara have also learned another lesson about collaboration: When their children have friends, they have fewer behavioral challenges. Do collaboration, reliable alliances, friendship, and positive behavioral support always combine to create good lives? No. But the aggregate effect of collaboration, reliable alliances, friendship, and positive behavioral supports is to increase the chances that children and families, and their professional partners, will have more enjoyable and more effective lives.

That is especially so when the families and their school partners take into account the "stovepipes" and "silos" that are inevitable parts of their lives. Stovepipes are geographically appropriate metaphors for discrete services that the Cortes and Berg families use in New York; likewise, silos are regionally appropriate metaphors for the many different services that the Doleman and Holley families use in Kansas. The challenge that each of these four families face is to ensure that there is an effective connection between all of the New York stovepipes or the Kansas silos. When services within schools and among school and other professional systems are in sync with each other, each service is more effective. Just consider what the consequences might be for Nicky and her family if her medical team did not interact with her teachers, or for Sean if his regular education teachers and special education staff blocked each other from making and implementing decisions about his education.

To support students in their achievement and performance, and indeed to support their families and the professionals who work with the children and the families, requires everyone to "connect to the main," to be less of an island.

INTRODUCTION

The partnership that emerges between families and professionals as they develop a student's individualized education program (IEP) or individualized family service plan (IFSP) continues as they implement the plan. Once students begin to receive the services that their IEP calls for, the goal of family-professional partnerships is to support a student's learning and development. In this chapter, we will describe how families and schools can be partners to achieve that outcome.

BENEFITS OF COLLABORATING WITH FAMILIES TO PROMOTE STUDENTS' ACHIEVEMENT AND PERFORMANCE

Before we begin our discussion of *how* families may be involved in their child's learning, we should reflect on why family-professional partnerships are important in promoting students' achievement and performance and recognize that the goal is not parent participation but student outcomes (Christenson & Sheridan, 2001). Families and school professionals have already discussed and agreed upon the outcomes by including them in the student's IFSP/IEP. Effective partnerships honor and encourage families' contributions to their child's learning and development and at the same time respect families' preferences for participation in their child's education.

Three decades of research on family participation in education tell us why effective parent-professional partnerships are essential. When parents engage with students in learning activities at home and in the community, children do better. Parental involvement in their child's learning contributes to increases in the following:

- Reading achievement (Chavkin, Gonzalez, & Rader, 2002; Faires, Nichols, & Rickelman, 2000; Hara & Burke, 1998; Shaver & Walls, 1998)
- Math achievement (Balli, Demo, & Wedman, 1998; Chavkin et al., 2002; Shaver & Walls, 1998)
- Positive attitudes toward school (Shumow & Miller, 2001)
- Attendance and retention (Henderson & Berla, 1994)
- Homework completion (Balli et al., 1998; Callahan, Rademacher, & Hildreth, 1998)
- Positive behavior at home and at school (Comer & Haynes, 1991; Sanders & Herting, 2000)

Children from all backgrounds and income levels benefit from family-professional partnerships.

Outcomes improve for gifted students, as well as students who experience difficulty learning. One study of family involvement in literacy learning found that students with the most difficulty experienced the greatest gains (Jordan, Snow, & Porche, 2000). Further, the benefits of parental involvement are likely to endure over time (Miedel & Reynolds, 1999).

Although most research on how parent involvement affects student learning took place in general education settings, the findings help shape the many ways that families of children with disabilities and teachers can work together to support student learning. Students with cognitive or behavioral challenges often have difficulty generalizing what they learn at school to home and community settings, making the home-school partnership even more vital.

The partnership practices of commitment and professional skills are particularly important in our efforts to work with families to promote student learning. Setting high expectations for students and being accessible to families are key practices in this process. One mother pointed out that working together to promote learning also benefits the individuals within the partnership:

> I didn't believe that there was actually a team. I thought it was Mark [her son], my husband, and I. Then there were the others who would be doing their own things but not necessarily helping us. I didn't think we were all going to actually work as a team, but we did. (Kincaid, Chapman, Shannon, Schall, & Harrower, 2002, p. 317)

We will discuss the five opportunities that parents and professionals have for working together to promote student learning in school, at home, and in the community: (1) fostering homework collaboration, (2) sharing information about student progress, (3) using assistive technology, (4) promoting friendships and community membership, and (5) providing positive behavior support.

COLLABORATING IN HOMEWORK

Traditionally, homework has been one of the activities that families, students, and schools have shared most often. School reform efforts such as No Child Left Behind (NCLB) have raised expectations for homework. As more and more students with disabilities participate in the general education curriculum, they are expected to complete work at home. For students with and without disabilities, homework is generally assigned to enhance achievement, to promote study skills, and, in some cases, to keep parents informed of their children's progress.

Parental involvement in student homework has been the focus of many studies. The benefits of having parents involved in homework are not limited to gains on achievement tests. A review of the research concluded that when parents support and become involved in their child's homework, students (1) are more likely to develop positive attitudes toward homework and learning, (2) feel more self-confident, and (3) take greater responsibility for completing their work (Hoover-Dempsey et al., 2001).

In general, students who have mild learning and behavioral disabilities benefit from completing their homework because their academic achievement improves (Epstein, Polloway, Foley, & Patton, 1993). However, there is little research on the role of homework for students with severe disabilities, particularly those who are in inclusive settings.

Although homework can support learning, students with disabilities often have more problems with homework than classmates who do not have special needs (Epstein et al., 1993; Gajria & Salend, 1995; Polloway, Epstein, & Foley, 1992). Students with disabilities may receive homework less consistently, but spend approximately 20 minutes more per night completing assignments than their peers without disabilities (Harniss, Epstein, Bursuck, Nelson, & Jayanthi, 2001). According to the Brown Center on Education Policy (2003), 83% of elementary students spend up to 1 hour on homework, and most secondary students spend between 1 and 2 hours each night on homework. The time demands associated with even usual homework assignments can be challenging for students with disabilities who often have difficulty sustaining attention and organizing time.

Key Issues Regarding Homework

Think about how homework completion can affect families. In chapter 3, we discussed the numerous family functions that already require time and attention in families busy lives. Your partnership with families is enhanced when you select strategies to support homework collaboration that match the families' preferences and resources. In the following section, we will discuss (1) family concerns about homework and (2) practical suggestions for homework collaboration.

Family Concerns About Homework.   Research on the perspectives of parents of academically gifted students indicates that their children complete homework with limited negative responses and without a great deal of help from their parents (Worrell, Gabelko, Roth, & Samuels, 1999). Students with disabilities, on the other hand, may require their families' assistance in completing homework. In this section, we will focus on the concerns of families who have children and youth with disabilities. Because homework rarely is given to students with severe disabilities, our focus will be on the concerns of parents of students with mild disabilities.

One study found that <u>parents may feel inadequate in helping their children with homework, particularly when they lack knowledge about the topic or information about the teachers' expectations</u> (Kay, Fitzgerald, Paradee, & Mellencamp, 1994). Consider the following parent's perspective on her child's homework:

> If I could actually see once in awhile how they're teaching him, then it might spill over into how I could do it at home. . . . When it comes to teaching my child, I feel like times have changed since I was in school, and I hate to teach him wrong. (Kay et al., 1994, p. 555)

What partnership practices can you draw on to respond to some of these concerns? Think back to chapter 9 on communication and chapters 2 and 3 on family interaction and family functions. What impact does the stress associated with homework have on parental and sibling interactions, on marital and extended family interactions, and on family functions?

Parents want comprehensive, two-way communication with teachers. They want assignments given to their children to be practical and individualized (Kay et al., 1994). Parents know that if homework is too difficult for their children to complete or the children consider it to be busy work, they are likely to lose any motivation to complete the homework. Parents and students prefer homework that involves concrete, hands-on projects that are interesting and engaging (Bryan & Sullivan-Burstein, 1998). Students complete their homework more often when the assignments are tailored to reflect their individual interests (Hinton & Kern, 1999). Because what may be easy for one student is difficult for another, effective teachers make reasonable modifications in homework assignments (ERIC/OSEP Special Project, 2001). These accommodations include adjusting questions, allowing alternative response formats, modifying the length of the assignment, providing peer tutors or study groups, providing learning tools, and giving fewer assignments. It also is helpful to provide tiered assignments targeted at a student's ability or interest level. For example, you can ask students to practice map-reading skills by using maps that contain more or less detail. In the following section, we will describe how you can collaborate with families and foster partnerships based on trust.

Practical Suggestions for Homework Collaboration

There are at least three ways to enhance homework collaboration: (1) create more opportunities for students, parents, general education teachers, and special education teachers to communicate with each other, (2) minimize family responsibility for homework, and (3) use strategies to improve homework practices (Epstein, Munk, Bursuck, Polloway, & Jayanthi, 1999; Harniss et al., 2001; Jayanthi, Sawyer, Nelson, Bursuck, & Epstein, 1995).

Create Communication Opportunities. Both teachers and parents want timely and consistent communication (Nelson, Jayanthi, Brittain, Epstein, & Bursuck, 2002). Figure 13-1 contains suggestions for communicating with parents.

Some elementary schools use communication folders as a way for students to carry information between school and

FIGURE 13–1
Tips for Communicating with Parents About Homework

- Do you teach students to use homework planners?
- Do you provide parents with teachers' names and their preferred times and methods for being contacted?
- Do you post homework assignments on a class or school Website?
- Do you give parents access to homework assignments by telephone/voice mail with the option for parents to leave messages if they have questions?
- Do you offer parents suggestions for assisting their children with homework?
- Do you communicate frequently with parents about homework assignments and students' progress?
- Do you use written forms of communication, such as notes, progress reports, and forms?
- Is there communication among all teachers to avoid homework overload?
- Do general education teachers have access to information on students' preferences, strengths, and needs related to homework modifications?
- Do you share homework expectations with students and families and agree on the consequences for incomplete homework?
- Do you teach students to graph their homework completion and use these graphs at parent-teacher-student conferences to discuss progress with parents?
- Do your students have access to homework hotlines?

Sources: Bryan & Sullivan-Burstein, 1998; Epstein, Munk, Bursuck, Polloway, & Jayanthi, 1999; Harniss, Epstein, Bursuck, Nelson, & Jayanthi, 2001; Jayanthi, Sawyer, Nelson, Bursuck, & Epstein, 1995.

home (Bos, Nahmias, & Urban, 1999), including announce-ments, notes, weekly school newsletters, and weekly home-work packets. The homework packets for students with disabilities are sometimes adapted for a particular student's strengths and needs. At higher grade levels, some students with disabilities meet with a homework "coach" to address organizational, study, time-management, and self-advocacy skills. The coach helps the student communicate with the various content teachers as well as with parents. "Con-tracts" for longer assignments are also helpful to students and parents in planning time lines and responsibilities.

Internet-based homework assistance centers may pro-vide a unique opportunity for promoting communication between students, families, and professionals (Salend, Duhaney, Anderson, & Gottschalk, 2004). Websites can be designed and used to suggest activities, explain assign-ments, offer resources, and provide guidelines on effec-tive homework practices.

Each of the communication strategies you learned in chapter 9 has relevance for homework collaboration. One mother pointed out how helpful an answering machine might be in exchanging information about homework:

> I am a single parent. I work all day long. By the time I ever get home, the teachers are gone. Why couldn't there be some sort of an answering machine at the school, so [that I could] dial this number to leave a message for the math teachers [and] dial this number for the English teachers. [The teachers] could probably answer me back and that might solve [these communication problems]. (Jayanthi et al., 1995, p. 217)

One comprehensive approach to homework partner-ships provided an opportunity for parents and middle-school students who were at risk of school failure to learn about self-management skills (Callahan et al., 1998). This approach required students to complete daily math as-signments by using self-monitoring, self-recording, self-reinforcement, and self-instruction. The students and parents were given separate training sessions. Results of the program indicated that homework completion and quality were significantly higher when the parents facili-tated this self-management approach than before inter-vention. Math achievement increased at a greater-than-anticipated rate, and students and parents were extremely positive about their involvement with the program.

In a more recent study, six middle-school students with emotional and behavioral disorders and their parents were taught the same self-management approach to com-plete homework (Cancio, West, & Young, 2004). The com-bined training provided for parents and students was associated with gains in homework completion and ac-curacy as well as a reduction in perceived homework problems for each of the students.

Create Options to Minimize Family Respon-sibility for Homework. Sometimes it may be advantageous to consider options for a student to com-plete homework outside the family setting, as one special education teacher pointed out:

> I have a situation where the mom cannot read and the girl wants to do her homework. She cannot help, so I modify her assignments. If I have a parent who either cannot read or chooses not to read, I take the responsibility on myself and modify things, so that the child can feel successful, feel like they are doing homework. (Jayanthi et al., 1995, p. 221)

In a growing number of communities, public libraries are offering homework assistance to students, with bene-fits ranging from improved study habits and grades to learning to cooperate with adults (Mediavilla, 2001). Other options to minimize parents' responsibility for sup-porting homework completion include providing less homework, arranging for peer tutoring, and providing homework assistance in study hall or after-school pro-grams (Epstein et al., 1999; Jayanthi et al., 1995). We encourage you to think about times when it may be most effective to reduce the amount of homework a stu-dent is required to complete. Be particularly mindful of whether your motivations are respectful of families' strengths and preferences, and whether your actions rein-force trusting partnerships. These questions may have rel-evance when you are working with a family whose skills or resources are such that they impact their involvement in their child's homework activities. You can affirm how a family values learning in a number of ways. For example, you can assist the family in finding someone to provide homework assistance or help them locate free materials in the local library (Christenson & Sheridan, 2001).

Improve Homework Practices. Approximately one fifth of the time students spend on schoolwork is at home. Teachers can help ensure positive homework expe-riences for students and their families by providing mean-ingful and individualized assignments, teaching students study skills, and providing parents with suggestions for setting up useful routines and practices (Bryan & Sullivan-Burstein, 1998; Epstein et al., 1999; Jayanthi et al., 1995; Salend, Elhoweris, & Van Garderen, 2003). Figure 13–2 contains suggestions for promoting positive homework experiences.

We encourage you to ask families about their experi-ences with their child's homework. This is a perfect op-portunity to be aware of the partnership principle of communication and apply the practice of listening. When you can actively listen and then respond to parents' ex-periences and concerns regarding homework, you are honoring and strengthening the partnership. To create a

FIGURE 13–2

Tips for Promoting Positive Homework Experiences for Students and Families

- Encourage families to designate a study area and regular study time at home.
- Develop a regular routine for giving assignments, and be consistent about when and how information is given.
- Provide parents with suggestions they may use to assist their children with homework.
- Provide students and parents with a list of major assignments at the beginning of the school year.
- Use homework assignments that involve families and students in carrying out projects at home.
- Send home all texts and materials needed for the assignment.
- Send home assistive technology devices the student uses in school.
- Develop a schoolwide policy on homework, and consider providing incentives to teachers who create individualized modifications.
- Discuss homework expectations and modifications with teachers, parents, and students at the student's IEP meeting and incorporate them into the IEP document.
- Teach students to manage their time effectively.
- Teach students study skills and learning strategies to increase their independent completion of homework.
- Use contracts with students to monitor completion of longer assignments.

Sources: Bryan & Sullivan-Burstein, 1998; Epstein, Munk, Bursuck, Polloway, & Jayanthi, 1999; Jayanthi, Sawyer, Nelson, Bursuck, & Epstein, 1995; Stormont-Spurgin, 1997.

responsive context around homework issues, you will need to individualize your approach for each family. Your respect for the family's preferences will build trust and support student achievement and performance.

SHARING INFORMATION ABOUT STUDENT ACHIEVEMENT AND PERFORMANCE

A second way to collaborate with parents to implement an IEP is to maintain ongoing communication about their child's achievement and performance and progress toward measurable annual goals. Reports cards, grading, and

progress reports are strategies for sharing that kind of information. NCLB requires schools to provide all parents with frequent reports on their child's progress and to specify when and how reports will be provided. The 2004 amendments to IDEA require schools to report the student's progress toward the measurable annual goals that are set out in the student's IEP. Traditionally, report cards are the primary means of providing information on student's progress.

Because growing numbers of students with disabilities are placed in general education, grading practices and methods of reporting grades have taken on increased significance. When grading systems are based on percentage cutoffs, students with cognitive disabilities are at a significant disadvantage. Given that grading is often at the discretion of general educators, collaboration among special educators, general educators, and families is necessary to determine grading criteria (sometimes called rubrics), grading adaptations, and methods for reporting student progress. A national survey of grading practices of elementary and secondary general education teachers found that special and general education teachers work collaboratively on grades about 40% of the time (Bursuck, et al., 1996).

The first step in collaborating with other teachers and families is to develop a shared understanding about the purpose of grading. Parents, teachers, and students may have different ideas about what grades mean (Munk & Bursuck, 2003).

One study asked parents of secondary students with disabilities and parents of students without disabilities to indicate how effectively report card grades met a set of specific purposes (Munk & Bursuck, 2001b). Both groups of parents believed that grades were important in communicating information about students' achievement, effort, and work habits. At the same time, both groups were skeptical about how effectively report cards met these purposes. Compared to parents of students without disabilities, parents of students with disabilities assigned more importance to grades as indicators of their child's strengths and needs, and assigned less importance to the role of grades in conveying information to postsecondary schools or employers. We encourage you to ask parents what they think the purpose is of report cards. Use this information as you develop grading policies and make decisions about individual grading adaptations. The survey questions included in Figure 13–3 can guide your discussion with parents.

Grading adaptations communicate information about a particular student's accomplishments. Because adapted or personalized grades are more precise measures of progress, they tend to increase the motivation of students

FIGURE 13–3

Gathering Information About Parents' Perceptions of the Purposes of Grades

> Ask parents to read or listen to the statements below. Ask them to indicate how important each purpose is to them in the grading of their children. Use the questions to begin a dialogue with families about grading.
>
> *I'm interested in knowing from the grades my child receives . . .*
>
> whether my child has improved in his/her class.
> how to help my child plan for his/her future.
> how hard my child is trying.
> what my child will do after high school.
> what my child needs to improve on to keep a good grade.
> what my child is good at and not good at.
> how well my child works with classmates.
> how much my child can do on his/her own.
> how my child's performance compares to other children's.
> how to help my child improve.
>
> *I would also like my child's grades to . . .*
>
> tell colleges and employers what my child is good at.
> motivate my child to try harder.

Source: Munk, D. D. (2003). *Solving the grading puzzle for students with disabilities* (pp. 23–24). Whitefish Bay, WI: Knowledge by Design.

with disabilities (Munk & Bursuck, 2001a; Ring & Reetz, 2002). If you use grading adaptations, you should describe them in a student's IEP, explain the basis of grading to students and parents early in the school year, and review your method throughout the year.

Researchers have identified a number of adaptations from which you can choose in collaboration with students and parents (Friend & Bursuck, 2002; Guskey & Bailey, 2001; Munk & Bursuck, 2001a, 2003). Ask yourself how the following adaptations relate to your own thinking about the purpose of grading:

- Prioritize and limit the number of assignments to be graded.
- Weight some assignments more heavily than others.
- Assign greater weight to effort.
- Base part of the grade on the processes or strategies the student uses to complete the assignment.
- Grade students on progress toward IEP goals.
- Grade on the basis of the student's improvement over time. By working with other professionals to create an open dialogue with families about grading, you will be

promoting partnerships that can lead to a high-quality education for a child.

In addition to grades given on assignments and report cards, progress reports provide families with timely feedback (Smrekar, 1993). These progress reports can be complex or simple; they can be sent home once a day, once a week, or once every few weeks; they can communicate about a single subject or area of development or about many. Lynch and Hanson (2004) suggest that when working with some families of different cultures, it may be helpful to provide information about their child's progress through cultural mediators, photographs, or videotapes. Videotapes have also been used in an early childhood program to involve parents in monitoring IEP objectives and to increase their awareness of their child's activities (Hundt, 2002). Remember to obtain the parents' permission before videotaping their child.

By sharing information about student progress in ways that respect families' preferences, you put into practice several partnership principles, including respect, communication, and equality.

SHARING DECISION MAKING IN THE USE OF ASSISTIVE TECHNOLOGY

A third opportunity for collaborating with families to support students' learning and development relates to assistive technology. IDEA classifies assistive technology as a related service (see chapter 6) and defines *assistive technology device* as any item, piece of equipment, or product system—whether acquired off the shelf, modified, or customized—that is used to increase, maintain, or improve a student's functional capabilities. (IDEA excludes any medical implant from the definition of "related service" and "assistive technology.") For example, if a student has difficulty holding objects, an adapted spoon becomes an assistive technology device. Assistive technology devices also include typing telephones for people who are deaf or hard of hearing and motorized wheelchairs for students who cannot walk. Assistive technology enables students to participate in everyday activities in school, at home, and in the community. The successful use of these devices rests largely on how families are involved in decisions about their child's use of assistive technology. In the following section, you will learn how to reach decisions about technology that are consistent with the family's goals, values, and lifestyle.

Accessing Assistive Technology

Assistive technology can be low-tech, such as communication boards or cards, or high-tech, such as a computerized speech recognition system. The IDEA definition includes off-the-shelf, adapted, or customized devices, thus creating many choices for the parents, student, and teachers. Selection of a device is an important decision for all of them. They will have already considered whether to use assistive technology when they are evaluating the student (chapter 11) or developing an IEP (chapter 13). If they include assistive technology in the student's IEP, the school must provide it, as it must provide all other related services listed in the IEP.

IDEA defines *assistive technology service* as a related service that assists the student in the selection, acquisition, or use of an assistive technology device. If the student, the family, or the school staff need training to use the device and the IEP includes the training as a related service, the school must provide the training or make sure that some other person or organization provides it.

As a teacher, you will observe when a student is unable to fully participate in or benefit from instruction. As a trusted partner, you can be instrumental in helping parents identify situations at home in which the student might benefit from the use of an assistive device.

Using Assistive Technology at Home

Assistive technology can make a significant positive impact on the lives of students with disabilities and their families (Angelo, 2000). Unfortunately, students and families do not always benefit from assistive technology (Parette, Brotherson, & Huer, 2000). Acquired devices are often underused or abandoned, particularly when the student is expected to use the device outside of school (Judge, 2002; Lahm & Sizemore, 2002; Parette, Van-Biervliet, & Hourcade, 2000). Rather than bringing the intended joy and independence to family life, assistive devices sometimes leave families feeling frustrated and dissatisfied (Jones, Angelo, & Kokoska, 1998).

Why does this occur? Usually, it is because parents do not have a meaningful voice in decisions about technology and because teachers accordingly make inappropriate recommendations. Think about what can happen when a teacher or other professional disregards the partnership practices of communication, respect, and trust. This mother's experience should be instructive:

> Yeah, when they first told me about it I had to fill out tons of paperwork. I didn't know who to call to inquire about it, the teachers totally took control of the whole thing and took it away from me when she got it. . . I wanted the books and liberator (an electronic communication device) right then and they told me no. It's gonna take us about a year to learn how to use it. We gotta keep it at school for about two or three weeks, and learn how to use it. I was really upset about that. I had to call the company to find out how much it cost, who funded it, who funded my daughter for it. How

did she even get it. You know it was a total breakdown from that point. (Parette, Brotherson, & Huer, 2000, p. 184)

There are two main reasons why parents do not use the assistive technology at home that their children have at school. First, some parents are unprepared or unable to carry out the responsibilities that teachers assign to them; they already have ordinary caregiving duties (Angelo, Kokoska, & Jones, 1996). These responsibilities include training to use and maintain the device, providing ongoing care and maintenance, helping their child use the device, and transporting the device to new locations.

Expectations about parent participation must be consistent with the family's resources and comfort in school-like settings (Kemp & Parette, 2000). Some parents do not have the time, child care, or other resources needed to attend training; other parents feel overwhelmed by the expectations imposed on them to support their child's use of technology. For one mother, simply handling the device posed a challenge: "The biggest concern I have right now is the weight of the device [Dynovox] . . . I couldn't have begun to even push the thing across the table, more or less carry it from room to room" (Parette, Brotherson, & Huer, 2000, p. 186).

The second reason parents may experience difficulties is that they may perceive the technology to be incompatible with the family's values, cultural background, and lifestyle (Parette, Brotherson, & Huer, 2000). Sensitivity and respect for a student's background is important in all interactions with families, but decisions about technology raise a particular set of issues:

- *Parents' desires for their children to fit in.* In studies involving African American families, some family members spoke of their concern about drawing negative attention to their child's disability through use of a device (Huer, 1999; Parette, Brotherson, & Huer, 2000).
- *Families' preferences about how their children communicate.* In a study of Mexican American families, many parents said they prefer that their children use sign language and speech instead of an augmentative device (Huer, Parette, & Saenz, 2001). Another study revealed that parents of African American children may prefer that communication systems with speech output reflect the vocabulary and dialects with which the children are familiar (Parette, Huer, & Wyatt, 2002).
- *The value families place on their children's independence.* Some parents place greater value on their child's dependence than do professionals from typical European American perspectives. For example, some Asian and Hispanic families do not necessarily support the use of technology to encourage their child's independence (Parette & McMahan, 2002).

- *The role of other family and community members.* Parents report that decisions about assistive technology need to consider with whom the student will want to communicate and socialize at home and in the community, as well as how the technology will be received by family and community members (Parette, et al., 2002).
- *Family's expectations about the immediacy of the benefits of the technology.* Families differ in how quickly they expect to have access to the device or how quickly they expect to see changes in their child's functioning once the device is used (Huer, 1999; Huer et al., 2001).

In the absence of ongoing communication with professionals, parents may feel frustrated and disappointed, abandon the technology, and begin to distrust the professionals. You must involve families in decision making from the outset and provide ongoing support to them to use the technology.

Involving Families to Make Decisions.   Initial discussions about assistive technology are opportunities to support families' preferences as well as understand and respect the influence of cultural and linguistic background in their decisions. Figure 13–4 sets out questions to guide your initial discussions with families. Notice how the questions reflect the communication strategies we discussed in chapter 9.

It is good practice to provide opportunities for families to see and use the technology being considered. Try to arrange for them to observe children using the device, and try out different devices with their children in the settings in which they will use the device (Judge, 2002). These opportunities can occur as part of the child's nondiscriminatory evaluation and transdisciplinary assessment (chapter 11). The partnership practice of empowering families, which is linked closely with the partnership principle of equality, provides families with a sound basis for making decisions about assistive technology and further solidifies trust.

Supporting Families to Use the Technology. Families need information, training, and other supports to enable them to use assistive devices at home. Families

FIGURE 13–4
Questions to Guide Discussions with Families About the Use of Assistive Technology

- Are you aware of what assistive technology is and how it might be able to assist your child?
- Are you and your child interested in using assistive technology at home?
- How might technology help your child be part of your family life? Community life?
- How, if at all, might technology improve your family's quality of life?
- What, if anything, about using technology concerns or frightens you?
- Is the use of assistive technology in harmony with your family values, culture, or lifestyle?
- Do you think that assistive technology will help your child to be more independent? Is it important to you that your child perform routine tasks independently?
- What do you think that assistive technology will do for your child? What benefits might you expect? How much time do you think it will take before you see changes?

- How do you think assistive technology will affect your home life? How do you think it will affect your other children? Other family members?
- What resources and supports would you need to use assistive technology in your home?
- What would be needed for you to use assistive technology outside your home?
- Do you think that using assistive technology outside of your home might make you or your child feel self-conscious or cause you or your child undue attention?
- What family members do you want consulted about technology decisions?
- How will use of technology add tasks to your family routine? What supports would help you to accomplish these tasks?
- What training might you need to use assistive technology? What supports would you need to devote time to the training? How do you prefer to learn new information?

Source: Adapted from Brotherson, M. J., Cook, C., & Parette, H. P. (1996). A home-centered approach to assistive technology provision for young children with disabilities. *Focus on Autism and Other Developmental Disabilities, 11*(2), 86–95. Copyright by Pro-Ed, Inc. Reprinted with permission. Parette, P., & McMahan, M. (2002). What should we expect of assistive technology? Being sensitive to family goals. *Teaching Exceptional Children, 35*(1), 56–61.

want information about the types of devices available, features of different devices, availability of vendor support, funding, and warranties (Parette, Brotherson, & Huer, 2000). They want that information in user-friendly formats in their native language, and they like demonstrations and hands-on learning (Parette, Brotherson, & Huer, 2000). Support groups made up of families who have experience with specific devices and families beginning to use the technology are helpful resources. Parents also need training, particularly in using, programming, and maintaining assistive devices (Parette, VanBiervliet, & Hourcade, 2000). Parents prefer that extended family members also receive training (Parette, Brotherson, & Huer, 2000).

Even when you make decisions with families and with careful consideration of their personal and cultural preferences, it is likely that changes within the student, family, or technology will require you to continue to be available to families. When families trust professionals to support them in decision making as well as in their use of technology, a unique opportunity exists to reinforce the partnership with families and to support student learning.

PROMOTING FRIENDSHIPS

As you learned in chapter 3, families want their children to have social relationships and are deeply concerned about the lack of friends or possible rejection in their children's lives. Recreational experiences and community environments are important to families. Fostering friendships and a sense of community for students and their families is yet another opportunity for parent-professional partnerships.

Enhancing Friendships

Parents clearly want their children to be accepted and valued members of a group, whether in home, school, or community life. One parent described what it would be like if her child were included at school:

> So I picture him sitting in a group at one of those tables with maybe four or five other children around him. And I picture them laughing and learning together. (Erwin & Soodak, 1995, p. 139)

It is not enough merely to place students with and without disabilities together and expect that everyone will feel included and make friends. How do educators work with families to create meaningful connections for students with disabilities within their classrooms, recreational activities, and neighborhoods? How can friendships develop and peers naturally advocate for each other when someone is not included?

One way would be to embrace the partnership principle of professional competence. By providing a quality education, continuing to learn, and setting high expectations, you will be able to explore with families the importance of friendship and discuss with them how friendships can best be achieved. Refer to chapter 3, particularly Figure 3–8, to review several strategies for being a partner with families to promote friendships among students. Then consider how you could use the following approaches and examples to promote friendships in your classroom:

- *Provide opportunities for friendships to develop.* Encourage and support student participation in activities that are fun, engaging, and accessible and use cooperative grouping during instruction to enable students to work together (Marr, 1997; Sapon-Shevin, 1999).
- *Teach about diversity.* Teach using an antibias curriculum, incorporate materials that are culturally diverse, and teach students how to respond to stereotyping and discrimination (Salend, 2001).
- *Teach about friendships.* Use children's literature to teach about friendships and embed the themes of friendship and social skills in your literacy or social studies curriculum (Falvey & Rosenberg, 1995; Forgan & Gonzalez-DeHass, 2004; Wilson, 1999).
- *Encourage students to participate in extracurricular activities.* Make information about after-school clubs and teams available to students and collaborate with other professionals to adapt activities to enhance participation (Salend, 2001).
- *Provide social skills instruction.* Ask students to role-play possible responses to social situations or listen to and interpret carefully constructed situations presented as "social stories" (Hartas & Donahue, 1997; Rogers & Myles, 2001).
- *Use peer support.* Prepare students to support each other as peer-tutors or help each other as "buddies" during noninstructional time (Copeland et al., 2002; Longwill & Kleinert, 1998; Turnbull, Pereira, & Blue-Banning, 2000).

Instructional practices that promote friendships are those that instill a culture of acceptance. Soodak and Erwin (2000) concluded that "when parents believed that they and their children were welcome and accepted members of the school and classroom community, effective parent-professional partnerships were possible" (p. 39). We encourage you to use the partnership practices associated with the principles of respect and commitment to facilitate students' friendships in school and in the community.

Fostering Parent Participation

Families also need to feel that they are an important part of the school community. Think about the families you have known or worked with in the past. Would they say they felt like valued members of their child's school community? Why or why not?

There are many ways to enhance families' participation and sense of community in their child's school. First, you might consider helping families connect with other families at school. As we discussed in chapter 10, the support that families find in one another is immeasurable. You might also review school policies or mission statements to see how building-level expectations contribute to families' perception of inclusion or exclusion. If you make membership a priority for children as well as their families, you are creating a powerful context for trust to flourish.

Providing meaningful opportunities for parents to attend and volunteer in school activities fosters partnerships with families and enhances their sense of community within the school. Are parents invited a couple of times each year for a performance, or are they encouraged to participate in a variety of meaningful activities throughout the school year?

By providing families with choices, professionals demonstrate their respect for families' preferences for participating in school activities and events. Specifically, professionals can create partnerships when families (1) attend school events, (2) contribute to classroom instruction, (3) contribute to other school tasks, (4) attend classes of their own, (5) participate in the parent-teacher organization, and (6) participate in family resource centers. Figure 13–5 lists examples of strategies that can be used within each of these options.

The choice to be involved must be made by the family. Parent involvement should be encouraged without causing embarrassment or shame. Families may differ from professionals in the value they place on involvement in school activities; cultural or language differences may make it difficult for families to be involved. Some families may lack the economic resources to participate.

What may be considered active participation by one group is viewed passive by another. For example, for some fami-

FIGURE 13–5
Opportunities for Parent Participation in School Activities

Opportunity for Participation	Illustrative Examples
Attending School Events	Attending an open house or back-to-school night
	Attending the school-sponsored book fair
	Attending season parties
	Attending school performances or concerts
	Attending school-run ball games
Contributing to Classroom Instruction	Developing instructional materials or equipment
	Tutoring individual students
	Participating in field trips
	Making a guest presentation in an area of expertise
Contributing to Other School Tasks	Supervising students in after-school activities
	Helping to organize school events, such as book sales or career days
Attending Classes	Attending evening classes for self-enhancement (for example, computer literacy, English as a second language, grant writing, cooking)
	Attending classes as a family
	Attending classes on child development
Participating in the Parent-Teacher Organization	Attending school- or districtwide meetings
	Participating on a committee (for example, the special education parent committee)
Participating in Family Resource Centers	Accessing information or resources
	Participating in parent support networks

lies, following the teachers' suggestions and making no demands is considered active participation; for others, involvement is conducting research on recommended practices in service delivery, asking questions, and constantly advocating for their child's needs in person and in writing. (Lynch & Hanson, 2004, p. 460)

Communicate with families to learn how much they want to be involved and how each family defines involvement. In addition, help them to access the resources they need to participate, such as transportation or child care. Figure 13–6 describes a literacy program developed for families who are homeless. As you read about this program, consider how the partnership practices of treating families with respect and affirming their strengths led to trusting relationships among the families and professionals.

A particular issue to consider when families of children with disabilities attend general school events is that they may not know many of the other families. Often, families come to know other families because their children are friends. You can welcome families into the school by increasing membership opportunities for them and their children. Consider the ideas presented earlier in this chapter as well as the strategies presented in chapter 3. Introduce the families of students with disabilities to other families, highlight their children's meaningful contributions to the class, and create opportunities for students and their families to make friends within the school and community. By using the practices associated with the partnership principle of commitment, you contribute to trust among families and professionals.

FIGURE 13–6
One Family at a Time

If you are a homeless parent, your child's education and even your own makes less of a difference to you than some basic necessities such as having a place to live, food on the table, and a reliable relationship with at least one adult who is involved with you and your child.

That's what Karen McGee learned in her role as reading coordinator of the Washoe County School District in Reno, Nevada. Naturally, Karen was concerned about the ability of district students to read.

She was especially worried about children whose families move frequently. These families are regarded as homeless because they do not have a single permanent address. They live in shelters or in trailer parks that rent on a week-by-week basis; they come to be known as "motel mothers."

It is often the case, Karen believed, that not only were her students deficient in their reading ability but so too were their parents. Their combined illiteracy, she was convinced, perpetuated a cycle of poverty. A solution, she hoped, would be to involve the students and their parents together in a reading program.

What she learned is that her aspiration was realistic but her strategies were ill-conceived. She had planned to provide transportation to school, reading instruction by teachers and volunteers, and guidance on how the parents could encourage their children to read at home. None of those strategies worked as planned.

Instead, parent involvement occurred and was sustained when Karen and her colleagues provided food; when they solicited parents' participation by advertising

an after-school program that was not focused on parent illiteracy (which stigmatizes parents) but was advertised and conducted as a "family fun night" in which reading instruction was only one of the activities; and when they established a personal relationship with the parents.

"We were dealing with survivors, and we had to admire their strengths," Karen concluded. To deal and to admire, Karen learned, resulted in a single bottom line: "Perhaps our most important discovery was that human relationships must precede academic pursuits."

Unless the district's staff could see that their challenge was not one of education but of seeing life through a different prism, then there would be no benefit to the children or their parents. These were, after all, parents who would say that they "can't distinguish between the living experience and the learning experience."

Accordingly, the district's staff faced a job of persuasion—persuading the parents to become involved in a school system. Given that they themselves were illiterate and on the economic margin of society, the staff's first task was to listen to the parents talk about "their living conditions, their children, their relationships (with other adults), and problems with the law." Then, and only then, did they offer something that was fun for both the parents and their children: reading strategies that kept the parents involved and that taught them to read and to guide their children to read.

It's really a matter of relationships, food, and fun. But mostly, relationships.

Source: Adapted from "One family at a time" by K. McGee, April 1996, *Educational Leadership*, pp. 30–33.

IMPLEMENTING POSITIVE BEHAVIOR SUPPORT

Partnerships with families that are well grounded in trust are particularly important to prevent situations in which students' behavior impedes their participation in school, at home, or in the community. In this section, we turn to the fifth opportunity for professionals to collaborate with families: partnerships to support students' positive behaviors.

Many factors have converged to place high priority on addressing problem behavior of students with and without disabilities. As you learned in chapter 6, two of the primary factors are (1) NCLB's emphasis on school safety and (2) IDEA's emphasis on positive behavior support. Fear of school violence has led to a dramatic rise in student expulsions and suspensions from school (Browne, Losen, & Wald, 2002), even as school-related violence has decreased (U.S. Department of Education and Department of Justice, 2004). School suspensions have risen nationally, from 1.7 million in 1974 to approximately 3.1 million in 1997 (U.S. Department of Education, 1999).

IDEA includes provisions on the role of schools in addressing the problem behavior of students with disabilities. IDEA protects students with disabilities from being disciplined for behavior that is a manifestation of their disability or is the direct result of the school's failure to implement the student's IEP (20 U.S.C. Sec. 1415 (k)(1)(E)), IDEA also requires that "in the case of a child whose behavior impedes the child's learning or that of others," the child's IEP team must consider the use of positive behavioral interventions and other strategies, and supports, to address that behavior (Sec. 1414 (d)(3)(B)(i)).

Positive behavior support is a problem-solving, data-based, and proactive orientation to maximize students' successful behavioral outcomes. Whereas the traditional behavior management approach views students as the problem, positive behavior support views systems, settings, and skill deficiencies as the problem. Thus, positive behavior support shifts the focus from "fixing" the individual to fixing the systems, settings, and skills.

The outcomes of positive behavior support are supportive systems, adaptive settings, and skill attainment enabling students to maximize their potential (Carr et al., 1999; Horner, Albin, Sprague, & Todd, 2000; Sugai, Horner, et al., 2000). Positive behavior support is an approach to maximize great expectations and affirm strengths while simultaneously responding to the needs of students and their families. One mother wrote of her family's experience in a home-school partnership to implement positive behavior support:

> The sweetest fruit of this successful partnership was that Samantha had gotten beyond violence. . . As Sam's life blossomed, our life together as a family began to open up as well. We purchased, for the first time in years, new furniture. We started to take Sam out with us. We went out to dinner, included her on shopping trips, and took her on a five-day vacation to California. It was fun to be with Sam. For the first time, we felt that we were becoming a family. (Fake, 2002, p 214)

Schoolwide Positive Behavior Support

Positive behavior support is designed to develop and maintain environments that honor and encourage positive and caring behaviors among all students. A schoolwide approach is emerging as an effective way to reach these goals (Turnbull et al., 2002). The National Center for Positive Behavioral Interventions and Supports (*www.pbis.org*) is taking the lead nationally in creating successful schoolwide models. Visit the Website to learn about the latest research.

As Figure 13–7 illustrates, schoolwide models generally offer three levels of positive behavior support: (1) universal support, (2) group support, and (3) individual support. The three levels provide a continuum of interventions that vary in the intensity of services, with far fewer students receiving the more intensive supports.

Level 1—Universal Support. Universal support provides clear expectations and positive feedback for all students across all classrooms and nonclassroom settings (for example, halls, cafeteria, playgrounds, buses). There are four key elements of universal support (Horner, 2000; Lewis & Sugai, 1999; Sugai, Horner, et al., 2000; Todd, Horner, Sugai, & Sprague, 1999):

- *Behavioral expectations are clearly defined.* These expectations are typically simple, positively framed, and few in number.
- *Behavioral expectations are taught.* Each of the behaviorally stated expectations must be explicitly taught so that students will know exactly what is expected of them.
- *Appropriate behaviors are acknowledged.* Schools need to build a positive culture in which students are positively affirmed at least four times as often as they are negatively sanctioned.
- *Program evaluations and adaptations are made by a positive behavior support team.* Schoolwide systems need guidance, and that guidance can best come from a collaborative team composed of administrators, teachers, parents, students, and community representatives.

Families are important members of the school's positive behavior support team in helping to develop, teach, and monitor schoolwide behavioral expectations. Parents

FIGURE 13–7

Schoolwide Framework for Positive Behavioral Support

Key Features	Universal Support	Group Support	Individual Support
Target group	All students	Some students	Fewer students
Settings	Classrooms and other school settings	Classrooms and other school settings	Classrooms, other school settings
			Multiple environments, including home and community
Data gathering	Interview school staff	Interview specific students	Functional behavior assessment of individual students in multiple settings
	Observations across school settings	Observe targeted behavior of specific students in school settings	
	Descriptive group statistics		Person-centered planning
			Interviews with student and family
Focus of interventions	Define, disseminate, and teach universal behavioral expectations	Implement self-management for targeted students	Provide individual support across multiple settings
			Develop collaborative partnerships with stake-holders to implement supports and leverage resources
Intensity	Limited	Moderate	Pervasive

are also important collaborators in following through at home with the school's expectations. In a national survey of more than 1,000 parents, one half reported that they would be "very comfortable" in helping the school decide its behavior and discipline policy, but only 20% have actually participated in this activity. Thus, many more families are available to assist in universal support than those who have actually participated (Farkas, Johnson, Duffett, Aulicino, & McHugh, 1999).

Community representatives can also serve on the school-based team, incorporating the same behavioral expectations in various community environments in which students participate—recreation programs, scouting, restaurants, religious organizations, and others. The more students receive consistent expectations across home, school, and community settings, the more likely they are to incorporate behavioral expectations across all aspects of their lives.

Universal support is meeting the needs of a substantial number of students who are decreasing their problem behavior and increasing successful behavioral outcomes

(Horner, 2000; Lewis & Sugai, 1999; Lewis, Sugai, & Colvin, 1998; Todd et al., 1999).

Schoolwide implementation of positive behavior support was explored in Central Middle School, an urban school in Kansas City, Kansas (Turnbull et al., 2002). Among the practices used to provide universal support to all students were the following:

- Codes of conduct were established that were consistent with specific shared behavioral expectations.
- Students were explicitly taught to use these behaviors.
- A referral/ticket system was implemented to reinforce desirable behavior.

After 2 years of implementing schoolwide supports, office discipline referrals decreased by 23%, time-outs went down by 30%, in-school suspensions were reduced by 12%, and 1- to 5-day suspensions decreased by 60%.

Level 2—Group Support. Group support moves beyond universal support to interventions that are implemented for a group of students in both classroom and nonclassroom settings. Level 2 support involves group and individual interventions, primarily at the classroom level, to students who are experiencing similar challenges in particular settings. Typically, educators gather information about the group through observations and interviews and then use the information to discern the patterns of behaviors within the group of students. For example, a teacher may ask: "When does my class have the most and least difficulty attending to schoolwork? Why do problems tend to occur during transitions?" Interventions are aimed at benefiting multiple students. For example, you may want to reteach a group of students how and when to meet specific universal expectations or you may rearrange the classroom to enhance communication or peer support.

How do family-professional partnerships enhance group support? Family members can contribute to the understanding of their child's behavior, offer suggestions for change, and help students work on generalizing the skills they are learning in school to community settings. The more that educators and families can agree on expectations, rewards, and other important elements of positive behavioral support, the more successful students will be in overcoming their behavioral challenges. Draw upon your partnership practices to enhance understanding of a student's behavior and promote a shared commitment to effect change.

Level 3—Individual Support. Educators provide individual support to students who can benefit from greater support than that provided through universal or group interventions. Individual support can occur solely in school or across multiple settings. Team decision making is at the core of individual support, and families are key collaborators.

Typically, the first step in providing individual support is for the student's IEP team and, if not already present, a specialist in positive behavioral support to conduct a functional behavioral assessment. A functional behavioral assessment usually involves collecting information through direct observation and through interviews with the student and others who spend significant amounts of time with the student. The purpose of the observations and interviews is to develop summary statements that describe specific behaviors, specific types of situations in which they occur, and the consequences that maintain the behaviors (Crone & Horner, 2003; O'Neill et al., 1997; Sugai, Lewis-Palmer, & Hagan-Burke, 2000). It is good practice to incorporate a functional behavioral assessment into the student's nondiscriminatory evaluation (see chapter 11) and IEP (see chapter 12).

Information drawn from the functional behavioral assessment becomes the foundation for planning individual-

ized interventions. There are numerous ways to support individual students, including changing conditions within the environment and teaching students effective ways to communicate or interact with others. Figure 13–8 sets out several suggestions for providing individual supports. Consider how they foster empowerment of students and families and demonstrate your respect for their individuality.

Families' involvement in providing individualized support to their children is pervasive. Research documents the importance of family-professional partnerships in carrying out a functional assessment and in developing, implementing, and monitoring a behavior intervention plan (e.g., Dunlap, Newton, Fox, Benito, & Vaughn, 2001; Peck-Peterson, Derby, Berg, & Horner, 2002). Family members have unique insights about the student, the situation, and the problem behavior. Just as parents know what brings out the best in their child, they also are likely to know what might trigger a problem behavior. In addition, many families already know ways to prevent problem behavior. This a perfect opportunity to use the partnership practices to affirm the families' strengths and foster their empowerment.

Family participation not only enriches understanding of the student's behavior, but also ensures that the selected interventions are consistent with the family's priorities, culture, values, and preferences. By honoring cultural diversity, you can achieve a fuller and clearer understanding of a student's behavior. For example, Chen and her colleagues described a situation in which a misunderstanding occurred when a teacher made an erroneous assumption about a student's refusal to eat lunch at school. Not until the teacher visited the child at home and observed the family eating sticky rice with their fingers did she realize that a change in school rules, not a behavior plan, was warranted (Chen, Downing, & Peckham-Hardin, 2002).

One meaningful way to involve families and community members in collecting information and decision making is by using person-centered planning (chapter 11). Person-centered planning is a tool for engaging families, community members, educators, and students in developing a vision plan to actively support students in achieving their dreams.

A review of more than 100 research articles published between 1985 and 1996 that investigated the behavioral outcomes of individuals with impeding behavior concluded (Carr et al., 1999):

- Positive behavior support was successful in achieving at least an 80% reduction in impeding behavior for approximately two thirds of the behavioral outcomes that were studied.

FIGURE 13–8

Tips: Individualized Support Strategies

- Alter the environment.
  - Accommodate students' environmental needs (e.g., attend to noises, light, and other sensory stimuli that may be distracting; provide quiet learning area).
  - Consider room arrangements and traffic patterns.
- Increase predictability and scheduling.
  - Use visual or written schedules to provide structure.
  - Prepare students in advance for changes and transitions.
- Increase choice making.
  - Encourage students to express their preferences and take them into account in planning instruction and environment supports.
  - Teach students specific skills in decision making and self-determination.
- Make curricular adaptations.
  - Adjust tasks and activities so that they are presented in formats that are consistent with students' strengths, needs, and preferences.

- Appreciate positive behaviors.
  - "Catch the student being good," and provide affirmation to students and families.
  - Teach student to use self-monitoring as a way to track their own success.
  - Maintain a 4-to-1 ratio of positive to negative statements.
  - Embed rewards within difficult activities.
- Teach replacement skills.
  - Teach students a different way to accomplish their purpose without needing to engage in the impeding behavior.
  - Teach students problem-solving skills so that they will know how to generate appropriate alternatives when they encounter problems.
- Change systems.
  - Work with other educators and families to develop state-of-the-art services and supports.
  - Work within your community to create inclusive opportunities in which students with impeding behavior can participate in a successful way.

■ The success of positive behavior support is substantially enhanced when a functional assessment is carried out as the basis for planning the intervention(s).

■ Positive behavior support is more effective when significant people (for example, educators and families) change their behavior as contrasted to when only the individual with impeding behavior changes.

■ Positive behavior support is more effective when the environment is reorganized.

■ Positive behavior support is more effective when it is carried out by significant people in the individual's life (for example, educators and families) than by people who do not have ongoing relationships with the individual (for example, researchers and clinicians).

■ Positive behavior support works just as effectively with individuals who have multiple disabilities as with individuals who have a single disability.

Many students benefit from individualized supports in school, at home, and in the community. However, for some children, change cannot occur unless the environment in which they live also changes. Conditions such as poverty, family health challenges, and impoverished neighborhoods play a powerful role in shaping students' behaviors. Supports and services for families impacted by social, economic, and health issues must be comprehen-

sive and coordinated. Integrated services provide an ideal context in which to embed individualized behavior support. Models are emerging that incorporate person-centered planning, positive behavior support, and coordinated supports and services to address issues impacting family life (for example, see Becker-Cottrill, McFarland, & Anderson, 2003).

Unfortunately, most schools still do not have comprehensive services. We hope you will use the partnership practices associated with the principle of advocacy to transform current discrete, segmented programs into ones that meet the holistic needs of students and families. In the final section of this chapter, you will learn about best practices in integrating services across numerous sectors. But first we will explore how professionals enhance students' learning and development within schools.

COORDINATING SERVICES WITHIN SCHOOLS

You have just learned about five opportunities for professionals to collaborate with families to support student learning and development. Professionals are also partners with each other, especially because students' IEP and IFSP teams must consist of various professionals who are usually from different disciplines. We now turn our attention to the critical role of partnerships among professionals in coordinating and implementing a student's IFSP or IEP.

Professional-professional partnerships are fundamentally no different than family-professional partnerships. Both are relationships in which individuals work together to reach a mutual goal. The partnership principles shape the interactions among team members. Whether professionals are providing services to students directly or indirectly, or whether they are coteaching or supporting students at different times or in different settings, professional partnerships need to be grounded in trust. Trust evolves as team members adhere to the principles of communication, respect, commitment, advocacy, equality, and professional competence. All members of the team (i.e., educators, therapists, paraprofessionals, and families) need to rely on each other and themselves.

Think for a moment how the partnership principles apply to your own professional partnerships. For example, have you achieved parity in decision making with other professionals with whom you have worked? Or have you experienced the inequity described by this professional:

> . . . One person on the team. . . saw his [the student's] issues as much more behavior than everyone else and she was basically consequencing behaviors instead of understanding the underlying mental illness. . . There was no one on that team who could convince her any differently. She just got very dug in and she felt she was the expert. . . So one of the things that makes a team function poorly is when somebody gets very territorial or very proprietary. (Blue-Banning, Summers, Frankland, Nelson, & Beegle, 2004, p. 177)

The key question in the implementation of an IFSP or IEP is how best to coordinate services to support the student's learning and development and to minimize the fragmentation or duplication of services and supports. According to teachers, service providers, and parents, the answer lies in effective professional-professional partnerships (Erwin & Rainforth, 1996; Giangreco, Prelock, Reid, Dennis, & Edelman, 2000; Snell & Janney, 2000a; Soodak & Erwin, 2000).

Researchers have identified practices that support professional partnerships and prevent fragmentation in service delivery (Friend & Cook, 2003; Giangreco et al., 2000; Snell & Janney, 2000b; Thousand, Villa, & Nevin, 2002). Three critical strategies for maintaining effective partnerships include (1) ensuring adequate time for planning, (2) regularly assessing team roles, responsibilities, and functioning, and (3) providing services to students in the classroom and other natural contexts.

Ensure Adequate Planning Time

Professionals need face-to-face communication to work within a common framework to benefit the student. However, one often-cited challenge to professional collaboration is finding sufficient time to meet (Friend, Reising, & Cook, 1993; Walther-Thomas, 1997). Because related service personnel may support students in more than one class or divide their time across schools, they have few opportunities for a common meeting time. Although it is critical for all team members to meet regularly, some teachers find it useful to meet individually with related service providers (Snell & Janney, 2000a). An alternative is for service providers to schedule themselves for longer blocks of time within a particular school to allow greater flexibility in their scheduling (Rainforth & York-Barr, 1997). This is difficult to do when therapists' schedules are developed after the school year begins. Thus, many administrators start the scheduling process several months before the start of a new school year to ensure that there is adequate planning time between professionals from various disciplines. Another way to create time to meet is to have assigned planning times overlap. Effective implementation of the student's IEP cannot occur unless everyone working with the student is on the same page. You may find it necessary to advocate for collaborative planning time in your school.

Assess Team Roles, Responsibilities, and Functioning

Team members bring different skills and knowledge to the partnership. Effective teams recognize these unique contributions and use them to benefit students. They are not limited by rigid disciplinary boundaries imposed within an "expert" model of service delivery. When team members trust each other, they can share their expertise and learn from each other. A general educator spoke of the mutual benefits of shared expertise:

> I need those people [team members] because they have the special education background that I don't have, to say those are his weak areas and these are the things we need to be doing for him. So I think it's good that they're there to balance me out; but actually, not to sound egotistical, I also think it's probably good that I'm here from the other point of view: To balance them out too . . . I think as a team we work really well. (Snell & Janney, 2000b, p. 486)

Paraprofessionals frequently play an important role in the education of students with disabilities. It is critical to consider how they will participate in implementing instruction and in communicating with other team members, including families. In a review of research involving paraprofessional support, Giangreco and Doyle (2002) concluded that the special education field may be relying too heavily on paraprofessionals in special education without providing them with sufficient training or a clear understanding of how they may best support students. Professionals need to achieve a balance between the use of paraprofessional support and the support of teachers, service providers, peers, and others. Collaborative teaming and effective communication is needed to implement each student's unique educational plan.

Provide Services Within the Classroom and Other Naturally Occurring Activities and Contexts

In chapter 3, we noted that providing services in naturally occurring contexts gives the students opportunities to participate in inclusive recreational activities. Providing related services within the context of the student's class, school, and home routines also enhances service integration and professional-professional partnerships. When related service providers work alongside teachers, professionals can share instructional decision making, model practices that can be used at other times, and modify instruction to address real-life situations (Giangreco et al., 2000; Rainforth & York-Barr, 1997).

In situations where services are poorly coordinated, teachers, parents, and students are left with the task of making sense of a fragmented educational program. One teacher noted how poor coordination and lack of communication affected a student in the general education class:

> By the end of the day, everybody I had talked to had said, "Here's something you need to be doing. Be sure you're doing this." And I had just gotten really frustrated and I thought: But he's just a little boy, when is he ever going to be with other kids? (Snell & Janney, 2000b, p. 484)

Parents suffer when coordination among teachers and service providers is poor or nonexistent. Some parents of young children with disabilities have had to assume roles that should have been carried out by professionals, largely due to poor coordination and the absence of trust (Soodak & Erwin, 2000). These roles included sharing information among teachers, therapists, and other team members to ensure consistency in their child's education, and arranging for specialized equipment and consultants. Where there is a lack of trust and poor coordination of services, parents may feel obliged to monitor their child's education to make sure it complies with the IEP. Professionals must honor their responsibilities and develop trusting partnerships with each other and with parents.

All service providers within and across programs need to work together in partnerships characterized by a commitment to students and families and trust in each other. We now turn our attention to those partnerships that extend beyond the school walls.

INTEGRATING SCHOOL AND COMMUNITY SERVICES

Throughout this book we have emphasized the importance of partnerships among individuals—primarily families and school professionals. You have just learned about the importance of professional-professional partnerships in implementing students' individualized programs. Partnerships also occur at the systems level when agencies providing different types of services to children and their families work together to accomplish mutual goals.

Schools and communities need to form partnerships for two reasons. First, education is necessarily a community responsibility. With an increasing number of children entering school with complex challenges and risks (Federal Interagency Forum on Child and Family Statistics, 2000) and children with disabilities being disproportionately exposed to conditions such as poverty and neglect (Fujiura & Yamaki, 2000; Sullivan & Knutson, 2000), it has become ineffective for schools to work alone in meeting the needs of students and their families.

Second, it is unreasonable to require family members to spend the often inordinate amount of time it takes to identify and access services within a fragmented system. Figure 13–9 describes how the quality of interagency partnerships can affect a family's experiences in accessing and benefiting from services. Consider how the family's trust in professionals was affected by the quality of the school-community partnerships.

Service integration is emerging as an alternative approach that provides comprehensive, seamless support for children and their families. The general education literature over the last decade has described various models of service integration. Two of the most frequently used terms are *full-service schools* and *community schools*. Many other terms are also used, including interprofessional collaboration, coordinated services, community-linked services, and school-linked services (Adelman & Taylor, 1997; Blank, Melaville, & Shah, 2003; Briar-Lawson, Lawson, Collier, & Joseph, 1997; Calfee, Wittwer, & Meredith, 1998; Coltoff, 1998; Dryfoos, 1998; MacKenzie & Rogers, 1997; Maguire, 2000; Raham, 1998). These approaches are substantial improvements over the typical situation of having services spread throughout the entire

FIGURE 13–9

Advocating for Systems Change: Taking Responsibility for Service Integration

Monica and Mark, both high school teachers, had dreamed of becoming parents for a long time when Lindsey joined their family. Lindsey was about 3 years old when Monica and Mark acknowledged her slow development, but her pediatrician comforted their fears by telling them that children develop at many different rates.

Monica and Mark enrolled Lindsey in a neighborhood child-care center when she was 4 so she could have more opportunities to learn to talk and play with friends. They asked the child-care center director what could be done to help her development. The director at the child-care center was very supportive, but she wasn't quite sure who should be contacted to start an evaluation. Monica and Mark finally found someone at the school system to ask for an evaluation. When the evaluation finally did happen, the team observed Lindsey for 40 minutes and concluded that she would be fine if given more time to adjust.

But Monica and Mark did worry. Lindsey couldn't answer a simple question; she spoke only a few words and couldn't follow simple directions. Lindsey's preschool teacher really liked Lindsey but felt that a speech and language therapist should be the one responsible for increasing her language. Monica and Mark felt their pleas for help were ignored; they felt alone and fearful of the future.

In the spring, Monica and Mark were finally able to write an IEP with the team. Mark and Monica wanted Lindsey to continue at the child-care center the following fall so that she could build on the friendships she had started. The preschool teacher wanted to work with Lindsey, but working with children with special needs, like Lindsey, wasn't even a part of her teacher education program. Monica sensed that asking for Lindsey to stay at the child-care center was like asking for the moon. The district did not have a history of placing children with special needs in community child-care programs. An administrator said that the district couldn't be expected to pay for Lindsey's preschool program in the community when there was a program for children with special needs in the school district.

Monica and Mark asked her about Head Start, a program that a friend of Lindsey's attended and was close to home. Monica remembers the director of special education telling her in amazement, "Don't you know that is a totally different program?" In the end, the team recommended reluctantly that Lindsey continue at the child-care center in the pre-kindergarten classroom with an early childhood special education consultant visiting with the teacher once a week. Mark and Monica would pay for the tuition at the center. Cost was an issue for them, but it was more important to help Lindsey maintain friendships. The team did not agree on the need for a paraprofessional at the child-care center. The team gave them some worksheets of activities and ideas for language development during the summer. Monica and Mark felt this was less than the level of support Lindsey needed to be successful, but reluctantly accepted the school's plan. They had no idea the amount of time and energy it takes parents to build partnerships with professionals and to be valued members of the team.

How might collaboration within the child-care program have changed the outcomes for Monica, Mark, and Lindsey? How would integrated delivery of services have improved their experiences? What could you do to advocate for change so that other families have access to the supports and services their children need?

community and requiring families to access and coordinate services on their own.

Full-service or community schools seek to provide quality education (for example, school-based management, individualized instruction, and team teaching). They link their students and staff to a vast array of other services provided by the school (for example, comprehensive health education and social skills training) and by community agencies within a school-based location (for example, immunizations, social services, and substance abuse treatment) (Calfee et al., 1998; Dryfoos, 2004; Raham, 1998).

Full-service or community schools have a single point of delivery, meet the holistic needs of the students within the context of their families, and provide whatever services are needed to enhance a child's success in school and in the community (Calfee et al., 1998; Dryfoos 2004). The schools and agencies providing integrated services do not merge; instead, they have mutually increased collaboration and coordination.

Community or full-service schools are growing throughout the United States (Blank et al., 2003). Although each school develops in response to the needs and preferences of its community, each strives to be a one-stop center for all education and community services. For example, one full-service or community school located in rural Vermont serves over 400 students, with more than half of them living in poverty (Maguire, 2000). In addition to a solid curriculum and high instructional expectations, multiple services include after-school programs, early childhood programs, health and wellness (e.g., medical care, healthy snack cart), parental involvement, and literacy. There are two mentoring programs. One provides credit to high school students for spending quality time with a student and the other involves local business owners mentoring a student every week.

Figure 13–10 includes a service matrix for another comprehensive, full-service school. Carefully review all of the different services reflected in this matrix. Most of the 24 services are located on one of the four school campuses. Additionally, some services are offered at a community center, a student's home, a child-care center, or a family center linked to the school. Students, their families, and other community members are able to use these services. This full-service school remains open 7 days a week, with many evening hours.

The emerging research on the effectiveness of community schools is quite promising. All the participants in a study examining 49 community school programs reported positive results on at least one outcome, including academic achievement, attendance, student behavior, or family well-being (Dryfoos, 2004). A report of an ERIC/OSEP special project concluded that full-service schools increase the use of services for children and their families and positively affect developmental outcomes for students living in high-risk situations (ERIC/OSEP Topical Brief, 2002).

What can teachers and other professionals do to make integrated services available to all students and their families? School-community partnerships are based on the same principles that promote trust within parent-professional and professional-professional partnerships.

First, there needs to be clear, honest communication. One representative from a local interagency coordinating council described the role of communication in the process of integrating services:

> It is not an easy process if you haven't started talking. So any disagreements or discussions that evolved were good. Because they needed to happen. . . The different people who were involved needed to be involved, needed the parents to hear their perspectives, and we needed the different kinds of agencies serving children. And we needed to all talk about these issues and open some doors. (Fowler, Donegan, Lueke, Hadden, & Phillips, 2000, p. 47)

Effective school-community partnerships require all individuals to communicate openly and to learn about each other's needs and preferences. Teachers and other professionals may be called upon to engage in conflict resolution when differences in vision and practice across agencies become stumbling blocks to collaboration (Park & Turnbull, 2003).

Professional competence is also important in establishing school-community partnerships. Teachers need to know and understand the community in which they work and the families of the students they teach (Blank, 2004; Blank et al., 2003; Park & Turnbull, 2003). In addition, teachers must be familiar with the services, supports, regulations, and funding available to families. At the very least, they need to know where to refer families to access information.

Full-service and community schools provide unique opportunities to partner with service providers throughout the community. The partnership principles of respect and equality should guide the development of these new relationships. Although locating integrated services on school grounds enables collaboration among the various professionals (ERIC/OSEP Topical Brief, 2002), issues of role clarification, space, and confidentiality can arise (Dryfoos, 1996). Be particularly mindful of power and equity as you move toward collaborative relationships with professionals in agencies that have a history of working independently.

Finally, teachers and other professionals need to embrace the practices associated with the principle of advocacy. School-community partnerships are emerging in response to a need to support families and enhance student learning and development. Keep your conscience primed to make sure the services and supports match the needs and preferences of the families, students, and the community. Broaden your alliances when different services or partnerships are warranted. Perhaps most important, advocate for systems change so that integrated rather than discrete services are provided to the families and students in your school.

Whether working with individuals from different disciplines within the same school, or across different agencies, working in partnership to implement the child's individualized education can bring positive and meaningful outcomes for everyone involved, particularly families.

SUMMARY

Parent-professional partnerships are essential for providing an effective individualized education to students with exceptionalities. First, students' learning extends

FIGURE 13-10
Service Matrix for a Real Full-Service School

Service	Description/Clientele	Location/Hours	Funding Sources
Adult education	Basic education and remediation for those adults aged 161 Undergraduate and graduate coursework	Middle School, Monday and Thursday, 5–8 PM College and enrichment classes by semester	• Adult Learning Center • Community schools • Community college • State university
Case work	Protective services, Project Vision Referrals for delinquency, foster care, developmental and economic services, alcohol/drug abuse, mental health, counseling, home visits	Middle School, weekdays	• State Department of Children and Families (DCF)
Child care	Free or reduced, subsidized child care for children aged 3 months to 12 years (some restrictions apply)	Appointments taken for location convenient to parent	• Children's Services
Community use of school facilities	Civic and parent groups apply for permission Available to all, free	Primary, Intermediate, and Middle Schools	• County School Board
Economic services	AFDC, Medicaid, food stamps: intake, screening, application, review Referrals to other community resources	Middle School, Monday through Friday, 8 AM–5 PM Appointments preferred; walk-ins accepted	• DCF
Educational opportunity center	Career options counseling and financial aid for students aged 191	Community Center, Tuesdays, 1–4 PM	• Community college
First call for help	Toll-free community resource information hotline	Available district-wide	• Center for Community Mental Health • United Way • Retired senior volunteers
Graduation enhancement program	Technology-based early intervention to promote student learning	Intermediate and Middle Schools	• County School Board
Health services	RN and psychologist: prevention, early detection, early intervention, and community referrals Mobile health unit Emergency food and clothing Affordable health insurance for school-age children	Intermediate and Middle Schools, Monday through Friday, school hours	• Supplemental School Health Grant: DCF and State Department of Education • Sacred Heart Hospital • Community resources • Healthy Kids Corp.

Service	Description/Clientele	Location/Hours	Funding Sources
Healthy kids	Affordable health insurance for children ages 3 to 19	Available district-wide Enrollment by toll-free number	• State legislature • Healthy Kids Corp. • County School Board • County commissioners • Blue Cross/Blue Shield Health Options
Home visitor high-risk infant program	Home visits by social worker for at-risk infants Training in parenting skills, immunizations, etc.	South end of county	• DCF
Job services	Employment service for job training and placement with computer access to regional job listings	Middle School, Monday through Friday, 8 AM–5 PM	• DCF • Private Industry Council (PIC) • Job Training Partnership Act
Juvenile Alternative Services Program (JASP)	Meaningful sanctions and services for certain juvenile offenders, and their families, designed to divert from judicial processing and to reduce incidence of law violations	Intermediate and Middle Schools	• DCF
Latchkey	State-licensed after-school programs until 6 PM school days and some holidays Summer camp program, 7:30 AM–6:30 PM	Primary, Intermediate, and Middle Schools Campers picked up and returned to Intermediate School	• Community schools • Parent tuition • Title XX funding for qualified families
Mental health counseling	Counseling for students and families Exceptional student education specialist Full-time therapist for emotionally or severely emotionally handicapped	Primary, Intermediate, and Middle Schools	• Center for Community Mental Health • Medicaid • Private Insurance
Parent involvement center	Educational and counseling materials available for checkout by parents for use with students at home	Primary, Intermediate, and Middle Schools	• Project Vision • National Foundation for the Improvement of Education (NFIE) • Junior League • Community resources • Parent-teacher association (PTA) • Parent advisory boards
Parent workshops	Hosted periodically during the school year for all interested persons	Primary, Intermediate, and Middle Schools	• Project Vision • Community resources • PTA • Parent advisory boards

FIGURE 13–10
(Continued)

Service	Description/Clientele	Location/Hours	Funding Sources
Prekindergarten	Head Start or early intervention programs for 4-year-olds Placement on space-available basis Some restrictions	Intermediate school	• Federal and state funding in collaboration with County School Board
Private Industry Council (PIC)	Employability skills for middle school, students age 16, and adults	Middle School	• PIC
Protective services	On-site investigator for abuse or neglect complaints through State Protective Services System's Abuse Registry	Middle School	• DCF
Research	Ongoing research activity supervised by state university	Primary, Intermediate, and Middle Schools	• Full-service schools • State university
Sheriff's department	On-site duty available for assistance with law enforcement issues, education, and prevention activities	Primary, Intermediate, and Middle Schools	• County Sheriff's Department • Full-service schools
Volunteers	Volunteers act as tutors, teacher helpers, mentors, etc.	Primary, Intermediate, and Middle Schools	• Retired senior volunteers • County School Board • Community Organizations
Women, infants, and children program	Offers nutrition counseling and supplemental food for prenatal and postnatal care and for children from birth to 5 years	Community Center, 1st Wednesday and 2nd Friday each month, 9 AM–3 PM	• PIC • Federal funding through County Public Health Unit

Source: From *Building a Full-Service School: A Step-by-Step Guide* (pp. 18–20), by C. Calfee, F. Wittwer, & M. Meredith, 1998, San Francisco: Jossey-Bass.

well beyond the 6-hour school day. Second, students and their families benefit when parents are meaningfully involved in their child's education in school, at home, and in the community. Consider the following points as you identify opportunities to partner with families to support the outcomes of student learning and development:

■ Families will have different preferences for the manner and extent of their involvement.

■ Effective communication with families is key to sharing priorities, goals, and expectations for student learning and development. Communicate often and honestly, and in ways that families consider useful.

■ Homework assignments and grading practices should be tailored to meet the needs of individual students and their families.

■ Shared decision making ensures that the assistive technology devices and other methods used to support achievement of a student's IEP goals are consistent with the family's culture and lifestyle.

■ Professionals can support student and family membership in the school and community.

■ When implemented systematically and in collaboration with families, positive behavior support can result in successful outcomes for students and their families.

■ Integrated services within schools and across service delivery systems ensure that supports and services comprehensively and holistically address student and family needs.

A shared commitment to student learning will enable you to work effectively with families to support their child's learning and development. As Figure 13–11 illustrates, the partnership practices will help you to choose actions that instill and maintain trust with the families.

REFLECTING ON THE VIGNETTE

1. What are the barriers to collaboration between each of the four families and the professionals who are their partners?
2. What suggestions do you have for overcoming those barriers?
3. What are the most effective strategies the families and their professional partners have used (based on reading the prologue and the preceding 12 chapters) to promote collaboration?

ENHANCING YOUR SELF-AWARENESS

Understanding the assumptions, skills, and knowledge you have about your own teaching and learning will help you form partnerships with families. How would you describe your learning experiences in and outside of school? As a teacher (or teacher-in-training), how comfortable are you in meeting the individual needs and preferences of children in your class? How do your own experiences help you find meaningful ways to involve families in their children's learning?

Homework collaboration

As a student, how do you complete academic assignments outside of school? What person or environmental supports do you need? How do you access help? Can you think of a time when you were particularly moved by the support you received from family members in completing schoolwork? Was there a time when an assignment added stress to your family life? What might have been done differently to change this situation?

Friendships and membership

Reflecting on your own school experiences, did you always consider yourself to be a valued member of the class? What did teachers do to help your relationships with other students? In this chapter, we addressed the importance of family membership. To what extent did your family consider themselves to be members of the school and community? What contributed to their feelings of membership?

Professional-professional partnership

Think back to a time when you worked collaboratively with others to accomplish a difficult task. Did you have sufficient opportunities to communicate with other individuals? Were the perspectives of all team members heard and respected? Was there equity among team members in decision making and in accountability? Did each team member possess the interpersonal skills and professional knowledge needed to participate? Were all team members available and accessible?

RESOURCES

1. National Parent Teacher Association (PTA)
   330 N. Wabash Avenue
   Suite 2100
   Chicago, IL 60611
   800-307-4PTA (4782)
   http://www.pta.org

   The PTA has excellent materials on general topics related to education, parenting, and special education. The National Standards for Parent/Family Involvement, developed in collaboration with Dr. Joyce Epstein, are available on the National PTA Website.

2. Family Center on Technology and Disability (FCTD)
   Academy for Educational Development (AED)
   1825 Connecticut Avenue, NW — 7th Floor
   Washington, DC 20009-5721
   202-884-8068
   http://www.fctd.info

   The Family Center offers a range of information and services on the subject of assistive technology to organizations and programs that work with families of children and youth with disabilities.

3. Positive Behavioral Interventions and Support Technical Assistance Center
   Behavioral Research and Training
   5262 University of Oregon
   Eugene, OR 97403-5262
   541-346-2505
   http://www.pbis.org

   The Technical Assistance Center on Positive Behavioral Interventions and Supports (PBIS) provides schools with information and assistance for identifying, adapting, and sustaining effective schoolwide disciplinary practices.

FIGURE 13–11

Creating Partnerships Through Trust Building: Selected Actions Leading to Trust and Distrust in Supporting Students'
Learning and Development

Partnership Principles and Practices	Issues	Actions Leading to Distrust	Actions Leading to Trust
Communication: Listen.	Family members share with you that they feel very embarrassed when they are in public and their child with problem behavior goes up to strangers and makes inappropriate remarks.	Tell the family that you are not embarrassed, and they should not be either.	Listen empathetically to what they are saying and ask what they think would be helpful in becoming more comfortable; ask if they have ever had the opportunity to talk with other families who face similar situations.
Respect: Honor cultural diversity.	A family who has been contacted to be involved in integrated services will not answer the door when someone makes a home visit, fearing loss of family privacy.	Decide that the family has "lost its chance" and drop them from a list of potential participants.	Arrange for someone from the family members' own cultural group to make contact with them, and recognize that building a trusting relationship may take significant time and effort.
Professional Competence: Provide a quality education.	A mother's partner (who is gay) is interested in helping the student in your class with homework, but she doesn't know the best way to go about it.	Ignore the partner because of your own values related to gay lifestyles.	Set up a dialogue journal with homework suggestions.
Equality: Foster empowerment.	The parent of one of your students has a chronic mental illness, and you are hesitant to include her as a classroom volunteer.	You ask the student if he thinks his mother is up to coming to school.	You call the mother, invite her perspectives on the kinds of school activities that would be especially meaningful to her, and make arrangements to respond to her priorities.
Commitment: Be sensitive to emotional needs.	Parents refuse to allow their teenager to go out during evenings or weekends because they are afraid of the impeding behavior that might occur.	Consider out-of-school issues to be outside the realm of your professional responsibility.	Facilitate friendships at school with peers, support the parents in using positive behavioral support with the student, and encourage them to include the student in evening and weekend classes.
Advocacy: Prevent problems.	Parents of a student with AD/HD are worried about the problems their child is having during after-school hours when they both are working and there is no one to provide child care.	Tell them that you strongly encourage them to take action before there is a serious problem with neighbors or others who live close by.	Provide them with information on the comprehensive school-linked services program and ask if they would like to receive information on community resources for after-school child care.

4. Coalition for Community Schools
   c/o Institute for Educational Leadership
   1001 Connecticut Avenue, NW, Suite 310
   Washington, DC 20036
   202-822-8405 X156
   http://www.communityschool.org

The Coalition advocates for community schools as the vehicle for strengthening schools, families, and communities so that together they can improve student learning.

Epilogue

THE SHARED NARRATIVES AND COMMON THEMES

There are common themes in the lives of Kenny Berg, Joesian Cortes, Nicky Doleman, Sean Holley, their families, and the professionals who have become their trusted partners.

Our disability is a family affair

Norma Cortes, Joesian's mother, sought help from United We Stand. There, she found Lourdes Rivera-Putz, mother of six (three of whom have disabilities); Martha Viscarrondo, mother of eight (one of whom has a disability); and Lori Rosenfeld (sister of a woman with a disability). With their help, Norma entered into mediation with Joesian's school administrators. At mediation, she met Emily Rodriguez, assistant principal of Joesian's school, and, as Lourdes describes it, "a Christian Latina, like Martha." Family, faith, ethnicity, and language all come together. Four strands link these people, creating a single unit that functions like a family, taking care of its members as though they were blood kin.

Similarly, the Doleman family reconstituted itself after Nicky was discharged from her first trip to the hospital. The initial act of reconstitution was the court's order designating Vera as Nicky's adoptive mother (and recognizing that she also is Nicky's biological grandmother). The second was the move that Vera's parents made from their small hometown near Greenville, Mississippi, to Vera's and Nicky's hometown of Lawrence, Kansas. The third was Charolette's successful re-entry into a normal life: job, education, and nurturing of Nicky. The fourth and final act of reconstitution was the enmeshment of all of the Dolemans into a single unit that cares for each other while especially centered on Nicky.

So it has been, too, with the Bergs and the Holleys. Not a single member of their family is untouched by disability.

The mobile serves its symbolic purpose: family members are linked to each other and inevitably are affected by and influence each other.

We are all survivors

No one outside his blood-related family has been more important to Kenny Berg than Carole Gothelf. She hired Kenny's mother, Clara; she befriended Kenny and became his and the family's advocate; she became his teacher and then the principal of his school. When asked, "What makes you so driven by justice?" she answers without hesitation: "We are all survivors." "Why," one asks her, "do you say that?" She answers: "When I was growing up in Brooklyn in the 1950s, many of my family's friends and neighbors had tattoos on their arms." These were no ordinary tattoos; indeed, they were unique. They were reserved for Jews (and political prisoners and people with disabilities) who had been held captive during World War II by the Nazis.

The tattoo of the Nazi concentration camps is a stigma, the negative connotation branded onto a person. So, too, is the person's disability. Both call out for justice. Carole responded in a just way to the Bergs, people of her faith. Ask Jake about justice, and he will tell you how he and his family fled from their native Poland, then to Russia, and then to France, all to avoid the pogroms. Ask Clara, and she will say that her family fled Europe and found safety in Montevideo, Uruguay. They know about justice. None of this is meant to minimize the enormity of the Holocaust by comparing it to the challenges facing people with disabilities. There is a huge difference in the scale and in the behavior of some and the suffering of others. The fact remains, however, that tattoos stigmatize, even as disability sometimes does, too. To survive the Holocaust is one matter, a life-and-death one. To survive and then prevail in service-delivery systems is quite another.

Lourdes and Norma also know about the stigma of place, language, ethnicity, and disability. The residual prejudice against people from Puerto Rico may not have played a role in Joesian's education, but it may have. The fact that Norma, his mother, does not speak English may have affected her ability to advocate for him until United We Stand took up her and Joesian's cause. The fact that Joesian does indeed have a slight speech-language impairment may have given many of his teachers a reason to overlook his need to learn to read rather than to attend to that need. In the Cortes family, "may have" plays a powerful role; the subtlety with which some people can discriminate on account of disability may have masked their intent to discriminate and, for a long time, the effects of their discrimination.

In her own way, Leia Holley, Sean's mother, also knows about the stigma of disability, and of the necessity for finding a person such as Tierney Thompson, Sean's teacher, whose instinct told her that she must never give up on Sean or Leia, no matter how hard the struggle.

Finally, there is Nicky's struggle simply to remain alive and the struggle of her family, physicians, and teachers to provide life-sustaining care and to add quality to her life.

We are always running

When Jake and Clara Berg and their families' lives were threatened, they ran away and sought life and toleration elsewhere. As a boy, Kenny needed help that was not available locally, so they placed him far away, in Boston, yet visited every weekend. As he aged out of school, they fled toward the one element that comforted and strengthened Kenny, the horses and Adriance Farm. Their origins and destinations were international and interstate.

When Norma Cortes became desperate, she ran from her plight to United We Stand. Her origins and destination were strictly intraborough: She never had to leave Brooklyn, once she came there from Puerto Rico.

When Vera Doleman's daughter Charolette realized, at last, that she must leave the father of her children, Nicky and Tavian, she fled into the arms of her mother and grandparents, who undertook their own journey from Mississippi to Kansas.

When Leia and Jamie Holley had a chance to locate in a school district of their choice, they gathered up Sean and JP and avoided a school district that they regarded as mediocre in preference for one that proved to be superior in every way.

Everyone flees from something and to something else. The challenge is to create the destination from which flight is unimaginable. That is a challenge that educators can meet if they understand about mobiles and families, about origins and destinations, about partnerships, and about trust.

We are the invisible "others"

For 2 years, Leia Holley fought to secure an appropriate education and a safe environment for her son Sean. Her fight was not against people but against a system that was inflexible and arguably indifferent to his needs. The system could have hired the paraprofessionals Sean's teacher needed, it could have included Sean in more of the general education program, and it could have communicated better with Leia. There were many "could haves" in the Holleys' lives.

So, too, the many teachers and administrators who disregarded the obvious fact that Joesian was not reading well could have referred him for an expert evaluation, could have offered him a different curriculum, and could have secured him a place in the Manhattan trade school operated by the Board of Education. But Joesian has been a victim of indifference. Many could have done something, but chose to do nothing.

Similarly, indifferent administrators at the New York City Board of Education refused to arrange for transportation for Kenny. Carole Gothelf, within a single day, made possible what others declined to create.

Each of these students, their families, and their close partners have been the victims of indifference. Many could have done something, but few chose to do anything. Why?

There is an indifference to the individual and a focus on the mass, the large numbers of students with disabilities. Or so it is said by the indifferent. Social utilitarianism, the greatest good for the greatest number, is their justification.

But what of individual utilitarianism, the greatest good for just one? To that, there is indifference. It is not a matter of resources, as Carole Gothelf, Emily Rodriguez, and Tierney Thompson proved. It is a matter of huge indifference, of looking the other way, of not seeing "the others."

Indifference is not universal; the many who chose to look away have their counterparts in the few who chose not to look away. Count Carole Gothelf, Beth Mount, and Arnie Mejia, Kenny's job coach, and the hired help at Adriance Farm are among those who do not look away. Include the women who run United We Stand of New York, the Raintree Montessori School and Woodlawn Elementary School staff in Lawrence, and Tierney Thompson and her dozen colleagues at Bonner Springs Elementary School among those who keep their eyes open and their attitudes determined.

We do fit and belong

Everyone fits somewhere. One of Kenny Berg's ideal fits—the environment that suits him beyond all others—is the water; the other, of course, is Adriance Farm. In the water, he finds perfect freedom. Just as he anchors himself to the ground when he gropes his way from place to place at the farm, so he anchors himself to the water, floating on its surface in perfect harmony with that element of nature. At the farm, in another environment nature, the animals do not know he is deaf and blind, and the farmhands do not care.

Joesian Cortes's perfect fit seems to be with his uncle, the plumber, and at the trade school where he is learning to be a plumber. Nicky Doleman's fit is in the environments where competence combines with compassion, in the preschools operated at the University of Kansas, in the Raintree Montessori School, and in Woodlawn Elementary School. Sean Holley's ideal fit is within the circle of his friends; if he does hurt himself or others, there is forgiveness.

Each family has a place where the fit between it and the world is good. Clara and Jake fit with Carole; Norma fits with Lourdes, Martha, and Lori at United We Stand; Vera fits, quite naturally, with her parents, sisters, and brothers, and Leia fits with Tierney and her colleagues.

A fit is not always with a natural environment. More often, it is with one or more people. Call the first fit a matter of ergonomics: designing the built or natural environment to the person. Call the second a partnership: designing a relationship in which each person can trust the other.

We have our natural and cultivated supports

A good partnership is similar to a product of nature. Like water, it can support you or drown you, as these families' lives show. Like the eggs that Kenny gathers from the chickens at Adriance Farm, however, the partnership is fragile; press too hard, and it breaks.

Leia Holley and Tierney Thompson know that; Leia pressed too hard on Tierney, and their partnership broke. That they reconstructed it is like an act of nature: so long as the relationship exists, so long as the chicken lives, there can be new eggs.

Clara Berg, on the other hand, found her own hard-boiled egg: Carole Gothelf had a shell that might crack, but her dedication to Kenny, Clara, and Jake remained intact.

In the Cortes family, Joesian's uncle trains him in the plumbing trade. Norma's daughter Tatiana translates for her when they attend Joesian's IEP conferences. By contrast, United We Stand and Emily Rodriguez are cultivated supports, deliberate partners.

In the Doleman family, the supports are the most natural of all. Grandmother and grandfather and sisters and brothers all rallied to the single cause of ensuring that Nicky and Tavion would have a safe, protecting, and loving home. At Raintree Montessori School, the cultivated support from teacher Pam Shanks and co-principal Illeana McReynolds undergirded the Doleman family.

We know about horrific catalysts and value the empathetic imagination

No one event always transforms a person's or family's life, but sometimes a single horrific event can do just that. Consider the emphasis that Clara and Jake Berg and Carole Gothelf ascribe to the Holocaust: It daily reminds them of the necessity for social justice. Consider, too, the consequences of abuse: It galvanizes Nicky's family in ways no other event could have.

No single event seems to have played such a fateful role in Norma Cortes's life; Joesian's gradual academic slide downward occurred over many years. Nor was there any one event that motivated Leia Holley, although Sean's seizure certainly called for immediate attention.

How did these families cope? There are many ways, but each family coped by having one or more reliable allies within the school system.

What characterizes those teachers and other professionals, those who became the families' partners? It is their empathetic imagination, their ability to understand, be aware of, be sensitive to, and vicariously experience the feelings, thoughts, and lives of another person.

We dream the impossible dream. We are idealists and romantics

The romanticism of Don Quixote enters the lives of these four families as an essential, vital, life-giving characteristic, as a flesh-and-blood imperative.

Clara and Jake Berg knew how much their son loved riding and grooming horses. Their dream, a farm community in which he would be welcomed with all of his perfections and imperfections, came to fruition when Kenny was hired at Adriance Farm.

Norma Cortes left school in San Sebastian, Puerto Rico, after completing the third grade; she knows little English and does not read it at all. Her goal for Joesian is that he will read and be able to be the firefighter or plumber that he wants to be.

Vera Doleman had a vision for Nicky and for Nicky's younger brother, Tavion. It was that they would be surrounded, as she herself was enveloped, in a loving family. Vera's was a dream of safety and protection.

Leia Holley expects Sean to have friends; after that, what he can do is less important than who he is and what he gives to others.

Just as Don Quixote had his dream, he also had his trusty squire, Sancho. So, too, these four families have their dreams and their allies. Romanticism is necessary, but in and of itself insufficient; realism requires partners.

THE FINAL LESSON

If we have been effective partners in the enterprise called education, you have learned and we have taught that there are abundant opportunities (created by law) for professionals to understand families and their children with disabilities; people possess extraordinary skills to become trusted and trustworthy partners. Beyond opportunities and skills lies the quality that we call the empathetic imagination; often that quality responds to the need for justice in our schools, community, and society. More than that, partnerships, trust, and the empathetic imagination are twice blessed: They bless those who seek them and those who are sought by the seekers. We hope you will be a seeker, for in being that you will become a recipient.

Rud Turnbull
Lawrence, Kansas
June, 2004

References

Abbott, D.A., & Meredith, W. H. (1986). Strengths of parents with retarded children. *Family Relations, 35,* 371–375.

Abery, B., & Zajac, R. (1996). Self-determination as a goal of early childhood and elementary education. In D. J. Sands & M. L. Wehmeyer (Eds.), *Self-determination across the life span: Independence and choice for people with disabilities* (pp. 169–196). Baltimore: Paul H. Brookes.

Able-Boone, H. (1993). Family participation in the IFSP process: Family or professional driven? *Infant-Toddler Intervention, 3*(1), 63–71.

Able-Boone, H., Sandall, S. R., Stevens, E., & Frederick, L. (1992). Family support resources and needs: How early intervention can make a difference. *Infant-Toddler Intervention, 2*(2), 93–102.

Abt Associates. (2002). *Study of state and local implementation of impact of the Individuals with Disabilities Education Act. Report on focus study I.* Bethesda, MD: Author.

Abudabbeh, N. (1996). Arab families. In M. McGoldrick, J. Giordano, & J. K. Pearce (Eds.), *Ethnicity and family therapy* (2nd ed., pp. 333–346). New York: Guilford Press.

Adams, K. S., & Christenson, S. L. (1998). Differences in parent and teacher trust levels: Implications for creating collaborative family-school relationships. *Special Services in the Schools, 14*(1/2), 1–22.

Adams, K. S., & Christenson, S.L. (2000). Trust and the family-school relationship: Examination of parent-teacher differences in elementary and secondary grades. *Journal of Psychology, 38*(5), 477–497.

Adelman, H. S., & Taylor, L. (1997). Addressing barriers to learning: Beyond school-linked services and full-service schools. *American Journal of Orthopsychiatry, 67*(3), 408–419.

Agosta, J., & Melda, K. (1995). *Supplemental security income for children with disabilities.* Washington, DC: Human Services Research Institute.

Agran, M., Snow, K., & Swaner, J. (1999). A survey of secondary level teachers' opinions on community-based instruction and inclusive education. *Journal of the Association for Persons with Severe Handicaps, 24*(1), 58–62.

Ainbinder, J., Blanchard, L., Singer, G.H.S., Sullivan, M., Powers, L. K., Marquis, J., & Santelli, B. (1998). A qualitative study of parent to parent support for parents of children with special needs. *Journal of Pediatric Psychology, 23,* 99–109.

Ainbinder, J., Blanchard, L., Singer, G. H. S., Sullivan, M., Powers, L., Marquis, J., et al. (1998). How parents help one another: A qualitative study of Parent to Parent self-help. *Journal of Pediatric Psychology, 23,* 99–109.

Ainge, D., Colvin, G., & Baker, S. (1998). Analysis of perceptions of parents who have children with intellectual disabilities: Implications for service providers. *Education and Training in Mental Retardation and Developmental Disabilities, 33*(4), 331–341.

Akey, T. M., Marquis, J.G., & Ross, M.E. (2000). Validation of scores on the psychological empowerment scale: A measure of empowerment for parents of children with a disability. *Educational and Psychological Measurement, 60*(3), 419–438.

Alan Guttmacher Institute. (1996). *Facts in brief: Teen sex and pregnancy.* Washington, DC: Author.

Algozzine, B., Browder, D., Karvonen, M., Test, D.W., & Wood, W. M. (2001). Effects of interventions to promote self-determination for individuals with disabilities. *Review of Educational Research, 71*(2), 219–277.

Al-Hassan, S., & Gardner, R. (2002). Involving immigrant parents of students with disabilities in the educational process. *Teaching Exceptional Children, 34*(5), 52–58.

Allen, R. I., & Petr, C.G. (1996). Toward developing standards and measurements for family-centered practice in family support programs. In G. H. S. Singer, L. E. Powers, & A. L. Olson (Eds.), *Redefining family support: Innovations in public-private partnerships* (pp. 57–89). Baltimore: Brookes.

Allen, S., Smith, A., Test, D., Flowers, C., & Wood, W. (2001). The effects of "self-directed" IEP on student participation in IEP meetings. *Career Development*

All references to IDEA are to the reauthorized law as passed by Congress in November 2004 and signed by the President in December, 2004 as P.L. 08-446. We presume that the law will be codified in the United States code in such a way that our references to the code are correct. As of the me this book goes to press, the law had not been codified.

for Exceptional Individuals, 24, 107–120.

Altshuler, S. J. (1997). A reveille for school social workers: Children in foster care need our help! *Social Work in Education, 19*(2), 121–127.

American Academy of Pediatrics. (2000). *Joint statement on the impact of entertainment violence on children.* Congressional Public Health Statement. Retrieved August 14, 2004 from www.aap.org/advocacy/ releases/ jstmtevc.htm

American Counseling Association Foundation. (1995). *The ACA code of ethics and standards of practice.* Retrieved June 8, 2001, from http://www.counseling.org/resources / ethics.htm

Angelo, D. H. (2000). Impact of augmentative and alternative communication devices on families. *Augmentative and Alternative Communication, 16*(1), 37–47.

Angelo, D. H., Kokoska, S. M., & Jones, S. D. (1996). A family perspective on augmentative and alternative communication: Families of adolescents and young adults. *Augmentative and Alternative Communication, 12*, 13–20.

APA Council of Representatives. (2003). *Resolution on the maltreatment of children with disabilities.* Retrieved August 14, 2004 from www.apa.org/pi/maltreatment.html

Aristotle. (2003). *The Nicomachean ethics.* (J. A. K. Thomson & Jonathan Barnes, Trans.) New York: Penguin Books.

Artiles, A. J., & Zamora-Duran, G. (Eds.). (1997). *Reducing disproportionate representation of culturally diverse students in special and gifted education.* Reston, VA: Council for Exceptional Children.

Avis, D. W. (1985). *Deinstitutionalization jet lag* (2nd ed.). Upper Saddle River, NJ: Merrill/Prentice-Hall.

Ayres, R., Cooley, E., & Dunn, C. (1990). Self-concept, attribution, and persistence in learning-disabled students. *Journal of School Psychology, 28,* 153–163.

Bahr, M. W., Fuchs, D., & Fuchs, L. S. (1999). Mainstream assistance teams: A consultation-based approach to prereferral intervention. In S. Graham & K. Harris (Eds.), *Teachers working together: Enhancing the performance of students with special needs* (pp. 87–116). Cambridge, MA: Brookline Books.

Bahr, M. W., Whitten, E., Dieker, L., Kocarek, C. E., & Manson, D. (1999). A comparison of school-based intervention teams: Implications for educational and legal reform. *Exceptional Children, 66*(1), 67–83.

Baier, A. C. (1986). Trust and antitrust. *Ethics, 96,* 231–260.

Bailey, D. B. (2001). Evaluating parent involvement and family support in early intervention and preschool programs. *Journal of Early Intervention, 24*(1), 1–14.

Bailey, D. B., Hebbeler, K., Scarborough, A., Spiker, D., & Mallik, S. (2004). First experiences with early intervention: A national perspective. *Pediatrics, 113*(4), 887–896.

Bailey, D. B., McWilliam, R. A., Darkes, L. A., Hebbeler, K., Simeonsson, R. J., Wagner, N., & Spiker, D. (1998). Family outcomes in early intervention: A framework for program evaluation and efficacy research. *Exceptional Children, 64*, 313–328.

Bailey, D. B., & Simeonsson, R. J. (1988). Assessing needs of families with handicapped infants. *Journal of Special Education, 22*(1), 117–127.

Bailey, D. B., Skinner, D., & Sparkman, K. L. (2003). Discovering fragile X syndrome: Family experiences and perceptions. *Pediatrics, 111*(2), 407–416.

Bailey, D. B., Skinner, D., Correa, V., Arcia, E., Reyes-Blanes, M. E., Rodriguez, P., & Skinner, M. (1999). Needs and supports reported by Latino families of young children with developmental disabilities. *American Journal on Mental Retardation, 104*(5), 437–451.

Baker, B. L., & Blacher, J. (2002). For better or worse? Impact of residential placement on families. *American Association on Mental Retardation, 1*, 1–13.

Baker, B. L., McIntyre, L. L., Blacher, J., Crnic, K., Edelbrock, C., & Low, C. (2003). Pre-school children with and without developmental delay: Behaviour problems and parenting stress over time. *Journal of Intellectual & Developmental Disability, 47* (4/5), 217–230.

Baker, B. L., with Ambrose, S. A., & Anderson, S.R. (1989). Parent training and developmental disabilities [Special issue]. *Monographs of American Association on Mental Retardation, 13.*

Baldwin, A. Y. (2002). Culturally diverse students who are gifted. *Exceptionality, 10*(2), 139–147.

Balli, S. J., Demo, D. H., & Wedman, J. F. (1998). Family involvement with children's homework: An intervention in middle grades. *Family Relations, 47*(2), 149–157.

Bandura, A. (1997). *Self-efficacy: The exercise of control.* New York: W. H. Freeman.

Barbell, K. (1996). *Foster care today: National and South Carolina perspective. Council on Child Abuse and Neglect. Foster Parent Recruitment and Retention Workshop.* Washington, DC: Child Welfare League of America.

Barlow, J., & Coren, E. (2000). Parenting programmes for improving maternal psychosocial health (Cochrane Review). In *Issue 3, Oxford: Update Software. Cochrane Library.*

Barlow, J., & Stewart-Brown, S. (2000). Behaviour problems and group-based parent education programs. *Developmental and Behavioral Pediatrics, 21*(5), 356–370.

Barr, M. W. (1913). *Mental defectives: Their history, treatment, and training.* Philadelphia: Blakiston.

Barrera, I., & Corso, R. M. (2002). Cultural competency as skilled dialogue. *Topics in Early Childhood Special Education, 22*(2), 103–113.

Barrie, W., & McDonald, J. (2002). Administrative support for student-le individualized education programs. *Remedial and Special Education, 23*(2), 116–121.

Batshaw, M. L. (2002). *Children with disabilities.* Baltimore: Paul H. Brookes.

Baum, N. (2003). Family quality of life: Canadian results from an international study. *Journal of Developmental and Physical Disabilities, 15*(3), 207–229.

Baumeister, A. A., Kupstas, F. D., & Woodley-Zanthos, P. (1993). *The new morbidity: Recommendations for actions and an updated guide to state planning for the prevention of mental retardation and related disabilities associated with socioeconomic conditions.* Washington, DC: U.S. Department of Health and Human Services.

Beach Center. (2000). *Unpublished research transcripts of focus groups.* Lawrence, KS: Beach Center on Disability.

Beach Center. (1999). Unpublished Transcripts. University of Kansas, Lawrence, KS: Beach Center on Disability.

Beach, R. (1996). Our children are getting the wrong message. In E. J. Erwin (Ed.), *Putting children first: Vision for a brighter future* (p. 29). Baltimore: Paul H. Brookes.

Bear, G. G., Juvonen, J., & McInerney, F. (1993). Self-perceptions and peer relations of boys without learning disabilities in an integrated setting: A longitudinal study. *Learning Disability Quarterly, 16,* 27–136.

Becker-Cottrill, B., McFarland, J., & Anderson, V. (2003). A model of positive behavioral support for individuals with autism and their families: The family focus process. *Focus on Autism and Other Developmental Disabilities, 18*(2), 113–123.

Beckman, A. A., & Brent, R. L. (1986). Mechanism of known environmental teratogens: Drugs and chemicals. *Clinics in Perinatology, 13,* 649–687.

Beghetto, R. A. (2001). Virtually in the middle: Alternative avenues for parental involvement in middle-level schools. *Clearing House, 75*(1), 21–25.

Behr, S. K., & Murphy, D. L. (1993). Research progress and promise: The role of perceptions in cognitive adaptation to disability. In A. P. Turnbull, J. M. Patterson, S. K. Behr, D. L. Murphy, J. G. Marquis, & M. J.

Blue-Banning (Eds.), *Cognitive coping, families, and disability* (pp. 151–164). Baltimore: Brookes.

Behrman, R. E. (Ed.). (2004). *The future of children: Children, families, and foster care.* Los Altos, CA: David and Lucile Packard Foundation.

Bell, M., & Stoneman, Z. (2000). Reactions to prenatal testing: Reflection of religiosity and attitudes toward abortion and people with disabilities. *American Journal on Mental Retardation, 105,* 1–13.

Bennett, J. M. (1985). Company, halt! In H. R. Turnbull & A. P. Turnbull (Eds.), *Parents speak out: Then and now* (2nd ed., pp. 159–173). Upper Saddle River, NJ: Merrill/Prentice-Hall.

Bennett, T., Zhang, C., & Hojnar, L. (1998). Facilitating the full participation of culturally diverse families in the IFSP/IEP process. *Infant-Toddler Intervention, 8,* 227–249.

Benson, B. A., & Gross, A. M. (1989). The effect of a congenitally handicapped child upon the marital dyad: A review of the literature. *Clinical Psychology Review, 9*(6), 747–758.

Benton Foundation. (1998). *About foster care, take this heart: The foster care project.* Retrieved August 14, 2004, from http://www.benton.org/publibrary/mtm/pages/aagtth.html

Bettelheim, B. (1950). *Love is not enough.* Glencoe, NY: Free Press.

Bettelheim, B. (1967). *The empty fortress: Infantile autism and the birth of the self.* London: Collier-Macmillan.

Billingsley, B. S. (2002). *Special education teacher retention and attrition: A critical analysis of the literature.* Gainesville: University of Florida, Center on Personnel Studies in Special Education.

Birenbaum, A., & Cohen, H. J. (1993). On the importance of helping families: Policy implications from a national study. *Mental Retardation, 31*(2), 67–74.

Blacher, J. (1984a). Sequential stages of adjustment to the birth of a child with handicaps: Fact or artifact? *Mental Retardation, 22*(2), 55–68.

Blacher, J. (1984b). *Severely handicapped young children and their families:*

Research in review. New York: Academic Press.

Blacher, J., & Hatton, C. (2001). Current perspectives on family research in mental retardation. *Current Opinion in Psychiatry, 14,* 477–482.

Blacher, J., & Lopez, S. (1997). Contributions to depression in Latino mothers with and without children with mental retardation: Implications for care-giving. *Family Relations: Interdisciplinary Journal of Applied Family Studies, 46,* 325–334.

Blackorby, J., & Wagner, M. (1996). Longitudinal postschool outcomes of youth with disabilities: Findings from the National Longitudinal Transition Study. *Exceptional Children, 62,* 399–413.

Blanchett, W. J. (2000). Sexual risk behaviors of young adults with LD and the need for HIV/AIDS education. *Remedial and Special Education, 21,* 336–345.

Blanchett, W. J. (2002). Voices from a TASH forum on meeting the needs of gay, lesbian, and bisexual adolescents and adults with severe disabilities. *Research and Practice for Persons with Severe Disabilities, 27*(1), 82–86.

Blanchett, W. J., & Wolfe, P. S. (2002). A review of sexuality education curricula: Meeting the sexuality education needs of individuals with moderate and severe intellectual disabilites. *Journal of the Association for Persons with Severe Handicaps, 27* (1), 43–57.

Blank, M., Melaville, A., & Shah, B. (2003). *Making the difference: Research and practice in community schools.* Washington, DC: Coalition for Community Schools, Institute for Educational Leadership.

Blank, M. J. (2004). How community schools make a difference. *Educational Leadership, 61*(8), 62–65.

Blue-Banning, M., Summers, J. A., Frankland, H. C., Nelson, L. L., & Beegle, G. (2004). Dimensions of family and professional partnerships: Constructive guidelines for collaboration. *Exceptional Children, 70*(2), 167–184.

Blue-Banning, M. J. (1995). [Unpublished raw data.]

Blue-Banning, M. J., Santelli, B., Guy, B., & Wallace, E. (1994). *Cognitive coping project: Coping with the challenges of disability.* Lawrence: University of Kansas, Beach Center on Families and Disability.

Blue-Banning, M. J., Summers, J.A., Frankland, H. C., Nelson, L. L., & Beegle, G. (2004). Dimensions of family and professional partnerships: Constructive guidelines for collaboration. *Exceptional Children, 70*(2), 167–184.

Blue-Banning, M. J., Turnbull, A. P., & Pereira, L. (2000). Group action planning as a support strategy for Hispanic families: Parent and professional perspectives. *Mental Retardation, 38*(3), 262–275.

Boggs, E. M. (1985). Who is putting whose head in the sand? (Or in the clouds, as the case may be). In H. R. Turnbull & A. P. Turnbull (Eds.), *Parents speak out: Then and now* (2nd ed., pp. 39–55). Upper Saddle River, NJ: Merrill/Prentice Hall.

Booth, T., & Booth, W. (2000). Against the odds: Growing up with parents who have learning difficulties. *Mental Retardation, 38*(1), 1–14.

Bos, C. S., Nahmias, M. L., & Urban, M. A. (1999). Targeting home-school collaboration for students with ADHD. *Teaching Exceptional Children, 31*(6), 4–11.

Boyce, S. (1992). Coping well with labelers of Down syndrome. *Down Syndrome News, 37.*

Boyd, B.A. (2002). Examining the relationship between stress and lack of social support in mothers of children with autism. *Focus on Autism and Other Developmental Disabilities, 17*(4), 208–215.

Braaten, E., & Felopulos, G. (2004). *Straight talk about psychological testing for kids.* New York: Guilford Press.

Braddock, D., Hemp, S., Parish, S., & Rizzolo, M. C. (2000). Growth in state commitments for community services: Significance of the Medicaid Home and Community-Based Services waiver. *Mental Retardation, 38*(2), 186–189.

Braddock, D., Hemp, S., Parish, S., & Westrich, J. (Eds.). (1998). *The state of the states in developmental disabilities.* Washington, DC: American Association on Mental Retardation.

Brannan, A. M., Heflinger, C.A., & Foster, E. M. (2003). The role of caregiver strain and other family variables in determining children's use of mental health services. *Journal of Emotional and Behavioral Disorders, 11*(2), 77–91.

Brantlinger, E. (1992). Professionals' attitudes toward the sterilization of people with disabilities. *Journal of the Association for Persons with Severe Handicaps, 17*(1), 4–18.

Brennan, E., & Freeman, L. (1999). Inclusive child care. *Focal Point, 13*(1), 1, 8–9.

Brennan, E. M., Rosenzweig, J. M., & Ogilvie, A. M. (1999). Support for working caregivers. *Focal Point, 13*(1), 1, 3–5.

Briar-Lawson, K., Lawson, H. A., Collier, C., & Joseph, A. (1997). School-linked comprehensive services: Promising beginnings, lessons learned, and future challenges. *Social Work in Education, 19*(3), 136–145.

Bricker, W. A., & Bricker, D. D. (1976). The infant, toddler, and preschool research and intervention project. In T. D. Tjossem (Ed.), *Intervention strategies for high risk infants and young children* (pp. 545–572). Baltimore: University Park Press.

Broderick, C., & Smith, J. (1979). The general systems approach to the family. In W. R. Burr, R. Hill, F. I. Nye, & I. L. Reiss (Eds.), *Contemporary theories about the family* (Vol. 2, pp. 112–129). New York: Free Press.

Brodzinsky, D. M. (1993). Long-term outcomes in adoption. *The Future of Children, 3*(1), 153–166.

Bronfenbrenner, U. (1990). Discovering what families do. In D. Blankenhorn, S. B. Ayme, & J. B. Elshtain (Eds.), *Rebuilding the nest: A new commitment to the American family* (pp. 27–38). Milwaukee, WI: Family Service American.

Brotherson, M. J. (2001). The role of families in accountability. *Journal of Early Intervention, 24*(1), 22–24.

Brotherson, M. J., Cook, C., & Parette, H. P. (1996). A home-centered approach to assistive technology provision for young children with disabilities. *Focus on Autism and Other Developmental Disabilities, 11*(2), 86–95.

Brotherson, M. J., & Goldstein, B. L. (1992). Time as a resource and constraint for parents of young children with disabilities: Implications for early intervention services. *Topics in Early Childhood Special Education, 12*(4), 508–527.

Browder, D. M., & Spooner, F. (2003). Understanding the purpose and process of alternate assessment. In D. L. Ryndak & S. Alper (Eds.), *Curriculum and instruction for students with significant disabilities in inclusive settings* (2nd ed., pp. 51–69). Boston: Allyn & Bacon.

Brown, F., Gothelf, C. R., Guess, D., & Lehr, D. H. (1998). Self-determination for individuals with the most severe disabilities: Moving beyond chimera. *Journal of the Association for Persons with Severe Handicaps, 23*(1), 17–26.

Brown, I., Anand, S., Fung, W. L.A., Isaacs, B., & Baum, N. (2003). Family quality of life: Canadian results from an international study. *Journal of Developmental and Physical Disabilities, 15*(3), 207–229.

Brown Center on Education Policy. (2003). *The 2003 Brown Center Report on American Education: How well are American students learning?* Washington, DC: Brookings Institution.

Browne, J. A., Losen, D. J., & Wald, J. (2002). Zero tolerance: Unfair, with little recourse. In R. J. Skiba & G. G. Noam (Eds.), (pp. 73–99). San Francisco: Jossey-Bass.

Bryan, T., & Sullivan-Burstein, K. (1998). Teacher-selected strategies for improving homework completion. *Remedial and Special Education, 19*(5), 263–275.

Bryk, A. S., & Schneider, B. (2003, March). Trust in schools: A core resource for school reform. *Educational Leadership, 60*(6), 40–45.

Buck v. Bell, 274 U.S. 200 (1927).

Buck, G., Polloway, E. A., Smith-Thomas, A., & Cook, K. W. (2003). Prereferral intervention processes: A survey of state practices. *Exceptional Children, 69*(3), 349–360.

Bui, Y. N., & Turnbull, A. (2003). East meets west: Analysis of person-centered planning in the context of Asian American values. *Exceptional Children, 38*(1), 18–31.

Bullis, M., & Cheney, D. (1999). Vocational and transition interventions for adolescents and young adults with emotional or behavioral disorders. *Focus on Exceptional Children, 31*(7), 1–24.

Burello, L., Lashley, C., & Beatty, E. (2001). *Educating all students together: How school leaders create unified systems.* Thousand Oaks, CA: Corwin Press.

Bursuck, W., Pollaway, E. A., Plante, L., Epstein, M. H., Jayanthi, M., & McConeghy, J. (1996). Report card grading and adaptations: A national survey of classroom practices. *Exceptional Children, 62*(4), 301–318.

Burton, S. L., & Parks, A. L. (1994). College-aged siblings of individuals with disabilities. *Social Work Research, 18*(3), 178–185.

Bush, G. W. (2001a). *Foreword: No Child Left Behind.* Retrieved February 23, 2004, from http://www.whitehouse.gov/ news/reports/no-child-left-behind. html

Bush, G. W. (2001b). *Overview: No Child Left Behind, President Bush's education reform plan.* Retrieved February 23, 2004, from http://www.ed.gov/nclb/ overview/intro/ presidentplan/page_pg3.html# execsumm

Butera, G., & Maughan, G. (1998). A place in the mountains: Rural homeless families in West Virginia. *Zero to Three, 19*(1), 24–30.

Butterworth, J., Gilmore, D., Kiernan, W., & Schalock, R. (1998). *Day and employment services in developmental disabilities: State and national trends.* Boston: Institute on Community Inclusion (UAP).

Buyse, M. L. (1990). *Birth defects encyclopedia.* Dover, MA: Center for Birth Defects Information Services.

Caldwell, J., & Heller, T. (2003). Management of respite and personal assistance services in a consumer-directed family support programme. *Journal of Intellectual Disability Research, 47*(4/5), 352–366.

Calfee, C., Wittwer, F., & Meredith, M. (1998). Why build a full-service school? In C. Calfee, F. Wittwer, & M. Meredith (Eds.), *Building a full-service school* (pp. 6–24). San Francisco: Jossey-Bass.

Callahan, K., Rademacher, J. A., & Hildreth, B. L. (1998). The effect of parent participation in strategies to improve the homework performance of students who are at risk. *Remedial and Special Education, 19*(3), 131–141.

Calloway, C. (1999). Twenty ways to promote friendship in the inclusive classroom. *Intervention in School and Clinic, 34*(3), 176–177.

Camarota, S. A. (2001). Immigrants in the United States—2000. *Spectrum, 74*(2), 1–5.

Campbell, P. H., Strickland, B., & La Forme, C. (1992). Enhancing parent participation in the individualized family service plan. *Topics in Early Childhood Special Education, 11*(4), 112–124.

Cancio, E. J., West, R. P., & Young, K. R. (2004). Improving mathematics homework completion and accuracy of students with EBD through self-management and parent participation. *Journal of Emotional and Behavioral Disorders, 12*(1), 9–22.

Canda, E. R. (1999). *Spiritually sensitive social work: Key concepts and ideals. Journal of Social Work Theory and Practice 1*(1), 1–15.

Caplan, P. J., & Hall-McCorquodale, I. (1985). Mother-blaming in major clinical journals. *American Journal of Orthopsychiatry, 55*(3), 345–353.

Carlson, E., Brauen, M., Klein, S., Schroll, K., & Willig, S. (2002). *Study of personnel needs in special education: Key findings.* Retrieved June 28, 2004, from http://ferdig.coe.ufl.edu/spense/Key Findings

Carnes, P. (1981). *Family development I: Understanding us.* Minneapolis, MN:

Interpersonal Communications Programs.

Carr, E. G., Horner, R. H., Turnbull, A. P., Marquis, J. G., Magito-McLauglin, D., McAtee, M. L., et al. (1999). *Positive behavior support as an approach for dealing with problem behavior in people with developmental disabilities: A research synthesis.* Washington, DC: American Association on Mental Retardation Monograph Series.

Carr, J. (1988). Six-weeks to twenty-one years old: A longitudinal study of children with Downs syndrome and their families. *Journal of Child Psychology and Psychiatry, 29*(4), 407–431.

Carter, B. (1999). Becoming parents: The family with young children. In B. Carter & M. McGoldrick (Eds.), *The expanded family life cycle: Individual, family, and social perspectives* (3rd ed.). Needham Heights, MA: Allyn & Bacon.

Carter, E. A., & McGoldrick, M. (1999). *Changing family life cycle: Individual, family, and social perspectives* (3rd ed.). Boston: Allyn & Bacon.

Certo, N. J., Mautz, D., Pumpian, I., Sax, C., Smalley, K., Wade, H. A., et al. (2003). Review and discussion of a model for seamless transition to adulthood. *Education and Training in Developmental Disabilities, 38*(1), 3–17.

Chaboudy, R., & Jameson, P. (2001, September/October). Connecting families and schools through technology. *Book Report,* 52–56.

Chan, S., & Lee, E. (2004). Families with Asian roots. In E. W. Lynch & M. J. Hanson (Eds.), *Developing cross-cultural competence: A guide for working with children and their families* (3rd ed., pp. 219–298). Baltimore: Paul H. Brookes.

Chavkin, N. F., Gonzalez, J., & Rader, R. (2002). A home-school program in Texas-Mexico border school: Voices from parents, students, and school staff. *School Community Journal, 10*(2), 127–137.

Chen, D., Downing, J. E., & Peckham-Hardin, K. D. (2002). Working with families of diverse cultural and linguistic backgrounds: Considerations for culturally responsive positive behavior support. In J. M. Lucyshyn, G. Dunlap, & R. W. Albin (Eds.), *Families and positive behavior support* (pp. 133-151). Baltimore: Paul H. Brookes.

Child Abuse Prevention and Treatment Act, Pub. L. No. 93-247, 42 U.S.C. 5101 § 3 (1974).

Children's Defense Fund. (1999). *The state of America's children yearbook.* Washington, DC: Author.

Child Welfare League of America. (2002). *Improving educational outcomes for youth in care: A national collaboration.* Washington, DC: Author.

Christensen, S., Ysseldyke, J. E., & Algozzine, B. (1982, July). Institutional constraints and external pressures influencing referral decision. *Psychology in the School, 19*(3), 341-345.

Christenson, S. L., & Sheridan, S. M. (2001). *Schools and families: Creating essential connections for learning.* New York: Guilford Press.

Cigno, K., & Burke, P. (1997). Single mothers of children with learning disabilities: An undervalued group. *Journal of Interprofessional Care, 11*(2), 177-186.

Clark, G. A., & Zimmerman, E. D. (1988). Views of self, family background, and school: Interviews with artistically talented students. *Gifted Child Quarterly, 32*(4), 340-346.

Clausen, J. M., Landsverk, J., Ganger, W., Chadwick, D., & Litrownik, A. (1998). Mental health problems of children in foster care. *Journal of Child and Family Studies, 7*(3), 283-296.

Cobb, H. B., & Horn, C. J. (1989, November). *Implementation of professional standards in special education: A national study.* Paper presented at the meeting of the Council for Exceptional Children, Birmingham, AL.

Code of Federal Regulations (C. F. R.) Sec. 300.500

Coker, C. C., Osgood, K., & Clouse, K. R. (1995). *A comparison of job satisfaction and economic benefits of four different employment models for persons with disabilities.* Stout:

University of Wisconsin, Rehabilitation Research and Training Center on Improving Community-Based Rehabilitation Programs.

Coleman, M. R., Gallagher, J., & Foster, A. (1994). *Updated report on state policies related to the identification of gifted students.* Chapel Hill: University of North Carolina, Gifted Education Policy Studies Program.

Coles, R. (1989). *The call of stories.* Boston: Houghton Mifflin.

Coles, R. L. (2003). Black single custodial fathers: Factors influencing the decision to parent. *Families in Society: The Journal of Contemporary Human Services, 84*(2), 247-258.

Coltoff, P. (1998). *Community schools: Educational reform and partnership with our nation's social service agencies.* Washington, DC: Child Welfare League of America.

Comer, J. P., & Haynes, N. M. (1991). Parent involvement in schools: An ecological approach. *Elementary School Journal, 91*(3), 271-277.

Cook, C. C., Brotherson, M. J., Weigner-Garrey, C., & Mize, I. (1996). Homes to support the self-determination of children. In D. J. Sands & M. L. Wehmeyer (Eds.), *Self-determination across the life span: Independence and choice for people with disabilities* (pp. 91-110). Baltimore: Paul H. Brookes.

Cook, R. S., Rule, S., & Mariger, H. (2003). Parents' evaluation of the usability of a web site on recommended practices. *Topics in Early Childhood Special Education, 23*(1), 19-27.

Cooper, C. S., & Allred, K. W. (1992). A comparison of mothers' versus fathers' needs for support in caring for a young child with special needs. *Infant-Toddler Intervention, 2*(2), 205-221.

Cope, D. N., & Wolfson, B. (1994). Crisis intervention with the family in the trauma setting. *Journal of Head Trauma Rehabilitation, 9*(1), 67-81.

Copeland, S., McCall, J., Williams, C. R., Guth, C., Carter, E. W., Presley, J. A., et al. (2002). High school peer buddies: A win-win situation. *Teaching Exceptional Children, 35*(1), 16-21.

Coren, E., Barlow, J., & Stewart-Brown, S. (2003). The effectiveness of individual and group-based parenting programmes in improving outcomes for teenage mothers and their children: A systematic review. *Journal of Adolescence, 26,* 79-103.

Council of State Directors of Programs for the Gifted and National Association for Gifted Children. (2003). *State of the states: Gifted and talented education report 2001-2002.* Washington, DC: National Association for Gifted Children.

Cousins, N. (1989). *Head first: The biology of hope.* New York: Dutton.

Covey, S. R. (1990). *The seven habits of highly effective people: Restoring the character ethic.* New York: Fireside/Simon & Schuster.

Crais, E. R., & Belardi, C. (1999). Family participation in child assessment: Perceptions of families and professionals. *Infant Toddler Intervention, 9*(3), 209-238.

Cripe, J., & Bricker, D. (1993). Family interest survey. In D. Bricker (Ed.), *Assessment, evaluation, and programming system (AEPS) for infants and children* (pp. 1-6). Baltimore: Brookes.

Crnic, K., & Booth, C. (1991). Mothers' and fathers' perceptions of daily hassles of parenting across early childhood. *Journal of Marriage and the Family, 53,* 1042-1050.

Crone, D. A., & Horner, R. H. (2003). *Building positive behavior support systems in schools: Functional behavioral assessment.* New York: Guilford Press.

Cuskelly, M., & Gunn, P. (2003). Sibling relationships of children with Down syndrome: Perspectives of mothers, fathers, and siblings. *American Journal on Mental Retardation, 108*(4), 234-244.

Dagirmanjian, S. (1996). Armenian families. In M. McGoldrick, J. Giordano, & J. K. Pearce (Eds.), *Ethnicity and family therapy* (2nd ed., pp. 376-391). New York: Guilford Press.

Dalzell, H. J. (1998). Giftedness: Infancy to adolescence—A developmental perspective. *Roeper Review, 20*(4), 259-264.

Damiani, V. B. (1999). Responsibility and adjustment in siblings of children with disabilities: Update and review. *Journal of Contemporary Human Services, 80*(1), 34–40.

Daniels, V. I. (1998). Minority students in gifted and special education programs: The case for educational equity. *Journal of Special Education, 32*(1), 41–43.

D'Antonio, W. V., & Aldous, J. (Eds.). (1983). *Families and religions.* Beverly Hills, CA: Sage Publications.

Darling, R. B., & Peter, M. I. (1994). *Families, physicians, and children with special health needs: Collaborative medical education models.* Westport, CT: Auburn House.

Davern, L. (2004). School-to-home notebooks: What parents have to say. *Teaching Exceptional Children, 36*(5), 22–27.

Davey, T., Penuel, W., Allison-Tant, E., & Rosner, A. (2000). The HERO program: A case for school social work services. *Social Work in Education, 22*(3), 177–190.

DeJong, L. (2003). Using Erikson to work more effectively with teenage parents. *Young Children, 58*(2), 87–95.

Demchak, M., & Greenfield, R. (2003). *Transition portfolios for students with disabilities; How to help students, teachers and families handle new situations.* Thousand Oaks, CA: Corwin Press.

Denny, M. K., Singer, G. H., Singer, J., Brenner, M. E., Okamoto, Y., & Fredeen, R. M. (2001). Mexican immigrant families' beliefs and goals for their infants in the neonatal intensive care unit. *Journal of the Association for Persons with Severe Handicaps, 26*(3), 148–157.

Deyhle, D., & LeCompte, M. (1994). Cultural differences in child development: Navajo adolescents in middle schools. *Theory into Practice, 33*(3), 156–166.

Diamond, K. E., & LeFurgy, W. G. (1992). Relations between mothers' expectations and the performance of their infants who have developmental handicaps. *American Journal on Mental Retardation, 97*(1), 11–20.

Diamond, S. (1981). Growing up with parents of a handicapped child: A handicapped person's perspective. In J. L. Paul (Ed.), *Understanding and working with parents of children with special needs* (pp. 23–50). New York: Holt, Rinehart, & Winston.

Dryfoos, J. (1996). Full-service schools. *Educational Leadership, 53*(7), 18–23.

Dryfoos, J. (1998). *Safe passage: Making it through adolescence in a risky society.* New York: Oxford University Press.

Dryfoos, J. (2004). *Evaluation of community schools: Findings to date. Coalition for Community Schools.* Retrieved July 3, 2004, from www.communityschools.org/evaluation/evalprint.html#effect

Dubus, P., & Buckner, J. (1998). A shelter is not a home: Homeless urban mothers and their young children. *Zero to Three, 19*(1), 18–23.

Duhaney, L. M. G., & Salend, S. J. (2000). Parental perceptions of inclusive educational placements. *Remedial and Special Education, 21*(2), 121–128.

Dunlap, G., Newton, J. S., Fox, L., Benito, N., & Vaughn, B. (2001). *Focus on Autism & Other Developmental Disabilities, 16*(4), 215–221.

Dunn, C. (1996). A status report on transition planning for individuals with learning disabilities. *Journal of Learning Disabilities, 29*(1), 17–30.

Dunst, C. J. (2002). Family-centered practices: Birth through high school. *Journal of Special Education, 36*(3), 139–147.

Dunst, C. J., Bruder, M. B., Trivette, C. M., Hamby, D., Raab, M., & McLean, M. (2001). Characteristics and consequences of everyday natural learning opportunities. *Topics in Early Childhood Special Education 21*(2), 68–92.

Dunst, C. J., Cooper, C. S., Weeldreyer, J. C., Snyder, K. D., & Chase, J. H. (1988). Family needs scale. In C. J. Dunst, C. M. Trivette, & A. G. Deal (Eds.), *Enabling and empowering families: Principles and guidelines for practice.* Cambridge, MA: Brookline.

Dunst, C. J., Hamby, D., Trivette, C. M., Raab, M., & Bruder, M. B. (2000).

Everyday family and community life and children's naturally occurring learning opportunities. *Journal of Early Intervention, 23*(3), 151–164.

Dunst, C. J., Herter, S., & Shields, H. (2000). Interest-based natural learning opportunities. *Young Exceptional Children Monograph Series, 2,* 37–48.

Dunst, C. J., Trivette, C., & Deal, A. (1988). *Enabling & empowering families: Principles and guidelines for practice.* Cambridge, MA: Brookline.

Dunst, C. J., Trivette, C. M., & Cross, A. H. (1986). Mediating influences of social support: Personal, family and child outcomes. *American Journal of Mental Deficiency, 90,* 403–417.

Dyson, L., Edgar, E., & Crnic, K. (1989). Psychological predictors of adjustment by siblings of developmentally disabled children. *American Journal on Mental Retardation, 94*(3), 292–302.

Dyson, L., & Fewell, R. R. (1989). The self-concept of siblings of handicapped children: A comparison. *Journal of Early Intervention, 13*(3), 230–238.

Dyson, L. L. (1993). Responding to the presence of a child with disabilities: Parental stress and family functioning over time. *American Journal on Mental Retardation, 98,* 207–218.

Dyson, L. L. (1997). Fathers and mothers of school-age children with developmental disabilities: Parental stress, family functioning, and social support. *American Journal on Mental Retardation, 102,* 267–279.

Dyson, L. L. (1998). A support program for siblings of children with disabilities: What siblings learn and what they like. *Psychology in the Schools, 35*(1), 57–63.

Dyson, L. L. (2003). Children with learning disabilities within the family context: A comparison with siblings in global self-concept, academic self-perception, and social competence. *Learning Disabilities Research & Practice, 18*(1), 1–9.

Eccles, J. L., & Harold, R. D. (1996). Family involvement in children's and adolescents' schooling. In A. Booth & J. F. Dunn (Eds.), *Family-school links: How do they affect educational outcomes?* (pp. 3–34). Mahwah, NJ: Erlbaum.

Einam, M., & Cuskelly, M. (2002). Paid employment of mothers and fathers of an adult child with multiple disabilities. *Journal of Intellectual Disability Research, 46*(2), 158–167.

Eisenberg, J. D. (2000). Chronic respiratory disorders. In R. E. Nickel & L. W. Desch (Eds.), *The physician's guide to caring for children with disabilities and chronic conditions.* Baltimore: Paul H. Brookes.

Elliott, D. J., Koroloff, M. I., Koren, P. E., & Friesen, B. J. (1998). Improving access to children's mental health services: The family associate approach. In M. H. Epstein, K. Kutash, & A. Duchnowski (Eds.), *Outcomes for children and youth with behavioral and emotional disorders* (pp. 581–609). Austin, TX: Pro-ed.

Emerson, J., & Lovitt, T. (2003). The educational plight of foster children in schools and what can be done about it. *Remedial and Special Education, 24*(4), 199–203.

Epstein, M. H., Munk, D. D., Bursuck, W. D., Polloway, E. A., & Jayanthi, M. M. (1999). Strategies for improving home-school communication about homework for students with disabilities. *Journal of Special Education, 33*(3), 166–176.

Epstein, M. H., Polloway, E. A., Foley, R. M., & Patton, J. R. (1993). Homework: A comparison of teachers' and parents' perceptions of the problems experienced by students identified as having behavioral disorders, learning disabilities, or no disabilities. *Remedial and Special Education, 14*(5), 40–50.

Erickson, R. (1998). *Accountability, standards, and assessment.* Washington, DC: Federal Resource Center, Academy for Educational Development.

ERIC/OSEP Special Project. (2001, Spring). *Homework practices that support students with disabilities. Research connections in special education* (no. 8). Reston, VA: ERIC Clearinghouse on Disabilities and Gifted Education.

ERIC/OSEP Topical Brief. (2002, September). *Full-service schools' potential for special education.* Reston, VA: ERIC Clearinghouse on Disabilities and Gifted Education and the Council for Exceptional Children.

Erikson, E. H. (1968). Identity: Youth and crisis, New York: Norton.

Erwin, E., & Brown, F. (2003). From theory to practice: A contextual framework for understanding self-determination in early childhood environments. *Infants and Young Children, 16*(1), 77–87.

Erwin, E., Soodak, L., Winton, P., & Turnbull, A. (2001). "I wish it wouldn't all depend upon me": Research on families and early childhood inclusion. In M. J. Guralnick (Ed.), *Early childhood inclusion: Focus on change* (pp. 127–158). Baltimore: Paul H. Brookes.

Erwin, E. J., & Rainforth, B. (1996). Partnerships for collaboration: Building bridges in early care and education. In E. J. Erwin (Ed.), *Putting children first: Visions for a brighter future for young children and their families* (pp. 227–251). Baltimore: Paul H. Brookes.

Erwin, E. J., & Soodak, L. C. (1995). I never knew I could stand up to the system: Families' perspectives on pursuing inclusive education. *Journal of the Association for Persons with Severe Handicaps, 20*(2), 136–146.

Essex, E. L., Seltzer, M. M., & Krauss, M. W. (1999). Differences in coping effectiveness and well-being among aging mothers and fathers of adults with retardation. *American Journal of Mental Retardation, 104*(6), 545–563.

Etscheidt, S. (2003). An analysis of legal hearings and cases related to individualized education programs for children with autism. *Research and Practice for Persons with Severe Disabilities, 28*, 51–69.

Etscheidt, S. K., & Bartlett, L. (1999). The IDEA amendments: A four-step approach for determining supplementary aids and services. *Exceptional Children, 65*(2), 163–174.

Evans, A. (2003). Empowering families, supporting students. *Educational Leadership, 61*(2), 35–37.

Everson, J. M., & Zhang, D. (2000). Person-centered planning: Characteristics, inhibitors, and supports. *Education and Training in Mental Retardation and Developmental Disabilities, 35*(1), 36–43.

Fadiman, A. (1997). *The spirit catches you and you fall down.* New York: Noonday Press.

Fagan, J. (1999). *Predictors of father and father figure involvement in pre-kindergarten Head Start* (White paper). National Center for Children and Families. New York.

Faires, J., Nichols, W. D., & Rickelman, R. J. (2000). Effects of parental involvement in developing competent readers in first grade. *Reading Psychology, 21*(3), 195–215.

Fake, S. (2002). Learning to collaborate as colleagues: Our key to success. In J. M. Lucyshyn, G. Dunlap, & R. W. Albin (Eds.), *Families & positive behavior support* (pp. 209–218). Baltimore: Paul H. Brookes.

Falicov, C. J. (1988). *Family transitions: Continuity & change over the life cycle.* New York: Guilford Press.

Falicov, C. J. (1996). Mexican families. In M. McGoldrick, J. Giordano, & J. K. Pearce (Eds.), *Ethnicity & family therapy.* New York: Guilford Press.

Falvey, M. A., Forest, M., Pearpoint, J., & Rosenberg, R. (1994). Building connections. In J. S. Thousand, R. A. Villa, & A. I. Nevin (Eds.), *Creativity and collaborative learning: A practical guide to empowering students and teachers* (pp. 347–368). Baltimore: Brookes.

Falvey, M. A., Forest, M., Pearpoint, J., & Rosenberg, R. L. (1997). *All my life's a circle.* Toronto, Ontario: Inclusion.

Falvey, M. A., Forest, M. S., Pearpoint, J., & Rosenberg, R. L. (2002). Building connections. In J. S. Thousand, R. A. Villa, & A. I. Nevin (Eds.), *Creativity & collaborative learning.* Baltimore: Paul H. Brookes.

Falvey, M. A., & Rosenberg, R. L. (1995). Developing and fostering friendships In M. A. Falvey (Ed.), *Inclusive and heterogeneous schooling: Assessment curriculum, and instruction* (pp. 267–284). Baltimore: Paul H. Brookes.

Families and Work Institute. (1994). *Employers, families, and education: Facilitating family involvement in learning.* New York: Author.

Farkas, S., Johnson, J., Duffett, A., Aulicino, C., & McHugh, J. (1999). *Playing their parts: Parents and teachers talk about parental involvement in public schools.* New York: A Report from Public Agenda.

Featherstone, H. (1980). *A difference in the family: Living with a disabled child.* New York: Basic Books

Federal Interagency Forum on Child and Family Statistics. (2000). *America's children: Key national indicators of well-being.* Washington, DC: Author. (ERIC Document Reproduction Service No. ED18816)

Feinberg, E., Beyer, J., & Moses, P. (2002). *Beyond mediation: Strategies for appropriate early dispute resolution in special education.* Consortium for Appropriate Dispute Resolution in Special Education (CADRE). Retrieved August 24, 2004, from http://www.directionservice.org/cadre/ beyond_med2002.cfm

Feldhusen, J., Van Winkle, L., & Ehle, D.A. (1996). Is it acceleration or simply appropriate instruction for precocious youth? *Teaching Exceptional Children, 28*(3), 48–51.

Feldman, M.A. (2004). Self-directed learning of child-care skills by parents with intellectual disabilities. *Infants and Young Children, 17*(1), 17–31.

Fennick, E., & Royle, J. (2003). Community inclusion for children and youth with developmental disabilities. *Focus on Autism and Other Developmental Disabilities, 18*(1), 20–27.

Ferguson, D. (1984). Parent advocacy network. *Exceptional Parent, 14,* 41–45.

Ferguson, D. (1998). Relating to self-determination: One parent's thoughts. *Journal of the Association for Persons with Severe Handicaps, 23*(1), 44–46.

Ferguson, P. M. (1994). *Abandoned to their fate: Social policy and practice toward severely retarded people in America.* Philadelphia: Temple University Press.

Ferguson, P. M., & Ferguson, D. L. (1993). The promise of adulthood. In M. Snell (Ed.), *Instruction of persons with severe disabilities* (4th ed., pp. 588–607). Upper Saddle River, NJ: Merrill/Prentice Hall.

Fidler, D. J., Hodapp, R. M., & Dykens, E. M. (2000). Stress in families of young children with Down syndrome, Williams syndrome, and Smith-Magenis syndrome. *Early Childhood Education Journal, 11,* 395–406.

Fiedler, C. R. (2000). *Making a difference: Advocacy competencies for special education professionals.* Boston: Allyn & Bacon.

Field, S., & Hoffman, A. (2002). Lessons learned from implementing the steps to self-determination curriculum. *Remedial and Special Education, 23*(2), 90–98.

Field, S., Martin, J. E., Miller, R. J., Ward, M. J., & Wehmeyer, M. L. (1998). *A practical guide for teaching self-determination.* Reston, VA: Council for Exceptional Children.

File, N. (2001). Family-professional partnership: Practice that matches philosophy. *Young Children, 56*(4), 70–74.

Finders, M., & Lewis, C. (1994). Why some parents don't come to school. *Educational Leadership, 51*(8), 50–54.

Fisher, D., Pumpian, I., & Sax, C. (1998). Parent and caregiver impressions of different educational models. *Remedial and Special Education, 19*(3), 173–180.

Fisher, R., & Ury, W. (1991). *Getting to yes: Negotiating agreement without giving in.* New York: Penguin Books.

Fisman, S., Wolf, L., Ellison, D., & Freeman, T. (2000). A longitudinal study of siblings of children with chronic disabilities. *Canadian Journal of Psychiatry, 45,* 369–375.

Fitzgerald, B. (1999). Children of lesbian and gay parents: A review of the literature. *Marriage & Family Review, 29*(1), 57–75.

Fitzgerald, J. (1997). Reclaiming the whole: Self, spirit, and society. *Disability and Rehabilitation, 19,* 407–413.

Flach, F. (1988). *Resilience: Discovering a new strength at times of stress.* New York: Fawcett Columbine.

Fleischman, H., & Hopstock, P. (1993). *Descriptive study of services to limited English proficient students.* Retrieved April 21, 2000, from http://www.ncela.gwu.edu/pubs/siac / descript/

Fleischmann, A. (2004). Narratives published on the Internet by parents of children with autism: What do they reveal and why is it important. *Focus on Autism and Other Developmental Disabilities, 19*(1), 35–43.

Fletcher, J., & Lyon, R. (1998). Reading: A research-based approach. In W. Evers (Ed.), *What's gone wrong in America's classrooms.* Palo Alto, CA: Hoover Institution Press, Stanford University.

Flouri, E., & Buchanan, A. (2003). The role of father involvement in children's later mental health. *Journal of Adolescence, 26,* 63–78.

Force, L. T., Botsford, A., Pisano, P. A., & Holbert, A. (2000). Grandparents raising children with and without a developmental disability: Preliminary comparisons. *Journal of Gerontological Social Work, 33*(4), 5–21.

Ford, D. (1998). The underrepresentation of minority students in gifted education: Problems and promises in recruitment and retention. *Journal of Special Education, 32*(1), 4–14.

Forest, M., & Lusthaus, E. (1990). Everyone belongs with the MAPs action planning system. *Teaching Exceptional Children, 22*(2), 32–35.

Forgan, J. W., & Gonzalez-DeHass, A. (2004). How to infuse social skills training into literacy instruction. *Teaching Exceptional Children, 36*(6), 24–30.

Forman, R. K. C. (Ed.). (1993). *Religions of the world* (3rd ed.). New York: St. Martin's Press.

Fowler, S. A., Donegan, M., Lueke, B., Hadden, D. S., & Phillips, B. (2000). Evaluating community collaboration in writing interagency agreements on the age 3 transitions. *Exceptional Children, 67*(1), 35-50.

Frankland, H. C. (2001). *Professional collaboration and family-professional partnerships: A qualitative analysis of indicators and influencing factors.* Unpublished doctoral dissertation, University of Kansas, Lawrence.

Frankland, H. C., Turnbull, A. P., Wehmeyer, M., & Blackmountain, L. (in press). An exploration of the self-determination construct and disability as it related to the Dine (Navajo) culture. *Education and Training in Mental Retardation and Developmental Disabilities.*

Frederickson, N., & Turner, J. (2003). Utilizing the classroom peer group to address children's social needs: An evaluation of the circle of friends intervention approach. *Journal of Special Education, 36*(4), 234-245.

Friedman, R. C. (1994). Upstream helping for low-income families of gifted students: Challenges and opportunities. *Journal of Educational and Psychological Consultation, 5*(4), 321-338.

Friedman, R. C. (2000). Families with gifted children. In M. J. Fine & R. L. Simpson (Eds.), *Collaboration with parents and families of children and youth with exceptionalities.* Austin, TX: Pro-Ed.

Frieman, B. B., & Berkeley, T. R. (2002). Encouraging fathers to participate in the school experiences of young children: The teacher's role. *Early Childhood Education Journal, 29*(3), 209-213.

Friend, M., & Bursuck, W. D. (2002). *Including students with special needs.* Boston: Allyn & Bacon.

Friend, M., & Cook, L. (2003). *Interactions: Collaboration skills for school professionals.* Boston: Allyn & Bacon.

Friend, M., Reising, M., & Cook, L. (1993). Co-teaching: An overview of the past, a glimpse at the present, and considerations for the future. *Preventing School Failure, 37*(4), 6-10.

Fujiura, G. T. (1998). Demography of family households. *American Journal on Mental Retardation, 103*(3), 225-235.

Fujiura, G. T., Roccoforte, J. A., & Braddock, D. (1994). Costs of family care for adults with mental retardation and related developmental disabilities. *American Journal on Mental Retardation, 99*(3), 250-261.

Fujiura, G. T., & Yamaki, K. (1997). Analysis of ethnic variations in developmental disability prevalence and household economic status. *Mental Retardation, 35*(4), 286-294.

Fujiura, G. T., & Yamaki, K. (2000). Trends in demography of childhood poverty and disability. *Exceptional Children, 66*(2), 187-200.

Fullan, M. (1999). *Change forces: The sequel.* London: Falmer Press.

Furey, E. M. (1994). Sexual abuse of adults with mental retardation: Who and where. *Mental Retardation, 32*(3), 173-180.

Furstenberg, F. F. (2003). Teenage childbearing as a public issue and private concern. *Annual Review Sociology, 29*, 23-39.

Gajria, M., & Salend, S. J. (1995). Homework practices of students with and without learning disabilities: A comparison. *Journal of Learning Disabilities, 28*(5), 291-296.

Gallagher, J., & Desimone, L. (1995). Lessons learned from implementations of the IEP: Applications to the IFSP. *Topics in Early Childhood Special Education, 15*(3), 353-378.

Gallagher, J., & Gallagher, S. (1994). *Teaching the gifted child* (4th ed.). Boston: Allyn & Bacon.

Gallagher, J. J. (1997). Least restrictive environment and gifted students. *Peabody Journal of Education, 72*(3&4), 153-165.

Gallagher, J. J., & Gallagher, G. G. (1985). Family adaptation to a handicapped child and assorted professionals. In H. R. Turnbull & A. P. Turnbull (Eds.), *Parents speak out: Then and now* (pp. 233-244). Upper Saddle River, NJ: Merrill/Prentice Hall.

Gallagher, P. A., Fialka, J., Rhodes, C., & Arceneaux, C. (2001). Working with families: Rethinking denial. *Young Exceptional Children, 5*(2), 11-17.

Gallagher, P. A., Floyd, J. H., Stafford, A. M., Taber, T. A., Brozovic, S. A., & Alberto, P. A. (2000). Inclusion of students with moderate or severe disabilities in educational and community settings: Perspectives from parents and siblings. *Education and Training in Mental Retardation and Developmental Disabilities, 35*(2), 135-147.

Gambetta, D. (1988). Can we trust? In D. Gambetta (Ed.), *Trust: Making and breaking cooperative relations* (pp. 213-238). Cambridge, MA: Basil Blackwell.

Gandhi, M. K. (1958). *Collected works of Mahatma Gandhi* (Vol. 22). New Delhi: Publications Divisions, Ministry of Broadcasting, Government of India.

Gans, L. (1997). *Sisters, brothers, and disability.* Minneapolis, MN: Fairview Press.

Garay, S. V. (2003). Listening to the voices of deaf students: Essential transition issues. *Teaching Exceptional Children, 35*(4), 44-48.

Garcia, C. A., & Kennedy, S. S. (2003). Back to school: Technology, school safety and the disappearing Fourth Amendment. *Kansas Journal of Law and Public Policy, 12* (2), 273-288.

Gardner, R., Cartledge, G., Seidl, B., Woolsey, M. L., Schley, G. S., & Utley, C. A. (2001). Peer-mediated interventions for at-risk students. *Remedial and Special Education, 22*, 22.

Gath, A. (1977). The impact of an abnormal child upon the parents. *British Journal of Psychiatry, 130*, 405-410.

Gaventa, W. C. (2001). Defining and assessing spirituality and spiritual supports: A rationale for inclusion in theory and practice. *Journal of Religion, Disability, and Health, 5*(2-3), 29-48.

Gavidia-Payne, S., & Stoneman, Z. (1997). Family predictors of maternal and paternal involvement in programs for young children with disabilities. *Child Development, 68*(4), 701-717.

Geenen, S., Powers, L., & Lopez-Vasquez, A. (2001). Multicultural aspects of parent involvement in transition planning. *Exceptional Children, 67,* 265-282.

Gelfer, J. I., & Perkins, P. G. (1998). Portfolios: Focus on young children. *Teaching Exceptional Children, 31*(2), 44-47.

Gelzheiser, L. M., McLane, M., Meyers, J., & Pruzek, R. M. (1998). IEP-specified peer interaction needs: Accurate but ignored. *Exceptional Children, 65*(1), 51-65.

Gerst, D. (1991). *Trevor is a citizen: Why grieve?* Unpublished manuscript.

Gettings, R. M. (1994). The link between public financing and systematic change. In V. J. Bradley, J. W. Ashbaugh, & B. C. Blaney (Eds.), *Creating individual supports for people with developmental disabilities* (pp. 155-170). Baltimore: Brookes.

Getzel, E. E., & deFur, S. (1997). Transition planning for students with significant disabilities: Implications for student-centered planning. *Focus on Autism and Other Developmental Disabilities, 12*(1), 39-48.

Getzel, E. E., Stodden, R. S., & Briel, L. W. (1999). *Pursuing postsecondary education opportunities for individuals with disabilities:* Manoa, HI: University of Hawaii.

Giangreco, M. (2001). Interactions among program, placement and services in educational planning for students with disabilities. *Mental Retardation, 39,* 341-350.

Giangreco, M. F. (1986). Delivery of therapeutic services in special education programs for learners with severe handicaps. *Physical and Occupational Therapy in Pediatrics, 6,* 5-15.

Giangreco, M. F., & Doyle, M. B. (2002). Students with disabilities and paraprofessional supports: Benefits, balance, and Band-Aids. *Focus on Exceptional Children, 34*(7), 1-12.

Giangreco, M. F., Prelock, P. A., Reid, R. R., Dennis, R. E., & Edelman, S. W. (2000). Role of related services personnel in inclusive schools. In R. A. Villa & J. S. Thousand (Eds.), *Restructuring for caring and effective education* (2nd ed., pp. 293-327). Baltimore: Brookes.

Gilhool, T. (1997, Spring). Tom Gilhool speaks out on significant accomplishments of parents as political advocates. *The Parent Movement: Reflections and Directions. Coalition Quarterly, 14*(1).

Gill, B. (1997). *Changed by a child.* New York: Doubleday.

Gilmore, S., Bose, J., & Hart, D. (2001). Postsecondary education as a critical step toward meaningful employment: Vocational rehabilitation's role. *Research to Practice, 7*(4), 1-4.

Gilson, S. F., Bricourt, J. C., & Baskind, F. R. (1998, March-April). Listen to the voices of individuals with disabilities. *Families in Society: The Journal of Contemporary Human Services, 79*(2), 188-196.

Glidden, L. M. (1989). *Parents for children, children for parents: The adoption alternative.* Washington, DC: American Association on Mental Retardation.

Glidden, L. M., & Johnson, V. E. (1999). Twelve years later: Adjustment in families who adopted children with developmental disabilities. *Mental Retardation, 37*(1), 16-24.

Glidden, L. M., Kiphart, M. J., Willoughby, J. C., & Bush, B. A. (1993). Family functioning when rearing children with developmental disabilities. In A. P. Turnbull, J. M. Patterson, S. K. Behr, D. L. Murphy, J. G. Marquis, & M. J. Blue-Banning (Eds.), *Cognitive coping, families, and disability* (pp. 173-182). Baltimore: Brookes.

Goals 2000: Educate America Act of 1994, P. L. 103-227, 20 U.S.C. § 5801 *et seq.*

Goddard, H. H. (1912). *The Kallikak family: A study in the heredity of feeblemindedness.* New York: Macmillan.

Goddard, R. D., Sweetland, S. R., & Hoy, W. K. (2000). Academic emphasis of urban elementary schools and student achievement in reading and mathematics: A multilevel analysis. *Educational Administration Quarterly, 36*(5), 683-702.

Goddard, R. D., Tschannen-Moran, M., & Hoy, W. K. (2001). A multilevel examination of the distribution and effects of teacher trust in students and parents in urban elementary schools. *Elementary School Journal, 102*(1).

Goldenberg, C. (2004) *Successful school change: Creating settings to improve teaching and learning.* New York: Teachers College Press.

Goldenson, L. H. (1965). *Remarks on the occasion of United Cerebral Palsy Associations' 15th anniversary.* Paper presented at the 15th annual meeting of the United Cerebral Palsy Associations, Los Angeles.

Goldstein, S., Strickland, B., Turnbull, A. P., & Curry, L. (1980). An observational analysis of the IEP conference. *Exceptional Children, 46*(4), 278-286.

Gollnick, D. M., & Chinn, P. C. (2002). *Multicultural education in a pluralistic society* (6th ed.). Upper Saddle River, NJ: Merrill/Prentice Hall.

Gomby, D. S., Culross, P. L., & Behrman, R. E. (1999). Home visiting: Recent program evaluations — Analysis and recommendations. *Future of Children, 9*(1), 4-26.

Gould, S. J. (1981). *The mismeasure of man.* New York: W. W. Norton & Co.

Goupil, G., Tasse, M. J., Garcin, N., & Dore, C. (2002). Parent and teacher perceptions of individualized transition planning. *British Journal of Special Education, 29,* 127-135.

Government Accounting Office. (2003). *Special education: Federal actions can assist states in improving post secondary outcomes for youth* (GAO-03-773). Washington, DC: Author.

Govier, T. (1992). Distrust as a practical problem. *Journal of Social Philosophy, 23,* 52-63.

Gowen, J. W., Christy, D. S., & Sparling, J. (1993). Informational needs of parents of young children with special needs. *Journal of Early Intervention, 17*(2), 194-210.

Gowen, J. W., Christy, D. S., & Sparling, J. (1993). Informational needs of parents of young children with special needs. *Topics in Early Childhood Special Education, 1*(2), 31-39.

Gowen, J. W., Johnson-Martin, N., Goldman, B. D., & Appelbaum, M. (1989). Feelings of depression and parenting competence of mothers of handicapped and nonhandicapped infants: A longitudinal study. *American Journal on Mental Retardation, 94*(3), 259–271.

Greenwald, R. (1997). *My son, my gentle son.* Tallmadge, OH: Family Child Learning Center.

Grigal, M., Quirk, C., & Manos, S. (1998). *MAPs as a planning tool: What works? What doesn't? Says who?* Paper presented at the TASH conference, Seattle, WA.

Grisham-Brown, J. (2000). Transdisciplinary activity-based assessment for young children with multiple disabilities: A program planning approach. *Young Exceptional Children, 3*(2), 3–10.

Grissom, M. O., & Borkowski, J. G. (2002). Self-efficacy in adolescents who have siblings with or without disabilities. *American Journal on Mental Retardation, 107*(2), 79–90.

Grossman, K., Grossman, K. E., Fremmer-Bombik, E., Kindler, H., Scheuerer-Englisch, H., & Zimmerman, P. (2002). The uniqueness of the child-father attachment relationship: Fathers' sensitive and challenging play as a pivotal variable in a 16-year longitudinal study. *Social Development, 11,* 307–331.

Grotevant, H. D., & McRoy, R. G. (1990). Adopted adolescents in residential treatment: The role of the family. In D. Brodzinsky & M. Schechter (Eds.), *The psychology of adoption* (pp. 167–186). New York: Oxford University Press.

Grove, K. A., & Fisher, D. (1999). Entrepreneurs of meaning: Parents and the process of inclusive education. *Remedial and Special Education, 20*(4), 208–215, 256.

Guidry, J., van den Pol, R., Keeley, E., & Neilsen, S. (1996). Augmenting traditional assessment and information: The video share model. *Topics in Early Childhood Special Education, 16*(1), 51–65.

Guralnick, M. J., Conner, R. T., & Hammond, M. (1995). Parent perspectives of peer relationships and friendships in integrated and specialized settings. *American*

Journal on Mental Retardation, 99, 457–476.

Guskey, T. R., & Bailey, J. M. (2001). *Developing grading and reporting systems for student learning.* Thousand Oaks, CA: Corwin Press.

Haffner, D. W. (1998). Sexuality education. *Social Policy, 28,* 76–78.

Hagner, D., Helm, R. T., & Butterworth, J. (1996). "This is your meeting": A qualitative study of person-centered planning. *Mental Retardation, 34*(3), 159–171.

Haller, E. J., & Millman, J. (1987). *A survey of Arc members* [Internal report]. Arlington, TX: The Arc.

Halpern, R. (1999). After-school programs for low-income children: Promise and challenges. *Future of Children, 9,* 81–95.

Halpin, A. W., & Croft, D. B. (1963). *The organization climate of schools.* Chicago: Midwest Administration Center of the University of Chicago.

Hammer, M. R. (2004). Using the self-advocacy strategy to increase student participation in the IEP conference. *Intervention in School and Clinic, 39*(5), 295–300.

Hannah, M. E., & Midlarsky, E. (1999). Competence and adjustment of siblings of children with mental retardation. *American Journal on Mental Retardation, 104*(1), 22–37.

Hanson, M. J. (1998). Families with Anglo-European roots. In E. W. Lynch & M. J. Hanson (Eds.), *Developing cross-cultural competence: A guide for working with young children and their families* (2nd ed., pp. 65–87, 93–126). Baltimore: Brookes.

Hanson, M. J. (2004). Families with Anglo-European roots. In E. W. Lynch & M. J. Hanson (Eds.), *Developing cross-cultural competence: A guide for working with children and their families* (3rd ed.). Baltimore: Brookes.

Hanson, M. J., Beckman, P. J., Horn, E., Marquart, J., Sandall, S. R., Greig, D., & Brennan, E. (2000). Entering preschool: Family and professional experiences in this transition process. *Journal of Early Intervention, 23*(4), 279–293.

Hanson, M. J., Horn, E., Sandall, S., Beckman, P., Morgan, M., Marquart, J.,

et al. (2001). After preschool inclusion: Children's educational pathways over the early school years. *Journal of Early Intervention, 68*(1), 65–83.

Hanson, M. J., & Lynch, E. W. (2004). *Understanding families: Approaches to diversity, disability and risk.* Baltimore: Paul H. Brookes.

Hara, S. R., & Burke, D. J. (1998). Parent involvement: The key to improved student achievement. *School Community Journal, 8*(2), 385–413.

Harden, B. J. (1997). You cannot do it alone: Home visitation with psychologically vulnerable families and children. *Bulletin of Zero to Three: National Center for Infants, Toddlers, and Families, 17*(4), 10–16.

Harniss, M. K., Epstein, M. H., Bursuck, W. D., Nelson, J., & Jayanthi, M. (2001). Resolving homework-related communication problems: Recommendations of parents of children with and without disabilities. *Reading and Writing Quarterly, 17*(3), 205–225.

Harris, V. S., & McHale, S. M. (1989). Family life problems, daily caregiving activities, and the psychological well-being of mothers of mentally retarded children. *American Journal on Mental Retardation, 94*(3), 231–239.

Harry, B. (1992). Making sense of disability: Low-income, Puerto Rican parents' theories of the problem. *Exceptional Children, 59*(1), 27–40.

Harry, B. (1992a). Developing cultural self-awareness: The first step in values clarification for early interventionists. *Topics in Early Childhood Special Education, 12*(3), 333–350.

Harry, B. (1992b). An ethnographic study of cross-cultural communication with Puerto Rican–American families in the special education system. *American Educational Research Journal, 29*(3), 471–494.

Harry, B., Allen, N., & McLaughlin, M. (1995). Communication versus compliance: African-American parents' involvement in special education. *Exceptional Children, 61*(4), 364–377.

Harry, B., Day, M., & Quist, F. (1998). "He can't really play": An ethnographic study of sibling acceptance and interaction. *Journal of the Association for Persons With Severe Handicaps* (JASH), *23*(4), 289–299.

Harry, B., Grenot-Scheyer, M., Smith-Lewis, M., Park, H., Xin, F., & Schwartz, I. (1995). Developing culturally inclusive services for individuals with severe disabilities. *Journal of the Association for Persons with Severe Handicaps, 20*(2), 99–109.

Harry, B., & Kalyanpur, M. (1994). Cultural underpinnings of special education: Implications for professional interactions with culturally diverse families. *Disability and Society, 9*(2), 145–165.

Harry, B., Kalyanpur, M., & Day, M. (1999). *Building cultural reciprocity with families.* Baltimore: Paul H. Brookes.

Hart, B., & Risley, T. R. (1995). *Meaningful differences in the everyday experience of young American children.* Baltimore: Paul H. Brookes.

Hart, D., Mele-McCarthy, J., Pasternack, R. H., Zimbrich, K., & Parker, D. R. (2004). Community college: A pathway to success for youth with learning, cognitive, and intellectual disabilities in secondary settings. *Education and Training in Developmental Disabilities, 39*(1), 54–66.

Hartas, D., & Donahue, M. L. (1997). Conversational and social problem-solving skills in adolescents with learning disabilities. *Learning Disabilities Research and Practice, 12*(4), 213–220.

Hasazi, S., Gordon, L., & Roe, C. (1985). Factors associated with the employment status of handicapped youth exiting from high school from 1979 to 1983. *Exceptional Children, 51*(6), 455–469.

Hasazi, S. B., Furney, K. S., & Destefano, L. (1999). Implementing the IDEA transition mandates. *Exceptional Children, 65*(4), 555–566.

Hastings, R. P. (1997). Grandparents of children with disabilities: A review. *International Journal of Disability, Development, and Education, 44,* 329–340.

Hastings, R. P., & Brown, T. (2002). Behavior problems of children with autism, parental self-efficacy, and mental health. *American Journal on Mental Retardation, 107*(3), 222–232.

Hastings, R. P., & Taunt, H. M. (2002). Positive perceptions in families of children with developmental disabilities. *American Journal on Mental Retardation, 107*(2), 116–127.

Hauser-Cram, P., Ericson-Warfield, M., Shonkoff, J. P., Wyngaarden-Krauss, M., Upshur, C. C., & Sayer, A. (1999). Family influences on adaptive development in young children with Down syndrome. *Child Development, 70*(4), 979–989.

Haviland, J. (2003). Time well spent: Determining what parents want in a parent meeting. *Principal Leadership, 3*(5), 50–53.

Heller, K. W., Gallagher, P. A., & Frederick, L. D. (1999). Parents' perceptions of siblings' interactions with their brothers and sisters who are deaf-blind. *Journal of the Association for Persons with Severe Handicaps, 24*(1), 33–43.

Heller, T., Hsieh, K., & Rowitz, L. (2000). Grandparents as supports to mothers of persons with intellectual disability. *Journal of Gerontological Social Work, 33*(4), 23–34.

Helm, D. T., Miranda, S., & Angoff-Chedd, N. (1998). Prenatal diagnosis of Down syndrome: Mothers' reflections on supports needed from diagnosis to birth. *Mental Retardation, 36*(1), 55–61.

Helsel Family. (1985). The Helsels' story of Robin. In H. R. Turnbull & A. P. Turnbull (Eds.), *Parents speak out: Then and now* (2nd ed., pp. 81–100). Upper Saddle River, NJ: Merrill/Prentice Hall.

Hemmeter, M. L., Joseph, G. E., Smith, B. J., & Sandall, S. (2001). *DEC recommended practices program assessment: Improving practices for young children with special needs and their families.* Denver, CO: Division for Early Childhood.

Henderson, A. T., & Berla, N. (Eds.). (1994). *A new generation of evidence: The family is critical to student achievement.* Washington, DC: Center for Law and Education.

Henry, J., & Purcell, R. (2000). Exploring the tensions: Being family-centered with parents who abuse/neglect their children. *Infant-Toddler Intervention: The Transdisciplinary Journal, 10*(4), 275–285.

Herman, S. E. (1994). Cash subsidy program: Family satisfaction and need. *Mental Retardation, 32*(6), 416–421.

Herman, S. E., & Marcenko, M. O. (1997). Perceptions of services and resources as mediators of depression among parents of children with developmental disabilities. *Mental Retardation, 35*(6), 458–467.

Herman, S. E., & Thompson, L. (1995). Families' perceptions of their resources for caring for children with developmental disabilities. *Mental Retardation, 33*(2), 73–83.

Heumann, J. (1997, Spring). Assistant secretary Judith E. Heumann. The parent movement: Reflections and directions. *Coalition Quarterly, 14*(1).

Hewitt, B. (2000). House divided. *People Weekly, 54,* 138–144.

Hinton, L. M., & Kern, L. (1999). Increasing homework completion by incorporating student interests. *Journal of Positive Behavior Interventions, 1*(4), 231–234.

Hoare, P., Harris, M., Jackson, P., & Kerley, S. (1998). A community survey of children with severe intellectual disability and their families: Psychological adjustment, career distress and the effect of respite care. *Journal of Intellectual Disability Research, 42,* 218–224.

Hodapp, R. M., & Krasner, D. V. (1995). Families of children with disabilities: Findings from a national sample of eighth-grade students. *Exceptionality, 5*(2), 71–81.

Hodge, K. A., & Kemp, C. R. (2000). Exploring the nature of giftedness in preschool children. *Journal for the Education of the Gifted, 24,* 46–73.

Holburn, S. (2002). How science can evaluate and enhance person-centered planning. *Research and*

Practice for Persons with Severe Disabilities, 27(4), 250–260.

Holburn, S., Perkins, T., & Vietze, P. (2001). The parent with mental retardation. In L. M. Glidden (Ed.), *International review of research in mental retardation* (Vol. 24). San Diego, CA: Academic Press.

Hollingsworth, H. L. (2001). We need to talk: Communication strategies for effective communication. *Teaching Exceptional Children, 33*(5), 4–8.

Holmes, J. G., & Rempel, J. K. (1989). Trust in close relationships. In C. Hendrick (Ed.), *Close relationships* (pp. 187–220). Newbury Park, CA: Sage.

Homes for the Homeless. (1992). *Who are homeless families? A profile of homeless in New York City.* New York: Author.

Hoover-Dempsey, K. V., Battiato, A. C., Walker, J. M. T., Reed, R. P., DeJong, J. M., & Jones, K. P. (2001). Parental involvement in homework. *Educational Psychologist, 36*(3), 195–209.

Hornby, G., & Ashworth, T. (1994). Grandparents' support for families who have children with disabilities. *Journal of Child and Family Studies, 3*(4), 403–412.

Horner, R. H. (2000). Positive behavior supports. In M. L. Wehmeyer & J. R. Patton (Eds.), *Mental retardation in the 21st century* (pp. 181–196). Austin, TX: Pro-Ed.

Horner, R. H., Albin, R. W., Sprague, J. R., & Todd, A. W. (2000). Positive behavior support. In M. E. Snell & F. Brown (Eds.), *Instruction of students with severe disabilities* (5th ed., pp. 207–243). Merrill/Prentice Hall.

Hornstein, B. (1997). How the religious community can support the transition to adulthood: A parent's perspective. *Mental Retardation, 36*(6), 485–487.

Howard, V. F., Williams, B. F., Port, P. D., & Lepper, C. (1997). *Very young children with special needs: A formative approach for the 21st century.* Upper Saddle River, NJ: Merrill.

Hoy, W. K., (2002). Faculty trust: A key to student achievement. *Journal of Public School Relations, 23,* 88–103.

Hoy, W. K., Hannum, J., & Tschannen-Moran, M. (1998, July). Organizational climate and student achievement: A parsimonious and longitudinal view. *Journal of School Leadership, 8,* 336–359.

Hoy, W. K., & Miskel, C. G. (2001). *Educational administration: Theory, research, and practice* (6th ed.). New York: McGraw-Hill.

Hoy, W. K., & Sabo, D. J. (1998). *Quality middle schools: Open and healthy.* Thousand Oaks, CA: Corwin Press.

Hoy, W. K., Smith, P. A., & Sweetland, S. R. (2002). The development of the organizational climate index for high schools: Its measure and relationship to faculty trust. *High School Journal, 86*(2), 12–38.

Hoy, W. K., & Sweetland, S. R. (2001). Designing better schools: The meaning and measure of enabling school structures. *Educational Administration Quarterly, 37*(3), 296–321.

Hoy, W. K., & Tarter, C. J. (1997). *The road to open and healthy schools: A handbook for change* (elementary and secondary school ed.). Thousand Oaks, CA: Corwin Press.

Huer, M. B. (1999). Focus group with parents with AAC devices. In H. P. Parette & A. VanBiervliet (Eds. Families, Cultures, and AAC), [CD-ROM] (pp. 194–228). Little Rock, AR: Southeast Missouri State University and University of Arkansas for Medical Sciences.

Huer, M. B., Parette, H. P., & Saenz, T. I. (2001). Conversations with Mexican-Americans regarding children with disabilities and augmentative and alternative communication. *Communication Disorders Quarterly, 22*(4), 197–206.

Hughes, C., Kim, J., Hwang, B., Killian, D. J., Fischer, G. M., Brock, M. L., et al. (1997). Practitioner-validated secondary transition support strategies. *Education and Training in Mental Retardation and Developmental Disabilities, 32,* 201–212.

Hughes, R. S. (1999). An investigation of coping skills of parents of children with disabilities: Implications for service providers. *Education and Training in Mental Retardation and Developmental Disabilities, 34*(3), 271–280.

Human, M. T., & Teglasi, H. (1993). Parents' satisfaction and compliance with recommendations following psychoeducational assessment of children. *Journal of School Psychology, 31,* 449–464.

Human Services Research Institute. (1995, May). *Supplemental security income for children with disabilities: An exploration of child and family needs and the relative merits of the cash benefit-program.* Salem, OR: Author.

Humphrey, K. R., Turnbull, A. P., & Turnbull, H. R. (in press). Perspectives of foster care providers, service providers, and judges regarding privatized foster care services. *Journal of Disability Policy Studies.*

Hundt, T. A. (2002). Videotaping young children in the classroom: Parents as partners. *Teaching Exceptional Children, 34*(3), 38–43.

Hunt, J. (1972). *Human intelligence.* New Brunswick, NJ: Transaction Books.

Hyun, J. K., & Fowler, S. A. (1995). Respect, cultural sensitivity, and communication. *Teaching Exceptional Children, 28*(1), 25–31.

Iceland, J. (2000). *The "family/couple/household" unit of analysis in poverty measurement.* Retrieved September 27, 2001, from http://www.census.gov/hhes/poverty/povmeas/papers/famhh3.html#2

Improving America's Schools Act of 1994, P. L. 103–382, 20 U.S.C. § 7425 *et seq.*

Individuals with Disabilities Education Act (IDEA), 20 U.S.C. Sec. 1412 (a) (12).

Individuals with Disabilities Education Act (IDEA), 20 U.S.C. § 1400 *et seq.*

Institute for Children and Poverty. (2001). *Deja vu: Family homelessness in New York City.* New York: Author.

Ivey, J. K. (2004). What do parents expect? A study of likelihood and importance issues for children with autism spectrum disorders. *Focus on*

Autism and Other Developmental Disabilities, 19(1), 27–33.

Jackson, C., Becker, S., & Schmitendorf, K. (2002). *Survey of satisfaction with resources related to deafness in Kansas.* Unpublished manuscript, University of Kansas, Lawrence.

Jackson, C.W., & Turnbull, A. (in press). Impact of deafness on family life: A literature review. *Topics in Early Childhood Special Education.*

Jackson, S. C., & Roberts, J. E. (1999). Family and professional congruence in communication assessments of preschool boys with fragile X syndrome. *Journal of Early Intervention, 22*(2), 137–151.

Jacob, N. (2004). Families with South Asian roots. In E. W. Lynch & M. J. kay (Eds.), *Developing cross-cultural competence* (3rd ed., pp. 415–439). Baltimore: Paul H. Brookes.

Jalali, B. (1996). Iranian families. In M. McGoldrick, J. Giordano, & J. K. Pearce (Eds.), *Ethnicity and family therapy* (pp. 347–363). New York: Guilford Press.

Janicky, M. P., McCallion, P., Grant-Griffin, L., & Kolomer, S. R. (2000). Grandparent caregivers I: Characteristics of the grandparents and the children with disabilities for whom they care. *Journal of Gerontological Social Work, 33,* 35–55.

Jayanthi, M., Sawyer, V., Nelson, J. S., Bursuck, W. D., & Epstein, M. H. (1995). Recommendations for homework-communication problems. *Remedial and Special Education, 16*(4), 212–225.

Jin, S., & Feldhusen, J. F. (2000). Parent identification of the talents of gifted students. *Gifted Education International, 14*(3), 230–236.

Joe, J. R. (1997). American Indian children with disabilities: The impact of culture on health and education services. *Families, Systems, and Health, 15*(3), 251–261.

Joe, J. R., & Malach, R. S. (2004). Families with American Indian roots. In E. W. Lynch & M. J. Hanson (Eds.), *Developing cross-cultural competence: A guide for working with children and their families*

(pp. 109–139). Baltimore: Paul Brookes.

Johnson, D. (2000). Teacher web pages that build parent partnerships. *Multimedia Schools, 7*(4), 48–51.

Johnson, D. R., Stodden, R. A., Emanuel, E. J., Luecking, R., & Mack, M. (2002). Current challenges facing secondary education and transition services: What research tells us. *Exceptional Children, 68*(4), 519–531.

Johnson, J. (2003). When it's your own child. *Educational Leadership, 61*(2), 30–34.

Johnson, J., & Duffett, A. (2002). *When it's your own child: A report on special education from the families who use it.* New York: Public Agenda Foundation. (ERIC Document Reproduction Service No. ED471033)

Johnson, J., Duffett, A., Farkas, S., & Wilson, L. (2002). *When it's your own child: A report on special education from the families who use it.* New York: Public Agenda.

Johnson, S. D., Proctor, W. A., & Corey, S. E. (1995). A new partner in the IEP process: The laptop computer. *Teaching Exceptional Children, 28*(1), 46–56.

Jones, G. R., & George, J. M. (1998). The experience and evolution of trust: Implications for cooperation and teamwork. *Academy of Management Review, 23*(3), 516–531.

Jones, S., Angelo, D., & Kokoska, S. (1998). Stressors and family supports: Families with children using augmentative and alternative communication technology. *Journal of Children's Communication Development, 20*(2), 37–44.

Jones, T. (2003). Conflict resolution quarterly, no. 3. Indianapolis, IN: John Wiley.

Jordan, G. E., Snow, C. E., & Porche, M. V. (2000). Project EASE: The effect of a family literacy project on kindergarten students' early literacy skills. *Reading-Research Quarterly, 35*(4), 524–546.

Jordan, L., Reyes-Blanes, M. E., Peel, B. B., Peel, H. A., & Lane, H. B. (1998). Developing teacher-parent partnerships across cultures: Effective

parent conferences. *Intervention in School and Clinic, 33*(3), 141–147.

Judge, S. (2002). Family-centered assistive technology assessment and intervention practices for early intervention. *Infants and Young Children, 15*(1), 60–68.

Kagan, C., Lewis, S., Heaton, P., & Cranshaw, M. (1999). Enabled or disabled? Working parents of disabled children and the provision of child-care. *Journal of Community & Applied Social Psychology, 9,* 369–381.

Kaiser, A., & Delaney, E. (1996). The effects of poverty on parenting young children. *Peabody Journal of Education, 71,* 66–85.

Kalyanpur, M., & Harry, B. (1999). *Culture in special education: Building reciprocal family-professional relationships.* Baltimore: Paul H. Brookes.

Kalyanpur, M., Harry, B., & Skrtic, T. (2000). Equity and advocacy expectations of culturally diverse families' participation in special education. *International Journal of Disability, Development and Education, 47*(2), 119–136.

Kalyanpur, M., & Rao, S. S. (1991). Empowering low-income black families of handicapped children. *American Journal of Orthopsychiatry, 61*(4), 523–532.

Kanner, L. (1949). Problems of nosology and psychodynamica of early infantile autism. *American Journal of Orthopsychiatry, 19,* 416–426.

Kaplan, L., & Girard, J. L. (1994). *Strengthening high-risk families.* New York: Lexington Books.

Kaplan-Sanoff, M. (1996). The impact of maternal substance abuse on young children: Myths and realities. In E. J. Erwin (Ed.), *Putting children first* (pp. 79–103). Baltimore: Brookes.

Karnes, M. B., & Teska, J. A. (1980). Toward successful parent involvement in programs for handicapped children. In J. J. Gallagher (Ed.), *New directions for exceptional children: Parents and families of handicapped children* (Vol. 4, pp. 85–109). San Francisco: Jossey-Bass.

Kasahara, M., & Turnbull, A. P. (in press). Meaning of partnerships: Qualitative inquiry of desirable family-professional partnerships. *Exceptional Children*.

Katz, L., & Scarpati, S. (1995). A cultural interpretation of early intervention teams and the IFSP: Parent and professional perceptions of roles and responsibilities. *Infant-Toddler Intervention, 5*(2), 177–192.

Katzen, K. (1980). To the editor: An open letter to CEC. *Exceptional Children, 46*(8), 582.

Kaufman, P., Kwon, J.Y., Klein, S., & Chapman, C. D. (1999). *Dropout rates in the United States: 1998.* Washington, DC: U.S. Department of Education, Office of Educational Research and Improvement.

Kaufman, P., Kwon, J.Y., Klein, S., & Chapman, C.D. (2000). *Dropout rates in the United States: 1999.* Washington, DC: National Center for Education Statistics.

Kay, P., Fitzgerald, M., Paradee, C., & Mellencamp, A. (1994). Making homework work at home: The parent's perspective. *Journal of Learning Disabilities, 27*(9), 550–561.

Kazak, A. E., & Marvin, R. S. (1984). Differences, difficulties and adaptation: Stress and social networks in families with a handicapped child. *Family Relations, 33,* 67–77.

Keim, J., Ryan, A. G., & Nolan, B. F. (1998). Dilemmas faced when working with learning disabilities in post-secondary education. *Annals of Dyslexia, 48,* 273–291.

Kelly, J. F., Buehlman, K., & Caldwell, K. (2000). Training personnel to promote quality parent-child interaction in families who are homeless. *Topics in Early Childhood Special Education, 20*(3), 174–185.

Kelly, K. M., Siegel, E. B., & Allinder, R. M. (2001). Personal profile assessment summary: Creating windows into the worlds of children with special needs. *Intervention in the School & Clinic, 36*(4), 202–211.

Kemp, C. E., & Parette, H. P. (2000). Barriers to minority family involvement in assistive technology decision-making processes. *Education and Training in Mental Retardation and Developmental Disabilities, 35*(4), 384–392.

Kincaid, D., Chapman, C., Shannon, P., Schall, C., & Harrower, J. K. (2002). Families and the tri-state consortium for positive behavior support. In J. M. Lucyshyn, G. Dunlap, & R. W. Albin (Eds.), *Families & positive behavior support* (pp. 309–328). Baltimore: Paul H. Brookes.

Kipnis, D. (1996). Trust and technology. In R. M. Kramer & T. R. Tyler (Eds.), *Trust in organizations:* Frontiers and theory and research (pp. 39–50). Thousand Oaks, CA: Sage.

Kirby, D. (2000). What does the research say about sexuality education. *Educational Leadership, 58*(2), 72–76.

Kirk, S.A. (1984). Introspection and prophecy. In B. Blatt & R. J. Morris (Eds.), *Perspectives in special education: Personal orientations* (pp. 25–55). Glenview, IL: Scott, Foresman.

Klein, S. D., & Kemp, J. D. (2004). *Reflections from a different journey: What adults with disabilities wish all parents knew.* New York: McGraw-Hill.

Kliebenstein, M.A., & Broome, M. E. (2000). School re-entry for the child with chronic illness: Parent and school personnel perceptions. *Pediatric Nursing, 2000*(26), 6.

Knoll, J. (1992). Being a family: The experience of raising a child with a disability or chronic illness. In V. J. Bradley, J. Knoll, & J. M. Agosta (Eds.), *Emerging issues in family support* (pp. 9–56). *Monographs of the American Association on Mental Retardation,* 18.

Kocinski, J. M. (1998). Foster care. *State Government News, 41*(4), 16–19.

Kolstoe, O. P. (1970). *Teaching educable mentally retarded children.* New York, Holt, Rinehart, & Winston.

Korenman, S., Miller, J. E., & Sjaastad, J. E. (1995). Long-term poverty and child development in the United States: Results from the National Longitudinal Survey of Youth.

Children and Young Services Review, 17, 127–151.

Koret Task Force. (2003). A report. *Education Next, 3*(2), 9–15.

Kozol, J. (1988). *Rachel and her children: Homeless families in America.* New York: Fawcett-Columbine/Crown.

Kozol, J. (1995). *Amazing grace.* New York: Crown Publishers.

Kramer, R. M., Brewer, M. B., & Hanna, B. A. (1996). Collective trust and collective action: The decision to trust as a social decision. In R. M. Kramer, T. R. Tyler (Eds.), *Trust in organizations: Frontiers of theory and research* (pp. 357–389). Thousand Oaks, CA: Sage.

Krauss, M., Mailick-Seltzer, M., Gordon, R., & Haig-Friedman, H. (1996). Binding ties: The roles of adult siblings of persons with mental retardation. *Journal on Mental Retardation, 34*(2), 83–93.

Krauss, M.W., Wells, N., Gulley, S., & Anderson, B. (2001). Navigating systems of care: Results from a national survey of families of children with special health care needs. *Children's Services: Social Policy, Research, and Practice, 4*(4), 165–187.

Kregel, J., Wehman, P., Seyfarth, J., & Marshall, K. (1986). Community integration of young adults with mental retardation: Transition from school to adulthood. *Education and Training in Mental Retardation, 21*(1), 35–42.

Kreutzer, J. S., Serio, C. D., & Bergquist, S. (1994). Family needs after brain injury: A quantitative analysis. *Journal of Head Trauma Rehabilitation, 9*(3), 104–115.

Kroeger, S. D., Leibold, C. K., & Ryan, B. (1999, September/ October). Creating a sense of ownership in the IEP process. *Teaching Exceptional Children, 32*(1), 4–9.

Kroth, R. L., & Edge, D. (1997). *Strategies for communicating with parents and families of exceptional children* (3rd ed.). Denver, CO: Love.

Kübler-Ross, E. (1969). *On death and dying.* New York: Macmillan.

Kunc, N., & Van der Klift, E. (1995). Voice In spite of my disability. Questions, concerns, beliefs, and practical advice about inclusive education. In J. Thousand & R. Villa (Eds.), *The inclusion puzzle: Fitting the pieces together* (pp. 163-164). Alexandria, VA: Association for Supervision and Curriculum Development.

Kupsinel, M. M., & Dubsky, D. D. (1999). Behaviorally impaired children in out-of-home care. *Child Welfare, 78*(2), 297-310.

La Greca, A. M., & Stone, W. L. (1990). LD status and achievement: Confounding variables in the study of children's social status, self-esteem, and behavioral functioning. *Journal of Learning Disabilities, 23,* 483-490.

Lahm, E. A., & Sizemore, L. (2002). Factors that influence assistive technology decision making. *Journal of Special Education Technology, 17*(1), 15-25.

Lake, J. F., & Billingsley, B. S. (2000). An analysis of factors that contribute to parent-school conflict in special education. *Remedial and Special Education, 21*(4), 240-251.

Lambie, R. (2000). *Family systems within educational contexts* (2nd ed.). Denver, CO: Love.

Lamme, L. L., & Lamme, L. A. (2001/2002). Welcoming children from gay families into our schools. *Educational Leadership, 59,* 65-69.

Lamme, L. L., & Lamme, L. A. (2003). *Welcoming children from sexual-minority families into our schools.* Bloomington, IN: Phi Delta Kappa Educational Foundation.

Lamorey, S. (2002). The effects of culture on special education services: Evil eyes, prayer meetings, and IEPs. *Teaching Exceptional Children, 34*(5), 67-71.

Landman, J. H. (1932). *Human sterilization: The history of the sexual sterilization movement.* New York: Macmillan.

Lanigan, K. J., Audette, R. M. L., Dreier, A. E., & Kobersy, M. R. (2000). Nasty, brutish. . . and often not very short: The attorney perspective on due process. In C. E. Finn, A. J. Rotherham, & C. R. Hokanson (Eds.), *Rethinking special education for a new century* (pp. 213-232). Washington, DC: Thomas B. Fordham Foundation/Progressive Policy Institute.

Lardieri, L. A., Blacher, J., & Swanson, H. L. (2000). Sibling relationships and parent stress in families of children with and without learning disabilities. *Learning Disability Quarterly, 23*(2), 105-116.

Lareau, A. (1987). Social class differences in family-school relationships: The importance of cultural capital. *Sociology of Education, 60,* 73-85.

Lareau, A. (1989). *Home advantage: Social class and parental intervention in elementary education.* Philadelphia: Falmer Press, Taylor and Francis.

Larner, M. B., Stevenson, C. S., & Behrman, R. E. (1998). Protecting children from abuse and neglect: Analysis and recommendations. *Future of Children: Protecting Children from Abuse and Neglect, 8*(1), 41.

Larry P. v. Riles, 343 F. Supp. 1306 (N.D. Cal. 1972), 502 F. 2d 1963 (9th Circ., 1974).

Larson, E. (1998). Reframing the meaning of disability to families: The embrace of paradox. *Social Science Medical Journal, 47*(7), 865-875.

Lee, I. M. (1994, June). *Collaboration: What do families and physicians want?* Paper presented at the international conference on the Family on the Threshold of the 21st Century Jerusalem: Trends and Implications.

Lee, Y. K., & Tang, C. S. (1998). Evaluation of a sexual abuse prevention program for female Chinese adolescents with mild mental retardation. *American Journal on Mental Retardation, 103*(4), 105-116.

Leff, P. T., & Walizer, E. H. (1992). *Building the healing partnership: Parents, professionals, and children with chronic illnesses and disabilities.* Cambridge, MA: Brookline Books.

Lehman, C. M., & Irvin, L. K. (1996). Support for families with children who have emotional or behavioral disorders. *Education and Treatment of Children, 19*(3), 335-353.

Leslie, L. K., Landsverk, J., Ezzet-Lofstrom, R., Tschann, J. M., Slymen, D. J., & Garland, A. F. (2000). Children in foster care: Factors influencing outpatient mental health service use. *Child Abuse and Neglect, 24*(4), 465-476.

Lesseliers, J., & Van Hove, G. (2002). Barriers to the development of intimate relationships and the expression of sexuality among people with developmental disabilities: Their perceptions. *Research and Practice for Persons with Severe Disabilities, 27*(1), 69-81.

Lessenberry, B. M., & Rehfeldt, R. A. (2004). Evaluating stress levels of parents of children with disabilities. *Exceptional Children, 70*(2), 231-244.

Levin, D. (1998). *Remote control childhood? Combating the hazards of media culture.* Washington, DC: National Association for the Education of Young Children.

Lewicki, R. J., McAllister, D. J., & Bies, R. J. (1998). Trust and distrust: New relationships and realities. *Academy of Management Review, 23*(3), 438.

Lewis, T. J., & Sugai, G. (1999). Effective behavior support: A systems approach to proactive school-wide management. *Focus on Exceptional Children, 31*(6), 1-24.

Lewis, T. J., Sugai, G., & Colvin, G. (1998). Reducing problem behavior through a school-wide system of effective behavioral support: Investigation of a school-wide social skills training program and contextual interventions. *School Psychology Review, 27*(3), 446-459.

Lian, M. G. J., & Fontanez-Phelan, S. M. (2001). Perceptions of Latino parents regarding cultural and linguistic issues and advocacy for children with disabilities. *Journal of the Association for Persons with Severe Handicaps, 26*(3), 189-194.

Lichtenstein, J. (1993). Help for troubled marriages. In G. H. S. Singer & L. E. Powers (Eds.), *Families, disability, and empowerment* (pp. 259-283). Baltimore: Brookes.

Lin, S. (2000). Coping and adaptation in families of children with cerebral palsy. *Exceptional Children, 66*(2), 201-218.

Lindle, J. C. (1989). What do parents want from principals? *Educational Leadership, 47*(2), 8A10.

Lindsay, G., & Dockrell, J. E. (2004). Whose job is it? Parents' concerns about the needs of their children with language problems. *Journal of Special Education, 34*(4), 225–235.

Logan, S. L., ed. (2001). *The black family: Strengths, self-help, and positive change.* 2nd ed. Boulder, CO: Westview Press.

Longwill, A. W., & Kleinert, H. L. (1998). The unexpected benefits of high school peer tutoring. *Teaching Exceptional Children, 27*(3), 52–55.

Lord, J., & Hutchinson, P. (2003). Individualized support and funding: Building blocks for capacity building and inclusion. *Disability and Rehabilitation, 18*(1), 71–86.

Lord-Nelson, L. G., Summers, J. A., & Turnbull, A. P. (2004). Boundaries in family-professional relationships: Implications for special education. *Remedial and Special Education, 25*(3), 153–165.

Loveless, T. (2003) The *Brown Center report on American education.* Washington, DC: Brookings Institution.

Lovitt, T. C., & Cushing, S. (1999). Parents of youth with disabilities. *Remedial and Special Education, 20*(3), 124–142.

Lucito, L. J. (1963). Gifted children. In L. M. Dunn (Ed.), *Exceptional children in the schools* (pp. 179–238). New York: Holt, Rinehart, & Winston.

Luetke-Stahlman, B., Luetke-Stahlman, B., & Luetke-Stahlman, H. (1992). Yes, siblings can help. *Perspectives, 10*(5), 9–11.

Lundgren, D., & Morrison, J. W. (2003, May). Involving Spanish-speaking families in early education programs. *Young Children,* 88–95.

Luscombe, A., & Riley, T. L. (2001). An examination of self-concept in academically gifted adolescents: Do gender differences occur? *Roeper Review, 24*(1), 20–22.

Lustig, D. C., & Akey, T. (1999). Adaptation in families with adult children with mental retardation: Impact of family strengths and appraisal. *Education and Training in Mental Retardation and Developmental Disabilities, 34*(3), 260–270.

Luterman, S. (1991). Counseling and the diagnostic process. In S. Luterman (Ed.), *Counseling the communicatively disordered* (pp. 80–82). Austin, TX: Pro-Ed.

Lynch, E., & Struewing, N. (2001). Children in context: Portfolio assessment in the inclusive early childhood classroom. *Young Exceptional Children, 5*(1), 2–10.

Lynch, E. W. (1998). Developing cross-cultural competence. In E. W. Lynch & M. J. Hanson (Eds.), *Developing cross-cultural competence* (2nd ed., pp. 47–86). Baltimore: Brookes.

Lynch, E. W., & Hanson, M. J. (1998). *Developing cross-cultural competence: A guide to working with children and their families* (2nd ed.). Baltimore: Brookes.

Lynch, E. W., & Hanson, M. J. (2004). *Developing cross-cultural competence: A guide for working with children and their families* (3rd ed.). Baltimore: Paul H. Brookes.

MacKenzie, D., & Rogers, V. (1997). The full service school: A management and organizational structure for 21st century schools. *Community Education Journal, 25*(3–4), 9–11.

MacMaster, K., Donovan, L. A., & MacIntyre, P. D. (2002). The effects of being diagnosed with a learning disability on children's self-esteem. *Child Study Journal, 32*(2), 101–108.

MacMurphy, H. (1916). The relation of feeblemindedness to other social problems. *Journal of Psycho-Asthenics, 21,* 58–63.

Madden, M. (22 December 2003). *The changing picture of who's on line and what they do.* Pew Internet & American Life Project. Available online at http://www.pewtrusts.com/pdf/pew_internet_yearend_2003.pdf (retrieved June 16, 2004).

Maddux, C. D., & Cummings, R. E. (1983). Parental home tutoring: Aids and cautions. *Exceptional Parent, 13*(4), 30–33.

Magaña, S. M. (1999). Puerto Rican families caring for an adult with mental retardation: The role of familism. *American Journal on Mental Retardation, 104*(5), 466–482.

Maguire, S. (2000). A community school. *Educational Leadership, 57*(6), 18–21.

Mahon, M. J., Mactavish, J., & Bockstael, E. (2000). Social integration, leisure, and individuals with intellectual disability. *Parks & Recreation, 35*(4), 25–40.

Malach, R. S., Segal, N., & Thomas, R. (1989). *Overcoming obstacles and improving outcomes: Early intervention service for Indian children with special needs.* Bernalillo, NM: Southwest Communication Resources.

Malka, M., & Meira, E. (1996). Loneliness, coherence, and companionship among children with learning disorders. *Educational Psychology, 16*(1), 69–79.

Mallow, G. E., & Bechtel, G. A. (1999). Chronic sorrow: The experience of parents with children who are developmentally disabled. *Journal of Psychosocial Nursing, 37*(7), 31–35.

Mank, D., Cioffi, A., & Yovanoff, P. (1997). Patterns of support for employees with severe disabilities. *Mental Retardation, 35,* 433–447.

Mank, D., Cioffi, A., & Yovanoff, P. (1998). Employment outcomes for people with severe disabilities: Opportunities for improvement. *Mental Retardation, 36,* 205–216.

Mank, D., Cioffi, A., & Yovanoff, P. (1999). The impact of coworker involvement with supported employees on wage and integration outcomes. *Mental Retardation, 37,* 383–394.

Mank, D., Cioffi, A., & Yovanoff, P. (2000). Direct support in supported employment and its relation to job typicalness, coworker involvement, and employment outcomes. *Mental Retardation, 38,* 506–516.

Mank, D., Cioffi, A., & Yovanoff, P. (2003). Supported employment outcomes across a decade: Is there evidence of improvement in the quality of implementation? *Mental Retardation 41*(3), 188–197.

Marcus, L. M. (1977). Patterns of coping in families of psychotic children.

American Journal of Orthopsychiatry, 47(3), 388–399.

Markward, M., & Biros, E. (2001). McKinney revisited: Implications for social work. *Children and Schools, 23*(3), 182–187.

Marr, M. B. (1997). Cooperative learning: A brief review. *Reading and Writing Quarterly: Overcoming Learning Disabilities, 13*(1), 7–20.

Marshall, N. L., Coll, C. G., Marx, F., McCartney, K., Keefe, N., & Ruh, J. (1997). After-school time and children's behavioral adjustment. *Merrill-Palmer Quarterly, 43,* 497–514.

Martin, J. E., Marshall, H. M., & Sale, P. (2004). A 3-year study of middle, junior high and high school IEP meetings. *Exceptional Children, 70*(3), 285–297.

Martin, J. E., Mithaug, D. E., Cox, P., Peterson, L. Y., Van Dycke, J. L., & Cash, M. E. (2003). Increasing self-determination: Teaching students to plan, work, evaluate, and adjust. *Council for Exceptional Children, 69*(4), 431–447.

Martin, S. S., Brady, M. P., & Kotarba, J. A. (1992). Families with chronically ill young children: The unsinkable family. *Remedial and Special Education, 13*(2), 6–15.

Marvin, R. S., & Pianta, R. C. (1992). A relationship-based approach to self-reliance in young children with motor impairments. *Infants and Young Children, 4*(4), 33–45.

Mason, C. Y., McGahee-Kovac, M., & Johnson, L. (2004). How to help students lead their IEP meetings. *Teaching Exceptional Children, 36,* 18–24.

Maxwell, E. (1998). "I can do it myself!" Reflections on early self-efficacy. *Roeper Review, 20*(3), 183–187.

McBride, S. L., Brotherson, M. J., Joanning, H., Whiddon, D., & Demmitt, A. (1993). Implementation of family-centered services: Perceptions of families and professionals. *Journal of Early Intervention, 17*(4), 414–430.

McConnell, S. (2001). Parent involvement and family support: Where do we want to go, and how will we know we are headed there? *Journal of Early Intervention, 24*(1), 15–18.

McGaughey, M. J., Kiernan, W. E., McNally, L. C., Gilmore, D. S., & Keith, G. R. (1994). *Beyond the workshop: National perspectives on integrated employment.* Boston: Children's Hospital, Institute for Community Inclusion.

McGill, D. W., & Pearce, J. K. (1996). American families with English ancestors from the colonial era: Anglo Americans. In M. McGoldrick & J. Giordano (Eds.), *Ethnicity and family therapy* (2nd ed., pp. 451–466). New York: Guilford Press.

McGoldrick, M., Giordano, J., & Pearce, J. K. (Eds.). (1996). *Ethnicity and family therapy* (2nd ed.). New York: Guilford Press.

McGonigel, J. J., Kaufman, R. K., & Johnson, R. H. (Eds.). (1991). *Guidelines and recommended practices for the individualized family service plan* (2nd ed.). Bethesda, MD: Association for the Care of Children's Health.

McHale, S. M., & Gamble, W. C. (1989). Sibling relationships of children with disabled and nondisabled brothers and sisters. *Developmental Psychology, 25*(3), 421–429.

McKnight, D. H., Cummings, L. L., & Chervany, N. L. (1998). Initial trust formation in new organizational relationships. *Academy of Management Review, 23*(3), 418–473.

McLaughlin, M. L. (1998). *Special education in an era of school reform: An overview.* Washington, DC: Federal Resource Center, Academy for Educational Development.

McNair, J., & Swartz, S. L. (1995). Local church support to individuals with developmental disabilities. *Education and Training in Mental Retardation and Developmental Disabilities,* 304–312.

McNamara, K., & Hollinger, C. (2003). Intervention-based assessment: Evaluation rates and eligibility findings. *Exceptional Children, 69*(2), 181–193.

McRoy, R. G., Grotevant, H. D., & Zurcher, L. A. (1988). *Emotional disturbance in adopted adolescents: Origins and development.* New York: Praeger.

McWilliam, P. J., & Winton, P. J. (1990). *Brass tacks: A self-rating of family-centered practices in early intervention.* Chapel Hill: Frank Porter Graham Child Development Center, University of North Carolina.

McWilliam, R. A., Lang, L., Vandiviere, P., Angell, R., Collins, L., & Underdown, G. (1995). Satisfaction and struggles: Family perceptions of early intervention services. *Journal of Early Intervention, 19*(1), 43–60.

McWilliam, R. A., Snyder, P., Harbin, G. L., Porter, P., & Munn, D. (2000). Professionals' and families' perceptions of family-centered practices in infant-toddler services. *Early Education and Development, 11*(4), 519–538.

Mediavilla, C. (2001). Why library homework centers extend society's safety net. *American Libraries, 32*(11), 40–42.

Mehan, H. (1993). Beneath the skin and between the ears: A case study in the politics of representation. In S. Chaiklin & J. Lave (Eds.), *Understanding perspectives on activity and context.* Cambridge, MA: Cambridge University Press.

Meyer, D. J. (Ed.). (1995). *Uncommon fathers.* Bethesda, MD: Woodbine House.

Meyer, D. J. (Ed.). (1997). *Views from our shoes.* Bethesda, MD: Woodbine House.

Meyer, D. J., & Vadasy, P. F. (1994). *Sibshops: Workshops for siblings of children with special needs.* Baltimore: Brookes.

Meyer, L. H., Park, H. S., Grenot-Scheyer, M., Schwartz, I. S., & Harry, B. (Eds.). (1998). *Making friends.* Baltimore: Brookes.

Michaud, L. F., Semel-Concepcíon, J., Duhaime, A. C. (2004). Traumatic brain injury. In M. L. Batshaw (Ed.), *Children with disabilities.* Baltimore: Paul H. Brookes.

Michaud, L. F., Semel-Concepcíon, J., Duhaime, A. C., & Lazar, M. F. (2002). Traumatic brain injury. In M. L.

Batshaw (Ed.), *Children with disabilities.* Baltimore: Paul H. Brookes.

Miedel, W. T., & Reynolds, A. J. (1999). Parent involvement in early intervention for disadvantaged children: Does it matter? *Journal of School Psychology, 37*(4), 379–402.

Miles, M. B. (1969). Planned change and organizational health: Figure and ground. In F. D. Carver & T. J. Sergiovanni (Eds.), *Organizations and human behavior* (pp. 375–391). New York: McGraw-Hill.

Miller, L. J., & Hanft, B. E. (1998). Building positive alliances: Partnerships with families as the cornerstone of developmental assessment. *Infants and Young Children, 11*(1), 49–60.

Miller, N. B. (1994). *Nobody's perfect: Living and growing with children who have special needs.* Baltimore: Paul H. Brookes.

Minuchin, S., & Fishman, H. C. (1981). *Family therapy techniques.* Cambridge, MA: Harvard University Press.

Mitchell, W., & Sloper, P. (2002). Information that informs rather than alienates families with disabled children: Developing a model of good practice. *Health and Social Care in the Community, 10*(2), 74–81.

Mokuau, N., & Tauiliili, P. (2004). Families with native Hawaiian and Samoan roots. In E. W. Lynch & M. J. Hanson (Eds.), *Developing cross-cultural competence: A guide for working with children and their families.* Baltimore: Paul Brookes.

Moon, S. M., Jurich, J. A., & Feldhusen, J. F. (1998). *Families of gifted children: Cradles of development.* Washington, DC: American Pysological Association.

Moore, K. A., & Vandivere, S. (2000). *Stressful family lives: Child and parent well-being* (B-17). Washington, DC: Urban Institute.

Morningstar, M. E., Turnbull, A. P., & Turnbull, H. R. (1995). What do students with disabilities tell us about the importance of family involvement in the transition from school to adult life? *Exceptional Children, 62*(3), 249–260.

Moseley, C. E., Gettings, R. M., & Cooper, R. (2003). *Having it your way: Understanding state individual budgeting strategies.* Alexandria, VA: National Association of State Directors of Developmental Disabilities Services.

Moses, K. I. (1983). The impact of initial diagnosis: Mobilizing family resources. In J. A. Mulick & S. M. Pueschel (Eds.), *Parent-professional partnerships in developmental disability services* (pp. 11–34). Cambridge, MA: Ware.

Mount, B. (1995). *Capacity works.* New York: Graphic Futures.

Mount, B., & O'Brien, C. L. (2002). *Exploring new worlds for students with disabilities in transition from high school to adult life.* New York: Job Path.

Msall, M. E., Bobis, F., & Field, S. (in press). Children with disabilities and supplemental security income: Guidelines for appropriate access in early childhood. *Infants and Young Children.*

Mull, C., Sitlington, P. L., & Alper, S. (2001). Postsecondary education for students with learning disabilities: A synthesis of literature. *Council for Exceptional Children, 68*(1), 97–118.

Munk, D. D. (2003). *Solving the grading puzzle for students with disabilities.* Whitefish Bay, WI: Knowledge by Design.

Munk, D. D., & Bursuck, W. D. (2001a). Preliminary findings of personalized grading plans for middle school students with disabilities. *Exceptional Children, 67*(2), 211–234.

Munk, D. D., & Bursuck, W. D. (2001b). What report card grades should and do communicate: Perceptions of parents of secondary students with and without disabilities. *Remedial and Special Education, 22*(5), 280–286.

Munk, D. D., & Bursuck, W. D. (2003). Grading students with disabilities. *Educational Leadership, 61*(2), 38–47.

Murphy, A. T. (1982). The family with a handicapped child: A review of the literature. *Developmental and Behavioral Pediatrics, 3*(2), 73–82.

Murphy, D. L., Lee, I. M., Turnbull, A. P., & Turbiville, V. (1995). The family-centered program rating scale: An instrument for program evaluation and change. *Journal of Early Intervention, 19*(1), 24–42.

Murray, C., Goldstein, D. E., Nourse, S., & Edgar, E. (2000). The postsecondary school attendance and completion rates of high school graduates with learning disabilities. *Learning Disabilities Research, 15,* 119–127.

Mutua, N. K. (2001). Importance of parents' expectations and beliefs in the educational participation of children with mental retardation in Kenya. *Education and Training in Mental Retardation and Developmental Disabilities, 36*(2), 148–159.

Myers, C. L., McBride, S. L., & Peterson, C. A. (1996). Transdisciplinary, play-based assessment in early childhood special education: An examination of social validity. *Topics in Early Childhood Special Education, 16*(1), 102–126.

Nagle, K., & Crawford, J. (2004). *EPRRI issue brief six: Opportunities and challenges: Perspectives on NCLBA from special education directors in urban school districts.* College Park, MD: Educational Policy Reform Research Institute.

Nagy, S., & Ungerer, J. (1990). The adaptation of mothers and fathers to children with cystic fibrosis: A comparison. *Children's Health Care, 19*(3), 147–154.

Naseef, R. A. (1997). *Special children, challenged parents.* Secaucus, NJ: Carol Publishing Group.

National Assessment of Educational Progress (NAEP). (2004). *2003 mathematics and reading assessment results.* Retrieved June 30 2004, from http://nces.ed.gov/ nationsreportcard/

National Association for Retarded Children (NARC). (1954). Blueprint for a crusade. In *Publicity and publications manual.* Washington, DC: The Arc.

National Association of Social Workers. (1996). *Code of ethics of the National Association of Social*

Workers. Retrieved June 8, 2001, from http://www.naswdc.org/ode/ethics.htm

National Center for Children in Poverty. (2003). *Low income children in the United States.* Retrieved April 6, 2004 from http://www.nccp.org/fact.html

National Center for Education Statistics. (1993). *Adult literacy in America.* Washington, DC: Office of Educational Research and Improvement, U.S. Department of Education.

National Center for Education Statistics. (1997). *Profiles of students with disabilities as identified in NELS: 88.* Washington, DC: Office of Educational Research and Improvement, U.S. Department of Education.

National Center for Education Statistics. (1999). *Digest of education statistics.* Washington, DC: U.S. Department of Education.

National Center for Education Statistics. (2000). *Dropout rates in the United States.* Washington, DC: U.S. Department of Education.

National Child Abuse and Neglect Data System (NCANDS) by the Children's Bureau, Administration on Children, Youth and Families in the Administration for Children and Families, U.S. Department of Health and Human Services. (2004). *Child maltreatment 2002: Reports from the states to the National Child Abuse and Neglect Data Systems— National statistics on child abuse and neglect.* Washington, DC: Department of Health and Human Services.

National Clearinghouse on Child Abuse and Neglect (NCCAN) Information. (2001). *The risk and prevention of maltreatment of children with disabilities.* Retrieved July 12, 2004, from http://nccanch.acf.hhs.gov/pubs/prevenres/ focus.cfm

National Clearinghouse on Child Abuse and Neglect (NCCAN) Information. (2004). *Child maltreatment 2002: Summary of key findings.* Retrieved July 12, 2004, from http://nccanch.acf.hhs.gov/pubs/factsheets/canstats.cfm

National Coalition for the Homeless. (2002, September). *How many people experience homelessness?* Retrieved

August 2, 2004, from http://www.nationalhomeless.org/numbers.html

National Council on Disability and Social Security Administration. (2000). *Transition and post-school outcomes for youth with disabilities: Closing the gaps to post-secondary education and employment.* Washington, DC: Authors.

National Council on Disability. (1995). *Improving the implementation of the Individuals with Disabilities Education Act: Making schools work for all of America's children.* Washington, DC: Author.

National Council on Disability. (2000). *Federal policy barriers to assistive technology.* Washington, DC: Author.

National Organization on Disability. (2000). *N.O.D./Harris Survey of Americans with Disabilities.* New York: Aetna, JM Foundation and Harris Interactive.

National Research Council. (2001). *Educating children with autism.* Washington, DC: National Academy Press.

National Research Council. (2002). *Minority students in special and gifted education.* Washington, DC: National Academy Press.

National Society for Autistic Children. (1977). *A short definition of autism.* Albany, NY: Author.

National Symposium on Abuse and Neglect of Children with Disabilities. (1995). *Abuse and neglect of children with disabilities: Report and recommendations.* Lawrence: University of Kansas, Beach Center on Families and Disability and Erikson Institute of Chicago.

Nelson, J. S., Jayanthi, M., Brittain, C. S., Epstein, M. H., & Bursuck, W. D. (2002). Using the nominal group technique for homework communication decisions: An exploratory study. *Remedial and Special Education, 23*(6), 379–386.

Nelson, L. G. L., Summers, J. A., & Turnbull, A. P. (2004). Boundaries in family-professional relationships: Implications for special education. *Remedial and Special Education, 25*(3), 153–165.

Nerney, T. (1998). The poverty of human services: An introduction. In T. Nerney & D. Shumway (Eds.), *The importance of income* (pp. 2–14). Concord, NH: Robert Wood Johnson Foundation.

Nicholson, J., Nason, M. W., Calabresi, A. O., & Yando, R. (1999). Fathers with severe mental illness: Characteristics and comparisons. *American Journal of Orthopsychiatry, 69*(1), 134–141.

Nicholson, J., Sweeney, E. M., & Geller, J. L. (1998). Mothers with mental illness: II. Family relationships and the context of parenting. *Journal on Psychiatric Services, 49*(5), 643–649.

Nicholson, J., Sweeney, E. M., & Geller, J. L. (1998a). Mothers with mental illness: I. The competing demands of parenting and living with mental illness. *Psychiatric Services, 49*(5), 635–642.

Nicholson, J., Sweeney, E. M., & Geller, J. L. (1998b). Mothers with mental illness: II. Family relationships and the context of parenting. *Psychiatric Services, 49*(5), 643–649.

Nissenbaum, M. S., Tollefson, N., & Reese, M. R. (2002). The interpretative conference: Sharing a diagnosis of autism with families. *Focus on Autism and Other Developmental Disabilities, 17*(1), 30–43.

No Child Left Behind Act of 2001, P. L. 107–110, 20 U.S.C. 6301 *et seq.*

Nosek, M. A., Howland, C. A., & Young, M. E. (1997). Abuse of young women with disabilities: Policy implications. *Journal of Disability Policy Studies, 8*(1–2), 157–175.

Obermayer, L. L. (2004). A special friend vs. a real friend. *TASH Connections, 30*(1–2), 18.

Oberti, C. (1993). A parent's perspective. *Exceptional Parent,* September, 18–21.

Oberti v. Board of Education of the Borough of Clementon School District, 995 F. 2d 1204 (3rd Cir. 1993).

O'Brien, J. (2002). Person-centered planning as a contributing factor in organizational and social change. *Research and Practice for Persons with Severe Disabilities, 27*(4), 261–264.

Ogletree, B. (2001). Team-based service delivery for students with disabilities. *Intervention in School & Clinic, 36*(3), 138–146.

O'Halloran, J. M. (1995). The celebration process [Fact sheet]. In *Parent articles 2* (pp. 195–196). Phoenix, AZ: Communication Skill Builders/The Psychological Corporation.

O'Hare, W. (2001). *Disconnected Kids: Children without a phone a home.* Ann E. Casey Foundation Kids Count Snapshot, available online at http://www.aecf.org/ kidscount/snapshot.pdf (retrieved June 15, 2004).

Oliver, J. M., Cole, N. H., & Hollingsworth, H. (1991). Learning disabilities as functions of familial learning problems and developmental problems. *Exceptional Children, 57*(5), 427–440.

Olson, D. H. (1988). Family types, family stress, and family satisfaction: A family development perspective. In C. J. Falicov (Ed.), *Family transitions: Continuity and change over the life cycle* (pp. 55–79). New York: Guilford Press.

Olson, D. H., McCubbin, H. I., Barnes, H., Larsen, A., Muxen, M., & Wilson, M. (1983). *Families: What makes them work?* Beverly Hills, CA: Sage.

Olson, D. H., Russell, C. S., & Sprenkle, D. H. (1980). Circumplex model of marital and family systems II: Empirical studies and clinical intervention. *Advances in Family Intervention Assessment and Theory, 1,* 129–179.

Olson, D. H., Sprenkle, D. H., & Russell, C. S. (1979). Circumplex model of marital and family systems I: Cohesion and adaptability dimensions, family types, and clinical applications. *Family Process, 18,* 3–28.

Olson, L. (2000). Finding and keeping competent teachers: Quality counts— Who should teach? *Education Week, 19*(18), 12–17.

Olsson, M. B., & Hwang, C. P. (2001). Depression in mothers and fathers of children with intellectual disability. *Journal of Intellectual Disability Research, 45*(6), 535–543.

O'Neill, R. E., Horner, R. H., Albin, R. W., Sprague, J. R., Storey, K., & Newton, J. S. (1997). *Functional assessment of problem behavior: A practical handbook* (2nd ed.). Pacific Grove, CA: Brooks/Cole.

Oregon Institute on Disability and Development. (2000). *Every child special—every child safe: Protecting children with disabilities from maltreatment: A call to action.* Oregon Institute on Disability and Development. Retrieved July 12, 2004, from http://www.ohsu.edu/research/ oidd/ oakspublication.cfm?style= moreaccess

Orsillo, S. M., McCaffrey, R. J., & Fisher, J. M. (1993). Siblings of head-injured individuals: A population at risk. *Journal of Head Trauma Rehabilitation, 8*(1), 102–115.

Orsmond, G. I., & Seltzer, M. M. (2000). Brothers and sisters of adults with mental retardation: Gendered nature of the sibling relationship. *American Journal on Mental Retardation, 105*(6), 486–508.

Orton, S. T. (1930). Familial occurrence of disorders in the acquisition of language. *Eugenics, 3,* 140–147.

Osofsky, J. D., & Thompson, D. (2000). Adaptive and maladaptive parenting: Perspectives on risk and protective factors. In J. Shonkoff & S. J. Meisels (Eds.), *Handbook of early childhood intervention* (2nd ed.). Cambridge, United Kingdom: Cambridge University Press.

Oswald, D. P., Coutinho, M. J., Best, A. M., & Singh, N. N. (1999). Ethnic representation in special education. *Journal of Special Education, 32*(4), 194–206.

(P.L. 94-142), amending Education of the Handicapped Act, renamed Individuals with Disabilities Education Act, (1975).

Palmer, S. B., & Wehmeyer, M. L. (2002). *Self-determined learning model for early elementary students: Parent's guide.* Lawrence, KS: Beach Center on Disability.

Parents in Action on Special Education (PASE) v. Hannon. 506 F.Supp. 831 (ND Ill. 1980)

Parette, H. P., Brotherson, M. J., & Huer, M. B. (2000). Giving families a voice in augmentative and alternative communication decision-making. *Education and Training in Mental Retardation and Developmental Disabilities, 35*(2), 177–190.

Parette, H. P., VanBiervliet, A., & Hourcade, J. J. (2000). Family-centered decision making in assistive technology. *Journal of Special Education Technology, 15*(1), 35–45.

Parette, P., Huer, M. B., & Wyatt, T. A. (2002). Young African American children with disabilities and augmentative and alternative communication issues. *Early Childhood Education Journal, 29*(3), 201–207.

Parette, P., & McMahan, G. A. (2002). What should we expect of assistive technology? Being sensitive to family goals. *Teaching Exceptional Children, 35*(1), 56–61.

Parish, S. L., Pomeranz-Essley, A., & Braddock, D. (2003). Family support in the United States: Financing trends and emerging initiatives. *Mental Retardation, 41*(3), 174–187.

Park, J., & Turnbull, A. P. (2001). Cross-cultural competency and special education: Perceptions and experiences of Korean parents of children with special needs. *Education and Training in Mental Retardation and Developmental Disabilities, 36*(2), 133–147.

Park, J., & Turnbull, A. P. (2003). Service integration in early intervention: Determining interpersonal and structural factors for its success. *Infants and Young Children, 16*(1), 48–58.

Park, J., Turnbull, A. P., & Park, H. S. (2001). Quality of partnerships in service provision for Korean-American parents of children with disabilities: A qualitative inquiry. *Journal of the Association for Persons with Severe Handicaps, 26*(3), 158–170.

Park, J., Turnbull, A. P., & Turnbull, H. R. (2002). Impacts of poverty on quality of life in families of children with disabilities. *Exceptional Children, 68*(2), 151–170.

Parsons, T. (1967). *Sociological theory and modern society.* New York: Free Press.

Pearman, E., Elliot, T., & Aborn, L. (2004). Transition services model: Partnersh for student success. *Education and Training in Developmental Disabilities, 39*(1), 26-34.

Peck-Peterson, S. M., Derby, K. M., Berg, W. K., & Horner, R. H. (2002). Collaboration with families in the functional behavior assessment of and intervention for severe behavior problems. *Education and Treatment of Children, 25*(1), 5-25.

Pena, D. (2000). Parent involvement: Influencing factors and implications. *Journal of Educational Research, 94*(1), 42-54.

Pennsylvania Association for Retarded Citizens (PARC) v. Commonwealth of Pennsylvania, (1971, 1972).

Petersilia, J. (2000). Invisible victims. *Human Rights, 27,* 9-12.

Petosa, R., & Wessinger, J. (1990). The AIDS education needs of adolescents: A theory-based approach. *AIDS-Education and Prevention, 2*(2), 127-136.

Petr, C. G. (1998). *Social work with children and their families: Pragmatic foundations.* New York: Oxford University Press.

Pizzo, P. (1983). *Parent to Parent.* Boston: Beacon.

Plucker, J.A., & Stocking, V. B. (2001). Looking outside and inside: Self-concept development of gifted adolescents. *Exceptional Children, 67*(4), 535-548.

Plucker, J.A., & Taylor, J.W. (1998). Too much too soon? Non-radical advanced grade placement and the self-concept of gifted students. *Gifted Education International, 13,* 121-135.

Polloway, E. A., Epstein, M. H., & Foley, R. (1992). A comparison of the homework problems of students with learning disabilities and nonhandicapped students. *Learning Disabilities Research and Practice, 7*(4), 203-209.

Poston, D., Turnbull, A., Park, J., Mannan, H., Marquis, J., & Wang, M. (2003). Family quality of life: A qualitative inquiry. *Mental Retardation, 41*(5), 313-328.

Poston, D. J. (2002). *A qualitative analysis of the conceptualization and domains of family quality of life for families of children with disabilities.* Unpublished doctoral dissertation, University of Kansas, Lawrence.

Poston, D. J., & Turnbull, A. P. (2004). Role of spirituality and religion in family quality of life for families of children with disabilities. *Education and Training in Developmental Disabilities, 39*(2), 95-108.

Powell, T. H., & Gallagher, P.A. (Eds.). (1993). *Brothers and sisters: A special part of exceptional families* (2nd ed.). Baltimore: Brookes.

Powers, L., Crowley, R., Decker, C., Dinerstein, R., Frattarola-Saulino, M., Harkins, D., et al. (2004). Self-advocacy, self-determination and social freedom and opportunity. In C. Lakin (Ed.), *Through new lenses: New theories and new evidence about family adaptation to children's disabilities.* Baltimore: Paul H. Brookes.

Powers, L. E., Sowers, J. A., Turner, A., Nesbitt, M., Knowles, E., & Ellison, R. (1996). Take charge: A model for promoting self-determination among adolescents with challenges. In L. E. Powers, G. H. S. Singer, & J.A. Sowers (Eds.), *On the road to autonomy: Promoting self-competence in children and youth with disabilities* (pp. 291-322). Baltimore: Brookes.

Prelock, P.A., Beatson, J., Contompasis, S. H., & Bishop, K. K. (1999). A model for family-centered interdisciplinary practice in the community. *Topics in Language Disorders, 19*(3), 36-51.

Preto, N. G. (1999). Transformation of the family system during adolescence. In B. Carter & M. McGoldrick, (Eds.), *The expanded family life cycle: Individual, family, and social perspectives* (3rd ed.). Needham Heights, MA: Allyn & Bacon.

Pretti-Frontczak, K., & Bricker, D. (2000). Enhancing the quality of individualized education plan (IEP) goals and objectives. *Journal of Early Intervention, 23,* 92-105.

Public Agenda. (2002). *When it's your own child: A report on special education from the families who use it.* New York: Author.

Pugliese, J., & Edwards, G. (1995). *Use of children's Supplemental Security Income (SSI) by families who have children with cerebral palsy or spina bifida.* Birmingham, AL: United Cerebral Palsy Association of Greater Birmingham.

Raghavan, C., Weisner, T. S., & Patel, D. (1999). The adaptive project of parenting: South Asian families with children with developmental delays. *Education and Training in Mental Retardation and Developmental Disabilities, 34*(3), 281-292.

Raham, H. (1998). Full-service schools. *School and Business Affairs, 64*(6), 24-28.

Rainforth, B., & York-Barr, J. (1997). *Collaborative teams for students with severe disabilities: Integrating therapy and educational services* (2nd ed.). Baltimore: Paul H. Brookes.

Ray, V., & Gregory, R. (2001). School experiences of the children of lesbian and gay parents. *Family Matters* 59, 28-34.

Rempel, J. K., Holmes, J. G., & Zanna, M. P. (1985). Trust in close relationships. *Journal of Personality and Social Psychology, 49*(1), 95-112.

Renwick, R., Brown, I., & Raphael, D. (1998). *The family quality of life project* (Final Report). Toronto: University of Toronto.

Research and Training Center on Community Living. (2002). *Children with disabilities: Social roles and family impacts in the NHIS-D.* Minneapolis: University of Minnesota.

Rhodes, R. L. (1996). Beyond our borders: Spanish-dominant migrant parents and the IEP process. *Rural Special Education Quarterly, 15*(2), 19-22.

Ricci, L.A., & Hodapp, R. M. (2003). Fathers of children with Downs syndrome versus other types of intellectual disability: Perceptions, stress, and involvement. *Journal of Intellectual Disability Research, 47*(4/5), 273-284.

Riley, B. J., Fryar, N., & Thornton, N. (1998). Homeless on the range: Meeting the needs of homeless families with young children in the rural west. *Zero to Three, 19*(1), 31-35.

Ring, M. M., & Reetz, L. (2002). Grading students with learning disabilities in inclusive middle schools. *Middle School Journal, 34*(2), 12-18.

Riordan, J., & Vasa, S. F. (1991). Accommodations for and participation of persons with disabilities in religious practice. *Education and Training in Mental Retardation, 26*(2), 151–155.

Roach, M. A., Orsmond, G. I., & Barratt, M. S. (1999). Mothers and fathers of children with Down syndrome: Parental stress and involvement in childcare. *American Journal on Mental Retardation, 104*(5), 422–434.

Roberts, C. D., Stough, L. M., & Parrish, L. H. (2002). The role of genetic counseling in the elective termination of pregnancies involving fetuses with disabilities. *Journal of Special Education, 36* (1), 48–55.

Roberts, R. (2000). Seizure disorders. In R. E. Nickel & L. W. Desch (Eds.), *The physician's guide to caring for children with disabilities and chronic conditions.* Baltimore: Paul H. Brookes.

Robinson, N. M., Weinberg, R. A., Redden, D., Ramey, S. L., & Ramey, C. T. (1998). Family factors associated with high academic competence among former Head Start children. *Gifted Child Quarterly, 42*(3), 148–155.

Robinson-Zanartu, C., & Majel-Dixon, J. (1996). Parent voices: American Indian relationships with schools. *Journal of American Indian Education, 36*(1), 33–54.

Rocco, S., Metzer, J., Zangerle, A., & Skouge, J. R. (2002). Three families' perspectives on assessment, intervention, and parent-professional partnerships. In J. M. Lucyshyn, G. Dunlap, & R. W. Albin (Eds.), *Families & positive behavior support* (pp. 75–91). Baltimore: Paul H. Brookes.

Rock, M. L. (2000). Parents as equals: Balancing the scales in IEP development. *Teaching Exceptional Children, 32*, 30–37.

Rodger, S. (1995). Individual education plans revisited: A review of the literature. *International Journal of Disability, 42*(3), 221–239.

Rodgers, R. H., & White, J. M. (1993). Family development theory. In P. J. Boss, W. J. Doherty, R. LaRossa, W. R. Schumm, & S. K. Steinmetz (Eds.), *Sources of family theories and methods: A contextual approach* (pp. 225–254). New York: Plenum.

Rogers, E. (2001). Functional behavioral assessment and children with autism: Working as a team. *Focus on Autism &*

Other Developmental Disabilities, 16(4), 228–232.

Rogers, M. F., & Myles, B. S. (2001). Using social stories and comic strip conversations to interpret social situations for an adolescent with Asperger syndrome. *Intervention in School and Clinic, 36*(5), 310–313.

Rogers-Dulan, J. (1998, April). Religious connectedness among urban African American families who have a child with disabilities. *Mental Retardation, 36*(2), 91–103.

Roggman, L. A., Boyce, L. K., Cook, G. A., Christiansen, K., & Jones, D. (2004). Playing with daddy and toys: Father-toddler social toy play, developmental outcomes, and Early Head Start. *Fathering, 2*(1), 83–108.

Romer, L. T., Richardson, M. L., Nahom, D., Aigbe, E., & Porter, A. (2002). Providing family support through community guides. *Mental Retardation, 40*(3).

Rose, L. C., & Gallup, A. M. (1998). The 30th annual Phi Delta Kappa Gallup poll of the public attitudes toward the public schools. *Phi Delta Kappan, 80*(1), 41–55.

Rotter, J. B. (1967). A new scale for the measurement of interpersonal trust. *Journal of Personality, 35,* 651–665.

Rousso, H. (1984). Fostering healthy self-esteem. *Exceptional Parent, 8*(14), 9–14.

Ruef, M. B., & Turnbull, A. P. (2001). Stakeholder opinions on accessible, informational products helpful in building positive, practical solutions for behavioral challenges of individuals with mental retardation and autism. *Education and Training in Mental Retardation and Developmental Disabilities, 36*(4), 441–456.

Rump, M. L. (2002). Involving fathers of young children with special needs. *Young Children, 57*(6), 18–20.

Ruppman, J. (2003). No child left behind: What it might mean for students with significant disabilities. *TASH Connections, 29*(10), 5–11.

Sabornie, E. (1994). Social-affective characteristics in early adolescents identified as learning disabled and nondisabled. *Learning Disability Quarterly, 17,* 268–279.

Safran, S. P., & Safran, J. S. (1996). Intervention assistance programs and prereferral teams: Direction for the twenty-first century. *Remedial and Special Education, 17*(6), 363–369.

Salembier, G., & Furney, K. S. (1997). Promoting self-advocacy and family participation in IEP and transition planning. *Journal for Vocational Special Needs Education, 17*(1), 12–17.

Salembier, G., & Furney, K. S. (1994). Promoting self-advocacy and family participation in IEP and transition planning. *Journal for Vocational Special Needs Education, 17*(1), 12–17.

Salend, S. J. (1998). Using portfolios to assess student performance. *Teaching Exceptional Children, 31*(2), 36–43.

Salend, S. J. (2001). *Creating inclusive classrooms: Effective and reflective practices* (4th ed.). Upper Saddle River, NJ: Merrill/Prentice Hall.

Salend, S. J., Duhaney, D., Anderson, D. J., & Gottschalk, C. (2004). Using the Internet to improve homework communication and completion. *Teaching Exceptional Children, 36*(3), 64–73.

Salend, S. J., Elhoweris, H., & Van Garderen, D. (2003). Educational interventions for students with ADD. *Intervention in School and Clinic, 38*(5), 280–288.

Sanders, M. G., & Herting, J. R. (2000). Gender and the effects of school, family, and church support on the academic achievement of African-American urban adolescents. In M. G Sanders (Ed.), *Schooling students placed at risk: Research, policy, and practice in the education of poor and minority adolescents* (pp. 141–161). Mahwah, NJ: Lawrence Erlbaum.

Sandler, A. G. (1998). Grandparents of children with disabilities: A closer look. *Education and Training in Mental Retardation and Developmental Disabilities, 33*(4), 350–356.

Sandler, A. G., & Mistretta, L. A. (1998). Positive adaption in parents of adults with disabilities. *Education and Training in Mental Retardation and*

Developmental Disabilities, 33(2), 123–130.

Sands, D., & Wehmeyer, M. (1996). *Self-determination across the life span: Theory and practice*. Baltimore: Brookes.

Sands, D. J., Spencer, K., Gliner, J., & Swaim, R. (1999). Structural equation modeling of student involvement in transition-related actions: The path of least resistance. *Focus on Autism and Other Developmental Disabilities 14*(1), 17–27.

Santelli, B. (1999). *Developing/expanding a statewide Parent to Parent program*. Lawrence, KS: Beach Center on Families and Disability.

Santelli, B., Poyadue, F. S., & Young, J. L. (2001). *The Parent to Parent handbook: Connecting families of children with special needs*. Baltimore: Paul H. Brookes.

Santelli, B., Singer, G. H. S., DiVenere, N., Ginsberg, C., & Powers, L. (1998). Participatory action research: Reflections on critical incidents in a PAR project. *Journal of the Association for Persons with Severe Handicaps, 23*(3), 211–222.

Santelli, B., Turnbull, A., Marquis, J., & Lerner, E. (1997). Parent to Parent programs: A resource for parents and professionals. *Journal of Early Intervention, 21*(1), 73–83.

Santelli, B., Turnbull, A., Marquis, J., & Lerner, E. (2000). Statewide Parent to Parent programs: Partners in early intervention. *Infants and Young Children, 13*(1), 74–88.

Santelli, B., Turnbull, A., Sergeant, J., Lerner, E., & Marquis, J. (1996). Parent to Parent programs: Parent preferences for support. *Infants and Young Children, 9*(1), 53–62.

Sapon-Shevin, M. (1999). *Because we can change the world: A practical guide to building cooperative, inclusive classroom communities*. Boston: Allyn & Bacon.

Satir, V. (1972). *Peoplemaking*. Palo Alto, CA: Science and Behavior Books.

Sattler, J. M. (2001). *Assessment of children: Cognitive applications* (4th ed.). LaMesa, CA: Jerome M. Sattler.

Schaffner, C. B., & Buswell, B. E. (1992). *Connecting students: A guide to thoughtful friendship facilitation for educators and families*. Colorado Springs: PEAK Parent Center.

Scheerenberger, R. C. (1983). *A history of mental retardation*. Baltimore: Brookes.

Scheetz, N. A. (2004). *Psychosocial aspects of deafness*. Boston: Pearson A and B.

Schleien, S. J., Green, F. P., & Heyne, L. A. (1993). Integrated community recreation. In M. E. Snell (Ed.), *Instruction of students with severe disabilities* (pp. 526–555). Upper Saddle River, NJ: Merrill/Prentice Hall.

Schleien, S. J., & Heyne, L. (1998, March/April). Can I play too? Choosing a community recreation program. *Tuesday's Child Magazine*, 10–11.

Schonberg, R. L., & Tifft, C. F. (2002). Birth defects, prenatal diagnosis, and fetal therapy. In M. L. Batshaw (Ed.), *Children with disabilities* (5th ed.). Baltimore: Paul H. Brookes.

Schorr, L. B. (1997). *Common purpose: Strengthening families and neighborhoods to rebuild America*. New York: Anchor Books Doubleday.

Schuman, A. (2002). Help or hindrance? Staff perspectives on developmental assessment in multicultural early childhood settings. *Mental Retardation, 40*(4), 313–320.

Scorgie, K., & Sobsey, D. (2000). Transformational outcomes associated with parenting children who have disabilities. *Mental Retardation, 38*(3), 195–206.

Scorgie, K., Wilgosh, L., & McDonald, L. (1998). Stress and coping in families of children with disabilities: An examination of recent literature. *Developmental Disabilities Bulletin, 26*(1), 22–42.

Scorgie, K., Wilgosh, L., & McDonald, L. (1999). Transforming partnerships: Parent life management issues when a child has mental retardation. *Education and Training in Mental Retardation and Developmental Disabilities, 34*(4), 395–405.

Scott, S. M., McWilliam, R. A., & Mayhew, L. (1999). Integrating therapies into the classroom. *Young Exceptional Children, 2*(3), 15–24.

Scotti, J. R., Nangle, D. W., Masia, C. L., Ellis, J. T., Ujcich, K. J., Giacoletti, A. M., et al. (1997). Providing an AIDS education and skills training program to persons with mild developmental disabilities. *Education and Training in Mental Retardation and Developmental Disabilities, 32*(2), 113–128.

Scott-Jones, N. (1993). Families as educators in a pluralistic society. In N. F. Chavkin (Ed.), *Families and schools in a pluralistic society* (pp. 245–254). Albany: State University of New York Press.

Seligman, M., & Darling, R. B. (1997). *Ordinary families, special children* (2nd ed.). New York: Guilford Press.

Seligman, M., Goodwin, G., Paschal, K., Applegate, A., & Lehman, L. (1997). Grandparents of children with disabilities: Perceived levels of support. *Education and Training in Mental Retardation and Developmental Disabilities, 32,* 293–303.

Seltzer, M. M., & Krauss, M. W. (1989). Aging parents with adult mentally retarded children: Family risk factors and sources of support. *American Journal of Mental Retardation, 94*(3), 303–312.

Senge, P. M. (1990). *The fifth discipline: The art & practice of the learning organization*. New York: Doubleday Currency.

Senge, P. M. (2000). *Schools that learn: A fifth discipline fieldbook for educators, parents, and everyone who cares about education*. New York: Doubleday.

Shafer, M. S., & Rangasamy, R. (1995). Transition and Native American youth: A follow-up study of school leavers on the Fort Apache Indian Reservation. *Journal of Rehabilitation, 61*(1), 60–65.

Shank, M. S., & Turnbull, A. P. (1993). Cooperative family problem solving: An intervention for single-parent families of children with disabilities. In G. H. S. Singer & L. E. Powers (Eds.), *Families, disability, and empowerment: Active coping skills and strategies for family interventions* (pp. 231–254). Baltimore: Brookes.

Shapiro, B. K., Church, R. P., & Lewis, M. E. B. (2002). Specific learning disabilities. In M. L. Batshaw (Ed.), *Children with disabilities* (5th ed., pp. 417–442). Baltimore: Paul H. Brookes.

Shapiro, D. L., Sheppard, B. H., & Cheraskin, L. (1992, October). In theory: Business on a handshake. *Negotiation Journal 8(4), 365–377.*

Shapiro, J., Blacher, J., & Lopez, S. R. (1998). Maternal reactions to children with mental retardation. In J.A. Burack, R. M. Hodapp, & E. Zigler (Eds.), *Handbook of mental retardation and development* (pp. 606–636). Cambridge, MA: Cambridge University Press.

Shapiro, J., Monzo, L. D., Rueda, R., Gomez, J.A., & Blacher, J. (2004). Alienated advocacy: Perspectives of Latina mothers of young adults with developmental disabilities on service systems. *Mental Retardation, 42*(1), 37–54.

Sharifzadeh, J. (2004). Families with Middle Eastern roots. In E. W. Lynch & M. J. Hanson (Eds.), *Developing cross-cultural competence: A guide for working with children and their families.* Baltimore: Paul Brookes.

Shaver, A.V., & Walls, R.T. (1998). Effect of Title I parent involvement on student reading and mathematics achievement. *Journal of Research and Development in Education, 31*(2), 90–97.

Shaw, J., Hammer, D., & Leland, H. (1991). Adaptive behavior of preschool children with developmental delays: Parent versus teacher ratings. *Mental Retardation, 29*(1), 49–53.

Shearer, M. S., & Shearer, D. E. (1977). Parent involvement. In J. B. Jordan, A. H. Hayden, M. B. Karnes, & M. M. Wood (Eds.), *Early childhood education for exceptional children* (pp. 208–235). Reston, VA: Council for Exceptional Children.

Shogren, K.A., & Rye, M. S. (2004). *Religion and individuals with intellectual disabilities: An exploratory study of self-reported*

perspectives. Unpublished manuscript.

Shumow, L., & Miller, J. D. (2001). Parents' at-home and at-school academic involvement with young adolescents. *Journal of Early Adolescence, 21*(1), 68–91.

Shumway, D. L. (1999). Freedom, support, authority, and responsibility: The Robert Wood Johnson Foundation national program on self-determination. *Focus on Autism and Other Developmental Disabilities, 14*(1), 28–35.

Sidel, R. (1996). *Keeping women and children last.* New York: Penguin Books USA.

Sileo, T., & Prater, M.A. (1998). Creating classroom environments that assess the linguistic and cultural backgrounds of students with disabilities: An Asian-Pacific-American experience. *Remedial and Special Education, 19*(6), 323–327.

Simmerman, S., Blacher, J., & Baker, B. (2001). Fathers' and mothers' perceptions of father involvement in families with young children with a disability. *Journal of Intellectual & Developmental Disability, 26*(4), 325–338.

Simon, J. P. (1996). Lebanese families. In M. McGoldrick, J. Giordano, & J. K. Pearce (Eds.), *Ethnicity and family therapy* (2nd ed., pp. 364–375). New York: Guilford Press.

Sindelar, P. T., Griffin, C. C., Smith, S.W., & Watanabe, A. K. (1992). Prereferral intervention: Encouraging notes on preliminary findings. *Elementary School Journal, 92*(3), 245–259.

Singer, G. H. S. (2002). Suggestions for a pragmatic program of research on families and disability. *Journal of Special Education, 36*(3), 148–154.

Singer, G. H. S. (2004). *A meta-analysis of depression in mothers of children with and without developmental disabilities.* Manuscript submitted for publication.

Singer, G. H. S., Glang, A., & Williams, J. (Eds.). (1996). *Children with acquired brain injury: Educating and supporting families.* Baltimore: Brookes.

Singer, G. H. S., Marquis, J., Powers, L., Blanchard, L., DiVenere, N., Santelli, B., et al. (1999). A multi-site evaluation of Parent to Parent programs for parents of children with disabilities. *Journal of Early Intervention, 22*(3), 217–219.

Singer, G. H. S., & Nixon, C. (1996). A report on the concerns of parents of children with acquired brain injury. In G. H. S. Singer, A. Glang, & J. Williams (Eds.), *Children with acquired brain injury: Educating and supporting families* (pp. 23–52). Baltimore: Brookes.

Single fathers with children increase by 25%. (1998, December 11). *The New York Times*, p. 22.

Sipes, D. S. B. (1993). Cultural values and American Indian families. In N. F. Chavkin (Ed.), *Families and schools in a pluralistic society* (pp. 157–174). Albany: State University of New York Press.

Skinner, D., Bailey, D. B., Correa, V., & Rodriguez, P. (1999). Narrating self and disability: Latino mothers' construction of identities vis-a-vis their child with special needs. *Exceptional Children, 65*(4), 481–495.

Skinner, D. G., Correa, V., Skinner, M., & Bailey, D. B. (2001). Role of religion in the lives of Latino families of young children with developmental delays. *American Journal on Mental Retardation, 106*(4), 297–313.

Smith, A., Dannison, L., & Vach-Hasse, T. (1998). When "grandma" is "mom": What today's teachers need to know (grandparent-headed households). *Childhood Education, 75,* 12–17.

Smith, J. D. (1985). *Minds made feeble: The myth and legacy of the Kallikaks.* Rockville, MD: Aspen Publications.

Smith, P. (2003). Self-determination and independent support brokerage: Creating innovative second-level supports. *Mental Retardation, 41*(4), 290–298.

Smith, P. A., Hoy, W. K., & Sweetland, S. F. (2001). Organizational health of high schools and dimensions of faculty trust. *Journal of School Leadership, 11,* 135–151.

Smith, S. W. (1990, September). Individualized education programs (IEPs) in special education—From intent to acquiescence. *Exceptional Children, 57*(1), 6–14.

Smith, S. W., & Brownell, M. T. (1995). Individualized education program: Considering the broad context of reform. *Focus on Exceptional Children, 28*(1), 1–12.

Smrekar, C. E. (1993). Rethinking family-school interactions: A prologue to linking schools and social services. *Education and Urban Society, 25*(2), 175–186.

Smull, M. W., & Harrison, S. B. (1992). *Supporting people with severe retardation in the community*. Alexandria, VA: National Association of State Mental Retardation Program Directors.

Snell, M. E., & Janney, R. (2000). *Teachers' guides to inclusive practices: Collaborative teaming*. Baltimore: Paul H. Brookes.

Snell, M. E., & Janney, R. (2000a). *Collaborative teaming: Teachers' guides to inclusive practices*. Baltimore: Paul H. Brookes.

Snell, M. E., & Janney, R. E. (2000b). Teachers' problem-solving about children with moderate and severe disabilities in elementary classrooms. *Exceptional Children, 66*(4), 472–490.

Snyder, E. P., & Shapiro, E. S. (1997). Teaching students with emotional/behavioral disorders the skills to participate in the development of their own IEPs. *Behavioral Disorders, 22*(4), 246–259.

Snyder, P., Thompson, B., & Sexton, D. (1993, April). *Congruence in maternal and professional early intervention assessments of young children with disabilities*. Paper presented at the annual meeting of the American Educational Research Association, Atlanta, GA.

Sontag, J. C., & Schacht, R. (1994). An ethnic comparison of parent participation and information needs in early intervention. *Exceptional Children, 60*(5), 422–433.

Soodak, L. C., & Erwin, E. J. (1995). Parents, professionals and inclusive education: A call for collaboration. *Journal of Educational and Psychological Consultation, 6*(3), 257–276.

Soodak, L. C., & Erwin, E. J. (2000). Valued member or tolerated participant: Parents' experiences in inclusive early childhood settings. *Journal of the Association for Persons with Severe Handicaps, 25*(1), 29–41.

Soodak, L. C., Erwin, E. J., Winton, P., Brotherson, M. J., Turnbull, A. P., Hanson, M. J., & Brault, L. M. J. (2002). Implementing inclusive early childhood education: A call for professional empowerment. *Topics in Early Childhood Special Education, 22*(2), 91–102.

Spiegel, H. M. L., & Bonwit, A. M. (2002). HIV infection in children. In M. L. Batshaw (Ed.), *Children with disabilities* (pp. 123–139). Baltimore: Paul H. Brookes.

Spinelli, C. G. (1999). Home-school collaboration at the early childhood level: Making it work. *Young Exceptional Children, 2*, 20–26.

Spradley, T. S., & Spradley, J. P. (1978). *Deaf like me*. New York: Random House.

Squires, S. (2000). Our family's experiences: An important outcome achieved. *Young Exceptional Children, 4*, 9–11.

Stainback, S., Stainback, W., East, K., & Sapon-Shevin, M. (1994). A commentary on inclusion and the development of a positive self-identity by people with disabilities. *Exceptional Children, 60*(6), 486–490.

Stainton, T., & Besser, H. (1998). The positive impact of children with an intellectual disability on the family. *Journal of Intellectual & Developmental Disability, 23*, 57–70.

Stallings, G., & Cook, S. (1997). *Another season* (1st ed.). Boston: Little Brown.

Steering Committee for the Federation of Families for Children's Mental Health. (1989, March). *Mission statement*. Alexandria, VA: Author.

Stein, M. A., Efron, L. A., Schiff, W. B., & Glanzman, M. (2002). Attention deficits and hyperactivity. In M. L. Batshaw (Ed.), *Children with disabilities*. Baltimore: Paul H. Brookes.

Stephens, K. R. (1999). Parents of the gifted and talented: The forgotten partner. *Gifted Children Today Magazine, 22*(5), 38–43.

Stodden, R. A., & Whelley, T. (2004). Postsecondary education and persons with intellectual disabilities: An introduction. *Education and Training in Developmental Disabilities, 39*(1), 6–15.

Stoller, E. P. (1994). Teaching about gender: The experiences of family care of frail elderly relatives. *Educational Gerontology, 20*, 679–697.

Stonehouse, A., & Gonzalez-Mena, J. (2001). Working with a high-maintenance parent. *Child Care Information Exchange, 142*, 57–59.

Stoneman, Z., & Waldman-Berman, P. (Eds.). (1993). *The effects of mental retardation, disability, and illness*. Baltimore: Paul H. Brookes.

Stonestreet, R. H., Johnston, R. G., & Acton, S. J. (1991). Guidelines for real partnerships with parents. *Infant-Toddler Intervention, 1*(1), 37–46.

Stormont-Spurgin, M. (1997). I lost my homework: Strategies for improving organization in students with ADHD. *Intervention in School and Clinic, 32*(5), 270–274.

Stowe, M. J., & Turnbull, H. R. (2001). Legal considerations of inclusion for infants and toddlers and for preschool-age children. In M. J. Guralnick (Ed.), *Early childhood inclusion: Focus on change*. Baltimore: Paul H. Brookes.

Strawser, S., Markos, P., Yamaguchi, B., & Higgins, K. (2000). A new challenge for school counselors: Children who are homeless. *Professional School Counseling, 3*(3), 162–171.

Strickland, B., & Turnbull, A. P. (1990). *Developing and implementing individualized education programs* (3rd ed., p. 50). Upper Saddle River, NJ: Merrill/Prentice Hall.

Strip, C., & Hirsch, G. (2000). Trust and teamwork: The parent-teacher partnership for helping the gifted child. *Gifted Child Today, 24*(2), 26–30.

Subotnik, R. F. (1999). Talent developed: Conversations with masters in the arts and sciences. *Journal for the Education of the Gifted, 22*(3), 298–311.

Sugai, G., Horner, R. H., Dunlap, G., Hieneman, M., Lewis, T., Nelson, C., et al. (2000). Applying positive behavioral support and functional behavior assessment in the schools. *Journal of Positive Behavior Intervention, 2*(3), 131–143.

Sugai, G., Lewis-Palmer, T., & Hagan-Burke, S. (2000). Overview of the functional behavioral assessment process. *Exceptionality, 8*(3), 149–160.

Sugai, G., Sprague, J. R., Horner, R. H., & Walker, H. M. (2000). Preventing school violence: The use of office discipline referrals to assess and monitor school-wide discipline interventions. In H. M. Walker & M. H. Epstein (Eds.), *Making schools safer and violence free: Critical issues, solutions, and recommended practices* (pp. 274–289). Austin, TX: Pro-Ed.

Sullivan, P. M., & Knutson, J. F. (2000). Maltreatment and disabilities: A population-based epidemiological study. *Child Abuse & Neglect: The International Journal, 24*(10), 1257–1273.

Sullivan, T. (1995). *Special parent, special child.* New York: G. P. Putnam and Sons.

Summers, J. A. (1987). *Defining successful family life in families with and without children with disabilities: A qualitative study.* Unpublished doctoral dissertation, University of Kansas, Lawrence.

Summers, J. A., Behr, S. K., & Turnbull, A. P. (1988). Positive adaptation and coping strengths of families who have children with disabilities. In G. H. S. Singer & L. K. Irvin (Eds.), *Support for caregiving families: Enabling positive adaptation to disability* (pp. 27–40). Baltimore: Brookes.

Summers, J. A., Behr, S. K., & Turnbull, A. P. (1989). Positive adaptation and coping strengths in families who have children with disabilities. In G. Singer & L. Irvin (Eds.), *Family support services.* Baltimore: Paul H. Brookes Publishing Co.

Summers, J. A., Boller, K., & Raikes, H. H. (2004). Preferences and perceptions about getting support expressed by low income fathers. *Fathering: A Journal of Theory, Research, and Practice About Men as Fathers, 2*(1), 61–82.

Summers, J. A., Dell'Oliver, C., Turnbull, A. P., Benson, H., Santelli, B., Campbell, M., & Siegel-Causey, E. (1990). Examining the individualized family service plan process: What are family preferences? *Topics in Early Childhood Special Education, 10*(1), 78–99.

Summers, J. A., Hoffman, L., Marquis, J., Turnbull, A., Poston, D., & Nelson, L. L. (in press). Measuring the quality of family-professional partnerships in special education services. *Exceptional Children.*

Summers, J. A., McMann, O. T., Kitchen, A., & Peck, L. (1995). *A qualitative study to identify best practices in serving families with multiple challenges: Using direct line staff as researchers.* Unpublished manuscript.

Summers, J. A., Templeton-McMann, O., & Fuger, K. L. (1997). Critical thinking: A method to guide staff in serving families with multiple challenges. In J. J. Carta (Ed.), *Topics in early childhood education* (pp. 27–52). Austin, TX: Pro-Ed.

Surís, J. C., Resnick, M. D., Cassuto, N., & Blum, R. W. M. (1996). Sexual behavior of adolescents with chronic disease and disability. *Journal of Adolescent Health, 19*(2), 124–131.

Swanson, M. (2002). *National survey on the state governance of K12 gifted and talented education, summary report.* ED471886.

Sweetland, S. R., & Hoy, W. K. (2000). School characteristics and educational outcomes: Toward an organizational model of student achievement in middle schools. *Educational Administration Quarterly, 36*(5), 703–729.

Swensen, A. R., Birnbaum, H. G., Secnik, K., Marynchenko, M., Greenberg, P., & Claxton, A. (2003). Attention-deficit/hyperactivity disorder: Increased costs for patients and their families. *Journal of American Academy of Child Adolescent Psychiatry, 42*(12).

Taanila, A., Järvelin, M. R., & Kokkonen, J. (1999). Cohesion and parents' social relations in families with a child with disability or chronic illness. *International Journal of Rehabilitation Research, 22*(2), 101–109.

Tagiuri, R. (1968). *The concept of organizational climate.* Boston: Harvard Graduate School of Business Administration.

Tasker, F. (1999). Children in lesbian-led families: A review. *Clinical Child Psychology and Psychiatry, 4*(2), 153–166.

Taunt, H. M., & Hastings, R. P. (2002). Positive impact of children with developmental disabilities on their families: A preliminary study. *Education and Training in Mental Retardation and Developmental Disabilities, 37*(4), 410–420.

Taylor, S. E. (1989). *Positive illusions: Creative self-deception and the healthy mind.* New York: Basic Books.

Technical Assistance Alliance for Parent Centers. (2003). *Parent centers helping families: Data outcomes 1997–2002.* Minneapolis, MN: Alliance National Center.

Tekin, E., & Kircaali-Iftar, G. (2002). Comparison of the effectiveness and efficiency of two response prompting procedures delivered by sibling tutors. *Education and Training in Mental Retardation and Developmental Disabilities, 37*(3), 283–299.

Terman, L. (1916). *The measurement of intelligence.* Cambridge, MA: Riverside.

Tew, B. J., Payne, E. H., & Lawrence, K. M. (1974). Must a family with a handicapped child be a handicapped family? *Developmental Medicine and Child Neurology, 18*(Suppl. 32), 95–98.

Thoma, C. A., Rogan, P., & Baker, S. R. (2001). Student involvement in transition planning: Unheard voices. *Education and Training in*

Developmental Disabilities, 36(1), 16-29.

Thomas, C. J. (1905). Congenital "word-blindness" and its treatment. *Ophthalmoscope, 3*, 380-385.

Thousand, J. S., & Villa, R.A. (2000). Collaborative teaming: A powerful tool in school restructuring. In R.A. Villa & J. S. Thousand (Eds.), *Restructuring for caring and effective education: Piecing the puzzle together* (pp. 254-292). Baltimore: Paul H. Brookes.

Thousand, J. S., Villa, R. A., & Nevin, A. I. (2002). *Creativity and collaborative learning* (2nd ed.). Baltimore: Paul H. Brookes.

Thurston, L. P. (1996). Support systems for rural families: Rationale, strategies, and examples. *Human Services in the Rural Environment, 20*(1), 19-26.

Timmons, J. C., & Whitney-Thomas, J. (1998). The most important member: Facilitating the focus person's participation in person centered planning. *Institute for Community Inclusion: Research to Practice, 4*(1), 1-4.

Timothy W. v. Rochester School District, 1st Cir. (875 F. 2d 954 1989).

Titiev, M. (1972). *The Hopi Indians of Old Oraibi: Change and continuity.* Ann Arbor: University of Michigan Press.

Tjosvold, D. (1997). Conflict within interdependence: Its value for productivity and individuality. In C. K. W. DeDreu & E. Van de Vliert (Eds.), *Using conflict in organizations* (pp. 23-37). Thousand Oaks, CA: Sage.

Todd, A. W., Horner, R. H., Sugai, G., & Sprague, J. R. (1999). Effective behavior support: Strengthening school-wide systems through a team based approach. *Effective School Practices, 17*(4), 23-37.

Todis, B., Irvin, L. K., Singer, G. H. S., & Yovanoff, P. (1993). The self-esteem parent program: Quantitative and qualitative evaluation of a cognitive-behavioral intervention. In G. H. S. Singer & L. K. Irvin (Eds.), *Support for caregiving families: Enabling positive adaptation to disability* (pp. 203-229). Baltimore: Brookes.

Todis, B., & Singer, G. (1991). Stress and stress management in families with adopted children who have severe disabilities. *Journal of the Association for Persons with Severe Handicaps, 16*(1), 3-13.

Traustadottir, R. (1991). Mothers who care: Gender, disability, and family life. *Journal of Family Issues, 12*(2), 211-228.

Traustadottir, R. (1995). A mother's work is never done: Constructing a "normal" life. In S. J. Taylor, R. Bogdan, & Z. M. Lutfiyya (Eds.), *The variety of community experience: Qualitative studies of family and community life* (pp. 47-65). Baltimore: Brookes.

Trute, B. (1995). Gender differences in the psychological adjustment of parents of young, developmentally disabled children. *Journal of Child Psychology and Psychiatry, 36*(7), 1225-1242.

Tschannen-Moran, M., & Hoy, W. (1997). Trust in schools: A conceptual and empirical analysis. *Journal of Educational Administration, 36*(4), 334-352.

Tschannen-Moran, M., & Hoy W. (2000). A multidisciplinary analysis of the nature, meaning, and measurement of trust. *Review of Educational Research, 70*(4), 547-593.

Turbiville, V., Lee, I., Turnbull, A., & Murphy, D. (1993). *Handbook for the development of a family friendly individualized service plan (IFSP).* Lawrence: University of Kansas, Beach Center on Families and Disability.

Turbiville, V., Turnbull, A.P., & Turnbull, H.R. (1995). Fathers and family-centered early intervention. *Infants and Young Children, 7*(4), 12-19.

Turbiville, V., Umbarger, G., & Guthrie, A. (1998). *Participation by fathers of children with and without disabilities in early childhood programs.* Unpublished manuscript, University of Kansas, Beach Center on Families and Disability.

Turbiville, V. P. (1994). *Fathers, their children, and disability.* Unpublished doctoral dissertation, University of Kansas, Lawrence.

Turbiville, V. P., Turnbull, A. P., Garland, C. W., & Lee, I. M. (1996).

Development and implementation of IFSPs and IEPs: Opportunities for empowerment. In S. L. Odom & M. E. McLean (Eds.), *Early intervention/early childhood special education: Recommended practices* (pp. 77-100). Austin, TX: Pro-Ed.

Turnbull, A., Edmonson, H., Griggs, P., Wickham, D., Sailor, W., Freeman, R., et al. (2002). A blueprint for schoolwide positive behavior support: Implementation of three components. *Council for Exceptional Children, 68*(3), 377-402.

Turnbull, A. P. (1988). Accepting the challenge of providing comprehensive support to families. *Education and Training in Mental Retardation, 23*(4), 261-272.

Turnbull, A. P., Blue-Banning, M., Behr, S., & Kerns, G. (1987). Family research and intervention: A value and ethical examination. In P. Dokecki & R. Zaner (Eds.), *Ethics and decision-making for persons with severe handicaps: Toward an ethically relevant research agenda.* Baltimore: Paul H. Brookes.

Turnbull, A. P., Blue-Banning, M., & Pereira, L. (2000). Successful friendships of Hispanic children and youth with disabilities: An exploratory study. *Mental Retardation, 38*(2), 138-153.

Turnbull, A. P., Blue-Banning, M., Turbiville, V., & Park, J. (1999). From parent education to partnership education: A call for a transformed focus. *Topics in Early Childhood Special Education, 19*(3), 164-171.

Turnbull, A. P., Blue-Banning, M. J., Anderson, E. L., Turnbull, H. R., Seaton, K. A., & Dinas, P. A. (1996). *Enhancing self-determination through group action planning: A holistic emphasis.* Baltimore: Brookes.

Turnbull, A. P., Guess, D., & Turnbull, H. R. (1988). Implications of biobehavioral states for the education and treatment of students with the most profoundly handicapping conditions. *Journal of the Association for Persons with Severe Handicaps, 13*(3), 163-174.

Turnbull, A. P., Patterson, J. M., Behr, S. K., Murphy, D. L., Marquis, J. G., & Blue-Banning, M. J. (Eds.). (1993). *Cognitive coping, families, and disability.* Baltimore: Brookes.

Turnbull, A. P., Pereira, L., & Blue-Banning, M. (1999). Parents' facilitation of friendships between their children with a disability and friends without a disability. *Journal of the Association for Persons with Severe Handicaps, 24*(2), 85–99.

Turnbull, A. P., Pereira, L., & Blue-Banning, M. (2000). Successful friendships of Hispanic children and youth with disabilities: An exploratory study. *Mental Retardation, 38*(2), 138–153.

Turnbull, A. P., & Ruef, M. (1996). Family perspectives on problem behavior. *Mental Retardation, 34*(5), 280–293.

Turnbull, A. P., & Ruef, M. (1997). Family perspectives on inclusive lifestyle issues for people with problem behavior. *Exceptional Children, 63*(2), 211–227.

Turnbull, A. P., Summers, J. A., & Brotherson, M. J. (1986). Family life cycle: Theoretical and empirical implications and future directions for families with mentally retarded members. In J. J. Gallagher & P. M. Vietze (Ed.), *Families of handicapped persons: Research, programs, and policy issues* (pp. 25–44). Baltimore: Brookes.

Turnbull, A. P., Turbiville, V., Jones, L., & Lee, J. (1992, Summer). A family-responsive approach to the development of the individualized family service plan. *OSERS News in Print*, pp. 12–15.

Turnbull, A. P., Turbiville, V., Schaffer, R., & Schaffer, V. (1996, June/July). "Getting a shot at life" through group action planning. *Zero to Three, 16*(6) 33–40.

Turnbull, A. P., Turbiville, V., & Turnbull, H. R. (2000). Evolution of family-professional partnerships: Collective empowerment as the model for the early twenty-first century. In J. P. Shonkoff & S. J. Meisels (Eds.), *Handbook of early childhood intervention* (pp. 630–648). Cambridge, England: Cambridge University Press.

Turnbull, A. P., & Turnbull, H. R. (1986). Stepping back from early intervention: An ethical perspective. *Journal of the Division for Early Childhood, 10,* 106–117.

Turnbull, A. P., & Turnbull, H. R. (1996). Group action planning as a strategy for providing comprehensive family support. In L. K. Koegel, R. L. Koegel, & G. Dunlap (Eds.), *Community, school, family, and social inclusion through positive behavioral support* (pp. 99–114). Baltimore: Brookes.

Turnbull, A. P., & Turnbull, H. R. (1996). Self-determination within a culturally responsive family systems perspective: Balancing the family mobile. In L. E. Powers, G. H. S. Singer, & J. Sowers (Eds.), *On the road to autonomy: Promoting self-competence among children and youth with disabilities* (pp. 195–220). Baltimore: Brookes.

Turnbull, A. P., & Turnbull, H. R. (1999). Comprehensive lifestyle support for adults with challenging behavior: From rhetoric to reality. *Education and Training in Mental Retardation and Developmental Disabilities, 34*(4), 373–394.

Turnbull, A. P., & Turnbull, H. R. (2001). Self-determination for individuals with significant cognitive disabilities and their families. *Journal of the Association for Persons with Severe Handicaps, 26*(1), 56–62.

Turnbull, A. P., Turnbull, H. R., Agosta, J., Erwin, E., Fujiura, G., Singer, G., & Soodak, L. (2004). Leaving no family behind: National goals, current knowledge, and future research. In C. Lakin (Ed.), *Keeping the promises: National goals, state-of-knowledge, and a national agenda for research on intellectual and developmental disabilities.* Washington, DC: Arc of the U.S.

Turnbull, A. P., Turnbull, H. R., & Blue-Banning, M. J. (1994). Enhancing inclusion of infants and toddlers with disabilities and their families: A theoretical and programmatic analysis. *Infants and Young Children, 72*(2), 1–14.

Turnbull, A. P., Turnbull, H. R., Shank, M., & Leal, D. (1995). *Exceptional lives: Special education in today's schools.* Upper Saddle River, NJ: Merrill/ Prentice Hall.

Turnbull, A. P., Turnbull, H. R., Shank, M., & Leal, D. (1999). *Exceptional lives: Special education in today's schools* (2nd ed.). Upper Saddle River, NJ: Merrill/Prentice Hall.

Turnbull, A. P., & Winton, P. J. (1984). Parent involvement policy and practice: Current research and implications for families of young severely handicapped children. In J. Blacher (Ed.), *Severely handicapped children and their families: Research in review* (pp. 377–397). New York: Academic Press.

Turnbull, A. P., Winton, P. J., Blacher, J. B., & Salkind, N. (1983). Mainstreaming in the kindergarten classroom: Perspectives of parents of handicapped and nonhandicapped children. *Journal of the Division of Early Childhood, 6,* 14–20.

Turnbull, H. R., & Stowe, M. J. (2001). A taxonomy for organizing the core concepts according to their underlying principles. *Journal of Disability Policy Studies, 12*(3), 177–197.

Turnbull, H. R., & Turnbull, A. P. (1978). *Parents speak out.* Columbus, OH: Charles E. Merrill Publishing.

Turnbull, H. R., & Turnbull, A. P. (1996). The synchrony of stakeholders: Lessons from the disabilities rights movement. In S. K. Kagen and N. Cohen (Eds.) *Reinventing early care and education: A vision for a quality system.* (pp. 290–305). San Francisco: Jossey-Bass.

Turnbull, H. R., & Turnbull, A. P. (2000). Accountability: Whose job is it anyway? *Journal of Early Intervention, 23*(4), 231–234.

Turnbull, H. R., & Turnbull, A. P. (2000). *Free appropriate public education: The law and children with disabilities* (6th ed.). Denver, CO: Love Publishing.

Turnbull, H. R., Turnbull, A. P., Shank, M., Smith, S. J. (2004). *Exceptional lives: Special education in today's school* (4th ed.). Upper Saddle River, NJ: Merrill/Prentice Hall.

Turnbull, H. R., Turnbull, A. P., & Wheat, M. (1982). Assumptions about parental participation: A legislative history. *Exceptional Education Quarterly, 3*(2), 1–8.

Turnbull, A. P., Summers, J.A., & Brotherson, M. J. (1984). *Working with families with disabled members: A family systems approach.* Lawrence: University of Kansas, Kansas Affiliated Facility.

Tuttle, D. H., & Cornell, D. G. (1993). Maternal labeling of gifted children: Effects on the sibling relationship. *Exceptional Children, 59*(5), 402–410.

U.S. Department of Commerce: Bureau of the Census. (1992). *Current population reports, series P-20, school enrollment.* Washington, DC: Author.

U. S. Department of Education. (1981). *Assistance to states for education of handicapped children: Interpretation of the Individualized Education Program (IEP).* Washington, DC: U.S. Government Printing Office.

U.S. Department of Education. (1990 January 9). Reading and writing proficiency remains low. *Daily Education News,* pp. 1–7.

U.S. Department of Education. (1992). *To assure the free appropriate public education of all children with disabilities: Fourteenth annual report to Congress on the implementation of the Individuals with Disabilities Education Act.* Washington, DC: Author.

U.S. Department of Education. (1995). *To assure the free appropriate public education of all children with disabilities: Seventeenth annual report to Congress on the implementation of the Individuals with Disabilities Education Act.* Washington, DC: Author.

U.S. Department of Education. (1996). *To assure the free appropriate public education of all children with disabilities: Individuals with Disabilities Education Act, Section 618.* Washington, DC: Author.

U.S. Department of Education. (1999). *The condition of bilingual education in the nation: A report to Congress and the President.* Washington, DC: Author.

U.S. Department of Education. (1999). *To assure the free appropriate public education of all children with disabilities.* Washington, DC: U.S. Department of Education.

U.S. Department of Education (2001). *National assessment of educational progress.* Washington, DC: National Center for Education Statistics.

U.S. Department of Education. (2001). *To assure the free appropriate public education of all children with disabilities: Twenty-second annual report to Congress on the implementation of the Individuals with Disabilities Education Act.* Washington, DC: Author.

U.S. Department of Education. (2001). *To assure the free appropriate public education of all children with disabilities: Twenty-third annual report to Congress on the implementation of the Individuals with Disabilities Education Act.* Washington, DC: Author.

U.S. Department of Education. (2001a). *Overview: No Child Left Behind, President Bush's education reform plan.* Retrieved June 10, 2004, from http://www.ed.gov/nclb/overview/intro/presidentplan/page_pg3.html#execsumm

U.S. Department of Education. (2001b). *To assure the free appropriate public education of all children with disabilities: Twenty-third annual report to Congress on the implementation of the Individuals with Disabilities Education Act.* Washington, DC: Author.

U.S. Department of Education. (2002). *To assure the free appropriate public education of all children with disabilities: Twenty-third annual report to Congress on the implementation of the Individuals with Disabilities Education Act.* Washington, DC: Author.

U.S. Department of Education. (2002). *To assure the free appropriate public education of all children with disabilities: Individuals with Disabilities Education Act, Section 618.* Washington, DC: Author.

U.S. Department of Education. (2002). *To assure the free appropriate public education of all children with disabilities: Twenty-fourth annual report to Congress on the implementation of the Individuals with Disabilities Education Act.* Washington, DC: Author.

U.S. Department of Education (2002a). *National assessment of educational progress.* Washington, DC: National Center for Education Statistics.

U.S. Department of Education. (2002b). *The facts about. . . good teachers.* Retrieved Oct. 30, 2003, from www.ed.gov/nclb/methods/teachers/teachers.html.

U.S. Department of Education. (2003). *More local freedom: Questions and answers on No Child Left Behind.* Retrieved October 30, 2003, from http://www.ed.gov/nclb/freedom/safety/creating.html#1

U.S. Department of Education. (2003). *Special education: Highlights of GAO-03-897, a report to the Ranking Minority Member, Committee on Health, Education, Labor and Pensions, U.S. Senate.* Washington, DC: U.S. Government Printing Office.

U.S. Department of Education and U.S. Department of Justice (2000). *Safeguarding our children: An action guide.* Washington, DC: Author.

U.S. Department of Education Office of Civil Rights. (1999). Projected student suspension rates values for the nation's public schools by race/ethnicity. *Elementary and Secondary School Civil Rights Compliance Reports.*

U.S. General Accounting Office. (2003, September). *Report to the Ranking Minority Member, Committee on Health, Education, Labor, and Pensions, United States Senate: Special education: Numbers of formal disputes are generally low and states are using mediation and other strategies to resolve conflicts.* Washington, DC: Author.

Uline, C. L., Tschannen-Moran, M., & Perez, L. (2003). Constructive conflict: How controversy can contribute to school improvement. *Teachers College Record, 105*(5), 782–816.

Ulrich, M. E., & Bauer, A. M. (2003). Levels of awareness: A closer look at communication between parents and professionals. *Teaching Exceptional Children, 35*(6), 20–23.

Uphoff, J. K. (1999). Religious diversity and education. In J. A. Banks & C. A. McGee-Banks (Eds.), *Multicultural education: Issues and perspectives* (3rd ed., pp. 108-128). New York: John Wiley & Sons.

Vacc, N. A., Vallecorsa, A. L., Parker, A., Bonner, S., Lester, C., Richardson, S., & Yates, C. (1985). Parents' and educators' participation in IEP conferences. *Education and Treatment of Children, 8*(2), 153-162.

Valdés, K., Williamson, B., & Wagner, M. (1990). *The national longitudinal transition study of special education students: Statistical almanac* (Vol. 1). Menlo Park, CA: SRI International.

Van der Klift, E., & Kunc, N. (2002). Beyond benevolence: Supporting genuine friendships in inclusive schools. In J. S. Thousand, R. A. Villa, & A. I. Nevin (Eds.), *Creativity & collaborative learning: The practical guide to empowering students, teachers, and families.* Baltimore: Paul H. Brookes.

Van Reusen, A. K. (1998). Self-advocacy strategy instruction: Enhancing student motivation, self-determination and responsibility in the learning process. In M. L. Wehmeyer & D. J. Sands (Eds.), *Making it happen.* Baltimore: Paul H. Brookes.

Van Reusen, A. K., & Bos, C. S. (1994). Facilitating student participation in individualized education programs through motivation strategy instruction. *Exceptional Children, 60*(5), 466-475.

Van Riper, M. (2000). Family variables associated with well-being in siblings of children with Down syndrome. *Journal of Family Nursing, 6,* 267-286.

Vaughn, S., Bos, C., Harrell, J., & Lasky, F. (1988). Parent participation in the initial placement/IEP conference ten years after mandated involvement. *Journal of Learning Disabilities, 21*(2), 82-89.

Vega, W., Hough, R., & Romero, A. (1983). *Family life patterns of Mexican Americans.* New York: Brunner/Mazel.

Veisson, M. (1999). Depression symptoms and emotional states in parents of disabled and non-disabled children. *Social Behavior and Personality, 27,* 87-98.

Voelker, S., Shore, D., Hakim-Larson, J., & Bruner, D. (1997). Discrepancies in parent and teacher rating of adaptive behavior of children with multiple disabilities. *Mental Retardation 35*(1), 10-17.

Vohs, J. R. (1993). On belonging: A place to stand, a gift to give. In A. P. Turnbull, J. M. Patterson, S. K. Behr, D. L. Murphy, J. G. Marquis, & M. J. Blue-Banning (Eds.), *Cognitive coping, families, and disability* (pp. 51-66). Baltimore: Brookes.

Vohs, J. R. (1997). Assistant secretary Judith E. Heumann. *Coalition Quarterly, 14*(1).

Voydanoff, P., & Donnelly, B. (1999). The intersection of time in activities and perceived unfairness in relation to psychological distress and marital quality. *Journal of Marriage and the Family, 61,* 739-751.

Vyas, P. (1983). Getting on with it. In T. Dougan, L. Isbell, & P. Vyas (Eds.), *We have been there* (pp. 17-19). Nashville, TN: Abingdon.

Walker, B., & Singer, G. H. S. (1993). Improving collaborative communication between professionals and parents. In G. H. S. Singer & L. E. Powers (Eds.), *Families, disability, and empowerment: Active coping skills and strategies for family intervention* (pp. 285-316). Baltimore: Brookes.

Walker-Dalhouse, D., & Dalhouse, A. D. (2001). Parent-school relations: Communicating more effectively with African American parents. *Young Children, 56*(4), 75-80.

Walther, J. B. (1996). Computer-mediated communication: Impersonal, interpersonal, and hyperpersonal interaction. *Communication Research, 23*(1), 3-44.

Walther-Thomas, C. (1997). Co-teaching experiences: The benefits and problems that teachers and principals report over time. *Journal of Learning Disabilities, 30,* 395-407.

Walther-Thomas, C., Korinek, L., McLaughlin, V. L., & Williams, B. T. (2000). *Collaboration for inclusive education: Developing successful programs.* Boston: Allyn & Bacon.

Wang, M., Mannan, H., Poston, D., Turnbull, A. P., & Summers, J. A. (in press). Parents' perceptions of advocacy activities and their impact on family quality of life. *Research and Practice for Persons with Severe Disabilities.*

Ward, S. (1996). My family: Formed by adoption. *Focal Point, 10*(1), 30-32.

Warfield, M. E. (2001). Employment, parenting, and well-being among mothers of children with disabilities. *Mental Retardation, 39*(4), 297-309.

Warfield, M. E., & Hauser-Cram, P. (1996). Child care needs, arrangements, and satisfaction of mothers of children with developmental disabilities. *Mental Retardation, 34,* 294-302.

Warfield, M. E., Krauss, M., Hauser-Cram, P., Upshur, C., & Shonkoff, J. (1999). Adaptation during early childhood among mothers of children with disabilities. *Journal of Developmental and Behavioral Pediatrics, 43,* 112-118.

Warren, F. (1985). A society that is going to kill your children. In H. R. Turnbull & A. P. Turnbull (Eds.), *Parents speak out: Then and now* (2nd ed., pp. 201-232). Upper Saddle River, NJ: Merrill/Prentice Hall.

Wehman, P., Bricout, J., & Kregel, J. (2000). Supported employment in 2000: Changing the locus of control from agency to consumer. In M. Wehmeyer & J. R. Patton (Eds.), *Mental retardation in the year 2000.* Austin, TX: Pro-Ed.

Wehman, P., Mank, D., Rogan, P., Luna, J., Kregel, J., Kiernan, W., et al. (2004). *Employment, productive life roles and income maintenance.* Baltimore: Paul H. Brookes.

Wehmeyer, M. L. (1998). Self-determination and individuals with significant disabilities: Examining meanings and misinterpretations. *Journal of the Association for Persons with Severe Handicaps, 23*(1), 5-16.

Wehmeyer, M. L. (2002). *Teaching students with mental retardation: Providing access to the general curriculum.* Baltimore: Paul H. Brookes.

Wehmeyer, M. L. (2003). Perspectives. *American Association on Mental Retardation, 41*(1), 57-60.

Wehmeyer, M. L., Agran, M., Palmer, S. B., Martin, J. E., & Mithaug, D. E. (2003). The effects of problem-solving instruction on the self-determined learning of secondary students with disabilities. In D. E. Mithaug, M. Agran, J. Martin, & M. L. Wehmeyer (Eds.), *Self-determined learning theory construction, verification, and evaluation.* Mahwah, NJ: Lawrence Erlbaum Associates.

Wehmeyer, M. L., Bersani, H., & Gagne, R. (2000). Riding the third wave: Self-determination and self-advocacy in the 21st century. In M. L. Wehmeyer & J. R. Patton (Eds.), *Mental retardation in the 21st century.* Austin, TX: Pro-Ed.

Wehmeyer, M. L., Morningstar, M., & Husted, D. (1999). *Family involvement in transition planning and implementation.* Austin, TX: Pro-Ed.

Wehmeyer, M. L., & Palmer, S. B. (2000). Promoting the acquisition and development of self-determination in young children with disabilities. *Early Education and Development, 11*(4), 465-481.

Wehmeyer, M. L., Palmer, S. B., Agran, M., Mithaug, D. E., & Martin, J. (2000). Promoting causal agency: The self-determined learning model of instruction. *Exceptional Children, 66*(4), 439-453.

Wehmeyer, M. L., & Sands, D. J. (1998). *Making it happen: Student involvement in education planning, decision-making, and instruction.* Baltimore: Paul H. Brookes.

Wehmeyer, M. L., & Sands, D. J. (Eds.). (1998). *Making it happen.* Baltimore: Paul H. Brookes.

Wehmeyer, M. L., & Schwartz, M. (1998). The relationship between self-determination, quality of life, and life satisfaction for adults with mental retardation. *Education and Training in Mental Retardation and Developmental Disabilities, 33*(3), 3-12.

Weicker, L. (1985). Sonny and public policy. In H. R. Turnbull & A. P. Turnbull (Eds.), *Parents speak out: Then and now* (2nd ed., pp. 281-287). Upper Saddle River, NJ: Merrill/Prentice Hall.

Weigel-Garrey, C. J., Cook, C. C., & Brotherson, M. J. (1998). Children and privacy: Choice, control and access in home environments. *Journal of Family Issues, 19*(1), 43-64.

Werner, E. E., & Smith, R. S. (1992). *Overcoming the odds: High risk children from birth to adulthood.* Ithaca, NY: Cornell University Press.

West, J. S. (1990). Educational collaboration in the restructuring of schools. *Journal of Educational and Psychological Consultation, 1*(1), 23-40.

Whitechurch, G. G., & Constantine, L. L. (1993). Systems theory. In P. G. Boss, W. J. Doherty, R. LaRossa, W. R. Schumm, & S. K. Steinmetz (Eds.), *Sourcebook of family theories and methods: A contextual approach* (pp. 325-352). New York: Plenum.

Wicks, A. C., Berman, S. L., & Jones, T. M. (1999). The structure of optimal trust: Moral and strategic implications. *Academy of Management Review, 24*(1), 91-99.

Willert, H. J., & Lenhardt, A. M. C. (2003). Tackling school violence does take the whole village. *Educational Forum, 67*(2), 110-118.

Williams, V. I., & Cartledge, G. (1997, September/October). Passing notes—to parents. *Council for Exceptional Children—Family Involvement in Learning,* 30-34.

Willis, W. (2004). Families with African American roots. In E. W. Lynch & M. J. Hanson (Eds.), *Developing cross-cultural competence: A guide for working with children and their families* (pp. 141-177). Baltimore: Paul Brookes.

Willoughby, J. C., & Glidden, L. M. (1995). Fathers helping out: Shared child care and marital satisfaction of parents of children with disabilities. *American Journal on Mental Retardation, 99*(4), 399-406.

Wilson, B. A. (1999). Inclusion: Empirical guidelines and unanswered questions. *Education and Training in Mental Retardation and Developmental Disabilities, 34*(2), 119-133.

Winton, P. J. (1992). Family-centered intervention: Words can make a difference. *Focus, 1*(2), 1-5.

Wood, W. M., Karvonen, M., Test, D. W., Browder, D., & Algozzine, B. (2004). Promoting student self-determination skills in IEP planning. *Teaching Exceptional Children, 36*(3), 8-16.

Woods, J. J., & McCormick, K. M. (2002). Toward an integration of child- and family-centered practices in the assessment of preschool children: Welcoming the family. *Young Exceptional Children, 5*(3), 2-11.

Worrell, F. C., Gabelko, N. H., Roth, D. A., & Samuels, L. K. (1999). Parents' reports on homework amount and problems in academically talented elementary students. *Gifted Child Quarterly, 43*(2), 86-94.

Wunsch, M. F., Conlon, C. F., & Scheidt, P. C. (2002). Substance abuse: A preventable threat to development. In M. L. Batshaw (Ed.), *Children with disabilities* (5th ed.). Washington, DC: Paul H. Brookes.

Yell, M. L., & Drasgow, E. (2004). *No Child Left Behind: A guide for professionals.* Upper Saddle River, NJ: Prentice Hall.

York, J., & Tundidor, M. (1995). Issues raised in the name of inclusion: Perspectives of educators, parents and students. *Journal of the Association for Persons with Severe Handicaps, 20*(1), 31-44.

Young, D. M., & Roopnarine, J. L. (1994). Fathers' childcare involvement with children with and without disabilities. *Topics in Early Childhood Special Education, 14*(4), 488-502.

Ysseldyke, J., & Olsen, K. (1999). Putting alternate assessments into practice: What to measure and possible sources of data. *Exceptional Children, 65*(2), 175-186.

Ysseldyke, J. E., Vanderwood, M. L., & Shriner, J. (1997). Changes over the past decade in special education referral to placement probability: An incredibly reliable practice. *Diagnostigue, 23*(1), 193-201.

Zafft, C., Hart, D., & Zimbrich, K. (2004). College career connection: A study of youth with intellectual disabilities and the impact of postsecondary education. *Education and Training in Developmental Disabilities, 39*(1), 45-53.

Zhang, C., & Bennett, T. (2003). Facilitating the meaningful participation of culturally and linguistically diverse families in the IFSP and IEP process. *Focus on Autism and Other Developmental Disabilities, 18*(1), 51-59.

Zigler, E., & Muenchow, S. (1992). *Head Start: The inside story of America's most successful educational experiment.* New York: Basic Books.

Zionts, L. T., Zionts, P., Harrison, S., & Bellinger, O. (2003). Urban African American families' perceptions of cultural sensitivity within the special education system. *Focus on Autism and Other Developmental Disabilities, 18,* 41-50.

Zirpoli, T. J., Wieck, C., Hancox, D., & Skarnulis, E. R. (1994). Partners in policymaking: The first five years. *Mental Retardation, 32*(6), 422-425.

Ziskin, L. (1985). The story of Jennie. In H. R. Turnbull & A. P. Turnbull (Eds.), *Parents speak out: Then and now* (2nd ed., pp. 65-74). Upper Saddle River, NJ: Merrill/Prentice-Hall.

Zoints, L. T., Zoints, P., Harrison, S., & Bellinger, O. (2003). Urban African American family's perceptions of cultural sensitivity within the special education system. *Focus on Autism and Other Developmental Disabilities, 18*(1), 41-50.

Zucker, L. G., Darby, M. R., Brewer, M. B., & Peng, Y. (1996). Collaboration structure and information dilemmas in biotechnology: Organizational boundaries as trust production. In R. M. Kramer & T. R. Tyler (Eds.), *Trust in organizations: Frontiers of theory and research* (pp. 90-113). Thousand Oaks, CA: Sage.

Zuniga, M. E. (2004). Families with Latino roots. In E. W. Lynch & M. J. Hanson (Eds.), *Developing cross-cultural competence: A guide for working with children and their families* (pp. 179-217). Baltimore: Paul Brookes.

Index